The COOK'S DICTIONARY and CULINARY REFERENCE

A Comprehensive, Definitive Guide to Cooking and Food

JONATHAN BARTLETT

CB
CONTEMPORARY BOOKS

Library of Congress Cataloging-in-Publication Data

Bartlett, Jonathan, 1931–
    The cook's dictionary and culinary reference : a comprehensive,
definitive guide to cooking and food / Jonathan Bartlett.
        p.   cm.
    ISBN 0-8092-3120-4
    1. Food—Dictionaries.   2. Cookery—Dictionaries.   I. Title.
TX349.B355   1996
641'.03—dc20   96-3055
                                                        CIP

Published by Contemporary Books
An imprint of NTC/Contemporary Publishing Company
4255 West Touhy Avenue, Lincolnwood (Chicago), Illinois 60646-1975 U.S.A.
Copyright © 1996 by NTC/Contemporary Publishing Company
Manufactured in the United States of America
International Standard Book Number: 0-8092-3120-4

18   17   16   15   14   13   12   11   10   9   8   7   6   5   4   3   2

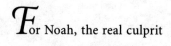For Noah, the real culprit

ACKNOWLEDGMENTS

No book of this sort is written in a vacuum. Too many people have contributed, some of whom I would like to thank here. If I have left some out (and I certainly have) it is not for lack of gratitude—simply a bad memory. First and foremost is my son Noah, who suggested the idea and has gracefully consented to my rather absurd dedication. Second would be the late Alexis Lichine, who hired me to contribute to his *Encyclopedia of Wines and Spirits* all those many years ago. His patience and forbearance (qualities most people who knew him would not credit him with) allowed me to figure out how to work on a book of this type.

Sally Taylor, Emeritus Professor of Botany at Connecticut College, and Edward Migdalsky of Yale's Ichthyology Department have been most helpful. If I have misinterpreted their comments, the fault is clearly mine.

Webster Scott, farmer extraordinary of East Lyme, Connecticut, has also been informative on what might be called leguminous matters (as well as supplying some excellent produce). To him my thanks also go.

And to the many others over the years, I recognize my debt.

INTRODUCTION

Cooking is usually described as both an art and a science. For the gifted professional this is undoubtedly true, but for most of us, it is uncertain science at best and, perhaps, more craft than art. This does not mean it must be slipshod or second-rate. Even among scientists, the number who achieve a Nobel Prize is small indeed, but no one would suggest that all the rest are purveyors of codswallop.

As is true of science, cooking also has its superstars, those special souls who have some innate sense for the taste and texture and presentation of foods, a flair for combining them in both traditional and innovative combinations, and an apparent inability to let whatever they are cooking go wrong (or perhaps an intuitive sense—honed by experience—for how to remedy it when it does). You will find such people in the kitchens of unbelievably expensive restaurants, in farmhouses and fishing camps, and in tiny kitchenettes in high-rise apartment houses. We can learn from them and pick up much that is useful from them, but unless we have the gift ourselves, we cannot quite reach their peaks. No matter. Much superb science is done by those who never attain Nobel status. And much fine cooking is done by simply paying attention and following the basic precepts—or breaking them judiciously.

Before we can pay attention to any details, we must have a sense for what those details consist of, for what our ground rules are. It is the purpose of this book to address these questions. It began as a guide to clarify the kinds of terms that appear in cookbooks and that are, or might be, unfamiliar to the novice or even the fairly experienced cook. What is a "blanquette," for example, or a "gallimaufry"? The book was not content to rest there. Common cooking terms—those terms we so easily forget or never bother to define with any accuracy—began to insert themselves. And how can you cook without food? So food crept in, too.

Following World War II and intensifying in the decades that followed, the diet of the average American expanded to include foods virtually unheard of previously—except perhaps in certain so-called ethnic neighborhoods. The crisp salad green arugula once appeared only at Italian greengrocers; today it can be found in a variety of outlets as well. And closer to home, catfish used to be pretty much confined to rural areas, especially in the South, and often fairly poor ones at that. Now they can be found in big-city supermarkets, even in wealthy areas. When we thought of tropical fruits, at one time we thought pretty much of bananas. Yet the variety of such produce seen today—avocados, mangos, kiwi, papayas, and star fruit just for starters—is overwhelming. Sometimes it is hard to know just how to deal with them. An aim of this book is to serve as a guide to these sometimes new, often unusual foods.

It is not the purpose of this book to be a cookbook. However, here and there you will find recipes of various sorts, thrown in pretty much at random. Some will be hardly more than suggestions of how to cook something; some will be more formal. Think of them as the salt that adds savor to the stew.

Abalone

Any of the mostly Pacific marine sea snails of the *Haliotis* genus. The abalone's large foot muscle (anywhere from 5 to 12 inches) is prized on both sides of the Pacific as a table delicacy. Its Atlantic counterpart is the ORMER. Abalone are expensive. They are becoming rare, are difficult to harvest, and must be worked over thoroughly before becoming edible. This involves slicing the tough muscle almost paper thin, then chilling it, and then pounding it into submission with a mallet. After that it is all delight.

Abalone is available fresh if you live in California, Mexico, or the Far East, but otherwise can be had canned or dried or frozen. Abalone is susceptible to baking, broiling, deep-frying, and sautéing. It is particularly effective in Chinese cooking, perhaps because so much Chinese cooking is of such short duration, and abalone toughens if it is overcooked—just see that it gets heated through.

Absinthe

A potent, banned alcoholic spirit of a greenish cast flavored chiefly with anise and wormwood (*Artemisia absinthium*) in great favor particularly among literary and military people—especially in France—from its development in the late 18th century until its prohibition in the 20th. Known as "the green muse," it had a debilitating, addictive, and often disastrous—even fatal—effect. The French poet Alfred de Musset missed so many meetings of the Academie Française that a colleague is said to have quipped that "he absinthes himself too much." The original absinthe formula was bought by the Pernod firm, which still makes an anise-flavored aperitif (as does the firm of Ricard) without the wormwood or its grim consequences.

Acerola

Also *Barbados cherry*. A West Indian shrub (*Malpighia glabra*) adaptable for home-growing in the southern United States. It produces a tart, cherrylike fruit with considerable vitamin C and is useful as juice or in preserves. It takes its name from its supposed resemblance to the Mediterranean AZAROLE.

Aceto Dolce

An Italian condiment consisting of bits and pieces of fruits that are preserved in vinegar and boiled-down grape juice and sweetened with honey.

Achiote
See ANNATTO.

Acid
A compound that helps give food a tart taste, keeps wines from insipidity, provides the tang of lemon and limes, and makes vinegar possible. And that's only for starters. Our foods would be dull and uninspired without acids, but in excess they can be brutal and many (of use in commerce and the laboratory rather than the kitchen) are lethal.

Acidophilus
A bacterium (*Lactobacillus acidophilus*) occurring naturally in milk but destroyed by pasteurization. It can be isolated and returned to milk, which will be labeled as such, i.e., "acidophilus milk." This type of milk is designed for those people who have a limited or nonexistent ability to digest the milk sugar lactose, which the acidophilus bacteria help consume.

Acidulated Water
Water to which an acid, such as lemon or vinegar, has been added. It is useful for such procedures as soaking beef or game kidneys or preserving the color of fruits or vegetables (apples or avocados, for example) or for cleaning aluminum cookware that has discolored from interaction with alkalis. A tablespoon of lemon juice or vinegar to a cup of water should be ample for most uses.

Acorn
The nut of the oak tree (*Quercus* spp.), used for flour by Native Americans and others (the peasantry of 19th-century Russia during famines or other times of deprivation, for example) and as a sort of coffee substitute, but probably of interest today only to the most dedicated forager. It has not been tried here. The acorn of the white oak (*Quercus alba*) is said to be edible as soon as it ripens, but other species of oak produce nuts so full of bitter tannin that they must be ground and leached and dried and roasted—all in all a cumbersome process—before becoming palatable.

Acorn Squash
A variety of SQUASH.

Ade
A beverage of sweetened water flavored with fruit, usually a citrus fruit. Lemonade is a prime example. Such drinks are particularly popular during the summer months.

Adobo
1. The national dish of the Philippines, probably derived from a Spanish wine and vinegar marinade. Like any meat dish of this sort its ingredients can vary, but

it usually consists of pork and sometimes chicken or seafood. The one essential ingredient is vinegar to add savor to the sauce.

2. A Mexican sauce based on vinegar and chili PEPPER.

Adzuki
Also *azuki*. An Oriental BEAN.

Agar
A gelatinous substance derived from certain types of red seaweed (*Chrondus* spp.). We used to call it *agar-agar* and the Japanese have always called it *kanten* and still do. Agar is useful in laboratories as a gelling agent and in food preparation as a vegetarian gelatin and stabilizer. The Chinese also use it in vegetable dishes and salads, despite its absence of taste.

Agaric
Also *champignon de Paris*. The MUSHROOM you are most likely to find at the vegetable counter.

Agave
A genus of evergreen plants that provides a number of products including hemp and the Mexican alcoholic beverages MESCAL (including TEQUILA) and PULQUE.

Age
To bring out taste enhancements and subtleties in foods by keeping them under controlled conditions of temperature and humidity for a given length of time. Fine wines are aged in barrels, then bottled, after which some of them continue to improve even for periods of decades, where ordinary wines tend to go sour and distilled spirits undergo no positive changes after being bottled. Beef and mutton are hung in cold rooms to develop their taste. And the best cheeses also need a little time to reach their potential.

Agen
A French PLUM mostly dried for prunes.

Agnolotti
Round or crescent-shaped RAVIOLI filled with meat.

Agrimony
A yellow-flowered European herb (*Agrimonia eupatoria*) of the rose family formerly used for making a sort of medicinal tea.

Agrodolce
An Italian sweet-and-sour sauce based on sugar cooked with vinegar and augmented with bay leaf, bitter chocolate, currants, and garlic along with the juices of the meat it is to accompany. It is frequently served with braised game.

Aioli

A garlicky MAYONNAISE favored in southern France, its ultimate place of origin being Provence. It is often served with cold vegetables—especially cold boiled potatoes—or cold poached fish or chicken. You make it as you would any mayonnaise except that you build it around lavish amounts of finely minced garlic; eight cloves are not too many for a cup of the sauce, which should have a pervasive aroma and cause a catch in the throat as it slides down.

Aji-no-moto

The Japanese name for MONOSODIUM GLUTAMATE.

Akee

A tricky fruit (*Blighia sapida*) widely grown in Jamaica, where it was introduced from West Africa in the 1790s by Captain Bligh (of *Bounty* fame). It is tricky in that it must be picked after the fruit (the edible portion is a part of the inner fruit, or aril) has opened. If picked before this, or if it is badly bruised, it is said to be toxic. Jamaicans serve it most notably as a breakfast dish with salt cod or scrambled eggs.

Akvavit

A variant spelling of AQUAVIT.

À la

See MODE.

Alaska King Crab

An enormous northern Pacific CRAB.

Albacore

A high-fat light meat of TUNA.

Albany Beef

Colonial American slang for STURGEON, which was, early on, so prevalent in the Hudson River (and others) that it was all but deemed too common for the discriminating palate, placing it with such other servile fare as lobster and salmon and shad. It shows, perhaps, that the French adage that says the more things change, the more they stay the same, just ain't necessarily so.

Alcohol

A spirit obtained by fermentation (wine and beer) or distillation (brandy, gin, rum, vodka, and whiskey). All manner of alcoholic spirits can be useful in cooking, whether for flavoring or flaming or both. Beer and wine are both excellent braising liquids, and all sorts of spirits can be advantageously added in small amounts at some point in the cooking process of many dishes. If added early enough, the alcohol evaporates, leaving only the taste behind. If a spirit such as a liqueur is added to ice cream, however, the alcohol remains intact and becomes an integral part of the dessert.

Al Dente
Italian for "to the tooth." A term used with pasta to connote that it is cooked just enough to give a little resistance when bitten into instead of being limp and over-done.

Ale
A form of BEER.

Alewife
A fish of the HERRING family.

Alfalfa
Also *lucerne*. A plant (*Medicago sativa*) widely grown for cattle fodder and hay; its SPROUTS are commonly used in salads and other dishes.

Alligator
A genus of reptile, one member of which (*Alligator mississippiensis*) inhabits fresh-water swampy areas of the southern United States. (The other is a native of China.) Although fairly rigidly protected by law, some alligators are harvested mainly for their hides, but also for their meat—at least locally. The tail is said to be the best part, being variously described as tasting like lobster or like veal. The fat, of which there is not much, is said to taste terrible.

Alligator Pear
A former name for AVOCADO.

Allspice
The berry of a Caribbean tree (*Pimenta dioica*), most notably grown in Jamaica, where it is known simply as *pimento*, not to be confused with the pimiento or pimiento PEPPER. The dried allspice berry is available whole or ground and imparts a suggestion of cinnamon, clove, and nutmeg combined. The ground variety is use-ful in baked dishes and curries and can be added to mayonnaise to be served, for example, with cold fish. The whole berries can profitably be added to stews or stocks.

Almond
A Mediterranean nut tree (*Prunus amygdalus*, sometimes listed as *Amygdalus com-munis*) widely grown in warm climates for its showy flowers and for the nuts them-selves, which can be eaten directly or used roasted, toasted, or raw in cooking and baking. Almonds can be found chopped, sliced, slivered, or whole as well as blanched or with their skins still intact. They are often sold in vacuum-packed containers, which makes sense inasmuch as their high fat content makes them perishable. If

you're going to keep them around awhile, put them in a tightly covered container and keep them in the refrigerator—or better yet, the freezer. In general, whole almonds keep better than the bits and pieces, and the unroasted keep better than the roasted.

Almonds go well in casseroles and with vegetables (especially snap beans) and go wonderfully with chocolate. Several fish dishes are flavored with almonds, including trout (although trout with almonds has its critics) and carp. A Balkan specialty is fried eel with almonds and paprika. Almonds also are used in stuffings, can be combined with milk and stewed onions for soup, or may be dusted over any number of dishes, up to and including shish kabob. They also appear as almond EXTRACT, MACAROON, MARZIPAN, NOUGAT, and PRALINE, and the Chinese are uncommonly fond of almond cookies. Almonds are often available smoked (sometimes hickory smoked) or covered with chocolate.

Almond Flour

A flour made from almonds that have been blanched and ground. Recipes dating back to medieval times use it as a thickening agent, as a flour replacement, as a base for cakes and puddings, and even as a coating for deep-fried foods.

Almond Milk

A medieval European almond-based liquid substitute for eggs and milk. It was used on fast days in an era when eating meat or dairy products could be a criminal offense. It was made by steeping ground almonds in hot water and then thoroughly straining out the almonds (2 ounces almonds to ½ cup water was suggested). The resulting liquid was also used to give desserts, soups, and stews a thicker, smoother texture.

Almond Paste

Blanched and ground almonds mixed with sugar and glycerin. Sometimes the ground kernels of peaches or apricots replace or augment the almonds. It resembles MARZIPAN but is less delicate.

Alum

In cookery, a salt of aluminum (usually potassium aluminum sulfate—$KAl(SO_4)_2 \cdot 12\ H_2O$—or ammonium aluminum sulfate—$NH_4Al(SO_4)_2 \cdot 12\ H_2O$) used in some double-acting BAKING POWDER. Its detractors claim it imparts a bitter taste and also that it is deleterious to the health.

Aluminum

A light, tough, heat-conducting metal excellent for use as COOKWARE and of inestimable culinary use when made into foil.

Amandine

Describes anything cooked with chopped or grated almonds. Trout amandine is perhaps the most widely known example.

Amaranth

A fairly widespread plant (*Amaranthus* spp.), varieties of which can be found from the tropics to southern Canada. Its leaves are used by foragers as a potherb, and its seeds can be ground into flour, which is available at health food stores as a newfound secret of the Aztecs. One package of flour contained a recipe for a delightful amaranth, oatmeal, and whole wheat bread, but, given the cost of the flour, it is not something one would put on the table every day.

An Oriental species (*Amaranthus gangeticus*), also known as *Chinese* or *Surinam spinach*, is sometimes homegrown as an ornamental and for its edible leaves, which are reminiscent of spinach and are used in the West Indian soup CALLALOU.

Amaretto

1. An almond-flavored LIQUEUR.
2. An Italian MACAROON.

Ambergris

A by-product of the sperm whale. Small amounts of ambergris have been used to enhance chicken and other dishes, but its main appeal seems to lie in its dubious reputation as an aphrodisiac. It commands high prices from makers of perfume. The chances of your finding any of this are slim unless you're a fabulously wealthy Chinese gourmet based in Hong Kong.

Amberjack

A fish of the JACK family.

Ambrosia

A dessert made of orange sections and sometimes such other fruit as bananas with slivers of coconut. There's nothing wrong with it, but it seems a far cry from the original ambrosia, which was what fed the gods of Mount Olympus.

American Cheese

It usually refers to a PROCESSED CHEESE, but can equally pertain to any of the traditional cheeses made in North America, from American Cheddar to Liederkranz, and all the fresh cheeses and goat cheeses being produced mostly by small cheesemakers in nooks and crannies of the United States and Canada.

Amontillado

A type of SHERRY less dry than fino but drier than cream.

Amoroso
A sweet dark SHERRY.

Anadama Bread
An American bread with a thousand "authentic" recipes, but about all that is sure is that among its ingredients are cornmeal and molasses. The legend behind its name is that of a Yankee farmer whose wife walked out on him, leaving him only a batch of cornmeal mush. He enriched it with molasses and perhaps some flour and yeast and made a bread, intoning the whole time "Anna, damn her." Somehow the bread became popular and still is, although you won't find it in any supermarket.

Anaheim
The mildest CHILI pepper. There is also a sweet pepper, anaheim mild, that is either green or red. It resembles a long, thin-skinned bell PEPPER.

Ancho
The dried version of the poblano CHILI pepper.

Anchovy
A fish (or fishes—the Engraulidae make up a large family) that for most of us comes exclusively out of a can, or perhaps a tube, like toothpaste. The important members of the family from the Western cook's standpoint are *Engraulis encrasicholus*, the European anchovy, which inhabits the Mediterranean and eastern Atlantic, and *Anchoa hepsetus*, the striped anchovy, in the western Atlantic. Relatives abound in other waters as well, especially around Southeast Asia.

Anchovies are eaten fresh here and there but really come into their own when canned and used to add zest to fish sauces. They can also be added (in very small amounts) to any form of braised or stewed meat. Anchovies are the basis for any number of sauces, including NUÓC-MAM and Worcestershire sauce. They are also processed into fish meal and oil.

Canned anchovies come in two varieties: flat and rolled. The rolled variety usually encircle a CAPER.

Andouille
A mild, lightly cured, and smoked French country sausage made with pork and tripe. It is often served grilled as a lunch dish or for picnics.

Andouillette
A smaller version of ANDOUILLE, except that it is not customarily cured or smoked but served fresh.

Angel Food Cake
A light and frothy white SPONGE CAKE.

Angel Hair
An exceptionally long, thin variety of PASTA.

Angelica
A widespread genus (especially *Angelica archangelica*) of herbs of temperate climates and with a flavor somewhat reminiscent of JUNIPER berries. Its stems and shoots are traditionally candied or used to sweeten fruitcakes, plum puddings, pastries, and preserves; the leaves are used for tea; and the root is ground for flour or used as a flavoring for cordials and bitters as well as vermouth and gin. Even so, angelica has the curious reputation of causing a distaste for alcoholic beverages. Angelica stems can also be stewed with rhubarb to complement and mitigate the rhubarb taste (without getting rid of it completely).

Angel Shark
An edible species of SHARK.

Angels on Horseback
An appetizer consisting of oysters wrapped in bacon, skewered, and then run under the broiler.

Anglerfish
See MONKFISH.

Angostura
The bark of either of two South American trees (*Galipea officinalis* and *Cusparia febrifuga*), which produces a bitter and tonic liquid. Also the name of a proprietary BITTERS.

Animelles
A French term for a sheep's testicles. At one time, they were in favor on the tables of French nobility and were served split, flattened, and sautéed.

Anise
A parsleylike plant (*Pimpinella anisum*) valuable for its seeds, which impart a taste similar to LICORICE. It is used in baking and can be added to fruits, fruit salads, carrots, coleslaw, and turnips. In addition, it forms the base for the liqueur anisette, which is also informed by fennel and coriander. The oil of anise is said to be poisonous to pigeons. Anise is not a replacement for the Chinese (and Mexican) flavoring STAR ANISE. Moreover, the bulblike vegetable often sold as anise or sweet anise is actually not anise but FENNEL.

Aniseed
The seed of the ANISE plant.

Anjou
A variety of PEAR.

Annatto
Also *achiote*. The seeds of a tropical tree (*Bixa orellana*). They are ground and used as a yellow or reddish coloring agent, especially in making butter and cheese. In some areas annatto is used as a substitute for SAFFRON, which is a great deal tastier but also far more expensive.

Annona
Generic name for the CHERIMOYA.

Antelope
Name given to various Afro-Asian mammals; however, the word also applies to the North American pronghorn (*Antilocapra americana*), considered by some as a superior variety of VENISON.

Antipasto
An Italian hors d'oeuvres course. It can range from a very simple offering of whatever the garden happens to hold at the moment, perhaps accompanied with a little salt or possibly a dip, to a more elaborate combination of hot or cold, fresh and cured meats, fish, and vegetables.

A.1.
A proprietary sauce devised to be used with meats. It is composed chiefly of tomatoes and vinegar with various flavorings (especially citrus) and is useful—as is CATSUP—for brightening up insipid or otherwise uninteresting servings.

Aperitif
The French equivalent of the cocktail. It usually consists of a deeply colored spirit-based beverage flavored with herbs of some sort and often tastes quite bitter. Some of those that are not dark-colored tend to turn cloudy when water is added. Various wines such as CHAMPAGNE, SHERRY, or a simple dry white wine (whether plain or mixed such as a KIR) also qualify as aperitifs. Like the cocktail, the aperitif is usually taken just prior to a meal.

Apollinaris Water
A mineral water from Germany. It is highly alkaline, somewhat bitter in taste, and contains carbonates of calcium, magnesium, and sodium.

Appelation d'Origine Contrôlée
Or *AOC*, a legally controlled place-name. A French term—other nations have their equivalents—certifying that the item so labeled is from the exact area specified in its name and adheres to various legal restrictions surrounding its production. It stems

from the conviction that certain commodities are the result of specific geographical or procedural accidents not able to be duplicated elsewhere.

The argument runs that Champagne, Parmigiano-Reggiano, Slivovitz, or Vidalia onions are not *types* that can be replicated—despite what their imitators say—but are instead the highly specific results of a certain place, its unique characteristics, and the manner of cultivation or processing that has grown up around them. In the words of the Swiss, anyone can put holes in their cheese; only in Switzerland can they put in the taste. It may sound arrogant, but it is based on the special conditions of Alpine climate, Alpine pasturage, the particular breed of cattle that feed in those pastures, the traditional methods of handling the milk, and the making and aging and general handling of the cheese. Adherents to the argument believe that the results are unique and should be protected from exploitation by imitators.

The concept can be carried too far and some historical perspective (beloved of the French and anathema to Americans) is called for. Some names are conducive to being AOC place-names, some are not. To the French, Cantal cheeses and Champagne wines are legally controlled whereas chicken Kiev, for example, and peach Melba are not. Chicken Kiev is not a chicken specially raised in the Ukraine, but one cooked in a style supposedly favored in Kiev; and peach Melba need not be limited to preparation by someone named Melba, but was simply created in honor of the operatic soprano Nellie Melba. Neither one has the geographical or historical implications of an AOC place-name any more than has a New York steak and are thus not susceptible to protection.

Appenzeller
A Swiss mountain-made firm cow's-milk CHEESE (both whole and skim milk versions are made) that is flavored with spices and cider or wine to give it a robust, fruity taste.

Appetizer
A snack (often a cocktail snack) or a first course for a meal.

Apple
An edible fruit of *Malus* spp. We seem to have an ambivalent approach to this fruit. It was the biblical apple that indirectly caused all our woes; it was the Greek apple of discord that brought about the Trojan War; and it was the early Church's apple of Sodom that looked so splendid on the outside but inside was nothing more than dust and ashes. It's almost enough to make you worry about apple pie. But that pie might just point to our salvation—the apple is all but sinfully good.

The apple is so good, in fact, that there is almost no end to the ways in which it can be used. We make apple cobblers and muffins and pan dowdys and pies and strudels and tarts and turnovers and upside-down cakes. We make butter and chutneys and dumplings and fritters and jellies and pickles and salads and sauces and soufflés. We make apple brandy and applejack and cider. We bake them and we candy them and we dry them and we fry them and we stew them. But no matter how many ways there are of preparing apples (one source estimated nearly two hundred, exclusive of such not strictly culinary ones as cider and juice and vinegar), perhaps our first love is for a fresh apple, preferably right off the tree.

However, the apple that is just right for eating off the tree may not be the apple that is just right for a pie or applesauce, which may not be the one for apple brandy. Some apples are recommended for all-around use, others for specific purposes; there is a potential problem here. All too often, an apple listed only as all-purpose can turn out to be merely mediocre at everything. Some of the apples you're likely to meet are:

Baldwin. A small, slightly acid late red apple applicable mostly to juicing and baking.

Cortland. An early red and very fine all-purpose apple with keeping qualities that make it available year-round.

Empire. A cross between red delicious and McIntosh. Crisp, juicy, and tasty.

Golden delicious. A variety somewhat similar to red delicious but somewhat later developing and both tastier and more versatile. You can not only eat it raw, but cook and bake successfully with it, too.

Granny Smith. A slightly puckery green apple from Australia (although also grown in the northwest United States) and perhaps, when it is properly ripened, the best all-around apple to be found in most markets today.

Gravenstein. A tart, all-around, very early yellowish-to-pink apple. Probably the best of the "summer" apples, but its season is brief.

Greening. A slightly tart green midseason apple good for all-around use but especially for cooking and baking.

Ida red. The largest of our apples, this one is a mild, somewhat pulpy apple favored by some for eating and excellent for baking.

Jonagold. A cross between Jonathan and golden delicious. A firm, sweet, juicy apple.

Jonathan. A slightly acid, medium-red, midseason, crisp eating and all-round apple. Get them freshly picked—they don't store with any distinction.

Macoun. A brief (it's usually gone by Thanksgiving) red apple with a pleasant, juicy bite. One of our better eating apples.

McIntosh. Perhaps the most prevalent (along with red delicious) red apple in most markets. It is slightly tart, is not a first-rate cooking apple, but is always available.

Milton. A small, mild, early red apple with green highlights.

Northern spy. A medium-large, tangy, midseason-to-late red apple flecked with green and good for almost any purpose.

Red delicious. A handsome, but somewhat bland and mushy, sweet red eating
apple, available most any time.

Rome beauty. A large firm red midseason apple appropriate for baking and for
pies and sauce.

Stayman. A medium-large, midseason apple, red with green highlights, crisp and
tangy; good for most purposes.

Winesap. A late-season dusky red apple with a juicy bite, good for eating, making applesauce, or baking.

When buying apples (or picking them, for that matter), select those that are firm
and brightly colored with no bruises. Bruises are apt to show up inside as unsightly
(and unsavory) mushy brown spots. Store them in a cool, dry place. It is not recommended that you leave apples sitting around your kitchen—they're prone to
mushiness if so treated. Instead, put them in a plastic bag with holes in it (many
supermarkets sell them this way) and store them in the vegetable drawer of your
refrigerator. If they're not quite ripe yet they will ripen, and if they are already ripe
they will hold, at least for a time, depending upon variety. Some people with school-
age children like to keep a few in a bowl just inside the door as a bribe to keep hungry kids away from less nutritious snacks, but only a few at a time need be removed
from storage for that purpose.

Apple Brown Betty

An early American dessert typically consisting of sliced apples, toasted breadcrumbs,
brown sugar, and perhaps cinnamon and nutmeg all baked together. Heavy cream
is sometimes offered with it.

Apple Butter

A preserve of apples that have been slowly cooked down with spices into a thick
gooey mass to be used as a spread.

Applejack

An American apple BRANDY.

Apricot

A tree that bears a small round peachlike fruit with yellow flesh by the same name.
It also has been identified as the original "apple" of Genesis, which might put the
Garden of Eden in the north of China, where the apricot (*Prunus armeniaca*) orig-
inated. Small and lush, it fares badly in commerce. An insufficiently ripe apricot is
flabby and lacks taste, yet once off the tree it quickly loses its distinction and becomes
ordinary. If you're an apricot buff, plant a tree or move closer to where they grow.
In the United States, this would be the West Coast (although they grow well in the
Middle Atlantic states roughly from Philadelphia through the Carolinas); otherwise,
France and sections of the Middle East are favorable grounds. A fair percentage of

the apricot harvest is canned (sometimes for juice or preserves), but most of it is dried. The dried fruit has many uses, one of them being as an addition to meat stews, a tasty secret known throughout North Africa and the Arab world and still relatively unpracticed elsewhere. Dried apricots can also be used to make a first-rate GLAZE for baked goods.

If you plan on picking apricots at your local market, make sure they have the full apricot color. A green one may or may not ripen. Ripen them at room temperature and refrigerate only those that are soft to the touch.

In China, the kernel of the apricot is used to flavor vegetable dishes, desserts, and a special soup. The catch is that in its raw state, the kernel of some apricots is toxic and must be boiled and then oven-dried to be made edible. Because these kernels superficially resemble almonds, they are sometimes known as *bitter almonds*.

Apricot Leather
A snack or trail food consisting of skinned and pureed apricots boiled down with sugar and poured into a cookie sheet or similar drying pan. It can be left in the sun to dry or placed in a low oven. The resulting sheet, which dries to the consistency of leather, is cut into thin strips for chewing when hunger, the need for energy, or simply the inability to leave it alone and untasted comes upon you.

Aquacate
A former name for AVOCADO.

Aquavit
Also *akvavit*. A Scandinavian spirit distilled from potatoes or grain (only the latter version is exported), flavored with various pleasant seeds and spices, most notably caraway seeds, and usually drunk chilled and straight.

Arborio
A type of RICE grown in Italy and used in RISOTTO.

Arbroath Smokie
A smoked HADDOCK similar to FINNAN HADDIE except that it is smoked whole, instead of split, and split only when ready to serve.

Arctic Char
A large CHAR of the far Northwest (Alaska and Canada).

Armadillo
A small mammal (of the family Dasypodidae) found in the southern United States and Central and South America that is noted for its bony, armorlike covering. It is eaten mostly in Texas and the Southwest, where its somewhat musky flavor is often complemented by spices or a hearty marinade. Of the various species of armadillo, the three-banded one (*Tolypeutes tricinctus*) is said to be the most succulent.

Armagnac

A first-rate French BRANDY distilled in the southwest corner of France, in the part that was once Gascony.

Aroma

A wine term for the lingering fragrance that a fine wine develops as it ages in the bottle.

Aromatic

A vegetable substance that gives a pleasing aroma and imparts a pungent taste is one definition of an aromatic, but some food experts then proceed to differentiate aromatics from herbs and spices, which seems like unnecessary hair-splitting. Aromatics would certainly include such herbs as basil and thyme; moreover, spices such as clove and nutmeg are nothing if not aromatic. However you want to define them, they add perfume to our dishes and pleasure to our dining.

Arrack

Also *arak* or *raki* or any of a number of other names. It designates a native spirit made anywhere from the eastern Mediterranean (where it may be flavored with ANISE) to Southeast Asia and is a combination of everything from dates to fermented grapes, palm sap, rice, or anything else that may be on hand. At the very least, it is usually both coarse and strong. Clearly, it is not a drink for the weak of heart (or liver).

Arrowhead

An aquatic plant (*Sagittaria* spp., especially *Sagittaria latifolia*) with roots that can be cooked like potatoes or dried for flour. They were much used by Native Americans, and related species are found in Chinese cooking. The tubers grow on roots at some distance from the parent plant, and one harvesting technique is to seek out caches stored away by muskrats. A drier way of acquiring them might be to check out an Oriental grocery, where they are sometimes available.

Arrowroot

A delicate starch derived from the roots of various plants, especially a tropical American herb (*Maranta arundinacea*), used as a thickener to replace flour or cornstarch or the like. It must be handled at a lower temperature than other starches, so don't let it boil. Use half the quantity you would add if you were using flour. Arrowroot is particularly useful for thickening clear liquids as it will not cloud up.

Arrowtooth Flounder

A large West Coast FLATFISH.

Arroz con Pollo
A Spanish dish, literally rice with chicken, or, as Anglos would say it, chicken with rice. It is generally augmented with green pepper and onion and tomato, sometimes capers and green peas, flavored with saffron, and moistened with white wine.

Artichoke
A thistle (*Cynara scolymus*), also called *French*, *crown*, and, on account of its globular shape, *globe artichoke*. It is not to be confused with the JERUSALEM ARTICHOKE or the CHINESE ARTICHOKE.

The artichoke has been cultivated for so long that we are not certain whether it is native to Europe or North Africa or both. Today, it is widely grown around the Mediterranean and in California. The usually fist-sized buds have slightly pointed, sharp-tipped leaves growing up around a head crowned by—at least as the bud matures—an inedible fibrous mass or *choke*. The leaves of the cooked artichoke are removed, and the fleshy ends scraped with the teeth. The choke then is removed and discarded, and the heart and bottom then eaten whole or stuffed.

Artichokes are most frequently boiled (vigorously, and with the lid *off* to avoid the development of a bitter flavor) and served with hollandaise sauce or butter and lemon juice. Some of the small ones are sometimes tender enough to eat whole— just trim the tops of the leaves to get rid of the tough parts and make sure you have artichokes with chokes so immature that they pose no problem in eating. These small artichokes can also be deep-fried. This treatment is adapted from the French and Italian techniques used for the violet Naples artichokes and for the tender French ones not readily available in the Americas. No matter how they are to be cooked, as soon as they are cut into, they will discolor unless dropped immediately into ACIDULATED WATER. The very tiniest artichokes in Italy are preserved and sold as hors d'oeuvres under the name *carciofini*.

You can get artichokes any time of the year, but they will be at their best, most plentiful, and (except when on special) cheapest in the late spring. Make sure the heads are firm and tight. If you must buy them in advance, keep them refrigerated in a plastic bag. Or cook them and store (refrigerated) in a covered container.

Artichoke Hearts
The defuzzed central core only—or sometimes these and the bottoms—of the ARTICHOKE. Artichoke hearts can be cooked and served as a vegetable, or marinated and used in or as a salad.

Arugula
Also known as *rugala*, *rucola*, and sometimes *rocket*. A tangy, mustardy salad green (*Eruca sativa* of the mustard family) much used in southern Europe and, until recently, found in North America almost exclusively in Italian neighborhoods. It can be a bit strong to be used by itself, but if added to other greens it can perk up a salad

immeasurably. Buy it just before you use it and wash it thoroughly. If you must keep it overnight, wrap it well in plastic and refrigerate it.

Asadero

A Mexican whole-milk CHEESE. The curd is cut, heated, and then pounded or kneaded and formed into loaves that vary from 8 ounces to 11 pounds. The name means "fit for roasting," indicating that it melts gracefully when heated.

Asafetida

A gum resin obtained from a plant (*Ferula* spp.) and used in Indian cooking for sautéing some vegetables. It can be found powdered or in lumps. Its taste is said to be strong (as is its smell) and to some people unpleasant, which is why most Indian cookbooks that call for it at all suggest that it can be left out.

Asiago

An Italian hard or grating CHEESE made originally from sheep's milk, but now more usually from cow's milk as is the North American version sold under the same name. When young and still soft, it makes an appealing table cheese.

Asian Pear

Several species of PEAR (*Pyrus* spp.) introduced into North America in the 1800s, but not widely marketed until the mid-20th century.

Asin

A mild and buttery Italian CHEESE made from cow's milk that has been allowed to curdle or sour. It comes in cylinders about 8 inches wide by 6 inches high and weighs in at about 14 pounds.

Asparagus

The succulent thin stalks (*Asparagus officinalis*) that signify spring. The stalks may be green or white (the white having been covered, sometimes with a mound of earth, to keep the sun from greening them), and there is an Italian variety with purple tips. Foragers have reported tasty wild asparagus, but it is thought to be escaped from abandoned farms and gardens, rather than being native.

Asparagus is first and foremost a spring phenomenon, and when encountered at other times of the year will be expensive in the extreme. Some stalks are thin and strawlike, others quite thick. Either can be good. Just make sure that the stalks have the full fresh greenness of the season, the tips are compact and closed, and there is no "woodiness" to them. Try to cook them the same day you buy them. (Otherwise keep them chilled in your vegetable drawer or wrapped in wet paper towels or plastic as they tend to dry out quickly.)

Various ways of cooking asparagus have been advocated here and there, including binding a bunch with a rubber band, setting it upright in the bottom of a double boiler with an inch or so of lightly salted water, covering it with the inverted top part of the double boiler, and letting it steam until just tender. (Special asparagus steamers are available to accomplish this if you have the storage space.) An alternate way is to cook it on its side in simmering, lightly salted water in a large frying pan. In any event, it is not recommended that you let it overcook.

Some cooks scrape the stems with a vegetable peeler, which makes a certain amount of sense especially if you are serving it to people who themselves have enough sense to hoist it in their fingers and eat the whole thing—or at least down to the point where the base begins to get stringy. Cold asparagus makes a splendid salad by itself, or it can be a revelation used in a cream of asparagus soup.

Aspartame
A proprietary artificial sweetener marketed as NutraSweet and Equal and used to replace saccharin or sugar. It has about the same amount of calories as sugar, but, as it is almost 200 times sweeter, it is used in much smaller quantity. Unlike saccharin, it tastes pretty much like sugar. Like saccharin, its safety is in considerable dispute.

Aspic
A meat jelly or gelatin (although it can be made with fish or vegetable stock as well) with which foods to be served cold are covered or glazed. It can also be flavored and served as is, as with tomato aspic.

Assam
A region of northeast India and Pakistan renowned for its TEA.

Asti
A wine center in the northern Italian area of Piedmont, known for its slightly sweet sparkling wines sold as Asti Spumante.

Atemoya
A tropical and semitropical fruit available in the late fall that is a cross between the CHERIMOYA (*Annona cherimola*) and the SWEETSOP (*Annona squamosa*). Light green on the outside, it has a pulpy white inside punctuated with a few scattered seeds. It has a light, creamy taste appropriate for eating right from the rind or using in fruit salads or compotes containing other, not too aggressively flavored, fruit.

Buy them when they are green and tender with no cracks or splits and eat them before they get too soft. As with other tropical fruit, such as bananas, atemoyas are best kept away from the refrigerator unless they are fully ripe.

Aubergine
A French (and British) term for EGGPLANT.

Auroch
A European bison or BUFFALO.

Auslese

A German term designating a wine made from selected bunches of grapes. If those grapes were individually culled from their bunches, the term would be BEEREN-AUSLESE, and if taken from specially selected overripe (and therefore sweeter) grapes, the label would read TROCKENBEERENAUSLESE. As the designation gets longer, the price gets higher.

Avgolemono

A Greek egg-and-lemon soup with rice. It can also be a sauce, in which case the rice is omitted.

Avocado

A plant (*Persea americana*) we received from the Aztecs but that has now migrated throughout the tropical world and into countless nontropical homes where people try—some actually with success—to make houseplants of them. At one time it was also known as *alligator pear*, from the tough, green, wrinkled skin of one widespread variety.

There are several different types of avocado, ranging in size from large eggs to near grapefruit. They include the Guatemalan variety, an early winter and spring spherical fruit with either a smooth green skin or a pebbly dark thick skin; the Mexican variety, which ripens in late spring and early fall, producing a slender, green, smooth, pear-shaped fruit; and the West Indian type, a late summer to early winter, dark-green variety with a leathery skin. They all share pretty much the same characteristics, however, and all are at their most buyable when their skins are uniform in thickness and color and have no blotches, spots, cracks, or dark indentations. To check for ripeness, hold the whole avocado in the palm of your hand and squeeze *gently*. If the whole fruit gives slightly, it is ready or nearly so. If it is hard, it is just not ready. Squeezing any other way is apt to induce bad spots in the fruit.

If you're planning to use your avocado immediately, choose one with a little give to it; otherwise, choose a hard one and keep it in a warm place until it ripens. Or put it in a paper bag or wrap it in foil until it softens. A ripe avocado can be kept briefly in the refrigerator, but refrigerating does an unripe one no good at all.

Avocados have a wonderfully buttery flesh that goes well in salads, make a fine GUACAMOLE, can be converted into soup, and, when the pits are removed, make a superb base for anything you want to stuff into them, although shellfish may just lead that particular parade. (For stuffing, the large varieties are preferable, as the smaller ones have smaller pits and thereby less space for your stuffing.)

Avocado bruises and discolors easily, so as soon as you have opened one up, squirt some lemon juice on it or rub it with the cut side of a lemon. Leaving the pit in place until the last minute also helps avoid discoloration, but not by much.

Azafran

A Spanish name for SAFFRON, but in North America it often refers to so-called Mexican saffron. Although Mexican saffron threads resemble the real thing in color and shape, the resemblance pretty much stops there. It is supplied not by the saffron plant, but by the SAFFLOWER, and is nowhere near as pungent in taste. It is, however, perfectly satisfactory if all you want is color.

Azarole

Also called *Neapolitan medlar* and *Spanish pine*. A Mediterranean tree (*Crataegus azarolus*) giving a sharpish, red-fleshed fruit something like a crab apple. It is used in preserves and marmalade.

Baba

A French cake impregnated with a liquor (such as rum, to make *baba au rhum*) or a LIQUEUR (such as KIRSCH).

Baba Ghanouj

Also *eggplant caviar*. A creamy, Oriental dip of pureed roasted eggplant mixed with garlic, lemon juice, olive oil, and TAHINI and garnished with parsley and sometimes black olives or tomatoes.

Baby Beef

Also called *pony beef*. A somewhat unhelpful term for a cut of BEEF you are not likely to see or to like much if you do see it. It is beef after the VEAL stage, but which is not yet matured into true beef—say three or four months to a year or so. It is meat that has lost the delicacy of veal but has not yet developed the robust flavor of beef. All in all, it tends to be stringy, tasteless, and tough—everything you don't want beef to be. Even so, a good measure of what we see as veal is indeed baby beef.

Baby Bel

A French CHEESE along the lines of BONBEL.

Bachelor's Button

See CORNFLOWER.

Backsteiner

A German CHEESE made from partly skimmed milk, shaped into bricks, and resembling LIMBURGER in taste.

Bacon

Cured and smoked meat from the flank portions of the pig. Bacon can be broiled, baked, or crisped in a dry frying pan; used to BARD lean roasts; or added to stews—such as COQ AU VIN—to increase viscosity and taste. Bacon is available sliced or in the slab for you to slice yourself (or sometimes as sliced slab bacon, giving you the best or worst of both). Different kinds of cures are marketed, and a good country-cured bacon may cost a bit more, but if not squandered on BLTs can be well worth the cost.

Bagel

A Jewish, doughnut-shaped roll traditionally smeared with cream cheese and perhaps embellished with lox or smoked SALMON. To give them their chewy but moist interior and crusty—even hard—exterior, bagels are boiled briefly before being baked. Some commercial bagels belie their heritage and have a tenderness that is appropriate for, say, Parker House rolls—another example, perhaps, of our desire for "authentic" food that tastes just like everything else.

Bagna Cauda

Also *bagna calda*. A northern Italian sauce of anchovies prepared in garlic-flavored oil and butter. The trick is to "melt" the anchovies without browning the garlic. The sauce is used as a hot dip for raw vegetables, especially CARDOON, but otherwise whatever is available—artichokes, carrots, celery, fennel—you name it. In some areas, white truffles may be added to the sauce.

Bagnes

A firm Swiss cow's-milk CHEESE suitable for making RACLETTE.

Bain Marie

A French utensil, often called a *water bath*, something like a DOUBLE BOILER, only not quite. It consists of a traylike device into which you put hot or simmering water and then one or more thin cylindrical pots. Some delicate concoction—a custard or a sauce, for example—goes into the pot, the pot goes into the bain marie, and everything stays warm or cooks without an excess of heat that might ruin the whole thing. You can fake a bain marie by using a roasting pan, so long as the water doesn't come so far up the sides of your pot that it spills into it. Or for a single small pot, try a CHAFING DISH.

Bake

To cook with dry heat in an enclosed space such as an OVEN. When applied to meat and poultry, the preferred term is ROAST, but the principle is the same. The word has also been extended to certain other uses. If you heat a number of large stones in a pit, lay wet seaweed over them, throw in clams and lobsters and corn and other good things, cover it all with canvas, and let it cook, purists say you are not baking but steaming. Purists or no, what you have is a CLAMBAKE.

Bake Blind

To bake—or partially bake—an unfilled piecrust. The crust will attempt to rise or dimple in the process. This is countered by making holes in it with a fork and weighing it down with dried beans or rice (reusable for this purpose but not much else). Foil or an extra pie plate on top of foil may also be used. The crust is then ready to receive a filling that needs little or no cooking.

Baked Alaska

A solid brick of ice cream placed on a bed of sponge or pound cake, topped with a meringue and perhaps some confectioners' sugar, and placed in a very hot (450°–500°F) oven just long enough to brown the meringue without melting the ice cream (about four minutes). A showy and satisfying dessert that looks far more difficult to make than it is. It can be made even more impressive by placing several empty eggshell halves in the meringue and, after taking it out of the oven, filling them with warmed brandy, setting the brandy alight, and serving the dish flambé.

Baked Beans

At one time almost the official dish of New England, at least on Saturday night. That's what you had for supper. The dish consists of dried beans soaked and simmered and placed in a special slope-shouldered bean pot with a piece of salt pork, brown sugar, and molasses, covered with water, and cooked throughout the day in a slow oven. It is traditionally served with BOSTON BROWN BREAD.

Bakers' Cheese

A CHEESE made from skimmed cow's milk and used to make commercial cheesecake and similar delights.

Baking Powder

A standard agent for making pastries and breads rise. It is useful for such items as, well, baking powder biscuits. What we buy today is called "double-acting" because it delivers part of its wallop immediately and then completes its one-two punch later on. A single-acting powder works right away and all at once, so that you almost have to add the powder with one hand and pop the whole thing in the oven with the other, or risk losing some of the powder's potency.

If you want to try a single-acting powder for yourself, mix two parts cream of tartar with one part baking soda and use double the amount of double-acting baking powder called for in your recipe. Add it just before you put your creation in the oven. Don't try to make it up in large batches—it doesn't keep (no baking powder keeps terribly well), and cream of tartar is expensive.

Baking Sheet

Another name for the ubiquitous COOKIE SHEET.

Baking Soda

Nothing more than good old household bicarbonate of soda, also called *sodium bicarbonate* ($NaHCO_3$). When combined with something acid—buttermilk, for example—it helps make batter rise. You will sometimes see suggestions that a little baking soda added to the cooking water will keep beans or peas bright green. Indeed this is so, but as the baking soda also removes vitamins, such a practice is now thought to be not so much a bad idea as a terrible one.

Baking Stone

A special flat stone that fits into the oven and on which bread dough is placed for baking. Like a quarry tile, it provides more reflective heat than a regular oven and more closely approximates the environment of a professional bakery oven. A baking stone (or a tile, for that matter) is set on the floor of a cold oven and heated up with the oven before the bread dough is put in place.

Baklava

An incredibly sweet Turkish pastry typically made with layers of PHYLLO dough, butter, and finely ground walnuts (or walnuts and almonds). It is baked in a slow oven and then drenched in a syrup of water and sugar (or honey, or both), dashed with lemon juice, and cut into diamond shapes and served at room temperature. Baklavas can also be made with other kinds of fillings.

Baldwin

A late red juicy eating APPLE.

Balm

An herb (*Melissa officinalis*) of the mint family, native to Europe but introduced to North America, where it has jumped the boundaries of regular gardens and gone wild. Because of the lemony scent of its leaves, it is also known as *lemon balm* and, because of its attraction for bees, as *melissa* (from the Latin word for honey). Balm is used in soups, sauces, and cold drinks such as iced tea as well as meat, fish, and poultry dishes.

Balsamic Vinegar

A specially made Italian VINEGAR.

Balsam Pear

See BITTER MELON.

Bamboo Shoots

The tender ends of various species of the bamboo tribe (Bambuseae), much used in Chinese cooking to give sweetness and crunch to stir-fried dishes and soups. Bamboo shoots (salted or unsalted—spring for the unsalted) come canned and are best used right away as they become tasteless and—even worse—limp if kept around very long after the can is opened (although they will keep for a while if you store them refrigerated in water and change the water frequently). They can also be found fresh (they must be parboiled or they will be toxic) in Chinese groceries and sometimes pickled. Rinse the latter before you use them. Certain bamboo leaves are also used in Oriental cooking as a wrapping for food that is to be grilled or steamed.

Banana

A long, narrow tropical fruit with a peel that encases a soft, pulpy center. Hindu legend has it that the banana (*Musa paradisiaca*), not the apple, was the forbidden fruit of Paradise, and that Adam and Eve covered their nakedness with banana leaves, which are probably a sight more seemly than mere fig leaves. The mainstays of banana growing today are Central and South America and, of the 30 or so varieties identified, only a very few are sent north. We see mostly the long yellow dessert banana and sometimes the shorter red ones. Despite variations in taste, the two can be treated pretty much the same.

Bananas for the most part are eaten fresh. Whether red or yellow, they are best when they have a full, consistent color somewhat flecked with brown—but not black—specks. The specks mean that the fruit is fully ripe and ready to eat (immature bananas do not share the high digestibility of ripe ones). Even if the banana looks a little brownish, very gently press it—if it isn't mushy, it may well be at the peak of its succulence. Black spots mean the banana has gone by and can be passed over.

Bananas can, however, be cooked, and not just slathered with ice cream, hot fudge sauce, nuts, and sprinkles and transformed into a banana split—excellent though that may be. There are other, less caloric ways of facing bananas. You can slice them thin and dry the chips for a nutritious, lightweight trail food. You can bake them—peel them, brush them with melted butter, sprinkle them with a little sugar, and place them in a buttered baking dish in a 350°F oven for 15–20 minutes. You can sauté them—peel them, brush them with lemon juice, roll them in crushed cornflakes, and cook them in butter. You can set them on fire—peel and poach them in vanilla-flavored syrup, then moisten them well with warmed brandy (or rum or other ardent spirit), light it all, and serve the dish flaming. They can be sliced into rounds and deep-fried as fritters; they can be coated with melted butter and grilled; they can be transformed into banana cream pie—these are just a few ways to use bananas other than simply peeling them and waiting for someone to upend himself on the peel.

The banana is related to the PLANTAIN but, unlike it, does not have to be cooked to be digestible. If you're going to keep bananas around for any length of time, store them at room temperature.

Banana Flower

The purple pointed heads of the maturing BANANA used in Southeast Asia as a vegetable and a garnish.

Banana Squash

A variety of SQUASH.

Banbury

1. A spicy (ginger, nutmeg) little pastry with candied fruit peel and dried fruit (especially currants or raisins) named for the small central English city where it first made its appearance.

2. A cheddarlike CHEESE, said to have been soft and rich, highly appreciated from the 17th until the 19th century, but seemingly no longer produced.

B&B

An after-dinner liqueur composed of equal parts of BRANDY and BENEDICTINE.

Banger

An English pork-and-breadcrumb sausage often served with mashed potatoes and thereby known as "bangers and mash."

Banneton

A small basket used for letting bread dough rise. When risen, the dough is turned out on a baking sheet and placed in the oven. When it emerges from the oven the surface of the baked bread will display the pattern of the basket.

Bannock

A large, round, flat unleavened bread of Scotland and England. It is made of oatmeal, wheat, or barley and is generally cooked on a griddle.

Banon

A French goat's-milk CHEESE that is cured in chestnut leaves, soaked in MARC, and set forth as small wrapped cylinders.

Bantam

A small domestic fowl originally from an area of western Java of the same name, but the term now refers to any diminutive fowl. The taste is similar to regular chicken, but more delicate, and the eggs—when you can find them—are about half the size of a standard chicken egg.

Baps

A Scottish buttermilk roll served at breakfast.

Barbados Cherry

See ACEROLA.

Barbaresco

A hearty dry red Italian table wine from the Piedmont region.

Barbecue

Originally an extravaganza at which an entire animal was spit-roasted out-of-doors; now almost anything—including an entire animal—cooked over a grill, preferably out-of-doors, with or without a spit.

Barbecue Sauce

A spicy, tomato-based sauce used for basting game or other meat or poultry that is being barbecued.

Barbe de Capucin

The French name for BELGIAN ENDIVE.

Barbera

A grapevine (*Vitis vinifera*) native to Italy's Piedmont region but widely planted elsewhere, as in California. It produces a full-bodied dry red table wine.

Barberry

A shrub of various species, especially the American or Allegheny barberry (*Berberis canadensis*) and common barberry (*Berberis vulgaris*), that grows clusters of small red berries highly fancied by birds and admired as the makings of an extraordinarily pleasant, tart preserve. If the berries are somewhat old, add some crab apple or apple jelly to supply the PECTIN that the berries no longer have. In New England, barberries were often put in other preserves to add tartness, and syrup made from the berries was mixed with water to serve as a cooling drink. Barberries grow wild—even obtrusively so—in New England and elsewhere in the northeastern sections of North America. A related plant, the Oregon grape (*Mahonia aquifolium*), is prevalent in northwestern North America.

Bard

To tie a thin slice of pork fat or beef suet that has been pounded flat (or, sometimes, blanched salt pork or bacon) around a piece of lean meat, poultry, or game to lubricate it and enrich its flavor during cooking. The barding fat (except sometimes bacon) is cut off and discarded before the roast is served.

Bardolino

A light, dry red Italian table wine from the area around Verona.

Bar-le-Duc

A fine, but very expensive, French red currant jelly from the town of the same name in Lorraine. It is often used in pastries or as a dessert topping.

Barley

One of the oldest known cereal grasses (*Hordeum vulgare*), grown largely for brewing BEER. It also contributes to WHISKEY and malt VINEGAR and is useful for soups such as SCOTCH BROTH. Barley comes in several forms including pot (or husked) barley with its outer layer removed, but its most common market form is pearled, in which the grains have been husked, polished, and rounded (and in the process stripped of much of their protein). It usually must be simmered for upward of half an hour before it can be used. Whole barley is usually available only in health food stores as are barley groats and barley flour (which is said to lend excellence to some kinds of cookies). Barley flour is also sometimes available as "patent," in which case it has been thoroughly milled for certain dietetic purposes. If you can find unhusked barley, you can make your own barley MALT. Sprout the unhusked kernels, dry the sprouts, grind them fine, and you have barley malt.

Barley Sugar

A mostly British confection of sugar boiled in barley water (barley ground and then simmered in water with a little salt) until hard and crisp. It was used as a digestive aid.

Barm

The yeast that forms on fermenting malt liquors, also known as *brewer's yeast*. It is used these days not for baking, but as a vitamin-rich food supplement.

Barm Brack

A traditional Irish yeast-risen bread flavored with candied fruit peel, raisins, and spices.

Barolo

A superior dry red table wine from Italy's Piedmont area.

Baron

A saddle of lamb or mutton, or a double sirloin of beef still joined at the backbone.

Baronet

A mild, buttery American cow's-milk CHEESE reminiscent of BEL PAESE.

Barquette

A small TARTLET pan in the shape of a flat-bottomed, double-ended boat; it may be fluted or plain. Barquette pastries are customarily filled with some savory mixture of cheese or chicken or shellfish or a vegetable (especially mushrooms) but can be adapted to a dessert by using a sweet filling.

Barracuda

A medium-sized game fish of warm, temperate seas. The great barracuda (*Sphyraena barracuda*) is not—except perhaps in extremity—used as food. Although it normally would make good eating, its flesh becomes toxic to humans if it contains the *ciguatera* toxin. Its more tropical relative, the guaguanche (*Sphyraena guachancho*), is highly thought of as a food fish in the West Indies, and a European relative (*Sphyraena sphyraena*) is also eaten as are the somewhat smaller species of the Pacific (especially *Sphyraena argentea*). Barracuda lends itself especially to grilling over charcoal or to baking, broiling, or smoking.

Barred Sea Bass
A saltwater BASS of the Pacific.

Barsac
A superb, naturally sweet French white wine from the region of BORDEAUX.

Bartlett
The familiar yellow PEAR of our markets. In Europe, it is known as the *Williams pear*.

Basil
An herb (*Ocimum basilicum*) native to India but associated today especially with French, Greek, and Italian food. It is a tasty and aromatic addition to vegetables, especially garlic and tomatoes, and is of great assistance to many casseroles and seafood dishes. Basil is also the herb behind PESTO, a robust sauce of Mediterranean Italy and the south of France. Basil grows well in kitchen gardens and window boxes, but get the green, not the purple, variety. It may not look as snappy, but it will have more taste.

Basmati
A variety of RICE originating in the Indian subcontinent in what is now Bangladesh.

Bass
The name for a number of fresh and saltwater fish.

> *Freshwater bass.* They come in several varieties and are all excellent panfish— and the easiest way to cook them is at streamside or along the bass lake; otherwise, they are good broiled or baked. In one category are:
>
> > • *Largemouth bass* (*Micropterus salmoides*). A fish found throughout the United States and through Mexico into Central America in ponds, lakes, and the like.
> > • *Smallmouth bass* (*Micropterus dolommieui*). A fighting gamefish now found virtually everywhere on the continent where the water is clear and the bottom rocky.
> > • *Spotted bass* (*Micropterus punctulatus*). A fish of the southern United States that is related, and similar in appearance, to the largemouth bass. It is found in sluggish water and deep ponds.
>
> In another category of freshwater bass are:
>
> > • *White bass* (*Morone chrysops*). A silvery fish that may reach three pounds. It is found pretty much throughout the United States, now that it has been

successfully introduced in areas where it was not native, but in numbers that vary from year to year.

- *White perch* (*Morone americana*). An olive-backed fish with silvery sides, considered by many to be about as good a panfish as you can find anywhere.
- *Yellow bass* (*Morone mississippiensis*). Similar to the white perch, the yellow bass is found generally in the central segment of North America from the Gulf of Mexico to the Canadian border.

Saltwater bass. There are quite a few of them, but of them all, the striped bass is king. It can be prepared by any method appropriate to fish and will reward you no matter how it is cooked. Other bass are not quite so versatile but are nonetheless rewarding in their own right.

- *Black sea bass* (*Centropristes striata*). A small—not much more than five pounds—delicate and tasty fish sold as whole fish, fillets, or steaks. A Chinese technique is to take the whole fish, make several slashes along the side, and then steam it with ginger, scallions, soy sauce, and tofu. Otherwise, it is recommended for baking and frying.
- *Barred sand bass* (*Paralabrax nebulifer*). A Pacific bottom-dwelling fish running up to about two feet in length.
- *Giant sea bass* (*Stereolepis gigas*). As the name implies, a whopper, running up to seven feet in length and 500 pounds in weight.
- *Kelp bass* (*Paralabrax clathratus*). An abundant Pacific gamefish of up to two feet in length, found especially, as the name implies, in beds of kelp.
- *Red grouper* (*Enpiephelus morio*). A fish of tropical and semitropical waters with lean, moist meat susceptible to any preparation suitable for other marine bass.
- *Sea bass* (*Dicentrarchus labrax*). The European (both Mediterranean and Atlantic) sea bass. Highly prized in its home waters, but deemed second to the black sea bass by some critics. In France, it is known as *loup de mer* and as *bar*.
- *Striped bass* (*Morone saxatilis*). One of the prime saltwater gamefish originally of eastern North America but introduced successfully to the Pacific as well (and to landlocked lakes), where it is a gamefish and not available commercially. Because of pollution and destruction of its habitat, it is rigidly controlled in many places, in hopes it will make a comeback. Unfortunately, stripers tend to inhabit areas where we choose to deposit some of the worst of our waste products—PCBs (a suspected cancer-causing chemical waste product) and the like—which has caused some authorities to suggest that we curtail our intake of these fish and others to suggest that we don't eat them at all. Consult your local wildlife and conservation people before taking your catch home.

• *White sea bass* (*Atractoscion nobilis*). Not a bass at all, but a croaker, with lean, firm, unassertive flesh suitable for broiling, grilling (if thick enough), poaching, or steaming.

Bassine

Either of two French cooking utensils, both extremely light and deep. One is flat-bottomed and used for deep-frying; the other is hemispherical and used for beating eggs and the like.

Baste

To pour a liquid over whatever it is you are roasting or broiling in order to moisten it and add flavor. The liquid can range from pan juices to melted butter, wine, fruit juices, or special elaborate basting concoctions, often whatever it was you marinated your food in beforehand.

Batter

1. The raw material of breads and pastries (and pancakes and waffles) once combined, consisting of flour and a liquid and whatever else your recipe has in mind. We used to "batter" such mixtures but now we only BEAT them. The process is the same—only the word has changed. A batter is thin enough to pour or scoop up and drop by the spoonful.

2. A coating, usually of breadcrumbs, cornmeal, flour, or something similar, to encase foods (especially chicken) that are to be deep-fried or otherwise cooked.

Batter Bread

A quick bread made without kneading—you beat it instead. Batter breads are coarser in texture and less certain of shape than kneaded breads, but they can be completed in two hours or less. In making them, you either increase the yeast or decrease the flour. Batter breads toast especially well.

Batterie de Cuisine

A French term for kitchen equipment: pots and pans, spoons and forks, whisks and bowls—all the toys that make cooking possible.

Bauerwurst

A coarsely textured, highly seasoned German sausage that can be sautéed or steamed.

Bavarian Cream

A dessert starting with a light custard sauce into which gelatin, lightly whipped cream, a flavoring (fruit of some sort is traditional), and sometimes additional egg yolks are folded before it is poured into a mold and chilled.

Baveuse

A French word used to describe an omelet that is still somewhat runny.

Bayberry

A small shrub (*Myrica pensylvanica* and *Myrica cerifera*) notable mainly for its small, grayish, waxy berries, which can be melted down into wax and molded into candles (they gutter themselves out almost completely, leave little if any drippings, and give off a soothing fragrance as they burn). The leaves of the bayberry and its relatives can be picked, dried, and used like a not-so-pungent BAY LEAF to season stews and the like.

Bay Leaf

The laurel leaf of the European tree (*Laurus nobilis*), but not of the American laurel. Its somewhat strong effect is all but indispensable for many cooking purposes, including as an ingredient of BOUQUET GARNI and in stews, soups, and sauces as well as stuffings. Cookbooks generally advise using it sparingly—too much so in the opinion of many, although in excess it can add bitterness to your dish.

Beach Plum

An eccentric relative of the PLUM (*Prunus maritima*). This one flourishes only in such seemingly infertile areas as sand dunes, especially from New Brunswick to Virginia. It produces fruit that can be red or purple or even yellowish and can be sweet and enticing or virtually inedible. It forms the basis of a clear tart jelly that goes well with pork, duck, or venison.

Bean

Do people read *Mr. Popper's Penguins* any more? If they do, they may recall how the family funds are dramatically depleted every time Mr. Popper has to shell out money for his improbable birds, causing Mrs. Popper to sigh and go to the closet for yet another can of beans. Beans, of course; "the poor man's meat." Beans have been feeding humankind economically for millennia, playing a role in human nutrition second perhaps only to cereal grains. One indication of the importance of beans is the way the nobility of ancient Rome took their family names from them—the Fabius clan from the faba or fava bean, for example, and Cicero from the chickpea (*cicer* in Latin).

One virtue of the bean plant is that it collects nitrogen, a building block of protein, and generously passes it along to those who eat it or to the soil into which it is plowed back. Bean protein in and of itself is not quite enough for adequate human nutrition, so people the world over have learned how to augment it—rice and beans, pasta and beans, wheat flour and beans (otherwise known as the Indian staple of CHAPATI and chickpeas) all bring the protein to levels able to maintain life and health.

Beans, of course, are available fresh, canned, frozen, and dried. Great steps have been taken in the way dried beans are presented to us. They still benefit from an overnight soaking in plenty of water (you can save the water to cook the beans in later or discard it as a stab at reducing the potential of flatulence). Some cooks still like to simmer beans until just tender—until you can blow the skin off one—before proceeding to the real cooking. Many others feel that the preliminary soaking is enough, that the additional precooking tends to make them mushy. If you're cooking beans for a cold salad, a pressure cooker combines both steps and accomplishes them in less than a half hour (just make sure you add a little salad oil to the water in your pressure cooker to calm the beans and keep them from foaming over). If the overnight soaking time disturbs you and you want to hurry things along a bit, take a huge pot and add two to three cups of water for each cup of beans, bring it all to a boil, let it boil two minutes, and then take the whole thing off the heat and let it stand, covered, for one to two hours.

Fresh beans are available in supermarkets year-round but are never so good as the ones that come from your own or a neighboring garden or farm stand. Indeed, in the off-season the frozen kind are often tastier and sometimes cheaper than what you find on the fresh counter—all in all a better deal.

Some of the beans you are likely to encounter include:

Adzuki bean (*Phaseolus angularis*). A small, red Oriental bean. It has a somewhat gritty consistency and is eaten boiled or sometimes ground into a sweetened paste for use in jellies and pastries.

Broad or *fava bean* (*Vicia faba*). A large white bean also called *horse bean* or *field bean*, somewhat similar to the lima bean but coarser, with an outer skin that is indigestible (except on young, fresh beans) and must be removed (blanching does the trick) before the rest of the bean is usable. It is also available dried and shelled.

Chickpea (*Cicer arietinum*). Usually available dried, the CHICKPEA is an important source of protein and even a staple of the diet for much of the world. It is beginning to find favor in North America, probably due to the growing influence of Hispanic cooking.

Common bean (*Phaseolus vulgaris*). This bean shows up in a whole panoply of varieties, some of which you may come across as:

- *Cannellini.* A large imported white kidney bean.
- *Chili bean.* A dark red bean used in chile con carne and other Mexican and Southwestern specialties.
- *Cranberry bean.* An attractively speckled pink bean with an inedible pod, used in soups, stews, and, when young, as a side dish.
- *Flageolet.* A small, delicate dried bean of France often served with lamb and used in CASSOULET. If it is not available, try navy or pea beans.

- *Great northern.* A mild white bean used often for baked beans.
- *Haricot.* French name for any bean. A *haricot vert* is green, a *haricot rouge* is red, and a *haricot blanc* is white. Haricots may be fresh or dried.
- *Kidney bean.* A large, deep red, kidney-shaped bean. It lends itself well to salads (add the dressing to the still-hot, drained beans) with basil, slices of red onion, and a vinaigrette dressing.
- *Marrow bean.* The largest of the round white beans.
- *Navy bean.* Larger than a pea bean and smaller than a great northern, it is a workhorse of the bean family for such dishes as baked beans, especially the canned variety.
- *Pea bean.* The smallest of the American white beans.
- *Pinto.* A pale pink bean with brown spots, much used in Southwestern cookery.
- *Snap bean.* The most common market bean, often referred to as a string bean (see below). A snap bean gets its name from its crispness when fresh. Test this by snapping one in half. If it snaps clean and resiliently instead of presenting a limp flaccidity, it is fresh and prime for eating. Snap beans can be green or yellow and are usually most flavorsomely cooked by steaming in just a very little water and then by dressing with butter or oil.
- *String bean.* The common, but dated, name for a snap bean. Previously, such beans had a stringy closure to the pod that ran down one side and had to be removed to make the bean palatable. You removed it by the simple but tiresome procedure of grasping the stem and pulling it down the side of the bean, repeating the process for each bean. Plant geneticists have long since bred this aspect out of the beans.
- *Turtle bean.* The black bean as used in black bean soup, the Cuban *Moros y Christianos* ("Moors and Christians," or black beans and rice), and the Brazilian national dish, FEIJOADA. It is earthy and flavorful and somewhat more assertive than other beans.
- *Wax bean.* The common name for the *yellow snap bean.*

Cowpea (*Vigna sinensis*). Also called the *black-eyed pea.* Despite its name it is more closely related to the bean than to the pea (although botanically all beans are a part of the family Leguminosae, the pea, or pulse, family).

Hyacinth bean (*Dolichos lablab*). Also called *lablab.* An Indian bean sometimes eaten fresh as a snap bean but more likely dried.

Lima bean (*Phaseolus lunatus* var. *macrocarpus*). Also called *butter bean.* A delicate white bean native to South America that comes in two sizes, the large, mealy forkhook and the smaller baby lima. It is available canned, dried, fresh, or frozen. Limas usually need something additional (some sort of cream sauce, bacon, or a ham hock, for example) to keep them from being uninteresting and bland.

Mung bean (*Phaseolus aureus*). A small (usually) green bean used mostly as a bean SPROUT, but also as the base for cellophane noodles. In the Philippines it is the basis for a nourishing soup and in India is ground into flour.

Pole bean (*Phaseolus coccineus*). A large green bean that grows up a supporting pole. It is tender, cooks quickly, and may only be available to home gardeners or those who have access to a farm stand.

Scarlet runner bean (*Phaseolus coccineus* or *Phaseolus multiflorus*). A favorite of the British, this bean has a pleasingly mottled pink-and-black hue and a tendency to "run," which is to set new plants wherever branch and leaf come into contact with the ground. To avoid letting it run, it is usually cultivated on poles. Easily available to gardeners, it is less accessible to supermarket shoppers. It develops long, large pods that are best picked and eaten before gaining their full growth, at which point they can be on the tough side. Scarlet runner beans are treated in the kitchen in the same way as snap beans.

Soybean (*Glycine max*). An Oriental staple for centuries, the SOYBEAN has become internationalized and has an extraordinary role to play in the kitchen. Soybeans are mostly found dried, but fresh-picked young ones can also be excellent; try them cooked up like lima beans, especially with a cream dressing.

Yard-long bean (*Vigna inguiculata*). When allowed to reach full maturity it will more closely attain a foot and a half than a yard. The young, immature ones are used as snap beans, the older ones dried.

Bean Curd
See TOFU.

Bean Paste
See MISO.

Bean Sauce
A Chinese sauce of fermented black or brown beans mixed with flour, water, salt, and, in some cases, hot chilis, garlic, and star anise. It is salty and pungent (and when augmented with chilis, obviously, hot). It comes in jars and if refrigerated after opening will keep virtually forever.

Bean Sprouts
The SPROUTS of various beans used in Oriental cooking and increasingly as an integral part of Western diets as well.

Bear

The largest of the carnivores and legal game in some areas. Bear (*Ursus* spp.) is usually compared to pork and must be cooked with the same care in order to kill the trichina parasite that infests both animals.

Unless the bear is very old, all the meat is said to be good, but the paws are the greatest delicacy; in Germany the front paws were once reserved for the very rich. No wonder. They were first skinned, then washed, salted, and put down with a boiled vinegar marinade for a few days, then removed so the bottom of the crock in which they were aging could be lined with chopped bacon, ham, and vegetables. The paws were then replaced in the crock and covered with bacon, the marinade, and some bouillon. The paws simmered seven or eight hours (with more bouillon added when it got low) and finally were cooled in their juices. Now they were ready to be cooked! The technique was to drain them well, slice them into four pieces, sprinkle them with cayenne pepper, cover them with lard, bread them, and grill them gently for a good half hour. You can prepare the sauce to go with them in just about the same length of time.

Bearberry

Various red berries of several northern shrubs (*Arctostophylos* spp.). The berries are said to be dry and uninteresting, although a handful might dress up a mixture of stewed fruit. They have the reputation of being highly attractive to the eastern black bear.

Béarnaise

A splendidly caloric French sauce, originally devised to accompany meats (filet mignon, for example) but frequently seen also with eggs, fish, poultry, and vegetables. It is made by cooking down vinegar (some authorities permit white wine instead) with shallots and herbs (chervil is recommended as is tarragon) until there is almost nothing left of it, then delicately whisking in egg yolks and a goodly amount of butter. A well-made sauce will have the consistency of mayonnaise and a taste all its own.

Beat

To blend, mix, and generally get additional air into whatever you have at hand. A number of nifty gadgets exist that help the process along, ranging from the fork or spoon to the whisk and from the rotary eggbeater to electric mixers, blenders, and food processors. The beater will have an effect on whatever you are beating. If you are making a soufflé or a meringue and need a finely beaten mixture, use a rotary beater or a whisk with small wires. For less demanding subjects, a coarser whisk will do. With the electric appliances, fineness is more a matter of how much time you take for your beating.

Beaten Biscuit

An unleavened biscuit of the southern United States that has lard as its base. The ingredients are mixed together, then beaten (traditionally with a mallet), folded over, and rebeaten, the process continuing until the batter snaps and crackles (but does not pop). Rounds are then cut out of the batter, pricked with a fork, and baked until crisp.

Beaujolais

A light, dry, generally red (there is some white) table wine from southern BURGUNDY, distinguished for its fruity flavor.

Beaune

A city in the Burgundy region of France, famous for its dry red and white table wines and as the linchpin of the Burgundian wine-growing area known as the CÔTE DE BEAUNE.

Beaver

An aquatic rodent (*Castor canadensis* in North America) that makes those interesting dams across streams that can thoroughly bollix up the landscape downstream. While beavers were originally hunted for their fur, they also formed a good part of the diet of the voyageurs and frontiersmen. They are not much eaten today, but once cleaned (they have some glands that must be removed) and given a good soak, they are said to make a delectable roast. The tail is traditionally a delicacy. There is also a European beaver (*Castor fiber*), which is smaller and scarcer than its American cousin.

Béchamel

A basic French WHITE SAUCE composed of flour stirred into heated butter and then mixed with warm milk. You can ring all manner of changes on it, depending upon what you wish to add—cheese, egg yolks, spices, or whatever.

Bêche-de-Mer

Another name for the TREPANG or *sea slug*.

Bee Balm

See OSWEGO TEA.

Beech

An American (*Fagus grandiflora*) and European (*Fagus sylvatica*) nut-bearing tree. The small nuts, midway in taste between the chestnut and the hazelnut, can be on the puckery side and, if so, benefit from being roasted. Otherwise, they may be made into a nut butter. They also produce a superior oil. Wild creatures also relish beech-nuts, and years when the crop is abundant often coincide with years when venison is especially plump and tasty. Beech leaves soaked in gin and then cooked up with sugar, brandy, and flavorings have been the basis for a homemade cordial in parts of Britain.

Beef

The meat we get from grown cattle, as opposed to VEAL, which comes from the young. Beef is the chief source of protein in North America, to the despair of vegetarians, who constantly point out how much protein we feed to our livestock and how little we get back on this nutritional investment. (To produce one pound of beef it takes seven to eight pounds of grain plus hundreds of gallons of often-scarce water.)

In the United States, beef is government inspected and rated according to quality and yield. The quality is reflected in the stamp that goes on the carcass (it is usually trimmed off by the time the meat arrives at the retail counter) and is of immediate concern to the consumer. (The yield repays the efficient stockman and benefits the consumer farther down the line, if at all.) The grades of beef are prime, choice, select, standard, commercial, utility, cutter, and canner.

Prime is the beef sold by specialty butchers and first-rate restaurants. It has the greatest amount of and most consistent "marbling" (or distribution of fat); is taken from beef critters with the best configuration and the firmest, most robust meat and best-looking fat; and, because it is so desirable, fetches the highest price. That price is further elevated if the meat is allowed to hang and age, which improves it mightily but runs up storage fees. And as the beef reduces in bulk while aging, the price per pound is further increased.

The next grade is *choice*. It's a little leaner than prime but still has enough fat to permit some aging. However, it doesn't age with the same distinction as prime. The bulk of the better cuts you'll find in your average butcher shop or supermarket will be choice.

Select (formerly *good*) and *standard* come a little farther down the ladder. There's nothing wrong with them; indeed, the word *select* was chosen to persuade more people to select cuts with that label. Good was considered not quite good enough. These cuts have less fat than have either prime or choice, which may make them healthier for the confirmed beef eater. Because of this leanness, they may have a little less flavor, and they won't be so juicy or tender. But unless you buy all your beef at a premium or carriage-trade butcher, you'll almost certainly be familiar with them. These are the cuts that you are likely to find as "house brands" or "specials."

The chances of finding the final four grades in a retail market are slim indeed. Some of them are used for ground beef and most of the rest for sausages, cold cuts, and canned beef products, although some will surface as the ribs and steaks that are sold in cut-rate steakhouses. They are mentioned here only for completeness.

When a beef carcass is butchered, it is divided into sides, each of which is then subdivided into a hindquarter and a forequarter. The forequarter has the following cuts:

Chuck. Includes steaks (boneless or not), a goodly amount of pot roasts, stew meat, and ground beef.

Rib. Can be cut into steaks or rib roasts.

Short plate. Ground beef.

Foreshank. Ground beef, soup, or stew.

Brisket. Can be made into corned beef, cut up for stew, ground, or used as fresh brisket for pot roasts.

Among the cuts to be taken out of the hindquarter are:

Round. Steaks including the *top round, bottom round, eye of round,* and *sirloin tip* as well as assorted boneless steaks, roasts, stew meat, and ground beef.

Loin. Club, T-bone, porterhouse, and sirloin steaks can be cut from the loin. It can also be removed from the bone as for filet mignon or chateaubriand.

Flank. Mostly ground beef except for the flank steak, considered by some the choicest morsel of them all. Flank is also used for London broil.

The best beef will have a bright red color and nearly white fat. Some beef is marked "lean" and is supposed to have less fat, but standards seem to change as to what defines a "lean" piece of beef. There are countless ways of cooking beef. You can broil, grill, or sauté chops, ground beef, and steaks; you can braise or roast the larger cuts; and you can make all manner of stews with beef. Beef (unless you plan to freeze it) is best bought within a day or so of your anticipated cooking time, especially if you are dealing with ground beef.

Beefalo

A cross between a bison and a Hereford or Charolais beef animal, bred to produce meat with the leanness of bison (or BUFFALO) and the flavor of beef.

Beefsteak Fungus

A wild MUSHROOM.

Beef Stroganoff

A Russian dish of thin strips of beef browned quickly in butter; combined with browned, thinly sliced onions; and augmented with a suspicion of lemon juice, a little mustard, and some sour cream (or yogurt). Mushrooms may or may not be included. It is often served with noodles, mashed potatoes, or sometimes with rice.

Beef Tea

Another term for beef BROTH.

Beef Wellington

A showy dinner presentation consisting of a tenderloin of beef roasted to very rare, cooled, then wrapped in puff pastry to which some FOIE GRAS and DUXELLES may have been added, and returned to the oven until the pastry is browned and the beef reheated but not overcooked.

Beer

The fermented beverage of grain, primarily malted BARLEY, augmented with water, hops, yeast, and sugar, among other additions. It is made of totally different grains in various parts of the world. Millet is used in areas of Africa, for example, and the Japanese make SAKE out of rice. (Any number of folk "beers" have been fermented out of the bark or twigs or roots of such plants as birch and sassafras among others, but as they are not made from grain they are technically not true beers.)

Beer plays a minor but useful role in the kitchen—over and above its place in washing down such foods as chili, pizza, and curry. It is a basis for soup, makes a fine liquid for bread-making or batter for deep-frying, and is indispensable for certain stews—such as the Belgian dish CARBONNADE FLAMANDE.

Among the kinds of beer you are likely to meet are:

Ale. At one time (but not in living memory), a form of beer fermented quickly and without hops, but now simply a variation on a theme of beers. Some ales, such as Stock Ale, were brewed to be stronger than regular beer, but this is rarely so now.

Bock beer. A traditional German beer brewed in small quantities in March from a mixture of barley and wheat. It is sweeter than regular beer, darker in color, and higher in alcohol. Bock beer, formerly available for a limited time each year, is now available year-round in the United States.

Lager. From a German word meaning to lie or rest. Originally, lager beer laid at rest while it fermented slowly, resulting in a light, pleasant, highly carbonated beverage. Now it refers to any light-bodied beer.

Pilsner. A distinctive lager beer from the Bohemian city the Czechs call Plzeň and the Germans call Pilsen.

Porter. A lighter form of stout with a creamy foam.

Stout. A dark, heavy ale strongly flavored with hops, very malty, and slightly sweet.

Beerenauslese

A German term for wine made from grapes that have been individually picked from bunches left on the vine until fully ripe, or perhaps a little more than ripe.

Beet

A plant that comes in four forms:

Chard (*Beta vulgaris* var. *cicla*). Usually seen as Swiss chard (although there are others), a vegetable with large yellowish, green, or red-tinged leaves with prominent ribs. Not perhaps the tastiest of vegetables, it can be appealing when steamed like spinach. Look for firm, crisp leaves with no yellowing.

Garden beet (*Beta vulgaris* var. *crassa*). A red (although there are gold and white varieties, too) root vegetable with a leafy green top, both parts of which are edible. Beet greens are especially good early in the year when the greens are young and tender; the roots are good anytime. When the beets are very young and the roots small indeed (roughly the size of marbles), the roots and tops steamed together make a splendid combination. Larger beets are used for pickles or for BORSCHT or can be boiled or baked (a cookery book from an earlier day recommended that before baking they first be washed in "ordinary brandy"). Cold cooked (or grated raw) beets can make an attractive and tasty addition to summer salads. When cooking beets, keep them intact, cut off the tops an inch or two above the red bulb and don't scrub them too hard—otherwise they will bleed. The nonred varieties, of course, have the advantage of not bleeding at all, but then they don't look so cheerful, either. Moreover, to obtain them, you'll probably have to grow them yourself. When selecting garden beets, see that they are smooth and firm with a deep red color.

Mangel-wurzel (*Beta vulgaris* var. *macrorhiza*). Also called *mangold* and grown as cattle fodder, although it can also feed (hungry) people.

Sugar beet. A variant of the garden beet with long, white roots that produce a sugar virtually indistinguishable from cane sugar.

Beetroot
A British name for BEET.

Beignet
A French FRITTER, or almost anything dipped in flour and deep-fried (although some beignets are baked). Some beignets have fillings of various sorts.

Beijing Duck
The politically accepted designation for PEKING DUCK.

Belgian Endive
The large, white, cylindrical, slightly bitter sprouts of the CHICORY plant (*Cichorium intybus*). It is also called *witloof* and may be used in salads or braised as a vegetable.

Bell
A green or red (or chocolate black, gold, purple, or yellow) sweet PEPPER.

Bellelay
A French CHEESE also sold as TÊTE DE MOINE.

Bel Paese

An Italian semisoft cow's-milk CHEESE also made (under license) elsewhere. It is mild and somewhat creamy. Italian Bel Paese carries a map of Italy on the label and is preferred by cheese lovers to those made elsewhere.

Beluga

A species of STURGEON sought after especially for its CAVIAR. (There is also a beluga whale, which is of course a mammal and which is not reportedly used for food except occasionally, perhaps, among the indigenous peoples of the Far North.)

Benedictine

A venerable and very sweet LIQUEUR originally brewed by monks of St. Benedict's order and still bearing on the label the Benedictine insignia D.O.M. (*deo optimo maximo*, "to God, most good, most great"). Because of its sweetness, it is often cut half and half with brandy to make a B&B (brandy and Benedictine).

Benne

See SESAME.

Bercy

A classic French fish sauce composed of white wine, shallots, butter, and concentrated fish stock.

Bergamot

   1. Also *wild bergamot*. A plant (*Monarda fistulosa*), otherwise known as *horsemint*, the leaves of which are used for tea.

   2. The Bergamot orange (*Citrus bergamia*), the essential oils of which are used in perfumery. The skin is used in the Italian preserve *mostarde di frutta*.

Bergamot Mint

A plant (*Mentha aquatica*) of the mint family. Its leaves have an aroma akin to BERGAMOT.

Bergkäse

A German word for certain types of CHEESE of mountain provenance, including FONTINA and GRUYÈRE.

Berry

A small, pulpy, edible fruit with seeds embedded within the pulp. They lend themselves to eating raw (especially just picked), with cream and perhaps sugar, with a little KIRSCH, in tarts and pies and muffins and shortcakes, atop vanilla or other ice cream, in compotes or fruit salads, or just about any other way the imagination can conjure up. The various berries can be found in this volume under their individual names.

What all berries have in common is a short separate life—they simply do not keep well once picked, which may explain in part the great popularity of pick-them-yourself berry farms.

Beurre Composé
A French term for COMPOUND BUTTER.

Beurre Manié
A French term for little bits of butter and flour rolled roughly into the size of peas and dropped into simmering sauces or stews to thicken them. An older way of thickening stews was to use the blood of the animal in question (you had to add a little vinegar to it right quick or it would coagulate and ruin everything), but experts now tell us that beurre manié does the job just as well with no difference in texture or taste. Whew!

The trick with beurre manié is to knead it together almost into a paste and then add it slowly as you stir. Slowly, because it takes a little while for the thickening action to take hold. When you have arrived at the thickness you like, let it simmer a few minutes to cook the "raw" taste out of the flour. Beurre manié might be described as a sort of "reverse" ROUX, in that you add it to the ingredients instead of adding the ingredients to it.

Bialy
A soft, chewy roll flavored with flakes of onion.

Bibb
A type of LETTUCE.

Bicarbonate of Soda
See BAKING SODA.

Bierkäse
Any strong CHEESE of the Limburger or Liederkranz persuasion, usually served with dark bread and beer.

Bifteck
The closest the French care to get to "beefsteak." According to French novelist Alexandre Dumas, it was introduced by British troops occupying Paris after the Battle of Waterloo in 1815, although Dumas considered the cut of meat used by the British for the purpose superior to that used then (and presumably now) by the French.

Bigarade

A tart ORANGE. It is at the base of *sauce bigarade*, a sauce built upon duck broth, sugar, the peel of a bigarade or Seville orange, and lemon juice, which is often served with duck.

Bighorn

A mountain sheep (*Ovis Canadensis*) of western North America. You will have to be a hunter (and a good one) or know one to be likely to feast on this. Those who have tasted prime roast wild mutton claim it has a taste and texture of surpassing excellence.

Bigos

A hearty hunters' game stew of Poland. It is made in a number of ways but typically with venison or whatever other meat a hunting party came up with, as well as other red meat, pork of various kinds, sauerkraut, tart apples, red or white wine, and perhaps a healthy jolt of vodka.

Bilberry

Nonspecific name for various berries related to the BLUEBERRY, sometimes even including the blueberry itself. In Europe, it is called the WHORTLEBERRY.

Billi Bi

An elegant, smooth soup of mussel broth, cream, and white wine apparently created for a customer at the restaurant Maxim's in Paris.

Biltong

A South African specialty of dried—but not sun-dried—meat. At its best, it has been compared with BUNDNERFLEISCH or Italy's fine air-dried HAM, PROSCIUTTO.

Bind

To add some agent to a dish in order to cement that dish together into a complete whole and to thicken and enrich it. Should you take some chopped meat, chopped carrot and onion, and some spices and mix them together you'll have a potentially interesting mixture. If you add a beaten egg, you will be adding a binder that will, when the whole thing is baked, pull those component parts into a coherent meatloaf. In addition to egg and egg yolk, milk and cream, gelatin, potato and potato flour, and breadcrumbs are commonly used as binders. BEURRE MANIÉ and ROUX are also effective binders in appropriate circumstances.

Bing

A fairly common large red sweet CHERRY.

Bird's Nest

In cooking terms, the nests that certain Chinese swifts (*Collocalia* spp.) construct along precipitous cliffs overlooking the South China Sea. These nests have a natural gelatinous consistency and are used for flavoring soup, poultry stuffing, or pastries. They are a beast to prepare, requiring an overnight soaking and then repeated washings and cleansing with peanut oil until the nests come completely clean. All this preparation, in addition to the dangers of climbing the cliffs to harvest them, make bird's nests expensive in the extreme.

Biscuit

A kind of quick, hot bread usually served for breakfast. Biscuits rely on BAKING POWDER rather than YEAST for rising and on a goodly amount of SHORTENING for tenderness. In British parlance, it refers to either a COOKIE or a CRACKER.

Bismarck Herring

A form of pickled HERRING.

Bison

The real name of the North American BUFFALO.

Bisque

A thick, smooth cream soup usually made with shrimp or other shellfish, but also sometimes prepared with vegetables, such as tomato.

Bitter Almond

An alternate name for the kernel of the APRICOT.

Bitter Melon

Also *balsam pear*. A Chinese vegetable (*Momordica charantia*) with a wrinkled, green, shiny skin that turns yellow as it further ripens. It somewhat resembles a cucumber and, like that vegetable, is prepared by removing the stem, halving it, and scooping out the seeds (which are said to be purgative when ripe). Unlike cucumber, the flesh of the bitter melon is then parboiled to offset its otherwise overly bitter taste. When cooked, it has a quininelike, almost minty taste and is used for soup or in stir-fried or braised dishes. If you run across one, select it if it is firm to the touch and of a goodly green color. It can be stored refrigerated for several weeks.

Bitters

A flavoring agent, usually quite bitter and pungent, concocted from herbs, leaves, roots, or rinds. Bitters are consumed plain or with water or in drinks, especially alcoholic drinks. Most bitters are sold under proprietary names.

Blackback Flounder

A variety of FLATFISH.

Blackberry

Various species of berry-producing plants of the genus *Rubus*—there are dozens of them. Foragers seek out their shoots in April and May to use in salads, but most of us wait until anywhere from June to August, when the fruit itself is fresh and ripe and sweet. This is also true of *dewberries* (or *trailing blackberries*), except that the dewberry tends to bear its identically elongated black berries (identical in taste and use, too) on long shoots that run along the ground rather than stand straight up, as the blackberry likes to do, and to set its fruit a little earlier than does the true blackberry.

When selecting blackberries, whether the small wild variety or the large market kind, the signs to look for are the same. Seek out plump, sleek, glossy-colored berries, clean and fresh-smelling berries exuding health and luster (no leaves or twigs or musty odors). If their black coats have taken on an air of fatigue or are turning gray, the game is over. Pass them by. And once you acquire your berries, use them. Blackberries do not keep with distinction.

Fresh blackberries are splendid with cream and sugar, although there are those who feel that cream does them no favor and that all they need is sugar. The small, wild ones—especially—are superb in jams and jellies. And any blackberry can be used in juice or pureed. The blackberry is in its element baked in a pie—particularly if you add just a suspicion, no more than the merest tablespoon, of crème de cassis. If you lack that, there are recipes for blackberry cordial that come highly recommended if a bit hazy in the details.

The only drawback to the blackberry is its large and pervasive seeds, which are a nuisance when they lodge between the teeth and keep some people from eating them at all.

Black Butter

In French, *beurre noir*; butter that has been slowly melted over low heat until brown (not black and certainly not burned), then enriched with capers, parsley, and vinegar (or lemon juice). If it's cooked to a slightly less deep color, it is brown butter, or beurre noisette.

Blackcap

Another name for BLACK RASPBERRY.

Blackcod

See SABLEFISH.

Blackened Fish

A cooking technique developed fairly recently by Cajun cooks. You take heavily seasoned fish fillets and cook them over high heat until charred. It is best done outdoors in a heavy skillet directly over the coals. Try to stay upwind.

Blackfish

See TAUTOG.

Black Pudding

See BOUDIN.

Black Raspberry

Also *blackcap*. A native American species (*Rubus occidentalis*) of RASPBERRY, generally put to the same uses as its more delicate-tasting, but tougher, red counterpart.

Black Sea Bass

A succulent saltwater BASS of the Atlantic.

Blackstrap

A type of MOLASSES taken from the end of the refining process. It is thicker and stronger (hoo boy, is it stronger!) in taste than regular molasses and has been traditionally used as cattle food and in industry. It is also available at retail outlets for those whose palates don't insist on blandness and has had various healthful properties attributed to it. A small amount added to a meat or game stew can affect it wondrously.

Black Tea

See TEA.

Black Walnut

A native American WALNUT.

Blade

Meatcutter's term for those cuts (including steaks) that come from the vicinity of the animal's shoulder blade.

Blanc de Blancs

A white wine, especially a CHAMPAGNE, made exclusively from white-skinned grapes. (Wines gain their color from the pigments in the skins that emerge during fermentation, so a white wine can be—and often is—made from juice that has been pressed out of red grapes and removed from the skins before fermentation begins.) A blanc de blancs Champagne is lighter in color than its sibling.

Blanch

1. To drop something briefly into merrily boiling water in order to loosen skin, to shell, to tenderize, to remove salt used as a preservative but not called for in the recipe at hand, or to enhance the color of vegetables to be served raw (or nearly so). The recipe will usually—or should—specify how long to blanch the item. Some foods are blanched by pouring boiling water over them. In some cases you will want to REFRESH the food you have blanched, but again your recipe should guide you.

2. An agricultural act by which the stems or sprouts of certain plants (asparagus, Brussels sprouts, cardoons, celery) are covered or otherwise kept from light in order to keep them white instead of allowing them to turn green.

Blancmange

A dessert most often made now with IRISH MOSS (although its medieval ancestor was a combination of chicken meat and rice or rice flour, and it was not served for dessert). It consists of milk and sugar simmered together with lemon peel and perhaps a beaten egg. This mixture is then poured over the Irish moss, cooled, and left to set in a mold. Cornstarch or arrowroot can be substituted for the Irish moss, and the dish can be modified with the addition of vanilla extract or fresh, canned, or frozen fruit.

Blanquette

A tender and delicate white stew, made usually from veal, sweetbreads, or the white meat of poultry. The meat is not browned beforehand, and the vegetables that are included tend toward onions and mushrooms rather than the heartier and more robustly colored vegetables found in so many other stews.

Blarney

A semisoft, mild Irish cow's-milk CHEESE. It is the Irish equivalent of Cheddar (unless Cheddar is the Anglo-American equivalent of Blarney).

Blend

To mix things together. The idea is to mix everything so thoroughly that any part of it will exactly resemble any other part.

In pastry-making, the term also refers to the process of cutting in, by using fingers, tandem knives, or a PASTRY BLENDER.

Blender

An electrical kitchen device consisting of a container with a set of sharp blades to amalgamate whatever you put into it to a certain degree of pulverization. Unlike a food processor, it doesn't work with solid materials alone but needs a little moisture to get its work done.

Blenny

Small, eel-like fish of the family Blenniidae, found right along the shore in Europe and North America. They can be deep-fried or used in soups and chowders.

Bleu

French for blue. It is applied to cheese, ROQUEFORT being the model, that has undergone fermentation, which results in the mold forming blue veins throughout the cheese.

Blind

See BAKE BLIND.

Blin

A small, thin buckwheat pancake often garnished with caviar, smoked salmon, or cheese. In Russia and Poland blini are traditionally served with sour cream as hors d'oeuvres.

Blintz

A Jewish version of the BLIN, it is a pancake filled with cheese, fish, fruit, jam, or potato and served with sour cream.

Bloater

In England, a lightly smoked HERRING. Bloater paste, a mixture of ground-up cooked bloaters and butter, is popular in Britain.

Blood Orange

A red-pigmented ORANGE.

Blood Pudding

Also called *blood sausage*. See BOUDIN.

Blowfish

A fish (*Spheroides maculatus*) that is a somewhat preposterous denizen of the American side of the Atlantic, at least of its warmer sections. One source lists them as ranging as far north as New York, but they are common off Connecticut, have been caught off Martha's Vineyard, and probably can be found considerably to the north of that, too.

Blowfish have the strange ability to puff themselves up to several times their normal size, presumably to make themselves too large to be swallowed, while at the same time elevating their scales to form thoroughly unpleasant, spiny prickles. There is not a great deal to eat on a blowfish—all that is eaten is the meat just around the spine—but what is there makes them worthwhile. The technique with a freshly caught blowfish is to grab it in a *gloved* hand, cut off the head just behind the eyes, then grasp the skin and pull it back revealing the spine and its meat. Cut off the entrails (which can be toxic), and you have what restaurants and fish markets like to call "sea squab." The meat of the blowfish, which is reminiscent of chicken, is first-rate broiled, deep-fried, or sautéed.

Blue

Cheesemaker's term for a cheese that has been fermented to allow the mold to form rich veins throughout the cheese. Most blue cheeses are made from the milk of cows or goats (although true ROQUEFORT is made from ewe's milk), and, while they are all reflections (but lesser relatives) of Roquefort, they are made elsewhere as well as in France. Very occasionally, farmhouse cheeses that are not in the blue-cheese category will form blue veins and will be snapped up and prized by cheese aficionados.

Blueberry

A North American berry cultivated commercially from North Carolina to Nova Scotia and westward to Michigan but with varieties that are found wild, in one form or another, in almost all parts of the continent. They include the *dry-land blueberry* (*Vaccinium pallidum*), which grows wild roughly from Maryland to Georgia; the *evergreen blueberry* (*Vaccinium ovatum*), of the Northwest; the *highbush* (*Vaccinium australe* and *Vaccinium corymbosum*), a berry grown for commerce; the *lowbush* (*Vaccinium angustifolium*), found especially in Maine and the Maritime Provinces; the *mountain blueberry* (*Vaccinium membranaceum*), a dark, almost black berry of the Cascades and Sierras; the *rabbiteye* (*Vaccinium askei*), a small, dark berry of the southern United States; and in Europe, the WHORTLEBERRY or *bilberry* (*Vaccinium myrtilis*).

Most commercially available blueberries are large—sometimes rivaling small grapes—and juicy. At times the smaller, wild varieties grown in northern New England, Canada, and the Adirondack Mountains of New York State are also to be found in markets. They are less uniform in size, less uniform in quality, and so much tastier as almost to be a whole different fruit.

Latch onto your blueberries, whatever their persuasion, when they look sleek and shiny and before they lose their glossy sheen and powdery bloom and turn mushy. Excellent plain, with cream, or covering ice cream (or plain or vanilla yogurt, for that matter), the large ones are less desirable in pies and muffins than the smaller ones, which tend to hold their shape better, instead of becoming blotchy as the big ones do. The big ones are fine, however, for shortcakes.

Blueberries are often confused with HUCKLEBERRIES, to the extent that in some areas the names are interchangeable. Botanical huckleberries, however, are of a totally different genus (*Gaylussacia*) and contain fewer but more prominent seeds.

Blue Crab

A common CRAB of North America's Atlantic coast.

Blue Dorset

Also *Blue Vinny*. A hard, white English skimmed cow's-milk CHEESE with a regular streak of blue running through it. It is quite rare except in its place of origin, the English county of Dorset.

Bluefish

A voracious, somewhat oily fish (*Pomatomous saltatrix*) of the North Atlantic, much prized by saltwater anglers for its rugged fighting ability as well as its fine taste. Captured blues tend to lose their edge especially quickly and are best cooked as soon after removal from the water as possible. Larger blues are best baked or broiled (broiling over charcoal is eminently satisfactory), but the smaller ones can be successfully sautéed and a tangy sauce, such as one made with mustard, can provide a fine complement to the fish.

There is a continuing controversy about blues and the extent to which they build up dangerous levels of PCBs (the apparently cancer-causing chemical waste product that pollutes so much of our seaboard). In general, we are advised not to eat the skin or the fatty dark parts of the fish (that's where the PCBs concentrate), to cook bluefish over fairly high heat (to leach out as much of the fat as possible), and not to eat more than one or two bluefish a week during the summer bluefish season.

Bluegill
A fairly common freshwater PANFISH (*Lepromis macrochirus*) found mainly in the southern United States.

Blue Mountain
A highly regarded COFFEE from Jamaica.

Bluepoint Oyster
Originally a small oyster from certain waters off New York's Long Island, but now the territorial aspect has been virtually eliminated, and it refers to just about any Atlantic oyster of a decent size.

Blue Vinny
See BLUE DORSET.

Blush Wine
Marketing jargon for ROSÉ.

Boar
A hog, but more generally applied to a wild boar (*Sus scrofa*), a formerly prevalent game animal once highly favored, especially around Christmastime. An Old World animal, it was introduced into North America, and you can still find boar in California and Texas restaurants and perhaps in other areas that specialize in exotic game.

Bobwhite
See QUAIL.

Bocconcini
A grooved PASTA tube similar to RIGATONI.

Bock
A dark BEER of German origin.

Bockwurst

A German sausage based on veal and pork and seasoned with parsley and perhaps cloves. It is sold raw and must be boiled and then browned to be made ready to eat. Bockwurst was traditionally served in the spring, the time in Germany when bock beer was available.

Body

A taster's term for a food or drink (especially wine) that is robust and mouth-filling. It need not be strong, so long as it has substance.

Bohea

An eighteenth-century type of TEA.

Boil

There are all sorts of scientific explanations for boiling, but it's enough to say here that it's the temperature at which most liquids cook most foods most efficiently. The boiling point varies with altitude, but, like most books, this one will assume that you're doing all your cooking on a boat in the mid-Atlantic on a calm day and leave it at that. Those accustomed to high-altitude cooking can probably write their own books and some of them have, which the unaccustomed might do well to consult if in need. For the rest of us, the temperature of the boiling point of water is 212°F.

However, boiling is not one simple action; instead, it can be described as a process that occurs through several distinct stages:

Preboiling. Little bubbles begin forming, signifying that the temperature has risen from wherever you started to about 160°–180°F. This is the temperature at which you might CODDLE an egg.

Simmering. Just—and only just—coming to a boil. Bubbles are forming on the bottom and sides of the pot but not breaking the surface. This begins when the water attains a temperature of about 185°F and reaches its plateau at about 205°F. To keep something in this condition for a sustained period takes an alert cook, a fine-tuned stove, and perhaps a little luck. (You might want to take the cover slightly off your pot or edge it away from the flame to control the temperature.) It is an ideal that is well worth trying one's patience and skill to achieve. This is the stage at which most boiled foods are—or at least are best—cooked.

Medium boil. This is what most of us get when we're trying to simmer but aren't paying enough attention. The temperature is hovering around 205°–210°F, and bubbles are rising to the surface and lightly breaking. It doesn't ruin most foods—unless they're delicate indeed—but what should be simmered emerges somewhat tougher and perhaps a shade less tasty.

Rolling boil. The water is bubbling up (and perhaps over) in a fine frenzy and enough steam is rising to cloud the glasses of the bespectacled. This degree of boiling (it's 212°F and there it will stay as long as there is water in the pot, although the steam is hotter) is appropriate for pasta and for boiling off excess liquid from broths and sauces. (Beware of doing this too close to a smoke alarm.)

When a recipe invites you to boil something, it traditionally means that you are to put that substance in cold water, bring the whole thing to the boiling point, then let it simmer until done—or until done enough for that part of your cooking process.

Boil Down

To let excess liquid boil off a sauce or a broth, for example. The aim is to concentrate and heighten the flavor while decreasing the volume. To *reduce*.

Boiled Dressing

A salad dressing usually containing milk or cream (or in some cases sour cream or yogurt) in addition to vinegar that is brought to a boil before being taken off the fire and chilled. It is appropriate for, among other uses, serving on COLESLAW.

Bok Choy

One of several Chinese cabbages (*Brassica chinensis*). It is quite similar to Swiss chard. This one has green leaves, white stems and ribs, and a mild taste and is available in regular or miniature (baby) sizes. Bok choy is good for soups and especially stir-fried dishes, where the crunchiness of the stems adds texture. For most purposes, the leaves can be cut into ribbons or bite-sized pieces and the stems into bite-sized pieces. Leaves and stems are best cooked separately, as the leaves cook faster.

Buy just enough bok choy for immediate use, and if you must store it, wrap it (unwashed) in plastic and refrigerate it for no more than three days.

Boletus

A genus of MUSHROOM including the French *cèpes* and the Italian *porcini*.

Bollito

A northern Italian stew, which might contain beef, a calf's head, a chicken, a ham, a tongue, and anything else that happens to be on hand, all cooked together in the same pot. The trick is to add each ingredient according to the time it takes to cook. The resultant broth will certainly be superb.

Bologna

A smoked and seasoned sausage of beef, veal, and pork. It is an excellent sandwich meat.

Bombay Duck

Not, of course, a duck at all, Bombay duck is a smelt-sized fish (*Harpodon nehereus*) caught off the coast of India (and elsewhere in southern Asia) and dried, salted to

be fried or grilled, and served with curries. It is sometimes available canned in specialty stores.

Bombe

A frozen, often fruit, dessert that is packed and layered. It was originally made in a
special spherical mold with fluted sides reminiscent of an old-fashioned bomb or
grenade.

Bonbel

A bland semisoft cow's-milk CHEESE made throughout the world by a French company that also produces Baby Bel and La Vache Qui Rit among its other cheese
products.

Bonbon

A candy with a covering of CHOCOLATE or FONDANT surrounding a center often containing fruit or nuts.

Bondon

A French CHEESE made from whole ewe's or cow's milk, salted, formed into small
cylinders, and consumed fresh.

Bone

To take the bones out of an animal, fish, or fowl or any cut thereof. A BONING KNIFE
is handy for such chores.

Bonefish

One of the great sport fishes of Florida (*Albula vulpes*). It is usually caught and
released. Its problem is summed up in its name—it is as bony as a shad but hardly
as good. Still, if you can handle the bones, you will find it quite palatable.

Boning Knife

A special, long-bladed (six to seven inches) knife. If one should come your way, coddle it—keep it sharp and use it sparingly for anything but its designed purpose. (Be
aware, however, that most professional butchers feel that boning is a chore for them,
not for the amateur.)

Bonito

A variety of TUNA.

Bonne Femme

A French cooking term meaning done in the fashion of the goodwife, or without
pretension. Meat and poultry *bonne femme* is braised in a closed casserole with
bacon and (usually) mushrooms and onions. Fish, especially sole, cooked *bonne
femme* is poached in white wine with shallots and served with mushrooms and pars-

ley. While neither sounds particularly difficult, sometimes it is the simplest things that are the most difficult to perfect.

Borage

A Mediterranean herb (*Borago officinalis*) sometimes grown for its ornamental flowers and for its cool, cucumbery taste. In France and Italy, its leaves are used in soups, salads, and vegetable dishes; in Germany it is often used along with dill; and in England and North America, the leaves and flowers may be added to cold drinks. The small, blue flowers can also be eaten raw in salads or candied.

Bordeaux

A world-famous wine-growing area of southwest France that produces dry red and white table wines, especially those of Graves, the Médoc, Pomerol, and Saint Emilion, and the sweet white wines of Barsac and Sauternes. Its finest specimens are sold bearing the name of the *château* (or *vineyard*—the château itself can refer to any building from a palatial structure to a dingy farmhouse) where the grapes were grown. A château-bottled Bordeaux (*mis au château*, in French) is one grown, made into wine, aged, and bottled on the premises and with an excellent chance of being superior to one bottled elsewhere. Red Bordeaux is also known as *claret*.

Börek

Turkish, and Middle Eastern in general, small packet of PHYLLO pastry filled with various stuffings—cheese, meat, vegetable—and served as an hors d'oeuvre or main course.

Borscht

It can be a stew, a rich mélange of beef or other meat and vegetables, sometimes with a sweet-and-sour tang, or it can be a delicate broth. However it is presented, borscht is always built around beets and always garnished with sour cream and sometimes a boiled potato.

Bosc

A russet-colored, flavorful PEAR.

Boston Brown Bread

A bread much appreciated in New England, made with rye and whole wheat flours and often some cornmeal, flavored with molasses and a few raisins, and steamed rather than baked; it is traditionally served with BAKED BEANS.

Boston Butt

A small HAM from the front shoulder (or leg).

Bottled in Bond

A phrase you're likely to see on whiskey, signifying that it is 100 proof, is at least four years old, and was bottled in a bonded warehouse. The excise tax is paid only upon its withdrawal from that warehouse.

Bouchée

A French term for a small patty shell filled with meats or fish and served as an hors d'oeuvre or appetizer.

Boudin

Also called *black pudding* or *blood pudding*. It is a type of sausage usually made around slaughtering time with the slaughtered animal's blood. *Boudin noir* (black sausage) is a French variation made with pork and the blood of the pig; *boudin blanc* (white sausage) is not made with blood and is more delicate, consisting of chicken with pork or veal, breadcrumbs, eggs, onion, and spices (chives and parsley). In France, black sausage is the traditional meal following the Christmas midnight Mass, although this writer, on his sole Christmas celebrated with a French family, was served quantities of delicious small eels sautéed in garlic and oil.

Bouillabaisse

The local fish stew or chowder of Marseilles, France and adjoining localities. Because of its excellence and renown, imitations have sprung up virtually the world over, while at the same time producing critics who claim that bouillabaisse can only be made in Marseilles with specific kinds of fish unobtainable elsewhere. Take your pick.

All bouillabaisse—even the imitations—must be made with several kinds of fish and, perhaps, shellfish. Opinions differ here, and a bouillabaisse is either authentic only if shellfish is included or only if it is not. In any case, several different kinds of fish, of varying textures and tastes, are essential, including an eel of some persuasion—conger eel in the Mediterranean, elsewhere, whatever is available. On its home grounds (or waters), it is unthinkable to make a bouillabaisse without a *rascasse*. This is a somewhat unpleasant-looking sea robin or scorpion fish (*Helicolenus dactylopterus*); the North Atlantic species is the blue mouth. A bouillabaisse is made with olive oil and tomatoes and saffron in addition to fish. Additional ingredients include onion and garlic and fennel, parsley and bay leaf and thyme, and some strips of orange peel.

To prepare this soup, you put all the ingredients except the fish in a large cookpot and heat them up. Then add the fish (cut up or whole depending upon the size of the fish, the size of the cooking utensil, and the whim of the cook) and cover it with water (or fish stock). Bring the water to a fast boil (some recipes specify adding already boiling water) and let it go at a fast clip for 10–15 minutes. Serve the fish in one bowl and the soup in another with a large slab of bread in the bottom of the bowl. True bouillabaisse eaters enrich it with a fiery sauce known as ROUILLE.

Bouillon

A clear soup or BROTH. It can be made with meat, fish, or vegetables, all of which are strained out before the soup can take the name of bouillon. Bouillon is often dehydrated and sold in small, pressed cubes or loose in packets, some of which can be salty to an irritating degree. However, there is at least one (somewhat pricey) low-sodium variety on the market.

Bounceberry

Also CRANBERRY. It does indeed bounce. In processing the berries, they are dropped down a chute with a series of four-inch baffles. Those that do not bounce over the baffles are discarded.

Bouquet

A wine term used to describe the first elusive perfume a wine emits upon its opening as opposed to the whiff of the grape that is FRUITINESS or the fully developed fragrance that is AROMA.

Bouquet Garni

A French term for about the most common form of herb seasoning, consisting of (usually) three to four sprigs of parsley, a sprig of thyme, and a bay leaf—although you can augment it any way you wish, perhaps with such additions as tarragon, peppercorns, allspice berries, lemon peel, or anything the dish you're cooking seems to crave. The herbs are typically wrapped in a single layer of cheesecloth, tied with string, and inserted into the dish. Cheesecloth is especially called for if you have no fresh herbs and are forced to fall back on dried ones and don't want them floating around in the finished dish.

Bourbon

A Kentucky WHISKEY made from a MASH containing at least half corn.

Bourride

A Mediterranean fish stew akin to BOUILLABAISSE. It has been suggested that what differentiates them is that bourride is made from white-fleshed fish only (no eel, for example), abjures the use of shellfish, and mixes AIOLI (instead of ROUILLE) into the broth.

Boursault

A soft French cow's-milk TRIPLE CREAM cheese.

Boursin

A CHEESE much like BOURSAULT but with added flavorings.

Bows
An American version of *farfalle*, Italian pasta shaped into butterflies or bow ties. Bows are usually made with egg-noodle dough, farfalle without eggs.

Box Cheese
A German cow's-milk CHEESE resembling BRICK. It comes in two varieties, a hard cheese made from whole milk, and a softer one made from partly skimmed milk. It is often flavored with caraway seeds.

Boxty Bread
An Irish bread made of mashed (cooked) and grated (raw) potatoes and hot milk with perhaps some flour and even baking soda. It is garnished with melted butter.

Boysenberry
A cross of blackberry, dewberry, and loganberry hybridized by the American horticulturist Rudolph Boysen sometime about 1920 and assigned to the genus *Rubus*. The bushes give off few berries, but those that are produced are jet black and absolutely enormous with soft seeds. In taste, the boysenberry resembles both the raspberry and the blackberry and can be used in the same ways as either one.

Braciola
In Italian cooking, very thinly sliced cuts of beef, stuffed with cheese and unsmoked ham (other variations occur, of course), sealed together or rolled up, dipped in egg and breadcrumbs, and sautéed in oil or, if thick, sautéed and simmered until tender.

Brains
Calves' brains are generally considered the best bet (although those of sheep, pork, and sometimes even beef cattle can also be found), but they must be as fresh as possible if they are to retain their choice and delicate qualities. Brains generally must be parboiled in ACIDULATED WATER and then quickly dropped into fresh, cold water to give the flesh firmness, after which they are ready for further cooking. This can consist of baking, broiling, frying, or scrambling (with eggs). They may also be enclosed in small pastries.

Braise
To cook meat or vegetables (or combinations of them) in a very minimal amount of liquid in a tightly closed container that ideally just fits the matter being cooked. It is helpful to marinate meat to be braised in ordinary wine with very thinly sliced carrots, celery, garlic, and onion for six or so hours, and then brown the meat. The meat can then be braised in the MARINADE.

Braising is a wonderful way of dealing with an old or tough piece of meat, and the aromas—even emanating from a closed container in a closed oven—will perfume any household during the several hours of cooking. It is wise, however, to check your dish from time to time and ensure that there remains enough of your braising liquid not only to do the job but also to give you the wherewithal for a sauce or gravy to go with your meat.

Bramble
An overall name for plants of the genus *Rubus*, which includes blackberries, boysenberries, dewberries, loganberries, and raspberries among its most important members.

Bran
The outer husk of grain. It is notable for its high fiber content and consequent laxative effect that apparently is salutary for the digestive system. Its principle use in the kitchen is in bread and particularly muffins, and its presence is highly trumpeted in commercial breakfast cereals.

Brandade
A specialty of southern France composed of pureed salt cod mixed with milk or light cream and olive oil and flavored with minced garlic. To make it, soak your shredded cod overnight, then let it simmer in water until tender. Drain well, and add to it a couple of cloves of crushed or minced garlic, then add, alternately, bit by bit, equal amounts of warm milk (or cream) and olive oil (only the best is what this dish insists upon) while stirring it vigorously (or running it through the blender or food processor) until it comes together into a pure white mixture the consistency of heavy cream. Most often it is served warm on toast although there are those who like it cold. It is also seen as *brandade de morue*, *morue* being French for cod.

Brandy
The alcoholic beverage distilled from fermented fruit juice, most notably fermented grape juice (or wine). In addition to its attraction as a beverage, brandy has its uses in the kitchen, especially if you wish to FLAME (and flavor) some food or other. Some of the names you are likely to encounter include:

> *Applejack.* American brandy distilled from apples, but most often diluted with grain neutral spirits, which cuts its cost almost as much as it cuts its quality. A *farm applejack* is made by freezing hard cider and tapping off for drinking whatever has not frozen.
>
> *Armagnac.* French brandy made from wine grown in Gascony, in southwest France.
>
> *Calvados.* French brandy distilled from apples grown in Normandy; it is the world's outstanding apple brandy.
>
> *Cognac.* French brandy made from wine grown in the Charente, in western France.

Fraise. Brandy distilled from strawberries. If it is labeled *fraise des bois*, it is made from wild strawberries.

Framboise. Brandy distilled from raspberries. If it is labeled *framboise sauvage*, it is made from wild raspberries.

Grappa. The Italian name for marc (see below).

Kirsch. Brandy made from cherries. The best has traditionally come from Alsace and from Germany's Black Forest.

Marc. Brandy distilled from grape residue after the grapes have been pressed for wine. Marc can also be made from other sources: *eau de vie de marc de cidre*, for example, is brandy distilled from the residue of cider pressings.

Metaxa. A slightly sweet brandy made from wine grown in Greece.

Mirabelle. Brandy distilled from the golden mirabelle plum; that from the old French province of Lorraine is especially good.

Napoleon. A meaningless—but amusing—term intended to imply excellence by invoking the Bonaparte name. You are supposed to believe that the brandy comes from the Napoleonic era and is thus old and superior. If it were true, after all this time, it would only be old.

Pisco. A brandy based on Muscat grapes from Peru—and in recent times Argentina, Chile, and Bolivia. It is put into clay containers and drunk young, sometimes in the form of Pisco Punch.

Poire. Brandy made from pears. It is often labeled *Poire William*, which is the European name for the Bartlett pear, and it is sometimes sold in bottles enclosing a tiny pear (the bottle, in which the pear comes to maturity, being slipped over the infant pear right on the tree).

Slivovitz. Yugoslav brandy distilled from plums. It has the same relationship to other plum brandies that Calvados has to other apple brandies.

Brant

A small species of WILD GOOSE.

Bratwurst

A German sausage of pork mixed with some breadcrumbs and flavored with grated nutmeg and other herbs (ginger and sage are possibilities). You can boil it, fry it, or run it under the broiler, but, as it usually comes fresh, it must be cooked somehow.

Braunschweiger

A light, more spreadable form of LIVERWURST.

Brawn

A sausage made of finely chopped pork (especially a pig's head) or pork and veal that is cooked, seasoned, spiced, and served cold, mixed together with its jelly. Also called *head cheese*. Brawn differs from a GALANTINE in that the latter is the meat encased in its jelly.

Brazier

A cooking utensil with a fairly thick bottom, a cover, and high sides. It is a compromise between a FRYING PAN and a CASSEROLE.

Brazilian Cherry

See SURINAM CHERRY.

Brazil Nut

An oily nut of a South American tree (*Bertholletia excelsa*) that is edible but extremely hard to crack unless the nuts are steamed for a few minutes. The shelled nuts are then dropped into boiling water for six or seven minutes, after which the inner skin can be removed. They can be roasted and salted or ground or chipped to enrich cookies or pastries of various sorts, or they can be added to stuffings to give a little crunch.

Bread

The staff of life, but how does one define it and why would anyone bother?

At its simplest, perhaps, bread is flour and water and yeast, kneaded together and baked. But bread without salt has very little savor, so better add some salt. And maybe while you're at it throw in some nuts, herbs, or other flavoring. And what kind of flour? Ordinary white flour is what most people think of, but that's only the beginning. Bread has been baked from a rich variety of flours including buckwheat, chestnut, corn, millet, potato, rye, and soybean. One West Coast Indian tribe laboriously prepared a flour from acorns to make their daily bread. So we'd better keep a weather eye on flour. Then there is water. Breads have been baked with all manner of liquids including milk, buttermilk, sour cream, and beer. So perhaps liquid should replace water in our definition. What about yeast? Unless we are willing to exclude from the world of bread the MATZO of the Jewish festival of Passover and the CHAPATI of the Indian subcontinent, we'd better be on the lookout here, too. But leavened breads have to be kneaded, don't they? Well, no. Batter breads are mixed together and beaten to a fare-thee-well and allowed to rise as they are baked. And other breadstuffs rise from the action of baking powder or even eggs thoroughly beaten to get as much air in them as possible. So that leaves us with baking. Try telling that to an elderly Mexican spreading a tortilla out on an open skillet over a hot fire.

Bread-and-Butter Pickle

A pickle usually made with cucumbers, onions, and various spices. Other vegetables have been used in home canning. The American food writer James Beard suggested zucchini.

Breadcrumbs
Bread, either fresh or dried, that has been cut into coarse pieces or finely grated. The dry varieties are widely available in foodstores (often with flavorings of various kinds—garlic or oregano, for example), but fresh breadcrumbs are better prepared at home. Breadcrumbs are called for in many recipes; just make sure you use the fine variety for coatings when frying or broiling and the larger coarser ones for stuffing. Freshly ground, soft breadcrumbs can also be used as a thickening agent.

Breadfruit
A large (up to eight inches) round fruit (*Artocarpus altilis*) only infrequently found in North American markets. Its flesh can be cooked in any of the ways that regular or sweet potatoes are prepared and must then be served hot or the texture becomes unpleasant. The taste is said to be reminiscent of bread. Cooked breadfruit can be adapted to other recipes and further preparation. For those who live in the tropical areas where these trees abound, breadfruit is one of the main staples of the local diet.

Bream
A large family (Sparidae) of European food fish related to the North American PORGY. The name is also applied to the bluegill, one of the most popular panfishes in the southern United States.

Brick
A salty North American semisoft whole-cow's-milk CHEESE that varies from mild to so assertive that it has earned the name of "the married man's Limburger."

Brie
A soft, creamy yellow, lightly rinded French cow's-milk CHEESE made in a section of the Île-de-France (the area around Paris) and neighboring Champagne but now also imitated widely around the world. At its best it will be labeled *fermier*, or farmhouse, and will be next to impossible to find or to afford if you should stumble over it. *Brie de Coulommiers* and *Brie de Meaux* are highly rated with *Brie de Melun*, a somewhat saltier version, slightly behind them.

Brill
A name applied to two unrelated FLATFISH.

Brillat-Savarin
A French cow's-milk TRIPLE CREAM cheese similar to Camembert and named for the celebrated 19th-century French gastronome Jean Anthelme Brillat-Savarin.

Brine
A solution of water heavily laced with salt and used for pickling or otherwise preserving. An 80 percent brine solution has been found to be standard in curing. The

old rule of thumb for producing it tells you to place a fairly small, fresh, unpeeled potato in the bottom of your container of water and start stirring in salt. When the potato comes to the surface you will have just about an 80 percent solution. An egg is said to work equally well.

Brinza

A soft, buttery, sometimes sharp Hungarian CHEESE made from ewe's milk, although that of the goat is sometimes added.

Brioche

An extraordinarily rich, yet light yeast bread of French origin enriched with a goodly amount of butter and eggs and baked in a round, flared, or fluted mold with a smaller round on the top. The dough can also take other shapes and can encase various fillings.

Brisée

The term *pâte brisée* is French for SHORT PASTRY.

Brisket

The meat from the breast of a BEEF critter, cut from under the first five ribs. It usually requires long, slow cooking and is the cut from which CORNED BEEF is made.

Brisling Sardine

A small sprat of the HERRING family.

Broccoli

A vegetable (*Brassica oleracea* var. *Italica*) made up of bunches of tightly closed, usually green buds growing out of a thickish stalk. Of eastern Mediterranean origin, broccoli has been cultivated in Italy since Roman times and has been passed along, especially to the United States where the Italian variety has found wide favor. A close relative of CAULIFLOWER, some varieties—especially one bearing a luxuriant head of deep purple flowerets—can be found marketed under either name.

When selecting broccoli, look for tight, compact heads of good color and well filled out flowerets. Stay away from heads that are bruised, have yellow spots, or are battered or flabby. In particular, avoid any that show buds that have opened up into yellow flowers. If the flowerets have already developed into small yellow flowers, the broccoli has passed its prime. Although many people find the stems (especially if peeled first) the tastiest part of the vegetable, you nonetheless don't want broccoli heads that are all stem to the detriment of tiny or nearly nonexistent flowerets. If you're not going to use your broccoli right away, refrigerate it in plastic—but not for more than two or, if you must, three days.

Broccoli can be cooked in any number of ways, but usually it is best dropped into simmering water until just barely tender before anything else is done with it. It then lends itself well to being sautéed with garlic or cheese and garnished with caper-flavored oil and vinegar. You can also steam broccoli, then REFRESH it and serve it as a cold vegetable or hors d'oeuvre with a dip.

Broccoli Rabe

Also *broccoli rab*, *raab*, *rape*, *rapini*, or *Italian turnip*. A plant (*Brassica napus*) of the mustard family used as a green. It has a bitterness that some welcome, others do not. You will find it as crisp, leafy, stalks perhaps with some yellow flowers. Check the stalks for toughness. Young, crisp stalks are fine, but large or woody ones are best avoided (cut them off if the rest of the green looks good) and stay away from leaves that are yellowed or look limp. If you steam them, chop them into bite-sized pieces, get the water boiling, drop in the stems, cook two minutes or so, and add the leaves. Another two minutes of cooking time will suffice, but should you like them less bitter, you can cook them longer (cook them long enough and they will probably come out bland). They go well with an oil and vinegar dressing and with sausages or other pork dishes.

Brochette

A French term for SKEWER; *en brochette* means cooked or served on skewers or both.

Brodetto

A fish soup of the Italian Adriatic coast centering around Ancona and Porto Recanati. As is the case of BOUILLABAISSE, the "real thing" cannot be made without the scorpion fish—*rascasse* in Marseille, *scorpena* or *scorfano* in Porto Recanati. The soup includes whatever other fish (and in some versions shellfish) is fresh out of the water and is made with olive oil, garlic, onions, tomatoes, and plenty of spices simmered with the spare parts of the fish to make a broth into which the chunks of the fish are added. The result is a thick mélange of fish parts in a flavorful broth, and, again like bouillabaisse, the broth is served over large slices of bread that are often fried in oil.

Broil

To cook over coals—sometimes referred to as grilling—or under the extremely hot broiling element of a conventional oven. The first broiling was doubtless done by impaling hunks of meat on sharp sticks and holding them over the fire until done (or done enough—depending upon the degree of hunger). Skewers and spits do this for us now.

Broiling, whether in a broiler or over coals, is an extremely popular cooking method, especially for steaks and chops, although some meats—veal, pork, and almost any game if cut thin—tend to dry out and turn tough before achieving doneness. Fish, conversely, broils well if carefully watched, as does poultry. Both benefit from being marinated for an hour or so prior to cooking and from basting with the marinade during cooking. And even steaks are best cut at least 1 to 1½ inches thick or you will risk having them dry out. You can also use the broiler to brown or crisp or glaze various foods before serving or before subjecting them to additional cooking.

Broiler

In poultry terms, a young chicken weighing 1 to 2½ pounds. A broiler-fryer will weigh as much as 3½ pounds.

Brook Trout

An esteemed game and food fish; a CHAR.

Broth

Broth is called by a variety of names—SOUP, *stock*, BOUILLON, CONSOMMÉ, or chicken, beef, or vegetable broth. All are the result of simmering (usually in plain, cold water for starters) some form of food until some or all of the taste (and nutrition) has passed from the food to the liquid. You might say that if the liquid is to be consumed as is, you are making soup; if it is to be used as a basis for a sauce or for cooking something else, you are making stock. (However, the utensil in which you cook it is not a broth pot but a stockpot.) Bouillon is another name for a clear meat broth, although the name is also extended to broths of poultry and vegetables. Consommé is a beef broth of a particular purity, delicately informed by root vegetables, usually fortified with gelatin, and sometimes augmented with additional flavorings; it is used for jellied soups and aspics.

Broths are tremendously useful in the kitchen, and it is reassuring to know that they freeze well (for up to about three months). While no serious, conscientious professional cook would make broth out of the carcass of a chicken or turkey roasted for the table (fresh, previously uncooked meat would be the basis instead), it is a time-honored economy elsewhere to do just that. If there is still some meat clinging to those bones, your broth will be even better. Just throw it all in the pot with some onion, carrot, perhaps some celery, a little thyme, and bay leaf, add water, and simmer it gently. When it has simmered long enough that the broth has taken on its color and taste, fish out the big pieces and strain the rest through a cheesecloth-lined colander. You will almost certainly think kindly of it during those long, cold stretches after Thanksgiving, say, when a warm soup at lunchtime restores the courage that the weather has so cruelly sapped. By the same token, the remains of a leg of lamb can be the basis for Scotch broth as a ham bone can be for pea soup.

Should you wish to make a broth—or stock—from scratch, one rule of thumb prescribes 1½ pounds meat, ½ pound bones, 1 tablespoon salt, and 2 cups chopped vegetables for each quart of water. All the solids, of course, and all particles of fat get strained out of the final product.

Brown

To form a crust on a piece of meat or vegetable—and enrich its flavor—by cooking it briefly in hot fat. Getting the fat good and hot, using very little of it, and having the patience to let the item become properly browned are the keys to success.

An alternative browning technique, especially for meats to be braised, is to DREDGE the meat and place it under the broiler until it takes on the deep brown color you want. Turn it from time to time so that it browns all over without overcooking.

Brownie

A rich, usually chocolate (although butterscotch and vanilla are also popular brownie flavors) cookie verging on a cake, sometimes enriched with nuts.

Brown Rice

Milled but unpolished RICE. It is more nutritious than white rice, as well as being tastier, and needs longer cooking time.

Brown Stock

A stock that has been made from bones roasted or SWEATED prior to being popped into the stockpot (see BROTH).

Brown Sugar

Originally, a sugar refined somewhat less strenuously than regular white sugar in order to retain more molasses. Now, it is refined white sugar treated with colored syrup to achieve whatever degree of darkness is wanted, resulting in a white sugar with a molassesy covering, which accounts for its richer taste and moister consistency. Indeed, you can counterfeit your own brown sugar, should you so desire. Put your molasses jar in warm water (to take the chill off it slightly and make the molasses runny) and then add 2 tablespoons molasses to ½ cup regular, granulated sugar and mix well. Your yield: ½ cup somewhat sticky brown sugar. Brown sugar is bulkier than white and needs to be tamped down forcibly when being measured.

Bruise

To smash something partially, such as a clove of garlic, a peppercorn, or whole allspice, to release flavor or facilitate peeling.

Brunch

A meal that commutes between being a late breakfast and an early lunch. It is usually intended to be quite leisurely and even perhaps elaborate, which makes it appropriate for a Sunday or other day of rest.

Brunoise

A French term for cutting food, especially carrots and celery and onions, into small dice and sometimes then sautéing them with ham (or butter) in the manner of a MIREPOIX.

Brunswick Stew

A stew originally from the southern United States usually made of squirrel and butter and onion and seasonings, but now more likely to be made with chicken. It is also apt to be embellished with tomatoes, lima beans, and okra.

Bruschetta

An Italian garlic bread. Slabs of bread are toasted, treated with garlic, and then drizzled with the best green olive oil available. It is customarily served warm.

Brussels Sprouts

A tiny cabbage-shaped vegetable (*Brassica oleracea* var. *gemmifera*) that grows on sprout-laden limbs of its plant, a relative of the cabbage. Freshly cut branches of brussels sprouts used as table centerpieces can give a festive look to the late-fall table, that being the time brussels sprouts are in season. Such branches are found increasingly in supermarkets as well as in farm markets and from those home gardeners who are able to salvage some harvest from any local deer, which happen to love the sprouting buds.

When buying brussels sprouts, look for the small-to-medium ones—the bigger ones tend to lose flavor—and stick with the green, avoiding the yellowing ones. You don't have to use them right up (they will keep for up to a week or so in a plastic bag or covered dish or in the vegetable drawer of the refrigerator). Before cooking them, it helps to remove any tough outer leaves and cut a cross in the stem end.

A bygone practice when cooking the sprouts was to drop them in boiling water and let them cook interminably. Most cooks today let them simmer no more than 10 minutes before draining them. If simmered about half that time and then sautéed over low heat in enough goose fat, olive oil, or butter to glaze them (cook them until the outsides are crisp and the insides bity and flavorful) they form a pleasant change of pace. No matter how you cook brussels sprouts, they are particularly good with chestnuts.

Brut

A French term for CHAMPAGNE that has not been sweetened, or at least not by very much. It is the driest Champagne made.

Bual

A variety of Portuguese MADEIRA.

Bubble and Squeak

A British combination of boiled beef, chopped cabbage, and mashed potatoes all fried together. The cabbage and potatoes combine on the effect that gives the dish its name.

Bûche de Noël

Also *Yule log.* A French Christmas jelly roll or GENOISE cake formed into a long log shape and usually frosted with a mocha icing applied to simulate the bark of a tree with knots here and there.

Bucheron

An extremely pleasant light French goat's-milk CHEESE usually flavored with herbs.

Buckeye

Also *horse chestnut* (*Aesculus* spp.). A fairly widespread North American tree, the nuts of which contain a bitter poison when raw but, when roasted, peeled, and leached with cold water for several days, can be made edible. The broken-up seeds and bruised branches of the red buckeye (*Aesculus pavia*) were said by the eminent botanist M. L. Fernald to have been tossed by Native Americans into small ponds and stirred around to so intoxicate fish that they would come to the surface and could be scooped up by hand.

Buckwheat

A plant of Siberian origin (*Fagopyrum esculentum* and *Fagopyrum tartaricum*) producing triangular seeds that can be ground into flour and used in breads (not alone, but in addition to other flours), pancakes, and some versions of SCRAPPLE. The Russians cook GROAT and call it *kasha*, which they use as a breakfast cereal, a side dish, or the basis for other dishes such as knishes (see KNISH). Russian blini (see BLIN) are made of buckwheat flour, whereas in parts of Italy, buckwheat flour is added to—or substituted for—cornmeal in making a variation on POLENTA. Once called "beech-wheat," it is not related to beech trees any more than it is to wheat, but is a member of its own botanical family (the Buckwheat). It is also grown by beekeepers for the taste its flowers impart to HONEY.

Buffalo

Any of a group of large ruminants. In most of the world, the term refers to the water buffalo (*Bubalus bubalis*), which is generally far too valuable as a draft animal to use for food, although Asians do put them to culinary use, too; in southern Africa, it refers to the dangerous Cape buffalo (*Syncerus caffer*), a game animal that might be eaten depending upon which of you ends up as hunter and which as hunted; in Europe it is the virtually extinct auroch (*Bison bonasus*); and in North America it is the bison (*Bison bison*), the great shaggy beast that once teemed across the Plains from Manitoba to Monterey. Bison, or buffalo (which is how you'll generally see it listed), is spasmodically available in butcher shops and restaurants here and there. Its meat is in demand because it is lean, containing not only less cholesterol than beef, but fewer calories as well. It is slightly closer in taste to beef (although somewhat sweeter) than it is to venison but lends itself well to venison recipes, especially those that call for a wine-based marinade or flavoring with juniper berries. It can also be substituted for beef or veal in almost any stew or chili dish. Just keep in mind that it will cook faster than the same amount of beef because of its lower fat content.

Bison have been crossed with beef cattle to produce hybrids known as beefalo and cattalo, which are also leaner than beef (but fattier than buffalo) and closer to it in taste.

Buffalo Berry

A handsome western North American berry (*Shepherdia argentia* and *Shepherdia canadensis*) akin to the BARBERRY. It is equally capable of being eaten raw, used as a summery fruit drink (especially if you wait until after the first frost), or made into a first-rate, pectin-rich preserve. Native Americans dried the berries to use them like currants.

Buffalo Chicken Wings

Deep-fried chicken wings (the tips removed) served with a hot, spicy sauce and blue cheese dressing, a recipe originating in Buffalo, New York.

Buffalofish

A Mississippi Valley fish (*Ictiobus* spp.), somewhat resembling CARP (even though it is actually a sucker) and usually found in smoked form, although when young, the fresh-caught flesh can be quite pleasant when cooked.

Bufflehead

A small, North American WILD DUCK (*Bucephala albeola*).

Bulb Baster

A plastic or metal basting device. It consists of a pointed tube with a suction bulb that fits on top. Squeezing the bulb draws liquid into the tube for release over whatever you wish to baste.

Bulgur

Also *bulghur*. Dehusked, whole-grain wheat that has been parboiled and cracked. It is useful in baking and can be substituted for rice or potatoes. It acts like a precooked CRACKED WHEAT, and the two can be used interchangeably.

Bullhead

Any of several varieties of CATFISH.

Bullock's Heart

See CUSTARD APPLE.

Bull Trout

The name notwithstanding, a CHAR.

Bully Beef

An English term for canned CORNED BEEF.

Bulrush

The CATTAIL. This bulrush is not, however, to be confused with the biblical bulrush, which is a papyrus.

Bun

A round, sweetened roll, like those that hamburgers are served on.

Bundnerfleisch

A wafer-thin, salt-cured sliced Alpine HAM, air-dried in the Swiss canton of Grisons.

Bundt Pan

A round, fluted TUBE PAN designed for baking a rich, dense, German coffee cake.

Buñuelo

A Spanish fritter batter into which all manner of foods may be dipped along the lines of a FRITTO MISTO. The Mexicans apply the name to a deep-fried pastry.

Burbot

A fish (*Lota lota*), known as *lote* in England and *lotte de rivière* in France (*lotte de mer* is the MONKFISH); *Lota maculosa* is the species found in North America. Burbot is a freshwater relative of the COD but is nowhere near so tasty. It is fairly common in lakes (including the Great Lakes) and ponds from the north-central United States to south-central Canada (as well as in Europe and Siberia). Bake it, broil it, or—if it is small enough—panfry it.

Burdock

Wild burdocks (*Arctium* spp.) have long been known to foragers who make good use of the leaves and roots and shoots as potherbs while trying to avoid the masses of sticky burs that cling to people and animals and are the very devil to remove. The root of the giant burdock (*Arctium lappa*) can now be found in Oriental stores, especially under its Japanese name, *gobo*. Burdock roots, somewhat resembling parsnips, will keep if stored damp in the refrigerator for no more than a few days. Shredded or sliced, they add flavor to soups and grains and stews.

Burgoo

1. A seaman's porridge made with oatmeal or sea biscuits and molasses.

2. A hearty meat and vegetable stew from Kentucky, originally made with squirrel but now with any meat (except squirrel, unless you supply it yourself) and often served at large public gatherings. According to one account, it is heavily flavored with Kentucky whiskey.

Burgundy
A wine-growing region of northeastern France producing relatively small amounts of some of the world's most prestigious dry red and white table wines. Burgundy embraces the Beaujolais, the Chablis, the Chalonnais, the Côte d'Or, and the Mâconnais. Burgundy has the reputation of producing hearty, full-bodied wines. This is true, but part of its output also qualifies as some of the world's most delicate and subtle.

Burnet
Also *salad burnet* and *garden burnet*. A European herb (*Sanguisorba minor*), the leaves of which are reputed to have a cucumbery flavor and are used in sauces, salads, omelets, cheese dishes, and herb-flavored vinegar. If you wish to try it, however, you'll probably have to grow it yourself. There is also a North American species (*Sanguisorba canadensis*), but apparently it has no gastronomic merit.

Burrito
In Mexican cooking, a TACO, the TORTILLA for which is made from wheat rather than corn flour.

Bustard
A family (Otididae) of game birds of southern Europe, Africa, Asia, and Australia, noted for their slowness of flight and succulence of flesh.

Buster Crab
A CRAB in the molt, busting out of its shell.

Butt
A cut of PORK, taken from the shoulder.

Butter
A firm emulsion made by churning milk or cream, used as a spread and in cooking and pastry-making. Butter has been considered such a glory of French cooking that "butter, butter, and more butter" was one French chef's answer to the secret of great cooking. And even though nutritionists have warned us to reduce our reliance on animal fats—of which butter is one—it is still almost indispensable in classic cooking. It is all but irreplaceable for baking, and many people feel that eggs and some other foods simply don't have the necessary taste when cooked in anything other than butter.

Butter comes to us in two forms, salted and sweet. Salted butter has a slight percentage of salt added, originally as a preservative but now because we are accustomed to the taste. Sweet butter has no additional salt. Butter has a tendency to burn, which is why it is a good idea to CLARIFY it before using it for cooking purposes.

Butter Bean

Another name for the lima BEAN.

Butter Cheese

Also *butterkäse* in German. A soft CHEESE with the consistency of butter, originally from Austria and Germany but now also made in North America.

Buttercream

A smooth and elegant pastry filling or frosting composed of butter, confectioner's sugar, egg yolks, and vanilla extract. There is both a cooked and an uncooked version.

Buttercup

A variety of SQUASH.

Butterfat

The fat that occurs naturally in milk and cream and that separates out for making butter. The higher the butterfat content of a dairy product, the richer that product will be.

Butterfish

Also *dollarfish*. A small, thin, rounded saltwater fish (*Peprilus* spp.) with silvery sides and a bluish back, usually running about 6–12 inches long. Butterfish are sweet and tasty panfish, and, like panfish everywhere, are at their best when panfried, although deep-frying is also indicated. The Pacific butterfish (*Peprilus simillimus*) sometimes masquerades under the name of *pompano*.

Butterfly

To cut something (such as a pork chop) almost in half and flatten it so that each half forms a mirror image of the other, as with a butterfly's wings.

Buttermilk

If you have your own cow you can make this yourself by saving the liquid left over from churning butter. Otherwise, the buttermilk you buy is ordinary skimmed milk (sometimes whole—check the label) soured by a special culture and, in some cases, enriched with tiny particles of butter mostly for cosmetic reasons. For cooking and baking, a dried buttermilk is available and handy to have on the shelf (or refrigerated once opened) as it doesn't turn bad if you don't use it all right away.

Butternut

    1. A native American WALNUT.

    2. A variety of SQUASH.

Butterscotch

A chewy candy and a rich sauce or flavoring excellent on ice cream (especially coffee ice cream); it is made from butter, brown sugar, water, and a smidge of vanilla extract. Sometimes corn syrup and cream are also included.

Butter Sole

A Pacific FLATFISH.

Button Mushroom

A small *champignon de Paris*, the regular MUSHROOM of commerce.

C

A common abbreviation for the CELSIUS (otherwise known as centigrade) temperature scale.

c.

A common abbreviation for MEASURING CUP.

Cabbage

A leafy vegetable (*Brassica oleracea* var. *capitata*), usually with a dense, compact head. A plant that has accompanied mankind throughout the ages and has often been dubbed "common" or "peasant fare" for its good service, it is a cousin to BROCCOLI, BRUSSELS SPROUTS, CAULIFLOWER, CHINESE CABBAGE, COLLARD greens, KALE, and KOHLRABI.

Although there are a great many varieties of cabbage, they pretty much boil down to three overall types: *smooth green*, *curly green* (or *Savoy*), and *red*. (You might bear in mind, however, that the red is often considered simply a differently pigmented variety of smooth green cabbage.) All three can pretty much be used interchangeably, although the Savoy is considered the most delicate.

Cabbage can be eaten raw or it can be boiled, braised, stuffed, used in salads (as in COLESLAW) or soup, or it can be pickled (as in SAUERKRAUT). The British have a way of steaming it, chopping it, combining it with beaten egg yolks and some butter and grated cheese, and topping it with breadcrumbs to be browned as a pie. Cabbage leaves can also be blanched and rolled for stuffed cabbage or as a replacement for grape leaves in DOLMA.

Good, heavy heads with well-colored, crisp leaves are the hallmarks of a sound cabbage. When using cabbage, remove any tough outer leaves and divide the cabbage into wedges, which you can then soak in water for up to an hour to make it firm and rid it of any pests. It is then ready for use.

Cabbage Palm

See PALMETTO.

Cabernet

Grape varieties (*Vitis vinifera*), usually either Cabernet Sauvignon or Cabernet Franc, that contribute to the great red wines of BORDEAUX. These vines are widely grown elsewhere, notably in California but also in other parts of Europe, in Australia,

South Africa, and South America, where they are capable of producing superior wines, often sold under their varietal name.

Cabillaud
A former term for COD fresh from the water, as opposed to dry or salt cod.

Cacao
A tree (*Theobroma cacao*) that produces CHOCOLATE.

Caciocavallo
A firm Italian cow's-milk CHEESE somewhat resembling Provolone.

Cactus Fig
See PRICKLY PEAR.

Caerphilly
Something close to the Welsh national cheese (although it is mostly made now across the border in England); this is a crumbly, firm white cow's-milk CHEESE with a bit of a salty tang. It is not a good keeper.

Caesar Salad
A salad of romaine lettuce, garlic, croutons, and Parmesan cheese with a dressing of olive oil, Worcestershire sauce, usually anchovies, and a raw egg. It was invented in 1924 in a restaurant in Tijuana, Mexico.

Café Brulot
A New Orleans specialty; strong coffee added to a mixture of citrus rind, spices, and sugar, heated up in a modicum of brandy and then lit.

Cajun
A style of cooking developed by the Acadians, survivors of a people of French descent who were brutally expelled from Canada by the English in 1755 and subsequently settled in the bayous of Louisiana. Cajun food runs to such dishes as ÉTOUF-FÉE, GUMBO, and JAMBALAYA. In recent years, BLACKENED FISH cooked quickly on a red-hot griddle and flavored with herbs and hot spices has become quite trendy, but although introduced by a Cajun chef it has no foundation in Cajun culinary history. Drawing on the bounty of the land where they settled, the Cajuns make large use of fresh-caught fish as well as game in their cooking. Hot sauces, such as TABASCO, are very much to the Cajun taste.

Cake
A term covering a wondrously bewildering variety of pastries and other good things to eat. (The term also applies to stuff that is dried and pressed into compact form, such as a "cake" of yeast.) Cake baking used to be considered extremely difficult, and some of the more specialized cakes still require the utmost skill and care in mea-

suring, mixing—indeed, in all aspects of preparation. On the cheerful side, however, reliable ovens, clearer directions, labor-saving mixes, and other shortcuts have brought most cakes well within the scope of all but the most distracted of cooks. A number of good, serious books on baking exist for those who wish to extend their range beyond the recipes you find printed on the backs of cake-mixture boxes.

Cake Flour
A finely milled, soft FLOUR suitable for cake baking. Unless you're planning on making fairly delicate cakes, you're probably just as well off using an all-purpose flour.

Cake Pan
Just as there are a great number of different types of cakes, so there are many types of cake pans. They range from the round or square ones used for birthday cakes and the like to molds in all sorts of fanciful styles. Some have a tube up the middle (*tube pans*) to allow more even heat all around the batter being baked as well as giving you a cavity in which to put a sweet gooey filling. What sort of cake pan to use? Only your recipe knows for sure.

Calabaza
Caribbean and Central, South, and (temperate) North American squashlike vegetable of the gourd family (family Cucurbitacaea) with a yellow skin and an orangy-yellow interior that is similar, its advocates tell us, to a highly superior pumpkin.

Calamari
See SQUID.

Calamint
An herb (*Satureja calamintha*) akin to SAVORY, used sometimes with vegetables (such as zucchini), game, and hearty dishes or to make tea.

Calamondin
A tropical tree (*Citrus mitis*) producing small, juicy, orange-red fruits used for fruit drinks and marmalade.

Calas
1. Nutmeg-flavored rice cakes eaten hot as a breakfast bread in New Orleans, where they were once colorfully hawked through the city by street vendors.

2. A picnic HAM.

Calendula
See POT MARIGOLD.

Calf
A young beef critter, aged from three months to two years when slaughtered. It is also sometimes referred to as BABY BEEF.

Calf's-Foot Jelly

An aspic made from simmering calves' feet until all the gelatin has been obtained. It can then be flavored and served. It was once highly thought of as a nutritious offering for those who were ailing or recuperating from ailments.

California Yellowtail

A fish of the JACK family.

Callalou

A West Indian soup and also the two different greens—TARO and the variety of AMARANTH known as *Chinese spinach*—that go into it, all of which are known by the same name. The soup consists of garlic, onion, salt pork, and a little thyme set cooking in chicken or fish stock. The greens are then added, and the whole dish augmented with okra and crabmeat and seasoned with salt, pepper, Tabasco sauce, and perhaps coconut milk. Food writer Nika Hazleton, in her *Unabridged Vegetable Cookbook*, allows that regular spinach and Swiss chard substitute very nicely for the two callalou greens.

Calvados

A French apple BRANDY.

Calzone

A variation on PIZZA. The typical pizza toppings are encased in baked or deep-fried dough instead of a flat pastry.

Cambric Tea

A youngster's substitute for TEA, composed of sweetened hot water with a dash of milk and perhaps a dollop of tea.

Camel

Camelus bactrianus and *Camelus dromedarius*, an Asian or African ruminant. It is eaten in North Africa and the Middle East and, according to one fastidious Frenchman, tastes like beef and smells like goat.

Camembert

The original Camembert is a soft-centered, slightly hard-rinded cow's-milk CHEESE from the village of the same name and its environs in the French region of Normandy. It is certainly one of the world's most famous cheeses and, as such, is imitated with varying degrees of success all over the world. The very best Camembert is made in the section of Normandy known as the Valley d'Auge and will be so labeled. At its finest, it is made from unpasteurized milk.

Camomile

See CHAMOMILE.

Campari
A reddish-brown proprietary Italian BITTERS.

Canada Goose
A common WILD GOOSE of North America (*Branta canadensis*).

Canadian Bacon
A cured and smoked meat from the loin of the pig. It is leaner and tastier than regular BACON and costs more.

Canadian Fish-Cooking Principle
A cooking method devised by the Canadian Department of Fisheries and generally accepted as the most authoritative word on the subject. Under these guidelines, a fish—any fish—is placed on its side and measured at its thickest part. A fresh fish is then cooked for 10 minutes per inch no matter what form that fish takes—whole, steaks, or fillets—and no matter what cooking method you plan on using. (In other words, if a fish measures one inch at its thickest, it would require 10 minutes of cooking time; if two inches, 20 minutes.) For poaching, you begin timing after the fish is in the simmering water and the water has returned to a simmer; if sautéing or frying, count on 10 minutes per inch or any fraction thereof; if baking, use a 450°F oven; if your fillets are rolled, measure them after rolling. The method also works for frozen fish if you cook the fish still frozen and double the cooking time—20 minutes per inch instead of 10.

Canadian Whiskey
A popular, light-bodied alcoholic spirit fermented in Canada from cereal grains under stringent government supervision.

Canapé
Any bite-sized, sandwich-style snack served at buffets, cocktail parties, or receptions.

Candied
A method of putting a GLAZE on vegetables such as yams by cooking them at least in part in a sugar syrup.

Candy
All those sugary confections that feed our "sweet tooth," rot our teeth, and lift our spirits. Few people seem to make candy at home any more, which is a pity. The homemade types are probably no better (or worse) for you than the commercial kind, but they're more fun and, with any degree of luck or skill, better tasting.

Candy Thermometer
A special thermometer, calibrated from about 40°F to anywhere from 375°F to 450°F. The best have some device for elevating the thermometer's bulb from the bottom of

the pan. Such devices are useful not only in making candy, but also when making jelly or checking the temperature when you are deep-frying something.

Cane Syrup

A very sweet, thick sugar-cane syrup.

Cannelini

A BEAN generally used in soups and stews.

Cannelloni

Hollow PASTA tubes stuffed usually with meat or cheese. Smaller versions are labeled *canelle* and even smaller, *cannelini*.

Cannoli

An Italian pastry shaped like a cylinder and filled with pastry cream (as with an ÉCLAIR, for example) or other sweet filling.

Canola Oil

See RAPESEED OIL.

Cantal

A hard, white cow's-milk CHEESE with a sharp taste, from the area of Cantal in the Auvergne in central France. It has been known (very occasionally) to develop an internal mold which gives it a light veining of blue, an addition to its name (it becomes Bleu de Cantal), and a premium to its price.

Cantaloupe

A widespread and popular MELON.

Canvasback

A large North American WILD DUCK (*Aythya valisineria*).

Cape Cod Turkey

A codfish dinner, presumably for Thanksgiving, but opinions vary as to whether it calls for a whole, fresh fish or for salt cod (there are recipes for both). In an area where turkeys were rare and cod both abundant and indispensable, it would seem only right to celebrate the harvest festival with the fish that had kept body and soul together the rest of the year.

Cape Gooseberry

See GROUND-CHERRY.

Capelin

See ICEFISH.

Capelli d'Angelo
Also ANGEL HAIR, a slim PASTA used in soups and side dishes.

Caper
A bush (*Capparis spinosa*) widely grown around the Mediterranean, the buds of which are picked and pickled to add zest to appetizers, sauces, salad dressings, stews, and other dishes that can use a little lift. Attempts are being made to establish the plant commercially in California.

Capon
A neutered male chicken weighing six pounds or more, usually quite a bit more. True capons are tender and juicy, but many butchers feel that modern poultry-raising techniques can produce ordinary roasters with similar qualities for significantly less money. They're almost right.

Caponata
A Sicilian appetizer. It consists of diced and sautéed eggplant added to onions that have been sautéed and then cooked down in oil and tomato puree with sugar and vinegar. This is then embellished with capers, black olives, and julienned celery and left to cool while the tastes mingle. Although it can be served either hot or cold, it is usually served at room temperature or slightly cooler. It can also provide an out-of-the-ordinary pasta sauce.

Cappelletti
A type of PASTA, served stuffed.

Cappuccino
An Italian espresso COFFEE served with a topping of frothy, hot milk or cream, often with spices as well as sugar.

Caprice des Dieux
A mild, oval-shaped French DOUBLE CREAM cow's-milk cheese widely imported into North America.

Capsicum
A genus of PEPPER that includes the sweet or bell peppers and CHILI peppers. Aside from the name, it bears no relationship to regular table or seasoning pepper.

Carambola
See STAR FRUIT.

Caramel
A flavoring, and also a candy, prepared by heating sugar until it turns to a brownish color—the degree of brown depending upon the length of time it was cooked. Liquid caramel is used as a flavoring. Solid caramel is the base for peanut brittle and

similar confections. Caramel candy has milk and butter added and presents a soft, chewy consistency.

Caramelize

To cook sugar to attain the consistency of CARAMEL. If you take about 2 parts water to 1 part granulated sugar, mix them together, and heat them over a very low flame, stirring constantly, you will ultimately achieve a rich, dark brown mixture (at which point you can take it off the stove and let it cool). This is caramel and represents the final stage in cooking sugar; it occurs when the sugar reaches a temperature of 360°F. A few drops of this mixture added to another dish will give that dish a dark color without any change in taste; the process is called caramelization.

Caraway

An annual herb (*Carum carvi*), the aromatic seeds of which have accompanied humankind so long that it is now only conjecture as to where caraway originally came from. Caraway seeds are used especially in rye bread and in cheese, but are also useful for flavoring seafood, pork dishes, and sauerkraut, and are found in the liqueur kümmel.

Carbonnade Flamande

A Belgian beef stew made by browning pieces of beef in a combination of oil and butter, then braising them with onions and garlic, some herbs (such as parsley and thyme), and a combination of beef stock and stout (or other strong beer).

Carciofini

A kind of tiny preserved ARTICHOKE served in Italy as an antipasto.

Cardamom

The fruit of an herb (*Elettaria cardamomum*) native to India and Sri Lanka. The marble-sized, straw-colored pod contains a mass of small, black, aromatic seeds somewhat resembling ANISE in taste. Available whole or ground (the whole is the better bet, as cardamom loses some of its savor on grinding), it is used in Indian cooking and in some Scandinavian pastries. A single seed will give a pleasant and distinctive flavor to a cup of after-dinner coffee. When using whole cardamom in cooking, break open the pods and add both the seeds and the pods to your dish. The pods will break up and amalgamate into the dish.

Cardoon

A Mediterranean thistle (*Cynara cardunculus*) related to the artichoke and cultivated for its stalk, which looks a little like a graying version of celery, and, to a much lesser extent, for its roots, which can be briefly boiled and served cold with oil and vinegar as an appetizer or in a salad. The stalks, shorn of leaves and destringed (as you would celery), can be cut into inch-long segments (they discolor when cut, so drop them into ACIDULATED WATER), parboiled for a few minutes or so (the very young, tender ones can also be used raw), then put into soups and salads or breaded and sautéed in oil and served, for example, with a tomato or cream sauce. They are also a fixture of a BAGNA CAUDA. You are far more likely to find cardoons in Europe than in the Americas. If you do find them, look for firm stalks (the outer leaves will probably be too tough to use) and keep them refrigerated, but not longer than a day or two.

Caribou

A large deer (*Rangifer tarandus*) of northern North America (identical to the European reindeer). It can be prepared like venison.

Carob

The pod of a Mediterranean tree (*Ceratonia siliqua*), used as a replacement for chocolate. It is a handy substitute if you are allergic to chocolate or consider it injurious to the health but, alas, is a pale imitation of the real thing. Those who grow their own (it takes a warm, dry, Mediterranean-like climate) state that the fresh fruit is sweet and chewy but that processing it into powder form is a chore. The pod is also referred to as *Saint John's Bread* on the theory that this, and not locusts, was what nourished Saint John the Baptist during his sojourn in the desert.

Carp

A freshwater fish (*Cyprinus carpio*) of Asian ancestry but now found throughout the world. Carp is especially important in Eastern Europe, where it is traditional for Christmas Eve, as well as in Asia, but it is also widely used in parts of Western Europe as well. (Large European estates often had a special carp pond to ensure a well-regulated supply.) Carp was introduced into North America in the 1870s and has since made itself completely at home in brooks and rivers all over the continent.

Unless you catch it yourself (angling and bow fishing are the most common methods), you are likely to find live carp in tanks in markets serving "ethnic" neighborhoods (Asian, Eastern European, Jewish) and you are most likely to find them during holiday seasons. Market carp usually range from 2 to 10 pounds (although they can grow considerably larger—up to 50 pounds or more), and generally the market will offer the whole fish instead of steaks or fillets. You can recognize a carp by its large, coarse scales, brown on top and a kind of garish dirty yellow on the sides.

Selecting carp is no different from selecting any fish, except that you're much better off if you buy it live and even take it home live (carrying it in a plastic bag like a goldfish, which is itself a relative of the carp). Getting it ready for cooking requires a little care. To skin it: Drop it into boiling ACIDULATED WATER while you count (slowly) to ten. Remove the fish and carefully behead it—but watch out for a gland just behind the head that you want to get rid of. Take hold of the skin and pull it off (use pliers if it helps), scales and all. You may then want to let the fish soak for a half hour or so in acidulated water to rid it of any "muddiness" it may have picked up from wherever it had been hanging out.

You're now ready to cook your carp. A large carp is often baked stuffed or with various trimmings (tomatoes, onions, paprika, and sour cream is the Hungarian way), braised (especially in beer or red wine and flavorings), or stewed (with eel, onions, garlic, and herbs in red wine). The late American food writer James Beard recommended cooking carp fillets according to the SPENCER METHOD.

Another time-honored method is carp in the Jewish fashion, in which the carp is sliced into even pieces and poached in stock and white wine, then removed from the liquid and reformed into the shape of the original fish. The cooking liquid is boiled down, augmented with olive oil and sometimes with almonds and raisins, and poured over the fish, which is served cold. Carp in a sweet-and-sour sauce is another technique that has found favor through the ages as has carp braised with blanched carrots and gingersnaps soaked in sherry.

Carrageen

See IRISH MOSS.

Carré

A French term for square; it is also a cheesemaker's term for any French cheese made in a flat, square configuration.

Carrot

Our domestic carrot (*Daucus carota* var. *sativa*) was developed from a wild (probably) European original that seems to have come full circle and escaped from cultivation to proliferate in North America as the plant known as Queen Anne's lace. This wild carrot has a root that can be edible but lacks the sweetness and nutritive value of the garden carrot. To begin with, the wild variety lacks the yellow carotene, the substance that gives garden carrots their high content of vitamin C.

Domestic or garden carrots can be found with long roots or short ones (baby carrots), the latter at first imported from Europe, then cultivated in Canada, and more recently grown in the United States. Carrots are brought to market either fresh, with their tops intact, or trimmed and packaged. Those with tops are fresher, but the tops must be removed upon purchase or on arrival at home, or the carrots will very quickly dry out. Packaged carrots are harder to judge, but they are best when they are firm, uncracked, unforked, and a bright orangey gold. (Carrots come in other colors, shapes, and sizes, too, but these will be seen rarely if at all in our vegetable markets.) They keep reasonably well in the refrigerator, if you have enough room for them.

Carrots are good cooked or raw; can be pressed for their juice; made into soup, salad, cake, or jelly; can be added to stews, meatloaves, and braised dishes; or cooked up in any number of ways to serve as a side vegetable.

Cascabel
A small, reddish-brown CHILI pepper running from mild to fairly hot.

Cashew
A nut of a tree (*Anacardium occidentale*) of the sumac family (poison ivy and all its kin) originally native to the Amazon but now most notably cultivated in India and Africa. It must be exposed to extreme heat (thoroughly charring the outside is one technique) to rid it of its oily secretions that would otherwise cause a nasty itchy rash. The processed nut can be eaten as is or roasted. Cashews are mostly used as a superior snack food as further cooking tends to turn them soft, although they are also useful in certain stuffings.

Casing
The "skin" of a sausage, traditionally made from the intestines of a pig or other meat animal (although most commercial casings are made of an edible substitute). Almost any good butcher will either have casings or can get them for you, should you decide to try your hand at sausage-making. A meat grinder with a sausage-stuffing attachment would be of great help.

Cassareep
The milky juices of the CASSAVA plant, boiled down (they are toxic raw), flavored with spices and sugar, and used as a flavoring, especially in the West Indies and Latin America.

Cassava
A starchy root (*Manihot esculenta*) and staple food of large areas of Africa, Southeast Asia, and Latin America. In Europe and North America it is known as TAPIOCA; other names for it include *yuca* in Latin America and *manioc* in sections of Africa. It grows prodigiously, keeps well if unharvested, but spoils very quickly once detached from the parent plant. It is made into FARINHA and is also used in breads and stews and in place of rice, except in North America, where it is mostly maligned as the chief ingredient of tapioca pudding. The juice is boiled down and used as a flavoring agent in the West Indies and Latin America under the name of CASSAREEP.

Casserole
A fairly deep, oval, round, or rectangular cooking vessel intended for oven cooking; also the name of any dish made in one. Casserole containers can be made out of any material that will hold and diffuse heat (including aluminum, cast iron, pottery, and stainless steel) and customarily have two small handles instead of the single, long type seen on frying pans. Casseroles are much appreciated for providing the cook the ability to cook a whole meal in one dish.

Cassia

The dried bark of an Oriental tree (*Cinnamomum cassia*) used in curries and as an inferior substitute for CINNAMON.

Cassis

A French word for black CURRANT (*Ribes nigrum*) and the name of the cordial (*crème de cassis*) made from it, which is used as a sweetener in drinks (including the aperitif known as KIR) and as a garnish for fruit-flavored ice cream (it's especially good with black raspberry). The name also applies, quite separately, to a wine made in Provence.

Cassoulet

A French casserole consisting of dried white beans, preserved goose (goose put down in gobs of its own fat to keep over the winter), sausage, and bits of lamb. Now that preserved goose is a luxury instead of the common means of keeping the meat from spoiling, leftover roast goose or duck is a handy substitute.

Castor Sugar

A British term for a SUGAR with a consistency somewhere between that of granulated and powdered sugar. If your recipe calls for castor sugar, use granulated.

Catawba

A once-popular North American wine grape (*Vitis labrusca*) giving a heavy, slightly sweet, white wine with a pronounced FOXY taste. An attempt to revive demand for a sparkling Catawba was made in the 1960s, but fortunately it quickly subsided.

Catchup

Another spelling of CATSUP.

Catfish

Almost any of a large family (Ictaluridae) of brackish water and freshwater fish. In the southern United States, catfish are almost a religion. They are easy to catch, are found everywhere, and are eaten apparently by everyone. In the Deep South they are deep-fried. Catfish can, of course, also be panfried, poached, or used in a stew in case you happen to be feeling heretical. You'll find the meat to be tasty, lean, and moist, though detractors say it lacks character. Some catfish give white meat, and there are also varieties that give meat with a reddish tinge.

However you decide to cook your catfish, skin it first. The Alabama method for doing this is to put the fish down on its belly and imagine a line on the side of the head running from the base of the skull down to just behind the pectoral fin (the one behind the gills). Place your knife on this line and slice just to—but not through—the backbone. Go back to the beginning of the cut and make two more slices, one on each side of the backbone and running all the way to the tail. Peel back the corners of the skin, cut around the top fin and cut it out. Now hold the fish in both hands, head in one hand, body in the other, and bring both hands sharply down and together, snapping the backbone. (On a monster-sized fish, you'll need your knee for leverage.) A strong tug should then remove the backbone, innards and all.

If you think hush puppies (see HUSH PUPPY) with your deep-fried catfish are a cliché, just give them a try and find out why the cliché came into being to begin with.

Catsup

A sauce, mostly based on tomato but sometimes made with a base of a number of other foods, including cranberries, grapes, guavas, mangoes, mushrooms, and walnuts. Commercial tomato catsup is usually a mixture of strained tomato liquid with an acid (such as lemon juice) that is flavored with salt, spices (including garlic or onion), some form of sweetener, and vinegar. Its sweetness helps mask the taste of much mediocre counter food.

Cattail

A marsh plant (*Typha latifolia*) described by wild food expert Euell Gibbons as a "supermarket in a swamp," in honor of its many uses. The leaves, roots, and stems are all edible and nutritious, and even the pollen can serve as a corn-flavored flour or flour stretcher.

Cattalo

A cross between a bison and a polled Angus beef animal, bred to produce meat with the leanness of bison (or BUFFALO) and the flavor of beef.

Caul

The lining of the lower intestine used as a CASING for sausages. Specialty butchers may have it or can order it, but some sausage makers suggest you try making sausages that can be cooked as patties before you embark on trying the cased variety. In Chinese cookery, caul is also used as a wrapping for foods to be deep-fried or steamed.

Cauliflower

A vegetable (*Brassica oleracea* var. *botrytis*) and relative of broccoli that is grown for its tightly closed, creamy white, undeveloped flowers rather than its leaves. These cauliflower heads are for the most part white, although the Mediterranean countries boast more colorful varieties, some of which are beginning to be cultivated in North America.

When you buy cauliflower, look for compact, dense heads—the whiter the better. If you see spots or blotches on them, look elsewhere. Once you get the vegetable home, trim off the base and any unwanted leaves and either leave the head intact or separate it into flowerets.

Cauliflower can be blanched and refreshed and served as a crudité, steamed and served with a cream or cheese sauce, mashed, pickled, dipped in batter and deep-fried, baked, or made into soup. Bear in mind that, like most vegetables, cauliflower does not reward overcooking.

It is not a great idea to buy cauliflower too far ahead of when you'll use it, as it tends to get somewhat rank as it ages. For storage (two or three days will do you no harm) keep it wrapped in plastic—if that's the way you bought it—or pop it into a plastic bag and put it in the vegetable drawer of the refrigerator.

Cavatelli
A noodle PASTA, curled up on itself.

Caviar
The prepared eggs (or *roe*) of the beluga, sevruga, sterlet, or sturgeon, all members of the sturgeon family, although the eggs of other fish such as cod, lumpfish, salmon, and whitefish sometimes borrow the name. Caviar is prepared by (lightly) kneading or beating the ovaries to loosen the eggs, straining them to dispose of extraneous tissue, then (very lightly) salting and usually pressing them for commercial packaging. Canned or bottled caviar is fairly widely available, but doesn't begin to compare to fresh.

The very best sturgeon caviar comes from the Caspian Sea, from Iran, Caucasia, and Kazahkstan, and it costs a mint. The common sturgeon of North American waters has been tried for caviar, but the fish is no longer common (overfishing and pollution seem to have diminished it) and not much seems to have come of the practice. The very best caviar consists of tiny—the smaller the better—eggs, gray rather than black in color and not too salty. (The most sought after is actually more amber than gray, is known as "imperial caviar," and is exceedingly rare.)

It is recommended that caviar, especially fresh caviar which must be kept chilled from the outset, be eaten chilled—preferably in a bowl nested into another bowl full of ice—ungarnished (except perhaps for a little lemon juice), and with a small, sterling silver spoon. The silver is used because it is inert (it imparts no alien taste) and because it is elegant, although in this case probably weighing in at considerably less value than the caviar you are putting in it. If you're not up to silver, bone is equally acceptable.

Cayenne
A CHILI pepper originally from Cayenne in the South American country of Guyana. It is one of the ingredients of cayenne pepper, now more popularly designated *hot red pepper.*

Cazuela

A flat, round, earthenware cooking vessel from Spain used for making PAELLA and similar dishes. As so often happens with containers such as this, the word is also applied to the hefty stew that is cooked in it.

Ceci

An Italian name for CHICKPEA.

Celeriac

Also known as *celery root*, *knob celery*, or *turnip-rooted celery*. It is a European celery (*Apium graveolens* var. *rapaceum*) grown for its edible root rather than its leaves. Celeriac is a brown knob that must be peeled. If you're using it raw, pop the peeled sections into ACIDULATED WATER right away or they will discolor. If you're cooking it, the peel comes off more easily after the cooking process. You can then slice, JULIENNE, or shred it for salad, soup, or dipping in batter for deep-frying. It is also used as a side vegetable. When choosing celeriac, pick a dense, hefty knob with plenty of weight for its size. Look out for any that look shriveled or soft. Pick one with some size to it, too, or you risk being left with a lot of peel and only a little root. Wrapped in plastic, it will keep for almost a week if refrigerated.

Celery

A useful vegetable (*Apium graveolens* var. *dulce*), the rib stalks and leaves of which are both edible. It is available in two forms, blanched (usually seen as *celery hearts*) and green, the difference being that the former is kept from light in order to keep it white, whereas the latter is greened by the sun, just like any other plant.

Celery leaves can be removed from the rest of the plant, cut up, and dried to give an herb that will add flavor to soups, stews, and meat dishes. The ribs can be eaten raw or cooked. In general, it is advisable to take any of the tougher outer stalks and use them for cooking, reserving the inner ones for more delicate duty. (Traditionally, these outer stalks were stringy and had to be destringed—you just pulled the strings off and threw them away—before they could be used. In practice, this is not always the case today, thanks to the stringless varieties developed by plant breeders.)

Celery can be cut into whirls or curls or stuffed to be served raw as an hors d'oeuvre. It can be baked, braised, deep-fried, or made into soup. Celery makes an interesting addition to stews or a tossed salad and is all but indispensable in adding both flavor and crunchiness to stuffings for fowl, shoulder of veal, or whatever you have that cries out for stuffing. Look for light green, crisp stalks with unwilted leaves. If you keep it damp enough, unused celery can be kept in a tightly closed plastic bag in the vegetable drawer of the refrigerator for quite a long time—weeks, not days. And if it goes limp on you, try putting it in cold water for an hour or two.

Celery Cabbage

See PE-TSAI.

Celery Root

See CELERIAC.

Celery Salt

A ground CELERY SEED mixed with table salt.

Celery Seed

A seed of the LOVAGE plant, related to celery. It is an ingredient of pickling spice and is useful for flavoring all sorts of meats (hamburgers and hot dogs, for example), fish, and vegetables as well as anywhere celery itself is useful.

Cellophane Noodles

Very thin, transparent Chinese noodles made from MUNG beans, with little if any flavor. They provide texture and a base for noodle dishes. Don't try to keep any cooked noodles around, though—they'll simply turn mushy on you.

Celsius

A temperature scale used by virtually everyone except Americans and even by American scientists, as opposed to a FAHRENHEIT scale commonly used in the United States. Also known as *centigrade*, the scale is named for the Danish astronomer Anders Celsius who first formulated it in 1742. If you have the temperature in degrees Fahrenheit and wish to convert it to Celsius, subtract 32 from your number and multiply the result by 5/9 (or by .556).

Cendré

A French cheesemakers' term for any CHEESE ripened in (usually edible) wood ashes, often the ashes from the trimmings pruned from grapevines.

Centigrade

The CELSIUS temperature scale.

Cèpe

A French MUSHROOM.

Cereal

The classic grains that have made up, and still make up, the staple diet of the vast majority of humankind—BARLEY, CORN, MILLET, RICE, and WHEAT. There are other cereals, of course, but none of quite such overriding nutritional importance. Among the runners-up might be included BUCKWHEAT, OAT, RYE, SORGHUM, and WILD RICE, and among recent rediscoveries AMARANTH and QUINOA. TRITICALE is a hybridized cereal grain that has come on the scene more recently. The word *cereal* has also come to cover the product of these grains when they are used as commercially prepared breakfast food.

Ceriman

Another name for the MONSTERA fruit.

Cero

A member of the MACKEREL family, its habitat ranges roughly from Massachusetts through the Gulf of Mexico and into the waters off northern Brazil. It is found in abundance off the Antilles, the Bahamas, and Florida.

Cervelat

A smoked pork (or pork and beef) sausage flavored with garlic, mustard, and other flavorings. A type of cervelat was at one time also made with eel.

Chabichou

A French goat's-milk CHEESE traditionally made in cone shapes, but commercially seen as cylinders or rectangles.

Chablis

A highly renowned French dry white wine from Burgundy, the best of which is sold with the name of its vineyard (as, for example, Chablis-Vaudésir), the rest simply as Chablis or, slightly farther down the scale, Petit Chablis. The name is also used for any more or less dry white wine (and sometimes even rosé) from anywhere other than France.

Chafing Dish

A nifty gadget for cooking or keeping things warm at the serving table, now mostly found at professional buffets. It consists of a pan (with cover) that fits into a basin of water (or water jacket), all suspended over a source of heat—alcohol or stove fuel. For cooking, the water jacket is removed and the pan exposed to the direct flame; for warming something or keeping it hot, the water jacket stays in place. The heat is regulated by a wick or a snuffer that can be adjusted from fully open (for hot fires) to fully closed (to turn it off) to anything in between.

Challah

A Jewish, slightly sweet, white, yeast-risen, light and eggy Sabbath bread with an egg-white glaze. It is commonly formed in the shape of braids.

Chalonnais

A French wine-growing region of southern Burgundy that produces extraordinarily pleasant red and white wines, which are generally a cut below the wines of the neighboring Côte d'Or. The region comprises the villages of Givry, Mercurey, Montagny, and Rully, but the name you will see most frequently on its wine labels will be CHARDONNAY, the name of the grape used for making the white wines.

Chalupa

A boat-shaped TORTILLA stuffed with just about anything you happen to have on hand. Mexicans use it as an appetizer.

Chamomile

A European plant (*Anthemis nobilis*) of the composite family (asters and all that), the leaves of which are aromatic and were much used by Victorian ladies (and also Peter Rabbit) to brew a tea thought to restore failing vigor. Herb gardeners sometimes also grow German or sweet chamomile (*Matricaria chamomilla*), which is similar if slightly stronger.

Champagne

The world's most famous sparkling wine. It comes from France's Champagne district, but the name has been appropriated for almost any sparkling wine anywhere. One of true Champagne's distinctions is that it is made by the "Champagne process," in which the sparkle is fermented into the wine right in the bottle. Lesser sparkling wines are often bulk-fermented (in large vats) or even charged with carbon dioxide, with a concomitant decrease in the quality of the final product. The better sparkling wines are labeled "Champagne process" or "*méthode champenoise*," except for true Champagne, which cannot legally be sold unless it is made that way, and thereby needs no further labeling.

The French label their Champagne according to the amount of sugar added to it. *Brut* is the driest, followed by *extra sec, sec, demi-sec*, and *doux*.

Champignon

A French term for MUSHROOM and also for a mushroom-shaped PESTLE used for working foods through a horizontal, or drum, sieve.

Chantelle

A CHEESE; a North American variation on BEL PAESE.

Chanterelle

A wild MUSHROOM.

Chaource

A French cow's-milk cheese from the Champagne district. It is similar to CAMEMBERT.

Chapati

A staple breadstuff of Northern India. Chapatis can be made by taking 1½ lb. (4 cups) coarse Indian wheat flour (half white and half whole wheat non-Indian flours are said to be a satisfactory substitute), a pinch of salt, and an ounce of clarified butter or ghee, working it into a dough with cold water, and leaving it to stand an hour or so. The dough is then formed into balls the size of tennis balls, rolled out (the Indians clap them between the palms of their hands) until flat, and finally baked on a hot griddle. Chapatis can also be made with rice flour, as is common in southern India where rice is the more abundant grain.

Chapon

A heel of bread rubbed with garlic and moistened with olive oil and vinegar. It is rubbed against the inside of a salad bowl in order to impart a little extra whiff of garlic, and can even be left in with the salad, just for tossing purposes—or longer if you wish to achieve a more intense tang of garlic.

Char

A species of fish so similar to TROUT that several of them are known popularly as trout whereas others may be termed salmon-trout. Together with GRAYLING, trout, and SALMON they are counted among the family Salmonidae. Char of various sorts are among the most sought-after gamefish, and nearly all of them grace the dining table (or camp kitchen) with flesh that is slightly pinker than trout. Like other salmonids, char seek cold water. As with trout, those you see in the market will be farm raised and tend to be inferior to those taken in the wild. Char may be cooked following any method appropriate for trout.

Among the more notable chars are:

Arctic char (*Salvelinus alpinus*). Found in northern waters including those of Alaska, Canada, Greenland, Iceland, Norway, and Siberia. A landlocked version is found in parts of Europe—including the Alps—where it is known as *omble chevalier*.

Brook trout (*Salvelinus fontinalis*). Also *speckled trout*. This fish likes cold running streams from Canada down the eastern coast of the United States and into Argentina. It is much more of a gamefish than a market fish, although its firm, mild flesh is appreciated at the table.

Bull trout (*Salvelinus confluentus*). A char of western North America, from Idaho up into Canada. More a gamefish than a table fish.

Dolly Varden (*Salvelinus malma*). A West Coast species found from Alaska down to Washington state. It's apparently a piscatorial washout—no great shakes as a gamefish and dullsville on the table.

Lake trout (*Salvelinus namaycush*). Found from Alaska down through the length of Canada into New York's Finger Lakes and the Great Lakes. A fine-flavored fish with market implications at least in the north.

Charbroil

To cook something over charcoal; GRILL.

Chard
A vegetable of the BEET family, more commonly known as *Swiss chard*.

Chardonnay
A French grapevine (*Vitis vinifera*) in wide use in Burgundy and, to a lesser extent, in Champagne. It is also grown all over the world. It is noted for the superior dry white wines it produces. It was previously known as Pinot Chardonnay, apparently because it was once thought to be related to the vines of the Pinot family.

Charlotte
A fairly small (although they come in different sizes), round mold, traditionally tin, with slightly sloping sides intended for cooking apple charlotte, a dessert consisting of slices of bread sautéed (or soaked) in melted butter and placed in the mold to form a lining, then topped with cooked, pureed, flavored apples augmented with apricots or apricot preserve, topped with more bread, baked, chilled, unmolded, and served at room temperature. Charlottes can also be made with ladyfingers instead of bread and with apricots, peaches, pears, or other fruit as well as filled with a fruit-flavored Bavarian cream. One made with ladyfingers and Bavarian cream would become a *charlotte russe*. The mold is equally handy for any food (Jell-O, for instance) that craves cooling in a mold. The word celebrates the heroine of Johann Wolfgang von Goethe's novel *The Sorrows of Young Werther*, a rousing popular success when it was first published in 1774.

Chartreuse
An ancient, herb-flavored, brandy-based liqueur available in two forms, green and yellow. The green is stronger, the yellow sweeter.

Chasselas
A table and wine grape (*Vitis vinifera*) of European origin producing a delicate white wine. It is grown especially in Germany and Switzerland.

Chateaubriand
A large (enough for two people), thick piece of the finest porterhouse steak, grilled and served with a BÉARNAISE sauce, in which shallots are cooked down in herb-flavored (tarragon, chervil, bay leaf) vinegar and wine, then enriched with egg yolks and butter, and finished off with a dash of lemon juice.

Châteauneuf-du-Pape
A full-bodied, deeply colored red wine of the French Rhône valley. A small amount of white is also made, but you'll probably have to go to France to find it.

Chaud-froid
A French term for a dish that has been cooked, glazed with aspic, and chilled.

Chayote

A tropical squash (*Sechium edule*) grown throughout South and Central America, the West Indies, and also in North Africa where it is used in COUSCOUS. About the size of an acorn squash or a very large pear, it is greenish-white to dark green in color, has one large seed, and yields a bland flesh that can be prepared like that of any other squash. When buying one, make sure it is firm, not squishy. You can keep it in the refrigerator for several weeks.

Checkerberry

Also called *teaberry* and *wintergreen*. A North American plant (*Gaultheria procumbens*) producing aromatic, red berries that mature in the late summer but remain on the plant throughout the winter, gaining in juiciness as they do. The leaves may be used for an herbal tea, and the oil obtained from it is used as a flavoring, as in wintergreen-flavored chewing gum.

Cheddar

A cheese originally of English origin but now a world citizen; indeed, English Cheddar is seldom seen in North American markets and is no better than (and often inferior to) some of the Cheddars made in Canada, New York State, and Vermont. It is technically a firm cow's-milk cheese with a full-bodied, mild to sharp taste (depending upon its age) and is either light cream-colored or dyed yellow (using annatto or sometimes marigold). It is without a doubt North America's favorite cheese and a highly versatile one, too; useful in cooking (WELSH RABBIT for example), for snacks, with crackers, and melted over hamburgers. It is so traditional with apple pie that many pie lovers consider that dessert incomplete without it.

The maneuver that gives a Cheddar its special consistency, known as cheddaring, is a technique of cutting and turning and stacking the curd after the whey has dripped out. This rids it of any residual whey and lends body to the final product.

Cheese

Essentially, it is artificially curdled milk, usually aged and sometimes flavored. The French statesman Charles de Gaulle is once said to have remarked on the impossibility of governing France, explaining that it is a nation so stubbornly independent that it has 246 separate types of cheese. Maybe so, but given the possibilities inherent in cheese-making, 246 individual, separate, usually aged and sometimes flavored varieties of artificially curdled milk represent but a drop in the bucket. The possible permutations are endless.

Cheese has been made from the milk of a rich variety of animals, including buffalo, cows, goats, reindeer, sheep, and (who knows?) maybe even llamas, yaks, and zebras. The type of animal, the food it eats, the climate it inhabits, the way the milk is treated, the yeasts in the air, the way the cheese is made and worked over, the amount of time it is aged, and the place where the aging occurs will all show up one way or another in the cheese, giving us a seemingly infinite number of possible cheeses.

That having been said, it remains that cheese can be broken up into four simple types: *soft*, *semisoft*, *firm*, and *hard*. Among the soft cheeses are the fresh cheeses, the cottage and cream cheeses, as well as such quick ripeners as Brie and Camembert and their followers, which are ripened by the addition of penicillin or some other mold or spore. The semisoft group embraces brick and Munster, Liederkranz and Limburger, Gorgonzola and Roquefort; they are ripened by bacteria or, with the blue cheeses, by a blue mold. Among the firm cheeses are Cheddar, Cheshire, Caciocavalla and Emmenthaler, Gruyère, and Jarlsberg. The hard cheeses comprise the grating cheeses—Asiago, Parmesan (or Parmigiano-Reggiano if it is the genuine Italian article), and Romano. Firm and hard cheeses are all ripened by bacterial action.

Cheesecake

An admirable, if caloric, dessert compounded of cream or cottage cheese with sugar, eggs, various flavorings, and—sometimes—sour cream, perhaps set in a graham-cracker crust and served cold. It can be made plain or with such additions as cherries, strawberries, or other fruits, or nuts. Although a form of it was held in high honor in ancient Greece, cheesecake seems to have reached its modern pinnacle in the 1920s in New York City, at a Broadway restaurant called Lindy's.

Cheesecloth

A finely meshed cotton cloth with a wide variety of applications, including holding cheese curd while the whey drips out of it. Other than that, it can hold herbs to flavor a soup or stew and make them removable, can be used to line a colander should you wish to strain a broth or soup, and is handy for cleaning up.

Cheese Straws

Strips of cheese-flavored pastry baked until crunchy, often served with soup.

Chef's Salad

It depends to some extent upon the chef, but customarily this salad includes greens augmented with strips of cheese, meat or poultry, and perhaps strips of vegetable as well as some hard-boiled egg.

Chenin Blanc

A wine grape (*Vitis vinifera*) originally from France's Loire Valley, where it is responsible for such wines as Vouvray. It is also grown elsewhere, especially in California, where it is capable of producing a moderately dry white wine of delicacy and grace.

Cherimoya

Also *custard apple*. A new-world fruit tree bearing a round, oval, or heart-shaped fruit. This tropical and subtropical plant (*Annona cherimola*), originally native to

Brazil, Equador, and Peru, has been described as the only fruit with the consistency of ice cream. Although they come in many different varieties, cherimoyas are all ripe when soft to the touch but free of any black spots. Choose fruit that sits in the hand with some authority, not one light for its size. Scoop the flesh out of the shell, get rid of the seeds, and use the fruit plain or in a fruit salad or COMPOTE or MOUSSE. Until they ripen, keep cherimoyas at room temperature; then, if you must, refrigerate them, but only for a day or so. You're better off eating them as soon as they become ripe.

Cherry

The name of a wide-ranging group of fruit trees, both wild and domestic. Most wild cherries are suitable only for ornaments or attracting birds (some seem to attract little more than loathsome tent caterpillars, however), although one bushy variety, the CHOKECHERRY, provides a fine tart jelly and upon a little doctoring with sugar syrup and brandy can be blended into a pleasing cordial. And the black or rum cherry (*Prunus serotina*) combines the virtues of an excellent hardwood tree with a fruit that, with the addition of tart apple, produces a rich, sharp jelly said to be first-rate.

Some cherries—the spectacular Japanese flowering cherry, for example—are cultivated for their blossoms. But the varieties of the cherries we use as fruits are numbered in the hundreds, sufficient to satisfy even the gluttonous. Cherries have a number of uses in addition to immediate table use, including being made into jams, jellies, and syrups. They can also be made into fruit brandy, known as KIRSCH, and distilled into the liqueur MARASCHINO. Basically there are two kinds of cherries—sweet and sour. Both are available fresh (in season) and canned. (That there are hybrids as well is of more interest to the nurseryman than the cook.)

Sour cherries (*Prunus cerasus*). These are your true pie cherries. In general, sour cherries are not overly pleasant when eaten out of the hand—although some meet this test more or less—being a little too acid for most of us. This, of course, is just what makes them suitable for cooking and especially baking. The drawback is that sour cherries need ripening on the tree for full development and begin losing their excellence almost immediately upon picking. This tends to restrict fresh sour cherries at their best to those with a tree or two or those with access to an orchard where they are grown. They are worth the search, but don't set them aside and save them for a rainy day. Get your cherries, bake your pie, and don't fool around. (The pie filling can, however, be frozen for future use.) And if you don't like pie, you can use sour cherries in a number of other ways. You can, as the Danes do, make them into soup. (Blend 2 cups of cherries simmered in water and a piece of lemon rind until soft with 1 cup raw cherries and season with a little lemon juice and sugar to taste.) Or you can use them to make cobblers, tarts, jelly, or sauce for pancakes or ice cream—or ice cream itself.

Sweet cherries (*Prunus avium*). Most of the cherries we see in the market are sweet and ready to be picked up and eaten. There are also spectacular ways to treat cherries, such as cherries jubilee, a dish in which cherries that have been simmered in sugar syrup are flamed with kirsch and brought to the table as a fiery extravaganza. Sweet cherries can be used in place of sour cherries in cooking so long as you reduce the sugar called for in the recipe and add lemon juice. On a more mundane note, cherries can also be pickled in vinegar for use as an hors d'oeuvre.

When selecting cherries, look—as usual with fruits—for plump, sleek ones, firm and shiny and with the stems still intact. Go for the dark ones and avoid any that are sticky. If you must keep them, pop them in plastic and refrigerate them. In most houses, they have a habit of disappearing fairly quickly.

Cherry Pitter

At its simplest, a device much like a pair of pliers, with an open basket on one end and a rod on the other. The cherry (or olive or other fruit to be pitted) fits in the basket, you press the handles together, the rod swings through the fruit, and the pit is forced out. There are other, more complicated gadgets to accomplish the same chore available at kitchen supply places.

Cherrystone

A grading, according to size, of the New England CLAM.

Cherry Tomato

A small, round red or yellow TOMATO.

Chervil

1. A delicate herb (*Anthriscus cerefolium*) much in favor among the French, where it is often included in FINES HERBES and BOUQUET GARNI and used to flavor soups, salads, and meats, although it must be added judiciously; boiling destroys its taste. Try chopping some chervil into your next hamburger before it goes on the grill. Otherwise it is a handy replacement anywhere parsley is called for, although the taste is more delicate. Chervil is only at its best when fresh (or frozen); fresh chervil loses its savor quickly and dried chervil has little or no effectiveness.

2. A root vegetable (*Chaerophyllum tuberosum*) used for soups and stews and also served like carrots. If you wish to try it, you'll almost certainly have to move to Europe or grow it yourself, assuming you can find the seeds somewhere.

Cheshire

A firm English cow's-milk CHEESE that somewhat resembles Cheddar but is moister and more crumbly. It comes, like the American flag, in red, white, and blue. White Cheshire is made from plain, uncolored milk and does not keep as well as its kin. Red Cheshire has coloring matter added to the milk, turning it to a deep orange color, and Blue Cheshire is essentially an accident—cheese that has developed a mold that gives it blue veins and increases its value and desirability among true cheese lovers. It is a rare and spontaneous occurrence but it does happen.

Chestnut

A nut-bearing tree (*Castanea*); it is totally unrelated to the horse chestnut (*Aesculus hippocastanum*), the raw fruit of which is inedible if not downright dangerous.

The roast chestnuts that used to be sold by street vendors for very little money and the masses of chestnuts that were once used to stuff birds of all sorts are not so widely found these days—not since the blight took most of the American chestnut trees. Chestnuts are still available from Europe, luckily, but they cost more now. They are still excellent in stuffings and still are incomparable pureed, mixed with brussels sprouts or red cabbage, or used in baking and for candies (*marrons glacés* or glazed chestnuts are one classic), and even for making chestnut soup. The good news is that the tree people think they have developed a blight-resistant American chestnut, so maybe the tree will make a comeback.

Handling chestnuts seems to cause problems. The easiest way to prepare them is to make a gash with a *sharp* knife in their rounded side and drop them in boiling water for 10 to 15 minutes. Peel them while still as hot as you can handle—or hotter—and if they are hot enough you should be able to get the brown inner skin as well as the outer part without too much fuss.

Dried chestnuts are available in some specialty stores, and chestnut flour can also be found. In remote parts of Italy where chestnuts were plentiful, they were used to make various breads, cakes, fritters, and scones.

Chèvre

A French word used for *goat* and, by extension, any goat cheese.

Chianti

A red table wine from Italy's Tuscany, but the name is now extended to denote all sorts of robust red wines from all sorts of places. Some Chianti was once sold in straw-covered bottles (called *fiaschi*); first-rate Tuscan Chianti never was.

Chicken

Certainly the world's foremost domestic fowl. What was once the Sunday dinner special has become a relatively inexpensive staple, and we're all probably the healthier for it. Anyone who remembers (or can find) range-grown chicken will grouse quite rightly that today's battery-raised chickens simply don't have the same taste. Still, there are ways of making chicken tastier by using marinades, spices, and other flavoring agents or by serving it with distinctive accompaniments.

One of chicken's greatest assets is its versatility. You can poach it or grill it or roast it or deep-fry it or sauté it or braise it; you can stuff it or leave it unstuffed;

you can serve it hot or reheated or cold; you can put it in stews and in salads; you can chop it or grind it or leave it in parts or cope with it whole. About the only thing you can't do is eat it raw—and there's probably somebody somewhere right now who is perfecting a chicken tartare that will make steak tartare take a backseat.

It is fortunate that chicken is so forgiving, for it is undeniably more healthful than most other forms of animal protein. If you remove the skin and all of the identifiable fat, it becomes a virtual health food. And even if you like a little crispy skin now and again, or find chicken fat an occasional worthy cooking medium, you're still ahead of the game, even if your margin has been reduced.

When you run across chicken in the market, you're apt to find it either whole or split up into parts. Whole chicken is clearly more economical, but the parts are often a great convenience, and it's certainly a better idea to pay a bit more for parts than to buy more than you need and let the rest go to waste (although chicken freezes easily enough).

Some of the market terms you're likely to meet in respect to chicken are:

Broiler. A young chicken weighing 1 to 2½ pounds.

Broiler-fryer. A young chicken weighing 1 to 3½ pounds.

Capon. A neutered male chicken weighing at least 6 pounds and usually quite a bit more.

Fowl. It used to mean a large female chicken of a certain age and undesirable for any use other than the stew or stockpot. This usage seems to have fallen by the wayside.

Fryer. A young chicken weighing 2½ to 3½ pounds.

Roaster. A chicken weighing 3 to 5 pounds.

Chicken-Fried Steak

A piece of beef (rarely top grade) dipped in batter and deep-fried, as you would chicken.

Chicken Kiev

A fillet of chicken breast pounded very thin, rolled around slivers of often herbed butter (the American food writer James Beard felt it works best if the butter is frozen first), sealed into a discreet package, dipped in flour, beaten egg, and breadcrumbs, and then deep-fried.

Chicken Tetrazzini

Diced chicken breast heated in a white sauce augmented with heavy cream, nutmeg, and a little sherry, poured over freshly cooked pasta, covered with breadcrumbs and grated cheese, and then run quickly under the broiler. The dish was created for the renowned soprano Luisa Tetrazzini, who thrilled operagoers, especially in San Francisco, around the turn of the century.

Chickpea

An almost universal legume (*Cicer arietinum*), used fresh or dried. It is ground into flour, added to salads and soups and stews, and even roasted and ground into a substitute for coffee, although the French novelist Alexandre Dumas tells us that nothing very good ever came of that. It is an important source of protein in many parts of the world. Prevalent from western Asia to the Mediterranean, it is gaining ground in North America as well.

Chickpeas are known by a variety of names, depending upon where you are. In much of the world they are called *pulse*, although that word is also used for other peas and beans. In Italy they are *ceci*; in Spain and Spanish-speaking countries they are *garbanzos*; in India they are *gram*. The best dried chickpeas available in North America come from Spain and are firm, wrinkled, and yellowish-white. If they have blemishes or seem all shriveled up, don't buy them. Chickpeas are also available canned; give these a good washing before you use them.

Chicory

A plant (*Cichorium intybus*) that provides roots that are dried and ground as a substitute for or addition to coffee, especially in France and French-influenced areas. The foliage of the young plants (and that of other variants of the species) is also sold as a slightly bitter salad green that closely resembles ENDIVE or ESCAROLE, including a red variety known as RADICCHIO. Some varieties of chicory provide the sprout-like heads that are blanched and sold as BELGIAN ENDIVE or *witloof*.

Chiffonade

To the French, sliced bits of lettuce or other greenery ribbons to use in or as a basis for soup. It can also refer to a salad dressing of olive oil and vinegar gussied up with sliced beets and hard-boiled eggs.

Chiffon Cake

A light, delicate cake using oil instead of the usual kinds of shortening (butter, lard, goose fat, vegetable shortening) and gaining its rising from beaten eggs and a little baking powder. The use of liquid shortening means that you don't have to CREAM the shortening with the sugar.

Chiffon Pie

A one-crust pie filled with a mixture of egg yolks and gelatin with a flavoring of some sort, often topped with whipped cream.

Chiles Rellenos

A Southwestern and Mexican specialty of hot chili peppers stuffed with cheese (Monterey Jack is appropriate), dipped in an egg-white batter, and deep-fried. They are often served with tomato sauce.

Chili

A variety of hot peppers (*Capsicum* spp.) native to the American Southwest and points south. They are not to be confused with the green or bell PEPPER. There are a number of kinds of chilis ranging in taste from docile and mild to hair-raising. The real heat in the chili is in the seeds and veins; thus it follows that these should be removed. Because the oils in chilis are both irritants and volatile, you are best advised, when deseeding or deveining truly hot peppers, to coat your hands with whatever inexpensive oil is on your cooking shelf and not under any circumstances to succumb to a desire to rub your eye until you have *thoroughly* washed your hands. (There seems to be a perverse compulsion to rub the eyes when slicing chilis—don't do it.) Chilis may be found fresh, dried, pickled, or simply put up in bottles, perhaps, with diluted vinegar. Some of the more familiar ones include:

Anaheim. The mildest of the chilis, it can be either green or red and resembles a long, thin-skinned sweet PEPPER.

Ancho. The dried version of the poblano (see below). It is much used in Mexican cookery.

Cascabel. A small, reddish-brown pepper ranging from mild to fairly hot (taste it to see). It may also be found dried.

Cayenne. An extremely hot green or red pepper from Guyana in South America, usually powdered and mixed with other chilis to form a hot spice, now more commonly referred to on spice racks as *hot red pepper*.

Fresno. An especially hot green or red pepper grown in California.

Guero. A yellow and extremely hot pepper.

Habanero. Extremely hot green, purple, or red chili widely used in the cooking of the Caribbean, Central and South America, and West Africa.

Jalapeño. About the hottest of the Tex-Mex chilis. It ranges from green to greenish-black and has been used not only in the dishes you might expect but also to flavor cheese, preserves, and even ice cream.

Paprika. A zesty, bright red pepper that can be sweet and mild or slightly hot. Dried and powdered, it is essential to a great deal of Hungarian cooking, and for flavoring purposes only Hungarian paprika will truly suit, although paprika is grown elsewhere, notably California and Spain. Other paprikas will give your dish its typically cheerful red color, but only the Hungarian paprika will provide the taste.

Pasilla. A long, lean, hot pepper you will find dried.

Poblano. A very dark chili in a triangle shape, not particularly hot but slightly bitter.

Serrano. More likely to be found in Mexico than in the United States, this green (occasionally red) chili is a good match in the hotness department for the jalapeño. Use sparingly.

Tabasco. Yes, there is a tabasco pepper (very hot, green or red, often sold in bottles), but it is not an ingredient of TABASCO SAUCE.

Tuscan. An Italian, small, light green pepper, often pickled in brine, and much fancied for antipasti.

Chili Bean

A dark red BEAN much used, in dried form, in Southwestern cookery.

Chili con Carne

Literally, Spanish for "chili (peppers being understood) and meat." A spicily hot dish you'll also see spelled *chile* and *chilli*. Often the merits of the spelling are debated as hotly as what degree of incandescence makes a chili worthy of its name. Chili is, depending on your source, either a chopped or ground meat dish (beef, as a rule) with garlic, onion, sweet pepper, tomato, and spices of all sorts (basil, coriander, cumin, cinnamon, fennel, and oregano are often present), all heavily flavored with hot chili peppers. The same mixture may also be augmented with cooked, dried kidney beans although this is disallowed in Texas. Unless you are a True Believer yourself, it's usually best to stay away from arguing about the ingredients and simply enjoy the food.

Chili con Queso

A Hispanic dip of cheese and chili pepper.

Chili Oil

Also *hot pepper oil*, *hot sauce*, *red oil*, and *red pepper oil*. Vegetable oil mixed with chilis, which give it its reddish hue. It is particularly useful in Chinese cooking, but only in extremely small amounts. Once again, it rewards refrigeration.

Chili Powder

A spice consisting of the ground-up pods of varieties of CHILI peppers augmented with other ingredients such as allspice, cumin, garlic, oregano, paprika, and salt. It comes in mild, hot, and three-alarm varieties. Since there are those who emphatically do not like it hot, chili dishes for company are often best spiced with a mild chili powder and served with optional hot peppers (such as dried, hot red pepper flakes) for those who prefer the more explosive combination.

Chili Sauce

A condiment found on supermarket shelves that resembles a cross between a sweet relish and tomato catsup; it can be excellent on hamburgers, but don't confuse it with chili pepper. It is made up of tomatoes augmented with bell peppers, perhaps some chili peppers, onion, vinegar, sugar, and spices.

Chill

Generally, to cool something off. Some pastry doughs must be chilled or they won't work right—wrap them in wax paper and pop them in the fridge for a half hour or so. Some bowls need to be chilled before you use them—place them in another bowl full of ice cubes and the bowl will remain dry, at least on the inside where it counts. Most white and rosé and some (but only a few) red wines reward your chilling them before serving. An hour or two in the refrigerator will usually do the trick, or you can use a specially designed wine cooler, a device (not the carbonated stuff they sell) large enough to hold the bottle upright in ice water up to about the shoulder of the bottle. Open the bottle before sticking it in the cooler.

Chilver

A yearling ewe and also its mutton.

Chimaja

A wild cherry (*Prunus ilicifolia*) native to Mexico. Its dried leaves and dried, ground roots are used in some Mexican and Southwestern dishes.

Chincoteague

An OYSTER from Chincoteague, Virginia. It is not anatomically different from other East Coast oysters.

Chine

The backbone of a meat animal, sometimes referring to a serving of that bone (or portion thereof) and its adjacent meat.

Chinese Anise

See STAR ANISE.

Chinese Artichoke

A tuber (*Stachys sieboldi*); also called *Japanese artichoke* and *crosne*. A white color when in the ground, a Chinese artichoke discolors quickly when removed from the earth. It has a taste that some find reminiscent of the regular ARTICHOKE, hence the name, and others identify more with the JERUSALEM ARTICHOKE. It is more likely to be served in Europe than in North America. Should you happen across one, make sure it is of a pure white color, firm to the touch, and use it as you would a Jerusalem artichoke.

Chinese Cabbage

There are quite a few varieties of Chinese cabbage, but the ones seen most widely in North American markets are BOK CHOY and PE-TSAI.

Chinese Celery Cabbage

See PE-TSAI.

Chinese Date
See JUJUBE.

Chinese Gooseberry
See KIWI.

Chinese Parsley
See CORIANDER leaves.

Chinese Spinach
See AMARANTH.

Chinois
A conical sieve that takes its name from a supposed resemblance to a Chinese coolie's hat. Either freestanding (in which case it needs a lip to grasp the bowl over which it is worked) or on a stand, it has an extremely dense mesh that requires the use of a pestle to work the food through.

Chinook
A king SALMON.

Chipirones
A Spanish term for SQUID. A Basque dish, *chipirones en su tinta*, or squid in their own ink, it consists of a small squid stewed in olive oil with garlic, onion, tomatoes, and spices, augmented with the inky fluid exuded by squid. Although it sounds a bit daunting, it can, when the squid are fresh, be superb.

Chipolata
A small, spicy sausage flavored with chives and other spices, sometimes including hot peppers.

Chipped Beef
Also called *dried beef* or *shredded beef*. Beef that has been shredded, pickled, smoked, and dried. (In earlier times it was air dried.) It is usually served creamed, traditionally for breakfast. Because of its saltiness, some people prefer to BLANCH it before cooking.

Chips
Vegetables, especially potatoes, that have been cut into thin, peeled slices that are then deep-fried. To the British, french-fried potatoes.

Chitterlings
Or *chitlins*. The internal spare parts of a hog, used, especially in the southern United States, as food. They may be simmered in tomato sauce or breaded and deep-fried.

Chive

An herb (*Allium schoenoprasum*) and a relative of the onion, used as a delicately oniony flavoring. Chives have a small, white bulb from which grow a mass of tubular leaves topped, when in bloom, with purple flowers reminiscent of clover. The leaves are cut off, snipped into bits, and added to vegetables, soups, salads, omelets (and other egg dishes), cream cheese, and, especially, cottage cheese. When mixed into a hamburger before grilling, they obviate any need to add onion slices to the burger. Chives grow well in herb gardens and in kitchen windows so long as they get some sun. There is also a flat-leaved variety, Chinese chives (*Allium tuberosum*), that has edible white flowers and a taste that a great many people find reminiscent of garlic.

Chlodnik

A Polish soup akin to BORSCHT, except that it also contains cucumber. It may also be augmented with veal, chicken, or shrimp.

Chocho

Another name for CHAYOTE.

Chocolate

A product of the cacao tree (*Theobroma cacao*), a tropical evergreen of South America and Mexico but introduced to West Africa, where the bulk of the world's chocolate supply is now grown. The beans of the tree contain kernels from which the chocolate is made. Removed from the pod, the beans are fermented, dried, roasted, and cracked, then ground into a paste known as chocolate liquor. This is then refined, the components being cocoa butter (as the oil is known) and ultimately cocoa powder. From these come various products that are all but gloriously addictive to many. Chocolate is available in several forms:

Chocolate syrup. Unsweetened chocolate mixed with sugar and some form of syrup (sugar or corn) and generally used to make chocolate milk. Don't try to use it instead of melted chocolate—it won't give the same results.

Cocoa. The dried powder used for a beverage or in cooking; it may be unsweetened, but don't count on it.

Milk chocolate. Cocoa butter, chocolate liquor, sugar, and milk solids, with perhaps some flavorings and preservatives. Originally, it seems to have been a gastronomic invention of the English.

Semisweet chocolate. Unsweetened chocolate with some sugar and sometimes other ingredients (including additional cocoa butter, flavorings, and preservatives).

Sweet chocolate. Unsweetened chocolate, chocolate liquor, sugar, and perhaps flavorings and preservatives.

Unsweetened chocolate. Pure chocolate with nothing added. It is the best bet
for cooking.

White chocolate. A mixture of cocoa butter, sugar, and vanilla flavoring but
without chocolate solids.

Chokecherry

A wild North American CHERRY (*Prunus virginiana*) known to foragers and once cultivated in Canada's southerly provinces for its astringent, tart fruit that is used in
jams, jellies, and homemade wines and cordials. Chokecherries are unwelcome
around peach orchards as they are carriers of a disease that afflicts those trees.

Cholent

A Jewish specialty, especially designed for the Sabbath, when cooking is impermis-
sible in Orthodox homes. It generally consists of a brisket of beef (or similar cut)
with soaked, dried beans and onions and potatoes and rich dumplings covered with
boiling water and simmered from late Friday night until the return from worship
on Saturday, when it is removed from the oven and served.

Chop

1. A meaty rib cut of an animal.

2. To cut something up to make it smaller. The technique varies. To chop parsley or chives, for example, the best approach is usually to snip them with a scissors—
yet we still call it chopping. Other operations are often best done on a cutting board
with a good heavy knife. This will range from *chopping* (fairly coarse, perhaps a half
inch square) through *dicing* (the size of a small set of gaming dice) to *mincing* (as
small as possible this side of a powder). Many laborsaving devices exist to do these
chores for you.

Chop Suey

An American (it was apparently first conceived in San Francisco) concoction along
the lines of Chinese cookery. It is made with beef and onions and celery and bean
sprouts flavored with Chinese sauces including soy sauce and served over rice.

Chorizo

A pork sausage of Spanish or Mexican origin spiced with moderately hot chilis and
flavored with garlic.

Choucroute

A French name for SAUERKRAUT. The Alsatian dish *choucroute garni* is composed of
sauerkraut augmented by various pork products—sausages, smoked pork chops,
unsmoked pork chops—and perhaps some goose or duck and carrots, onions, and
juniper berries (although the way Alsatian sauerkraut is cured, these berries are
incorporated in the process) into a meal that is a feast in itself.

Choux Pastry
See PUFF PASTRY.

Chowchow
A mustard pickle, often used with CURRY.

Chowder
A word that seems to go back to an old French word, *chaudière*, defined as a metal receptacle for warming, boiling, or cooking. That certainly sounds like what we use to cook chowders in today, and what we put into that receptacle generally results in a hearty seafood soup or stew. Various other ingredients qualify a dish as a chowder, including some vegetables, especially corn. In New England, where chowder is taken seriously, salt pork is the one universal ingredient, or used to be.

Chow Mein
A version of CHOP SUEY but served over noodles instead of rice.

Christmas Pudding
See PLUM PUDDING.

Chrysanthemum Pot
See FIRE POT.

Chub
Also called *cisco*. A mixed bag of small freshwater fish related to the WHITEFISH and usually sold smoked, but the name is also sometimes given to the totally unrelated TAUTOG.

Chuck
The meat of a beef critter's shoulder and part of its neck; usually the least expensive cut and often an excellent value. Not the most tender cut, it is mostly used for ground meat, steaks (such as London broil), stew meat, and pot roasts.

Chufa
A fairly widespread weed (*Cyperus esculentus*) found almost everywhere, with edible tubers somewhat resembling peanuts. Chufa roots have been found in such diverse places as the tombs of Egyptian pharaohs, on Ethiopian and Spanish dining tables, and in the kitchens of American foragers. They can be dried and eaten, roasted to make a coffeelike beverage, candied, ground into flour, and coaxed into giving a milky liquid said to be much appreciated in Latin America. It has been grown as food for pigs, but grows in such a rampant and obtrusive way that farmers and gardeners generally detest it.

Chutney

A condiment of Indian origin made generally on a MANGO base, although other bases are also used, including apples, cranberries, mint, peaches, and tomatoes. Spices are added to it, and it is often made in the sweet-and-sour fashion, balanced between vinegar and sugar.

Cicely

A European herb (*Myrrhis oderata*) sometimes called *sweet cicely*, *sweet chervil* (it's only distantly related), and *myrrh* (it is unrelated to the magi's gift of the New Testament, which referred to a perfume). Both seeds and leaves were once used as flavorings and in salads (it is said to resemble a stronger version of CHERVIL), but the plant seems to have fallen into disfavor.

Cider

At one time it meant the fermented juice of apples—unfermented juice was referred to as *sweet cider*—but nowadays what used to be sweet cider is generally called cider and what used to be cider is now *hard cider*. Unless you get your sweet cider from the orchard, it will most likely have some sort of preservative in it to keep it from beginning to ferment. (Some supermarkets carry dated jugs of cider, but check the label for the presence or absence of elements introduced by sources other than nature.) Hard cider is more difficult to obtain (unless you make it yourself—for which you're supposed to have a license), but many wine and spirit shops can get it for you even if they don't stock it. Cider is also made into a useful vinegar and is the starting point for apple BRANDY.

Cilantro

See CORIANDER.

Cinnamon

An aromatic spice of historic dimensions. It would be next to impossible to count the ways in which we use cinnamon. You might start your day with cinnamon toast, but where to go from there? Curries, pastries, soups, stews, and hot toddies all benefit from a little cinnamon as do so many other delectable things. The bringer of all this joy starts its career as the bark of an Oriental evergreen (*Cinnamomum zeylanicum*), which gets stripped off, cut into the small curls we buy (or powdered and sometimes stretched with inferior materials such as cassia), and shipped the world over. The footsteps of cinnamon, to mix the metaphor slightly, form the caravan trails of antiquity and the sea lanes of today.

Cioppino

A Californian fish stew of uncertain origin—the American food and wine expert James Beard, who grew up in the West, felt that it arose among Portuguese fishermen; others give it an Italian origin. In any event, it is made with one or several kinds of fish augmented with clams, mussels, crab, dried mushrooms, garlic, onion, parsley, and tomato, of course, as well as green pepper and lots of hearty red wine. Toasted or fried bread, especially sourdough bread, makes a fine accompaniment. A feast!

Cisco

Also CHUB. A small, herringlike (but no relation to the herring) fish (*Coregonus* spp.) of the Great Lakes, akin to whitefish. You can prepare it as you would trout.

Citric Salt

See SOUR SALT.

Citron

1. The fruit of a small tree (*Citrus medica*) resembling a lemon. Its rind is candied and sold for use in baking.

2. A pickle or preserve made from the rind of a variety of watermelon (*Citrullus vulgaris* var. *Citroides*).

Citrus

A genus of plants that includes CITRON (definition 1), grapefruits, lemons, limes, oranges, and their kin, which are referred to collectively as citrus fruits. They are covered in this volume under their individual headings.

Civet

A French stew of a game animal such as rabbit, hare, or muskrat and, at one time, the lamprey eel. (It has no connection, however, with the inedible animal known as civet cat.) A civet traditionally is made with red wine, small onions, mushrooms, and the blood of the animal in question to BIND it.

Clabber

A thick, curdy beverage of sour milk, much appreciated in the Old South and in parts of Central Europe. Pasteurized milk will not "clabber" the way the old, whole milk used to (it spoils first), but a contemporary clabber can nonetheless be approximated by adding vinegar or lemon juice to milk (1 teaspoon to 1 cup milk) and letting it stand in a warm place for a half hour or so. Clabber can also serve for the buttermilk a recipe calls for but that you forgot to buy.

Clafouti

A pastry from the region south of Limoges in south-central France; it is thick and made from eggs, flour, and sugar poured over (and topped with) pitted cherries (or other fruit). More sugar is added, and it is eaten either hot or cold.

Clam

Worldwide, there are some 12,000 species of marine clam, ranging in size from almost too small to be noticed to a huge monster that, should you step in one by mistake, could easily claim your leg as it closes its shell. So far, there seems to be no record of this happening. Fortunately, only a relative handful among this profusion are of culinary interest.

There also exist freshwater clams, but the ones that concern us here are all marine species, living mostly in sand or mud.

Clams are popular in North America, but nowhere near so as lobster and shrimp. They are eaten "on the half shell," which means raw, but less so than formerly, inasmuch as so many of the waters we dig them out of have become so polluted as to make raw shellfish a health hazard. They are also cooked in a number of ways— truly fresh, deep-fried clams, for example, make a mockery of the packaged offerings sold from supermarket frozen food shelves. Clam chowder occurs as two styles, MANHATTAN CHOWDER and NEW ENGLAND CHOWDER. Clams can also be baked—the meat ground up, enhanced with, perhaps, breadcrumbs and cheese and spices; made into a cocktail dip, fritters, and hash; panfried (breaded or not); baked in a pie (a specialty of New York State's Long Island); or steamed. Steamed clams usually make use of the soft-shell variety, but hard-shell clams are also excellent cooked this way.

When selecting clams, make sure the shells are tightly closed. If they seem slightly open, give them a rap. If they are open (or won't close when rapped) pass them by. They are dead or dying. Do not try to keep them in water—they will use up all the oxygen and die. Put them in a container in the back of the refrigerator. They will keep for a couple of days this way, though it seems footless to acquire clams just to store them away for future use. Once they've been shucked (a CLAM KNIFE is handy here) they will keep up to three or four days.

There is a variety of commercially available clams, depending upon where you happen to be, as well as others a good forager might find. Some of them you might run across include:

American quahog (*Mercenaria mercenaria*). Ranges from the Gulf of Saint Lawrence to the Gulf of Mexico and has been introduced to California and Europe. This species includes the *cherrystone* and the *littleneck*, which are classified according to size. Anything over three inches in diameter ranks as a *quahog*. They can be tough, which is why they are usually chopped up for use in a chowder.

Cherrystone clam. A young (two–three inches in diameter) American quahog (see above).

Geoduck (*Panopea generosa*). Pronounced "gooey-duck." A large Pacific clam found from Alaska to Baja California. It is huge (up to 13 pounds, about half of which is neck) and is difficult to find fresh except right at the coast. The

neck is usually chopped for chowder and the body used otherwise. It can
be found canned and frozen.

Giant clam (*Tridacta gigas*). Not something you're likely to run across unless
you're hanging around the Indian Ocean. It runs up to 500 pounds, and the
muscle is considered a delicacy when you can find it.

Littleneck. A young (up to two inches in diameter) American quahog (see
above).

Pacific littleneck (*Protothaca stamenea*). No relation of the Atlantic littleneck,
this one is a popular food clam throughout its range, which is the whole of
the North American Pacific Coast.

Pismo clam (*Tivela stultorum*). A flavorful clam of California, once abundant
but now endangered.

Razor clam (*Siliqua* spp. and *Ensis directus*—the common Atlantic razor clam).
They are shaped like an old-fashioned straight razor and have the ability to
dig fast and deep when alarmed. Except for foragers, only the Pacific species
is usually to be found, and then mostly in its northern range. California has
a ban on harvesting them. Pacific razors are used mostly for fried clams,
but reward the cook who has enough imagination to use them in other ways
as well.

Southern quahog (*Mercenaria campechiensis*). Closely related to the *American
quahog* (see above), it overlaps in habitat and also ranges farther south. It
is not so sought after, but can be used in the same ways as its northern relative.

Steamer clam (*Aya arenaria*). A soft-shell clam originally of Atlantic waters
(Labrador to North Carolina) but introduced to the Pacific as well. It is
steamed and served with its broth.

Surf clam (*Spisula solidissima*). Found along the Atlantic Coast from Nova Scotia to the Carolinas in open, sandy beaches roughly where the surf breaks.
It is a tough customer and is used mostly for canning. Related surf clams
are also found on the West Coast and, indeed, worldwide.

Washington clam (*Saxidomus nuttalli*). This clam and the related *smooth Washington clam* (*Saxidomus giganteus*) are found commercially, especially in
British Columbia, and range as far south as Baja California.

Clambake

A traditional shoreline feast, especially in New England. Customs vary, but generally, a huge pit is dug in the sand, lined with stones, and as much brushwood as can
be found is thrown in and lit. The fire is topped with seaweed, and clams, lobsters,
potatoes, onions, ears of corn, and any fish you can lay your hands on are thrown
in, covered with more seaweed and a tarpaulin, and left to cook. The secret, of

course, lies in knowing just when to add each ingredient so everything is ready at the appropriate time.

Clam Broth
A liquid used in small amounts when steaming clams augmented with the juices they emit in the cooking. The warm broth, poured out into cups or mugs, goes nicely with the steamers.

Clam Juice
Clam broth bottled and sold in both fish stores and supermarkets. It is a handy substitute for fish broth.

Clam Knife
A sturdy utensil to keep you from slicing yourself up while opening a live clam. It is a blunt knife with a rounded blade that you slide between the clam's shells and rotate to sever the muscle that keeps the shells shut.

Claret
Any red wine of BORDEAUX.

Clarify
To separate the clear, liquid part of a mixture from the solids. Unsalted butter is clarified by heating it slowly and then decanting the clear liquid top off the solids below, while coffee, when camp-boiled with all the grounds in it, is clarified by dropping eggshells into it so that the grounds form around the eggshells and drop to the bottom. So it doesn't work perfectly—everything tastes better outdoors anyway.

Clary
An herb (*Salvia sclarea*) with characteristics resembling both MINT and SAGE, grown in some North American gardens but otherwise hardly seen. It is used to flavor egg dishes, pastries, and wine and is one of the herbs that give flavor to Italian VERMOUTH.

Classic Cooking
A concept of cookery embracing elaborate and beautifully presented dishes mostly of French origin but also including dishes especially from Austria, Italy, and Russia. Such dishes frequently require rich sauces, some of them of such complexity that few but highly trained professional cooks, with plenty of time and patience (and skill), can do them justice. Even simple dishes were adapted to the classic style. For example, BORSCHT—which doubtless began as a simple peasant beet soup—was transformed by the French master chef Auguste Escoffier, whose version calls for six separate vegetables (including, of course, beets), several herbs, a base of an extremely complicated consommé, some brisket of beef, and some "partly roasted duck." It was more the richness of classic cooking than its complexity, however, that led to the introduction in the 1970s of NOUVELLE CUISINE.

Clay Cooking

One of the oldest of cooking methods. At its most primitive—and still used today in camp cooking—the fish or fowl to be cooked is covered with fresh, wet clay (the real stuff—not what you get in kids' playsets) and put in, on, and under hot coals until deemed done. The now hardened clay is broken off, taking scales or feathers with it, and a tasty morsel, its juices intact, is left behind. Pieces of meat can, of course, also be cooked by this method. A number of clay cooking pots are available for use in modern ovens, and recipes also exist for baking bread in a plain pottery flowerpot. (It works, all right, but have a care—flowerpots are typically made with clays that contain lead, which is toxic.)

Cleaver

See MEAT CLEAVER.

Clementine

A small tangerine, a variety of ORANGE.

Clod

A British meatcutter's term for a cut from the shoulder or neck of a beef animal, or what Americans usually call CHUCK. (In Britain, it technically refers to the hanging folds of a beef critter's neck.)

Clotted Cream

See DEVONSHIRE CREAM.

Cloudberry

A northern type of RASPBERRY (*Rubus chamaemorus*) with a large berry that starts out pink, changes to amber, and matures into a soft, juicy, yellow fruit with a somewhat mucilaginous texture. It is favored for baking in Scandinavia.

Cloud Ear

A Chinese MUSHROOM.

Clove

1. A pungently aromatic, dried bud of an East Indian tree (*Eugenia aromatica*), now grown widely in Africa. Sold ground as well as whole, cloves enhance all manner of soups and stews, meats (such as ham), pastries, hot drinks such as mulled wine, and, when stuck into an orange, they form a pomander for keeping linen cabinets and their contents fresh and sweet smelling. A whole clove will have a potency better than its ground counterpart, especially if the ground one has been open to the air for any length of time.

2. A segment of a head of GARLIC.

Club Sandwich

A double-decked sandwich composed of three pieces of toast with mayonnaise and layers of bacon or chicken or lettuce or tomato or turkey or anything else that seems appropriate, either alone or in combination.

Club Steak

A rib steak—the rib meat of the animal in question with the bone removed.

Coagulate

Simply to clot, clump, or curdle. It's what your blood does when you nick yourself with a paring knife, and that's good as it stops the bleeding. It's what oil and egg yolk do when you combine them too fast in making mayonnaise, and that's a shame. (Try opening another egg and beating the coagulated mixture into it, but this time adding more slowly and beating harder.) Coagulation makes CHEESE possible.

Coalfish

Another name for *pollack*, a member of the COD family.

Coat

To encase food in a protective covering, such as batter, before frying or sautéing something.

Cob

Also *cobnut*. British variety of HAZELNUT.

Cobbler

1. A sweetened drink of wine or spirit with citrus fruit.
2. A deep-dish fruit pie with only a top and no bottom crust.

Cobia

A large, brown, tropical fish (*Rachycentron canadum*) of global distribution, also called *crabeater* and *sergeant fish*. The Atlantic varieties can be seen as far north as Massachusetts in summer. It is not presently a commercial fish but specimens are caught from time to time, especially in the Chesapeake Bay and the Gulf of Mexico. Its meat is firm, moist, and tasty. Try baking a small one or grilling steaks of a larger one.

Coca

A plant (*Erythroxylon coca*) of the Andes and West Indies. It is the source of cocaine and, once its narcotic qualities have been removed, of COLA beverages.

Cochineal

A red dye made from a parasitic insect (*Dactylopius coccus*), once believed to be the seed of the plant it lives on. The dye is used in pastries and some stews and in making liqueurs. It is under scrutiny as a possible carcinogen.

Cocido

A hearty Spanish meal in a single stew, derived from the equally hearty OLLA PODRIDA, consisting of a combination of all or some of the following: beef, chicken, ham, salt pork, and sausage; vegetables such as cabbage, carrots, leeks, and potatoes; chickpeas; and the broth in which they were all cooked. The meal is traditionally served with the broth first, followed by the vegetables, sometimes augmented with an AIOLI sauce, and last the meat. With a sturdy red wine, who could ask for—or even contemplate—anything more?

Cock-a-Leekie

A Scottish soup of chicken and leeks, sometimes thickened with oatmeal.

Cockle

A European shellfish (especially *Cardium edule* but there are others) generally used in a sauce or eaten raw in the same way as oysters. Cockles, along with mussels, were what the ill-fated Molly Malone, of Irish ballad fame, sold from her barrow through the streets wide and narrow of the fair city of Dublin. There are cockles on the American side of the Atlantic and in the Pacific, too, but except for some taken from Puget Sound, they are not much used for seafood in North America.

Cockscomb

A fleshy crest on the head of a male chicken or other related bird. You used to blanch it for a few minutes, poach it for 25 minutes, and then rub off the outside skin with a heavy towel. You could then use it as a garnish for certain extremely fancy, classic dishes that nobody makes any more. Cockscombs were also sautéed in butter with the liver, gizzards, a little garlic and onion, cream, seasonings, and Worcestershire sauce, after which they were served on rice. Unless you have your own chicken coop, however, you're not going to find them anywhere. Like chicken feet, cockscombs are made of a spongy tissue that serves as a repository for disease-bearing germs, and they've been effectively taken off the market as a result.

Cocktail

A traditional premeal drink, originally of North America and now of the world at large, although in many places it has been supplanted by, for example, a glass of white wine. It usually consists of a strong, mixed, alcoholic drink, served cold. The word also applies to a mixture of fruits or seafood served as a first course, especially at a catered banquet.

Cocktail Sauce

A commercial preparation typically consisting of chili sauce, horseradish, lemon juice, and Tabasco, often served in restaurants with seafood cocktail or oysters.

Cocoa
1. Variant spelling of CACAO.
2. Pulverized CHOCOLATE, especially as used as a beverage.

Cocoa Butter
A vegetable oil obtained from cacao beans, the source of CHOCOLATE.

Coco de Mer
A nut (*Locoicea maldivia*) resembling an outsized coconut (some 18 inches long by 5 inches thick); it grows only on a couple of islands in the Seychelles island group in the Indian Ocean.

Coconut
The fruit of the remarkable coconut palm (*Cocos nucifera*), a tropical tree that seems to contain virtually everything needed to sustain life. From its roots (dried and ground for a coffeelike beverage) through its trunk (building supplies and furniture), the husk of its fruit (mattresses), its leaves (thatch for roofs), the dead wood and stalks (firewood), the covering for its fruit (cups, bowls, spoons, and buttons as well as valuable copra), and its sap (fermented into a lightly alcoholic beverage), the tree is a hospitable one even before you get to its culinary uses.

As for the nuts of the coconut palm, they provide a nourishing and easily digested milk, a useful vegetable oil, and a meat that can be used fresh (if you are on the spot—it won't ship), dried (*desiccated* is the usual term), or powdered for munching, baking, candy-making, or flavoring curries or other dishes. It does, of course, have drawbacks—for a vegetable oil, it is uncommonly high in fatty acids, and coconut is not a "complete" food in that it calls for serving with some form of vegetable or dairy product to flesh it out nutritionally.

Coconut Milk
The "milk" of the COCONUT obtained by grating the meat and pressing out the liquid in it. It is used in most of the ways milk is used.

Coconut Oil
An oil obtained from the COCONUT.

Coconut Syrup
A syrup of coconut milk and caramelized sugar used as a sweetener, especially in Thai cooking.

Cocotte
A French DUTCH OVEN.

Cod

This large, white-fleshed fish is just about the premier food fish in Western history, rivaled only by the HERRING. (About twice as much fish of the herring family is taken each year, but a great deal of it is used for other than human consumption.) Essentially a North Atlantic fish, cod is eaten not only on both sides of that ocean, but along the Mediterranean, in the Caribbean, throughout Africa, and on the Indian subcontinent. There are species and other kin of cod to be found in the Arctic, Mediterranean, and Pacific oceans, but generally in lesser numbers. One species, the BURBOT, prefers freshwater. Those various cousins notwithstanding, almost all commercial cod is taken from the cold waters of the North Atlantic.

Much of the ubiquity of cod can be traced to the Portuguese. Intrepid sailors, they transported their taste for cod with them on their travels—to Gloucester, the cod capital of Massachusetts; to Goa, on India's Malabar Coast; to the West Indies and South America, where they colonized Brazil; and, of course, home to Iberia. Wherever they went—and it was just about everywhere—they left a heritage of cod. Clearly, fresh cod will not stand the journey from the waters off Newfoundland to India without help, and to provide that help, most cod was salted or dried or both. Traditional terms to describe cod in its various forms include:

Cabillaud. Old name for cod fresh from the water.

Dry cod. Cod that has been salted and dried.

Green cod. Cod that has been salted but not dried.

Stockfish. Cod that has been dried but not salted.

Among the great attributes of cod, aside from the staggering quantities that are removed from the sea each year, is the variety of cooking techniques to which it lends itself. Indeed, cod and its relatives can be used raw for SUSHI, or can be baked, boiled, broiled, fried, grilled, sautéed, steamed, or made into chowder. It can be rendered into fillets or steaks or prepared whole—stuffed or unstuffed—and is usable down to its cheeks, tongues, and sounds (or swim bladders). It can be treated with a variety of sauces or none at all. In addition to being dried and salted, it can be canned, flaked, frozen, or shredded. The fish is so useful, in fact, that there is even an old sea chantey that tells how the deprived denizens of Cape Cod made use of all the parts of their regional fish ("Cape Cod girls they have no combs," one verse relates, "they comb their hair with codfish bones").

Cod comes from a large family comprising some 120 species, only a few of which, fortunately, concern us here. Some of the more important members of the cod family and its relatives include:

Atlantic cod (*Gadus morhua*). The most prevalent member of the family, this one generally runs three feet or so in length (mature ones can run up to six feet, but are rarely seen this large) and averages about 3 to 15 pounds in weight. It has a mottled, brownish color tinged with green, is distinguished

by its barbels or hairs hanging down from its chin, has a whitish line running down its side, and has a white belly.

Cusk (*Brosme brosme*). A highly streamlined fish, the cusk has a dorsal (or back)
fin that seems to merge right with the tail and the ventral (stomach) fin to
ring the whole rear portion of the fish, top and bottom. Although a white-
fleshed fish and a relative of the cod, cusk has a certain amount of oil in its
flesh and is best baked or broiled. The name is also sometimes used for the
BURBOT.

Gray cod. Or Pacific cod (see below).

Greenland cod (*Gadus ogac*). A northerly member of the family, somewhat
smaller (under two feet in length) than its Atlantic relative, this one sticks
closer to shore and shallower water. Some experts consider it simply an
Atlantic cod subspecies. It is found mostly as a dried fish in Scandinavia.

Haddock (*Melanogrammus aeglefinus*). In the market, the haddock will usually
be slightly smaller than the cod and have a darker color, a black instead of
more-or-less white line down its side, and a black mark on its shoulder. Haddock is generally considered tastier and more delicate than cod and is often
preferred to cod in making a New England fish chowder.

Hake (*Merluccius merluccius*). A streamlined, blue-to-gray species of the cod
family. Hakes abound the world over. Hakes most likely to be found in a
North American market are the silver hake (*Merluccius bilinearis*), the
Atlantic hake (*Merluccius albidus*), the red hake (*Urophysis chuss*), the white
hake (*Urophysis tenuis*), and the Pacific hake (*Merluccius productus*). Culinarily they are similar and can be treated like cod.

Ling (*Molva* spp.). A long, slim fish mostly of extreme northern waters with a
green or brown back, often with white marbling. It is caught and dried in
Iceland and Scandinavia. In the United States, what the fish anglers call ling
is usually red hake, although the name is also sometimes applied to the BUR-
BOT. The so-called LINGCOD is not a cod.

Pacific cod (*Gadus macrocephalus*). The Pacific version of the Atlantic cod, usually smaller than its Atlantic cousin (reaching a maximum of about three
feet) but otherwise pretty similar. It roams over an area from the Arctic Circle to the southern part of California on one side of the ocean and to the
west coast of Korea on the other. A desire to secure fisheries for Pacific cod
helped spur the United States to purchase Alaska from the Russians in the
1860s.

Pacific whiting. The Pacific hake (see Hake, above).

Pollack. On the European side of the Atlantic, a brown or dark green fish (*Pollachius pollachius*) growing to two feet or so and mostly taken by anglers.
In eastern North America, a dark-colored greenish fish (*Pollachius virens* but

also called *coalfish*, *green cod*, and *saithe*) that can grow up to 3½ feet in length but is seen mostly by coastal anglers as a small (roughly six-inch) panfish. Pollack is not quite as good eating as cod, but it is acceptable enough, although on coastal Maine they once tended to throw them back or feed them to the cat. In western North America, the walleye or Alaska pollack (*Theragra chalcogramma*) is prevalent but is mostly fished for by the Japanese.

Scrod. Originally a small (under 1½ feet and less than about two pounds) cod, but the name extends to any related fish of about the same size.

Tomcod. A miniature cod lookalike rarely attaining a foot in length and found along both coasts. The Atlantic tomcod (*Microgadus tomcod*) is a fish of inlets and estuaries; the Pacific tomcod (*Microgadus proximus)* is often found farther out to sea. Both are favorites of anglers, but only the Pacific tomcod has commercial importance.

Whiting. A bland but popular European fish *(Merlangus merlangus)*. Its most striking presentation is the French method of *merlan en colère* or "irate whiting," whereby the whole fish is fried and curled up with the tail threaded through the eye socket. In North America, the name refers sometimes to the silver hake and sometimes to a different WHITING altogether.

Coddle

A method of soft-boiling (especially an egg) without letting it actually boil. You put the egg in water at a temperature of approximately 180°F and leave it for 10 minutes, by which time it will have taken on a slightly creamy consistency. Another method is to slip the egg into simmering water and remove the pan from the flame immediately. After 10 to 15 minutes the egg will be coddled. Coddled eggs have always been considered more easily digested than eggs cooked otherwise.

Coeur à la Crème

A lush dessert of sweetened, flavored cream cheese whipped until light, augmented with heavy or sour cream, and then molded in a small china or wicker heart-shaped mold and chilled. It is turned out of its mold and served with a sauce made from fresh berries, especially strawberries. A Valentine's Day special.

Coffee

Petroleum is not the only all-but-universal gift Arabia has given the world—there is also the coffee bean, which is the seed of an evergreen shrub that is brewed into a hot drink. Legend has it that this bean was first noticed by an Arabian goatherd whose attention was called to it by the actions of his goats after they had been munching on the plant. He tried it himself, liked it, and spread the word, and life has not been the same since.

In actual fact, the most widely used coffee bean, *Coffea arabica*, is not originally indigenous to Arabia—Ethiopia seems a better bet—and the use of the coffee bean predates Arab experimentation. However, earlier African use did not include brewing it into a beverage—that was the gift the Arabs presented to the world sometime around A.D. 1000. Arabia and Africa are no longer, of course, the main sources of coffee. The plant was, often by devious means, introduced to Java, the West Indies, South America, and other areas. Fine coffees come from all these places today, not excluding Arabia—as does a lot of mediocre stuff, too.

There are other species of coffee than *arabica*. These shrubs are hardier and less demanding as to growing conditions, but of inferior fruit. In North America there will be some *Coffea robusta* mixed into blends, but probably no *Coffea liberica*, a plant found in the lowlands of Liberia, that is not of much interest away from its roots. Whatever the coffee, the beans must be allowed to ferment slightly—but not too much—before they can be of use. They may be fermented dry, either still on the trees or picked and spread out, or they may be subjected to the wet, or washed, process. Best-quality coffee is usually a result of the wet process, except for some Arabian and Ethiopian offerings that are still dried on the tree.

Coffee is categorized initially by its place of origin. Some of the names you are likely to encounter include:

Blue mountain. See Jamaican below.

Brazilian. Although enormous amounts of coffee are grown in Brazil, not much
    is retailed as Brazilian, and if it is, you will know that it is (or ought to be)
    arabica coffee grown in Brazil and not much more.

Colombian. A great deal of coffee in North America comes from Colombia, all
    of it of the *arabica* variety, and most of it very good indeed. The most highly
    regarded comes from the areas of Armenia, Manizales, and Medellín.

Excelsior. A grade of Colombian coffee reflecting the size of the bean (fairly
    large), not the quality of the coffee (usually quite good).

Jamaican. The very best is Jamaican blue mountain, and it will be expensive in
    the extreme but worth the money for the true (if well-heeled) coffee fancier.
    The coffee is both famous and scarce. Jamaican mountain coffee will not
    be the same but might be worth the try. However, all but a tiny fraction of
    Jamaican coffee is sold to Japan, and, in any case, more coffee labeled
    Jamaican is sold than is grown in Jamaica.

Harrar. The most highly rated Ethiopian coffee, grown largely on wild *arabica*
    shrubs; little of it is to be seen in North America.

Java. The Indonesian island that gave coffee its American nickname. Little Java
    coffee is available today, but the real thing is an *arabica* coffee with a rich
    taste and heavy body. Much that is seen is mixed with Mocha to make
    Mocha-Java.

Kenya AA. The highest grade of Kenyan coffee with a delicate, smooth flavor. It is an *arabica* coffee much prized in Europe and the United Kingdom.

Kona. A flavorful, full-bodied, *arabica* coffee from Hawaii produced in relatively small amounts.

Mocha. A full-bodied, smooth, tangy coffee from Yemen produced in quite small amounts, much of which is blended with Java to make Mocha-Java.

Before coffee can be used as we use it, it must be roasted. This was once accomplished at home and was known as "parching." Only as much coffee as was needed was doled out, often into a covered frying pan, where the beans were slowly heated, while being constantly stirred, until they attained the right color and were roasted through. Now, of course, coffee is roasted commercially, although home roasting devices can still be found. If you wish to parch your own coffee, and have the time and the skill to do so, you will have more control over what you drink. However, given the virtues of the breathing devices that let the roasted coffee release its gases into the atmosphere without allowing additional air into the sealed container, you probably won't be gaining all that much. And blended coffee is usually vacuum packed, ensuring a certain amount of freshness. Once opened, coffee is best kept in the refrigerator or freezer, whether you're dealing with whole roasted beans or ground coffee.

Coffee does not get stronger the more it is roasted—although sometimes it almost seems to taste that way; instead, it gets darker and changes taste slightly. The degrees of darkness, starting with the lightest, include city or American roast, Brazilian roast (which signifies not that the coffee was grown in Brazil but that it is roasted in the way favored there), Viennese roast, French or New Orleans roast (to which chicory is sometimes added), Spanish or Cuban or French-Italian roast, and Italian or espresso roast.

Once coffee is roasted, it will keep its savor for a decent interval; but once ground, that taste and aroma and all the goodness that we hope for from coffee dissipate quickly. Buying whole, roasted beans and grinding them just before use is probably the best way of ensuring a first-quality brew. Next is buying fresh-roasted coffee and having it ground before your eyes, but only in an amount you expect to use fairly quickly. Vacuum-packed ground coffee will be as good—or as miserable—as the blend you buy.

Coffee can be brewed in various ways. The simplest is camp-boiled coffee. You take fresh water and either pour the coffee into it and bring it to a boil (this is considered heresy by coffee connoisseurs, but it has its advocates) or, more conventionally, drop the ground coffee into the boiling water, reduce the heat, and let it all simmer until it attains the color and aroma of coffee as you like it. There are problems here with the grounds. They can be left in and the coffee gently decanted off them; they can be clarified with white of egg and eggshells; or they can be filtered out. Only the last guarantees that your coffee will be limpid. Historically, camp coffee was replaced by the percolator, which sent boiling water up a tube and allowed it to trickle down through the coffee grounds to settle back in the original container as coffee. Of course, the water at some point is passing through already brewed grounds, which does nothing good for the quality of the coffee. Percolators emit a satisfying gluggy noise (which may have been the inspiration for the sounds made by the marvelous machine in the 1950s movie *The Man in the White Suit*) and perfume their surroundings with the aroma of coffee, but don't produce much more than a barely adequate cup.

The percolator gave way to various filtration systems and to the drip pot, ancestor of many modern coffee machines, in which the coffee is placed in a container—such as a filter—and boiling water is poured through it. The French *café filtre*, by which a special coffee-holding metal top with perforated bottom is placed over the cup and boiling water poured through it, is a variation on this. Another device for making coffee is the Turkish *ibrik*, a tall, long-handled pot of brass or copper that is wide at the bottom, tapers as it rises until flaring just before the top, which has a lip. Finely ground coffee is boiled in the *ibrik* with sugar and sometimes spices and poured into small cups in such a manner as to include a foamy topping. And there are also espresso machines, in which live steam—or steam and hot water or milk combined—is forced through the coffee grounds to produce a strong, quickly achieved brew.

Coffee Cake
A sweet, rich bread, sometimes augmented with fruit, nuts, or spices, sometimes yeast-risen, otherwise leavened with BAKING POWDER or BAKING SODA and usually served warm at breakfast time.

Cognac
A French BRANDY. At its best, it provides the standard against which all other brandies are measured.

Coho
A species of Pacific SALMON.

Cointreau
An orange-flavored after-dinner liqueur.

Cola
Probably the most prevalent soft drink of North America if not the world. It consists of a highly sugared (or artificially sweetened), carbonated concoction based on some variation of the KOLA nut with additional flavorings.

Colander

A large metal or plastic (more rarely ceramic) container perforated with holes on the bottom and along the sides, useful for draining pasta and all sorts of other foods too large or too clumsy for a sieve. A dishtowel-lined colander is also useful for straining soups and stocks.

Colby

A mild, firm Cheddar-style cow's-milk CHEESE developed in Colby, Wisconsin, but now made all over the world.

Colcannon

An Irish dish of mashed potatoes and cabbage or kale cooked up in hot milk with onion, butter, and seasonings. Parsnips may be mashed into the potatoes.

Cold Cuts

Sandwich meats—various bolognas, salamis, and similar sausage and sausagelike delicatessen fare.

Cold Duck

An inexpensive sweetish combination of red and white sparkling wines appropriate, perhaps, for beach picnics.

Coleslaw

A tart and refreshing salad of shredded cabbage mixed up with various other good things (green pepper and caraway seeds, for example) and dressed with mayonnaise or, especially, BOILED DRESSING.

Collard

A broad, dark-colored variety of KALE (*Brassica oleracea* var. *acephala*) related to the cabbages and originating somewhere around the eastern Mediterranean. It is probably most widely appreciated in the southern United States, where it is generally cooked long and slow with some form of smoked or salt pork. While collard greens keep reasonably well, they're best obtained shortly before use. Good green leaves, not nibbled by insects, are your hallmarks.

Collop

1. A small cut of meat from the animal's back, sometimes in a slice, sometimes minced; if whole, it might be beaten to tenderize it.

2. A slice of bacon.

Comfrey

An herb (*Symphytum officinale*) once prized by the British for its medicinal use (helping to heal broken bones was one) but now out of favor for such purposes. Imported to North America, it has gone wild and is now largely used by foragers who pick the young leaves to use as greens. It is also dried to make herbal tea.

Common Crab
The European CRAB.

Common Cracker
A crisp, thick, hard, unsweetened wheat cracker once found everywhere in New England but now uncommon even there. Among its uses is being crumbled into a New England chowder.

Compote
A simple but often elegant dessert of fruits, berries, or a combination, cooked or fresh, enlivened or not with wine or other spirits (rum, kirsch or other fruit brandy, and aquavit are often used), prepared according to what's in the market, on the trees, or on hand.

Compound Butter
Small globs of butter that have been worked with some flavoring substance such as anchovies or garlic or tarragon or whatever will do your dish the most good. Garlic butter is, of course, mandatory for garlic bread; otherwise compound butters tend to be used as garnishes.

Compté
A French cow's-milk CHEESE similar to, and pretty much interchangeable with, GRUYÈRE.

Conch
A marine mollusk (*Strombus gigas*) found in warm waters from North Carolina through the Caribbean and pronounced *konk*. It is incredibly tough unless properly dealt with, which usually includes beating it with a mallet. It is generally eaten raw (in a salad), breaded and deep-fried, used in a chowder or gumbo, or marinated in lime juice. It is sometimes misreferred to as WHELK.

Conchiglie
An Italian PASTA in the shape of a conch shell. They are more readily known as "shells" and come in various sizes.

Concord
A North American GRAPE variety (*Vitis labrusca*) first identified in 1843 in the garden of one Ephraim Bull in Concord, Massachusetts. A heavy producer of fruit, its grapes are applicable for grape juice and jelly but, due to their lack of sugar, cannot be used for wine without massive infusions of additional sugar, which renders the wine coarse. Its wines also have an extremely strong, innate FOXY taste. Concord

grapes nonetheless contribute to North American kosher wines and are used for some other vinous purposes, but not with any great distinction.

Condensed Milk
Evaporated MILK with added sweetener.

Condiment
Anything we add to food to enhance its flavor or give it more savor. Catsup, chutney, mustard, and even the onion we put on our hamburgers are condiments. Condiments differ from seasonings in that seasonings are generally added by the cook during the cooking process, while condiments are added just before eating and at the discretion of each individual diner.

Confection
Candy or any similar sweet item, formerly called *sweetmeat*.

Confectioners' Sugar
The most powdery grade of sugar with an addition of cornstarch. It is used in baking, candy-making, and other culinary disciplines, where its fineness and ability to soak up liquids is an asset.

Confit
A French term for meat (usually, but not restricted to, pork and goose) cooked in its own fat and then put down in a crock and covered completely with the same fat. It was a handy way of preserving food for the winter before more modern methods of preservation were developed. Preserved goose (*confit d'oie*) is an ingredient of the CASSOULET made in the city of Toulouse, France.

Congee
A Chinese porridge (it can be as thick or as thin as you like) of rice augmented with fish or fowl or whatever happens to be available when it is being made.

Conger
A sea eel (*Conger conger*) of northern Europe and the Mediterranean. It is one of the many fish used in a BOUILLABAISSE. There are other species of congers, but they are not generally used for food.

Conpoy
Chinese dried sea SCALLOP with a rich, distinctive flavor and a prohibitive price tag. Conpoy may occur as a separate, long-simmered dish or may be used to enrich soups and stews. Because of their expense, they are more likely to be encountered at formal banquets than anywhere else.

Conserve

A sweetened preserve made like a jam but often containing more than one kind of fruit.

Consommé

Another name for a classically clear BROTH, except that commercial consommé generally has additions such as flavorings and gelatin—to assist you should you use it for making aspic or jellied consommé. If the meat that is the base of the consommé is simmered in a previously prepared broth—rather than plain water—the result is referred to as a *double consommé*. The same result can be obtained by boiling down a consommé to half its volume, thus increasing its taste. Although beef is the most common base, consommés are also made from other meats, including game, poultry, seafood, and turtle.

Convection Oven

A specialized oven in which the hot air is continuously circulated around the food being cooked. It cooks faster than a regular OVEN, not as fast as a MICROWAVE OVEN.

Converted Rice

A RICE that has been PARBOILED. It has been steeped in water, steamed, then dried and milled. This increases the vitamin content but generally increases cooking time, too.

Cook

1. To prepare food artistically as well as scientifically. Technically the term refers only to foods that are treated with some form of heat, but in practice we use it for any food preparation—even peeling an orange.

2. A person who prepares food.

Cookie

A sweet baked good prepared from a basic dough but varied almost infinitely by the sizes and shapes it can be given, by flavorings, by the various additions to it, and by the cooking method (most are baked but some are fried).

Cookie Cutter

A gizmo used to cut cookie dough or pastry into various shapes—rounds, ovals, Christmas trees, Scottie dogs, stars, and what-have-you. Some mind-boggling ones are made as a roller with a handle; you roll it over your dough and it leaves in its wake a miraculous variety of different shapes.

Cookie Sheet

A flat, thin, metal sheet with slightly raised edges. Use them for baking cookies, biscuits, or bread or place them under anything that might overflow in the oven and bollix up the surface (the cookie sheet is usually easier to clean than the oven floor) or for any other use that springs to mind.

Cooking Wine

A misnomer. Wine experts and food experts alike will tell you that a wine not good enough to drink is a wine not good enough to cook with. This does not, of course, mean that you should take your expensive, rare French vintage and decant it into a sauce. A sauce can just as well be made with a lesser, more moderately priced bottle, albeit a drinkable one. And again, the better the wine, the better a sauce is apt to be, and a bad wine will guarantee a bad sauce.

When you're using table wine in stews, it's often a good idea to heat it almost to the boiling point, then set fire to it, rotating the pan gently to let it burn most fully before adding it to the rest of the ingredients. This burns off the alcohol (and the harshness that can accompany a winy dish if the wine is uncooked), leaving only the taste, which is what you wanted in the first place. In addition to table wine, any FORTIFIED WINE will especially lend itself to cookery. Watch out for "cooking sherry," though. Traditionally, it was mediocre sherry generously laced with salt to discourage the kitchen help from making inroads into it. The same can be said for commercial "cooking wine."

Cookware

The various pots and pans and other devices we use as cooking utensils. What the original cookware of our ancestors was, we cannot, of course, be sure. Conjecturally, it was a casing of mud or clay around whatever it was that was being placed in the fire, as camp cooks use clay even today, especially for fresh-caught fish. This would have led to the development of clay pots and the craft of pottery. Early pots had to be smeared with some plant pitch to make them waterproof, and the development of the watertight glazed pot made a significant contribution to cookery. With the Iron Age, humankind was able to concoct metal pots, the descendants of which abound in kitchens to this day. Many of us swear by our iron cookware—but due to its weight, we often swear at it, too. Fortunately, there are alternatives, each of which has its strengths and its weaknesses.

The materials we see in cookware today (aside from TEFLON, which is a special case) are primarily aluminum, copper, enamel, glass, iron, pottery, steel, or tin.

Aluminum. A tough, strong, extremely light material that holds heat well and conducts it almost as well as copper. It is usually used alloyed with some other metal. Its main drawback is its tendency to interact with acids and give some foods a darkish color and an off taste. It will also interact with alkalies (perhaps in your tap water) and become discolored itself.

Copper. It conducts heat beautifully, cools quickly when removed from the heat (thus giving you close control over your cooking), and looks perfectly splendid (unless it is neglected). However, as it interacts with just about every-thing it comes into contact with, it can produce surface chemicals that are toxic. Manufacturers get around this by coating the inside of the pot (the cooking surface) with silver, stainless steel, or tin. Aside from the problem of keeping it clean, copper is also expensive.

Enamel. An enamel covering over cast iron or other base provides pretty good heat conduction and no possibility (unless you chip through the enamel) of interaction with the food being cooked. You can't brown your food so well in enamel as you can in its cast-iron equivalent—it tends to cook before it browns—but it makes a handsome braising vessel that comes proudly to the table.

Glass. It used to be that glass cookware required a mat between the vessel and the burner to prevent the heat from causing breakage. Modern glasses, such as Pyrex, now go directly on the burner without fuss. They are amusing—and instructive—as they provide the opportunity to see just when a liquid starts to boil, for example. But the glass conducts the heat just through the surface directly over the heat source; it can't spread it around the way metal does. And it can still break.

Iron. It can be cast into molds or drawn into sheets and then made into uten-sils, but the latter are often too thin to heat evenly. Cast iron is heavy. It soaks up heat slowly and cools off slowly, making it wonderful for slow-cooked dishes. But aside from its weight, cast iron rusts, pits, and needs inti-tial "curing" and proper care.

Pottery. This refers to cooking devices made essentially from wet clay put through an ordeal by fire to give it permanence and shape. It includes earth-enware and stoneware (the difference is of importance to the potter, not the cook) and, in its most extravagant form, porcelain. Mostly this is spe-cialty stuff—Spanish paella dishes, for example, or bean pots, or clay mar-mites and terrines, or the clay cooker that goes by the trade names Römertopf and Schlemmertopf. Pottery is slow to heat, slow to cool, and highly breakable. And these special devices take special handling that calls for them to be thoroughly soaked in cold water and placed, with contents, in a *cold* oven. This calls for some adjustment in timing your recipes.

Steel. Steel itself is not all that great a medium for cookware unless it is stain-less steel. This is steel (and chromium and sometimes other metals) that somehow forms a chemical film over its whole surface and protects it from any interaction with the outside world. It will remain bright and shiny and will not react with the foods cooked in it. But it simply doesn't conduct heat very well. In reaction to its lack of conductivity, stainless steel is, like alu-minum, usually used in combination with another, more conductive metal.

Tin. Tin is what tinkers used to tinker with. Tin is extremely soft—too much so to be used for an ordinary pot. Its virtue is that it seems to be unaffected by any cooking element other than heat. It won't rust or pit, it doesn't react adversely to any foods you put in it, and it forms an even coat on whatever other metal—such as copper—you want to add it to. A tin-lined copper pot is ideal for delicate work, such as special sauces. So long as you don't leave a tin-lined pot unattended over a heat source, you should have no problems with it. It will discolor, but this is in its nature and need not be addressed in any way. To get it shiny and bright would result in stripping off the tin, and the darker color holds the heat better anyway.

Coon

1. An aged, sharp North American form of CHEDDAR cheese.
2. A RACCOON.

Coot

Some of the most common shorebirds (*Fulica* spp.) in northeastern waters and once considered food of sorts. Efforts to eat coot (the breast meat only) have usually been defeated by the extreme fishiness of its taste, although brave attempts have been made to tame it with onions and turnips on the one hand and unsweetened chocolate on the other.

Coq

The French word for *rooster*.

Coq au Vin

A French casserole of chicken parts cooked in red wine with mushrooms and small onions. Some bacon or salt pork is often added, and the chicken may be flamed with brandy. Using a goodly amount of wine and cooking it down drastically imparts the dish's characteristic flavor.

Coquille

A French term for *shell*, such as the scallop shell in which the dish of scallops simmered in wine and known as *Coquilles St. Jacques* is traditionally served. The term is also used for dishes made in the shape of shells.

Coral

In the kitchen—as in the lobster boat—the roe of the lobster, so named for the distinctive color it attains when cooked. It is highly fancied by lobster lovers. The name can also be applied to other, similarly colored, roes, such as that of scallops.

Cordial

A spirit akin to, and often synonymous with, a liqueur.

Core

The seedy, central portion of a fruit such as an apple; also to remove that portion.

Corer

A device designed to remove a CORE.

Coriander

Also *cilantro* and *Chinese parsley*. A tangy green herb (*Coriandrum sativum*) some-what resembling Italian parsley in looks but not in taste—it is considerably stronger and more pungent (from the time of the ancient Greeks it has had the reputation of smelling like bedbugs—however they smell—although this seems to apply only to bruised, unripe seeds) and, to many of us, altogether delightful. It is widely used in Oriental and Mexican cooking but can sometimes be difficult to find other than in Oriental or specialty markets. Coriander doesn't keep well, so when you buy it fresh, make sure it isn't wilted. Bring it home, pick out the discolored leaves, and store what you're not using refrigerated in a plastic bag, but don't count on keeping it more than a few days. The dried seeds are used in baked dishes, in cheese, in cur-ries, and as a flavoring for cordials, gingerbread, and gin.

Corkscrew

A device for getting a cork out of a bottle. It consists of a wire spiral to penetrate the cork and a handle of some sort to lever the cork out. The most effective corkscrews have an open spiral, one with a central shaft into which you can intro-duce a toothpick or a match. To be most effective, the cross-section of the spiral shaft, or worm, should be square rather than round, and the worm itself should have rounded edges for a better grip on the cork. Otherwise you are more likely to have a gimlet and an easy time digging the corkscrew into the cork, but a frustrating time extracting it.

Corn

A cereal grain, specifically indigenous to the New World. Originally (and in Great Britain still) it meant grain of any sort, so when Keats's poem pictured Ruth "in tears amid the alien corn," don't think of her as weeping in some Biblical equivalent of Iowa. (In fact, the Old Testament makes it quite clear that Ruth and Naomi showed up just in time for the barley harvest, and Keats would have known that perfectly well.)

Only in America is the word corn used solely for *Zia mays*, which everyone else calls *maize*. (In America, maize is usually reserved for Indian corn with its vividly colored red, blue, and black—even purple—kernels.) In honor, no doubt, of its American origin, corn in the kitchen is pretty universally called corn—not maize or anything else, no matter where that kitchen is.

Corn is a plant of many uses. In North America it is a summer ritual to have corn on the cob—either shucked and dropped in boiling, unsalted water just long enough to heat it through or unshucked, soaked in water, and placed right on the coals to steam in its own husk—often with butter and salt, although fresh-picked corn doesn't really need either one. Cut in sections, it can be dropped into long-simmered stews, a specialty in, for example, Argentina. Taken off the cob, corn figures in chowders, fritters, puddings, and soufflés, and it can be dried for hominy, ground into cornmeal, pressed for its oil, processed for its starch, or used in a rich variety of other ways.

Although varieties of corn have been developed that do not shed their goodness almost instantly upon picking, corn is still best when as fresh as possible. Second best is corn that has been kept cool and moist. The larger ears provide bulk to satisfy appetite, but the smaller ones—and the smaller kernels—are often tastier.

Clearly, you don't want to buy corn that's been sitting around any length of time, and you're best off if you can get it picked that same day. For casseroles and other dishes for which corn is simply another ingredient, the frozen variety (and perhaps even canned corn) should be eminently suitable. Otherwise, fresh, fresh, fresh is the watchword.

Cornbread

A quickbread using cornmeal instead of, or together with, regular flour. Cornbread is a staple of both New England and the South. It can be baked, cooked on a griddle, or deep-fried. Cornbreads can be found with a variety of flavorings ranging from cheese, for example, to molasses.

Corn Dog

A hot dog dipped in cornmeal batter and deep-fried. It is usually served on a stick.

Corned Beef

Also *pickled beef*. It was originally cured by the use of large grains of salt called *corns* in making the pickling brine. The degree of cure is often open to question. New England boiled dinner is traditionally made with a cut of beef that has been left in the brine for a comparatively short time, resulting in only a light cure. Because some corned beefs receive a more thorough curing, some recipes call for soaking or blanching the meat before anything else is done to it.

Cornell Bread

A bread recipe worked out as a means of enhancing nutrition. It is essentially a white bread enriched with dried milk solids, soy flour, and wheat germ.

Corn Flour

A flour made from cornmeal by being more thoroughly bolted (or sieved). It is useful in baking and as a thickener (you mix it up with a little cold water first) and can be found in health food stores. A special corn flour, known as MASA, is used in making a tamale.

Cornflower

Also called *bachelor's button*. This strikingly blue flower (*Centaurea cyanus*) was once mashed with sugar in a mortar and pestle by French pastry chefs to give a blue color to such items as custards and creams.

Cornhusker

A bland, firm cow's-milk cheese of the midwestern United States, comparable to CHEDDAR.

Cornichon

A tiny French pickled GHERKIN, often served as an hors d'oeuvre.

Cornish Game Hen

See ROCK CORNISH HEN.

Corn Liquor

Also *moonshine* and *white lightning*. A spirit distilled from a corn mash, sometimes illegally. The legal version tends to be somewhat raw, but has its admirers.

Cornmeal

Corn kernels that have been dried and ground into a meal. Cornmeal is available in both yellow and white varieties—the color comes from the original corn kernels with little or no difference in taste although the white may not be so rich in vitamin A—and in blue in parts of the Southwest and some health food and specialty stores elsewhere. Cornmeal is used in baking (muffins, for example, and cornbread) and also to make cornmeal mush (American) and polenta (Italian). Sometimes available is stoneground cornmeal, which many find tastier than the regular. An eye-catching stunt is to dredge chicken in blue corn, fry it, and use it in a chicken salad.

Corn Oil

A cooking or salad oil obtained from corn. It is healthfully low in saturated fats but has little taste. On the other hand, it can be heated quite hot before it breaks down and is thereby a good bet for frying and sautéing.

Corn Pone

A Southern specialty of deep-fried (or sometimes baked) cornbread, classically made of white cornmeal, bacon fat, salt, and boiling water and served as a side dish.

Corn Salad

See LAMB'S LETTUCE.

Cornstarch

The starchy part of corn removed and reduced to a powder. It is used to thicken desserts, sauces, and innumerable Chinese dishes, although in the last case too much of it is apt to impart a cheap, glossy look. Mix it with a little cold water before you use it to avoid lumps.

Corn Syrup

A sweetener made from corn, used especially in candy-making and some pastries. It comes in light and dark varieties, the difference being an extra step taken in making the dark or amber type to caramelize it.

Correct

To taste your dish before you serve it to assess the seasoning and see that it is to your liking. Why cookbook writers almost universally assume that you've somehow goofed it, and the seasoning must now be "corrected" before the dish can be considered palatable, is best left to someone else to explain.

Cortland

An early red all-purpose APPLE.

Cos

Another name for romaine LETTUCE.

Costmary

Another herb (*Chrysanthemum majus*) you're going to have to grow yourself or do without—and if you decide to grow it, watch it like a hawk or it will run wild and crowd out everything else. Costmary is useful in soups and meat dishes and for an infusion into a tea as well as for any use that TANSY, which it resembles, is put to.

Costolette

An Italian term for CUTLET. Italians claim that the Milanese way of cooking cutlets—dipping them in egg and breadcrumbs and frying them in butter—was the inspiration for the Viennese *Wiener schnitzel*.

Cotechino

An Italian pork sausage seasoned with cloves and nutmeg. It is usually simmered at length before serving with dried beans or lentils.

Côte de Beaune

A wine-growing area of France, the southern half of Burgundy's CÔTE D'OR and producer of some of the world's most acclaimed dry red and white table wines. Among its most prestigious vineyards are Le Corton, Corton-Charlemagne, Montrachet, and some other vineyards of the communes of Aloxe-Corton, Beaune, Chassagne-Montrachet, Meursault, Pommard, Puligny-Montrachet, Savigny-les-Beaune, and Volnay.

Côte de Nuits
A wine-growing area of France, the northern half of Burgundy's côte d'or and producer of some of the world's most acclaimed dry red and, to a much smaller extent,
white table wines. Among its most prestigious vineyards are Bonnes Mares, Cham-
bertin, Chambertin-Clos de Bèze, Clos de la Roche, Clos des Lambrays, Clos de
Vougeot, Clos Saint Denis, Clos de Tart, Echézeaux, Grands-Echézeaux, La Tâche,
Musigny, Richebourg, and Romanée Conti. Other outstanding vineyards are found
in the villages of Chambolle-Musigny, Fixin, Flagey-Echézeaux, Gevrey-Chambertin,
Morey-Saint Denis, Nuits-Saint-Georges, Prémeaux, and Vosne-Romanée.

Côte d'Or
The "Golden Slope" of France's Burgundian wine-growing region, comprising about
a 35-mile stretch of some of the world's most extraordinary vineyards. The region
is divided into the côte de nuits to the north and the côte de beaune to the south.

Côtelette
A French term for CUTLET.

Côtes du Rhône
Red, white, and rosé, often sturdy wines grown along the Rhône River in south-
eastern France. Some of the more specific wine names include CHÂTEAUNEUF-DU-
PAPE, Côte Rotie, Hermitage, and the rosé wines of Tavel.

Cotriade
A fish stew from France's Brittany region. It is made from the day's catch—including as many different varieties of fish as possible—stewed up with potatoes, onions,
bay leaf, and thyme and served over a chunk of crusty bread.

Cottage Cheese
A form of clotted milk or near-cheese found under various names (including *pot
cheese* and *farmer's cheese*), originally representing the thrifty farmer's approach to
using up soured milk.

Cottage cheese has any number of uses. Apart from its value plain (or with
chives, watercress, lemon juice, fruit preserves, or whatever pleases your palate), it
is used as a filling for pancakes, as an ingredient of cakes, or graced with canned
fruits (a pear or an apricot) as a weight-reducing salad.

If you want to make your own cottage cheese, try heating 5 cups of milk to a
temperature of 100°F, stir in 1 tablespoon of buttermilk and 2 teaspoons (or equivalent) of RENNET, cover, and leave it a couple of hours in a warm place to set. When
it is set, cut it into half-inch cubes and reheat it to 100°F, stirring all the time, and
then let it stand another 15 minutes. Ladle it gently into a colander lined with cheesecloth and let the whey drain out of it for 10 minutes or so, then hold it under the
cold-water tap to rinse the last of the whey away. The drained curds can then be

placed in a bowl and "creamed" by adding a little light cream or yogurt or they can be salted should you so desire. Eat it up within two to three days—this is home-made and has no preservatives.

Cottage Pie
A SHEPHERD'S PIE made with beef instead of lamb.

Cottonseed Oil
A vegetable oil made from the seeds of the cotton plant (*Gossypium* spp.) and used mostly in the food-packing industry as a less expensive substitute for olive oil.

Coulibiac
A hot fish pie of Russian origin. In Russia, it is traditionally made with sterlet, when you can get it, but salmon is apparently a worthy substitute as is any form of perch, pike, or whitefish. The pie filling also embraces hard-boiled eggs, mushrooms, and shallots along with kasha, rice, or semolina.

Coulis
It started out meaning the pan juices of any fish, game, meat, or poultry (especially if they could be used as a soup) and now refers to any thickened sauce or, by some mysterious French leap of logic, to a kind of bisque or thickened soup made with shellfish.

Coulommiers
One of the better examples of BRIE cheese.

Country Captain
An American adaptation of an Indian chicken stew of which there are dozens of vari-ations. In addition to chicken, it seems to include, in all its manifestations, curry powder, garlic, green pepper, and onions, is garnished with currants and almonds, and is served with rice. The "captain" of the title would seem to have been a native Indian officer, or Sepoy, serving with the British Army in India.

Coupe
A French term for a whole collection of extremely fancy SUNDAES.

Courgette
An English name for ZUCCHINI.

Court-Bouillon
A liquid used to simmer fish. It typically includes, in addition to fish bones and water, varying amounts of wine or vinegar, vegetables such as onion and carrot, and herbs including thyme and bay leaf. The term can be—but rarely is—applied to broth for meat or vegetables.

Couscous

A North African form of hard durum wheat (see FLOUR), typically steamed with meat, fish, fowl, and/or vegetables. It is sometimes sweetened and prepared as a dessert.

Couscousière

A utensil made for cooking COUSCOUS. It consists of a large, wide-bottomed pot narrowing at the top and a smaller upper pot with holes punched in the bottom and a loosely fitting cover. The meat, vegetables, herbs, and liquid all go in the lower pot and simmer, creating a tasty broth. The couscous grain goes into the upper pot, which is stacked atop the other. The steam, rising through the perforations into the upper pot, circulates through the couscous, cooking it and flavoring it simultaneously. Meat, vegetables, and grain are all served together.

A couscousière can be faked by taking a large pot and placing a colander on top, sealing it in place with plenty of aluminum foil. In either case, make sure that the whole upper container is clearly above the level of the simmering liquid. Otherwise the bottom of the couscous will simply get wet and the steam will not be able to circulate through as it should.

Cowberry

A mountain CRANBERRY.

Cowpea

A bean also called *black-eyed pea*.

Cowslip

In England, a spring wildflower (*Primula veris*), the blossoms of which are used for homemade wine, much as the DANDELION is. In North America, this flower is most likely the marsh marigold (*Caltha palustris*), a buttercup-like swamp flower. Cowslip leaves, when blanched in several washings of boiling water to rid them of their acrid taste, are said to provide a flavorful green.

Crab

A marine crustacean that is fairly plentiful in the waters off both coasts of North America, in intertidal zones and estuaries, and also, of course, found in prolific variety worldwide. Although they are widely eaten, they are generally not quite so highly prized elsewhere as they are in North America. There is also a marine critter known as a crab, which is actually more closely related to spiders and scorpions than to true crabs; this is the *horseshoe crab* (*Limulus polyphemus*), which is apparently edible, although it might take quite a few to make a meal. Crabs are marketed fresh—as either hard-shell or soft-shell—as well as frozen and canned. Some of the terms you're apt to encounter when dealing with other than fresh, whole crabs are:

Backfin. Meat from the back of the crab. It is in smaller pieces than meat simply labeled lump (see below); crabmeat labeled backfin lump is the most delicate meat the crab can offer.

Claw meat. As the name implies, meat from the claw; it is brownish and may not be so desirable if color is important. Otherwise it is just as tasty and should be less expensive.

Flake meat. Crab meat in small bits and pieces, culled from the shell after the larger pieces are lifted out.

Imitation crabmeat. Flavored, processed, and textured fish paste treated to make it appear as much like crab as possible. If you're not familiar with fresh crab or throw enough flavorings into it (as you might for a spicy seafood salad), you might not notice the difference. If it prices out at anywhere near the cost of real crab meat, however, it is, of course, a rip-off.

Lump meat. Large clumps of solid white body meat.

Prepared crabmeat is useful for many recipes including bisques, casseroles, cocktails, crab cakes, curries, salads, soufflés, and soups—in fact just about any use other than an old-fashioned Maryland (or San Francisco) crab boil, in which live crabs are boiled and served on tables with paper "tablecloths" and mallets. The crab is then pried out of its shell and eaten at the table, traditionally with quantities of cold beer (or chilled white wine).

When confronted with fresh crabs, the first move is to boil them, either in salted water, water to which you add a little vinegar, or water enriched with CRAB BOIL SPICE. Techniques here differ. Blue crabs are generally dropped live—and lively—into merrily boiling water. Dungeness crabs are routinely dispatched by turning them on their back and either stabbing them in the nerve centers with an icepick or laying the sharp edge of a knife along the midline and banging it with a hammer or mallet or whatever heavy object is handy. It can then be cleaned and cooked (or cooked and cleaned). In either case, the crab is best if allowed to boil 10 minutes for a blue crab, somewhat longer for a Dungeness, less if a quite small species. Once cool, the crab can be served whole or cleaned for whatever use is wished.

When cleaning a cooked hard-shell crab, twist off and crack the claws to allow access to the claw meat. Take off the crab's back and then the spongy tissue underneath (including the gills or "dead man's fingers"), split the body, and remove the meat. If the crab is uncooked, take off the shell and scrape away the interior portions. You can, if you wish, cut the crab in half and crack the claws (and, if a Dungeness crab, the legs). Boil.

When coping with a soft-shell crab, try to get those that are still quite small and as soft as possible (the shells grow back fairly quickly). If the fish market hasn't cleaned them, either ask them to or fix them yourself. Kill them by inserting an icepick or knife just behind the eyes, then lift up the twin points on each side of the back and take out the gills. Cut the head off just behind the eyes and squeeze out the sand sac. Turn the crab on its back and remove the apron. Soft-shells are frequently rolled in seasoned flour and sautéed in butter to be served with parsley and lemon, but there are other excellent ways of coping with them, including broiling.

There are various types of crabs and names for stages of crab life that occur here and there. Among them are:

Alaska king crab (*Paralithodes brevipes*, *camtschatica*, and *platypus*). Huge (they can measure nine feet from tip to tip) northern Pacific crabs, mostly seen as frozen legs (which can be two feet long themselves).

Blue crab (*Callinectes sapidus*). The common crab, weighing about a pound, of the western Atlantic and the Gulf of Mexico, and particularly Chesapeake Bay. Alan Davidson in his magisterial *North Atlantic Seafood* reports that it has also become successfully established in the Mediterranean as well. Most of the crabs we see in American markets are blue crabs. From the standpoints of both quantity and taste, the blue crab is compelling. It is at its best during the summer and late summer months.

Buster crab. A blue crab that is in the molt, "busting" out of its shell.

Common crab (*Cancer pagurus*). The crab of Europe's side of the Atlantic, treated much as you would blue crab.

Dungeness crab (*Cancer magister*). The premier crab of the Pacific coast, weighing upward of two pounds. They are, of course, available fresh on the West Coast (where, among other ways, they may be boiled and cracked and served with a tarragon mayonnaise). They are also frozen and canned.

Jimmy. A male blue crab (see above).

Jonah crab (*Cancer borealis*). You won't find this one in a fish market, but you might come across it along the more northerly Atlantic coast. Treat it like a small blue crab.

King crab. In addition to the Alaska king crab, there are also the California king crab (*Paralithodes californiensis* and *Paralithodes rathbuni*) and the golden king crab (*Lithodes aequispinus*). Should you run across one of them, treat them as you would the Alaska species (see above).

Rock crab (*Cancer irroratus*). Another East Coast crab, it is smaller than the Jonah but otherwise pretty similar. Again, you'll have to catch it yourself. Its West Coast counterpart, which is also not (or at best very rarely) commercially marketed, is *Cancer antennarius*.

Snow crab (*Libinia emarginata*). It is also known as the spider crab, but marketmen thought the name too rich for the consumers' stomachs and switched it.

Stone crab (*Menippe mercenaria*). This is the highly esteemed and quite expensive Southern stone crab, found along the coast from North Carolina around to Texas and most famous in Florida, particularly the Keys. Only the claws are eaten—the crab is caught, one claw is removed, and the crab is replaced in the water to grow a new one. The claw is boiled and cracked open, and the meat eaten with mayonnaise or a tangy butter after being removed from its shell with an oyster fork or (as many of us prefer) fingers.

Crab Apple

Any member of mostly extremely hardy, mostly wild fruit trees of the genus *Malus* (especially *Malus coronaria*) notable for their flowers and for their extremely sour fruit that can be made into jams and jellies. Crab apples can also supply the PECTIN for fruits deficient in it that are being made into preserves and jams.

Crab Boil Spice

A largely Southern combination of spices—allspice, bay leaves, cayenne pepper, cloves, coriander seed, dill seed, and mustard seed are in one commercial combination—added to the water in which crabs are to be boiled. Its makers are also inclined to recommend it for lobster.

Cracked Wheat

Wheat kernels that have gone through a preliminary cracking or milling but have not been subjected to the full process that results in regular wheat flour.

Cracker

Essentially flour and water and perhaps a little salt, baked until dry and crisp. As a first stage up, milk can augment or replace the water, and after that almost anything goes. The family includes sea biscuits, soda crackers, and every type of sweetened and flavored cracker used for snacks and pick-me-ups. Crumbled, they become CRACKER MEAL.

Cracker Meal

Unsweetened crackers broken into small crumbs and used for breading chops or cutlets or other foods as well as for topping dishes to be run under the broiler. It is suitable for any use when a fine equivalent of breadcrumbs is called for.

Crackling

The odds and ends left over from TRYING OUT (or rendering) pork fat. Crackling that is not wanted for any other purpose can be used in bread, especially cornbread.

Cranberry

Also *bounceberry*. A small, tart, red berry that is synonymous with sauce and the Thanksgiving turkey (although most cranberries are used for juice these days). Cape Cod seems to have the stranglehold on commercial or bog cranberries, although the plant (*Vaccinium macrocarpon*) grows wild in bogs from Nova Scotia to North Carolina and westward through Michigan to Oregon and Washington.

There is also a northern or European cranberry (*Vaccinium oxycoccus*) that bears small, edible berries as well as the *mountain cranberry* (*Vaccinium vitisidaea*), also called *lingonberry*, and an unrelated high-bush shrub (*Viburnum trilobum*, also called *squawbush*), which produces scads of handsome scarlet, cranberry-like berries that can be transmuted into first-rate jams or jellies.

When buying fresh bog cranberries, look for firm, almost bulletlike, shining red berries with a lustrous coat. Avoid any that are dull-colored or soft. If you're not using them right away, refrigerate or freeze them. At 0°F or lower they will keep quite nicely until the next season's crop comes on the market.

One pound of berries will equal about a quart and will cook down to slightly more than 3 cups of sauce. Of course, sauce is not the only end product of cranberries. They make a tasty jelly and even a zesty cold soup; they go well in breads, muffins, and cakes; they make an interesting addition to applesauce; they make a widely available juice or juice cocktail; and they lend themselves especially well to cranberry pie.

Cranberry Bean
A BEAN with a pink pod.

Crappie
A variety of PANFISH.

Crawdad
A folk name for the CRAYFISH.

Crawfish
A saltwater shellfish of the family Palinuridae, also called SPINY LOBSTER and *langoustine* and resembling the LOBSTER except that it lacks the massive claws. Crawfish are found from the Mediterranean northward to England and along the coasts of South America and South Africa, but only fitfully along the North American coastline. Some find their way to market as frozen *South African lobster tails*, *rock lobster*, and other names. The name is sometimes interchangeable with the freshwater CRAYFISH. It is cooked like lobster.

Crayfish
A freshwater shellfish of the Astacura tribe, prevalent in Europe and western North America, and to a much lesser extent in eastern North America. Crayfish are prepared in a number of ways, but most popularly are boiled (or poached) in a COURTBOUILLON and washed down with beer (or, in northern Europe, AQUAVIT). Many other ways exist of cooking them, of course, including using them in a BISQUE, in the preparation of which it is traditional to cook the whole carcasses, crush them, strain the liquid, and add it to enrich the soup.

Cream

1. The fatty part of milk. It is found in markets as light cream or heavy cream (or whipping cream), light cream being appropriate for use in coffee and some cooking, heavy cream being appropriate for cooking and whipping.

2. To reduce something to the consistency of cream by mashing it against the side of a mixing bowl with a fork, spoon, or spatula—or running it slowly through a blender or food processor. Butter and sugar are the most likely candidates to be creamed together, and the twin keys to success in doing it by hand are patience and an aching hand and wrist. Keep at it and remember, you can't overdo it.

Cream Cheese

A mildly acid, rich CHEESE useful for spreads and for cheesecake. Victorian expert on food and cookery Mrs. Isabella Beaton referred to it as "cream dried sufficiently to cut with a knife."

Creamer

1. A cream pitcher.
2. A nondairy preparation to replace milk or cream in coffee.

Cream of Tartar

A white powder (potassium tartarate) that forms inside barrels in which wine has fermented. It is a component of single-acting BAKING POWDER and is also useful in helping egg whites keep their form when beaten.

Cream Puff Pastry

A versatile pastry dough made from butter, water, flour, eggs, and salt. It is used as a vehicle for any number of fillings. It can be filled with chocolate or other flavorings for cream puffs, éclairs, or profiteroles or stuffed with some form of fish or chicken for hors d'oeuvres or a light snack. Its French name, *pâte à chou*, signifies "cabbage (shaped) pastry" on account of the spherical form the small mounds of dough explode into when baked.

Cream Sauce

See WHITE SAUCE.

Cream Sherry

A heavily sweetened SHERRY.

Crema Dania

Also *Danica*. A Danish soft cow's-milk CHEESE developed as a Scandinavian variation on BRIE, but without the soft center.

Crème

A French word for *cream*. The word also denotes a particularly sweet LIQUEUR. Crème de menthe, for example, is a sweet peppermint liqueur, crème de banane a sweet banana-flavored one.

Crème Brûlée

A custardy French dessert (although Jane Garmey in *Great British Cooking: A Well Kept Secret* contends that it is a variation on an 18th-century British invention) consisting of caramelized sugar that is poured into an individual custard dish and allowed to harden; you then pour in custard and cook it as you would any custard and let it chill. When you are ready to serve it, top it with yet more caramelized sugar, run it under the broiler (to set and harden the topping), and serve it forth.

Crème Caramel

A French dessert composed of a custard that is baked in a mold lined with caramelized sugar, then allowed to cool. The dish is then inverted and the mold removed. It is served cold.

Crème Chantilly

1. Sweetened whipped cream with a little vanilla added for flavoring.
2. A white soft Scandinavian cow's-milk CHEESE more properly called *Hablé Crème Chantilly*.

Crème Fraîche

A French term for a thick, flavorful form of matured cream. Crème fraîche is not readily available in North America, but can be quite nearly approximated by adding 1 tablespoon buttermilk, sour cream, or yogurt to 1 cup heavy cream, heating it almost to the boiling point, then letting it stand, covered, in a warm place for 24 hours, or until it gets thick. You can refrigerate it at this point and it will keep for 4 to 5 days.

Crème Pâtissière

See PASTRY CREAM.

Crenshaw

A particularly succulent MELON.

Creole

1. A style of cooking most notably practiced in Louisiana. It derives largely from a mixing of French (and Spanish) and African traditions grafted onto New World circumstances and foodstuffs.
2. A kind of CHEESE formed by a mixture of CLABBER and heavy cream; it was once sold by street vendors in New Orleans and is reportedly still to be found in Louisiana in commercial form.

Creole Mustard

A hot Louisiana mustard enlivened with horseradish.

Crepe

A thin and delicate French pancake made of an egg-and-flour batter to which is added a little salt or, if a sweet crepe is desired, a little sugar. Crepes can be filled or flavored with almost anything edible (fruits or berries and cheese are popular). The most famous variation, Crepes Suzette, is flavored with orange liqueur.

Crépinettes

A designation for a family of small, flat French sausages made from pork or lamb or fowl (or whatever is handy) and grilled before serving.

Cress

A mostly British term for a number of pungent salad greens of the mustard family, especially *garden cress* (*Lepidum sativum*), the very young sprouts of which are often mixed with young mustard greens and served as mustard and cress either as a salad or as a sandwich filling. The word is also often used to designate WATERCRESS.

Crimp

To use a fork to press the edges of an unbaked piecrust against the rim of the pie plate to seal in the filling and provide a traditional decoration. If you don't want to use a fork, use your fingers, but you just won't get the same decorative effect.

Crisp

To bring life back to slightly limp vegetables by letting them soak in cold water before cooking them. If they were not too tired to begin with, crisping does exactly what the word implies.

Croaker

A game and food fish (*Micropogon undulatus*) that is a member of a family that has an urge to be heard (one relative is the DRUM). Croakers make an odd, croaking sound out of the water and perhaps in it as well. Among the recommended cooking methods are broiling and panfrying.

Croissant

A rich French roll in the shape of a crescent, usually made from a dough in the PUFF PASTRY style. Croissants and coffee laced with milk form the basic middle-class French breakfast.

Croque-Monsieur

Just about the ultimate in a ham-and-cheese sandwich. Thin slices of ham and Gruyère cheese are placed on thinly sliced, buttered bread and browned in butter until golden.

Croquette
A small pastry roll or cone filled with a seasoned mixture of chopped meat, chicken, vegetables, or fish, and then dipped in egg, breaded, and deep-fried.

Crosne
A CHINESE ARTICHOKE.

Cross-Hatch
To weave strips of piecrust across the top of a one-crust pie to provide a lattice-like effect.

Crottin
Also *crottin de Chavignol*. The traditional small, hard, dry goat's-milk CHEESE made around the village of Chavignol, southwest of Paris. The word *crottin* is a somewhat earthy, affectionate nickname; it signifies (goat) droppings.

Croustade
A shell made by hollowing out a square or round slab of bread and stuffing the cavity with a creamed and seasoned mixture (fish, chicken, meat, or vegetable) and baking the whole creation until the crust is browned and crisp.

Croûte
A French term for *crust*. It refers to any food (chicken, fish, ham, beef, elaborate pâtés) that has been completely encased in pastry. The dish is then referred to as *en croûte* except in the case of beef, when it can be called BEEF WELLINGTON.

Croutons
Diced breadcrumbs toasted or fried in butter, goosefat, or other fat and used as a garnish in soups, salads, and other dishes.

Crown Roast
An elegant roast of lamb or pork that consists of the ribs, removed from the backbone, trimmed, turned meat side inward, and tied to form the shape of a crown. The center is often filled with a chopped meat preparation and the end of the ribs are covered with paper frills to keep them from burning.

Crudité
A French term for a raw or very quickly blanched vegetable served, usually with a dip, as an hors d'oeuvre or appetizer.

Cruet
A utensil for holding oil, soy sauce, or other condiment for use at the table, often designed as two vessels in one for holding oil and vinegar.

Cruller

A spicy DOUGHNUT formed into a cylinder and frequently twisted.

Crumb

1. See BREADCRUMBS.

2. A baker's term for the texture of a slice of bread. Most breads call for a fine crumb, but cornbread, for example, usually benefits from a coarser crumb.

Crumpet

An English tea bread similar to a muffin but cooked on a griddle rather than baked. It is cooked only on one side, which results in a top riddled with small holes. Crumpets are at their best when freshly toasted and slathered with incredible amounts of butter and jam. If you happen to be British, you will know that a particular protocol has built up around the acceptable eating of crumpets; but if you're not, you'll probably enjoy them anyway, especially if you slather them with sufficient butter and jam.

Crush

To break up by rolling or pounding as you would nuts, seeds, or bits of bread (to make breadcrumbs).

Crust

The thick, hard, or browned surface of a cooked item of food, such as the outside of a loaf of bread or the top and bottom of a pie or tart.

Crustacean

The name for a grouping of animals with hard, crustlike shells. Among their ranks are crabs, lobsters, and shrimp.

Crystallize

To preserve a fruit, for example, or an edible flower with sugar syrup.

Cubanelle

A longish, medium-sized sweet PEPPER. It can be green, red, or yellow.

Cube

To cut or DICE into small squares.

Cubeb

A relative (*Piper cubeba*) of black pepper, formerly used as a seasoning and as a medicinal.

Cube Steak

A thin cut of beef that has been put through a device that prints cube-shaped markings on it, helping to break up the fibers and tenderize it.

Cucumber

A member of the gourd family (*Cucumis sativus*). There are several types of cucumbers, ranging from the long English variety to the spiny Asian kind to the fairly recently developed seedless ones; they also embrace the garden cucumbers including the gherkin, which is best for pickling (especially the French CORNICHON). Although most of the ones we see are green, cucumbers also come in yellow and in white.

Market cucumbers come with their rinds covered with a waxy finish (to hold in moisture and preserve them) that cannot be removed except by peeling. Since a part of the taste of a cucumber is in the rind (although most of it is in the seeds), the full appreciation of a cucumber is restricted to people with a garden, or access to one, although the wax is edible if you like that sort of thing. Buy cucumbers that have a fresh, green color and a good, solid firmness and are fairly small and evenly shaped. Keep in mind that an unwaxed cucumber is neither deeply green nor shiny. With a tight layer of plastic wrap around them, cucumbers will keep for a week refrigerated, but they're better if you use them right up.

Most cucumbers are pickled or used in salads, but they also lend themselves to sautéing, deep-frying, stuffing and baking, and forming a major component of a hot cream or cold summer soup.

Cuisine Minceur

Sometimes called *lean cuisine*. A cooking trend developed in the 1970s by French chef Michel Guérard. Its premise was the avoidance of butter, cream, and other rich ingredients in order to enhance health yet promote elegant dining.

Cullen Skink

A soup made with FINNAN HADDIE.

Cumberland Sauce

A classic sauce for game composed of lemon and orange juice, lemon and orange rind, red currant jelly, port wine, and mustard. It is frequently left to settle overnight and is served at room temperature.

Cumin

An ancient spice (*Cuminum cyminum*), originally out of Egypt but now successfully cultivated all over. It adds a tang to curries and chilis and is useful in flavoring sauces, sausages, soups, and stews and is excellent over rice. Cumin is an ingredient of a number of mixed spicings. The hearty split-pea soup that can brighten the winter doldrums is all the better for a pinch of it.

Cunner

A small, coastal, commercially unimportant fish (*Tautolabrus adspersus*) similar to the TAUTOG, only smaller and found from Newfoundland to the Chesapeake, but most common along the New England coast. Cunners can be a pretty good PANFISH, although most anglers throw them back as too bony.

Cup

See MEASURING CUP.

Cupcake

A small cake baked in an individual cupcake mold and usually given some form of ICING. Cupcakes are traditional fare at children's birthday parties.

Curaçao

An orange-flavored LIQUEUR originally made on the island of the same name. It is of assistance in flavoring orange soufflé or duck à l'orange.

Curd

The solid part of milk; it is that part of the milk that solidifies when milk curdles and when RENNET is added to it to make cheese.

Curd Cheese

See COTTAGE CHEESE.

Cure

To preserve fish or meat. Drying, salting (also known as *corning*, as in corned beef), and smoking are time-honored techniques. Curing goose and pork in their own fat was once widespread, especially in France and Germany.

Currant

1. The dried fruit of a small European GRAPE, used especially in baking. The name is a variation on Corinth, the Greek city from which the first such currants were shipped and still an important source of currants today.

2. The fruit of either of two related plants of European origin, one (*Ribes sativum*) giving red (and sometimes white) currants, the other (*Ribes nigrum*) bearing black currants. There are also black currants native to North America (chiefly *Ribes Americanum*), with a somewhat musky berry that calls for cooking, and several varieties of the red, all of which are of more interest to foragers than to marketers.

Red currants—when dead ripe—are mostly transformed into preserves (including a notable one from Bar-le-Duc in northeast France) or used in pastries. They can also be eaten either off the bush, dusted with sugar and refrigerated for an hour or two as a dessert, or crushed and mixed with water to form a soothing drink. White currants are sweeter and less acidic than red. Fresh red and white currants have an abundance of pectin and high acidity, making them excellent partners for jelly-making with low-pectin fruits. And for many people, red currant jelly is to venison as mint jelly is to lamb.

Black currants are less widely grown. They are mostly used in jams and jellies and as the base of the French liqueur CASSIS; in the British Isles, they are highly favored for pastries.

Currants are not so widespread as they once were, in part because their cultivation is discouraged. They harbor a fungus that is devastating to the white pine, an important timber resource and ornamental tree.

Curry

An Indian complex of flavorings and also any food made with it. Curry powder is a mixture of a number of dried herbs and spices (usually incorporating various amounts of such spices as caraway seeds, cardamom, chili, cinnamon, clove, coriander, fenugreek, mustard seed, pepper, and turmeric), but curried dishes are often further enhanced with additional spicing, according to the taste of the server. Curries are usually considered spicily hot, but some—especially those originating in northern India—are not in the least bit so, taking their flavoring more from such mild herbs as cinnamon than the chilis more favored to the south.

Curry Paste

Curry ingredients submerged in oil (or GHEE). If you don't plan on grinding your own curry powder each time you cook a curry, the paste is a better bet than commercial powder. It will keep longer and retain more of the taste and aroma of the ingredients than will powder, which tends to go flat reasonably quickly. It is available in Oriental markets and specialty stores, and if enough people show interest, the supermarkets will not be far behind.

Curry Powder

A commercial preparation of curry herbs and spices. If it is labeled "Madras," it will be slightly hotter or more pungent that otherwise. However, since curry powder loses its edge once the can is opened, don't plan on keeping it around more than about two months. Try the curry paste or, better yet, grind your own.

Cusk

A fish of the COD family.

Custard

A mixture of egg and milk, sometimes with sweeteners and flavorings, cooked in a double boiler or baked. Temperature control is crucial to custard-making, a stove-top temperature of 165°–170°F being about ideal while a low oven setting (follow your recipe but check the oven control's accuracy with your oven thermometer) is necessary and the use of a BAIN MARIE is generally recommended. Custards are served as desserts and also form the basis for ice cream and for many succulent fruit pies and tarts.

Custard Apple

Also *bullock's heart*. A tropical tree (*Annona reticulata*) related to the CHERIMOYA, bearing spherical greenish fruit with sweet, juicy, creamy white flesh encompassing a fair number of inedible seeds. It is often used in iced drinks. The name is also applied to the cherimoya and to the PAWPAW.

Cut In

In pastry-making, to blend shortening with flour. See PASTRY BLENDER.

Cutlet

A fine, thin slice of meat (lamb, pork, or veal) taken from the neck or leg. Cutlets are often dipped in beaten egg and breadcrumbs and are either broiled or fried. Poultry breeders are also marketing chicken and turkey cutlets that can be cooked much like their meat counterparts.

Cuttlefish

A mollusk (*Sepia officinalis*) similar to SQUID. In Europe, cuttlefish are usually served deep-fried with a garlic sauce, and, in the Orient, used mostly dried as a flavoring for soups.

Cymling

A variety of SQUASH.

Dab

A European FLATFISH. In North America, the name is also used for the yellowtail flounder.

Dace

A small freshwater European fish (*Leuciscus leuciscus*) or any of several North American fishes resembling it. Dace can be cooked like SMELT.

Daikon

An Oriental RADISH (*Raphanus sativus* var. *longipinnatus*). It is most generally seen as a long white root—up to a foot long—but there are also varieties that are more turnip-shaped. It has a sharp but somewhat sweet taste and is used raw (grated or shredded into salads) or pickled. The leaves can also be steamed as a vegetable.

Dal

Also *dhal*. The Indian word for a pulse (lentil, pea, or bean) that has been dried and split, like split peas. Dal often accompanies curries, where it is cooked, most traditionally, with spices and garnished with browned onion slices.

Damson

A small, tart PLUM (*Prunus institia*), used especially for preserves.

Danablu

See DANISH BLUE cheese.

Danbo

A firm, mild Danish cow's-milk CHEESE with holes in it, slightly resembling SWISS CHEESE. It is sometimes flavored with caraway seeds.

Dandelion

Those little yellow flowers (*Taraxacum officinale*) that bloom all over your lawn each spring. If you harvest the leaves (but not from your lawn unless you avoid the use of pesticides and similar compounds unhealthy to humans) you will have a slightly bitter-tasting green that fits well into a salad or can be cooked like spinach or turnip greens. To continue the spinach comparison, dandelion greens make an excellent substitute for spinach in a fish florentine (which is fish on a bed of spinach) using freshly caught perch or other panfish combined with freshly picked dandelion leaves. Lacking the opportunity to accomplish all that, you can buy cultivated dandelion greens in most markets in the spring and will doubtless find them more tender even than the wild variety. You may note that dandelions also enjoy a resurgence in the fall, but don't get carried away. Fall dandelion greens have all the excitement you might expect from an equal amount of meadow grass.

If the leaves don't interest you, collect the flowers—steep them in water, drain them, boil the liquid with sugar and orange and lemon rind, pour it into a crock and add yeast. After it has fermented, bottle it, then put it in a cool, dark place and don't touch it for six months. When you do open it, you will (or ought to) have dandelion wine. Or you can simply drop the blossoms into a lightly beaten egg, then into cornmeal, and sauté them in oil for a slightly different snack or garnish.

Danish Blue
A blue-veined, white Danish cow's-milk CHEESE intended to compete with Roquefort.

Danish Pastry
A rich pastry made from a yeast-risen dough and filled with any one of a variety of cheeses or custard or fruits or spices or nuts or what-have-you.

Dâo
Robust red and white Portuguese wines from the hill country between Lisbon and Oporto.

Dariole
The English say it is an old English word for a kind of Chaucerian cheesecake; the French that it is a medieval French almond pastry. There is today a kind of small, cylindrical French mold used for an almond pastry called a dariole.

Darjeeling
An Indian TEA.

Dash
A scant ⅛ teaspoon—an amount too small, or needed in too unspecific an amount, to be more precisely measured or specified.

Dasheen
See TARO.

Date
The fruit of the date palm (*Phoenix dactylifera*). Dates are happiest growing in dry, semiarid conditions, producing their best fruit in the Near East and North Africa and in desert portions of Arizona and California. In addition to providing a good finger-food snack, dates are good in breads and cakes, are made into DATE SYRUP,

and are also chopped up for use in salads. (Dates have also been made into a wine that is considered quite speedily intoxicating.)

Dates are sold fresh or dried. When selecting fresh dates, look for plump, golden fruit that is glossy and smooth. They may be found either pitted or unpitted. If your recipe calls for sliced dates, chill them thoroughly before slicing. And if you use them in baking, give them a coating of flour before adding them. It will keep them from clumping together. If you get fresh dates, wrap them in plastic and keep them refrigerated for as long as two weeks. Dried dates will keep well for months, longer if refrigerated.

Date Syrup

A syrup used in Middle Eastern cooking. It is made by generously covering fresh, plump, good-quality dates with boiling water and leaving them to soak for three hours. The dates are then brought just to a simmer for five minutes or so and let cool, at which point they are pressed through a fine sieve, cheesecloth, or muslin towel and cooked very slowly for two hours or until thick. Date syrup is then used as a sweetener for yogurt, dolmas, or pickles; mixed up with chopped walnuts and bits of bread as a dessert; or generally used as a Western cook might use corn syrup or molasses.

Daube

A French stew, usually beef but occasionally made with other meats or fowl. A daube is braised in red wine (or white—especially for rabbit or gamebirds) with vegetables (carrots, onions), a piece of salt pork or streaky bacon, and spices and then cooked very slowly for a very long time. The dish takes its name from the pot, or *daubière*, in which it was originally cooked, modern examples of which are available from places that specialize in expensive cookware, especially of the imported variety.

Day Lily

Originally a garden plant, the day lily (*Hemerocallis* spp.) has jumped the garden walls and can be found along roadsides and in open places all over North America. Gather the buds when they are full and fat, just before they open into freckled yellow-orange flowers. Drop them briefly into boiling water, and serve hot with butter and salt as a side vegetable. Or stir-fry them in oil with water chestnuts in the Chinese manner.

Decant

To very gently pour a liquid—such as a fine old wine—from one bottle to another to separate the clear upper fluid from the murkier stuff and its solids (sediment) below. The latter are, if you've done it deftly, left behind.

Decoction

A fancy, and fortunately rare, term for the liquid left over from boiling (more properly, simmering) meats and vegetables. Most of us prefer to say soup or broth or even vegetable water. The Lord alone knows where you're going to run across this word.

Deep-Fat Fry

To fry by immersing something in extremely hot fat until it becomes crusty on the outside and moist and cooked inside—usually not very long. All manner of foods can be cooked this way, notably french-fried potatoes, onion rings, Southern fried chicken, DOUGHNUTS, and CRULLERS. It is also a technique that seems especially efficacious for fish. The cooking fat (typically lard, oil, or shortening) is usually reusable (strain it and keep it in a cool place), and there are reports from the Deep South of fat being used a number of times before it is considered ready to impart its full flavor. Cooking fat that has been used for fish, however, will impart a fishy taste to anything cooked in it afterward and is best clearly labeled and kept specifically for that purpose.

Deep-Fat Fryer

A pot for DEEP-FAT FRYING. It should be plenty deep and, ideally, wider at the top than the bottom. With it you'll need a wire basket with a handle. The food to be cooked is placed in the basket, lowered into the hot fat, then retrieved by raising the basket as soon as the food is done. You can fake it all with a huge pot and a sizable sieve, but if you're going to do this sort of cooking frequently, you're better off investing in the real thing.

Deer

Any of various animals of the family Cervidae, the most prevalent in North America being the mule and the whitetail deer, and also the antelope, caribou, elk, and moose. The meat of all of these is commonly referred to as VENISON. Waverley Root, in his monumental book *Food*, warns that at least at one time and place, some Chinese menus included "household deer," or what we know as rat.

Deglaze

To collect all the little bits of meat and poultry left over in the pan after browning, sautéing, broiling, or roasting by adding a little liquid (red wine, sherry, stock, among others), mixing it all up (scraping the bits from the pan's surface if that seems appropriate), letting it boil up together, and using it as gravy or as the basis for a gravy or sauce.

Degrease

To skim off the excess fat from something, for example, a soup or stew. One strategy that is especially useful for stews, because they tend to improve on being reheated the second day anyway, is to put the dish in the refrigerator. Just before reheating it, spoon out the solid fat that has risen to the surface and formed a thick white layer. Take a little care (use your fingers if you have to) so that the small pieces of vegetables or meat remain with the stew instead of being rejected with the excess fat.

Dehydrated
Dried. Dehydration is a time-honored method of preserving food. Sun-dried foodstuffs (such as tomatoes) are available as are devices for doing your own dehydrating. Fruits, herbs, meats, and vegetables of all sorts can be dried at home, thus making a dehydrator a handy gadget, especially for the home gardener.

Delmonico Steak
Alternate name for SHELL STEAK.

Demi-Sec
A term that, when applied by the French to Champagne, does not mean—as the translation would suggest—"half-dry," but actually quite sweet.

Demitasse
A small cup in which after-dinner coffee is served. It is about half the size of a regular coffee cup.

Dende
A west African and South American oil made from palm nuts. The culinary variety is made from the whole nut, is of an orangy-red color, and has a strong flavor. You can fake it by adding paprika to olive oil, letting it sit for a half hour, then straining out the paprika (cheesecloth makes a convenient strainer).

Derby
A bland, light-colored English cow's-milk CHEESE; a variant flavored with sage is a British Christmas tradition.

Dessert Wine
A sweet wine intended for serving with or just after a sweet dessert or in midafternoon as an alternative to tea. The term embraces sweet table wines (such as SAUTERNES) as well as FORTIFIED WINE.

Devein
To remove the dark "vein" or intestinal column that runs along the back of a shrimp. You don't have to worry about small shrimp, but would be well advised to devein the larger ones—otherwise you may have to cope with some grit. Either a sharp knife or a special deveining tool is appropriate.

Deviled
Hot, hot, hot—or at least highly spiced (cayenne pepper, mustard, and hot sauces such as Tabasco are the usual suspects).

Devil's Food Cake
A rich chocolate cake.

Devonshire Cream
A British form of clotted cream whereby fresh, whole, unpasteurized milk is allowed to set and then heated until a skin forms on the top. It is then skimmed and gently warmed until thickened, at which point it presents a yellow, crusty top and a rich, creamy, and very tasty underpart. Should you have some unpasteurized milk handy and wish to try making Devonshire cream, you had best seek out a good, specific recipe.

Dewberry
A plant closely akin to the BLACKBERRY except that it trails along the ground instead of growing upright. Its fruit resembles blackberries in almost all respects and is used in exactly the same ways.

Dhal
A variant spelling of DAL.

Dice
To cut something into pieces smaller than something chopped but larger than something minced. See CHOP.

Diet
To try to lose weight; also the method used to lose weight. The tiresome truth seems to be that virtually all foods—in sensible amounts—are diet foods and that the management of weight demands getting into the dreary habit of eating food in moderate, balanced amounts. Good luck!

Digestive
Digestive biscuits were slightly sweet whole wheat crackers similar to graham crackers popular in England and the United States in Victorian times, and still to be found among traditionalists today. The French *digestif* refers to brandy or liqueur taken after dinner in the forlorn hope that it will aid the digestion as much as it does the disposition of the diner.

Dill
An herb (*Anethum graveolens*) that gives the name and flavor to dill pickles. And that is by no means all. The spidery green fronds of fresh dill combine incomparably with salmon (as in GRAVLAX) and shrimp and go well in potato or macaroni salad. Indeed, dill enhances almost any vegetable as well as egg dishes and all manner of soups, stews, and casseroles. However, dill is best added toward the end of the cooking time. Dried dill is sold as dill weed; the seeds are also sold and resemble CARAWAY SEEDS, with which they can be virtually interchanged.

Dilute
To add liquid to thin or cut the strength of something.

Dim Sum
Assorted fried or baked Chinese dumplings filled with pork or seafood and served with rice balls and pastries. They are served as appetizers and as snacks.

Diplomat
An elegant dessert based on ladyfingers soaked in KIRSCH, set on a base of crystallized fruits, and layered with soaked dried fruits and BAVARIAN CREAM.

Dirty Rice
A Cajun dish of rice cooked with chicken gizzards and livers; it takes its name from the coloration the rice receives from this combination. It will probably also contain celery, garlic, onion, pepper, and various spices as well.

Dittany
Also *Maryland dittany* (*Cunila origanoides*). A member of the mint family used to replace CHERVIL, MARJORAM, or THYME and brewed into tea by native Americans. There is also an unrelated herb known as *Cretan dittany* (*Origanum dictamnus*), a relative of marjoram.

Divinity
A form of FUDGE made with stiffly beaten egg whites, sugar, and, usually, nuts.

Dock
See SORREL.

Dogfish
The most common species of the small sharks, found in cool to cold waters in both the Atlantic and Pacific with close relations elsewhere. There is a smooth dogfish (*Mustelis canis*), relatives of which are consumed in the Mediterranean area, and one with spines that can give you a nasty sore, the spiny dogfish, sand shark, or spurdog (*Squalus acanthias*). Considered "junk fish" by many anglers (most of whom have never tried it), both species of dogfish lend themselves well to deep-frying and can also be successfully baked. How you're going to get through that tough, sandpapery hide is another problem altogether. If you should want to try one, be sure to skin it first.

Dollarfish
See BUTTERFISH.

Dollop
A very small amount.

Dolly Varden
Although it is called a trout, it is actually a species of CHAR.

Dolma
A stuffed vegetable, from the Turkish word for "stuffed." In the West, it usually refers to stuffed GRAPE LEAVES.

Dolphin
1. DORADO.
2. A sea mammal (Delphinide family) once apparently used as food but not according to any available recent record.

Dorado
A fish (*Coryphaena* spp.) of worldwide distribution in tropical and warm, temperate waters much prized everywhere including Hawaii, where it is called *mahimahi*. Its firm, rich meat is excellent filleted or steaked and can be cooked almost any way that fish can be cooked, including being popped into a chowder. The fish is also known as *dolphin*, although it has no connection whatsoever with the true dolphin, which is a mammal.

Dory
See JOHN DORY.

Dot
To put small bits and pieces of something (especially butter) on top of a dish generally just before you pop it into the oven. The butter (or whatever) then melts evenly over the whole top.

Double Boiler
Two pots in one, really, with the smaller one designed so that it fits neatly into the larger—tight at the top, looser elsewhere—but dangling down with an inch or so of space to spare at the bottom. The bottom pot simmers water, and ingredients that need gentle, indirect cooking or heating are placed in the upper pot. The cooking action results from the steam swirling around the upper pot. Either half can be put over a direct flame, although you may want to use the upper pot only over a gentle one.

Double Cream
A cheesemaker's term for a fresh cheese, usually of cow's milk, with its dry components consisting of at least 60 percent fat.

Double Gloucester
A mellow, golden (or red if colored with ANNATTO), rich British cow's-milk CHEESE that has been compared to an extremely fine Cheddar. It has become exceedingly

hard to find and will be exceedingly expensive if you do. Critics think a good one well worth both the search and the price.

Dough
The raw material of breads and pastries after the BATTER stage. Dough has had the yeast added and kneaded in, and the whole mass has formed a cohesive lump, ready to be cooked—or perhaps left to rise.

Doughnut
Essentially a small, round, deep-fried cake, often with a hole in the middle. The hole is said to have been added (or subtracted) by a dyspeptic sea captain looking for a way to cook his fried cake more thoroughly and thereby render it somewhat more digestible.

Doughnut-making takes a deft hand (too much handling toughens doughnuts) and a sharp eye on the temperature of the cooking fat (below 360°F they soak up too much fat and get soggy; above 375°F they break down chemically). Once a doughnut is mastered, you can sugar it, fill it with jelly, leaven it with yeast (to make raised doughnuts), or ignore the doughnut shape entirely and braid it into crullers or any shape that fits your mood.

Doux
A winemaker's term meaning "sweet," except in the case of CHAMPAGNE, in which case it will be very sweet indeed and will seldom, if ever, be seen in North America.

Dove
Any of various pigeons (of the family Columbidae) that are classified as game in some areas, songbirds in others. In areas where they proliferate and destroy crops, doves are both fair game and good eating whether roasted (spit-roasting is popular), braised, or broiled (usually with a strip of bacon over it to offset the leanness of the meat). In general, the young (known as *squab*) are best broiled or grilled whereas the older ones tend to be tough and need longer cooking.

Dover Sole
A name for two kinds of FLATFISH: the delicate true sole of northern European waters and a Pacific flounder, also of excellent culinary quality.

Dragée
A small, sugar-coated nut (almond, usually) as well as a tiny colored candy, usually silvered, used for decorating pastries.

Dragon's Eye
See LONGAN.

Drain

To separate a solid from a liquid, often by pouring the whole thing into a colander or sieve.

Drambuie

A Scottish cordial based on Scotch whisky and flavored with honey and herbs.

Draw

To remove entrails, as of a game bird.

Dredge

To coat lightly, usually with flour, cornmeal, sugar, etc., depending upon what you and your recipe have in mind. Of the recommended techniques, you can place everything in a paper bag and shake vigorously (if you have a couple of pounds of meat chunks, however, you're obviously not going to want to shake them all at the same time—do it in batches) or you can place the coating material on a plate and dip the items to be dredged in it until the desired amount is achieved. There are also devices like a salt shaker with a handle for sprinkling a coating on food. The size of the holes vary according to whether you're planning to use it for flour, sugar, cinnamon, or whatever.

Dress

To get something ready for cooking. Game animals are dressed by being gutted, bled, and sometimes skinned and decapitated. Birds are gutted and defeathered. Fish don't get dressed—they get cleaned and scaled—except to ready them for smoking, in which case they may be HOG DRESSED.

Dressing

1. Another word for STUFFING.
2. Salad dressing.

Dried Beef

See CHIPPED BEEF.

Dripping Pan

A container placed beneath a food being broiled, grilled, or smoked in order to catch the juices dropping from it or the liquid being used for basting. You can DEGLAZE the drippings and add them to the feast.

Drippings

The fat that drips from a roast or from cooking bacon or sausages. It's mostly a British term. Drippings from pork products provide the pork or bacon fat in which so many other dishes are cooked; beef drippings are essential to making YORKSHIRE PUDDING and TOAD-IN-THE-HOLE and other Britannic specialties.

Drizzle

To spatter drops of a liquid over a food in a somewhat slapdash way, as by shaking them off a fork.

Drop Cookie

A cookie, the batter for which is dropped from a spoon onto the baking sheet.

Drum

An informal name for a family of fish (Sciaenidae) with the ability to work the muscles of their air bladder to make a resonant noise. The drums include the croaker as well as the black drum (*Pogonias cromis*)—found from New York south—and the red drum or channel bass (*Sciaenops ocellata*). The black drum is held to be no great shakes as food while the red drum is well thought of and can be prepared as you would a striped BASS.

Drupe

Also called *stone fruit*. A fruit or nut with a single seed contained in a hard shell, surrounded by pulp, and enclosed by a skin. Almonds, apricots, cherries, peaches, nectarines, and plums are all drupes.

Dry

1. To preserve a food by removing the moisture from it. Peas and beans come to mind as does fish of various sorts. Jerky is a way of preserving meat by drying it. A modern variation on this age-old technique is freeze-drying.

2. Refers to a wine in which all the sugar in the grape juice has been converted into alcohol.

Dry Cod

A COD that has been both salted and dried.

Dublin Bay Prawn

See NORWAY LOBSTER.

Dubonnet

A French proprietary APERITIF.

Duck

A swimming bird with short neck, short legs, and webbed feet. Most domestic ducks that you see are Long Island ducklings and are fat, containing a goodly amount of waste in proportion to the edible meat. In some areas Muscovy ducks are available— especially around Chinese enclaves and usually from live-poultry markets. Larger, meatier, and with a much darker and tastier meat, they more closely resemble goose than they do regular ducks. Wild ducks are, of course, normally available only to hunters.

Most ducks are sold either frozen or thawed (in which case refreezing is not recommended) and weigh about five pounds. When choosing a duck or duckling, there is not much to perceive if the bird is frozen, other than to avoid freezer burn or a build-up of ice around the bird (which can show that it has been in the freezer an uncommonly long length of time). Fresh duck is best when it is plump and glowing with health—when the fat is pure white and the flesh has a little spring to it when you poke it with your finger.

Duck is most commonly roasted, although broiling can give excellent results as can grilling (preferably on a constantly rotating spit beside the flame to avoid having the fat drip into the flames and flare up). Other ways to cook duck include pressing (a gastronomic stunt best left to restaurants unless you really want to spring for the enormously expensive duck press it calls for), braising (often with turnips), or even deep-frying as you would chicken. Because of the fattiness of the bird, an orange sauce often accompanies it.

Many cookbooks recommend that fatty birds such as duck and goose be roasted in a pan of water or be pricked all over with a fork and placed in a pan with a little boiling water for a half hour or so to leach out the fat. Another technique is to remove whatever fat you can and drain off the excess from time to time during the cooking process. With a little judicious basting at the end, the skin still comes out brown and crisp.

Duckling
A young duck of 2½ to 5 pounds.

Duck Sauce
Also called *plum sauce*. A Chinese condiment made of sweetened plums (Asian plums are actually more closely related to apricots) and flavored with vinegar and pepper. It can be found on the table of virtually any Chinese restaurant and is used to accompany PEKING DUCK as well as pork and spare ribs.

Dulse
A northern seaweed (*Rhodymenia palmata*) used as a condiment in Scotland and recommended for shredding into salads or as a flavoring agent for cold fish. Dried dulse is generally available at health food stores. In general, dried dulse needs to be soaked for a couple of hours in water, after which it is simmered in milk seasoned with salt and pepper before it is ready to be used.

Dumpling
A dumpling is essentially dough—baking powder, eggs, flour (or breadcrumbs or mashed potatoes or rice or a combination of them), milk, and salt, with the eggs either beaten intact or separated and whites and yolks added separate. Dumplings can be made plain or can enclose other food and are cooked in gently simmering

broth. The crucial point in preparing dumplings is not to crowd them as you drop them into the broth and to keep the cover on the pot for the entire time the dumplings are cooking. Anyone who has ever dipped a piece of doughnut into a steaming cup of coffee has doubtless yielded to the same impulse that resulted in the first dumpling. So universal is this impulse that virtually all cultures have some form of dumpling, whether they're called DIM SUM or GNOCCHI or QUENELLES or whatever.

Dundee Cake
A Scottish fruitcake topped with almonds that are added in the middle of the baking time so as to become brown without burning.

Dungeness
A Pacific Coast CRAB.

Dunlop
A firm Scottish cow's-milk CHEESE similar to Cheddar but white and with less holding power.

Durian
A fruit of a tree (*Durio zibethinus*) native to Southeast Asia, especially Indonesia and Malaysia. It is roughly the shape of a football with the thorny hide of a pineapple, is of an olive green exterior that slowly changes to yellow, and has a creamy interior with yellow seeds that can be roasted. The flesh has a sweet taste like a mixture of bananas and figs. It must be an acquired taste for the odor has been described as penetrating and sulfurous and even as smelling like sewage. Fresh durians can only be transported by air (on those airlines that will accept them), which makes them expensive indeed, but they can be had canned.

Durum Wheat
A hard variety of WHEAT used largely for PASTA.

Dust
To put a light coat of flour, sugar, etc., on something. It is like DREDGING only not as extreme.

Dutch Cocoa
COCOA that has been treated to make it less acid; in the process it also becomes darker, milder, and more soluble.

Dutch Oven
Originally the heavy iron pot that hung from a crane in the fireplace and sometimes the small apertures in the sides of early fireplaces in which food was placed to cook or keep warm. In modern parlance, it varies from a casserole to a roasting pan to a

slow-cooking well. Its most common sense seems to be an iron or glazed pot with handles and a cover used either for cooking on top of the stove or in the oven.

Duxelles

Mushrooms that have been chopped extremely fine, twisted in a cloth (to squeeze out the moisture), and browned in butter with onions and shallots, then left to cool for use as a flavoring or stuffing. The French gastronome who called himself Ali Bab beautifully described it as "mushroom hash."

Ears

Pig's ears are all that you're likely to see. They can be pickled briefly in brine and then simmered for a half hour or so, rolled in butter and breadcrumbs (or a hot, deviled sauce), and broiled or fried. They have a most satisfying, crunchy yet gelatinous consistency.

Earthenware

Pottery COOKWARE.

Earth Nut

In England, a small tuber (*Buniun flexuosum*) that grows in woody places and is eaten raw. Otherwise, another name for PEANUT.

Eau de Vie

A French term for a distilled spirit.

Eccles Cake

A small English tea cake made of PUFF PASTRY filled with currants and other dried fruit and, originally, mint leaves.

Éclair

A rich French pastry; éclairs are finger-shaped pieces of CREAM PUFF PASTRY with a cream or custard filling and a layer of icing on top.

Edam

A firm or semihard mild Dutch cow's-milk CHEESE, always presented as a round, red-covered ball.

Edirne

A soft white Turkish ewe's-milk CHEESE.

Eel

A saltwater fish that spends most of its life in either fresh or brackish water (see also CONGER and MORAY). Eels hatch somewhere in mid-Atlantic, in the vicinity of the Sargasso Sea. While still quite small, they migrate to the streams of their parents, those with European parents (*Anguilla anguilla*) heading east, those with North American parents (*Anguilla rostrata*) heading west, apparently ending up in the same stream those parents came from. They then moon around in those waters until it's time to head back to sea to spawn, which may be a matter of up to 20 years, during which time they grow to a length of four feet (if European) or two to three feet (if American) and take on a black or dark green cast.

It is a well-kept secret in the New World (but not the Old) that eels are delicious. True, fresh eels must be skinned, and that can seem a little daunting at first. Try making an incision around the neck, slicing down along the backbone, and then, holding the head in one hand and the rest of it in the other, breaking the backbone. The skin should unzip quite handily. Once the backbone and intestines are removed you have nothing but edible meat. If you have caught the eel yourself or bought it live, either cook or freeze it fairly quickly after killing it—eel is so rich a fish it will turn on you more quickly than do leaner specimens.

One classic way of cooking eel is to roll it in flour and panfry it in a little oil or oil and garlic. Or it can be breaded and sautéed or sautéed and then simmered in tomato and white wine. Eel can be poached—simmered in water with celery and green pepper, for example, or in a green sauce of sorrel and other green herbs. Or it can be baked. Or stewed. There is also a mention of a sausage that was made of eel and carp, seasoned, smoked, and simmered in white wine and enclosed in a fish casing. And as an appetizer or elegant opening course, there is always smoked eel. Why so little eel is consumed in North America remains one of the great mysteries.

Egg

The reproductive unit, especially of chickens, contained in a oval shell. Except for bringing water to a boil, cooking an egg is considered about the simplest kitchen chore there is. And so it can be—but getting it right may be something else again. Eggs are versatile. They can be baked, boiled, fried, poached, or scrambled; they can be eaten raw; they can be added to pastries and other baked goods; they can be transformed into omelets or soufflés; they can be used as a thickener or to bind other ingredients together; they can be used as a coating agent for foods to be deep-fried, broiled, or sautéed; they can be used to clarify soup, wine, or coffee; they are an emulsifying agent that allows us to make such sauces as mayonnaise. The list of the uses of the egg is long indeed. But if the egg is a bummer, all this versatility is footless.

The primary responsibility of an egg is to be fresh. (This does not, of course, apply to Chinese PRESERVED EGG.) Egg experts inform us that we can actually tell how fresh an egg is by immersing it in cool water. If it lies flat, it is fresh. If it tilts a bit, it is less fresh. And if it stands on its end, get rid of it. Over the centuries, people have figured out ways of keeping eggs more or less usable for up to about five weeks. Coating them with paraffin or a gooey substance known as water glass preserved them, but did not make them any more appetizing. (They might serve for making cookies or coating pieces of fish to be fried, but you wouldn't want one for breakfast.) Nowadays such practices are confined largely to people making transoceanic passages in small boats, and even so they usually prefer their eggs to be powdered, which takes up less space and gives slightly more attractive results.

In the last analysis, of course, the freshness of your egg will depend upon the market where you buy it. There are other criteria in selecting eggs over which you can exercise slightly more control: grade and size. (Color is another factor, but this reduces to personal preference as there is no difference in taste between brown and white eggs.) Eggs are graded AA, A, and B. In the market, AA and A are about all you'll see. In AA, the extra letter signifies extra quality (larger yolks, primarily). Buy the better grade if you're not going to use the eggs right away or if you are planning them for a dish where presentation is important. Eggs are sized as jumbo, extra large, and large. These terms refer to weight, a dozen jumbo eggs weighing 30 ounces, whereas extra large eggs will weigh 27 ounces and large eggs, 24.

An egg cooks better if it's at room temperature than if fresh out of the refrigerator (although it separates more easily if cold). If you're pushed for time, however, you can step around this hurdle by running your egg briefly under warm water before cooking it. (This helps keep the egg from cracking, which you can also do by taking a stout needle or pin and gently pushing it in one end of the egg.)

Always store eggs—cooked or uncooked—in the refrigerator and don't wash them. Washing opens the pores in the shell and invites foreign matter, from refrigerator odors to bacterial invasion. You don't need either.

All the above presupposes that you are looking into hens' eggs; there are others—duck, goose, and quail, for example, plover in Europe, and perhaps ostrich in South Africa, and even some varieties of sea turtle (thereby putting at further risk an already endangered species). Duck and goose eggs tend to be stronger and somewhat oilier than those from the hen, plover and quail somewhat more delicate.

Eggah
An Arab version of an omelet, consisting of a firm mixture of various meats or vegetables (or both) held together by the egg and either cooked on the stovetop or baked. It can be eaten either hot or cold (or anywhere in between).

Egg Cream
A beverage containing neither egg nor cream, although both may have been in it originally. It is native to New York City, where its ingredients include milk and seltzer water and either chocolate or vanilla syrup (or both). Devotees insist that it be made with Fox's U-Bet brand of syrup and argue forcefully as to the traditional site of the best examples of the egg cream mixer's art. Manhattan's Second Avenue near St. Mark's Place is one of the leaders, but this is hotly contested by inhabitants of the city's other boroughs.

Egg Foo Yong
An omelet with chicken or meat or seafood and Chinese vegetables.

Eggnog

A drink compounded of milk, eggs, and sugar, beaten together with whatever else the occasion calls for. Rum and brandy are favorite ingredients of eggnog as are freshly grated nutmeg and sometimes vanilla. For a Christmas or New Year's eggnog, the ingredients may be mixed several weeks before the drink is to be consumed and then allowed to age in a cool place. Mixing or shaking it every day or so helps keep it together so that the perishable parts don't separate out and spoil.

Egg Piercer

A handy kitchen device often of plastic consisting of a fixed needle inside an indented case. You place the large end of your egg in the indent, press gently, and the needle makes a tiny hole in the egg. This keeps the egg from cracking during hard or soft boiling. A stout needle and a steady hand can bring about the same result.

Eggplant

A sufficiently versatile vegetable (*Solanum melongena* var. *esculentum*). There is a variety that is not only egg-shaped but also white, but we don't see it in our markets all that much. Most of the eggplant we see are purple and pear-shaped, although very small, fingerlike ones are becoming more readily available. There is also a zebra-striped variety that can be used in the same ways as the purple. Others that are seldom seen have yellow or red exteriors. The eggplant itself is botanically a berry of Asian origin although the last way we would use it is as a berry.

When selecting eggplant, look for glossy skins without blemishes or scars. Avoid any that are shriveled or spotted or spongy. A small or medium eggplant is preferable to a huge one, and try to get those that have a little heft to them. At one time, a spokesman for Balducci's, a New York City purveyor of produce and other good things, was quoted as saying that the preferred eggplant has a longish slit on its rounded end, rather than a round scar. No one else seems to have commented on this phenomenon, but you might want to keep it in mind. And try to buy or otherwise acquire them just before you are ready to use them. Don't keep them more than a day or two in the refrigerator—and don't put them in a bright, warm place at any time.

For most uses, eggplant is peeled and sliced and piled up with a sprinkling of salt under a heavy weight to drain for a half hour or so. This rids it of any bitter juices that may have accumulated in it, after which it is ready to cook. (An exception is eggplant that is boiled, which rids it of the bitterness automatically; there are, however, few—some, but few—occasions for boiling eggplant.)

Eggplant lends itself to grilling, especially since its peak season is in August, which in most of North America is prime barbecue time; simply slice it and dribble some decent olive oil on it and place it over the coals, next to the steak, or cut it in chunks and skewer it between the tomatoes and the lamb for kabobs. It can also be stuffed, baked, or broiled, or it can be fried, deep-fried, or stewed, and it seems to have an affinity for olive oil and garlic. Some of the truly classic eggplant dishes, in addition to eggplant parmigiana, include BABA GHANOUJ, CAPONATA, IMAM BAYELDI, MOUSSAKA, and RATATOUILLE.

Egg Roll

A Chinese snack consisting of filling (meat, seafood, vegetables) wrapped in a thin layer of dough, then deep-fried, panfried, or steamed. Egg roll skins can be made up in batches and frozen, or bought ready-made and already frozen. Thaw them completely before using them. If the batter was made without eggs, the result is referred to as a *spring roll*. They are usually smaller and more delicate than regular egg rolls and are thought to have originated in New York City's Chinatown, where they were served to guests to mark the Chinese New Year, which is celebrated in the spring.

Eggs Benedict

An extravagant dish, not highly favored by modern nutritionists, consisting of a toasted English muffin each half of which bears a slice of Canadian bacon (or ham), a poached egg, and a topping of hollandaise sauce. It is generally served for brunch or as an elegant breakfast, although it is also likely to turn up on lunch menus.

Egg Timer

A miniature hourglass timed for three minutes. You turn it over and when the sand has run through, your soft-boiled egg is ready. A useful tool if the alarm of a mechanical timer offends the ears in the early morning.

Egg Wash

A mixture of egg white (or yolk) beaten with water to brush on baked goods to give them a glossy sheen.

Egri Bikavér

"Bull's Blood of Eger," a robust Hungarian red table wine from the town of Eger, in the mountains northeast of Budapest.

Elbow Macaroni

Semicircles of hollow PASTA that come in various sizes.

Elderberry

A fruit of a genus of shrubs or trees native to both the New World (*Sambucus canadensis*) and the Old World (*Sambucus nigra*). Although elderberries grow wild throughout North America, there have also been successful attempts to cultivate them, resulting in larger yields and smaller seeds. Most elderberries, however, are still picked in the wild—along fence rows and in lonely fields and woodlots.

The somewhat pungent dark black berries are eaten off the bush (in which case they can be a disappointment), made into pies or tarts, juiced, made into syrup, or (with the addition of crab apples to supply needed PECTIN) made into jelly. While fresh elderberries can have a distinctive taste found disagreeable by many, they can be simmered with a small amount of sugar and lemon rind and the result either used as is or canned or frozen for later use.

Elderberries can also be made into wine, as can the attractive white flowers that precede them. The flat flower clusters can also be dipped in batter and sautéed, although it seems a waste unless you have so many plants that the berries that would otherwise develop from them won't be missed.

Election Cake

A yeast-risen, loaf-shaped cake stemming from New England (Hartford, Connecticut, is usually given the credit), containing dried figs and raisins and reportedly baked on election day as a reward for those voters voting a straight ticket. Sometimes candied fruits, nuts, and either brandy or sherry complement the ingredients.

Elephant Garlic

A hybrid form of GARLIC developed from a cross between garlic and onion. It is larger, even much larger, than garlic (hence the elephant) and sufficiently mild almost not to qualify for the name garlic.

Elk

A large Eurasian deer (*Alces alces*). The name is also used for the *wapiti* (*Cervus canadensis*) or American elk, although the European elk is more closely related to the MOOSE. The meat of both true elk and wapiti is considered choice VENISON.

Elver

A young EEL.

Emincé

In the day of the late-nineteenth-century gastronome Brillat-Savarin, anything finely minced. Now, it refers to slices of leftover roast or braised meat (or poultry) warmed up and served in a sauce.

Emmental

Also *Emmental Français*. French imitation of EMMENTHALER.

Emmenthaler

The quintessential Swiss CHEESE, complete with the holes (cheesemakers call them "eyes"). It is a firm, nutty cow's-milk cheese much imitated but never with complete success. It seems that to achieve its best, the cheese needs the combination of grass, water, and Alpine air that only Switzerland can provide. The cheese takes its name from the Emme River (Emmenthal means "Emme Valley"), which flows through central Switzerland. The holes are pockets of gas that come about through fermentation as the cheese ages and the flavor develops. Properly aged Emmenthaler costs more than those for which this timing is stinted and tastes far better, too.

Empanada
A Spanish and Mexican turnover, filled with meat or shellfish and vegetables, deep-fried, and commonly covered with tomato sauce. A sweetened version is also made, sometimes filled with fruit.

Empire
A crisp and tasty eating APPLE.

Emulsion
A liquid—or semisolid—in which globules of fat are distributed evenly throughout. Mayonnaise is an emulsion.

Enamelware
A type of COOKWARE.

Enchilada
A Mexican dish of tortillas dipped in sauce, fried, then filled with meat or cheese or chicken, rolled up, and baked, usually with additional sauce poured on top.

Endive
A salad green (*Cichorium endivia*) akin to CHICORY and sometimes sold as ESCAROLE. It consists of curly leaves surrounding a lighter green core. It is not to be confused with BELGIAN ENDIVE.

English Muffin
A round, fairly flat breakfast bread "baked" on a griddle or frying pan and toasted before eating. It is traditionally broken open with a fork, rather than cut with a knife, to give a rough, grainy texture to the surfaces taking the butter or jam.

Enokitake
A Japanese MUSHROOM.

Entrecôte
A French cut of meat equivalent to a sirloin or rib steak.

Entree
Originally, it referred to a course served after the fish and before the meat at a many-coursed French formal meal. Rice pilafs, pâtés of various sorts, fish or shellfish pies, or meats or poultry with a sauce are included among possible entrees. In North America, the word refers to the main course of any meal.

Epazote

A widespread, pungent herb (*Chenopodium ambrosioides*) used dried in bean dishes and soups, especially in Mexican cookery.

Epigramme

In classic cuisine, a way of cooking lamb. Boned pieces of breast of lamb are cooked, then cooled under a press. These pieces, together with lamb chops of the same size and shape, are then dipped in egg and breadcrumbs and either broiled or sautéed.

Epoisse

A French (from the region of Burgundy) soft cow's-milk CHEESE sold in a rounded shape about four inches wide by two to three inches high.

Ermite

A soft blue-veined Canadian cow's-milk CHEESE.

Erwtensoep

A hearty Dutch pea soup with pork products and root vegetables. It is at its best if eaten on the day after it is made.

Escabeche

An Iberian specialty consisting of fish dipped in hot olive oil and then cured in an olive oil and vinegar marinade flavored with carrot, garlic, onions, and various spices, much as GRAVLAX is cured in lime juice.

Escalope

A French term for a piece of meat (especially veal) or fish sliced very thin, further flattened, then fried quickly in butter or oil.

Escargot

A French term for SNAIL.

Escarole

Another name for ENDIVE, a curly-headed slightly bitter salad green (*Cichorium endivia*) similar to CHICORY.

Espresso

A dark, flavorful Italian after-dinner (or midmorning or late-afternoon or whenever) COFFEE. It is made in a special machine that forces a mixture of steam and hot water through a special blend of coffee, often brewed at double strength. There are simpler devices that come up with a close approximation of the real thing.

Esrom

A Danish cow's-milk CHEESE resembling PORT SALUT.

Essence

1. A highly condensed flavoring agent. It is prepared by cooking fish, herbs, meat, poultry, or vegetables with only enough water to keep them from burning until all their juices have been released and boiled down to about half the original volume. They combine tremendous concentration of flavor with very little bulk. A little of such essence will add considerable flavor to whatever it is added to.

2. EXTRACT.

Étouffée

A Cajun dish of either shrimp or crayfish cooked with onions and peppers and sometimes tomatoes on the base of a ROUX or butter or margarine. Given the Cajun outlook on cooking, a roux would seem more traditional.

Evaporated Milk

A canned MILK that has had about 60 percent of its liquid content removed by evaporation.

Excelso

A Colombian COFFEE that receives its name from the size, not the quality, of the beans. Nonetheless, the quality is generally quite high.

Extract

An essential oil of a substance such as almond or lemon or vanilla dissolved in alcohol and used sparingly in baking.

Extra Sec

A term used for CHAMPAGNE signifying that a small amount of sugar has been added to the wine. It is not so dry as *brut* but drier than *sec*.

F
Common abbreviation for degrees FAHRENHEIT.

Faba Bean
Another name for the fava or broad BEAN.

Faggot
A traditional hearty English pork sausage, originally made with pork innards, bread-crumbs or oatmeal, and spices. Faggots are cut into squares and are served hot or cold.

Fahrenheit
A TEMPERATURE scale most widely used in North American cookery, as opposed to the CELSIUS scale generally used elsewhere. It was devised in 1714 by Gabriel Daniel Fahrenheit, a German physicist. To convert Celsius to Fahrenheit, simply multiply the number by ⅗ (or by 1.8) and add 32.

Fairy Ring
A type of edible wild MUSHROOM that grows in circles (or rings) in fields and pastures.

Faisandage
A French term for fowl, game, or red meat in general that has been left out to hang until it is distinctly "high." It is not subjected to the temperature and humidity controls that enhance the quality of prime beef. The name derives from *faisan*, or pheasant, a bird once thought unworthy of the table if not treated this way.

Falafel
Also *felafel*. A Middle Eastern (especially Egyptian) specialty composed of dried, soaked, and minced fava beans (or chickpeas) with garlic, onions, parsley, and spices (coriander, cumin, pepper, salt), reduced to a paste, sometimes leavened with baking powder or yeast, and deep-fried. There is at least one prepared mix on the market if prepared mixes are to your taste.

Falernian Wine
A wine of the ancient Romans grown north of Naples and lavishly praised by such writers as the poet Horace. There is today an Italian wine known as Falerno from

roughly the same area, but it is negligible (unless you happen to own a piece of the vineyard).

Farce

Also *farci*; it is French for FORCEMEAT.

Farfalle

A PASTA in the shape of butterflies or bows. In North America it is usually made with an egg dough, in Italy, seldom, if ever. There are also *farfallettes* and *farfallini*, which are smaller, and *farfalloni*, which are larger.

Farfel

A Jewish specialty consisting of an egg and barley dough that is chopped or grated and added to soups and stews.

Farina

1. A flour made from a hard, but not a durum, wheat.
2. Any fine meal or flour.
3. A proprietary breakfast cereal.

Farinha

A floury meal made from CASSAVA. In South America, it is toasted, grated, and sprinkled over all manner of dishes as a condiment.

Farmers' Cheese

See COTTAGE CHEESE.

Fat

Fats in the kitchen include the animal fats—bacon fat, beef drippings, butter, goose fat, lard—on the one hand and OIL and the hydrogenated vegetable shortenings on the other. Animal fats can be used to BARD or to LARD as well as to serve as a heating medium. In baking, the fat—or SHORTENING—produces tenderness. For deep-frying, consult your recipe for the amount of heat needed. Vegetable shortenings attain about 370°F, lard about 400°F, and vegetable oil about 450°F before they begin to burn and mar the flavor.

Fatback

The strip of fat from a pig's back or loin used fresh in the southern United States, but otherwise available cured. A blanched piece of salt pork can be substituted.

Fava Bean

A BEAN popular in Europe and the Near East, less so in North America.

Fecula

Essentially potato flour, but also any flour made from ARROWROOT, CASSAVA, CHEST-
NUTS, or other vegetables. Fecula is used like flour or cornstarch for thickening
soups and sauces.

Fedelini

Very fine PASTA tubes somewhat like ANGEL HAIR. It is disputed whether the origin
of the name is "faithful," from *fedele*, or "wiry," from *filo* ("wire").

Feijoa

A tubular fruit two to three inches long and an uninteresting green in color but with
a compelling aroma. Feijoa (*Feijoa sellowiana*) is native to southern Brazil and environs but now is mostly exported from New Zealand, although it is grown to some
extent in California as well. Inside the thin skin is a layer of white flesh enclosing a
pulp studded with almost imperceptible seeds. It has a pineappley taste.

Feijoas are best when fully ripe (they can be bitter if unripe). Pick them when
they are soft to the touch, and if you have one that's not quite ready, leave it at room
temperature and check it daily. Feijoas are good eaten raw or in fruit salads or other
mixtures, pureed, stewed, or—especially if you can grow your own shrub—made
into jelly or jam.

Just to make matters confusing, feijoas are sometimes referred to as *pineapple
guavas*, although the true GUAVA is little more than a distant and far superior relative.

Feijoada

Brazil's national dish—a feast that when made with all the trimmings begins with
black turtle beans and includes beef, sausage, tongue, smoked and fresh pork (including the feet, ears, and tail), and bacon simmered together with onion and garlic and
chilis, sprinkled with FARINHA, and served with rice. If all of the ingredients are not
available, it is made with such meats as the cook can lay hands on. The beans and
rice and farinha are always a part of it.

Fell

The paperlike outer covering of a leg of lamb. When roasting lamb, there is no need
for, nor anything gained by, removing the fell except that doing so allows you to trim
some of the lamb's excess fat.

Fendant

A wine grape (*Vitis vinifera*) of Switzerland responsible for some pleasant dry white
wines and some slightly sparkling ones, which are sold under the same name; elsewhere it is known as CHASSELAS.

Fennel

A plant of Mediterranean origin (*Foeniculum vulgare*) that is used as a vegetable and as an herb. It resembles both LICORICE and ANISE but is more subtle than either. The plant can be found in North American gardens and has also taken root on its own. The variety that is cultivated for table use is *Foeniculum vulgare* var. *azoricum*, known as *finocchio* and as *sweet fennel* or *Florence fennel*. Although regular wild fennel has similar characteristics, it does not develop the same tasty bulbous root.

Finocchio consists of a white, licorice-scented bulb and feathery leaves. If you buy it whole, keep the feathery tops on until you're ready to use the bulb, then cut them off at the top of the bulb. Trim the base and use it raw (or parboil it first) as a CRUDITÉ with a little oil and vinegar or as a salad. The fennel bulb can be blanched and simmered in butter or other fat and dressed with cream, cheese, or gravy. The dried leaves have a particular affinity for fish and also pork and can be used in any recipe in which dill is appropriate. Fennel seeds contribute to pies and enhance breads and rolls and roast fowl and contribute greatly to such Italian delicacies as sausages flavored with fennel and garlic (and sometimes pepper). The fronds and stems of the plant can be dried and used as a fuel over which to cook fish or fowl, but especially fish. A widespread way of approximating the taste of fish grilled over burning fennel twigs is to spread a goodly amount of dried fennel leaves and stems over the nearly broiled fish and then flame it with brandy.

Fenugreek

An Asian herb (*Trigonella foenumgraecum*) with a slightly bitter seed used in Indian and Persian cooking, especially for making CURRY. Ground fenugreek seeds are also used to make an artificial maple flavoring for ice cream and candies.

Fernet-Branca

A proprietary Italian BITTERS, thought to ease the strain of a hangover.

Feta

A soft white Greek ewe's-milk CHEESE with a slightly salty tang. As it has no rind, it is generally kept in a briny solution. Feta made with cow's milk is now widely made outside of Greece. It perks up salads and contributes to many Greek and other Balkan dishes.

Fettucine

An Italian term for *small ribbon*. A ribbon-shaped egg PASTA, usually about ¼-inch wide. Its most famous manifestation is almost certainly Fettucine Alfredo, which originally was a combination of fettucine, lots of sweet butter, and a massive infusion of freshly grated Parmigiano-Reggiano cheese. It has since been augmented with cream and black pepper, and sometimes with such additions as garlic, ham, peas, and nutmeg.

Fiber

In nutritional terms, the indigestible ingredients of plants that are essential to a sound diet as an aid to digestion and excretion of waste. Fibrous foods include dried beans, bran (both oat and wheat), fruit, oatmeal, whole wheat, and vegetables (both root and leafy).

Fiddlehead Fern

A stage in the development of the ostrich fern (*Pteretis nodulosa*) and also the bracken (*Pteridium* spp.) and royal (*Osmunda regalis*)—although the latter plants are under study for having a carcinogenic potential. The desirable stage is the early one when the fronds of the young ferns attain a height of five inches or so with their tops in the form of a crosier or tight coil that resembles the upper part of a violin. Fiddleheads can be steamed like asparagus and eaten with salt and a little butter or even with various sauces such as hollandaise.

Fiddleheads grow in damp and woody places and along roadsides. In New England and Nova Scotia—where they are thought highly of—they can usually be found during the period around Easter. They are also available in markets for a period of a few weeks. In selecting fiddleheads, choose those with tight heads and, if possible, with a dark green color. If the heads are limp and uncurled, don't bother with them. Once you get them home, rinse them and trim off all but about an inch of the tail extending from the coil. Rub off any fuzz or scales that may be on the fern. If the prices seem insane (they can vary widely even in the same area and on the same day), try to schedule a trip to a moist woodlot to pick your own. Consulting a good guide to ferns might be a wise initial step.

Field Mushroom

A wild MUSHROOM that is most similar to the regular commercial variety.

Field Salad

Another name for LAMB'S LETTUCE.

Fig

A fruit of a tree (*Ficus carica*) of Mediterranean origin (probably somewhere in Asia Minor) now widely grown in California, Texas, and Louisiana. Figs are available canned, dried (some 90 percent of the crop is dried), fresh, or preserved in syrup. When selecting fresh figs, pick those that are soft to the touch but sweet smelling— older figs tend to ferment, giving off a characteristic odor as they do. Sometimes figs form a "bloom" on the skins that can easily be wiped off and is no cause for concern. But if the skins show distinct brown or gray spots, the fruit has passed its prime.

Fresh-picked figs can be eaten as is, especially when a sweet dessert is called for. Or they can be chilled and served as an hors d'oeuvre with thinly sliced ham or cheese. Canned and dried figs are used in desserts and in baking, especially fruit-cakes—indeed the "plums" in plum pudding were originally, in fact, figs, as in the old Christmas carol request to "bring us a figgy pudding." The dried variety usually benefits from being soaked or simmered (for 20 minutes or so) before being used. Fresh figs are best refrigerated, dried ones kept tightly packaged.

There are a variety of figs available commercially. The one generally accepted as the best of them is the Smyrna, which is imported from Turkey, as is the small wasp (*Blastophaga grossorum*) essential to its pollination. It is a large white-fleshed fruit. Others commonly seen are the Kadota (small, with yellowish-green fruit) and the Mission (purplish-black), introduced into California by the Spanish.

Figpecker

Any of a variety of Old World warblers (*Sylvia* spp.) that commonly feed on figs or grapes. In North America, they would be classified as songbirds and thereby protected from being used as food. In other places, however, they are usually grilled in vine leaves.

Filbert

See HAZELNUT.

Filé

A powder made from the dried leaves of the sassafras tree (*Sassafras albidum*) and used in GUMBO. If added after the gumbo is taken off the fire, it mixes in obediently and enhances the flavor. If added while the gumbo is still cooking, it forms a gelatinous goo that gums up everything.

Filet

A French term for FILLET.

Filet Mignon

A thick piece of BEEF cut from the small end of the TENDERLOIN.

Fillet

Also *filet*. A piece of meat (especially beef tenderloin) or fish that has been skillfully removed from the bone. In the case of fish, the skin may or may not be left on (with small fish, removing the skin may cause the fillet to disintegrate).

Filo

See PHYLLO.

Fin

The stabilizing membranes of certain forms of marine life. Some fins, such as that of the SKATE and some forms of SHARK, are highly prized in culinary circles.

Fine

1. A French term for the house brandy of a French bar (or bistro), sometimes called *fine maison*.

2. In brewing beer or wine-making, the removal of extraneous particles to make the final product clear. This is done by adding eggshells or a form of clay and letting the particles settle, or simply by filtering.

Fines Herbes

Anything that's prepared with a flavoring of chopped herbs—chervil, chives, tarragon, for example—always including and sometimes limited to parsley. Also the combination itself.

Finish

1. In the kitchen, the final touches you put on your culinary masterpiece before serving it forth. This may range from preparing the sauce, to glazing the ham, to simply tasting what you've accomplished to see if the seasoning is up to your expectation.

2. The diet fed to a domestic food animal prior to slaughter.

Finnan Haddie

Haddock that has been lightly smoked to a rich golden yellow color in a way that apparently originated in a Scottish fishing port called Findon (but apparently pronounced Finnan), where haddock were split, salted, and then smoked, originally over a peat fire. It is now prepared in any number of places. Finnan Haddie can be soaked if necessary (to get the salt out) and then poached and served with mashed potato and butter or with a cream sauce either as a breakfast, a lunch, or a light dinner. It can also be prepared with butter, milk, onion, and mashed potato, as a smoky chowder known to the Scots as Cullen Skink. It is not easy to find these days, but some fish markets stock it in the freezer.

Fino

A light and dry cocktail SHERRY.

Finocchio

See FENNEL.

Fire Pot

Essentially, an elaborate Chinese CHAFING DISH in which food is cooked at the table, especially in cold weather when the heat of the cooking helps send warmth through the dining area. It is an expensive metal device (frequently made of brass) consisting of a pot in which you can build a fire (charcoal, alcohol) with a funnel going up the middle much like an oversized tube pan. The funnel vents off the heat while the container around it holds gently simmering stock into which the diners dip thinly sliced bits of meat, poultry, seafood, or vegetables until cooked to their liking. A fondue pot or chafing dish should make an effective substitute. In some special Chinese banquets, white chrysanthemum petals are strewn over the broth as a decorative garnish leading to an alternate name for this device, *Chrysanthemum Pot*.

Fish

Most of the fish we buy is frozen, or was until shortly before we bought it. There's nothing wrong with frozen fish. It won't be as good as one caught fresh (less moist, for example, perhaps tougher) but it will certainly be better than a fish that's been sitting around for slightly too long in a fish-market display case. And it saves you the need to decide if the fish is fresh enough for your taste. Moreover, checking on freshness is becoming increasingly difficult as more and more fish markets fillet (or steak) everything before putting it on display. A whole fresh fish is becoming something of a rarity.

Should you happen across a fish market that displays the whole fish, look for bulging, clear eyes; reddish-colored gills; bright scales clinging close to the body; firm, springy flesh that jumps back into place when you prod it gently with your finger; and, above all, no offensive or strong smell. If the fish meets all these tests, you might almost have caught it yourself. But obviously, if the fish is filleted, the only tests left to you are springiness of flesh (to make sure it hasn't dried out) and the smell test.

When you get the fish home, wrap it well and refrigerate it until you're ready to use it. If it is frozen, keep it in the freezer or let it thaw in the microwave or refrigerator (not on the kitchen counter—the fish gets mushy that way).

The amount of fish you are going to need will depend on how you buy it. Fresh fish is traditionally sold whole, drawn, steaked, or filleted. The whole fish is just that—exactly as it came from the water. Allow 1 pound per person (except for panfish of under a pound for which ½ pound or one fish per person should suffice). If the fish is drawn—whole but scaled and gutted, head and tail on or off—allow ½ pound per person. For a large steak, one with a fairly hefty bone, ⅓ pound should be ample, and if the steak has very little bone, ¼ pound. A quarter of a pound per person also ought to fill the bill for fillets.

Many recipes will call for white-fleshed fish or lean or fatty fish. In general, dry, lean, or white-fleshed fish are those that have their oil concentrated in the liver; oily fish have their oil distributed throughout. White-fleshed fish include brook trout, cod, haddock, flatfish, perch, smelt, and tilefish; oily fish include bluefish, eel, herring (including shad), mackerel, rainbow trout, salmon, and tuna.

Fish can be eaten raw (as SASHIMI or SUSHI), or cooked in any of a number of ways including baking, broiling, frying, grilling, poaching, and steaming (not to speak of the wonderful fish chowders, soups, and stews that have evolved over our fish-eating past). For cooking exclusive of soups and stews, the Canadians have evolved a method of timing that seems to work to perfection (see CANADIAN FISH-COOKING PRINCIPLE) and a researcher for the United States government also evolved the SPENCER METHOD for cooking fillets.

Individual fishes and fish dishes will be found under their separate names in this volume.

Fish and Chips

Originally, a British fast-food item composed of deep-fried fillets of fish served with french fries, and often flavored with malt vinegar. They were commonly bought from a stand, where they were served wrapped in a newspaper. (Devotees in London claimed that the newspaper selected had an influence on the taste.) It is now, of course, internationally known and widely available in restaurants and the frozen-food sections of supermarkets.

Fish Flour

Also called *FPC* (fish protein concentrate). A product composed of dried and chemically treated fish (originally red hake of the COD family) ground to a fine, nearly tasteless and odorless powder. As the powder is practically pure protein, it can be used as an additive to foods in protein-poor countries. Because it is composed of the whole fish (innards and all), it does not meet U.S. standards and cannot be sold in the United States.

Fish Maw

The air bladder of certain kinds of fish, dried, sliced, and used in a variety of Chinese dishes. It provides a pleasant spongy texture and has the ability to absorb the flavorings around it, although it has little of its own.

Fish Poacher

Not someone who filches fish, but a dandy, usually high-priced device that is long and narrow with high sides and a remarkable, perforated rack with handle. The whole fish—head and tail included—fits on the rack and gets covered with liquid and poached. The rack can then be removed from the poacher, the fish from the rack, and the whole fish in all its glory served forth.

Five Bitter Herbs

Symbolic herbs which the Jews use in the Seder dinner to celebrate Passover. They are coriander, horehound, horseradish, lettuce, and nettles.

Five Spices

A Chinese combination of cinnamon, cloves, fennel, star anise, and Szechuan peppercorns. It is used—sparingly—in roasting meat and poultry, as well as in some braised dishes.

Flageolet

A delicate kind of BEAN widely appreciated by the French, especially when served with lamb.

Flake

1. A test for whether fish is done. When it has cooked to the point where it breaks or "flakes" easily when lightly jabbed with a fork, it is done.

2. A way in which the big food processors prepare grain by passing it through metal rollers to flatten it and then cutting it into smaller flakes. Another name for it is rolled, as opposed to steel cut, in which process the grains are slashed into small bits but not flattened.

Flaky

Describes a sufficiently dry piecrust that easily breaks off in flakes, or large pieces.

Flambé

A French term for FLAME.

Flame

To impart flavor and sometimes spectacular effect by adding warmed alcohol (usually a brandy of some sort but also whiskey or even gin if you want to impart a junipery taste) to a dish and setting it on fire. If you have a gas stove, you can put your small amount of alcohol into a soup ladle and, warming it gently over the flame, pour it over your dish and light it, turning the pan with a rolling motion to keep it alight as long as possible. If you have an electric stove, put the alcohol in a small pan and place it over a moderate burner until you see the first bubbles. Then pour it on and light it.

Flaming can be done to burn off the alcohol from a table wine that is to be added to a stew or piece of meat to be braised, to impart taste to a gravy such as the pan juices in which you have sautéed a medallion of beef or venison, or to make a stunning presentation at the table, as you might with a plum pudding. If you are bringing the flaming dish to the dining table, add a scant teaspoon of granulated sugar to the brandy before you light it, and it will burn with a cheerful blue flame.

Flan

1. A one-crust pie (or tart) baked in a straight-sided, bottomless ring (flan ring) that is removed before the flan is served. (Flan and flan ring are, of course, put on a cookie sheet to bake.)

2. A sweet custard dessert.

Flank

The underpart of a beef critter, below the ribs; from it come flank steak, stew meat, hamburger, and London broil.

Flapjack
See PANCAKE.

Flatbread
A thin, crispy, Scandinavian, crackerlike bread, usually based on rye flour.

Flatfish
Flatfish are fish that have adapted to life at the bottom of the sea. Lying flat on the sea bed, the mature fish have eyes only on one side of the head (there are right-eyed and left-eyed species) and when at home have an uncanny ability to dig themselves partway into the sand and, using their coloration as camouflage, vanish from sight. If you catch one or find a whole one in the market, you will note its almost oval shape, its white underbelly (which is anatomically its side, not its belly), and its dark, often mottled upper side. Flatfish range in size from minuscule (if you catch one of these, throw it back) to the huge Atlantic halibut, which can—but almost never does—run to some 800 pounds (the Pacific halibut runs almost as large but not quite).

By far the most important of the flatfish are the *soles*, only one of which is to be found in North American waters. Its slight culinary interest is indicated by its name—hogchoker. To offset this lack, some North American flounder have been nicknamed sole. It is important to know that just because a fish is called sole it won't necessarily be sole, but if it is sole, it will be better than any other flatfish (although some would give this palm to the turbot).

Except for the very largest flatfish (halibut is usually sold as steaks, for example), flatfish are filleted. They can be baked, broiled, poached, or sautéed and can be cooked alone or with mussels and shrimp or stuffed with crabmeat and rolled or treated with almost any advantageous sauce. They can be used in long-simmered dishes, such as stews, only with great care as they tend to fall apart with long cooking (add them, if at all, only at the end). Small ones can be cooked whole (often skinned first); one technique is to sauté the skinned fish quickly in butter then dab it with breadcrumbs and poach it half awash in dry vermouth in a 450°F oven until the breadcrumbs are browned. The cooking liquid can be reduced and enriched with butter to serve as a sauce.

Although it is wise to bear in mind that names vary according to local usage and prejudices, some of the flatfish you might come across include:

Arrowtooth flounder (*Atheresthes stomias*). The Pacific's answer to the quite similar Greenland turbot.

Blackback flounder. Occasional name for a small (less than three pounds) winter flounder (see below).

Brill (*Scophthalmus rhombus*). A European relative of the turbot (see below) only not so highly favored. The name is frequently used in North America for the windowpane flounder.

Butter sole. A tasty Pacific flounder (*Isopsetta isolepsis*) found from Alaska
through southern California.

Dab (*Limanda limanda*). A smallish European flatfish related to the North
American yellowtail flounder (see below). The name is also used for other
species of flatfish, including the American plaice (see below).

Dover sole (*Solea solea*). The true Dover, or Channel, sole is found mainly in
the North Sea and the Bay of Biscay and if served fresh in North America,
will have been flown in (otherwise it is frozen). It sets the standard that no
other flatfish can quite attain. The name is also used for an excellent Pacific
flounder (*Microstomus pacificus*).

Flounder. Any of several flatfish, one of which, the European flounder
(*Platichthys flesus*), is found in northern European waters and others in the
Americas. Although they are generally considered inferior to sole, they are
usually sold under that name.

Fluke (*Paralichthys dentatus*). Also called *summer flounder* from its proclivity
to come toward shore in warm weather and retreat to the ocean depths in
winter. Generally considered a superior flatfish.

Fourspot flounder (*Paralichthys oblongus*). Resembles a small fluke with four
spots on the upper side. It's only a so-so table fish.

Gray sole. Frequent market or restaurant name for the witch flounder and sometimes winter flounder. (See below.)

Greenland halibut. A name, disallowed by U.S. fishery officials, for the Greenland turbot (see below).

Greenland turbot (*Rheinhardtius hippoglossoides*). A northerly fish similar to halibut, sometimes found smoked.

Halibut (*Hippoglossus hippoglossus*). The largest of the flatfish and a major
source of food in Europe and in North America. Its lean, firm, mild meat
lends itself to baking, broiling, frying, poaching, and steaming.

Hogchoker (*Trinectes maculatus*). A true sole that is caught in brackish waters
from Cape Cod to Central America but rarely attains legal "keeper" size. It
has a readily identifiable stripe along its back crossed by several more stripes
going across its body. It was at one time netted along with herring to serve
as food for pigs, who found the hard scales indigestible. The rest of the
fish—what there is of it—is said to taste fine.

Lemon sole (*Microstomus kitt*). A highly thought of and important European
food fish; the name is also used for the North American winter flounder
(see below).

Pacific halibut (*Hippoglossus stenolepsis*). The Pacific edition of the Atlantic halibut and just as important as a food fish.

Pacific sanddab (*Citharichthys sordidus*). A tasty flounder found from the far north to Baja California.

Petrale sole (*Eopsetta jordani*). A large and excellent flounder of California waters.

Plaice (*Pleuronectes platessa*). An important European food fish that is most commonly fried but can be cooked in other ways as well. There is also an *American* or *Canadian plaice* (*Hippoglossoides platessoides*) caught in large numbers off Canada and to a lesser extent northern New England, most of which is sold as dab or simply flounder or even sole.

Rex sole (*Glyptocephalus zachirus*). A widespread Pacific fish of cold to moderate waters.

Rusty flounder. The yellowtail flounder (see below).

Sole. Primarily the Dover sole (see above) but the name is used for any small flatfish, usually filleted. Waverley Root, in *Food*, reports that a true sole (should you be faced by the whole fish) has a rounded snout, all the others a pointed one.

Summer flounder. The fluke (see above).

Turbot (*Psetta maxima*). A highly prized European flatfish, rated second (but not by everybody—some rate it higher) only to Dover sole.

Windowpane flounder (*Scophthalmus aquosus*). An extremely thin (it is virtually translucent when held to the sun) flounder of eastern North America, sometimes called *brill*. This fish is more likely to be caught by anglers than found commercially.

Winter flounder (*Pseudopleuronectes americanus*). The common flounder of eastern North America from Labrador to the Chesapeake and beyond. A typical fish will reach a foot in length and weigh 1 to 2 pounds although they can come bigger.

Witch flounder (*Glyptocephalus cynoglossus*). A small but flavorful flounder found on both sides of the Atlantic and often sold in North America as *gray sole*.

Yellowtail flounder (*Limanda ferruginea*). A yellow-tailed species found from Labrador to Virginia and often referred to as *yellow dab*, although much of it is served in fish markets and restaurants as fillet of sole. It is one of the better flounders.

Flatten

To beat a piece of meat with a mallet, the side of a plate, the flat side of a knife or cleaver, or whatever comes to hand in order to make it thin and also to break up the tissues, thus tenderizing the meat.

Fleuron

A small piece of pastry cut into some decorative shape and used as a garnish.

Flip

A spiced and sweetened drink (often based on sherry) made with a beaten egg. It is not much seen any more.

Flitch

A whole side of bacon.

Floating Island

1. Whipped, sweetened egg whites poached in vanilla-flavored milk and served in a custard sauce.

2. A chilled dessert consisting of a liqueur-soaked sponge cake layered with jam and nuts and currants, topped with whipped cream, and set in custard.

Flounder

Certain varieties of FLATFISH.

Flour

The common denominator of breads and pastries. When we think of flour, we usually think of wheat flour. But flour can be—and probably has been—ground from the seeds and nuts of almost any plant anyone can think of. A list of some of the more common flours might help:

Barley. Barley meal (slightly coarser than regular flour) and barley flour are sometimes added to breads for texture and variety.

Buckwheat. Most notably used in pancakes, including Russian blini, but also an ingredient of some versions of SCRAPPLE.

Chickpea. Also called *gram* flour. It is used in India for CHAPATIS and other Indian breads.

Corn. Used in baking, in cooking, and as a thickener and sometimes a stretcher in sausage-making.

Potato. Mostly used as a thickener. Potato (and sweet potato) bread and rolls are made with wheat flour and mashed or pureed potatoes (although Irish Boxty Bread is made with both mashed cooked and grated raw potatoes).

Quinoa. A plant much like a cereal grain used more as a side dish than for baking, but also amenable to bread-making.

Rice. Mostly used in addition to other flours for a taste and texture difference.

Rye. After wheat, the most important of the bread flours. It makes a traditional dark, dense, long-lasting loaf. Because rye is somewhat lacking in gluten (see Wheat, below), it is usually made with some wheat flour as well. Rye flour can be light or dark, depending upon how stringently it has been processed. The darkest has the most bran in it.

Soy. Often added to breads to give an extra nutritional boost (soy is, after all, rich in protein).

Triticale. A "new" flour (it was developed in 1875, but in a pretty primitive form until tinkered with and finally popularized in the 1960s) from a plant hybridized from wheat and rye. It is a productive crossbreed and does well in poor or worn-out soils, but while its flour has somewhat more rising power than rye, it has far less than wheat and seems more appropriate for an unleavened staple such as chapatis than as a contribution to conventional, yeast-rising, Western breads.

Wheat. Wheat flours fall initially into two categories: soft and hard. A major difference between them is how much of the highly elastic protein known as gluten they contain, hard having more gluten, soft more starch. Gluten has the ability to expand mightily and is what makes bread rise. The softer, starchier flours bake into a more tender, less chewy result and are preferable in pastries, although European critics (hard wheat being largely a North American offering) maintain that soft wheat makes a better-tasting bread. Commercial millers blend hard and soft to attain whatever end they are offering. Among some of the terms you're likely to meet are:

- *All-purpose.* A blend of hard and soft wheats with bran and germ removed, calculated to fill the needs of both pastry cook and breadmaker. Each manufacturer tries to maintain a blend that is the same year after year, but each one differs somewhat from that of other makers, so the experts advise us to try a flour and, if it doesn't give a result we like, try another. When we hit on one we like, stick with it. All-purpose flour may be bleached or bromated or it may not—the label (by law) will inform you.

- *Bleached.* Chemically treated to make it look whiter, which it does. It will also probably contain aging agents said to enhance its baking properties. These maneuvers, however, reduce the gluten content, decreasing the attractiveness of bleached flour for yeast-rising bread. It will also have had all its nutrients removed and some put back in to "enrich" it.

- *Blended.* Like all-purpose flour, it is blended to meet the baking demands of a presumed audience.

- *Bread.* An unbleached but bromated flour with slightly more gluten than regular all-purpose. It can be used in other ways, but it is intended for baking bread.

- *Bromated.* Treated with potassium bromate, an agent intended to smooth out the finished product.

- *Cake.* The most refined of the soft-wheat flours. The average amateur cook can usually make do with all-purpose.
- *Durum.* A hard-wheat flour, usually available only at health food stores. If you make your own pasta, you'll probably be interested in latching onto some.
- *Enriched.* White flour to which the millers have restored some of the vitamins and minerals that were removed in the milling process. It doesn't apply to whole wheat flour, which still has its own nutrients more or less intact.
- *Fortified.* Same as enriched.
- *Gluten.* A flour specially prepared from white flour to remove the starch. Heavy on protein but light on the B vitamins, it can be made into bread for people on low-starch diets or added to rye or other more-or-less gluten-free flours to help them rise. Small amounts added to nut or raisin breads can lead to more even distribution of those heavier elements throughout the bread.
- *Graham.* A coarsely ground whole wheat flour, named for its developer and advocate, Dr. Sylvester Graham.
- *Instant-Blending.* Also called *quick-mixing* depending upon manufacturer's preference. A thoroughly processed, lump-free flour for making gravies and sauces or sprinkling over food you want very lightly floured. It costs extra, as you would expect.
- *Pastry.* Finer than all-purpose but not so fine as cake flour.
- *Self-Rising.* Technically this is a mix, as it is all-purpose flour with baking powder added. Baking powder tends to lose its potency after being exposed to air, so this flour is not a good bet to keep around any length of time after it has been opened.
- *Semolina.* A pale, low-gluten pasta flour made from durum wheat.
- *Whole wheat.* Flour ground from the entire wheat kernel, containing most of the components that are processed out in the milling of white flour. It is more nutritious but not so rich in gluten as white flour, nor does it last so well. Don't keep it around too long—use it up! And if you must hang on to it, keep it refrigerated.

Flour

To cover lightly with any dry coating such as flour, cornmeal, breadcrumbs, or whatever, flavored or not. See DREDGE.

Flowers

Medieval cooks made great use of flowers in their dishes. Rose petals, primroses, and violets were all worked into various dishes as well as drinks. Carnation petals were so appreciated as a garnish in drinks that they were given the name "sops in wine." In modern times, marigolds, nasturtiums, and squash blossoms may sometimes be found. Other flowers are equally edible, but infrequently seen.

Fluke

A variety of FLATFISH.

Flummery

An ancient British dessert in which oatmeal and the water in which it has been soaking are boiled until thickened, and then augmented with a variety of flavorings among which might be cream, raisins, sugar, and, perhaps, almonds and sherry. It is eaten cold.

Flute

Another word for CRIMP.

Flying Fish

A group of fishes of the family Exocoetidae found far out to sea in tropical waters around the world. Why these fish glide out of water is not known. Because flying fish are attracted by light, seamen often set lanterns in appropriate waters at night and in the morning pick up any fish that have landed on board. Other than deep-frying, there seem to be few recipes for them. There are also some types of SQUID that are able to propel themselves for brief glides out of the water, a bit of information probably first brought to general awareness by the crew of the raft *Kon Tiki* that crossed the Pacific in 1947.

Focaccia

A flat Italian bread, originally unleavened and griddle-cooked, now generally made with yeast and oven-baked. Italian focaccia may be made with butter, lard, or olive oil, but olive oil (other oils impart oiliness without savor) seems most appropriate. Focaccias are sometimes informed with rosemary, sage, or thyme and some may include a topping, as of onions or tomatoes much like a pizza—or just plain salt.

Foie Gras

The specially fattened liver of a goose (and less frequently duck). Foie gras is considered one of the great delicacies and is both uncommon and expensive. Most foie gras is rendered into pâté which can be very good indeed (or totally indifferent), but which never approaches the original in quality or taste.

Most of the best foie gras comes from Alsace and is distinguished by its weight (a single liver can weigh over two pounds, or a tenth of the weight of the whole goose), by its color (a good one is creamy white with pink overtones), and by its texture (firm!). As if it weren't expensive enough on its own, foie gras lends itself to being flavored with TRUFFLES. The French, quite naturally, have developed a number of ways of cooking foie gras (if it is cooked, it will almost certainly be from a goose liver—duck liver tends to fall apart). To taste any of these, you will most likely have to go to France and be prepared to shell out a good down payment on the National Debt. You will probably find it worth the expense.

Fold

To mix together, very gently indeed. Take egg whites, for example, which you have beaten to a froth and wish to incorporate into the rest of your ingredients. Lay them quietly on top of your mixture and with the aid of a spatula or spoon gently cut down through the middle of it all until you touch the bottom of the bowl. Scrape your spatula or spoon delicately along the bottom of the bowl, then up the side and over the top, burying the egg whites under the bottom ingredients. Turn the bowl slightly and repeat. Folding replaces stirring for dishes that would be disturbed by too much commotion.

Fondant

A granulated sugar paste used to glaze or ice pastries. Fondants can also be flavored with liqueurs, or essences, or whatever seems appropriate.

Fondue

1. Originally a Swiss concoction of cheese melted in flavored wine and eaten by dipping into it chunks of day-old crusty bread held on long forks. Swiss fondue is a delightful offering for informal dining—just make sure the cheese you use is not a processed cheese, which tends to produce an oiliness on the top of the dish that a natural cheese does not. A "glug" of wine and a handful of grated cheese (Emmenthaler or Gruyère is traditional) per person has been prescribed as the way to do it, the dish being prepared in front of everyone in a special fondue pot—known as a *caquelon*—which has been rubbed with a clove of garlic beforehand. (If you have no access to a caquelon, try a chafing dish.) The cheese is usually augmented with a teaspoon or so of flour and a tablespoon or so of KIRSCH is traditionally added toward the end. Should the mixture become too thick, you just add more wine (but warm or at least at room temperature).

Swiss fondue was so well received that embellishments came about inevitably. Most are variations on the Chinese FIRE POT, in which a communal pot is put simmering in the middle of the table and diners have a selection of foods—beef (fondue bourguignonne) or vegetables, for example, and even seafood and fruit—to dip into it until the food is done to their liking. A number of sauces and condiments are set around for everyone to savor at their pleasure. And the famous gourmet Brillat-Savarin developed his own variation, Fondue au Fromage, composed of scrambled eggs and grated Gruyère cheese. It seems a far cry from the original meaning of the word—fondue comes from the French word meaning melt—but provides a lot of pleasant dining nonetheless.

2. A French puree of vegetables (carrots, celery, tomatoes, for example) cooked slowly in butter or oil.

Fonduta

An Italian FONDUE made with FONTINA cheese.

Fontina

An Italian cow's-milk CHEESE made in Piedmont. It resembles a softer Gruyère, albeit with smaller holes and a richer taste. Its creamy texture lends it to melting, as in FONDUTA. Other fontinas are made elsewhere but lack some of the richness of the original.

Food Mill

A hand-operated kitchen gadget for mashing, pureeing, or ricing. In one variety, the food is placed in a container with a mesh bottom while a curved metal blade (on a handle) grinds it through the mesh, leaving behind any extraneous matter. Because of the blade's curve, reversing it causes it to unstick any food that threatens to settle in and gum up the mesh.

Food Processor

With its various blades and disks, a food processor will grate, grind, slice, mince, mix, or puree, and some are equipped with a dough hook to knead your bread dough for you. After the proper attachment is installed, and the ingredients are dropped down a hollow chimney, a button is pressed, and all your sins are taken away. By varying the blade and the way the ingredient is inserted, you can determine whether it will come out julienned, in rounds, or in chunks. It is undoubtedly the one machine that has liberated the cook from incredible drudgery.

Fool

An English dessert of pureed, sometimes cooked fruit (especially berries and particularly gooseberries), cooled and mixed with whipped cream (2 parts cream to 1 of fruit puree is standard). It is normally served cold in sherbet glasses.

Forcemeat

Stuffing. A mixture of finely chopped (or minced) and highly seasoned ingredients appropriate for almost anything stuffable.

Fortified Wine

A wine to which brandy has been added to stop fermentation or simply to raise the alcoholic content (or both at the same time). As the yeasts that ferment sugar into alcohol stop working when the alcoholic content reaches a certain level (anywhere from 7 percent to 16 percent), the early addition of brandy ensures that some of the grape sugar remains as sugar while simultaneously boosting the alcohol somewhat.

The classic fortified wines, all of which are useful as COOKING WINE, are Madeira, Marsala, port, sherry, and vermouth.

Fortune Cookie
A plain, somewhat tasteless cookie enclosing a piece of paper with a fortune, saying, or would-be clever remark printed on it. It is a specialty of American Chinese restaurants.

Four Spices
See QUATRE-EPICES.

Fowl
Technically any sort of bird, but in the kitchen the term is often restricted to a mature female chicken of any size or weight that is suitable for soup or stew.

Fox Grape
A native American grape (*Vitis labrusca* for the most part) with a taste characteristic defined as FOXY.

Foxy
A wine characteristic called, for reasons unknown, foxiness. This inexact term refers to the distinctively pungent taste and aroma of the grapes and wines native to eastern North America. They are perhaps most characterized by the Concord grape and its products. The introduction of hybrids and the ability to grow European grapes successfully in eastern North America have diminished the importance of native grape varieties for use in wine-making.

FPC
See FISH FLOUR.

Fraise
The French term for strawberry and also the clear BRANDY distilled from it. *Fraises des bois* are wild strawberries, which can also be distilled.

Framboise
The French term for raspberry and also the clear BRANDY distilled from it. *Framboise sauvage* is the term for wild raspberry, which can also be distilled.

Frangipane
An almond-flavored cream or custard used with pastries.

Frankfurter
Also *hot dog*. An all-time favorite in the sausage family, without which major league baseball and summer picnics would become pale imitations of themselves. The original, German hot dog, or *Frankfurter würstchen*, was made with salted and spiced

minced beef and pork. Hot dogs today can be made from beef, or from beef and pork or poultry or veal, at times stretched with milk solids or soy flour. All-beef franks may not legally be "stretched," and Kosher franks must contain only rabbinically approved beef and seasonings.

Frappe

Essentially, a milkshake, especially in the environs of Boston, Mass., but pretty much now gone the way of the dinosaur. It consists of milk, some form of flavoring, and ice cream, although at one time it might also have included an egg, all combined and thoroughly mixed.

Frappé

1. A drink composed of a liqueur poured over shaved ice.
2. A dessert of thick fruit juice or syrup frozen until mushy.

Freeze Dry

To preserve food by freezing it in a vacuum and removing the moisture. The most commonly seen freeze-dried commodity is most certainly instant coffee.

Freezers

The freezing point is 32°F or 0°C. Most home freezers are best kept a bit under that temperature, especially as they tend to warm up a bit each time the door is opened and every time something unfrozen is placed in them for storage. If you can keep your freezer full, or nearly so, it will work more efficiently than if partly empty. Foods to be frozen require tight packaging to seal out any air; otherwise they are subject to *freezer burn*, a condition resulting in a whitish or grayish appearance, loss of moisture, and deterioration of quality.

French Bean

See string BEAN.

French Colombard

A French white wine grape (*Vitis vinifera*) widely grown in California. In France it is mostly used for distilling into COGNAC, but in California it develops into a pleasant, dry white wine, often sold under the name CHABLIS.

French Dressing

A traditional French salad dressing, or *vinaigrette*, consists of 3 parts olive oil, 1 part wine vinegar, salt and pepper, and, perhaps, some minced parsley. The salt is added to the vinegar and beaten severely, after which the oil—with the pepper freshly ground into it—is also added. The parsley is then strewn on top and stirred in. From there on almost anything goes—anchovies, capers, cheese, chives, garlic, mustard, and even sugar have been added to French dressing, as have tarragon and chopped sweet pickles. Walnut or vegetable oils of various sorts often replace the olive oil.

French Frying

See DEEP-FAT FRYING.

French Toast

Also known as *German toast* and *pain perdu*. Slices of bread that have been dipped in milk and beaten egg, panfried, and served with jam, jelly, or other sweet topping.

Freshwater Clams

Not clams at all, but mussels of the family Unionidae. They are edible but not much eaten and have been described as sweet and succulent when young, becoming chewy as they mature.

Fresno

A particularly hot, short green or red CHILI pepper grown in California.

Friar

A juicy PLUM suitable for snacks or preserves.

Fricandeau

In classic cooking, a choice cut of veal rump steak that is larded, braised, glazed, and served forth in a form so tender it can be cut with a spoon. The term can, however, also refer to braised fillets of fish.

Fricassee

A stew made with a white sauce based on meat stock. It is applicable to light-colored meats and fowl, including chicken, rabbit, sweetbreads, and veal. If the meat is not browned, it becomes a white fricassee or blanquette; a brown fricassee is made with meat browned beforehand.

Fried Rice

An Oriental way of using leftover cooked pork or chicken or what-have-you. Whatever you're using is cut small and heated in a little oil. An egg is often broken over it and whisked in, after which cooked rice (and sometimes soy sauce) is mixed into the whole thing, which is served hot and informally.

Frill

A decorative paper sleeve slipped over the end of a lamb chop or the bones of a crown roast to prevent burning when cooking.

Fritatta

An Italian omelet incorporating meat, seafood, or vegetables. It is turned in the cooking process, but not folded over, as you would fold a French omelet.

Fritter

A batter or a food dipped in that batter that is deep-fried or sautéed.

Fritto Misto

An Italian term for *mixed fry*. It is a wonderful and accommodating meal of bits of fish, meat, poultry, or vegetables (or any combination thereof) dipped in batter and deep-fried. One approach is to cut everything to the same size and shape so that once it is put in batter and cooked, it is impossible for the diner to know in advance just which delicate morsel is about to be consumed. The dish is as appropriate with leftovers as it is with fresh foods.

Frog's Legs

As the name implies, the legs of the frog (*Ranus* spp.). The French have the reputation of being the great eaters of frog's legs, but that's only because the British caught them at it and, being appalled at the sight, called everyone's attention to it. Actually, frog's legs are—or were—also much prized in rural North America and are still in favor with those who live near froggy ponds and with people on fishing trips. Such expeditions often arrive in camp when it's too dark to fish, but just right for taking a flashlight out for frogs.

One simple way to prepare frog's legs is to sever the feet and soak the legs in milk or cold water for an hour or so, then dry them and dredge them with flour. Brown a good clove of garlic in clarified butter, remove the garlic (the taste will all be in the butter anyway), sauté the frog's legs in the garlicky butter, and serve hot. Frozen frog's legs are also available but are hardly worth the expense. Even at their best, frog's legs tend to resemble a bland piece of chicken.

Fromage

A French word for *cheese*. For example, *fromage de tête* is head cheese (see BRAWN).

Frost

To put frosting on a cake. Where frosting and ICING change places is mostly a matter of semantics. Frosting is thicker than icing, not nearly so liquid, and will stay in place when slathered on. In either case, a good spatula is a great help. The word is also used for the icy glaze that forms on the outside of a glass filled with crushed ice.

Frozen Yogurt

A form of yogurt frozen to resemble—and compete with—ice cream. It has a slightly more acid tang than ice cream and ranges from quite soft to very hard. Some of it is delightful, but don't fall for the line that it's good for you. It's not bad, but it's not a health food, unless you crave a frozen dessert and have been instructed to avoid the fat in ice cream.

Fructose

A fruit sugar or levulose. Because of its makeup, it is allowable for diabetics. You can find it either granulated or in liquid form, but it is sufficiently different from regular sugar (glucose) to make it unworkable in any recipe not designed for it.

Fruit

Generally speaking, the soft enclosure that holds the ovary of a tree or plant. Actually, what we normally think of as fruit does not always fit the botanists' definitions. For example, zucchini (which we use as vegetables) are fruits, but oranges (which we use as fruits) are not. Whether a specific plant is a true fruit or not is, of course, of little, if any, concern in the kitchen. What counts is whether the fruit is good and what it is good for. In this volume, individual fruits will be found under their appropriate headings.

Fruit Butter

A spread made by stewing fresh fruit with sugar and spices.

Fruitcake

A dark, spicy, usually festive (as a wedding cake, for example) cake incorporating fruit and nuts and often made with brandy, rum, or other spirit. Holiday fruitcakes usually profit from some aging from the time they are baked until they are eaten. With the exception of wedding cakes, fruitcakes are not iced, but instead are frequently decorated with candied fruits and nuts.

Fruit Cocktail

An appetizer, frequently seen at banquets, consisting of chopped up citrus and other fruits, and usually topped with a maraschino cherry.

Fruit Cup

A cold dessert consisting of fruits and sometimes nuts cut small and served in syrup or some form of fruit LIQUEUR.

Fruit Drinks

Fruit-flavored beverages for which U.S. government regulations specify, somewhat loosely, how much actual fruit juice must be contained.

Artificially flavored fruit drink. No minimum, but "artificially flavored" must appear on the label.

Fruit ade. Must contain at least 15% fruit juice, except for lemon-and-lime, for which the minimum is 12.3%.

Fruit drink. Must contain at least 10% juice, except for lemon-and-lime, for which the minimum is 6%.

Fruit-flavored drink. Need not contain as much as 10% juice.

Fruit juice. Must contain at least 30% juice.

Fruit punch. Must contain at least 10% juice, except for lemon-and-lime, for which the minimum is 6%.

Fruitiness

A wine term referring to the fresh grapelike perfume emanating from certain young wines. Most fruity wines are best drunk young before this quality begins to fade.

Fruits de Mer

A French term for a serving of assorted seafood, especially shellfish, either cooked or raw, usually presented as a first course.

Frumenty

Also *furmenty.* An old English form of whole wheat porridge flavored with milk, sugar, salt, eggs (or egg yolks), and, perhaps, saffron.

Fry

1. The young of fish.

2. To cook in butter or lard or oil. There are three basic techniques of frying: DEEP-FAT FRYING, panfrying or SAUTÉING, and STIR-FRYING.

Fryer

In poultry terms, a young chicken weighing 2½–3½ pounds.

Frying Pan

Also *skillet.* A heavy-bottomed flattish pan for browning, sautéing, omelet-making, and other uses. (The hero of one old folk song used his for washing his face.)

Fudge

A semisoft confection made from brown or white sugar, butter, cream, and evaporated milk (or plain water) and flavored usually with either chocolate or vanilla, but sometimes with ginger, glazed fruits, maple syrup, nuts, or orange. While a beginners' specialty, fudge is not all that easy to get right and may take some practice.

Fumé Blanc

Also *blanc fumé.* A French white-wine grape otherwise known as SAUVIGNON. It is a specialty of a French wine-growing region along the Loire River where its wine is likely to be labeled Blanc Fumé de Pouilly.

Fumet

A French term for ESSENCE.

Funnel Cake

A Pennsylvania Dutch specialty, often hawked at street festivals and county fairs. As batter is poured through a funnel into hot fat it takes the shape of deep-fried spirals. Funnel cakes are usually served topped with jelly, sugar, or syrup.

Furmint

A wine grape (*Vitis vinifera*) that produces TOKAY.

Fusilli

A PASTA in the form of twists of spaghetti, somewhat in the shape of a corkscrew. It is recommended for dishes incorporating thick, creamy sauces.

G
Also *gm*. Common abbreviation for GRAM.

Gado Gado
An Indonesian specialty of chilled vegetables (perhaps beans, bean sprouts, cabbage, cucumber, scallions, tomatoes), quartered hard-boiled eggs, and pineapple, with chili peppers and a peanut sauce.

Gal.
Common abbreviation for GALLON.

Galantine
An elegant preparation of meat, poultry, or fish that has been stuffed and beaten (or pressed) into a desirable shape, coated with gelatin, and served cold. A showy achievement, it is best left to professionals and to only the most highly skilled of home cooks.

Galette
A round, thin, French cake made of flaky pastry and having some sort of stuffing. The best-known example is the *galette des rois* (galette of the kings), a sweet pastry filled with jam, whipped cream, and one bean (bringing luck to whoever finds it). It is traditional for the Feast of the Epiphany (January 6) commemorating the arrival of the Three Kings at the manger in Bethlehem.

Galingale
A European plant (*Cyperus longus*) with an edible, somewhat gingery root. It was highly favored in medieval England but seems to be pretty much forgotten today.

Gallimaufry
A medieval chicken stew cooked in wine or VERJUS and flavored with cinnamon and ginger. The name has also been applied to a shoulder of mutton that was boned and cooked with various herbs, then sewn back into its skin. Gallimaufry has since degenerated into a catchall description for any misbegotten stew.

Gallon
A standard unit of liquid measure equivalent to 4 quarts. The American gallon contains 3.785 liters; the Imperial gallon contains 4.545 liters.

Gamay

A grapevine (*Vitis vinifera*) responsible for the French dry red table wines of the Beaujolais district of BURGUNDY as well as wines grown elsewhere, especially California.

Game

Birds and animals generally taken by hunting, whether supplied that way or raised specifically for the table.

Gammelost

A soft, blue, skim cow's-milk CHEESE from Norway, sometimes aged in juniper-flavored straw.

Gammon

A British term originally for the foreleg of a pig, smoked or not; BACON generally.

Ganache

A French pastry filling of semisweet chocolate and heavy cream.

Gar

1. Any of several North American freshwater fish (family Lepisosteidae) with long and slim bodies, thick scales, and elongated snouts. Gar are equipped with numerous, very sharp teeth. Their flesh is edible, if dry, and comparable to PIKE. However, their eggs are toxic.

    2. NEEDLEFISH.

Garam Masala

An Indian food flavoring consisting of several spices. It varies from kitchen to kitchen, but a representative north Indian one might include 5 tablespoons caraway seeds, 1 tablespoon cardamom seeds, 1¾ tablespoons ground cinnamon, 1¾ table-spoons ground cloves, 6 tablespoons coriander, and 6 tablespoons peppercorns. The ingredients are picked over to remove any husks and then ground coarsely together. If kept in a tightly lidded jar, garam masala will keep not indefinitely, but for a good, long time before losing potency. (A south Indian example would be more likely to be made up of some combination of chili peppers, cumin, and fenugreek.)

Garbanzo

See CHICKPEA.

Garbure

A traditional vegetable (mostly) stew or soup from southwest France. The twin demands made by a garbure are that the water remain boiling throughout the cook-ing process and that the finished product be thick enough that a spoon placed in its middle stands upright.

The manner of cooking garbure is to get a large amount of water boiling in an earthenware pot, then begin adding ingredients according to availability and cooking time. Sliced peeled potatoes, broad beans, peas, snap beans, shredded cabbage, and parsley, thyme, marjoram, and garlic for flavoring are added; at the last minute, a chunk of pork or goose previously preserved in its own fat is thrown in. Since preserved pork and goose are not perhaps daily items outside southwest France, a meaty ham bone, a smoked ham hock, or a slab of bacon can serve as a replacement. Finally, the dish is thickened further with slices of day-old bread.

Garden Burnet
See BURNET.

Garlic
A pungent cousin of the onion and one of the most popular and misunderstood of foods. Garlic (*Allium sativum*) comes in heads, each consisting of a number of separate segments known as cloves, each of which is enclosed in its own paperlike covering. If the covering is removed and the garlic pressed or mashed, its potency is released in full. If the papery covering is left on and the garlic clove is boiled or simmered, the potency disappears completely, leaving a slightly sweet, nutlike remainder with a subtly pleasant taste and no aroma—either from the dish or on the eater's breath. If the clove is peeled, chopped, and cooked, it will release a goodly part of its potency, but far less than if mashed. Once you have sautéed garlic, you might as well remove it from the pan as it loses its taste to the cooking medium (or you can add it later in the process, after whatever else you are browning is mostly done).

When buying garlic, look for sturdy, solid heads that are unshriveled and not in any way discolored. You are best advised to buy the loose variety—or pluck off what you need from braided garlic hanging on a string—rather than those that come packaged in a box with a plastic window. These have been known to be stale and old, but you have no way of telling that until you get them home. Once at home, don't refrigerate garlic—just leave it alone in a dry, dark place. Traditionally, it is supposed to hasten the ripening of bananas and other produce kept in its immediate proximity—and this does indeed seem to work.

There are several varieties of garlic. There is regular American garlic, the strong, pungent bulb so many know and love. There is Mexican garlic and Italian garlic, both not so pristinely white and not so strong, either. There is elephant garlic, a particularly mild—some would say bland—fairly recent entry on supermarket shelves. There are the wild varieties, such as field garlic (*Allium vineale* and *Allium oleraceum*) that grows in meadows and mars the flavor of milk given by the cows grazing on it. Foragers find some wild varieties usable, others too strong, leaving an odor on the breath that lingers long after the taste has gone. However, wild garlic (*Allium canadense*) and wild leek (*Allium tricoccum*) are both quite highly thought of.

Garlic is used mostly as a flavoring for almost anything—salads and roasts and vegetables and spaghetti and cheese (a clove of garlic is considered essential to any self-respecting Swiss FONDUE) and garlic bread and garlic soup, in which as many as 40 cloves of garlic are called for and which comes out as gentle as a lamb (which is also good with garlic). Not everyone likes it, of course. There are those who feel that a day without garlic is a day wasted, whereas others prefer to avoid it completely. And vampires, we are told, flee from the very presence of it.

Garlic-Mustard
A tall plant (*Alliaria officinalis*) that grows wild in fields and near stands of trees and shrubs. It imparts just the taste you would expect it to and has been used in salads and stuffings.

Garlic Powder
Powdered, dehydrated garlic. It adds a suggestion of garlic that is particularly useful when concocting something that only needs the merest suspicion of it.

Garlic Press
A small kitchen device for dealing with garlic if you don't want to smash it, peel it, and chop it up with a knife. A garlic clove (unpeeled if the press is any good) is placed in a basket with a mesh on one side and a lever-activated plate on the other. When closed and pressed, the garlic—but not the peel—is extruded through the mesh. Because the pressed garlic comes out in smaller bits than if you chopped it all by hand, it has more surface area and the taste seems correspondingly greater, so you can use less garlic. The best presses have a removable basket for easier cleaning (although it is also easier to lose).

Garlic Salt
Salt flavored with dehydrated garlic. It is useful—in great moderation—for such picnic fare as carrot sticks or celery, but is no substitute for the real thing. It has a tendency to impart a tinny taste to your fare. Better by far is to rub a cut clove of garlic in some coarse table salt and use that.

Garnish
An edible trimming added to a dish to make it look more attractive, impressive, or mouthwatering.

Garum
A condiment of historic interest only, or so we may hope; it was made for ancient Romans (who flipped out for it) from the sun-dried entrails of various small, anchovy-like fish. Its closest modern equivalent is the Vietnamese NUÖC MAM.

Gayette

A baked Provençale sausage made of equal amounts of pork liver and fresh bacon with garlic and seasonings. It is served cold as an hors d'oeuvre.

Gazpacho

A Mexican salad masquerading as soup. A good gazpacho will have at the least a lot of chopped tomatoes, cucumbers, onions, and peppers together with oil and vinegar and some toasted croutons. It is at its glorious best served icy cold and eaten with a spoon out of soup bowls.

Gefilte Fish

A Jewish specialty consisting of fish (usually yellow pike and whitefish but sometimes carp) that has been boned and chopped with carrot, celery, egg, green pepper, matzo meal, onion, and salt and pepper. This mixture is formed into balls, simmered lengthily in a broth prepared from the fish bones, and then cooled in its broth. It is characteristically served cold with horseradish. At one time it was stuffed ("gefilte") back into the skin of the fish for cooking, and perhaps we should be grateful that this practice seems to have gone by the boards.

Gelatin

A thickening substance which when mixed with hot water congeals to a jelly. Most commercial gelatin is derived from animal by-products (skin, cartilage, sinews), but a vegetarian version made from AGAR is also available, as is one made from mushrooms. Gelatin obtained from fish products is called ISINGLASS. Unflavored and unsweetened gelatin, used for most cooking purposes, should not be confused with the sweetened and flavored gelatins intended as desserts.

Gelato

An Italian version of ice cream made with egg yolks, milk, and a sweetener. It is firmer than American ice cream and usually not as sweet.

Gem Pan

A small muffin pan.

Generic

In general, a food product having a nonproprietary (brand) name. The term is specifically used to designate a wine that is advertised as having the same characteristics as some well-known model, for example, Burgundy. The original model is made only in the French region of that name, but the name Burgundy has been used to designate heavy red table wines—some good, some pretty awful—grown all over the world. Chablis and Chianti are also names that are—to the original growers— pirated with considerable frequency. Labeling wines according to the grape variety that goes into them (VARIETAL wines) is one step away from the use of generic names. So is the addition of the place where the wine was grown and made, as in the California counties of Napa and Sonoma, which have long been seen on wine labels and are generally recognized as worthy of respect in their own right.

Genever

See HOLLANDS.

Genoise

A delicate, extremely rich, French sponge cake. It serves as a base for many elegant desserts.

Gentian

A flowering plant of the *Gentiana* genus, it is mostly used as an ornamental, except in France and Switzerland, where it is used as a flavoring. The flowers may be used to flavor cordials and liqueurs, and the root of one (*Gentiana lutea*) has been used medicinally and is distilled for liqueurs and aperitifs (see APERITIF), the most notable of which is the French proprietary aperitif Suze.

Geoduck

A large (up to five pounds) CLAM (*Panope generosa*) of the Pacific Coast; it is a privilege to report that the name is pronounced "gooey-duck." Unless you live in the neighborhood, however, you're not likely to see it except possibly in cans. The geoduck is anatomically unable to close its shell completely; once out of the water, it spills out its liquids and dies before it can be delivered to any but the closest markets.

Germ

The part of a CEREAL seed that sprouts, thus forming the new plant. Germ is rich in nutrients, but also has a great deal of oil that tends to turn rancid. Hence, most flours have had the germ removed, which is a pity when you consider that a great deal of the flavor of wheat (and consequently of bread) is in the germ. Wheat germ is widely available (refrigerated) in health food stores and more widely in vacuum-packed bottles, which must be refrigerated after opening. It can be found both toasted and untoasted and may be added to bread dough; used in place of breadcrumbs in meatloaves, stuffings, or coatings; or sprinkled over plain yogurt to give it a crunchy texture. If you're going to use it instead of breadcrumbs, be advised that it burns at a lower temperature.

German Toast

Another name for FRENCH TOAST.

Géromé

A French, soft or semihard, whole cow's-milk CHEESE resembling MÜNSTER.

Gervais
A French cream CHEESE from Normandy, originally named for its developer but now pretty much a generic name for any soft, creamy cheese.

Gewürztraminer
A grapevine (*Vitis vinifera*) producing a spicy, dry white wine especially in the French region of Alsace but also grown elsewhere.

Gex
A French, hard, blue-veined, cow's-milk CHEESE. It has been compared to STILTON.

Ghee
An Indian version of clarified butter.

Gherkin
A small variety of CUCUMBER (*Cucumis anguria*) used for pickles. It also refers to various immature larger cucumbers used for the same purpose.

Giant Clam
A monstrous great CLAM of the Indian Ocean.

Giant Sea Bass
A saltwater BASS.

Giblets
The liver, heart, and gizzard of poultry; the term is sometimes extended to refer also to the cockscomb, feet, neck, and wing tips. Giblets are generally used to make gravy and broth, although the liver—especially goose liver—is often saved for some other, presumably more noble, purpose. (Besides, it tends to turn bitter if boiled.)

Gigot
A French term for leg of lamb or mutton.

Gild
To brush something with egg yolk to give a golden color, as with pastry.

Gill
1. The breathing apparatus of fish. Gills must be "pulled," or removed, if the head is to be used to make fish stock, or they will impart a harsh bitterness.

2. An archaic unit of liquid measure amounting to ½ cup which comes to 4 fluid ounces (11.8 centiliters) U.S. or 5 fluid ounces (14.2 centiliters) Imperial. An Imperial gill measures out to ⅝ U.S. cup.

Gin
A spirit distilled from grain and flavored with juniper berries. Although mostly used for drinking, it has kitchen uses too, including as a substitution for rice wine

in Chinese recipes and for flaming dishes that might profit from a whiff of juniper. The kitchen choice is the clear style known as London gin. There is also a Hollands gin, or genever, that is stronger tasting and not of much use culinarily.

Ginger

Also *ginger root*. A spice (*Zingiber officinale*) of Asian origin found fresh, candied, powdered, and preserved. Ginger is used especially in Chinese cooking and in curries, but is also useful for any number of other purposes. (There is also a North American herb known as *wild ginger*, *Asarum canadense*, the dried root of which is said to impart a gingery tang, but as the plant is a somewhat endangered one, it is best left alone.)

Fresh ginger is available in most markets as twisty roots, known as "hands." Choose plump, light-colored, firm pieces and keep them refrigerated (ginger dries out and gets stringy with age). Once you've cut a piece, wrap the rest in plastic and refrigerate again, or peel it and drop it in a small jar of vodka. It will not only keep, but will impart some of its savor to the vodka, which can also be used as a flavoring agent. Ginger can also be frozen, in which case it grates more easily.

Peeled fresh ginger, whole or grated, enhances the taste of many sauces—teriyaki, especially—and is also a great help to stews, braised meats, and even some fish dishes. Ginger can also be peeled, chopped, and put through a garlic press to give ginger juice, called for in some (especially Chinese) recipes.

Candied, or crystallized, ginger (sometimes called stem ginger in that the portion closest to the stem is the choicest and most tender part) is not as popular as it once was, but is still available here and there. It is simmered in syrup and preserved in sugar, or it may be packed in a red syrup, in which case it will be quite sweet. The sugar or syrup can be used for sauces and marinades.

Powdered ginger has far less potency than fresh and is used in baking (gingerbread is an obvious example) and can also substitute for the fresh when roasting meats—simply rub the roast with powdered ginger when preparing it for cooking. Otherwise, it is not a satisfactory substitute for fresh.

Ginger Ale

A highly sweetened nonalcoholic carbonated beverage flavored with ginger.

Ginger Beer

A mostly British, usually nonalcoholic, carbonated beverage that is fairly strongly flavored with ginger.

Gingerbread

One of the oldest favorites among spicy cookies, breads, and cakes. Ginger, honey, and molasses still flavor the gingerbread-men cookies we see at Christmas as well as the elaborate houses constructed from gingerbread cookie dough and decorated with icing. Gingerbread as cake is another favorite; it is often served with whipped cream or the winy sauce described by writer M.F.K. Fisher (brown sugar, butter, and dry sherry in equal parts, beaten together over heat, but never enough to bring it to a boil). The French have their own version of gingerbread, known as PAIN D'EPICE, but the spicing does not always include ginger.

Gingersnap
A very thin ginger-and-molasses-flavored cookie.

Ginkgo Nut
The fruit of the ginkgo tree (*Ginkgo biloba*). It is sold dried or canned and is used in Chinese recipes for poultry, soup, and vegetables and by the Japanese to make cookies. Dried gingko nuts must be shelled and blanched before being used.

Ginseng
A plant (*Panax quinquefolium*) beloved of the Chinese and other Oriental peoples who attribute all manner of healthful, and indeed aphrodisiac, qualities to it. For medicinal purposes, the root is dried and shredded; for culinary purposes, the leaves are brewed into tea and sometimes steeped in some form of alcoholic drink to be used as a pick-me-up.

Girdle
A British term for GRIDDLE.

Gizzard
An internal organ of poultry that grinds food up. It is used in giblet gravy and can be made into a stew with the hearts and kidneys, but it is tough and needs long, moist cooking. Unless you like grit in your gravy, it is a good idea to slice open the gizzard and clean out anything in it before setting it to simmer.

Gjetost
Perhaps the Norwegian national CHEESE. It is a sweet, golden-brown cheese originally made from boiled goat's-milk whey, although it now comes more often from a mixture of whey from cow's milk and goat's milk.

Glace de Viand
An extremely concentrated meat EXTRACT used sparingly as a flavoring agent.

Glandular Meats
Yet another dreadful term for VARIETY MEATS.

Glasswort
See SAMPHIRE.

Glaze

A liquid brushed on food in order to impart, when heated, a high glossy sheen. Egg or egg white (usually mixed with a slight amount of water) can be used to enhance the crust of bread or pastry; apple or red currant jelly to glaze fruit tarts; apricot jam to glaze ham; and a little bit of last-minute sugar sprinkled on sautéing carrots, onions, or turnips will glaze them nicely.

Globe Artichoke

A French or regular market ARTICHOKE.

Glögg

A Scandinavian fruit, spirit, or wine punch served hot and often spectacularly flamed before serving.

Gloucester

An English cow's-milk CHEESE somewhat akin to Cheddar. It comes in two incarnations: single and double. Single Gloucester is smooth and yellow and has a mild taste. Double Gloucester is colored red (with ANNATTO), is firmer than single Gloucester and slightly crumbly, and has a richer, slightly more acid taste.

Glucose

A form of fruit sugar useful in making some jams and candies because it does not crystallize. It can be had powdered or in liquid form as CORN SYRUP.

Glühwein

See MULLED WINE.

Gluten

A protein in FLOUR, which releases the gas that enables bread dough to rise and expand. The amount of expansion varies with the flour—and its gluten content. Commercial gluten flour is processed specially to reduce the flour's starch content and retain its gluten.

Glutinous Rice

A starchy variety of RICE much favored by the Chinese.

Gnocchi

An Italian DUMPLING of pasta or potatoes, filled with almost anything and served with or without a sauce as an appetizer or a main dish.

Goat

Capra spp. Not an item in great demand in most of North America, goat (especially the flesh of an adult male, incredibly tough and having a highly unpleasant aroma) can be found in markets catering to Indians and West Indians who use it in curries and for roasting. Kid, a young goat, is similar to lamb and can be treated in the same ways. Goat's milk is usually available in health food stores.

Goat Cheese

Any CHEESE made from goat's milk. Long a favorite of Europeans, goat cheese (*chèvre* to the French) became something of a fad among trendy North American diners and expanded its base of appreciation when everyone else found out how good it can be. In addition to the imported varieties, goat cheese is now being made in small dairies throughout North America, but especially in New England.

Goatfish

A name given to various species of red MULLET.

Gobo

The Japanese name for BURDOCK.

Godiveau

In classic French cooking, a FORCEMEAT, the important ingredients of which are veal and veal kidneys.

Golden Berry

Another name for GROUND-CHERRY.

Golden Delicious

A yellow APPLE conducive to cooking or eating raw.

Golden Syrup

A sweet, British cane-sugar syrup that is used to sweeten desserts and sauces and as a filling for tarts. If you need a substitute, use a light corn syrup.

Goldeye

A North American freshwater fish (*Hiodon alosoides*) that ranges from northern Canada to the Great Plains. It is served smoked—notably in Canada.

Goober

Also called *goober pea*. A PEANUT.

Goose

Any of the large birds of the family Antidae. Most geese are found in the frozen-food sections of our markets, although sometimes a fresh one—usually only if ordered in advance—will be available. If it is frozen, thaw it in the refrigerator (allow two days for this and don't refreeze it once it has thawed). Geese will run anywhere from 5 to 20 pounds, but generally the 8-to-10-pound bird is the best bet. It will be younger—and tenderer—than the bigger one and will have enough meat to make it all worthwhile. This does not, of course, apply to a WILD GOOSE, which you would be well advised to accept at any weight that is offered to you.

Goose is not economy fare. The percentage of meat to total weight does not begin to rival that of a turkey or even a chicken, but its advocates claim that the meat of a goose is otherwise unrivaled by any domestic bird. Although goose is quite fatty, the fat can be leached out and rendered into a prime cooking or baking medium, so all is not wasted. Goose is also made more expensive by U.S. federal regulations concerning the dressing of fowl. Machines through which chicken and turkeys sail easily are baffled by the tough pinfeathers of geese, which mandate a lot of costly hand labor before the birds meet U.S. standards. Thus, what was once an economy bird has become a latter-day luxury item.

The usual way of cooking one's goose is to roast it, generally with some form of fresh or dried fruit stuffing or sometimes with sauerkraut. Goose can also be roasted in the Alsatian manner, in which it is stuffed with sausages and served with sauerkraut that has been flavored with the goose drippings. In England, goose was traditionally stuffed with onions and sage and roasted on Michaelmas Day (September 29) to commemorate the dinner that Queen Elizabeth I was eating when she received word of the victory over the Spanish Armada.

Cookbooks often recommend that goose and duck—because of their fattiness—be pricked all over and parboiled in water or else roasted over a pan of boiling water. An alternative that works wonders with goose is to rub a little goose fat on the bottom of the roasting pan, into which you place the goose on its side. Roast the goose at 425°F and draw off the fat every quarter hour as the bird cooks. After the first hour the bird can be turned to its other side. After an additional hour, it can go on its back and be kept there until done (about 2½ hours total roasting time, subtracting any time spent draining the fat off). By the end of the second hour, or maybe a little earlier, the fat has pretty well gone out of the bird. To keep it from drying out completely it can be basted instead with equal parts goose fat, orange juice, and port.

Roasting, of course, is not the only successful way to cook goose. Braising is also called for, and the sausage-and-sauerkraut accompaniment is, if anything, even better this way. Goose is also distinguished by being smoked or it can be conserved by being preserved in a CONFIT.

Gooseberry

A thorny, berry-producing plant of the *Ribes* genus related to the CURRANT. Those native to Europe *(Ribes grossularia)* have proved difficult to grow successfully in North America, but native American species (including *Ribes hirtellum*) yield berries that are similar, more acid, and somewhat smaller than their English counterparts (which can be as large as eggs). Crosses between the two have also been developed.

Gooseberries are either green or red, usually with a fuzzy skin, and range in taste from quite sweet to extremely acid. They are made into fools and tarts, can be eaten right off the bush (if they're not too tart), or used for a sauce (mackerel with goose-berry sauce is notable). Because fresh gooseberries are so uncommon in North America, most of what we see is canned.

Gooseberries were popular in early New England but fell out of favor some time early in the twentieth century, in part, certainly, because they harbor a disease that is devastating to white pine. Those of us who harbor white pines in our yards would consider it downright unneighborly should anyone around us engage in raising gooseberries, no matter how good they are.

Goosefish
See MONKFISH.

Gorgonzola
A creamy, strong, Italian cow's-milk CHEESE from Lombardy with a whitish interior streaked with veins of blue. It has an odor that can develop into something over-powering. Gorgonzola comes in wrapped triangles and is useful for many occa-sions—it goes well with fruit and good red wine, for example, and, melted with an equal amount of butter and a healthy slug of brandy, it makes a rich and highly caloric spaghetti sauce.

Gorp
A trail food consisting of dried ingredients—grains, nuts, fruit (especially raisins), and seeds might go into it, pretty much at the gorp-maker's discretion. The aim is to quell appetite and provide instant energy.

Gosling
A young (up to 6 months) GOOSE.

Gouda
A Dutch, semisoft-to-hard, bland, whole or partly skim cow's-milk COHEESE, cov-ered with red wax and often served at breakfast.

Goulash
A classic Hungarian meat stew, often combining paprika, sauerkraut, and sour cream in a delicate balance with beef, lamb (originally mutton, most likely), pork, or veal. However, the name has been extended to cover any stew with various and often undetermined ingredients.

Gourd
A hard-shelled fruit of the family Cucurbitaceae, which includes cucumbers, mel-ons, squash, and pumpkins. Most gourds, however, are inedible and are cultivated for their curious, variegated shapes and coloration. The ones we see are *Cucurbita pepo* var. *Orifera*.

Gourmandise
Cheese lovers often consider this more a cake than a cheese, although it starts with a cow's-milk cheese that is embellished with either cherry extract or KIRSCH and sometimes topped with nuts.

Graham Cracker
A thin whole wheat cracker made according to the nutritional theories of the nineteenth-century American food reformer Dr. Sylvester Graham. Graham crackers (and graham cracker flour) are quite widely used as a crust for cheesecake and certain types of pies.

Graham Flour
A whole wheat FLOUR.

Gralloch
A game term meaning to gut; originally applied to deer, it now covers any game animal.

Gram
1. A standard unit of measure equivalent to .035 ounce.
2. A Southeast Asian term for the CHICKPEA and its various products, especially the flour made from it.

Grana
The Italian word for grain, but gastronomically referring to the so-called granular, or grating, cheeses. These are cheeses that often start out as regular table cheese, but after two or more years harden and become appropriate for grating. ASIAGO and PARMIGIANO-REGGIANO are a couple of outstanding examples.

Granadilla
See PASSIONFRUIT.

Grand Marnier
A very sweet, orange-flavored liqueur similar to CURAÇAO. It makes a superb CREPE, is excellent with duck, and is a superior flavoring agent for baked goods.

Granita
A form of SHERBET that has had the beating process omitted during its freezing. Instead of coming out as a firm solid mass, it results in a kind of flavorsome slush.

Granny Smith
A popular, green-colored, highly versatile APPLE.

Granola

Originally, a homemade breakfast cereal inspired by the increased interest in health foods during the 1960s. A typical granola might consist of dried fruit, nuts, seeds, and grains (especially oats, but also sometimes augmented with millet or rye or soy or wheat germ or any combination thereof). It was all treated with some unsaturated fat, perhaps some honey or other natural sweetener, and baked into a cohesive whole. When buying commercial granola, you would be well advised to read the ingredients on the label and see to what extent it conforms to the original.

Granulated Sugar

A grade of SUGAR in daily use.

Grape

A fruit of the grapevine. There are numerous types of grape that grow in various places around the world, but only two broad categories need concern us here—the European varieties (*Vitis vinifera*) and those native to North America (especially *Vitis labrusca* and *Vitis riparia*, but there are others). Broadly speaking, European grapes produce all the world's prestigious wines as well as providing table fruit and raisins. North American grapes are used for some wines (especially sparkling wines), juice, soda, preserves, and munching as well as adding to fruit salads and compotes. Wines made from native American grapes have a distinctive taste and aroma, referred to— apparently for want of a better description—as FOXY. Included among European varieties are those native to or developed in the Near East, where Arab agronomists, obedient to the Muslim prohibition on alcohol, turned their talents to developing superior table and raisin grapes.

That grapes grow wild in North America has been known at least since the voyages of Leif Ericson. Most that are seen in markets will have a bluish skin, a pronounced taste, and fairly prominent seeds. The skin separates quite easily from the pulp, giving them the name "slipskin." European varieties (most European grapes we see in North American markets are actually grown in California or South America) have a skin and pulp that is more of a piece. Seedless versions of many of them have also been developed. Such grapes may be any color—from white through yellow and green to red and purple and even black.

In selecting grapes, look for solid, unblemished colors and plump, firm fruit that is securely attached to the stems. Shriveled, opaque, or moldy berries are best avoided. Grapes will keep for a few days at room temperature, longer if refrigerated. Wash them just before using.

Grapefruit

A semitropical citrus tree (*Citrus paradisi*) that most likely developed out of the similar but less desirable SHADDOCK. The large round fruit (although sometimes slightly flattened at top and bottom) is white or pink (or even deep red and sometimes bronze) and has a distinctive tart taste overlying a residual sweetness. It takes its name not from any kinship in taste to the grape, but because early ones grew in great clusters, looking for all the world like gargantuan grapes. And a wine was once made from grapefruit, but it seems to have gone by the boards.

Most of the world's grapefruit is grown in the United States, in Florida and Texas primarily. While generally eaten at breakfast—often halved or as juice—grapefruit have other applications as well, including in fruit salads, as dessert (the sweeter varieties, at least), and as an ingredient of marmalade.

Choose grapefruit that are firm to the touch, free of soft spots or indications of rotting, smooth-skinned, and either flat at the ends or round. Thin skins are preferable to thick ones (the fruit will be juicier). Grapefruit will keep at room temperature for up to a week or so. Put them in the refrigerator if you plan on keeping them longer than that.

Grapefruit Knife
A thin, slightly curved, serrated knife intended for delicately removing the segments from the half grapefruit presented to you at the table.

Grape Leaves
The leaves of grapes used as wrappers for stuffings. Any kind of grape leaves can be used so long as they are picked while young and tender. They are blanched and drained and stuffed and baked, then left to cool before serving. One stuffing includes lamb chopped with rice and vegetables (and perhaps pine nuts and parsley), often given a slight boost with lemon juice. Grape leaves are available in bottles from specialty grocers and some supermarkets. They come packed in brine, so you will probably wish to wash them pretty well.

Grappa
A robust form of Italian BRANDY.

Grate
To reduce such ingredients as raw vegetables, cheese, nuts, etc., to small chunks or even a fine powder by rubbing them over some sort of raspy surface. Modern blenders and food processors are wonderful at relieving us of much of this chore.

Gratin
Also *au gratin*. To finish a dish by covering it with a crust, usually cheese and breadcrumbs, and putting it in the oven or under the broiler until it browns. Also any dish so finished.

Gravenstein
An early, all-round APPLE.

Graves

A French wine-growing area of the prestigious BORDEAUX region, noted for some of the world's most acclaimed dry red and white table wines. Among its best known vineyards are Château Haut-Brion, Château La Mission Haut-Brion, Château Haut-Bailly, and Château Pape Clément.

Gravlax

A Swedish dish of raw salmon cured with dill, pepper, salt, and sugar. It may be served with a VINAIGRETTE dressing flavored with dill and mustard.

Gravy

A type of sauce that ranges from the pan drippings from a piece of meat or poultry (plain or thickened with flour or some other element) to elaborate sauces based on those pan juices.

Gray Cod

Another name for the Pacific COD.

Grayling

A freshwater fish of the Salmonid family, akin to TROUT. The European grayling (*Thymallus thymallus*) is said to leave the water bearing with it a scent of thyme. A small fish (up to four pounds), it can be lightly poached or otherwise cooked in any way suitable for trout. The North American species include the Arctic grayling (*Thymallus signifer*), MONTANA GRAYLING (*Thymallus montanus*), and MICHIGAN GRAYLING (*Thymallus tricolor*). In addition to making good eating, they are also prized as sports fish.

Gray Sole

Usually the WITCH FLOUNDER, but the name is used to refer to other FLATFISH as well, particularly the WINTER FLOUNDER.

Grease

To lubricate a cooking utensil—pot, pan, baking sheet, mixing bowl, or whatever—with some form of oil or grease, such as bacon fat, butter, goose fat, lard, or vegetable oil of some sort.

Great Northern Bean

A large, white, dried BEAN.

Green Bean

A frequent market name for the green snap BEAN.

Green Cod

1. Another name for POLLACK.
2. Codfish that has been salted but not dried.

Greengage
A group of sweet, yellowish-green types of PLUM.

Greening
A tart, green APPLE suitable for cooking or baking.

Greenland Cod
A northern COD.

Greenland Turbot
A northern FLATFISH similar to halibut.

Greenling
A food fish (*Hexagrammos decagrammus*) of the Pacific, found especially off the coast of Washington. Although its meat has a greenish tinge, it turns white on cooking. Greenling can appropriately be broiled, panfried, poached, or steamed.

Green Onion
Another name for SCALLION.

Green Peppercorns
Peppercorns that have been picked before becoming fully ripe; because they tend to spoil earlier than do black or white PEPPER, they are often freeze-dried. Green peppercorns are less pungent than is the more mature spice.

Greens
A useful catchall phrase for all sorts of leafy potherbs and salad ingredients.

Gremolada
A garnish of finely chopped garlic, parsley, and lemon zest used especially with OSSO BUCO.

Grenache
A grapevine (*Vitis vinifera*) capable of making a sweet wine in southern France and Spain and a more or less dry rosé in California.

Grenadine
A sweet, thick, sometimes alcoholic, pomegranate-flavored syrup.

Griddle
A flat, usually iron pan with no—or almost no—sides for use over direct heat. If it has three legs (for fitting over a campfire), it is called a *spider*.

Griddle Cake
See PANCAKE.

Grill

To BROIL something, especially over charcoal.

Grilse

A young, usually male SALMON weighing in at three to five pounds. Grilse are fish that have returned prematurely from the ocean to the river in which they were hatched. You'll never find the term in a fish market, but you might be lucky enough to catch one.

Grind

To render something into a powder or at least very small pieces. The mortar and pestle and various specialized grinders have long been available. Today they are augmented by many heaven-sent modern kitchen appliances.

Grinder

1. Any device designed to GRIND up food.
2. A HERO sandwich.

Grissini

See SALT STICK.

Grits

Ground HOMINY. A specialty of the southern United States, grits are boiled into a type of cornmeal mush and served as a side dish, especially at breakfast, or chilled until firm and then fried.

Groat

The crushed, hulled kernel of a grain, such as buckwheat. They come in varying degrees of grindings, from coarse to quite fine.

Grog

To the British Navy it meant simply RUM, but the term now refers to a variety of hot, spiced, and sweetened rum drinks usually favored on cold winter nights.

Ground-Cherry

Also *Cape gooseberry, golden berry, husk-tomato,* and *winter cherry*. It is a close relation of the TOMATILLO. The fruit of various species of the genus *Physalis*, it comprises a golden or greenish berry that grows in a papery husk like a Chinese lantern (indeed, the decorative Chinese lantern plant, *Physalis alkekengi*, is also a close relation). Native ground-cherries are found mostly in the southern United States; imported ones generally come from New Zealand.

Imported ground-cherries are available in the spring and early summer, and domestic ones can be foraged for (or home grown) mainly during the summer. Look for a yellowish or orangy color. They store remarkably well—indeed the name winter cherry refers to the berry's wintering-over qualities, even at room temperature, so long as the husk is left intact. Ground-cherries are especially favored for preserves, but they are also good eaten as they are (peel back the husk, wash the berry, and enjoy) or they can be added to baked goods such as muffins and pies used to enliven sauces for chili or for white meats (poultry and veal).

Groundnut

1. A British name for PEANUT.

2. A North American vine (*Apios tuberosa*) with an edible but not very interesting tuber that can be boiled in salted water like a potato. It is recommended that it be eaten while still hot.

Grouper

A large number of tropical and semitropical saltwater fishes of the Serranidae or BASS family. Small ones can be cooked whole, otherwise they are usually steaked and baked, broiled, grilled, or generally cooked as you would sea bass. With some North American species you will want to remove the skin, due to its strong flavor.

Grouse

Widely distributed game birds, sometimes inaccurately referred to as partridge. They include the blue grouse (*Dendrapagus obscurus*), ruffed grouse (*Bonasa umbellus*), sage grouse (*Centrocercus urophasianus*) Scotch grouse (*Lagopus scoticus*), and spruce grouse (*Canachites canadensis*) among grouses; the rock ptarmigan (*Lagopus mutus*), white-tailed ptarmigan (*Lagopus leucurus*), and willow ptarmigan (*Lagopus lagopus*) among ptarmigans; and the greater and lesser prairie chickens (*Tympanuchus cupido* and *Tympanuchus pallidicinctus*). There are other relatives, but these pretty much cover the more widespread ones. Their meat is dark and delicate, that of the breast being the most favored. Grouse are typically covered with strips of bacon or other barding fat, roasted, and served on slices of toast. Because grouse are seldom acquired in large numbers, one per person seems about all that can be expected, but if you can provide more it would not be wasted on any self-respecting grouse lover.

Gruel

Any thin, even watery, porridge (originally oatmeal).

Grunion

A Pacific fish (*Leuresthes tenuis*) that you don't catch, you pluck. Each year at spawning time the fish approach the beach and flip themselves out of the water on the lap of the incoming high tide, dig a hole in the sand, and deposit their eggs, relying on the next wave to return them to safety. While they are floundering about, they can be simply plucked from the sand and put in a basket. Grunion can be baked or broiled or fried or otherwise cooked as you would SMELT.

Grunt

1. A sizable family (Pomidasidae) of tropical and semitropical marine fish of Caribbean and Atlantic waters. They can be baked or broiled or grilled as with any other fish.

2. A spiced and sweetened fruit or berry dessert with a biscuit-dough crust of uncertain etymology, except that it seems to overlap with the buckle, PANDOWDIE, and SLUMP.

Gruyère

A Swiss (but also French), Alpine, hard cow's-milk CHEESE somewhat resembling EMMENTHALER, but firmer, with a slightly more pronounced bite, and containing smaller holes. Processed imitations are made elsewhere, but bear little resemblance to the original.

Guacamole

An avocado preparation used as a filling for a TACO or TOSTADO in Mexico and as a dip farther north. It consists of avocado mashed with onion, tomato, lemon juice, and various flavorings, such as chili, garlic, coriander, a mixture of these and others.

Guaguanche

A Caribbbean variety of BARRACUDA.

Guava

A yellowish-green fruit of a tropical tree (*Psidium guajava*) of South America and the Caribbean. Guavas can be eaten fresh (by themselves or with a little sugar and a dollop of rum or brandy) or made into a stew or a paste, or mashed and flavored with port or spices and heaped over pancakes, or—as they do in the Philippines— slowly stewed in coconut milk. They are also made into a highly acclaimed sweet jelly. A kindred tree (*Psidium cattleianum*), known as the *strawberry guava*, gives smaller, white-fleshed fruit, and a lesser member of the guava family, the pineapple guava or FEIJOA, borrows the name but doesn't taste as good.

When guavas are not quite ripe they can smell somewhat rank, but this develops into a more entrancing, indeed enveloping, aroma at which point the guava should be eaten or kept—in or out of the refrigerator—for no more than a day or two. As with all tropical fruits, guavas do not respond kindly to being refrigerated before they are ripe.

Gudgeon

A European freshwater fish (*Gobio gobio*), related to the carp, with a mixed culinary press—there are those who recommend it and those who do not.

Guero

An extremely hot, yellow CHILI pepper.

Guinea Fowl

Also *guinea hen*. A somewhat pricey domestic fowl (*Numidia meleagris*), originally of African origin. Slate gray and nondescript, it acts—as do geese and peacocks—as a "watchdog," setting up a raucous screech when anyone approaches. Except in specialty butcher shops, guinea fowl must usually be special ordered well ahead of delivery time.

The flesh of the guinea fowl is lean and dry and as dark as that of a game bird. If roasted, the bird is best barded with bacon or suet, or spitted and cooked over a grill using some sort of sauce for basting; guinea fowl can also be braised.

Guinea Pig

A rodent (*Cavia cobaya*) native to South America where they were bred originally for food and where they may still be eaten. They were quite popular in the British Isles at one time but now are used as laboratory animals or pets.

Guinness

A proprietary STOUT originally brewed in Ireland but now licensed elsewhere as well.

Gull

Any of a family of aquatic birds (Laridae) with a strong taste of fish which helps keep people from eating them. In the British Isles, gulls' eggs are highly thought of, but do not seem to have much attraction elsewhere.

Gum Arabic

A substance used as a gelling agent, especially in confections. It is exuded by various species of acacia, including *Acacia arabica* and *Acacia senegal*.

Gumbo

1. See OKRA.

2. A stew of Cajun origin containing OKRA or flavored with FILÉ powder. Gumbos can contain fish, shellfish, meat, fowl, vegetables, or combinations seemingly of all of these, although one tradition seems to exclude beef. One account describes a gumbo as starting with a roux of flour and lard that is cooked infinitely slowly (at least an hour) until it turns a rich, dark brown but never black. To this is added whatever you've acquired—fish, game, poultry, meat, maybe some oysters or a sausage or two, some vegetables, and ultimately the okra or filé powder to thicken it. (There is also a vegetarian version, *gumbo z'herbes* or *green gumbo*.) Perhaps it's fair to define gumbo as any thick, dark, delicious stew from Louisiana that includes among its ingredients either okra or filé powder or both.

Gum Tragacanth

A substance used as a gelling agent. The gum seeps naturally from a Middle Eastern plant (*Astragalus gummifer*) and is collected and dried into a powder that will swell when water is added to form a gooey gelatinous mass.

Gurnard

A family (Triglidae) of odd-looking food fishes of northern European and Mediterranean waters. In North America, it is known as SEA ROBIN.

Habanero

An extremely hot CHILI pepper that looks much like a bell pepper. It comes in green, purple, and red. It is used in the cooking of the Caribbean, Central and South America, and West Africa.

Hackberry

Also called *sugarberry*. A tree (*Celtis occidentalis*) prevalent from southern Canada southward. It provides a cherrylike fruit that, particularly after a hard frost, has a sweet, datelike taste.

Haddock

A fish of the COD family.

Haggis

A Scottish sausage consisting of a sheep's stomach (or sheep's tripe) stuffed with the chopped heart, liver, and lungs of the animal as well as some suet, oatmeal, and onions. This is then seasoned and sewed up and simmered for hours.

Hake

A fish of the COD family.

Halibut

A large and culinarily important FLATFISH.

Halvah

A sweet, flaky baked dessert of Balkan or Near Eastern origin consisting of crushed almonds or sesame seeds that are mixed up with honey or other sweet syrup. Other ingredients may be added according to the whim of the maker.

Ham

A cured and smoked upper part of the hind leg of a pig; in practice, the word has been extended to cover various other parts of the animal, including the foreshoulder (picnic ham) or, indeed, any part that has been cured and smoked. Conversely, a fresh leg of pork is sometimes referred to as "fresh ham."

Hams are available with or without the skin, bone in or partially boned or bone out, ready to eat or in need of some or a lot of cooking, and even smoked but not cured. Most commercial ham has had water added (up to 10% of the weight of the fresh meat) and will say so on the label. Originally, the curing and smoking process dried out a ham and water was added to make it juicier. This tradition continues because meatpackers like the idea of selling you a juicier (and heavier) ham.

The taste of the ham is established by the way it is cured, which in turn is generally named for the place where that style of curing originated. Some of the types of ham include:

Bayonne (*jambon de Bayonne*). A ham cured in a village outside Bayonne in southwest France. It is usually sliced very thin and served raw as an hors d'oeuvre but is sometimes added to dishes to be cooked. *Larousse Gastronomique* warns that it should not be boiled.

Butt or Boston butt. The upper shoulder, usually boneless.

Country-style. A usually dry-cured (salt but not brine), wood-smoked ham aged for as little as six months or as long as a year and a half. Mass-produced country-style hams are made somewhat differently and are available pretty much anywhere, but the old-fashioned kind does not meet federal meatpacking standards and can only be sold where it is made. A country-style ham may be covered with a layer of green mold that is as much a badge of authenticity as anything else. It does no harm and scrapes off easily enough. Because of the amount of salt used in the cure, such hams must be soaked for a day or more and blanched in boiling water before the serious cooking begins. The usual treatment for such hams is to skin them and boil or bake and often glaze them. They usually will come with pretty explicit instructions.

Danish. Imported, canned hams that are cured in the same way as bacon and are best prepared according to the instructions on the can.

Paris (*jambon de Paris*). A lightly smoked (or unsmoked) French ham more in the American style than is usually true of French hams. It is cooked before eating.

Parma. Prosciutto (see below).

Picnic. The foreshoulder.

Prague. Traditionally smoked over beechwood; must be cooked before eating.

Prosciutto. Dry-cured and air-dried Italian ham. It is sliced thin and eaten raw or added to dishes to be cooked. Most prosciutto sold in the United States is domestic and has the advantage of being boneless and easy to slice, but it isn't as good as the original.

Ready-to-eat. An American ham that is cured very lightly and with water added. Although it is edible as is, taking the skin off and roasting it for 10 or 15 minutes to the pound in a 450°F oven usually renders it more presentable. It may be glazed before roasting or not, depending upon your preference.

Smithfield. A mass-produced country-style ham from Smithfield, Virginia. The
   commercial version of country-style ham. It comes with explicit and excellent instructions.
Westphalian. A German ham that is said to be cured with the smoke of juniper
   bushes; it is sliced thin and eaten raw.
York. An English style of lightly cured ham.

A widespread way of cooking a cured and smoked ham is to soak it overnight
(longer if it is a country-style, heavily salted ham) then cover it with fresh water
and simmer it gently—never allowing it to come to a full boil—for 25 to 30 minutes
per pound. Remove from the water and skin the ham, taking off all the excess fat
as you do so. It can now be served warm. If it is to be served cold, restore it to its
bath and let it cool. If the ham is to be roasted, simmer it for 20 minutes per pound
before skinning it, then glaze it and roast in a 400°F oven for 45 minutes or so, basting from time to time.

Ham lovers don't have to spring for the huge whole joint to indulge their
taste. Slices of ham are also sold—country-style as well as regular—and can be
fried (and served with RED EYE GRAVY) or broiled. Recipes for ham also include
croquettes and mousse and salads and soufflés and many other ways of dealing
pleasurably with it.

Hamantaschen

A Jewish, three-cornered pastry replete with honey, nuts, poppy seeds, and raisins—
or alternatively apricot or, more likely, prune butter. It symbolizes the hat of Haman,
the enemy of the Jews, who got his just deserts on the gallows in the biblical book
of Esther. Hamantaschen is a feature of the feast of Purim, which celebrates the victory of Esther over the genocidal Haman.

Hamburger

There are about as many theories on cooking hamburgers as there are people who
cook them, but forming chopped beef into a patty and frying it in butter or other
fat (or broiling it) is the base of it. Hamburgers can be served on buns or not, with
or without onion, with the addition of chopped chervil or chives mixed in, or
topped with cheese or bacon or both—the sky's the limit.

Hamburger—or any chopped meat for that matter—can be used as the basis
for any number of dishes from meatloaf to MOUSSAKA to a beefy version of SHEP-
HERD'S PIE (usually referred to as COTTAGE PIE).

Hamburg Parsley

A variety of PARSLEY with an edible root.

Hand Cheese

A Pennsylvania-Dutch sour cow's-milk CHEESE made with skimmed milk and originally shaped by hand. It is hearty and strong and sometimes flavored with caraway seeds.

Hang

To age meat by letting it hang in a cool, controlled environment until it becomes tender and succulent. Custom butchers routinely hang their meat until they consider it ready for sale. As it loses bulk during the aging process, aged meat is commensurately more expensive. Freezing seems to have much the same effect as hanging. Kosher meat is not hung, as Jewish dietary laws prescribe that it be eaten too soon after butchering.

Hangtown Fry

Several legends surround this dish, but all revolve around Placerville, a city near Sacramento. During the Gold Rush the community was known as Hangtown. It was either some desperado's last supper or the answer to a newly rich miner's request for the most expensive dinner in town. It consists of oysters and eggs cooked together (sometimes with butter and cream) into some sort of pancake.

Hard Sauce

A heavy and highly caloric sauce traditionally served with the Christmas plum pudding. It is typically made by thoroughly beating one part butter and two parts fine sugar with brandy, rum, or lemon juice, and then chilling it until it is indeed hard. The British call it *brandy butter* or *rum butter*. Many who enjoy plum pudding for their Christmas feast replace the hard sauce these days with vanilla ice cream.

Hardtack

A seaman's name for ship's biscuits, represented today by PILOT CRACKERS and by the thin, crisp flat breads from Scandinavia.

Hare

An animal of the genus *Lepus* similar to the RABBIT and treated the same way in the kitchen, although some authorities consider it at its best very fresh, very young, and spit-roasted.

Haricot

A French word for BEAN.

Harira

An extraordinarily hearty Moroccan stew combining meat (beef, lamb, mutton) with root vegetables, legumes, and spices. It is served during the holy month of Ramadan. During that month, Muslims are enjoined from eating during daylight hours and are certainly ready for something robust when night falls.

Harissa

An all-but-incandescently hot Tunisian CHILI pepper sauce used to flavor COUSCOUS. It can be made by pureeing soaked red chili peppers with garlic, salt, and a few caraway seeds and other spices and preserving it all in a little olive oil. It can also be found in some Middle Eastern markets and health food stores.

Harrar

A first-rate Ethiopian COFFEE available mostly in Japan, and rarely in North America.

Hartshorn

A primitive baking powder and smelling salt that apparently was originally made from stags' horns. It is now available (mostly in pharmacies) as a carbonate of ammonia.

Hasenpfeffer

A German dish whereby a rabbit is jointed and marinated (completely covered) in equal parts of water and vinegar (enriched with onion and carrot and bay leaf) for two days, after which it is first browned and then simmered. Sour cream is added toward the end and the dish is served on toast.

Hash

To chop up small, as you would in making the dish also known as hash, which consists of leftovers usually augmented with potatoes and onions and sometimes other ingredients. Meat, fish, and poultry often profit from being cut to the size of regular gaming dice when being prepared for hash.

Hasty Pudding

An ancient and quickly made dessert consisting of flour (cornmeal in North America, wheat flour in Britain) with butter, milk, spices (bay leaf, mace, nutmeg), and some form of sweetening such as honey or molasses. It is dotted with butter, covered with cinnamon, and popped under the broiler until brown.

Haunch

A hindquarter of an animal, usually—in this context—venison.

Havarti

A pale, mild, semisoft skimmed cow's-milk Danish CHEESE with a great many tiny holes. Aging gives it some tang.

Haw

    1. Red haw, the fruit of the HAWTHORN.

    2. *Black haw* or *stagbush* (*Viburnum prunifolia*). A tree or shrub found from New England westward to Kansas and south to the Gulf of Mexico giving small, blackish fruit in a flat-topped cluster, usually eaten right off the tree.

Hawthorn

A flowering shrub (*Crateagus* spp.) found in both the Old and New Worlds, which bears small, red berries capable of being made into jelly.

Haybox

An early form of slow cooker. It typically consisted of two boxes, one of which nested inside the other. The dish to be cooked was brought to a boil in a closed iron pot and placed in the smaller box with hay stuffed all around it. This box was placed in the larger one, again with hay stuffed all around it, and closed. The whole thing was then covered with a blanket or an old piece of oilcloth or whatever and left until the food was considered done.

Hazelnut

The hazelnut (*Corylus americana* and *Corylus cornuta*) and its relatives, including the European filbert (*Corylus maxima*) and the English cobnut (*Corylus avellana*), are all members of the same family and have the same uses, differing mostly in place of origin and in size and shape. They are of much greater culinary importance in Europe than North America.

The nuts become ripe in late August (around August 22, the Feast of Saint Philibert, for whom the filbert is named) and are available whole or dried. Whole hazelnuts (they look a little like acorns) can be put out with an assortment of nuts for between-meal or after-dinner munching. They are far better, however, roasted for use in cooking. Hazelnut butter is a fine—if extravagant—replacement for peanut butter and will occur whether you want it or not if you grind hazelnuts too cavalierly. To avoid this, either toast them slightly first to give them a little crispness or put them in a bag and run a rolling pin over them. A food processor or blender will do the trick—especially a food processor—but again take care you don't inadvertently achieve nut butter. Hazelnuts go particularly well in rich Viennese-style pastries and also blend happily with chocolate. Hazelnuts can also be grated for dusting over fish dishes. You may also run across hazelnut oil, but use it sparingly—it is not only expensive, but also strong.

Hazelnuts are hardly cheap (they are generally available mostly in specialty stores), but unshelled they keep practically forever. Shelled and roasted hazelnuts should be kept refrigerated in some form of airtight container.

Head

The whole head of an animal has been served in bygone times, such as the boar's head that enlivened many a British Christmas dinner some centuries ago until wild boars became extinct in the British Isles. Lamb and mutton are still served entire at Balkan and Middle Eastern feasts, and those who partake of them often consider the meat from the head as among the choicest parts. Fish heads are often prized as a base for a fish stock, but only if the gills have been removed; otherwise they impart a bitter taste.

Head Cheese
See BRAWN.

Heart
Because the heart is essentially a muscle (there are some blood vessels that you will want to remove if the butcher has not done so already), it can be tough and is thus best braised, especially with root vegetables such as carrots, onions, and turnips. Veal heart is what is most frequently seen. Heart meat does not profit from sitting around aging—get it fresh and use it fast. (It will, however, freeze well.)

Hearts of Palm
See PALMETTO.

Hedgehog
A small, spiny European mammal (*Erinaceus* spp.) said to taste like young pork and amenable to recipes for pork.

Herbs
Various plants, the shoots, leaves, seeds, or roots of which are used as flavorings. They fall into three often overlapping categories: *potherbs*, or plants that are cooked and used primarily as vegetables, such as beets, dandelion greens, kale, or spinach; *salad herbs*, or plants that are used uncooked, such as arugula or chicory; and *sweet herbs*, or plants that are used to impart their flavor or fragrance to a dish as it cooks, such as basil or thyme. Herbs may be fresh or dried (the latter are more powerful); they may be used as a marinade or added anywhere during the cooking time from the very beginning to near the end; and they may be used alone or in combination with others. They are discussed in this volume under their separate headings.

Herkimer
An American white, crumbly, Cheddar-style, cow's-milk CHEESE with a sharp flavor, from Herkimer County, New York.

Hermit
A spicy, chewy New England cookie, much like a BROWNIE, with a goodly amount of chopped fruits and nuts in it. Its keeping qualities are such that seafarers in the sailing-ship era were said to stow hermits away for munching at odd moments during their voyage—which could last for months or, if whaling, years.

Hermitage
A vineyard producing dry red and white table wines from France's Rhône Valley, near the towns of Tain l'Hermitage and, to a lesser extent, Crozes l'Hermitage

(it being a time-honored French practice to tack on to the town's name that of its most prestigious vineyard).

Hermit Crab
A curious sort of shell-less crustacean (families Paguridae and Parapaguridae) that inhabits the shells abandoned by "real" shellfish. Hermit crabs are edible (apparently you cook them as you would shrimp) but don't seem to whip up much gastronomic excitement.

Hero
Also *grinder* or *submarine sandwich*. A sandwich—meats and cheeses of various sorts with lettuce and tomatoes and mayonnaise or oil and vinegar—wrapped up in a long loaf of Italian bread.

Herring
An abundant family of important saltwater and anadromous fish more often found smoked or canned than fresh. In its largesse, it provides us with the following:

Alewife (*Alosa pseudoharengus*). A small, shadlike herring that comes up into the streams and rivers of North America as far south as the Carolinas each year about April, or following the smelt run. Alewives can be prepared in the same way as Atlantic herring, but don't count on their being so flavorful.

Atlantic herring (*Clupea harengus*). Perhaps the leading member of this finny tribe, the Atlantic herring can be found from the waters off Russia or northern Canada to the mouth of the Mediterranean where they are pursued by bass, bluefish, cod, mackerel, shark, tuna—and fishermen. Ashore, these fish are mostly found canned as sardines (see below) or salted or pickled and may be put up in sour cream or wine sauce. *Bloaters* are fresh-cured English herring; *kippers* are fat, cold-smoked herring from Scotland; *maatjes* are fat, young herring from Denmark; *rollmops* are fresh fillets of herring rolled around gherkin, onion, and pepper, skewered with a toothpick, and placed in a jar with spices and vinegar; *schmaltz* are fat, mature herring from Germany. *Bismarck herring* are pickled in white wine and vinegar and flavored with carrot and onion as well as salt and pepper.

Blueback herring (*Alosa aestivalis*). A species almost identical to the alewife.

Menhaden (*Brevoortia tyrannus*). Also called *bunker*, from the New Amsterdam term "mossbunker," or shad. An oily fish, it is most probably what Squanto used to enrich the hillocks in which he taught the Pilgrims to plant corn. It is still largely used for fertilizer today although some schools may end up in nets in Down-East Maine and get canned as sardines. According to the fish and cookery expert Alan Davidson, menhaden have been prized off Cape Hatteras for their roe, which reaches its peak just as their migrations take them into those waters. In New England in summer, they are often driven into shallow bays where they consume all the oxygen, die in droves, and cause an unholy stench.

Pacific herring (*Clupea pallasii*). The Pacific subspecies of the Atlantic herring with a range on both sides of the ocean from northwestern Alaska to Baja California on the one side and Russia to the Yellow Sea on the other.

Pacific sardine (*Sardinops sagax*). A member of the herring family found throughout the Pacific in varying numbers, some of which end up in the canning factories.

Pilchard (*Sardina pilchardus*). The grown version of the European—but not North American—sardine. In Spain and Portugal pilchards are grilled and, as is true of any grilled fish, they taste better when done over glowing coals.

Sardine. In European waters, the young of the pilchard (see above); in eastern North America, any member of the herring family unfortunate enough to fetch up in a sardine fisherman's net; and in the west, a Pacific sardine (see above). Most sardines in North America show up in cans, but if you come across a mess of sardines or fresh herring being sold as sardines, you might try grilling them, seasoning them, perhaps, with a little fennel, and flaming them with warm brandy just before serving.

Shad. To many, the unchallenged champion of the herring family is the American shad (*Alosa sapidissima*), acclaimed both for its flesh and its roe. It is native to eastern North America, but was introduced with great success to the West in the late 1800s. Shad spawn in vast numbers in tidal rivers and streams. Their season is a short one—in the Connecticut River it is figured at mid-April to late May—and the delicacy of their flesh is only marred by the multiplicity of their bones. Boned shad is plentiful (in season) but whole shad is also available for those who enjoy wrapping the fish tightly in foil and baking it for 2–5 hours in a very slow (250°F) oven, during which time the bones disintegrate and become edible. Too little cooking by this method results in too-evident bones; too much in a dried-out fish. But whoever said there were no risks in the search for perfection? There are other species of shad highly favored elsewhere along the Atlantic and Mediterranean and their bywaters.

Sprat (*Sprattus sprattus*). A small European herring found from Scandinavia to the Mediterranean. Small ones are often canned and marketed as Brisling sardines.

Whitebait. A small fish that is fried and eaten whole, innards and all. Whitebaits are traditionally small herring of various sorts but in North America can include massive infusions of SILVERSIDES (also called *shiners*) or sand eels, neither of which are herring at all.

Hervé

A Belgian soft, cow's-milk CHEESE made variously from whole and partly skim milk, often flavored with herbs. It bears a resemblance to LIMBURGER.

Hibachi

A Japanese charcoal grill. Because they tend to be quite small, hibachis are favored by apartment dwellers with fireplaces.

Hickory

A group of American trees (of the genus *Carya*) with edible nuts, the most notable of which is the PECAN. Hickory nuts are highly favored in baking. Hickory wood is of considerable importance in barbecuing and smoking foods.

Hickory Salt

Also *hickory-smoked salt*. Includes salt that has been smoked over hickory coals as well as salt or monosodium glutamate mixed with hickory ashes or the equivalent in artificial flavoring.

Highball

A tall drink usually of whiskey poured over ice with water or soda.

Hippocras

A medieval beverage of red wine heavily sweetened, spiced (one source calls for sugar and cinnamon to predominate), and served hot.

Hips

See ROSE HIPS.

Hochepot

A fatty, thick Belgian or French soup or stew like a POT-AU-FEU, but made with several different kinds of meat (beef, lamb or mutton, pork, and especially some form of bacon or salt pork) and vegetables. The broth is generally served separately from the solids.

Hock

1. Any white wine from the Rhine Valley of Germany.
2. An ankle or shank of a domestic animal, especially the pig.

Hoecake

A Virginia version of JOHNNYCAKE, a cornmeal cake originally baked on the blade of a hoe.

Hog

A domestic PIG.

Hog Dress

1. In game parlance, an animal that has been bled and gutted but not usually skinned or had the head and feet removed.

2. To remove the head, tail, and entrails of a fish and flatten it somewhat as a part of its preparation for smoking.

Hogfish

Also known as *hog snapper* (not to be confused with the hogchoker, which is a FLAT-FISH). A brown-to-crimson fish (*Lachnolaimus maximus*) ranging from North Carolina to the Caribbean. Although said to be better than average culinary fare, it is also said to be occasionally toxic—depending, it would seem, on what it has been eating. It is generally cut into steaks for baking or broiling or—if small enough—panfrying.

Hogget

A British term for a YEARLING LAMB.

Hogplum

A small, oval fruit (*Prunus umbellata*) native to Florida and South Carolina with soft, tart flesh. If you should find it, use it up right away either as is or in a mixture of other fruits. Or put it in jams and jellies.

Hoisin Sauce

A Chinese sauce and condiment made of soy beans, chili, garlic, and spices. It is used to marinate and cook duck, shellfish, and spareribs, for example, and is served at the table with a number of dishes. It is sold in cans and jars and once opened keeps seemingly forever in the refrigerator.

Hollandaise Sauce

A classic French sauce consisting of melted butter mixed with beaten egg yolks and flavored with lemon juice and salt and pepper. Usually, a small amount of the butter is melted, the egg yolks gently added, and the remainder of the butter slowly beaten in before the flavorings are added. Because all this is a delicate operation, it is generally accomplished in a double boiler over not-quite-boiling water.

Holland Pepper

A cone-shaped PEPPER that can be black, orange, purple, or yellow and serves as an expensive stand-in for regular bell pepper. Such peppers are grown hydroponically in Holland, which accounts for their elevated price tag.

Hollands

A strong, assertively flavored, Dutch GIN that is drunk straight or over ice rather than compounded in a mixed drink.

Home Fries
Peeled and sliced potatoes fried usually with sliced or chopped onion.

Hominy
Whole, hulled corn treated with lye (soaking it in water with wood ashes is traditional) to rid it of its bran and germ (which are discarded) and ground. The remainder is called samp and can be further ground into hominy grits.

Homogenize
A term applied primarily to milk (but also to other commodities such as some salad dressings). It is a process by which the fat globules in milk are broken up and redistributed evenly throughout instead of rising to the top in the form of cream.

Honey
The earliest sweetener except in North America, where the European honey bee was not introduced until the 1600s. (Before the European explorations, honey-giving bees in the Americas were strictly tropical and produced a sometimes hazardous honey. For most Native Americans, the early sweeteners were fruits and berries and maple syrup.)

Honey has been cherished for millennia (the Old Testament promise of plenty was "milk and honey") and has had a number of uses in addition to being a table sweetener. The confections of the Near East—such as BAKLAVA and HALVAH—as well as the *pain d'épice* of France owe their sweetness to honey. Fermented honey—or mead—was prized in northern Europe (wine was preferred in the south, as it still is) until the advent of cane sugar. And honey is still a highly prized sweetener today, even if mead is no longer much found.

The flavor (and color) of any honey depends upon the flowers from which the bees are collecting the nectar they use in making that honey. (The honey collected in Classical times from Mount Hymettus, near Athens, was said to gain its legendary flavor from the wild thyme on which the bees grazed.) Among today's examples, buckwheat honey is dark colored and full of flavor as opposed to blueberry honey, which is light in color and delicate in taste. Much honey sold in regular markets is either a blend or is clover honey (stemming from a variety of alfalfa rather than that clover that occasionally exhibits four leaves). Both are light colored and quite unobtrusively sweet. But special honeys are available in specialty stores and from apiaries.

Honey is sold either in the comb or extracted. Comb honey is increasingly rare as it is tricky to handle, difficult to ship, and dismays many consumers by the unfamiliar but perfectly edible waxy pieces of comb that are part of it. (It has also been suggested that it is more difficult for processors to gussy up with additives and stretchers and other "improvements.") Extracted honey is what we normally see in bottles or those handy squeeze jars on our supermarket shelves.

The extracted honey we buy is usually in liquid form, put up in airtight bottles right after it has been centrifuged, strained, or otherwise separated from the comb and stabilized. Honey can also be found in granulated or crystallized form or as something in between. Comb honey is generally sold in little boxlike squares. Check it to see that all the cells are capped and contain honey rather than pollen or emptiness, that the cappings are all dry and unstained, and that the honey is of a consistent color.

Honey can be pesky in the kitchen, especially in baking. It has the quality of picking up moisture, which means that in humid weather a frosting may end up overly moist even though the same amount of honey works perfectly well in a spell of dry weather. This property may not bother you in some other circumstances, however, and may well be an advantage in making some kinds of bread or fruitcake. Honey is a runny substance, but just how runny will depend on the temperature. Cold weather—and age—will cause it to crystallize and turn milky. This is no cause for alarm. Simply warm it up—but keep the temperature moderate. Put the whole container in a pot of water at about 140°F until the honey is clear. Anything higher than that can cause the honey to deteriorate. Or microwave it at full power for half a minute or so. And don't be concerned if the honey starts to granulate again when it cools off. Let it be until you need it and then warm it up again. When measuring honey, try coating your measuring spoon with vegetable oil (the honey will glide right over it instead of sticking to the spoon, thus allowing you an accurate measure).

Honeybell
Also *Mineola tangelo*. A sweet, red-fleshed, bell-shaped orangelike fruit available during the winter months.

Honeydew
A variety of MELON.

Honey Mushroom
An edible wild MUSHROOM that takes its name from its color rather than its taste.

Hoppin' John
A dish of black-eyed peas and rice usually with a little slab bacon or salt pork. It is native to the Deep South, where it is traditionally eaten on New Year's Day.

Hops
A plant (*Humulus lupulus*) of Europe and Asia but which has been introduced into North America; its fruit is a major ingredient in making beer. Hops also put out tender sprouts each spring that are gathered and prepared like asparagus, often under their French name, *jets de houblon*. You are unlikely to find them in most markets, but if you do, dash right home with them and use them at the next feasible meal cooked as you would cook asparagus.

Horehound

A plant (*Marrubium vulgare*) of the mint family. It is used to flavor candies, cough drops, and cordials, and it has also been used for making a country wine.

Hors d'Oeuvre

Any of the various foods we use as a preface to a meal. Hors d'oeuvres may consist of small sandwiches, CRUDITÉS, stuffed eggs, or any other small delicacy aimed at whetting the appetite.

Horse

An animal (*Equus caballus*) only intermittently used as food. This may be in part because horses are not raised for that purpose and tend to be tough and in part for sentimental reasons. Horsemeat is in many respects similar to beef, but somewhat sweeter.

Horse Chestnut

See BUCKEYE.

Horse Mackerel

A fish of the TUNA family. The term is applied to the *bluefin* (or *giant*) *tuna*.

Horseradish

A European perennial plant (*Armoracia lapathifolia*) naturalized in the northeastern United States and southern Canada. Its roots provide a lively and peppery condiment. Most horseradish is sold grated and preserved in vinegar to accompany cold meats such as pot roasts or tongue as well as seafood dishes such as shellfish cocktails and GEFILTE FISH. Or it is used to transform regular mustard into CREOLE MUSTARD. Fresh horseradish is also available, and if you grate it yourself, you may wish to mix it with lemon juice instead of vinegar. If you buy it fresh, you'll be wise to wrap it in plastic and refrigerate until ready to use it, then peel it. It is not recommended that you cook horseradish, as doing so takes all the taste away. Regular bottled horseradish is neutral in color, but it is also found colored red with beet juice.

Hot Cherry

A round, somewhat hottish CHILI used mostly for pickling.

Hot Cross Bun

A sweet, yeast-risen bun containing currants and decorated with a sugar-syrup in the shape of a cross. It is traditional breakfast fare for Good Friday.

Hot Dog

See FRANKFURTER.

Hot Pepper Oil

Oil—olive, soy, or other vegetable oil—flavored with CHILI peppers and used in Chinese (especially Hunan and Szechuan) and Italian cookery.

Hot Pot

Also known as *hotch-potch* or even *hodgepodge*. An English version of IRISH STEW.

Hot Red Pepper

A name applied to what was once pretty universally called CAYENNE pepper.

Hot Sauce

See CHILI OIL.

Houx

A very rare Alsatian spirit made by distilling holly berries and sugar. Its rarity is only matched by its cost.

Hubbard

A variety of winter SQUASH.

Huckleberry

A genus of wild berry (*Gaylussacia*) similar to the BLUEBERRY with which it is virtually interchangeable and to which the name is often applied. The botanical huckleberry can be identified by its ten prominent seeds. (The blueberry has many more seeds, but they are so unobtrusive you would be hard put to know they are there.) The *common* or *black huckleberry* (*Gaylussacia baccata*) is also slightly more acidic than the blueberry.

Hull

To remove the outer covering of something, as the green stem part of strawberries, the shells of nuts, or the outer leaves and silk of corn.

Humble Pie

Originally the *umbles* or innards of a deer. As the gentry reserved the choicer cuts of venison for themselves, they bestowed the heart, liver, and other entrails to the help, who frequently prepared them as a pie. The help may have gotten the last laugh, as usual, giving the gentry the concept that developed into the British staple, beef and kidney pie.

Hummus

An Arabic word for CHICKPEA. It is usually seen in North America as a puree of chickpeas and garlic with mint or parsley, a little lemon juice, and perhaps some olive oil. Add a little sesame paste or oil (TAHINI) and it becomes known on its home grounds as *hummus bi tahini*.

Hungarian Peppers

There are two of them: *Hungarian red*, used mostly for PAPRIKA, and *Hungarian sweet*, a long, waxy, mild, sweet yellow PEPPER.

Hush Puppy

A Southern specialty of cornmeal mixed with butter, eggs, and milk and perhaps some chopped onion and deep fried. The name is said to derive from the practice of slipping an occasional one to the dogs to keep them quiet during mealtime.

Husk Tomato

See GROUND-CHERRY.

Hyacinth Bean

An Indian BEAN eaten dried or fresh.

Hydrogenated Fat

A fat (vegetable oils, particularly) that has been treated with hydrogen to transform it from a liquid to a semisolid. It makes a more spreadable product and improves keeping qualities. Margarine is a good example.

Hydromel

In classical Greece and Rome, a beverage of honey diluted with water. The word also referred to honey fermented into MEAD.

Hyssop

A member of the mint family (*Hyssopus officinalis*) with pungent, slightly bitter leaves formerly used in salads and as a condiment. It is now grown mostly as an ornamental and for its oil, which is extracted and used in making liqueurs. It is also the source of a superior honey.

Ibex

A European mountain goat (*Capra* spp.), now exceedingly rare, but once hunted fairly routinely for its meat. Also a wild goat of Asia Minor (*Capra aegragus*) considered the ancestor of the contemporary domestic goat.

Ice

1. Frozen water.
2. A dessert that can be defined as ice cream without the cream. Ices are generally made of water or fruit juice sometimes fortified with sugar or egg whites or the fruit itself and frozen. If the mixture is stirred several times during the freezing, unwanted ice crystals are less likely to form in it.
3. To chill something.
4. To apply ICING to something.

Iceberg Lettuce

A widespread market LETTUCE.

Ice Cream

Ice cream is essentially an amalgam of milk (or cream or a combination of both), sugar, flavoring, and salt (and sometimes eggs) mixed together as it freezes to form a uniform consistency that is firm and free of annoying icy crystals. Commercial ice cream, of course, has stabilizers and other extraneous matter added, including air (a certain amount of which is necessary but which in excess can increase the bulk, decrease the price, and do nothing in particular to help the quality).

Credit for the invention of ice cream is often given to the Florentine kitchen help brought by Catherine Medici to France when she married Henri II in 1533. Maybe so, but America in the nineteenth century is where it reached its full fruition.

Among the variations on ice cream are GRANITA, SHERBET, and WATER ICE.

Icefish

Also *capelin*. A small Arctic fish (*Mallotus villosus*) somewhat resembling SMELT and often found dried.

Iceland Moss

A gray or brown lichen (*Cetraria islandica*) of the extreme north but also found as far south as Pennsylvania. It is boiled, dried, ground into powder, and used in baking or boiled with milk to make jelly, especially for invalids. Available mostly in health food stores.

Ice Milk
A dessert similar to ICE CREAM except that it contains considerably less butterfat and slightly less food solids per gallon.

Ice Plant
A showy, southern, decorative green (*Mesembryanthemum crystallinum*), with fleshy, spinachlike leaves that gleam like ice crystals in the sun. The slightly pungent leaves can be cooked like spinach or chopped into soups, but if not used almost immediately after picking they will dry out.

Icing
The sweet and decorative topping for a cake. Classically, it must be white, but in practice it applies to any topping, usually a thin one. Thicker toppings are then referred to as frosting.

Ida Red
A large red APPLE that is excellent for baking.

Iguana
A tropical American lizard (of the family Iguanidae) species which ranges from one to five feet in length. Iguanas were a staple of the pre-Columbian diet and remain popular table fare from the U.S. Southwest through South America. They are typically skinned and then roasted or charcoal broiled.

Imam Bayeldi
A Turkish eggplant dish the name for which has been translated as "the imam fainted," referring, so the story goes, to a Muslim priest (or imam) who fainted over the dish either because it was so incredibly delicious or because the amount of oil in it made it unacceptably extravagant for his parsimonious nature (or perhaps a combination of both). The dish, which is served cold, consists of eggplant stuffed with a puree of spiced onions and tomatoes. It is stewed long and slow in a covered pan with enough olive oil to come about half way up the sides of the eggplant.

Imperial Measure
A system of weights and measures originated for the British Empire. It is slightly heftier than the American system and can cause disruptions in recipes if adjustment for it is not made. It has been supplanted in its place of origin by the metric system.

Indian Corn
A term for the more vividly colored (red, blue, black or multicolored) varieties of CORN.

Indian Cress

See NASTURTIUM.

Indian Pudding

A New England dessert composed of cornmeal and molasses to which may be added milk and eggs, spices, sugar, and berries or an apple or pear. It is then baked long and slow and served hot with whipped cream or—more usually—vanilla ice cream. Indian pudding can be particularly welcome as darkness advances on a chill autumn evening.

Infuse

To place herbs or other ingredients in hot liquid in order to pass their flavor to that liquid. You are making an infusion when you brew tea.

Inkfish

See CUTTLEFISH.

Inky Cap

Any of several varieties of wild MUSHROOM.

Instant Rice

A prepared rice that cooks in minutes but does not approach regular rice in taste or texture.

Invert Sugar

A form of sugar brought about by heating sugar syrup with an acid (lemon juice, for example) or an enzyme, thereby breaking the sugar (sucrose) into two simpler sugars (glucose and fructose). Invert sugar blends more easily into breads, candies, and syrups. It is sold in liquid form.

Irish Coffee

A concoction of hot, strong coffee (and sugar for those who like their coffee that way) laced with Irish whiskey and topped with whipped cream.

Irish Mist

A LIQUEUR composed of Irish whiskey and honey; the Irish version of DRAMBUIE.

Irish Moss

Also called *carrageen* or *carrageen moss*. Two types of red algae or seaweed (*Chondrus crispus* and *Gigartina mamillosa*) found along the coasts of the North Atlantic from New England and the Maritime Provinces to England and especially Ireland. Most of what is harvested commercially goes into a gelatin used to stabilize such products as beer and ice cream or is used as a stretcher for low-caloric fast food. Some gets into kitchens (mostly through health food stores). It is soaked and then boiled in milk or water and the strained liquid used for desserts such as BLANCMANGE and for thickening seafood soups and chowders.

Irish Soda Bread
An Irish bread made with oatmeal and wheat flour and leavened through the interaction of buttermilk and baking soda. It is sometimes flavored with caraway seeds and currants.

Irish Stew
An Irish RAGOUT of lamb, onions, and potatoes.

Irish Whiskey
A smoky, dry, malt WHISKEY produced in Ireland.

Ironware
A variety of COOKWARE.

Irradiation
A method of treating food with radiation as a means of killing microorganisms or insects as well as promoting shelf life. The foods so treated include pork (to kill the trichina parasites responsible for trichinosis), various fruits and vegetables including potatoes (to stop sprouting), and wheat and flour and spices (for insect control). The irradiation of milk is also under discussion. These foods do not themselves become radioactive in any way, but changes in their chemical structure may not be entirely beneficial.

Isinglass
A gelling agent extracted from the swim bladder of the sturgeon. Other agents have taken its place.

Italian Sausage
A coarse pork sausage that comes in two varieties, sweet and hot, the hot having had hot pepper added to it. It is also often flavored with garlic and fennel and is first-rate fresh off the barbecue grill.

J

Jack

1. A California cheese also called MONTEREY JACK.

2. A family of tropical and subtropical marine fishes (Carangidae) including amberjacks, jacks, pompanos, and scads. Some of the important fish of this family are:

Amberjack (*Seriola dumerili*). Also called *greater amberjack*. A game and food fish of the warmer sections of the Atlantic.

Bar jack (*Caranx ruber*). An Atlantic fish esteemed in the Caribbean. It is frequently found smoked.

California yellowtail (*Seriola dorsalis*). Also called *yellowtail*, as are so many similarly colored fish. Found along the Californian and Mexican coasts, it can be found smoked or canned as well as fresh and is good broiled or baked with herbs and white wine. Skin it before you cook it and take off any dark-colored meat.

Florida pompano (*Trachinotus carolinus*). A premier food fish of the South, it is found from South Carolina to Brazil and in the Gulf of Mexico. It is most frequently baked or broiled.

Jack mackerel (*Trachurus symmetricus*). A jack of the Pacific from Baja California to Alaska. Much of it is canned, although it can also be cooked as you would cook MACKEREL.

Palometa (*Trachinotus goodei*). An Atlantic game species favored as a panfish.

Paloma pompano (*Trachinotus paitensis*). The Pacific pompano found from California to central South America. It is similar to its Atlantic relative both as a fish and as food.

Scad (*Trachurus trachurus*). Although not a first-rate food fish, it can be baked, fried, or cooked over coals.

Jackfruit

A fruit of a tropical tree (*Artocarpus heterophyllus*) related, but inferior, to the BREADFRUIT.

Jackrabbit

Any of various hares (*Lepus* spp.) of the American Southwest with long ears (they were originally called "jackass rabbits"). They can be cooked like RABBIT, but tend to be tough unless very young.

Jaffa
A superior, sometimes expensive ORANGE from Israel.

Jalapeño
About the hottest of the Tex-Mex CHILI peppers, jalapeños range from dark green to greenish-black. They are used not only to give savor to Tex-Mex dishes but have been used to flavor everything from Cheddar-cheese spread to ice cream as well as preserves.

Jalousie
A small, flaky, French pastry filled with almond cream and topped with jam.

Jam
A thick fruit or berry spread made from pieces of fruit, sugar, and pectin.

Jamaica Plum
A small reddish or brownish tropical fruit (*Spondias purpurea*) resembling a plum-sized mango. It has a sweet, slightly sharp taste and can be used in fruit salads or compotes. Don't plan on keeping it around more than a day or so.

Jambalaya
The American food expert James Beard seemed to feel that the name for this Cajun or Creole stew derived from the French word *jambon,* "ham." Certainly an authentic jambalaya (if there is such a thing) would seem to have ham or some other form of cured pork along with the Tabasco sauce, rice, chicken, vegetables, and perhaps shrimp that are its other mainstays.

Jambo
Also *jambos, jambu,* and *rose apple.* A semitropical, ornamental shrub or tree (primarily *Eugenia jambos,* although there are similar relatives) with a sweet, pear-shaped fruit that can be eaten right off the tree (or shrub) or made into preserves. If you find any commercially, you have every right to be mildly astonished.

Jansson's Temptation
A casserole of layers of anchovies, onion, and potato cooked in butter and cream for which its namesake, a religious zealot, is said to have forsworn his vows of austerity and pigged out. It is something of a Scandinavian, fishy equivalent of a NANTUCKET FIREMAN'S SUPPER.

Japanese Artichoke
See CHINESE ARTICHOKE.

Japanese Horseradish
See WASABI.

Japanese Medlar
See LOQUAT.

Jarlsberg
Norway's answer to the Swiss cheeses, EMMENTHALER and GRUYÈRE.

Java
A source of COFFEE; also a popular nickname for it.

Jelly
    1. Meat or fish or poultry stock that congeals—or hardens—as it cools into a colorless, gelatinous substance; ASPIC.

    2. A clear spread made from the juice of various fruits and sugar either by the action of the naturally occurring fruit substance PECTIN or by the use of additional pectin.

Jelly Bean
A small, chewy candy that comes in any number of colors and flavors. Jelly beans were the favorite snack of former President Ronald Reagan.

Jellyfish
Not in any sense of the word a fish, jellyfish are free-swimming, gelatinous invertebrates and only resemble fish in that they both live in water. Jellyfish vary in size from pinheads to six to seven feet in diameter and are 99 percent water. The Chinese have a way of drying a variety of jellyfish (*Rhopilema esculenta*) and preparing it cold for summer dishes. It is slightly chewy with no particular taste. It is usually found dried and shredded and requires several hours soaking but no further cooking or it is apt to toughen. It may be added to cucumber and DAIKON, dressed with vinegar and sesame oil, and served as a salad.

Jelly Roll
In Britain, *Swiss roll*. A popular cake made by baking a special, somewhat runny batter in a jelly roll pan. The pan, much like a heavy COOKIE SHEET, has slightly higher sides in order to hold the batter poured into it. The cake is then spread with jelly while it is still hot and rolled up like a log with the jelly inside. It is sometimes then sprinkled with sugar.

Jerky
A meat—originally venison, but now mostly beef—that has been cut into strips, salted, and dried. It is used as a trail food.

Jerusalem Artichoke
A small edible tuber. Its formal name is *Helianthus tuberosus* and it's not from Jerusalem, nor is it an artichoke (although it resembles one somewhat in taste); it is

a kin of the sunflower, which is doubtless why there seems to be a move afoot to rename it SUNCHOKE. (The Jerusalem in the name has been said to be a corruption of *girasole*, Italian for sunflower, although that derivation seems to have been exploded in favor of the Dutch *Ter Neusen*, a town from which the vegetable was early on exported to England, easily switched to the more familiar "Jerusalem" just as asparagus is so often hawked as "sparrow grass.") Once the knobbed root is peeled, it is easy to prepare and can be eaten raw or cooked and served just like any root vegetable. If you wish, the root can be steamed and the skin rubbed off after cooking. Jerusalem artichokes make good soup, and you can also find noodles made of the flour milled from them. They have a tendency to dry out, and people who grow their own leave them heaped in mounds outside all winter. It would be wise not to buy them too far ahead of the time of use and to refrigerate them in a plastic bag until that time comes.

Jewfish

A type of giant sea BASS (*Epinephelus itajara*) attaining a length of eight feet and weighing up to 700 pounds. Found in the western Atlantic from Florida to Brazil, including the Gulf of Mexico and the West Indies. It is an excellent table fish at whatever size you find it.

Jew's Ear

A *cloud ear fungus* or MUSHROOM.

Jicama

A tropical root vegetable (*Pachyrhizus tuberosus*) looking a little like a sandy-colored ball with a white interior. Despite its bland flavor it is useful to replace water chestnuts, to give crispness to Chinese stir-fried dishes, or used raw in salads to add texture. The name, being of Latinate origin, is pronounced "HEE-ca-ma."

   The best jicama is thin skinned and somewhat juicy (dig your nails into it to check it). You can keep jicamas for two to three weeks in the refrigerator, but once they're cut, wrap them in plastic and use them by the end of the next day.

Jigger

A bartenders' measure classically of 1½ ounces, but doling out variously 1, 1½, or 2 liquid ounces.

Johannisberg Riesling

A wine grape (*Vitis vinifera*) so-called in California to differentiate it from other "rieslings" to which it may or may not be related. This is the grape that is responsible for the fine white wines of Germany's Rhine district and France's Alsace. It does well in California, too, but is such a light bearer that it is not overly popular with grape growers.

John Dory

A remarkably ugly but extremely tasty fish (*Zeus faber*) of the eastern Atlantic and Mediterranean with a relative (*Zenopsis conchifera*) with the same common name off North America and yet another (*Zeus capensis*) in southern waters. The fish has a large "thumbprint" on its sides which tradition says was put there by St. Peter himself, giving the fish the alternate name *St. Peter* or *St. Peter's fish*. The John Dory yields fillets that can be treated like those of a flounder or sole or used in fish stews.

Johnnycake

A Rhode Island cornmeal cake. Although authentic recipes for it differ drastically, it would seem to have been made with cornmeal, water, and salt and to have been embellished with such additions as butter and eggs and baking powder as the frontier moved westward and coastal life grew less rigorous. Its Southern counterpart is the Virginia HOECAKE.

Jonagold

A firm, juicy, red APPLE.

Jonah

A small CRAB available mostly to foragers.

Jonathan

A tart, midseason, all-round APPLE.

Jugged

A word referring to a stew generally of game with mushrooms and onions and originally cooked in earthenware or stone, using the blood of the animal in question to BIND it. Jugged hare is the most common example of it.

Jujube

    1. Also called *Chinese date*. It is an Oriental shrub, *Zizyphus jujuba*, now cultivated in California as well. It gives a yellow, datelike fruit often preserved in syrup or made into jelly or dried. Jujubes are also used in Chinese cooking. A Mediterranean variety, *Zizyphus lotus*, provides most of the jujubes seen in Europe.

    2. A small, fruit-flavored gumdrop or lozenge.

Julep

Originally a Persian sweetened drink, it is now best known as a Southern combination of mint and Bourbon whiskey mixed up with a small amount of sugar and a huge amount of crushed or cracked ice, culminating in a strong libation that is served in a frosted glass. Historically, there have been other juleps besides the mint julep, but most of them have dropped out of sight over the years.

Julienne

To cut—as carrots, celery, cooked chicken-breast meat—into matchstick-sized pieces. Ideally, these pieces would be of the same diameter and length as a thick, old-fashioned wooden kitchen match.

Juneberry

See SERVICEBERRY.

Juniper

A hardy evergreen (*Juniperus communis*), the aromatic and slightly bitter dried berries of which are used to flavor stews (especially pork and venison, although there also exist recipes for a medieval corned beef flavored with juniper) and other dishes (it goes nicely with bluefish) and in making gin.

Junket

A mixture of milk and sugar set with RENNET powder. It can take the form of a sweetened dessert, a drink, or a pudding.

Jus

A French term for pan juices, as in the phrase *au jus*, referring to meat or poultry served just with its own pan juices.

Kabob

Turkish for "broiled meat," and originally the meat would almost certainly have been mutton. *Shish kabob* is "skewered broiled meat," and we are as apt to use lamb as anything else, sometimes alternating it on the skewer with chunks of onion and green pepper, cherry tomatoes, mushrooms, or other vegetables. It is usually a better idea to skewer and grill the vegetables separately, as their cooking times and the time it takes to broil the meat are not necessarily the same.

Kaffir Corn

See SORGHUM.

Kahlúa

A Mexican coffee-flavored LIQUEUR.

Kaki

A Japanese PERSIMMON.

Kale

A curly-leafed, strong-tasting form of cabbage (*Brassica oleracea* var. *acephala*), although it does not form heads as cabbage does. Two varieties are common, one very curly with bright green to greenish-yellow leaves, the other green with a bluish tinge.

Kale is most plentiful during the winter months and was favored exactly because it was available when other greens were scarce. Buy good, robust-looking leaves and cook them soon after buying them. Kale will not reward your letting it sit around unused any more than it will reward your overcooking it. Cut away the tough parts and cut up and cook the rest in just enough boiling water to cover but for no more than about 5 minutes.

Kangaroo

About the only part of this Australian marsupial (of the family Macropodidae) that is reportedly used as food is the tail, which can be prepared in the same way as OXTAIL.

Kanten

A Japanese term for AGAR.

Kasha

A Russian name for roasted, dehulled BUCKWHEAT and for dishes made with it.

Kasseri

A Greek CHEESE made from either ewe's or goat's milk. It begins as a firm cheese, but as it matures it hardens into one that can be grated.

Kedgeree

An Anglo-Indian dish of fish in a cream sauce with curry powder that is served with rice. It has evolved into a rice-and-fish combination in which about equal parts of rice and leftover fish (some salt fish is sometimes included), some hardboiled egg, a small amount of white sauce, and perhaps some grated cheese are combined with curry powder in ways that—as with any leftover—are dictated by whatever is available. It is typically served hot.

Kelp

Essentially, it is seaweed. There are a number of different varieties of seaweed gathered in various parts of the world for culinary purposes. The Irish gather IRISH MOSS, and both the British and the Japanese gather LAVER, which the Japanese dry, process, and call KOMBU.

Kelp Bass

A Pacific Coast saltwater BASS.

Kenya AA

The top of the line of Kenyan COFFEE. It is highly regarded.

Ketchup

Another spelling for CATSUP.

Kettle

A large, lidded pot with a handle (or bail) used for boiling water (as a tea kettle) or for making soups or stews or various other dishes. Kettles were originally made of iron, which gave excellent cooking properties and was long lasting, but posed problems of weight. Iron kettles can still be found—and are still useful—but many kettles today are made of aluminum, enameled metal, or steel. Another name for it is DUTCH OVEN.

Key Lime

A small LIME from the Florida Keys. It is particularly renowned as the base of Key lime pie.

Kg

Abbreviation for KILOGRAM.

Kid

A young GOAT.

Kidney

An edible internal organ, veal kidneys and lamb kidneys being the most tender and flavorsome. (Beef and pork kidneys are sometimes available and require a preliminary soaking and blanching as well as slightly longer cooking.) Most kidneys found in today's markets are frozen, which is probably a good thing because a kidney that has been allowed to go off even slightly can be quite unappetizing.

When preparing kidney, remove any skin and cut out the white central part. If the kidney is strong (if it has an unpleasant aroma), soak it in either ACIDULATED WATER or milk for an hour or so, then slice it thin and either sauté it in a little butter or broil it fairly quickly—kidneys do not profit from being overcooked—and serve it perhaps with a mustard sauce. Kidneys are also excellent served over SPOON-BREAD or served up in a beef-and-kidney pie. The stronger kidneys can be grilled or stewed and any that might be left over can be put to excellent use chopped up in an omelet. Kidneys also benefit from being cooked in MARSALA.

A kidney cut into small cubes and added with the rest of the meat can also contribute a fine flavor to a stew, especially a game stew, in which case the kidney of the animal in question is the likely candidate.

Kidney Bean

A large, dark red, kidney-shaped BEAN.

Kielbasa

A Polish sausage, usually of pork but sometimes beef or turkey; it is garlic-flavored, often hickory-smoked, and typically sold in large links in the form of a lopsided O. Although precooked, it profits from being heated up or browned before serving.

Kilogram

A metric system unit of weight equivalent to 2.2 pounds.

Kimchee

A Korean pickled cabbage usually with exceedingly hot peppers, but everyone in Korea makes kimchee and everyone makes it individually, so it varies widely. The dish is, by government decree, a South Korean National Treasure and is available canned and sometimes in plastic bags in many North American markets.

King Crab

A large CRAB of northern Pacific waters and any of its subspecies.

Kingfish

In eastern North America, generally the king MACKEREL or *cero*, although technically the name belongs to several members of the croaker or drum family, including the northern kingfish (*Menticirrhus saxatilis*), found along the Atlantic and Gulf coasts, and the southern kingfish (*Menticirrhus americanus*), which overlaps its northerly relative and extends its range as far south as Argentina. On menus or in fish markets, these fish will usually be listed as WHITING. In the West, kingfish may refer to either of two species, the California corbina (*Menticirrhus undulatus*) and the white croaker (*Genyonemus lineatus*), both highly regarded, especially as panfish.

Kipper

Short for kippered HERRING.

Kir

A French APERITIF named for a left-wing World War II resistance hero who became known as the "red" mayor of Dijon, the Abbé Félix Kir. It traditionally consists of a Burgundian white wine made from the Aligoté grape (although any reasonably austere, dry, white wine will fill the bill nicely) augmented with just a suspicion of crème de CASSIS. Too much cassis will make it overly—even cloyingly—sweet.

Kirsch

Also *kirschwasser*. A clear, white fruit BRANDY distilled from small wild European cherries (and their pits) especially in Germany, Switzerland, and Alsace. The finest is traditionally that of Germany's Black Forest, although the French and Swiss would naturally dispute this.

Kiss

1. A cookie made from a miniature mound of MERINGUE with various flavorings.
2. A small commercial chocolate candy.

Kiwi

1. A flightless bird of New Zealand (*Apteryx* spp.) perhaps once used as food by the Maoris.
2. Also *kiwi fruit* or *Chinese gooseberry* (*Actinidia chinensis*), though most of ours come from New Zealand and, more recently, California. It is, moreover, no relation to the conventional, botanical gooseberry. You can remove the fuzzy skin and

eat it plain—like any other fruit—for its flavor of strawberries and melons and tangerines, roast it with meat or add it to fruit compotes or any such concoction of your
choosing, or bake it into a tart. Kiwis are recommended for meat dishes because,
like papayas, they contain an enzyme that breaks down protein and thus helps tenderize meat either in cooking or as a marinade. It also precludes using kiwis in jams,
as its enzymes will also keep the jam from setting.

A ripe kiwi will be slightly soft when you touch it and will keep at room temperature for 2 or 3 days.

Kloster
A soft, German, cow's-milk CHEESE somewhat resembling a mild Limburger.

Knackebrod
A hard, thin bread (more like a large cracker) baked from rye flour, dating from the
sailing-ship days when it was made as a ship's biscuit. You can still find it (mostly
imported from Sweden) in specialty stores and a few supermarkets.

Knackwurst
An alternate spelling of KNOCKWURST.

Knaidlich
A Jewish dumpling made of matzo meal and eggs and poached in chicken soup in
which it is also traditionally served. Knaidlichs can be plain or stuffed.

Kneading
A key operation in bread-making. The aim is to take a batch of perhaps slightly sticky
bread dough and work it into a firm, cohesive, slightly springy, almost elastic ball
that can be set aside and allowed to rise. Kneading is usually done on a wooden or
marble breadboard coated lightly with flour (to avoid sticking). You can do it with
one hand or two, depending upon your own preference. The basic technique is to
set the mound of dough before you, curl up the end closest to you, and fold it over
and away from you, pushing it into the middle. Then give the dough a quarter turn
and repeat. Keep on doing this until you get the effect called for. Don't try to be
careful or tentative or gentle with it—give it a good workout. One effect of the kneading is to break up the gluten in the flour which will then combine with the yeast,
form carbon dioxide gas, and cause the bread to rise. Any well-constructed recipe
will give you a pretty clear notion how much kneading is called for before you start.
Some kitchen appliances have an attachment known as a bread hook that can do
this chore for you, and for a pretty penny, you can obtain a bread-making machine.
All you do is add the ingredients, press a few buttons, and wait for the finished loaf—

all the mixing, kneading, rising, and baking is done automatically. It's certainly more convenient, but it does take the fun out of it.

Knife

A cutting instrument consisting of a blade attached to a handle. Certainly among the most useful kitchen utensils are the knives—plural because there are different knives for different uses. A well-equipped kitchen will have at the very least a broad-bladed French knife (for vegetables), a carving knife, a ham slicer, a paring knife, and a serrated knife (for bread and other soft commodities, such as tomatoes).

Knish

A baked or deep-fried packet of bread dough stuffed with any of several fillings, the most common of which are potato and buckwheat (KASHA).

Knob Celery

See CELERIAC.

Knockwurst

A German sausage made from pork and beef, flavored with garlic and cumin, and resembling a fat hot dog in shape. It is typically boiled or fried or grilled.

Knuckle

A HOCK or ankle of a domestic animal. The knuckle one sees most often is that of the pig, often smoked and served with sauerkraut.

Köfte

Turkish meatballs or anything so shaped; they are widespread in various guises from the Mediterranean to Southeast Asia. Köfte may be fried or broiled.

Kohlrabi

Also called *turnip cabbage*. A German vegetable (*Brassica oleracea* var. *gongylodes*), the leaves, stems, and bulb of which are equally edible. The leaves, when young, can be steamed like spinach and the stem and bulb are either sliced or julienned for salad, or steamed and dressed with butter and lemon juice and seasoned with parsley and chives. (Or with sour cream and dill.)

When kohlrabi is young and fresh, the outer rind can be pierced with a fingernail. If it is tougher than that, think twice before springing for it. It may be too old. You're also probably better off avoiding it if the bulbs exhibit checks or cracks or if the stems and leaves seem droopy. And stick to bulbs that are no more than three inches across and still tender. As much of the taste resides in the rind, you are best advised to pare the vegetable only after cooking it.

Remove the stems from the leaves and store them separately in plastic bags in the refrigerator. The stems and bulbs will last as long as a week if you're lucky, the leaves for no more than a day or so.

Kolacky

A rich, sweet, yeast-risen bun from Eastern Europe, usually circular in shape with a dent in the middle for a filling that may contain poppy seeds or some form of fruit.

Kola Nut

A tropical nut (*Cola nitida*) used as stimulant in Africa and the West Indies.

Kombu

KELP that has been dried and processed and either rolled into clear sheets or powdered. It is used as a flavoring agent in Japanese cooking.

Kona

A superior COFFEE from Hawaii.

Kosher

Food that is selected, prepared, and served according to Jewish dietary laws.

Koumiss

Also *kumiss*. A Tatar specialty of fermented, sour mare's milk. In its original form it was apparently pretty frightful, and a modern move to approximate it with a yogurt base seems to have gone by the boards, although recent travelers to Mongolia report koumiss is still a staple there.

Kreplach

A Jewish dish of noodle dough stuffed with cottage cheese or meat and simmered in chicken stock. In a sense, Jewish ravioli.

Kuchen

Any German yeast-risen cake.

Kudzu

An Oriental vine (*Pueraria thunbergiana*) that has become naturalized in the southern United States. The plant has roots that can be boiled and eaten or processed for their starch (useful as a thickener for delicate sauces), but agriculturally it is also a terrible, indeed disastrous, pest.

Kugelhopf

A sweet, yeast-risen bread from Central Europe embellished with currants (or raisins) and almonds. It is baked in a fancy, fluted tube pan known as a kugelhopf pan.

Kumiss

See KOUMISS.

Kümmel

A sweet, white LIQUEUR distilled from grain or potatoes and flavored with caraway seeds and cumin; it is a traditional favorite in the Baltic region.

Kumquat

A tiny, bright yellow, Oriental citrus fruit (*Fortunella* spp.) about the size of a cherry but with the taste of a sweet orange. It is found especially during December and January and is used for preserves and eaten fresh or in a fruit salad or compote. Kumquats also come canned in a sweet, heavy syrup as a dessert. When buying fresh kumquats, look for a bright orange color (and store them in the refrigerator). If they have a greenish cast, pass them by.

Kvass

A Russian beer, usually home-brewed, made from rye, barley, and malt and having a minty or cranberry flavor.

L
Common abbreviation for LITER.

Lacer
A metal SKEWER used to close the vent of a bird or other object being roasted to keep the stuffing inside. Once the lacers are in place, you take a piece of string and secure and tie it just like a shoelace. When the roasting is done, snake out the lacers and throw away the string.

Ladle
A deep-bowled spoon on a long handle for dispensing liquids, especially soup.

Lady Apple
A very small red or yellowish-to-red APPLE with a slightly tart taste, of particular use as a garnish.

Ladyfingers
   1. A delicate variation on sponge cake, eaten with a topping or ice cream or used as a basis for more elaborate concoctions such as BAKED ALASKA or CHARLOTTE.
   2. A British term, used in the plural (i.e., "ladies' fingers"), for OKRA.

Lager
A light BEER.

Lake Herring
See CISCO.

Lake Trout
A sport and food fish classified as a CHAR.

Lamb
The meat of a young sheep under the age of a year (or before it develops its permanent teeth) and weighing typically 80 to 120 pounds, from which will come some 40 to 70 pounds of usable meat. Meat from an animal older than that is referred to as YEARLING LAMB (*hogget* in Britain) and later on as MUTTON. The most delicate lamb is milk-fed, meaning it is taken before it is weaned, and gives a pure white but somewhat flavorless meat, usually at great cost. As it ages, it gains weight and flavor but loses something in tenderness. American lamb is "finished," as the trade term some-

what inelegantly puts it, on grain, whereas most imported lamb has been fed only grass. Grain-fed lamb is the more tender of the two. The French have a special category known as *pré-salé* or *salt-meadow lamb* (also mutton). This refers to animals that have been raised in seaside meadows and gain a distinctive flavor from this salty pasturage.

In the United States, lamb is not highly favored, consumption of it running well behind beef and pork and even trailing veal. Indeed, Americans consume some ten times as much fish as they do lamb. Americans also tend to prefer their lamb well cooked (critics say dried out) as opposed, say, to the French custom of serving it still pink and rosy.

Select lamb that is light in color, fine grained, and firm to the touch. Look for fat that is a creamy white with some give to it—yellowish fat denotes mutton rather than lamb whereas fat that is brittle suggests too much storage time in the freezer.

The cuts of lamb most likely to be seen are the breast, chops, leg, shoulder, and— from specialty butchers, anyway—perhaps saddle. Lamb is excellent barbecued, boiled (more an English than a North American practice), braised, sautéed, stewed, or roasted. Leg of lamb is sometimes boned and rolled (and stuffed) and sometimes boned and flattened into a shape reminiscent of a butterfly and called by that name.

Lambrusco

An Italian wine grape (*Vitis vinifera*) vinified into a somewhat sweet (some would say mawkish), highly aromatic, often slightly sparkling red wine.

Lamb's Lettuce

Also known as *mâche, corn salad*, and *field salad*. A European salad green (*Valerianella olitorio*) with a mild, somewhat nutlike flavor, available to gardeners, foragers (it was brought into North America early on), and frequenters of highly expensive, specialty greengrocers. It is sold in small bunches and is only worth buying if it is fresh and sparkling green. Wash it well, trim the roots, and use as you would bibb lettuce or cook it briefly as you would spinach.

Lamb's Quarters

A wild potherb (*Chenopodium album*) related to spinach and tasting something like it.

Lamprey

A primitive jawless fish resembling an eel (chiefly *Petromyzon marinus*), found in saltwater and in lakes, rivers, and streams. In North America it is best known as a voracious destroyer of food and game fish, especially in the Great Lakes. In Europe, it was formerly eaten (England's King Henry I is said to have died from having eaten too many eel), but now this is rare except perhaps in the Bordeaux region of France where *lamproies à la Bordelaise* can still be found. (The dish consists of lampreys stewed up mainly with leeks and red wine, although white wine substitutes for red on rare occasions.) Lamprey is said to have little taste of its own—albeit being slightly fatty—but to reflect favorably on any sauce added to it.

Lancashire

An English, crumbly, mellow, farm CHEESE that lends itself well to melting and is somewhat reminiscent of CHESHIRE.

Langouste

A French term for CRAWFISH.

Langoustine

A French term for NORWAY LOBSTER.

Langsat

A peach-sized fruit of a southeast Asian tree (*Lansium domesticum*) with a velvety outside and white, slightly bitter flesh, usually eaten raw. Langsats are very rare outside of a few Oriental markets.

Langue de Chat

Literally, French for cat's tongue, but don't let it throw you. It refers to a crisp, dry, French cookie sometimes covered with chocolate, and sometimes layered with a filling somewhat like a particularly elegant Oreo cookie. It gets its name from its supposed resemblance to the tongue of a cat.

Lapwing

See PLOVER.

Lard

1. Rendered pork fat. Lard is useful for deep-fat frying, for baking, and for sautéing, but keep in mind its high saturated-fat content. In the days of cholesterol unconsciousness lard was used for making the flakiest piecrusts. The best-quality lard is known as *leaf lard* and comes from the area just around the kidney.

2. LARDING.

Larding

A process in which strips of fat are threaded into cuts of meat to lubricate the meat as it cooks. Larding can be accomplished by making slits in the meat with a sharp knife and sliding bits of pork fat, bacon, or beef suet into it (keep the knife in the incision and press down on it to keep the incision open, then slide the piece of larding meat right down the blade) or by using a LARDING NEEDLE. Larding is called for especially with veal and venison roasts, which otherwise tend to be dry on account of their leanness.

Larding Needle

A needle, conveniently enough, for LARDING meat. Larding needles come in two varieties. One is a 6–8-inch-long hollow needle tapering to a sharp point. The chilled LARDOON gets packed into the hollow part and the needle is stuck through your roast, parallel to the grain, and comes out the other side with the lardoon left behind.

The other variety (20 inches long or so) is larger and looks like a knife with its blade fashioned into a half-moon and again coming to a very sharp point. The strip of fat is laid in the trough of the half-moon, the needle is stuck through the meat, and while the end of the trough is held secure, the needle is gently withdrawn, resulting in a piece of meat with a strip of larding running clean through it. With additional larding strips you can form rows, staggered rows, circles, or whatever you please, and when you slice the roast, each piece will carry its design like stigmata.

Lardoon

Also *lardon*. The long, thin strip of fat used in LARDING. Chilling lardoons before inserting them into your roast helps keep them intact and makes them easier to handle.

Largemouth Bass

A freshwater BASS.

Lark

Any one of a large, international family (Alaudidae) of songbirds. In Europe, larks are sometimes eaten, and indeed, the French village of Pithiviers in the château country of the Loire Valley is renowned, among its other gastronomic specialties, for its lark pâté. In North America, larks are songbirds and as such are protected by law from such indignities.

Lasagna

An Italian specialty of long, broad noodles—sometimes with one or both edges cut into a curly or rippled pattern—softened in boiling water, often sautéed with some tomato paste, then layered with cheese, meat, poultry, or some combination of these with tomato or tomato/meat sauce. It is ultimately baked or sometimes steamed.

Latke

A Jewish potato pancake. It is traditionally served during the festival of Hanukkah.

Laurel

A European BAY. The leaves of the eastern North American or mountain laurel (*Kalmia angustifolia*) are toxic whereas those of the California laurel (*Umbellularia californica*) are edible but of lesser quality than the European bay.

Lavender

A variety of mint (*Lavandula officinalis*) used more as an aromatic cosmetic than in cookery. However, the dried (or fresh) leaves are sometimes brewed for drinks and can be used (sparingly!) in marinades. They were once, apparently, used in aspics.

Laver

An edible seaweed (*Porphyra laciniata*) used pickled in Britain and also known by its Japanese name, *nori*. Nori is used in SUSHI and as a flavoring, especially for soup. Foragers gather it along the seacoast; others find it dried in health food stores. Before using it, soak it for an hour or so and it will just about double in size.

There is also a *green laver* (*Ulva lactuca*) used as a cooked vegetable and flavoring.

Lb.

Common abbreviation for POUND.

Leavening

Also *leavening agents*. The agents that make bread rise and impart lightness; YEAST, BAKING POWDER, and BAKING SODA are the most common, although angel food cake, for example, is actually leavened by beating air into egg whites.

Lebkuchen

A spicy German Christmas cookie made with both honey and brown sugar (or molasses) and flavored with nuts and candied fruits. It is often produced in fanciful designs. Lebkuchen are best made a month or so in advance of the time they are to be served and left to age.

Leek

The national emblem of Wales and the "poor man's asparagus" of France, but the next thing to a luxury item in North America. Leeks (*Allium porrum*) are related to onions and have a sweet, mild oniony flavor that goes particularly well in soups (such as COCK-A-LEEKIE or VICHYSSOISE), potato dishes, and stews. In Europe, leeks may be braised and served as a separate vegetable.

Leeks are long (six to eight inches is usual) and cylindrical and topped with leaves that are best trimmed off before use. To clean them (they can be full of grit) trim the leaves and make a slit through the center of the leafy end, cutting down about an inch and a half. Then make another cut at a right angle to the first (to form a +) and bend back the layers of leek and rinse well. If grit persists, you may have to increase the penetration of the slits.

Leeks are at their best when not too big (they get tough) and when they have clean white bottoms and unwilted tops. You can keep leeks for a few days if you trim off the roots and tops and hold them, swathed tightly in plastic wrap, in the refrigerator.

There is also a *wild leek* (*Allium tricoccum*) found from Canada to the midsection of the United States that is considered one of the milder and sweeter examples of the wild onion.

Lees

A heavy sediment deposited by young wines as they take on age. The wine is "racked" (or essentially decanted) off the lees as a part of its clarification. Some extremely old, fine wines also develop a deposit—lees—and must be decanted to rid them of this unwanted distraction.

Legume

A family (Leguminosae, the pea or pulse family) of edible plants second in nutritional importance only to the cereal grains. Legumes are, broadly speaking, podbearing plants, and among them are the various varieties of BEAN and LENTIL and PEA.

Leicester

A hard, mild but tangy, English, usually partly skimmed cow's-milk CHEESE with a flaky consistency and a high reputation among cheese lovers.

Lemon

A citrus fruit (*Citrus limon*) of Asian origin but now grown in great quantity in California and imported from Chile, Italy, and Spain. Although always oval, lemons range somewhat in size and in thickness of rind. In addition to whole lemons, dried lemon peel and lemon juice (frozen or otherwise processed) are available.

Culinarily, lemons have many uses. The slightly sour taste adds to seafood and salads, replaces vinegar in many instances, flavors ice cream and yogurt, informs lemon meringue pie, makes a respectable pickle, and is, of course, indispensable in lemonade. The rind—or zest—of lemon is also a prime flavoring agent. In North Africa, lemons are cured for a month or so in salted lemon juice (with or without spices) and used to flavor all manner of stews and salads.

In selecting lemons, look for even shapes and unbruised skin. Thin-skinned lemons will give more juice for their weight than those with thicker skins.

Lemonade

A thirst quencher compounded of water, sugar, and lemon juice—either plain or carbonated. It can be served hot or cold.

Lemon Balm

See BALM.

Lemon Curd

A pastry filling (although it can also be used as a bread spread) consisting of the juice and rind of several lemons poured over a copious amount of sugar and augmented with a goodly amount of butter and beaten eggs. It was all cooked over a low fire until it thickened and began to bubble but removed before it curdled. It was then refrigerated for later use. It can also be found commercially.

Lemongrass

A tropical grass (*Cymbopogon citratus*), the fresh or dried lemony leaves of which are much used in Southeast Asian cooking.

Lemon Sole

A European FLATFISH of northern waters; in North America, the name is also applied to the winter flounder, especially the larger specimens.

Lemon Squash

A British soft drink akin to LEMONADE.

Lemon Thyme

A species (*Thymus serpyllum* var. *vulgaris*) of THYME with a slightly lemony flavor and aroma.

Lemon Verbena

Also called *verbena*. A shrub (*Lippia citriodora*) of South American origin much cultivated in France for its lemon-scented leaves which are used in moderation for flavoring salads, soups, stews, and braised dishes, or as a general all-round seasoning.

Lentil

A versatile legume (*Lens esculenta*) of great antiquity (it may have been the basis of Esau's "mess of pottage" in the Old Testament) used widely in the Near East and Southeast Asia, more sparingly elsewhere. The lentil most commonly found in North America is the European variety, which is slightly smaller than a pea bean and green or greenish brown in color. Lentils available on the Indian subcontinent, however, can be bright yellow or green or red and can more closely resemble rice in form. Lentils make a superior salad and soup, are compatible with tomatoes and kielbasa in a casserole, can be used as a side dish, and are the basis for the DAL of the Indian subcontinent.

Lettuce

A garden vegetable *Lactuca sativa* that serves—among other virtues—as the basis for our green salads. Lettuce is generally available in four varieties: *butterhead* (or *Boston*), *iceberg, leaf,* and *romaine* (or *cos*). Botanists group butterhead and iceberg together as "head" lettuce, but for kitchen use, they are more conveniently separated.

The butterheads (*Lactuca sativa* var. *capitata*) comprise Boston and Bibb. Boston lettuce has a green, smooth, not overly compact head with a tender, buttery taste. Its close relative, Bibb lettuce (developed by a 19th-century amateur American horticulturist, John Bibb), is smaller, darker, more delicate, and harder to find. Both make exceptional salads but must be treated with a certain amount of respect as they will bruise easily. Iceberg or crisphead (also *Lactuca sativa* var. *capitata*) has tightly closed heads and except for the heart has little flavor. In addition, it lacks some of the nutritional assets of other lettuces. Nonetheless, in part because it can be packed compactly and ships well, it is by far the most widely grown and largest selling lettuce in North America. Leaf lettuce (*Lactuca sativa* var. *crispa*) comes in a number of types, but the ones you'll see in the markets will almost exclusively be loose-leaf red or green lettuces, also amenable to salads. Romaine (*Lactuca sativa* var. *longifolia*) has a longer, cylindrical head and a slightly tougher leaf. It is best for salads when it is still small (no more than six inches tall) and still relatively tender, but it does incontrovertibly add crunch to your salad. There is one other, ancient, variety of lettuce but it's unlikely you'll see it in North America except perhaps in Chinese markets: asparagus or stem lettuce (*Lactuca sativa* var. *angustana*). It forms an enlarged, slightly phallic-looking stalk which is eaten instead of the leaves.

In addition to its use in salad, lettuce can be braised, creamed, or made into soup. However, salad is our most frequent use of lettuce. Since the leaves can be dirty as well as delicate, lettuce is best washed gently in warmish water, then dried thoroughly. A centrifugal salad spinner has replaced the dishtowels and paper towels that once seemed a requisite to getting rid of the water and drying the lettuce sufficiently for it to accept the dressing. In general, it is usually best to rip the dried lettuce into bits with your fingers and not to add the dressing until you're ready to toss and serve. The salad might get soggy otherwise.

Look for lettuce that is unbruised, unwilted, and of a robust color. Avoid any with leaves that are browning along the tips. When you get it home, rinse it off, wrap it in plastic, and refrigerate for a couple of days if you must. As with most fresh produce, lettuce is best served as soon after purchase as is feasible.

There are also various salad greens that, although not lettuce, serve to augment or complement lettuce. They include ARUGULA, CHICORY, ENDIVE, ESCAROLE, and RADDICHIO.

Level

An instruction for measuring ingredients when cooking or baking; it signifies a quantity that does not exceed the height of the measuring device, whether spoon or cup. The easiest way to ensure this is to run a flat knife gently over the completely full spoon or cup to trim off any excess. Bear in mind, however, that some cups (especially glass and plastic cups) are not designed to be completely filled but have marks indicating various measures; leveling must be accomplished by eye in such cases.

Leveret

A young HARE of two to four months.

Leyden

A Dutch, hard, partially skimmed cow's-milk CHEESE flavored with cumin and sometimes caraway seeds and cloves, but otherwise resembling GOUDA.

Liaison

A French term for THICKENING or giving body to such a dish as a soup or stew.

Licorice

A European plant (*Glycyrrhiza glabra*), the bittersweet-tasting roots of which can be made into a sticky, chewy candy and dried to produce a flavoring with characteristics similar to (but stronger than) ANISE and FENNEL.

Liebfraumilch

A popular name for what is most frequently a pleasant but ordinary German white wine.

Liederkranz

A mild, soft, aromatic cow's-milk CHEESE made in the United States and modeled after LIMBURGER.

Lights

The lungs of an animal. They are not ordinarily sold for human consumption in the United States.

Lillet

A proprietary French wine-based APERITIF.

Lima Bean

See BEAN.

Limburger

A semihard, strong-smelling, cow's-milk CHEESE that originated in Limbourg, Belgium, but is replicated under this and other names elsewhere.

Lime

A small, oval, green (although some are more yellow than green) citrus fruit (*Citrus aurantifolia*) that provides a juice ranging from tart to sour. Most of the limes we see are so-called Persian limes, which are greener and larger than the Mexican or Key counterpart. Both pulp and rind are useful, as they provide a bold flavor. Limes are used in a variety of ways—as the base of a SEVICHE, in sherbet, as a limeade, in mixed drinks (as a gimlet), and in the renowned Key lime pie, for example.

In general, the Mexican lime (including the Key lime) is smaller and yellower than the Persian, and aficionados maintain it has considerably more taste and subtlety. There are those who claim that a Key lime pie (built upon lime juice, condensed milk, and eggs) can only be made with Key limes. Others are less finicky. Try it both ways and decide for yourself.

Limequat
A cross between a KUMQUAT and a LIME.

Limpa
A sweet, Scandinavian rye bread flavored with anise, cumin, or fennel and perhaps cardamom, but also informed with grated orange peel.

Limpet
A single-shelled mollusk that can be found clinging to rocks along both the Atlantic and Pacific shorelines. The Pacific owl limpet (*Lottia gigantea*) is the largest variety and is gathered along the coast of northern Mexico. Limpets in the western Atlantic are small and usually overlooked, whereas those on the eastern shores and in the Mediterranean (*Patella* spp.) are larger and have been gathered and cooked by coastal dwellers since prehistoric times. They are reputed to have some qualities of an oyster and to be usable in any recipe calling for cooked oysters.

Ling
1. A fish of the COD family.
2. A LINGCOD.
3. A COBIA.

Lingcod
A Pacific fish (*Ophiodon elongatus*) unrelated to the COD. It is a superior firm and flavorsome food fish that is usually sold as steaks or fillets and can be baked or braised or poached. Although the fresh fish tends to have a greenish cast, it turns a reassuring white when cooked.

Lingonberry
A Scandinavian variant of the cowberry or mountain CRANBERRY.

Linguica
A Portuguese sausage of cured and roughly ground pork flavored with various spices, especially garlic and often including paprika.

Linguine
A spaghetti PASTA in the shape of a long, narrow, slightly flattened noodle. It is often served with a clam sauce.

Linzertorte
A rich and elegant Viennese pastry replete with almonds or hazelnuts and raspberries.

Liptauer

A cheese spread originating from a Hungarian ewe's-milk CHEESE, but now made from the milk of either a cow, ewe, or goat. It can have all manner of flavorings, including caraway, onion, and paprika, and ranging also to anchovies, capers, and chives.

Liqueur

A sweet, usually strong alcoholic spirit flavored with some form of fruit or herb. According to one definition, a liqueur differs from a CORDIAL in that, technically, a liqueur is distilled with the flavoring substance already in it, whereas a cordial has the flavoring added to the spirit after distillation. In practice, the two overlap so as to make distinctions unprofitable if not meaningless.

A spirit such as a framboise or a kirsch or an exemplary aged Cognac or Armagnac—often referred to as liqueur brandy—is not a liqueur but a BRANDY.

Liquor

1. Overall name for any distilled alcoholic beverage.

2. Any liquid, for example the juices of a shellfish, in which vegetables or meat has been braised or boiled.

Litchi

The official name for this fruit (also spelled lychee) is *Litchi chinensis* and you *may* find it fresh in Oriental markets during the summer months. The fruit starts out rose colored but turns to brown as it matures and develops a rough and brittle skin. The litchi is noted for its remarkably sweet, firm but juicy, jellylike pulp. But keep in mind that it loses its excellence quickly when removed from the tree. You may also find it canned. Aside from eating litchi plain, you can serve it as dessert, add it to fruit salads, or find a Chinese recipe in which it is used for a sauce or with fried fish.

Dried litchi nuts (often also called litchi) are a different ballgame—black and chewy and reminiscent of raisins—but despite the name they are not a nut. (In fact, the stone around which the chewy fruit resides is not an edible one.) It has been suggested that eating a dried litchi nut gives you about as much of an impression of the fresh fruit as a prune tells you of the juicy flavor of a fresh plum.

Liter

A standard unit of liquid measure equivalent to 1.06 quarts by the United States system or 1.8 quarts using the British Imperial system.

Littleneck

A gradation of CLAM.

Liver

The largest of the mammalian internal organs and a subject that engenders both great admiration and great disdain. Anyone who has been inflicted with institutional fried liver and bacon (usually cooked to the consistency and appeal of shoe leather) has every reason never to wish to confront such a dish again. Yet liver, sliced thin and skillfully cooked, can stand up with the best of foods.

The liver you are most likely to see is calf's liver, although that of beef, lamb, and pork may also come on the market from time to time. They are all wildly nutritional—lots of iron and protein and vitamins. (Liver was once prescribed for people with severe iron-deficiency anemia for its high iron and vitamin B_{12} content.) The liver of younger animals seems preferable to those of older ones partly for nutritional purposes and partly because they are more tender and require less cooking. Poultry (especially chicken) liver is also widely available and lends itself to a number of uses. And the greenish liver of the lobster (also called *tomalley*) is much prized by lobster fanciers.

Mammalian liver is most frequently sautéed, although it can be baked or braised or broiled or made into dumplings. Chicken livers appear in different parts of the menu. They can be scrambled with eggs for breakfast; they can be seasoned with a little Tabasco, wrapped in bacon, and put under the broiler to serve as an hors d'oeuvre; they can be sautéed or broiled for lunch or dinner (marinate them first in Teriyaki sauce, grill them on skewers, and you have *rumaki*). All these dishes can be made with duck liver, too, should you find any.

Of course, liver in its most elegant culinary incarnation comes in the form of FOIE GRAS and *pâté de foie gras*, the specially fattened livers of selected geese and the pâté that is made from them. Other delectable pâté and terrines (see TERRINE) are also made mostly from calf's or pork liver, and there's hardly a roadside restaurant in France that does not feature its own *pâté maison*, often served with the tiny pickles that the French call *cornichons*.

A great deal of liver is sold frozen (butchers claim that it is easier to slice liver thin when it's frozen) but some can be fresh, again usually sold in slices. Make sure it's bright and moist, with a clean, healthy smell. If it hasn't been frozen previously, you can keep it in your freezer until needed; otherwise wrap it in plastic, refrigerate it, and use it as soon as you can.

Liverwurst

Also *braunschweiger*. A liver SAUSAGE composed of pork liver with such additions as cardamom, onion, pistachio nuts, and pepper. It is sometimes sold smoked and sometimes fresh.

Loaf Pan

A deep, rectangular pan useful for cooking bread or for meat or vegetable loaves.

Lobster

Perhaps the most prestigious of shellfish. Although lobsters of sorts are found in most oceans of the world, the two most important species are the American (*Homardus americanus*) and the European (*Homardus gammarus*), although a case can be made for the NORWAY LOBSTER and the SPINY LOBSTER as well.

American lobsters are taken from the Atlantic Ocean between the Maritime Provinces and New England (although lobsters also inhabit the coasts of the Carolinas). And while lobster fishing is important elsewhere, the most productive areas for the American lobster are Nova Scotia and Maine, in part because the colder the water it comes from, the better the lobster will taste. The habitat of the European variety runs from northern Europe to the Mediterranean.

While alive, a lobster runs from nearly black to dark green to a cold blue and turns red only upon cooking. Lobsters suitable for the table start at 1 to 1½ pounds but can get much bigger, although they seldom get the chance to do so. Because lobsters grow out of the hard shell, or carapace, that encloses them, they must shed that shell annually. When they do, they become unworthy of the table because their flesh swells with water and all taste leaves them. Once the new shell begins to harden, however, the SHEDDER is still unfit to be shipped but on the spot can be sweet and delicious and often less expensive than the more desirable hard-shells. Lobsters are always at their best immediately upon removal from their home waters; "with the dew still on" is the way Maine poet R. P. T. Coffin put it. Once out of the water—even if placed in a tank—it's downhill all the way.

When buying a live lobster, make sure it is fresh and lively. Pick it up—or have the fishseller pick it up (most lobsters today have their claws secured by stout rubber bands to keep them from mangling or removing a finger)—and watch to see that the critter waggles its legs and tail and clearly shows its displeasure. If buying cooked lobster, pick it up and heft it. If it feels light for its size, it may not have been strictly fresh when it was cooked. Another test for the same thing is to uncurl the tail. If it springs right back to the curled position, the lobster was fresh. If not, it is suspect.

There are many approaches to cooking lobster. Coastal experts scoff at the injunction to cook the lobster in plenty of boiling water. A lobster, they maintain, is better off steamed, thus allowed to cook mostly in its own juices. Whether steamed or boiled, what water does go into the kettle is salted, unless seawater is used, in which case additional salt becomes unnecessary. In either case, lobsters must be placed *live* in the water (the impact of the steam or water results in virtually instant death despite some reflex muscle action that seems to have them flailing about in the kettle). Ten minutes is ample for steaming a lobster weighing about a pound.

Broiled lobster calls for a different technique. Place the lobster belly down on a hard surface and insert a sharp knife between the body and the tail to sever the spinal cord, killing the lobster quickly. Flipping it over on its back, you then open the belly and remove the intestines and spongy lungs. The liver (green) and roe (red—also known as coral) are removed and set aside. They are among the lobster's greatest culinary delicacies.

In addition to simply steaming (or boiling) and broiling lobster, other ways to prepare them exist. Lobster stew calls for fresh lobster, rich milk, fine butter, and a dollop of heavy cream—and two days' aging if you can stand waiting that long. Lobster in NEWBURG sauce is often preferred (especially if the lobster is not at its freshest), and lobster salad and lobster rolls (lobster salad in a hot dog bun) are delightful extravagances. In soups, lobsters are prepared as lobster BISQUE and used in BOUILLABAISSE and other chowders. Lobster thermidor is a fancy way of preparing lobster with a white sauce, mushrooms, wine, and a covering of cheese, but most lobster lovers feel that the lobster tends to get lost in the trimmings. The French have a *lobster américaine* (or sometimes *armoricaine*) in which pieces of lobster are sautéed in olive oil and then simmered with onion, tomatoes, and spices. The mixture is returned to the shells and dressed with a sauce of the boiled-down cooking liquid enriched with butter and the coral of the lobster. Most coastal North Americans consider it unnecessarily gaudy for the North American species, but you might want to consider it if you're ever presented with a Mediterranean specimen.

Locust Bean
See CAROB.

Loganberry
A hybrid berry (*Rupus loganobaccus*) from California, an apparent cross between a DEWBERRY and a RASPBERRY and named after its developer, Judge James H. Logan. Loganberries look like blackberries but bear a closer resemblance in taste to a tart raspberry. They are used in exactly the ways that blackberries are used except that they are seldom found fresh. Most loganberries are made into preserves or canned.

Loin
The upper midsection of a meat animal; from it come steaks and chops and the prized tenderloin.

Loire
A wine produced in an area extending eastward from the mouth of the Loire River in France, including red, white, and rosé, sweet and dry, semisparkling, and still wine (there is also some sparkling wine of negligible quality). The recognized regions include Anjou, Coteaux de la Loire, Jasnières, Muscadet, Pouilly-sur-Loire, Quincy, Reuilly, Sancerre, and Touraine. Perhaps the most renowned wine is the Touranian wine Volnay.

London Broil
A strictly American cut of beef taken from the flank. It is usually on the tough side and is grilled or charcoal-broiled and sliced quite thin and on a slant.

Longan

Also *dragon's eye*. A fruit of an East Asian tree (*Euphoria longana*), similar to the LITCHI but not so delicate.

Longhorn

A term for an American CHEDDAR, specifying shape, not quality. It is six inches around by thirteen inches long and weighs twelve to thirteen pounds.

Long White Potato

A long, thin, elliptical POTATO from California, amenable to boiling and panfrying.

Loofah

A gourd (*Luffa aegyptiaca* or *Luffa acutangula*), the vascular skeleton of which is widely used (especially in Great Britain) as a bathroom sponge (it is a wonderful back scrubber). When alive it is also used as a versatile vegetable related to the cucumber. The young fruit can be eaten cooked (as you would zucchini) or raw, and the flowers can also be deep-fried or simply picked raw for salads.

Lop Cheong

A spicy Chinese pork SAUSAGE.

Loquat

A small, sweet golden fruit (*Eriobotrya japonica*) sometimes called *Japanese medlar*, but nonetheless of Chinese origin, now grown in southern Europe, Israel, the Far East, Florida, and California. It tastes like a cross between an apple and an apricot. Because they decline so quickly off the tree, loquats are rarely at their best away from their growing areas. Perhaps because of this characteristic, they are largely used for preserves, although when properly fresh they are considered superior for eating raw, in fruit salads, or in pie.

Louisiana Hot Sauce

A proprietary sauce made up of chilis with salt and vinegar—much like an incandescent Tabasco.

Loukanika

A Greek pork and beef sausage informed with allspice, cinnamon, garlic, and especially orange peel.

Lovage

An Old World herb (*Levisticum officinale*, also known as *wild parsley*), the roots of which are candied like those of ANGELICA. The leaves are used as a flavoring for soups and main dishes. Despite its nickname, its taste more nearly resembles a strong version of celery than it does parsley.

Lox
See smoked SALMON.

Luau
A gala Hawaiian feast usually featuring a whole roast pig, POI, tropical fruits, and much dancing and gaiety.

Lucerne
See ALFALFA.

Luffa
An alternate spelling of LOOFAH, based on its biological classification.

Luganega
A lightly spiced, Italian pork SAUSAGE, sometimes flavored with cheese.

Lukewarm
A temperature that is tepid or moderately warm. Try a drop on the inside of your wrist. If it feels neither measurably hot nor cold, it will pass for lukewarm, always assuming that you yourself are at room temperature. Bread-makers must be aware of temperature because yeast actively depends on it. Some yeasts will curl up and die if you add water that is too hot for them—lukewarm is just fine. Other yeasts, such as the dried kind you get in small packages, seem able to handle a little more heat.

Lumache
A PASTA in the shape of a snail's shell. Like all such pasta, it is suited to heavy sauces, especially those containing chunks of meat or seafood.

Lumpfish
A gray-green North Atlantic fish (*Cyclopterus lumpus*) found from New Jersey to Brittany. Although its edibility is debated (apparently the female becomes virtually inedible after egg laying whereas the male is good any time), its major importance is as a provider of roe for lumpfish CAVIAR.

Lumpy
Having small clumps of some ingredient not smoothly integrated into the rest. It often refers to something such as batter, dough, soup, or mashed potatoes that has not been kneaded or mixed enough. Eliminating the problem is sometimes a matter of adding the lump-making ingredient more slowly, or sometimes of beating, mixing, or stirring longer or more strenuously. And with mashed potatoes, you might try boiling them a little longer to make them a tad more malleable.

Lychee
An alternate spelling of LITCHI.

Maatjes
A variety of cured HERRING.

Macadamia
A luxury nut (*Macadamia ternifolia*) originally native to Australia but transplanted to Hawaii in the 1890s. A difficult nut to crack, it must undergo strenuous processing before it can be shelled so as to be available as a costly and delicious cocktail snack, dessert nut, or flavoring for sauces.

If you buy macadamia nuts whole, place them on a cookie sheet in a 200°F oven for 30 minutes, then put them on a firm surface, cover them with a towel, and bash them with a hammer to open them. Then pick out all the little pieces of shell and roast the nutmeat until it's done (but not burned) and ready to eat. Enjoy!

Macaroni
Any of a group of hollow PASTA tubes either straight or cut into one of a rich variety of shapes.

Macaroon
A rich, crusty, elegant cookie based on almond paste, sugar, and white of egg, although coconut is also sometimes added. The best versions come from France and Italy. Macaroons can be baked plain or flavored with any number of substances.

Mace
The outer covering of the NUTMEG, used as a spice in its own right. (It contributes a taste combining elements of both nutmeg and cinnamon.) Mace comes either in thin, lacy "blades" (all but impossible to find) or as a reddish powder (available just about anywhere spices are sold). Mace is particularly useful for flavoring cherry pie, whipped cream, seafood, poultry, and stuffing.

Macédoine
A French term for a mixture of chopped fruits or vegetables that may be cooked or raw.

Macerate
A fancy term meaning to STEEP or SOAK.

Mâche

See LAMB'S LETTUCE.

Mackerel

A food fish common to temperate and tropical waters the world over. An oily fish, it is only at its best (and a very fine best that is, too) when all but instantly fresh out of the water. It excels when grilled over coals (perhaps with a gooseberry, mustard, or rhubarb sauce) or baked or poached. The French have a method of poaching it in a baking dish in white wine with some carrot and onion and herbs, and flavoring it with a little vinegar and lemon juice. The dish (*maquereau au vin blanc*) is then chilled and served cold. Varieties of mackerel include:

Atlantic mackerel (*Scomber scombrus*). The familiar mackerel of North American markets.

Cero (*Scomberomorus regalis*). Found roughly from Massachusetts through the Gulf of Mexico down to northern Brazil, but it is especially abundant in the Antilles, Bahamas, and the waters off Florida. It is delicate and lends itself to broiling or especially charbroiling.

Jack mackerel (*Trachurus symmetricus*). Actually not a mackerel but a JACK.

King mackerel (*Scomberomorus cavalla*). Common in the waters of the southern United States and often marinated in lemon or lime juice before cooking.

Pacific mackerel (*Scomber japonica*). The widespread mackerel of the Pacific, different from its Atlantic counterpart in ways of interest only to the scientist, not the cook.

Spanish mackerel (*Scomberomorus maculata*). A larger relative of the Atlantic mackerel found in the waters and fish markets all along the Atlantic coastline. It is a big enough fish to provide steaks as well as whole fish and fillets.

Tinker mackerel. The early, young members of the Atlantic persuasion, still small enough to qualify as panfish.

Wahoo (*Acanthocybium solandri*). A large tropical mackerel, slightly less oily than its northern relatives and commonly served as steaks.

Mâcon

A French city and center of the Mâconnais wine region, an area of southern BURGUNDY, known especially for its white wines usually marketed by the varietal name Chardonnay.

Macoun

A crisp, tasty eating APPLE with a fairly short season.

Macrobiotic Diet
A health diet based on the Oriental principle of yin and yang—yin personifying all that is feminine, dark, cold, and wet, yang everything masculine, light, hot, and dry, together embodying everything that is. By balancing yin foods with yang, the macrobiotic diet aims at prolonging life and health. The diet is long on cereals, grains, fish, and vegetables while generally staying away from animal protein.

Madeira
1. A sweet FORTIFIED WINE that takes its name from the Portuguese island of its origin, although that name has been widely borrowed for similar wines made elsewhere. It is just about the best of the fortified wines for cooking, giving a richness, after the alcohol has burned off, that blends wonderfully with veal and with kidneys, among other foods, without imparting excessive sweetness.

A common designation for Madeira is Rainwater, meaning only that the product is probably dry and certainly pale and may or may not be Portuguese—and there are some Rainwaters that are very good indeed. There are four types of traditional (Portuguese) Madeira, all named for the grape from which they are made:

Bual. A full, sweet, dark-brown dessert wine.

Malmsey. A rich, full-bodied after-dinner wine.

Sercial. A dry, aromatic Madeira and the traditional accompaniment of turtle soup.

Verdelho. A wine similar to Sercial but somewhat sweeter and considerably rarer.

2. In British usage, a cake informed with lemon and a piece of citron, but having no connection with the wine of the same name except that the two were often served together.

Madeleine
A delicate, scallop-shaped French tea cake best known for stirring the childhood memories of novelist Marcel Proust, which culminated in his work, *Remembrance of Things Past.*

Madrilène
A jellied CONSOMMÉ flavored with tomato. It can be served hot, but usually it is cold. Either way, lemon wedges make an appropriate accompaniment.

Maguey
A Mexican name for AGAVE.

Mahimahi
A Hawaiian name for DORADO.

Maize

A name used, except in North America, for CORN.

Mako

An edible species of SHARK.

Malaga

A sweet, dark-colored, FORTIFIED WINE from Spain.

Malanga

A mealy tropical tuber (*Xanthosoma* spp.) also known as *yautia* and *tannia*, which is similar to (and often confused with) TARO. Malanga is important in Caribbean cookery and in West Africa. The green leaves and tubers are both used (the greens sometimes known as *callaloo*). Buy malanga tubers when they are firm to the touch and use them up in a day or two. Malangas are often simply peeled and boiled or can (with restraint) be dropped into soups and stews, especially spicy ones.

Mallard

A WILD DUCK.

Mallow

Several varieties of European herbs (family Malvaceae) imported into North America, the best known of which is the MARSHMALLOW. Mallows are used in Europe as a flavoring for cheese.

Malmsey

A type of MADEIRA wine.

Malt

A germinating cereal—usually barley—or one that has germinated, been dried, and then powdered. Syrup from barley malt—or the dried malt itself—is useful in baking as a mild sweetener and to activate yeast. Otherwise, malt is particularly important in brewing beer and making malt vinegar.

Malted Milk

A mixture of dehydrated milk with malted barley or wheat that is added to milk and taken either chilled or warm. Add ice cream and perhaps some chocolate or vanilla syrup and you have a classic drugstore malted.

Malt Liquor

A BEER with a relatively high alcoholic content.

Mamiglia

A Romanian version of POLENTA.

Mammee

Also *San Domingo apricot*. A Caribbean and South American fruit (*Mammea americana*), which when ripe has a taste suggestive of apricot. Before it is ripe, while it is still green, the taste is more akin to a tart apple. It has a brown, leathery skin and yellow-to-creamy flesh. The mammee is eaten raw, in compotes, in fruit salads, and in ice cream.

Mammee Sapote

A somewhat bland relative of the SAPODILLA occurring in Central America and Southeast Asia. It is not to be confused with the unrelated MAMMEE.

Manatee

Also *dugong*. Tropical, herb-eating aquatic mammals (*Trichechus* spp.). They are slow, inoffensive, and sufficiently dim-witted that they are endangered along the coastline of the southeastern United States where they tend to get fouled up in the propellers of passing boats, often with fatal results. They have served as food—prepared as steaks or stews—and are reputed to have a porklike taste.

Manchego

A crumbly Spanish CHEESE apparently once made with ewe's milk but now also with cow's milk. It has a rich, nutty flavor.

Manchet

A white bread of medieval times, made from only the finest wheat flour and reserved for nobility. It was sometimes the wafer offered at Mass, although one source reports manchet was served to the master of the house while God was provided only with "chet," the next step down in quality.

Mandarin

Also *tangerine*. An orangelike fruit (*Citrus reticulata*) with an extremely loose skin, making it easy to peel. It is smaller and generally sweeter than the regular orange and has ends that are slightly flattened.

Mandoline

A slicing machine for getting thin, even slices of vegetables (such as potatoes) or firm-fleshed fruits (such as apples). It consists of a board with an adjustable blade over which you pass the material to be sliced. In some cases, there is a blade for simple slicing and a blade for ripple cutting (as for french fries). Mandolines range in price from quite inexpensive to outrageous. In the latter case you may be better off spending your money on a food processor, unless you simply like expensive toys.

Mangel-Wurzel

A field version of the BEET used as cattle fodder. The very young mangel-wurzel may be prepared as you would young beets, although no one seems to have worked up much enthusiasm for it.

Mange-Tout

A French name of the sugar snap PEA.

Mango

A marvelously aromatic tropical fruit (*Mangifera indica*) that comes in all sorts of sizes and shapes and colors but turns up most usually as an approximately round (although sometimes kidney shaped), green or yellow or red (or a combination of these), soft, almost pulpy, orange-fleshed fruit. You can occasionally get a dud, apparently, the taste of which has been compared to turpentine, but persevere—the ripe, well-selected mango encloses a wealth of soft, juicy, seductive flesh that is at least a match for any fruit in the world.

When selecting a mango look for unblemished, taut skin with some give to it and no blotches or soft spots. Sniff the end and reject any with no aroma or an unpleasant one. As with any tropical fruit, keep it at room temperature until it is ripe and then eat it—refrigerate a fully ripe mango only if you must and then not for more than a day or so (although pureed mango freezes well). If a mango is not ripe when you open it up, don't heave it—poach it in a little sugar syrup and have it for dessert.

Mango has a variety of uses. It can be used as a dessert fruit either alone or with other fruits; it can be added to fruit cocktails and salads and curries; it can be made into pickles and preserves and as such is a prime ingredient for CHUTNEY. Mango lovers will certainly be able to add to this list.

Mango Squash

See CHAYOTE.

Mangosteen

A small, juicy, east Asian (Malaysia and environs) fruit (*Garcinia mangostana*) with a taste of both peach and pineapple. You're not likely to find it in North America, but this too may change.

Manhattan

A cocktail popular especially in the 1940s and still with its admirers. It consists usually of two parts whiskey (rye whiskey classically, but bourbon or a blend is often substituted) to one of sweet vermouth. There is also a dry manhattan which uses dry instead of sweet vermouth.

Manicotti
An American version of Italian cooking, consisting of wide pasta tubes stuffed with cheese or a cheese-meat combination, swathed in tomato sauce, and baked.

Manioc
See CASSAVA.

Manteca
A CHEESE from Basilicata, an area toward the toe of the Italian boot. It is a bland, usually cow's-milk cheese (although buffalo's milk was at least once used) surrounding a heart of pure butter. It was prized in this sunny clime as a way of preserving butter without refrigeration.

Mantis Shrimp
Another name for SQUILLA.

Manzanilla
A light, dry Spanish cocktail wine that, although not grown in the traditional SHERRY area (it comes from Sanlúcar de Barrameda, a dozen miles from sherry's bailiwick, Jerez de la Frontera), is accorded the official place name sherry.

Mao Tai
A potent Chinese spirit distilled from SORGHUM. It can be taken straight (if you have the stamina) or used in cookery. If you have none on hand, gin makes an adequate substitute.

Maple Sugar
A residue left from boiling down MAPLE SYRUP until the liquid is all but gone, leaving a sweet, granular candy behind.

Maple Syrup
A boiled-down sap of the sugar maple and relatives (*Acer* spp.), used as a sweetener and flavoring agent. Maple trees with the ability to store sufficient sugar to be tapped successfully only flourish in northeastern North America, where sugaring is both a cottage industry and big business.

Maple syrup is marketed either as pure maple syrup (which may be "pure" or may be artificially flavored) or as maple-flavored. (In the latter case it will be corn syrup or honey or some other flavoring with a little maple added and should cost less than authentically pure syrup.) In addition to being used on pancakes or biscuits or ice cream, maple syrup is an extravagant delight in pecan pie. An old custom (predating our acid rains) is to pour the still-hot, freshly made syrup over clean snow and let it congeal. The resulting candy was said to be accompanied by small pickles and has been described as delicious but hard on the teeth.

Maple syrup is graded by the U.S. government. Grades include: AA or Fancy, light amber colored and mild; A, medium amber and mellow; B, dark amber and hearty; C, dark and robust.

Maraschino
1. A cherry LIQUEUR originally from Yugoslavia.
2. An artificially colored and flavored cherry used as a garnish.

Marble Cake
A pastry that has alternating veins of light and dark dough, intended to resemble marble stone.

Marbled
A term describing meat that is flecked with small, evenly distributed dots of fat. It is a characteristic only of the best cuts of meat, especially beef.

Marc
A French form of BRANDY.

Marennes
A variety of French OYSTER, named for the port where they are cultivated. Some of them, due to the chlorophyll they ingest from a type of algae in their home waters, take on a distinctly green color and a somewhat coppery taste.

Margarine
Also *oleomargarine*. A cooking fat and spread, originally made with animal fats (but now made with vegetable oils) that started out as a butter substitute but has become an entity of its own. Margarines come in the usual panoply of sticks and tubs and may be whipped (more air added for easier spreading, but substituting this for regular margarine in a baking recipe is asking for disappointment at the very least) or mixed with butter. There's a liquid margarine in a plastic bottle that might be handy over a charcoal grill if your refrigerator has space for it. All margarine calls for refrigeration.

Marigold
See POT MARIGOLD.

Marinade
A tenderizing and flavoring liquid in which food, especially meat, fowl, or fish is soaked before cooking. Marinating time varies from a half hour or so for flavoring to a full week (refrigerated) for both flavoring and tenderizing certain cuts of game or making sauerbraten. Effective meat marinades commonly contain an acid—wine, vinegar, lemon juice—for tenderizing and an oil to lubricate a dry meat. A meat marinade may be used as a basting liquid to moisten meat during cooking. Because

of the acid content, marinades are best contained in something other than aluminum ware.

Marinara Sauce

An Italian tomato sauce, usually meatless, flavored with garlic and onions and oregano, sometimes some green peppers, and conceivably a touch of anchovy. Meat can be added at the cook's discretion.

Marinate

To soak something in a MARINADE.

Marjoram

Two herbs, sweet marjoram (*Majorana hortensis*) and pot marjoram (*Majorana onites*) of the MINT family, closely related to OREGANO but somewhat gentler (sweet marjoram being the most fragrant). Marjoram is used in a BOUQUET GARNI, in stuffings, and in soups, stews, and salads and is particularly compatible with chicken and lamb and veal. The Germans use it in sausage-making and refer to it as *wurstkraut*, or sausage plant (literally "sausage cabbage").

Marlborough Pie

A one-crust pie that originated in Massachusetts, apparently as a contribution to the Thanksgiving Day festivities. It is an apple pie, flavored with lemon juice and nutmeg, but made with sauced instead of sliced apples.

Marlin

A superior game fish (*Makaira* and *Tetrapturus* spp.) of tropical and temperate waters. Its flesh has been described as similar to SWORDFISH and can be cooked according to any method appropriate for that fish. It is, however, exceptional when smoked. Marlin caught in the western Atlantic may not legally be sold.

Marmalade

Originally a QUINCE jelly, but now a preserve made from almost any citrus fruit (including pieces of the fruit and rind). It characteristically has a tangy sweet-and-sour taste. The vast majority of present marmalades are made from Seville oranges, but lime and even ginger varieties are sometimes available.

Marmite

A covered pot usually with slightly bulging sides (tapering toward the top) made of porcelain, earthenware, or metal. It may be used to make stock, soups, and stews of various sorts—the kind of food you crave on a chilly midwinter evening.

Marmot

A genus (*Marmota*) of burrowing rodents perhaps most notably including the WOODCHUCK.

Maroilles

Or *marolles*. A soft, French, cow's-milk CHEESE with a reddish rind, a yellowish paste, and an assertive aroma. It is made, by French law, only in certain areas in northeast France, where it was developed a millennium ago.

Marron Glacé

A CHESTNUT that has been peeled, poached, and preserved in vanilla-flavored sugar syrup. Very pricey indeed.

Marrow

1. The inner part of an animal's long bones. It is not much eaten in North America, except perhaps in the Italian veal stew known as OSSO BUCO. At one time, and especially in Europe, the marrow bones were split and cooked, and then the marrow was removed and spread on toast. It was considered digestible, tasty, and wholesome.

2. In British terminology, although more properly known as vegetable marrow, a summer SQUASH.

Marrow Bean

A large white BEAN.

Marsala

A FORTIFIED WINE from around the city of the same name in western Sicily, but which has been adopted for use by similar wines made elsewhere. At its outset a dry wine, although this variety is less frequently found. Most Marsala has been sweetened. Marsala is used as an aperitif, is a premier cooking wine, and is essential to the Italian dessert ZABAGLIONE.

Marshmallow

A candy originally made from the gelatinous gum extracted from the roots of the marshmallow plant (*Althaea officinalis*) but now made from egg whites and corn or other syrup with added gelatin. In addition to toasting them over a campfire, you can also use marshmallows in cake fillings and frostings. Commercially available marshmallow cream is a first-rate (and tasty) stabilizing agent for chocolate fudge.

Foragers can still find the marshmallow plant, but almost exclusively along the East Coast. Wild food expert Euell Gibbons reported that the water in which marshmallow roots were boiled could be whipped up into a handy vegetarian substitute for egg white.

Marsh Marigold

A wild North American plant (*Caltha palustris*) often referred to as cowslip.

Marsh Rabbit

Also *marsh hare*. A fancy name for a MUSKRAT.

Martini

Probably the most prevalent cocktail of the 1940s and 50s. It consists of gin (later vodka) and dry vermouth in varying ratios. Three parts gin to one part vermouth was generally considered a conservatively "dry" martini, with the less the vermouth, the greater the degree of dryness. Often garnished with a lemon twist, green olive, or cocktail onion.

Marzipan

Almonds that have been ground up and prepared with sugar and egg white. Marzipan is often brightly colored with vegetable dye and can be used as icing or filling for pastries, or it can be made into little cakes and candies in all sorts of fanciful shapes and sizes.

Masa

A Mexican corn flour specially treated with limewater (water to which a salt of calcium has been added) and used for making tortillas. A special dehydrated version, *masa harina*, is available in some supermarkets.

Mascarpone

Also *mascherpone*. A cream-style CHEESE from northern Italy and Switzerland often flavored with lemon juice and tasting somewhat like a slightly acid RICOTTA. It makes a handy cheese spread and can be the basis for a superior cheesecake.

Mash

    1. To reduce something to a pulp, as mashed potatoes.

    2. Grain steeped in water and ready for fermentation (the starch converts to fermentable sugar) and subsequent distillation into an alcoholic spirit. If some of the previous batch of already fermented mash is added as a starter, the result is SOUR MASH.

Maslin

A medieval European bread made from a mixture of rye and wheat flour. It was the common bread for most people in the Middle Ages, white bread being a luxury for the rich.

Mastika

A Greek aperitif (from the island of Chios) distilled from brandy and flavored with gum mastic, the resinous exudation from a small tree (*Pistacia lentiscus*).

Maté

Also *yerba maté* and *Paraguay tea*. A tea brewed from the buds, leaves, and shoots of a South American holly (*Ilex paraguayensis*). It is not all that common in North America but can sometimes be found in health food stores. There is both a green (somewhat mouth-puckering) and a roasted (earthier) version.

Matelote

A French fish stew, usually quite rich, made with dry red or white wine and often containing eel. It is a stew containing freshwater fish except in Normandy, where salt-water fish (often including conger eel) are used, cooked up in butter and cider.

Matsutake

An expensive and rare Japanese MUSHROOM.

Matzo

Also *matzoh* and (plural) *matzoth*. A Jewish, unleavened bread made of wheat flour and water only (although flavored varieties are available for nonliturgical purposes). It attains liturgical importance at the Passover Seder, the ritual dinner commemorating the Exodus from Egypt when the Jews had no time to make yeast-risen bread and carried with them matzos instead. Matzo flour is also made into meal and dumplings (matzo balls) flavored with onion, egg, seasonings, and chicken fat.

Mavrodaphne

A wine grape (*Vitis vinifera*) of the eastern Mediterranean (especially Greece) and the rich, red, syrupy, sweet dessert wines made from it.

Mayapple

A wildflower (*Podophyllum peltatum*) widespread over most of eastern North America with white, somewhat odorous, cup-shaped flowers; also called *mandrake* for its supposed resemblance to that Old-World plant. Its lemon-shaped fruit, thought "mawkish" and "insipid," by some, has been praised by others as a source of marmalade or as juice added to lemonade. It has also been made into a drink with sugar and MADEIRA. Only the fruit is edible.

Mayonnaise

An uncooked dressing of emulsified oil, egg yolk (or whole egg), lemon juice or vinegar (or both), and flavorings. In the days before the blender and food processor, mayonnaise was tedious to make (the oil had to be amalgamated into the egg yolk literally drop by tiresome, individual drop until the emulsifying was well on its way). Commercial mayonnaise came as a godsend. Present-day commercial mayonnaise can have so much added to it that sometimes it barely seems to resemble the original concept. And blender or food processor mayonnaise is quick and very nearly foolproof, although given the possibility of some eggs containing salmonella, commercial egg substitutes may be preferable to fresh eggs for this purpose.

Any number of changes can be rung on mayonnaise, ranging from the addition of green herbs (for green mayonnaise) to garlic (for AIOLI) to fruits, cheese, horseradish, sour cream, or anything that might enhance the dish at hand.

Maypop

See PASSIONFRUIT.

May Wine

A German beverage consisting of sweetened Rhine (or Moselle) wine and Champagne (in Germany, probably SEKT), flavored with WOODRUFF and garnished with wild strawberries or sometimes with pieces of pineapple. May is the month when—in Germany, at any rate—the woodruff develops its flavorsome buds and leaves (the unopened buds are the most flavorful) but before it flowers and loses its culinary edge. An approximation of the real thing can usually be found bottled wherever wines are sold.

McIntosh

A red, all-round APPLE available most anytime.

Mead

Also HYDROMEL. A fermented drink made of honey, mead was known to the Greeks and was popular in medieval Europe, especially in the British Islands. Even the French soaked pears in mead to serve as dessert. Commercial mead is still occasionally available as a specialty item.

Meal

1. A cereal grain ground up but not bolted (or sieved) as fine as flour.

2. Anything ground up to the consistency of a coarse powder—bones, dried fish, whatever, often used for fertilizer rather than foodstuff.

Mealy

1. A term used to describe something having the dry characteristics and consistency of meal. For example, an Idaho potato will have a "mealy" consistency when cooked, especially when compared to an Eastern one (Maine or Long Island).

2. A term referring to flour, grain, or dried vegetables that sat around long enough to have small insects (known as mealy worms) form in the container. There's little to be done at this stage except perhaps donate it to the bird feeder.

Measuring Cup

A standard unit of measure. The American cup contains 8 fluid ounces, .24 liter; the British or Imperial cup has 10 fluid ounces, .28 liter.

Meat

The flesh of animals, although it started out meaning solid food as opposed to drink. (The edible parts of nuts and shellfish also trade on the name.) Most of our meat comes from domestic animals, from which we derive beef, kid, lamb, mutton, pork, rabbit, and veal, and most of that is from the muscle tissues. These provide us our chops and roasts and steaks. There are also the nonmuscle servings of meat, the VARIETY MEAT or brains and kidneys and the like.

In addition to domestic animals, game animals provide meat for some people. Venison is probably the most widespread, whether from antelope, elk, mule deer, whitetail deer, or, occasionally, moose. Furred game was the meat of the original settlers, and all manner of it—bear or beaver or muskrat or squirrel or woodchuck— can still be found on some North American dining tables. For the most part, this book will address itself to domestic fare, which is what most of us can expect to find. The various meats are treated under their individual headings.

Meatballs

Ground meat rolled into small rounds, often augmented with breadcrumbs, egg, herbs, and spices—often spiced according to national preference, a Turkish meat-ball differing from a conventional North American one, for instance—and then fried, grilled, or poached.

Meat Cleaver

A hefty cutting tool for splitting whole carcasses or cutting up large pieces of meat; it is also useful for removing the head and feet of freshly killed fowl. Oriental cooks wield smaller cleavers to accomplish everything from slicing vegetables to cutting parsley into a veritable powder. Their skill, speed, and agility with the cleaver is out-standing, but imitating them is not recommended for the unpracticed.

Meat Hammer

A hammer with gridlike teeth on one side and either a flat side or grooves on the other, used for tenderizing and flattening meat such as veal cutlets for scallopini or chicken breasts for certain types of suprême. The meat is covered with waxed (or other) paper and pounded with the flat side. The toothed side is used for tenderiz-ing otherwise tough cuts of meat.

Meatloaf

A perennial favorite consisting of ground meat (beef, pork, veal, sometimes all three, or ground chicken or turkey) mixed with all manner of flavorings—breadcrumbs, egg, green pepper, herbs, diced garlic or onion, and yogurt are all possibilities—and then baked. Meatloaf is eaten either hot or cold and is sometimes accompanied by horseradish.

Meat Tenderizer

A commercial powder containing an enzyme (PAPAIN is much used) to break down the tissues of a tough piece of meat. Pounding with a meat hammer and marinat-ing can give the same effect.

Meat Thermometer

A cooking tool for ascertaining the interior temperature of a piece of roasting meat to give the cook an idea of when it is properly done. Some such thermometers are inserted in the roast as it enters the oven and stay in until it is done. The best (because they are more accurate) consist of a thin probe with a dial and are inserted briefly toward the end of the cooking time (the reading is given almost immediately) and then the instrument is removed. They can be reinserted (and re-removed) as necessary if the roast requires more cooking time.

Medallion

Also *médaillon* in French. A term for food—especially meat—that has been cut into rounds or ovals. Medallions are usually taken from one of the pricier cuts, such as the tenderloin.

Medlar

A small round dark brown fruit popular in Europe and introduced fairly early into North America, where the tree (*Mespilus germanica*) flourishes from Louisiana to southern Ontario. Medlars are picked when they are still hard and inedible, usually after the first frost, and left to soften until they appear almost rotten. Their slightly acid flavor has been described as "winy," and they are more likely to be made into jelly than eaten whole. The LOQUAT is sometimes called the Japanese medlar.

Médoc

An area of France's BORDEAUX wine-growing region producing some of the world's most prestigious red table wines. Its most outstanding growths include Château Lafite-Rothschild, Château Latour, Château Margaux, and Château Mouton-Rothschild (although Château Haut-Brion, on the other side of Bordeaux in GRAVES, was included by the vineyard classification of 1855 among the leaders of the Médoc hierarchy and still retains that courtesy title).

Melba Toast

A thin slice of toast, crispy and browned throughout in a very slow oven. It was named for the turn-of-the-century Australian soprano Dame Nellie Melba.

Melilot

A European sweet clover (*Melilotus officinalis*) fed to rabbits being raised for the table (to make them taste more like their wild brethren); the dried leaves can be brewed as a tea, added to some Swiss cheeses, and used to impart a sort of vanilla-like flavor to soups and stews.

Melissa

See BALM.

Melon

A family (Cucurbitaceae) of edible gourds of probably Persian origin, generally eaten raw as a breakfast food, an appetizer, or a dessert (and also used for flavoring a liqueur of sorts). Melons are at their tastiest when chilled (but not paralyzed with cold) before serving.

Choosing a melon can be something of an adventure. In general, melons are ripe when they have a sweet aroma at the end where they were removed from the vine, when the area around that exit scar is slightly soft, and sometimes when they darken a little in color. When dealing with muskmelons, especially, if the severed end shows definite signs of scarring or cutting, the melon was picked before it was completely ripe and will be inferior. These varieties of melons are excellent if removed from the vine once they are fully ripe (when they will all but drop off by themselves), but if plucked while still unripe, will never attain any further distinction. If you're planning on opening a melon and not using it all up right away, wrap the remainder securely in plastic before refrigerating it, or you're apt to have everything around it smelling melony.

Melons are pesky to classify, as they all seem to interbreed quite cheerfully across any lines of classification that mere mortals can devise for them. However, some sense might be made by looking at them as follows:

Bitter melon (*Momordica charantia*). A Chinese melon used as a vegetable. See BITTER MELON.

Cantaloupe (*Cucumis melo* var. *cantalupensis*). Just to make life difficult, these are *not* the melons known in North America as cantaloupes, which are muskmelons (see below). The true cantaloupe (much seen in Europe) has a warty or scaly rind and usually orange (sometimes green) flesh and a pleasant aroma.

Casaba. A winter melon (see below).

Honeydew. A winter melon (see below).

Muskmelon (*Cucumis melo* var. *reticulatus*). These have a netted skin and include those melons sold in North America as cantaloupe. The netting (the excellent food writer Waverley Root reports that the French term for this is "embroidery") is usually somewhat raised above the melon's skin and the orangy or greenish flesh is tasty and aromatic. Muskmelons, particularly, reward being used as quickly as possible after removal from the vine.

Persian. A variety of muskmelon (see above).

Watermelon (*Citrullus vulgaris*). The summer picnic favorite with its long, oval crocodile-green outside, its pink flesh, and its flat seeds for children to use for spitting contests. Actually, not all watermelons are green (some are yellow) and many do not even share the familiar long, oval shape (some are round). They all taste about the same, though, and all can be selected on the basis of a regular shape, a slightly dullish color (no sheen!) and a satisfying "thunk" when tapped (a hollow sound is a sign the melon is not ripe). Watermelon is also the basis of a standard pickle.

Winter melon (*Cucumis melo* var. *inodorus*). Hard-rinded melons that come in a variety of descriptions—some smooth, some with ridges, some pebbly. They come with green or orange or white flesh and only lack the aroma so associated with, for example, muskmelons. (Premier examples of winter melon include casaba and honeydew.) There is also a Chinese WINTER MELON that is used as a vegetable.

Melt
To dissolve a solid or semisolid into a liquid or near-liquid state, as you might with the butter you're planning to put on your popcorn.

Menhaden
A fish of the HERRING family, too oily for most culinary purposes.

Menudo
Originally a Spanish tripe and calf's-foot stew from Andalucia, it is also a Mexican stew of tripe, calves' feet, and whole hominy, cooked with chili peppers, garlic, and onions and traditionally served on New Year's Day.

Meringue
Essentially, it is stiffly whipped egg whites and sugar baked quickly at a moderate temperature (350°F) as a dessert topping or somewhat more lengthily at a lower temperature (225°F) for individual candies.

Essentials of meringue-making entail using a spotlessly clean bowl for whipping (no trace of oil or egg yolk, which bespeaks a bowl made of something other than plastic, which is almost impossible to get completely unoily), adding the egg white only a little at a time, and ceasing the whipping when the froth stands in thin "peaks." Overbeating results in lumpy foam and requires a fresh start with new eggs. Mysteriously, whipping the whites in a copper bowl leads to a better output—more stable, harder to overbeat—but so does the addition of a bit of cream of tartar.

Merlot
A wine grape (*Vitis vinifera*) that provides softness and grace to the distinguished wines of BORDEAUX and other areas. It is widely grown in Italy and California, giving a pleasant, perfumed wine that is best drunk quite young.

Mescal
A colorless, rough Mexican liquor distilled from the Mexican century plant (*Agave tequilana*) used in the making of TEQUILA. The name is also used for any spirit fermented or distilled from various Mexican cacti.

Mesclun

In France's Côte d'Azur, a salad of young, somewhat bitter spring potherbs. Elsewhere, any similar salad.

Mesost

A soft, light-brown, Swedish cow's-milk CHEESE with a slightly sweetish taste, reminiscent of Norwegian GJETOST.

Mesquite

A spiny shrub or small tree (*Prosopis* spp.) of the Southwest and Mexico. Its aromatic wood is used for outdoor barbecues.

Metate

A Mexican flat stone providing a surface for grinding corn for tortillas and other culinary uses.

Metaxa

A slightly sweet Greek BRANDY.

Metric System

A system of weights and measures used practically everywhere in the world except the United States, where it is used only in scientific work.

Meurette

A freshwater MATELOTE from Burgundy. The stew balances the somewhat oily fish it uses (always including some eel) with the acidity of the red Burgundian wine that also goes into it.

Mexican Saffron

See SAFFLOWER.

Mexican Sage

See OREGANO.

Meze

A Greek rendition of HORS D'OEUVRE.

Mezzani

An Italian term for medium. It refers to medium-thick macaroni PASTA of varying lengths, often preferred for a baked dish.

Microwave Oven

An OVEN designed to cook with electromagnetic waves. Microwave ovens come with different amounts of power: most range from 600–700 watts although some are 400–500 and others 1,000–1,200. Cooking times will, naturally, vary according to the amount of power. In addition, a well-designed microwave will have different power controls, thus allowing the cook to choose between cooking on full power, defrosting on far less power, and otherwise adjusting the power according to the desired result.

Microwave cooking offers some tremendous advantages—notably speed—along with a few disadvantages—for example, difficulty browning such foods as roasted meat and toasted bread. For such basics as thawing frozen foods quickly and boiling, steaming, or poaching, the microwave is, of course, unrivaled. To confine it only to such duties would be to underuse this highly flexible and useful instrument. The time it takes to master the idiosyncrasies of the microwave as against conventional ovens is nothing compared to the time saved in the cooking process. There are dishes one would avoid cooking in a microwave. Certain French-style pot roasts, or daubes, achieve their excellence in part by the slow intermingling of the various ingredients over the course of hours of simmering and, in part, by the anticipation fueled by the heady aroma that pervades the house when the dish is cooking. By accomplishing the cooking in an hour and a half in the microwave, you surrender part of the joy of cooking to the expedient of speed. The sacrifice may be worth the cost, but perhaps not always.

Mignonette

1. A French combination of coarsely ground black and white pepper.
2. A summer SQUASH.
3. Another name for *médaillion* or MEDALLION.

Milfoil

See YARROW.

Milk

Nature's most nearly perfect food, but a mixed blessing at best if you're allergic to it or, as can occur with maturity, lose the ability to digest it. Most milk is supplied by cows, although goat's milk is available in some places, and buffalo's milk and ewe's milk (from sheep) is used here and there for making cheese. Milk is not only a perishable but also a delicate food. When heating it—for soup or sauce or whatever—use a double boiler or only a low-to-medium flame. Too much heat is harmful to it. Try stirring it or covering it when cooking it; the skin it forms will come about more slowly, and there are valuable nutrients in the skin.

Some of the labels you're apt to encounter at the dairy counter may include:

Acidophilus. Milk that is first pasteurized then recultured with the acidophilus lactobacillus (a bacteria naturally occurring in milk but killed by pasteurization). The restored bacilli destroy milk sugar, or lactose, and the milk is designed for people whose ability to digest lactose is impaired or nonexistent. Acidophilus milk sours more quickly than regular milk.

Buttermilk. Pasteurized low-fat or skim milk with a special culture added to give it the slightly acid tang expected of buttermilk. Raw buttermilk (the leavings of the cream after the butter has been churned) is said to be available in a few scattered health food stores.

Certified milk. Raw milk sold only under stringent health conditions. It is not legally available in all states of the United States and because the certification is not recognized by the federal government (it is under the authority of the American Association of Medical Milk Commissions), it cannot be shipped across state lines.

Condensed milk. Heavily sweetened evaporated milk (see below).

Dry milk. Pasteurized milk from which all the water has been removed. It may be made from whole or low-fat milk, as specified on the label.

Evaporated milk. Canned milk from which about 60 percent of the water has been evaporated.

Half-and-half. Pasteurized or ultrapasteurized milk and cream together; it contains more than 10 percent but less than 20 percent milk fat.

Homogenized milk. Milk that has been subjected to a process that reduces the fat globules to about a quarter of their original size and makes the milk's consistency the same throughout. Unhomogenized milk has a thick clotting of cream at the top which can either be spooned off or, by shaking the bottle vigorously, distributed throughout the milk, but not particularly evenly.

Low-fat milk. Pasteurized milk with a fat content under 2 percent.

Pasteurized milk. Milk treated by pasteurization to remove any disease-bearing organisms.

Powdered milk. Milk that has had virtually all the water evaporated. Because it is made from low-fat milk and because the volatile elements have all been removed, powdered milk is pretty dull stuff if mixed with water for drinking. It is best used for baking.

Skim milk. Milk containing no more than 0.5 percent milk fat.

Raw milk. Unpasteurized milk, allowed to be sold only from specifically licensed and carefully monitored dairies. See certified milk.

Ultrapasteurized. A relatively new variation on PASTEURIZATION in order to prolong the product's shelf life (but whatever else it does is still under debate). Ultrapasteurized milk sealed in aseptic containers can last up to three months without refrigeration, but once the package is opened it must be treated just as you would treat ordinary milk.

Milk Punch

A spirituous beverage made of milk, sugar, various spices (such as nutmeg), and some form of alcohol such as rum (or whiskey), often fortified with brandy and perhaps embellished with ice cream, stirred to a smooth texture, and served cold.

Milk Shake

A strictly North American soda fountain specialty of milk, some form of flavoring syrup, and ice cream, thoroughly shaken (or put through the blender) until smooth.

Milk Toast

White bread, toasted and buttered, onto which is poured warm milk, salt, and pepper. The incomparable American writer on food M. F. K. Fisher described it as being "for the Ill, Weak, Old, Very Young, or Weary."

Milkweed

A common wild plant (*Asclepias syriaca*) that gives off a milky juice when cut. Native Americans used the blossoms and the extremely young, tender buds as a flavoring agent and thickener. They must either be dried or else washed several times with boiling water or they will be unacceptably bitter.

Mille-Feuille

A French pastry (the name means "thousand leaves") made of numerous thin layers of puff pastry with a creamy icing in between, similar to a NAPOLEON.

Millet

A cereal grain (*Panicum miliaceum* and related species) cultivated since ancient times for the not especially tasty flour milled from its seeds as well as for the seeds themselves. Millet is available in the hulled form mostly in health food stores and can be used in whole-grain baking or as a rice substitute. It is of particular importance as a staple grain in Africa, where the plant's ability to thrive in soils too waterless for most crops renders it indispensable.

Milt

Also called *soft roe*. The sex glands and sperm of a male fish, the male equivalent of ROE. It is usually prepared by cleaning off the blood vessels and poaching it in lemon-flavored water.

Milton

A mild early red APPLE.

Mimosa

1. A salad strewn with chopped, hard-boiled egg yolks spread out so as to resemble a mimosa flower.

2. A concoction of Champagne and orange juice, often served at brunch.

Mince

To chop something really fine but not quite reduce it to powder.

Mincemeat

Originally it was meat that was indeed minced, i.e., chopped into very small, fine pieces. That was not, of course, all that was done to it. It was enriched with fresh and dried fruits (apples, for example, and raisins), spices, and rum or brandy or Madeira (or all three), and set down to age for use during the dreary winter months when fresh food was unobtainable. That was the origin of our present-day mince pies and other delicacies containing mincemeat.

Mincemeat is no longer necessarily—or even very often—made with meat. The venison or beef that formed its base has been replaced in many recipes with dried fruits (especially apples, apricots, cherries, pears, and raisins) or vegetables (such as tomatoes). The British style is to make traditional mincemeat with beef fat (suet) and no additional meat, American and French to make it with beef fat and additional minced meat. Mincemeat (whether the original style or essentially meatless) is most notably used as a pie filling.

Mineral Water

A bottled water taken from springs that contain purportedly health-giving minerals. Mineral waters are now frequently served as a replacement for alcoholic drinks or sodas under a number of names: Poland Springs and Saratoga among those from the United States; Apollinaris, Evian, Perrier, and Vichy Celestins among the better-known imported varieties. Mineral water may be still or sparkling.

Minestrone

A nourishing Italian vegetable soup with pasta and dried beans, sometimes including meat or poultry, and generally topped with grated cheese, but like all soups of this kind it tends to contain whatever the cook has at hand when it comes time to make the dish. Long simmering tends to blend the ingredients together and give it a velvety texture.

Minnow

Any very small fish usually used, if at all, for bait but sometimes a candidate for WHITEBAIT.

Mint

Any plant of the genus *Mentha* but especially APPLEMINT, BERGAMOT MINT, PENNY-ROYAL, PEPPERMINT, and SPEARMINT.

Mint's pleasant fragrance and mild tanginess are perhaps best known in mint juleps and in the mint sauce so frequently served with lamb. It also contributes great flavor to fresh green peas or carrots; it is widely used in the Near East and North Africa for tea and in soups; and its oil is used or synthesized for chewing gum and ice cream and various different kinds of candy. Crème de menthe is a sweetened LIQUEUR that is flavored with mint.

Minute Steak

An extremely thin, often scored, slice of beef that is usually cooked very briefly (one minute per side) over very high heat.

Mirabelle

A BRANDY distilled from the sweet, yellow mirabelle plum (*Prunus cerasifera*). If it is labeled "Mirabelle de Lorraine," it is a superior spirit made from plums grown around the French cities of Nancy and Metz and nowhere else. Mirabelle is an *alcool blanc* or colorless fruit brandy. The mirabelle plum is also used as a somewhat bland dessert plum and for making excellent tarts and preserves.

Mirepoix

A mixture of—usually—carrot, onion, celery, and a little ham, diced and cooked in butter until tender. It is used as a flavor enhancer for meats and shellfish, often serving as the bed on which such foods are braised and, after the fat has been taken off, blended to serve as a gravy or sauce.

Mirin

Also *rice wine*. A slightly sweet Japanese rice-based cooking wine used especially as a glaze for broiled foods and as a flavoring in basting sauces. If you don't have any, try a medium-dry sherry, a white vermouth, or—in a pinch—a shot of gin as a replacement.

Miroton

A French stew made of slices of boiled beef layered with onions and reheated in an onion-flavored sauce.

Miso

A fermented soybean (barley, chickpeas, and rice can also be its base) paste usually augmented with salt and a cereal grain. It is used in Japanese cooking in many forms and is often seen in soup. Misos come in a variety of strengths and flavors. Generally speaking, the darker the color, the stronger the taste. When adding miso to a hot liquid, mix a little of the liquid into the miso first, then pour it all back in.

Mix

To blend things together until all the elements become pretty much one unit.

Mixed Grill

An elaborate spread for a late, formal breakfast, brunch, or luncheon. It would consist typically of several different types of broiled meats—bacon, kidneys, lamb chops, and sausages, and less frequently brains or sweetbreads—served together with grilled tomato halves and mushrooms. Eggs may be but are not traditionally included in the assortment.

Mixer

1. A kitchen device designed to take the drudgery out of mixing your foods. Fixed mixers stand on a base on the kitchen counter and have removable beaters and sometimes attachments for grinding meat or making fruit juice. The much smaller portable mixers also have removable beaters but can be held in one hand and stored in a kitchen drawer.

2. Any liquid such as soda, tonic, water, or suchlike to be added to a long alcoholic drink.

Mocha

1. A superior variety of Arabian coffee bean or anything flavored with it.

2. A flavoring of coffee mixed with chocolate or cocoa.

Mock Turtle Soup

A soup intended to imitate the taste and gelatinous quality of turtle soup but made with a calf's head and other meats (bacon, ham, a veal knuckle) as well as various spices and vegetables. It is flavored with Madeira or sherry.

Mode, à la

French for "in the style of." If you cook tripe the way they do in the ancient French city of Caen, for example, you will have *tripes à la mode de Caen*. Sometimes the word "mode" is omitted; if you see *à la parisienne*, read it as if it were written *à la mode parisienne*. *Beef à la mode* (with no further qualification) refers to a large piece of beef braised in red wine with vegetables. Sometimes another meat, such as venison, is substituted for the beef, which would then cause the dish to be renamed, for example, venison à la mode.

The term is also joyously used for a piece of pie served with a generous scoop of ice cream, and for this purpose vanilla ice cream is the only acceptable choice and apple pie the only base for it.

Molasses

Originally, it was whatever was left over when all the attainable sugar had crystallized out of the juice of the sugar cane. (Beet molasses is a possibility although an unpleasant one, as it turns out. A limited amount of an excellent, albeit very light, molasses is also made from SORGHUM.)

There are essentially three levels of quality in molasses-making. In the first, the liquid is taken with a little realizable sugar still left in it—this is "first" (and best-quality) molasses, the grade intended for table use; "second" molasses has less sugar—its most prevalent use is in mixes and other prepared foods; and a "third" (or strong-tasting BLACKSTRAP) molasses has little if any crystallizable sugar left in it and has applications in industry, as animal food, and for some kitchen uses. The molasses we are most likely to see in our kitchens these days, however, is generally first molasses mixed with some form of cane syrup (it gives a lighter and more consistent product).

Before cane sugar became so widespread, molasses was a prime sweetening agent, although today it is used as much for flavor as for its saccharine effect. It is prized in baking (when substituting, one cup of molasses equals about three quarters of a cup of granulated sugar and adds about two and a half ounces of liquid that must be subtracted from some liquid element in the recipe). It is a mainstay in such dishes as baked beans and SHOOFLY PIE and can be used for flavoring cookies and bread (especially whole-meal breads) and in icing for cakes. Molasses is also the basis for RUM.

Some molasses bottles are labeled "unsulfured" (or "sulfured"). This is because, in the past especially, sulfur dioxide was used in the making of some molasses to lighten the color, but in so doing it imparted a noticeable sulfurous taste. Sulfur is not much used any more.

Mold

1. The somewhat fuzzy growth that appears on overage foods. To Sir Alexander Fleming it may have opened the way for penicillin, and there are molds that ferment wine and beer and give certain cheeses their character, but for most of us it is a nuisance or worse. Some molds, such as that forming on country hams or on bacon, can be scraped off and nothing is lost. Other moldy foods (breads, fruit) must simply be thrown out. Proper storage inhibits mold.

2. A form or utensil used to give a specific shape to a food or dish which is heated or chilled to induce it to take on that shape.

Mole

No, not that pestiferous nuisance that makes hillocks on your lawn, but a smooth Mexican sauce based on chili peppers with spices and vegetables and, in the case of *mole poblano*, a little unsweetened chocolate. It frequently accompanies poultry and meat dishes.

Mollusk

Shellfish, broadly speaking, but the term also includes the SNAIL. Edible examples include the ABALONE, CLAM, COCKLE, CONCH, LIMPET, MUSSEL, OCTOPUS, OYSTER, PERIWINKLE, SCALLOP, SQUID, and WHELK.

Monkey Bread

An unusual, sweet, yeast-risen coffee cake or sweet bread with considerable eggs and butter. After the first rising, the dough is pinched off into golf-ball-sized pieces, rolled in brown sugar and currants, and piled into a tube pan for an additional rising and baking. How it got its name is anyone's guess.

Monkfish

Also *anglerfish* and *goosefish*. A somewhat bizarre fish (*Lophius americanus* and *Lophius piscatorius*), looking like a cross between a shark and a ray, inhabiting the Atlantic and adjacent waters. The tail of the fish yields a white meat that has the firmness and texture of lobster, for which it is sometimes substituted but not always with attribution. Monkfish has little taste of its own but admirably reflects whatever it is prepared with. The name is also applied to a species of edible shark.

Monosodium Glutamate

Also called simply *MSG* or by its trade name, *Accent*. A flavor enhancer of Oriental origin, it is much used in Chinese and Japanese cooking (in Japan it is called *aji-no-moto*). Although it has little if any taste of its own, it seems to highlight the flavor of the food to which it is added. Some people seem to have an adverse reaction to too much of it, complaining of dizziness, facial tightness, shortness of breath, and chest pains, all of which tend to dissipate shortly after their onset.

Monstera

Also *ceriman*. A rare and unlikely climbing plant (*Monstera deliciosa*) found in tropical climes and elsewhere in greenhouses. It is noted for its long, leathery leaves and for its unusual, scaly, green, banana-shaped fruit. When developing, the fruit is not only hard to get at, but also mildly toxic and terrible tasting. Once ripe, the scales drop from it (piecemeal), revealing a soft, white fruit with a taste veering between pineapple and banana. It will doubtless be most difficult to find, except perhaps in Florida.

Monterey Jack

A bland, semihard, cow's-milk CHEESE first made in the late nineteenth century in Monterey, California. It melts well and often includes flavorings such as chilis (especially jalapeño) or garlic. A hard version (dry Jack) is also made as a grating cheese.

Montilla

A dry Spanish cocktail wine akin to SHERRY, especially a MANZANILLA.

Montrachet

1. A Burgundian vineyard producing some of the world's most celebrated dry white wines.

2. A soft, creamy, white goat's-milk CHEESE from the Burgundian region of France. It is commonly rolled into small "logs" which are themselves frequently dipped in edible ashes.

Moo Goo Gai Pan

A Chinese dish of boneless chicken, stir-fried with mushrooms and flavored with garlic and ginger.

Moonfish

A small, thin fish (*Selene* and *Vomer* spp.) found off the coast of New York and southern New England, off the coast of Europe, and in the Mediterranean. It is sometimes used as a not particularly generous panfish. The name also applies to the OPAH.

Moonshine

An illegally distilled whiskey, specifically CORN LIQUOR; it is a specialty of areas of the southern United States. Sophisticated buyers of moonshine try to differentiate between those who drink their own product and those who know too much about how it was made to be willing to take that risk.

Moose

The moose (*Alces americana*) is North America's largest member of the deer family, licensed for hunting only under stringent conditions but providing copious quantities of flavorful venison. The moose is closely related to the European ELK (*Alces alces*) but not the American elk, or wapiti.

Moose Milk

An alcoholic beverage and reportedly the drink of choice of those who banded together in the 1930s to invent the sport of frostbite dinghy racing. It consists of one part coffee, two parts milk, and five (or more) parts rum and can be served hot, cold, or lukewarm.

Moo Shu

A Chinese stir-fried pork dish with eggs, ginger, lily buds, and scallions, served in an incredibly thin pancake (*moo shoo pancake* or *Peking doily*).

Moray

Also *moray eel*. The morays are a family (Muraenidae) of somewhat dangerously ill-tempered, tropical marine eels that inhabit rocky crevices and coral reefs. The Mediterranean moray (*Muraena helena*) was highly prized by the Romans and is used today—if at all—as a replacement for CONGER eel in BOUILLABAISSE.

Morel

An edible MUSHROOM.

Morello

A dark-colored sour CHERRY.

Mortadella

A large Italian SAUSAGE of ground pork with cubes of beef and pork fat, flavored with coriander and usually some form of spirit. In the United States, it is essentially a variation on bologna.

Mortar

The container part of a mortar and pestle, in which spices and nuts and other ingredients are ground into powder. The blender and food processor have pretty much supplanted it.

Moselle

A white wine made from grapes grown along the banks of the Moselle river in Germany.

Mostarda di Cremona

Also *mostarda di frutti*. An Italian chutneylike condiment consisting of whole, small fruits (apricots, cherries, pears, plums) and slices of melon, put up in a sugar syrup and flavored with mustard oil and garlic. It is used to accompany cold boiled meats, poultry, and fish, especially eel.

Mountain Oyster

See PRAIRIE OYSTER.

Moussaka

A dish of Balkan origin (its exact birthplace being hotly disputed among Greeks, Romanians, Turks, and perhaps others). It consists of sautéed ground meat (beef, lamb, mutton, veal, venison—and even sometimes fish) layered with sautéed eggplant slices and tomato sauce; it is topped with a white sauce, flavored with cheese and usually nutmeg and cinnamon, and then baked. In one variation, the eggplant is replaced by artichoke bottoms.

Mousse

Either a rich, usually frozen (or at least cold) dessert built around whipped cream or a light and airy soufflélike dish.

Mousseline

A sauce, dish, or preparation into which whipped cream or beaten egg whites have been introduced. Sometimes a HOLLANDAISE or MAYONNAISE may be so augmented and merit the addition of the name.

Mozzarella

In its place of origin—Naples—this is a soft, somewhat tasteless cheese made from buffalo's milk that is transformed upon cooking into a flavorful addition to the dish at hand (such as pizza). It is also made with cow's milk, with less spectacular results. Elsewhere, it is a cow's-milk cheese with a rather rubbery consistency that melts extremely well and is used once again for pizza and other dishes that need a topping of melted cheese.

MSG

An abbreviation for MONOSODIUM GLUTAMATE.

Muddler

A bar accessory consisting of a glass rod with a flat end. It is useful for such chores as crushing the mint and sugar cube in a mint julep or pressing the juices out of the citrus fruit in an OLD-FASHIONED.

Muenster

Also *Münster*. A French cheese also spelled MUNSTER.

Muesli

A breakfast cereal (and snack or trail food) of Swiss origin beloved of health food aficionados. It consists of various amounts of raw or toasted cereals (such as rolled oats), dried fruit (especially apples and to a lesser extent lemons), and nuts. Raisins or currants are also frequent additions, as is wheat germ.

Muffin

A small quickbread usually flavored with berries or bran or cornmeal or something similar, leavened with baking powder, and mixed just enough to distribute the ingredients evenly but not enough to make it tough. Muffins are generally served hot at breakfast (although there are some that are more appropriate at dinner). They are baked in muffin tins. Unlike regular muffins, the ENGLISH MUFFIN (which is leavened with yeast) is precooked on a griddle and toasted before eating. In England, however, a muffin is a tea cake.

Muffin Tin

Or *muffin pan*. A frame of small cuplike indentures used for making muffins and cupcakes. An early variation with smaller indentations was known as a *gem pan*.

Mugwort

A Eurasian herb (*Artemesia* spp.) related to wormwood; it is the informing flavoring of ABSINTHE. The slightly bitter, dried leaves of mugwort were once used as a flavoring for a variety of dishes, including soups and stews.

Mulberry

Perhaps best known as the source of the favorite food of the Chinese silkworm, mulberry trees exist in varieties that produce fruit edible by people too, unless the birds get them first. (They have been described as a first-rate method of diverting birds from more valuable crops such as raspberries.)

Of the various mulberries, the most prevalent are the Chinese (*Morus alba*, the one used for silkworms), which gives white and also black berries, and the red mulberry (*Morus rubra*). There is also a black mulberry, *Morus nigra*, which gives black fruit but, while abundant in Europe, is not widely grown in North America. Some mulberries will produce fruit probably best left to the birds, although it may be usable in preserves or tarts. Others produce sweet, lush black or white or red-to-purple fruit that clamors to be eaten right off the bush. Mulberries are so perishable that you do indeed have to eat them virtually off the bush, so you're not likely to find them commercially—you pretty much have to grow them yourself. If you should grow them, you can use the fresh fruit for pies or, with some slightly tarter fruit, make them into jelly.

The name is also sometimes applied to the flowering raspberry (*Rubus odoratus*), an ornamental shrub with inedible fruit, but this usage is considered dead wrong by botanists.

Mule
The offspring of a female horse and a male donkey, apparently considered a delectable substitute for horsemeat in areas where horsemeat is eaten.

Mull
To heat a drink such as beer, cider, or wine and enrich it with spices (cloves, cinnamon) and sweeteners. A hot, mulled drink can be a very present comfort on a cold evening.

Mullet
White-fleshed food fish of salt, brackish, and (to a lesser extent) fresh tropical or temperate waters with a worldwide distribution. The red mullets, which are actually goatfish (*Mullus barbatus* and *Mullus surmuletus*), are found mostly in the Mediterranean. They have been praised since classical times, and many recipes recommend they be poached in various liquids and served with various delectable sauces.

The common mullets of North America are the striped or jumping mullet (*Mugil cephalus*) and the white or silver mullet (*Mugil curema*). North American mullets generally are baked or broiled or fried or grilled rather than poached or steamed.

Mulligan Stew
A catchall stew of meat or fish and vegetables reputed to have its origins in the hobo camps of the United States, from the turn of the century through the Great Depression. Clearly, it encompassed whatever anyone could come up with.

Mulligatawny
A peppery Anglo-Indian chicken (or oxtail) soup flavored with curry and other spices and frequently garnished with hardboiled eggs. In its heyday, it was considered one of the glories of Anglo-Indian cuisine.

Mung
An Oriental BEAN largely used for its sprouts. In India, mung beans are used in the same way as split peas or lentils and are also ground into flour.

Munster

A creamy semisoft cow's-milk CHEESE of Alsatian origin (but widely copied else-where) sometimes spelled Münster (or Muenster), as if it were German. It is extremely mild and sometimes flavored with cumin or caraway seeds.

Muscadet

A dry white wine made from grapes grown around the mouth of France's Loire River. The best of it will carry the label Muscadet de Sèvre et Maine. Muscadet is often recommended as an accompaniment for oysters or other shellfish and is considered best when chilled, but not numbingly so. Like so many dry white wines, it is best consumed young (say, one to three years old).

Muscadine

Either of two varieties (*Vitis rotundifolia* and *Vitis munsoniana*) of North American GRAPE, otherwise known as the *scuppernong*, that makes a good—if somewhat strong—table grape. It is most prevalent in the southeastern United States. By adding vast amounts of sugar, a wine of sorts can be made from it, and it has been widely used for preserves. The late wine expert Frank Schoonmaker did not consider the muscadine a true grape and considered its wine to be more akin to a cordial than a wine.

Muscat

A group of related grape varieties (*Vitis vinifera*) used as a table grape and for mak-ing raisins and wine. With their characteristic "musky" taste and aroma, they con-tribute to wines ranging from the prestigious sweet wines of France's Sauternes to the sometimes good, but sometimes all but sickeningly sweet, wines of lesser climes.

Muscatel

A wine made from MUSCAT grapes. Some muscatels can be rich, soothing dessert wines, some simply inexpensive, inferior highly alcoholic products sometimes referred to as "sneaky pete."

Muscovy

A species of duck (*Cairina moschata*) native to an area ranging from Mexico to Brazil and almost resembling a goose rather than a Long Island duck. It may be found most frequently at live-poultry markets in or near Chinese neighborhoods (where real food is not only requested but demanded). It has darker meat and is less fatty and more tasty than the ducks you usually encounter, but must be eaten young or it acquires an unpleasant musky taste.

Mush

Cornmeal boiled in water (or milk) to be served as a cereal or to be cooled, cut into pieces, and fried as a side dish. POLENTA might be described as a form of cornmeal mush.

Mushroom

For the purposes of the kitchen, an edible fungi. There are plenty of inedible ones and a discouraging number that are toxic. If you're not a mycologist (a fancy name for mushroom expert) do not go out and pick your own unless you have an expert at your side. The novelist Robert Graves reported that after eating a poisonous mushroom, its victims proclaimed, just before they died in agony, that they had never tasted anything so delicious. Fortunately, there are plenty of edible mushrooms, many of which are sheer gastronomic wonders.

Mushrooms appear in odd places and in a myriad of incarnations. Many we like to eat crop up in dank woodlands, grow on rotting wood, or suddenly appear in woodlots or grassy meadows. Others show up in the vegetable departments of our local markets. And when they are good, they are very, very good.

Mushrooms are a peculiar phenomenon. They have no leaves, no roots; they are unable to synthesize chlorophyll (which is what makes plants green) and are in effect parasites on other organic material. They have little if any nutritional value, although they do provide texture and taste. The most common ones we see, the French *agaric mushroom* or *champignon de Paris*, are more or less umbrella shaped and range in color from cream to white to tan. They are among the gilled mushrooms and, like most other commercially available mushrooms, are available canned (mushrooms do not adapt to canning with any distinction) or dried or fresh.

When you are buying conventional mushrooms in the market, look underneath the cap and check the gills. If they are closed, the mushroom is fresh. If they are open and black, the mushroom is probably over the hill. Closed gills suggest a fresher—and more appetizing—mushroom, but if they are slightly open but not yet black, they are often tastier but lack delicacy (chop them up and drop them in the stew but only at the last minute). They are usually sold in plastic containers with holes here and there. Don't stop up the holes—but keep the mushrooms dry and let them breathe, even when refrigerated. Damp mushrooms tend to go bad quickly. It is, however, a better idea to buy those that are not prepackaged and select the ones that appeal to you.

The use of mushrooms depends upon the ingenuity of the cook. There are mushroom aficionados who can make a meal of them—from the appetizer through the main dish to the salad and the dessert—even the wine that goes with it and the cordial that follows. Most of us are not that versatile, alas.

It would be impossible to describe every edible mushroom within the confines of a volume such as this. However, some of the ones you might encounter—either at the market or in company with someone who knows the field—might include:

Beefsteak fungus (*Fistulina hepatica*). A liver-shaped, quite red, juicy mushroom with a buff underside considered excellent when fresh, often used raw in salads.

Button mushroom. A small champignon de Paris (see below).

Cèpe (*Boletus edulis*). The French name, but in any country this is as good a wild mushroom as you're going to find. A large (six inches or so in diameter), variable in color from grayish to tan, somewhat elusive mushroom found mostly (if at all) in the spring and fall. Cèpes are more available dried than fresh and enlighten all manner of soups and stews and stuffings.

Champignon de Paris (*Agaricus bisporus*). The common mushroom of commerce (although we are seeing more and more wild mushrooms in our markets).

Chanterelle (*Cantherellus cibarius*). A broad, bright yellow wild mushroom that seems to grow better in Europe than in North America; the European specimen has an aroma likened to that of ripe apricots that its American counterpart somewhat lacks. Use chanterelles as a flavoring in other dishes or as a side dish by themselves. (Freshly picked chanterelles may be a pain to wash.)

Chinese black mushroom (*Lentinus edodes*). The Chinese cousin of the Japanese shiitake (see below). It's not black but more likely brown or buff and is sold dried. Soak these for 25 minutes or so and add them to Chinese dishes or cook them in broth with soy sauce and sherry as a side dish.

Cloud ear fungus (*Auricularia polytrica* or *Auricularia auriculajudae*). Also called *tree ear* and *wood ear* for its propensity for growing on decaying wood and sometimes *Jew's ear* from the second scientific name. A Chinese mushroom or fungus sold dried. It has a delicate flavor and a slight "bite." Soak a little of it (it expands up to five times its original size), wash it well, cut it in pieces, and add it to soups, stir-fries, and stews.

Enokitake (*Flammulina velutipes*). Sometimes simply shortened to *enoki*, which is technically the tree on which it grows. A Japanese mushroom consisting of a long white stalk with a slight bulb at the top. Rinse enokitakes well and use them in salads, soups, and simmered dishes, but when cooking them, add them only at the last minute.

Fairy ring (*Marasmius oreades*). A somewhat bell-shaped brown (fading to yellowish-white with age) mushroom that grows in rings in grassy meadows, but make sure you have the right one, for there are others that resemble it that are not pleasant.

Field mushroom (*Agaricus campestris*). A close relative of the mushroom of commerce, it can be found here and there, sometimes in rings, sometimes in incomplete rings, usually in grassy ground. Use it as you would a commercial mushroom.

Honey mushroom (*Armillaria mellea*). In Latin *mellea* means honey, but the name refers not to the taste but to the color of the mushroom. It is a thin, fleshy disk that occurs in cleared land, forests, and orchards and is a menace to living trees. Apparently, it sends stringlike growths beneath the soil that attack the roots of neighboring trees, ultimately killing them. (In their final agony, such trees are said to give off a phosphorescence that must take a nocturnal passerby with some astonishment.) In Italy, these mushrooms are pickled in vinegar and oil and served forth in the winter season.

Inky cap (*Coprinus atramentarius*). There are other inky caps, but this one is the "common" one. A fleshy bell-shaped mushroom that grows pretty nearly anywhere. Good but only when fresh and young; as a warning, it often causes nausea if taken before, with, or after an alcoholic beverage.

Matsutake (*Armillaria edodes*). A Japanese mushroom that is thick, meaty, and dark brown. You probably won't find matsutakes outside of Japan, and even there they will be expensive in the extreme. If you run across a recipe calling for them, use oyster mushrooms instead.

Morel (*Morchella esculenta*). One of the favorites of gastronomes, this dome-shaped mushroom, two to four inches high and with a honeycomb texture, has an earthy, nutlike flavor. Sauté it in butter and the devil take the cholesterol.

Oyster (*Pleurotus ostreatus*). A soft, moist, peppery, shell-shaped mushroom with white flesh and a gray to white to brown exterior. It grows on rotting tree trunks in parts of Asia, Australia, Europe, and North America. When young, before it gets overly tough, it is used in casseroles and soups and stir-fried dishes or is stewed. It is an interesting stand-in for the regular, commercial mushroom.

Porcini. An Italian name for cèpe (see above).

Portabella. A large, brown, beefy mushroom found in most supermarkets. It would call to mind the description of mushrooms as being "the poor man's beefsteak," except that the portabella is considerably more expensive per pound than is beef.

Puffballs (*Bovista, Calvatia, Lycoperdon,* and *Vascellum* spp.). A whole gamut of mushrooms large and small, ranging from white to purple, that when squeezed emit their spores like a cloud of dust. Most of them are eminently edible, but only when they are still young enough that the interior is a pure white. Slice them and sauté them or chop them and pop them into whatever dish you're making that might profit from them.

Rodman's mushroom (*Agaricus rodmani*). Practically a twin, culinarily speaking, of the *champignon de Paris*.

Shaggymane (*Coprinus comatus*). Another of the inky caps (see above). It grows in rich earth and waste lots and when young is tender and succulent. Try it sautéed on toast.

Shiitake (*Cortinellus shiitake*). A Japanese mushroom akin to the Chinese black mushroom (see above) and usually sold dried. If you come across a fresh one, cut a slice in the top to ensure the inside will be as thoroughly cooked as the outside.

Muskellunge

A hard-fighting freshwater fish (*Esox masquinongy*) of the Great Lakes and upper Saint Lawrence River. It is a relative of the PIKE and can be cooked in similar ways.

Muskmelon

One of the major varieties of MELON.

Muskrat

A fur-bearing, aquatic rodent (*Ondatra zibethica*) of North America. Though sought for its fur, it is also taken for its meat, which may be called by its Cajun name, "marsh rabbit" or "marsh hare." Muskrat meat is similar to rabbit and lends itself to the same cooking methods.

Muslin

An indispensable fabric for the kitchen. Not only is it useful as a dishtowel and for general mopping up, a muslin towel lining a colander is ideal for straining out extraneous matter in soups and stews. Home cheesemakers find muslin useful to hold the curd of milk cheese while the whey drips through. Once used, the muslin can be rinsed and run through the washing machine and emerge as good as new.

Mussel

A saltwater mollusk highly prized in Europe but somewhat scorned in North America, where it is sometimes marketed as a "mussel clam" in an effort to increase its popularity.

The most common North American mussel is the blue mussel (*Mytilis edulis*), found in large quantities on the East Coast. The western mussel (*Mytilus californicus*) is prone to infection from certain types of plankton, especially those that cause the so-called red tide, and is not harvested between May and October, the months when the plankton are most likely to appear. (The mussels themselves seem unaffected by this infection, but become poisonous to those who eat them.) Fortunately, cultivated mussels are available that are not subject to this affliction. The more robust horse (or red) mussels (*Modiolus* spp.) are also seen along the West Coast and in eastern Canada.

Unlike so much other shellfish, mussels are not recommended to be eaten raw (although this is still fairly common in parts of Europe). Before cooking them, they must be cleaned of any sand or mud and be separated from their "beard," or *bissus*, a fibrous growth they use to cling to the rocks and pilings where they live. (Wild mussels can be particularly pesky in this respect, with the last vestiges of the beard often being best ripped out with a pair of pliers.) When cleaning mussels, drop them into a pan of water and discard those with open shells and ones that float. Wash them in several rinses of water and pull off the beard.

Select mussels just as you would clams—look for moist, intact shells with no strong odors. Don't try keeping them covered with water (they'll drown); instead, refrigerate them in a container of some sort covered with a wet cloth. They should keep that way for a couple of days anyway, so long as the cloth remains wet.

Blue mussels are usually steamed open (commonly in white wine or perhaps cider) and then served with or without their shells in a CHOWDER, PAELLA, RISOTTO, or similar dish. They may also be prepared as *moules marinières*, in which the mussels are steamed in wine with onion and herbs and then served with one or both shells intact and with the strained broth, enriched with a little butter and minced parsley, poured over them. The whole marvelously messy dish is sopped up with plentiful chunks of French bread. The larger varieties can also be breaded and fried. Craig Claiborne, when he was food critic for *The New York Times*, went on record as believing that Billi Bi, a cream of mussel soup, is about as close to perfection as a soup can get. Canned mussels, plain or smoked and packed in oil, make an advantageous cocktail snack.

Must

A grape (or other fruit) juice that is not yet fermented into wine.

Mustard

Various plants of the mustard family that are used as a potherb, in salads, as a seasoning (especially for curries), and as a condiment. There are other, nonculinary, uses (such as mustard plaster) outside the scope of this book.

Mustards are the standard bearers for the large botanical family that also includes turnips and cabbages. The varieties that give us the mustard we use as a condiment are black mustard (*Brassica nigra*) and white mustard (*Brassica alba*), the names coming from the color of their seeds.

Mustard seeds are used in Indian cooking—the whole black seeds are dropped into the hot oil and make a popping sound when the oil is sufficiently hot. Mustard ground into a condiment comes in various guises. Regular, or ballpark, mustard is the slightly sweet, tart, light brown addition to our hot dogs and similar foods. It is made from white mustard with some vinegar and turmeric among its seasonings. Imported mustards are usually tangier. All start with powdered mustard seeds that are then mixed with vinegar, grape juice, beer, or some other agent and spiced to give them their own identity. German (such as Düsseldorf) mustard, for example, is often sweeter and spicier than French (such as Dijon or Meaux) and many mustards come in smooth or somewhat coarse ("country style") varieties. English and Chinese mustard is sold as a dry powder; add cold water and let it sit for 10–15 minutes while the flavor develops. Both tend to be stronger, even considerably stronger, than the other varieties, with the Chinese generally leading the list for pungency and strength.

Mustard Greens

The leaves of the MUSTARD plant, used as a potherb. There are several varieties, including *Brassica alba*, or white mustard. Chinese mustard (*Brassica juncea*) sports large, dark leaves with a pungent taste; the very youngest leaves are used in Chinese soups and stir-fried dishes. In North America they will be found, if at all, in Oriental markets. A British mustard (*Sinapis alba*) is grown to be harvested when only a few inches tall and used in mustard-and-cress sandwiches. Unless you grow it yourself, it's not likely to be available in North America. What is grown in North America is a mustard plant (*Brassica japonica*) that produces leaves ranging from smooth with a white midriff to curly and bright green. All bear small bright yellow flowers and are most likely to be in the markets during the winter months.

Select mustard greens that look fresh and not wilted and use them up in a day or so. You can wrap them in plastic and refrigerate them for several days, but don't wash them until you're ready to use them. Then wash them well and use the smallest leaves to accompany other greens for salad or simmer them for 10 minutes or so in salted boiling water and serve them with melted butter or bacon bits. You can also sauté or steam them.

Mutton

The meat of an adult sheep, roughly one to five years old. In the United States, mutton gives way almost entirely to LAMB, which is preferred in the belief that mutton is tougher and has a rank, gamy taste. Prime mutton is similar to lamb with slightly more fat content and a richer taste. Also like lamb, good mutton is close grained and firm to the touch, although the meat before cooking is (or ought to be) bright red and the fat will be more on the yellow than the white side. Removing all the outer fat will often keep mutton from developing any of that unwanted gaminess.

Mutton is sometimes seen in restaurants in the form of the English mutton chop, a thick slab of tenderloin that is traditionally broiled. Otherwise, mutton may be boiled, braised, roasted, or stewed. If the mutton is to be roasted, it usually benefits from a little aging, as with the finest grades of beef.

Muttonfish

A name applied to several fish. Included is a mottled yellowish or gray foot-long or slightly larger species (*Macrozoarces americanus*) of the North Atlantic and its European equivalent (*Zoarces viviparus*), known as eelpout in Britain. There is said to be a move afoot to market these fish as *ocean sole*. Muttonfish is also the name for two more southerly species, one a delectable snapper (*Lutjanus analis*), also called *mutton snapper*, the other a grouper (*Alphestes afer*), also called *mutton hamlet*, of some importance in the West Indies. Both can be cooked according to any recipe appropriate for bass.

Mutton Snapper

A MUTTONFISH.

Myrtille

A French term for the BILBERRY and distilled into a rare but delectable fruit brandy, *eau de Vie de Myrtille*.

Mysost

A soft Scandinavian light-brown CHEESE from the whey of cow's milk. It has a slightly sweet flavor and is far and away the favorite cheese of Scandinavia.

Nacho
A Mexican snack consisting of a tortilla chip topped with melted cheese and chopped CHILI.

Namaycush
The species name for the lake trout, a CHAR, also known as *togue*.

Nam Pla
A strong, pungent sauce made in Thailand by fermenting fish in salt and drawing off the ensuing liquid, which is used like soy sauce. The Vietnamese variation is known as *nuöc mam*.

Nanking Cherry
A usually ornamental, cherrylike tree (*Prunus tomentosa*) with small, red, edible fruit usually left for the birds but occasionally used in preserves.

Napa
    1. A valley of California where some of the best table wines of that state (and of North America as a whole) are produced.
    2. CHINESE CABBAGE.

Napoleon
A light and tender pastry consisting of three layers of puff pastry with a cream filling. It may be drizzled with chocolate, frosted, or sprinkled with powdered sugar.

Nasi Goreng
An Indonesian specialty consisting of spiced fried rice with various vegetables and meats, poultry, or shellfish. It is traditionally washed down with beer.

Nasturtium
A flowering plant of South American origin that comes in two varieties, one (*Tropaeoleum majus*) a climber, the other (*Tropaeoleum minus*) a dwarf much used along the edges of gardens. The young shoots and leaves of the dwarf variety give a peppery taste to soups and sandwiches, and its attractive flowers are slightly more peppery as well as visually attractive in salads. In England, where the leaves are sometimes called *Indian cress*, the immature seeds are pickled as a substitute for CAPERS.

Natal Plum

A South African shrub (*Carissa grandiflora*) imported into areas of North America (and Hawaii) where there is little or no frost. It produces a white, star-shaped flower and a scarlet, plumlike fruit suitable for pies and preserves and sauces.

Navarin

A French lamb (or mutton) stew, traditionally made with onions and potatoes. If the word *printanière* is added, so are carrots, turnips, and green peas.

Navel Orange

A variety of eating (as opposed to juice) ORANGE.

Navy Bean

A small BEAN usually found dried.

Neapolitan Medlar

Another name for AZAROLE.

Neat

1. Old English name for ox, now used almost exclusively to refer to neat's-foot jelly, meaning the jelly made from the foot of an ox, or more likely, a calf.

2. Plain, unadulterated, as whiskey straight, with no water or mixer.

Nectar

Originally, it was the food of the gods of Mount Olympus but has since been reduced to a thick, sweet, even syrupy juice extracted from such fruits as apricots and peaches.

Nectarine

Essentially, it is a naturally defuzzed PEACH. There seems to be some disagreement as to whether the nectarine is a naturally occurring phenomenon or came about as a cross between a peach and a plum. However, in addition to being smoother, nectarine fruit generally runs smaller than peaches and is more highly colored as well as firmer. Nectarines can be used in the same way as peaches, with the advantage that they need not be peeled. Just wash them well. Select nectarines as you would peaches—look for a healthy skin without greenish highlights, a little give without being mushy, and no blemishes or spots.

Needlefish

A name for a fish with a long, beaklike mouth such as the saury or the gar, but more specifically one of the family Belonidae, mostly warm-water marine species, although they are sometimes found as far north as Cape Cod. Needlefish are edible, although not too many people are aware of this, and can be cooked like PIKE. According to Alan Davidson's *North Atlantic Seafood*, the backbone may turn bright green during cooking, but this is in the nature of the beast and nothing to be alarmed about. If you dislike green, you may wish to remove the backbone before cooking the fish.

Negus

An eighteenth-century hot drink compounded of wine (principally PORT) with water, sugar, lemon juice, and nutmeg. James Boswell, the eminent writer and biographer of Dr. Samuel Johnson, enjoyed it prior to retiring for the night.

Nelis

Also *winter nelis*. A variety of late PEAR.

Neroli

An oil extracted from orange blossoms; also an orange-flavored almond pastry.

Nesselrode Pudding

An extraordinarily rich iced or frozen French dessert originally consisting of custard flavored with chestnuts and laced with maraschino liqueur. Other ingredients include whipped cream, raisins and currants soaked in Malaga wine, and candied fruits, with a garnish of glazed chestnuts.

Nettle

A prickly pest of a plant (*Urtica*); it is covered with stiff hairs that give a hefty jolt like a bee-sting when you brush up against them. Only the new tips of the nettle as it first pokes out of the ground in the spring are picked (and wearing gloves to pick them is highly recommended). Washed under running water, they can be sliced into a kettle with the water they were washed in still clinging to their leaves and cooked like spinach. (Cooking does away with the sting.) Or they can be made into a cream soup or a pudding as the Scots do. The tender new spring growth of the bull or cat briar (*Smilax glauca*) can be used in the same way.

Neuchâtel

A Swiss canton noted for its table wines, most of which are of the dry, white persuasion.

Neufchâtel

A soft, French, cow's-milk cream CHEESE from Normandy. The American rendition is moister than the original and has less butterfat.

Newberg

A sauce for various dishes but most frequently associated with LOBSTER. It consists of butter, brandy, cream, egg yolks, and wine (Madeira or sherry).

New England Boiled Dinner

A meal of corned beef and cabbage. In New England, the preference is for a lightly corned piece of beef or one that has been blanched to rid it of some of its saltiness.

It is simmered with root vegetables (carrots, onions, parsnips, potatoes, and turnips) and a piece of salt pork. Cabbage is added toward the end of the cooking time, and the dish is usually served with beets that have been cooked separately. The leftovers are chopped up and served in a beet-colored mélange known as RED FLANNEL HASH.

New England Chowder

A fish, clam, or corn CHOWDER containing salt pork. It is usually thought that a New England clam chowder differs from the New York (Manhattan) style by restricting the vegetables to onions and potatoes. This is only partly true; the essential ingredient of New England chowder is the salt pork, as crucial to the cookery of New England as fatback is to that of the South.

New York Chowder

A clam CHOWDER augmented with aromatic vegetables such as celery and tomatoes, neither of which is used in the traditional New England version.

New York Steak

See SHELL STEAK.

New Zealand Spinach

A plant (*Tetragonia expansa*) originally from New Zealand and Australia but now cultivated just about anywhere, especially in places that get too hot for spinach to thrive. The leaves are somewhat like spinach only slightly more bitter. This is a green you're more likely to grow than see in your supermarket.

Niter

Also *nitre*. See SALTPETER.

Nockerl

An Austrian DUMPLING. In addition to the regular variety, there is also a lighter, sweetened variety to accompany fruit dishes.

Noisette

1. A French term for hazelnut or the color of hazelnut, as with butter that has been cooked until light brown.

2. Small, round pieces of fine meat, especially the tenderloin or the eye of a chop.

Nondairy Creamer

An imitation dairy product composed of oils with a high content of saturated fat (coconut or hydrogenated vegetable) with various things to sweeten and preserve it. It is not a good bet for those with cholesterol worries.

Nonpareilles

In France, small CAPERS preserved in vinegar.

Nonpareils

1. Sprinkles—variously colored grains of sugar used to decorate pastries and ice cream.

2. Small chocolate disks sprinkled with tiny, white sugar candies.

Noodles

PASTA made with egg and usually presented in ribbon shape in a variety of sizes, although it can be bent or rippled, folded or curled. Simply because pasta is of Italian origin does not mean that all types of pastas are Italian or Italian inspired. There are many other varieties from other places, including Asia, and in addition to wheat flour, noodles are made here and there from bean curd, buckwheat, cornstarch, rice, and even seaweed.

Nopal

A fruit of the PRICKLY PEAR.

Nopales

Also *nopalitos*. A Mexican specialty that has been steadily moving north. It consists not of the fruit but of the oval leaves, known as paddles, of various varieties of cacti (*Opuntia* spp.). The taste has been compared to a slightly tart green bean with a touch of asparagus and its slippery consistency to that of okra. To use nopales, peel off any "eyes" or prickles, trim the edges, then simmer them lengthily with herbs, onions, tomatoes, and a little oil and vinegar. You may also steam them or sauté them quickly, perhaps scrambled with eggs. They also add a comforting crunch to salads.

Buy nopales when they are crisp and green and still fairly small. If you get them fresh, they will keep, in plastic, refrigerated, for a week or more.

Nori

A Japanese name for dried LAVER.

Northern Spy

A midseason, excellent, all-round APPLE.

Norway Lobster

Also *Dublin Bay prawn* and *scampi*. A shellfish (*Nephrops norvegicus*) found along the Atlantic coast from Iceland to the mouth of the Mediterranean and into the Adriatic. Running some 10 inches long, its coloration is pink to orange-red with red and white striped claws. In Europe, especially the British Isles where they may be either fresh or frozen, Norway lobsters are steamed and shelled and dipped in lemony melted butter or otherwise into mayonnaise; grilled with olive oil; or used in the equivalent of a shrimp cocktail. Alan Davidson explains, in his *North Atlantic Seafood*, that the name Dublin Bay prawn came about when Irish fishermen returned from their voyages having picked up some Norway lobster on the way. The street vendors gave them the name because the Dublin Bay fishing wharves were where they went to buy them.

Nougat

A candy made of roasted almonds, pistachios, or hazelnuts and sugar syrup or honey. Originally, it was made with walnuts. White nougat (made with the addition of white of egg) is most frequently seen, although nougat can also be colored.

Nouvelle Cuisine

A style of cooking ("new cooking," to the French) that arose in the 1970s. It stressed lean and light foods in smallish quantities and emphasized vegetables—often quickly cooked to ensure crispness—and sauces that were boiled down rather than enriched with butter and flour. It marked a departure from the traditional, rich dishes of French CLASSIC COOKING.

Noyau

A French liqueur concocted by steeping cherry or peach pits in alcohol sometimes also flavored with the oil of almonds. It has an almondy flavor and is either colorless or slightly pink.

Nuöc Mam

A pungent, salty Vietnamese sauce (a variant of NAM PLA) made from fermented fish, one of many such sauces found in Asian countries. It is used much as is soy sauce.

Nurse Shark

An edible species of SHARK.

Nut

A fruit seed that is surrounded by a tough, woody casing and a membranous inner one. Nuts have been part of the diet of the human race as long as there has been one and are still greatly enjoyed whether eaten alone or used to enliven dishes as simple as spaghetti or as impressive as a Viennese pastry, or pressed for oil. Nuts can be used ground or whole as well as blanched, plain, or roasted. In popular usage, the word is also used to designate all manner of kernels and pods (peanuts, for example) and seeds. The various nuts will be treated under their individual headings in this volume.

Nut Butter

Peanuts, of course, come to mind right off. It's hard to imagine growing up in the United States without peanut butter, whether you buy it or make it yourself (you'll probably have to add a little peanut oil to it to civilize it and make it usable). However, butters have been made from other nuts as well, especially cashews, Brazil nuts, and hazelnuts.

Nutcracker

A device for cracking nuts. There are many designs ranging from levers to screw presses to a simple hammer to pound open the recalcitrant object. You can also use a special grinder or mill.

Nut Grass

See CHUFA.

Nutmeg

A most useful and versatile spice. It is the nut of an Oriental tree (*Myristica fragrans*). To reach the kernel, the nutmeg, the outer covering of the fruit (which itself is eaten in areas where the tree is grown) is stripped away, and the lacy MACE covering is removed. The nut is dried and may be shipped whole or ground. Most nutmeg is sold ground, but if you grate it yourself, you'll get a fresher, spicier taste (if you don't, make sure you buy the ground nutmeg in very small amounts and don't keep it too long—if the aroma is weak, the spice will be too, and it should probably be replaced).

Nutmeg is useful in pies and other baked goods, can be added to fish and meat and game, is helpful to poultry, is excellent in cheese dishes such as soufflés, and does wonders with vegetables, especially spinach. Nutmeg is also traditionally grated over eggnog or milk punch and is indispensable in a great many Near Eastern and Balkan dishes.

Nutmeg Grater

A special, fine-mesh grater used for nutmeg. Nutmeg graters come in many different shapes and sizes, and some antique ones are made of materials ranging from tin to sterling silver, although modern ones are tin or stainless steel. One modern type resembles a pepper mill but is somewhat unwieldy and hard to keep clean (not that any of them is a picnic in this respect). The old-fashioned pierced-tin (or steel) model may still be as good as any, with its curved surface and hole in the back in which to store your nutmeg. Some graters will even hold more than one nutmeg.

Oat

A cereal grain (*Avena sativa*) of central European origin, but probably adopted most lovingly in Scotland. It can be made into a flour of sorts, but as that flour contains no gluten, it isn't by itself of much use in bread-making. The form that is most frequently seen in the kitchen is generally *rolled oats*, the oats having been steamed and flattened, cut into flakes, and sometimes processed for quick or instant cooking. Steel-cut oats are the oat kernels (or groats) sliced small and may be labeled "Scotch" or "Irish" or "Irish Style." The whole kernels themselves are also sometimes available. Rolled and steel-cut oats and groats are not interchangeable except perhaps as a breakfast cereal and even then need different cooking times (usually specified on the label).

In addition to furnishing breakfast, oats make a wonderful contribution (in both taste and texture) to breads, cookies, crackers, and oatcakes and were used—at least by the northern Celts—as a thickener for soups and stews. You can also find quick-cooking rolled oats that cook in as little as five minutes (although with some loss of flavor and texture) and which are interchangeable in recipes for regular rolled oats. Instant oats are another question. As they are slightly precooked, they are useful only as a cereal. Oat bran has also been widely acclaimed as a provider of dietary fiber.

Oatmeal

The OAT in its most usual processed (or hulled) form, steel cut, and cooked as a porridge. In Britain, oatmeal comes in four sizes: coarse, medium, fine, and pinhead. If your recipe calls for any of the smaller sizes, use a grinder or food processor to refine whatever you have.

Oca

An edible plant (*Oxalis crenata* and *Oxalis tuberosa*) native to Peru. It produces small tubers looking something like irregularly shaped walnuts. If fresh picked, the tubers are toxic, but after drying are used like new potatoes or—after further drying—like dried figs.

Ocean Perch

A fairly large (up to three feet in length) orange or reddish ocean fish (*Sebastes* spp.) or any of its relatives or lookalikes; together they comprise a wealth of firm, bland fish fillets open to any variation of fish cookery.

Octopus

An eight-armed, soft-bodied sea creature; the common octopus of eastern North American waters is *Octopus vulgaris*, that of the west, the enormous *Octopus dolfleini* (with arms outstretched it can attain 16 feet). Neither one seems to be much in demand as food except in neighborhoods inhabited by people of Asian or Mediterranean origin, people who know a good thing when they taste one. A freshly caught octopus can be tough indeed, and the larger it is, the tougher you can expect it to be; one technique to combat this is to bash the beast against a handy rock 80 or 90 times or take a baseball bat to it. Long simmering also tenderizes it. Small octopuses are used in all manner of fishy salads and stews, and those of any size are often stewed with white wine or olive oil and pepper or tomatoes. They can also be stuffed and braised or cut into rings and deep fried.

Oeufs à la Neige

Egg-shaped bits of meringue poached in sweetened milk and served in a thin custard sauce as an elegant French dessert.

Offal

One of several unsatisfactory terms for those innards and assorted spare parts of an animal used in cooking, this one being taken from British usage. Other unsatisfactory terms (there are no satisfactory ones) include glandular meats, organ meats, and VARIETY MEATS.

Oil

A fat, in current usage mostly of vegetable origin, that is liquid at room temperature and used in cooking and salad dressings. Common oils include canola, corn, olive, peanut, safflower, sesame, and soy, but oils are made from other plants including almonds, walnuts, coconuts, and cottonseed. Shellfish oil, the shells and carapaces of shellfish beaten smooth with a mortar and pestle, mixed with an equal weight of olive oil, and most carefully filtered, is used to season sauces such as mayonnaise or added to fish salads.

Oils vary in taste and in nutritional qualities. OLIVE OIL also comes in various grades, the best (from the first pressing) being labeled "extra-virgin."

Oils of animal origin are used for purposes other than cooking. Fish liver oil is considered a health or vitamin supplement, and whale oil—once indispensable as a lamp fuel—is now used, if at all, as a lubricant of fussy machinery.

Oiseaux sans Tête

French term for fillets of meat—usually beef or veal—stuffed with sausage or bacon, breadcrumbs, onions, and seasonings. They are rolled, browned, and simmered in liquid (beer or beef stock). The French term means "birds without heads."

Oka

A semisoft, Canadian, cow's-milk CHEESE made by Trappist monks in the small town of the same name. The monks brought the recipe from France in 1881 and have been producing the cheese ever since. It bears a resemblance to PORT-SALUT.

Okra

Hibiscus esculentus, also called *gumbo*. Somewhat fingerlike pods (the British call them ladies' fingers) widely used in Africa, the West Indies, and the southern United States. (Indeed, the best that have greeted this writer so far were bought young and fresh and small from a farm stand on a lonely, dusty stretch of Florida road.)

Okra is often spurned because of the gluey, even slimy, texture it can present (this can be as much a by-product of its preparation as it is of the vegetable itself), although that mucilaginous quality is actually one of okra's virtues and enables it to thicken whatever you're cooking with it. Pick it young (three inches long at most—the bigger ones get woody) when it is still bright green and retains some snap in the stem. Stay away from those pods that are limp or scarred in any way. You can keep okra, refrigerated and in a plastic bag, for a day or so and you can also buy it canned (so-so) or frozen (it freezes well). Unless you want okra for its thickening effect, don't cut the pods. Keep them whole and don't overcook them. If, on the other hand, you plan on using okra as a thickener for a soup, stew, or GUMBO, by all means cut the pods. The liquid will leach out and your soup or stew will benefit from it.

In addition to thickening stews and gumbos, okra is often served fried lightly in just a little oil, served up with tomatoes and corn (a classic combination), stuffed and fried as is done in India (run your thumb down the pod and clean out all the seeds, then pinch in the stuffing bit by bit), or dipped in batter and french fried.

Old-Fashioned

A cocktail made of WHISKEY (rye for purists, otherwise bourbon or blended) and water poured over a small cube of sugar with a dash of bitters in a special flat-sided glass (known as an old-fashioned glass) and graced with a slice of lemon or orange as a garnish. A maraschino cherry may also be added.

Oleomargarine

Also *oleo*. Former name for MARGARINE.

Olive

A fruit (more properly berry) of the olive tree (*Olea europaea*). Like most fruits, it consists of pulp surrounding a pit. But where the pulp of most fruits is largely water, that of the olive is largely oil, and olives are valued especially for OLIVE OIL.

The olives we see in the market come essentially in two forms: green and ripe, representing the two extremes of ripeness—green olives are still unripe; black olives are fully so. Neither one is edible as it comes off the tree (they are too bitter) but must be cured in some manner first, usually by soaking them in lye, then pickling them in brine or salt. They are then usually packed in some solution of brine, oil, or vinegar. If you run across olives that are tan or even red, they represent the stage in the ripening process at which they have been picked. Think of them as variations on green olives, although the riper they are the better they are suited to cooking—like the fully ripe, black ones. Green olives are often allowed to ferment before being packed for shipment, giving them slightly more tang than you can expect from black ones. A prime example are those known as Spanish olives. They are frequently employed as a snack or as a garnish—with a filling of some sort—to decorate a dry martini. Fully ripe black olives can be found in a shriveled state, cured in brine, or large and plump for garnishing, cooking, or simply munching. It is the black olive that informs so many Greek, Italian, Provençale, and other Mediterranean dishes.

Olive Oil

The oil expressed from the OLIVE. The first, gentle pressing produces "virgin," or in these overblown days "extra-virgin" oil, which is light and yellowish and retains a whiff of the fruit. The second pressing results in a slightly more greenish oil of not quite such delicate quality as the first, and with further pressings the quality declines steadily. Keep olive oil away from light or it may turn rancid on you.

Olla Podrida

Also *cocido* and *puchero*. The national dish of Spain. Like all dishes of this sort, its contents depend somewhat upon what is at hand, but it customarily has beef or pork and chicken augmented with chickpeas and chorizo sausage and every conceivable vegetable in season at the time of its making. It is cooked in the traditional Spanish earthenware cookpot, the OLLA.

Oloroso

A sweet, fragrant, full-bodied SHERRY.

Olympia

An OYSTER of the North American West Coast.

Ombre

A European GRAYLING (*Thymallus thymallus*) related to chars, salmon, and trout, caught only in rivers, never in lakes.

Omelet

The classic omelet is of the French style: eggs whisked with butter, salt, and some form of liquid (cream, milk, water) and cooked over fairly high heat in an OMELET PAN or the equivalent until the outside is firm and slightly crusty and the inside still a mite runny (or *baveuse* as the French have it). It is usually folded over in half or in thirds. From then on, the variations become all but infinite.

Omelets can be flavored with herbs or cheese, stuffed with all manner of foods (chicken, chicken liver, shellfish, vegetables), sweetened for dessert, enriched with chocolate or fruit or combinations of them, and even served flaming. Omelets can be made with eggs beaten together, or with yolks and whites beaten separately, and the whites folded in, which borders on the SOUFFLÉ. Producing any sort of omelet that ranks higher than simply serviceable takes a little practice, but once mastered becomes simplicity itself.

Other nations besides France, of course, have omelets, too. The Italians have their FRITATTA, the Arab world its EGGAH, and as they both concern eggs that are beaten and heated to a firm mass, they can qualify as omelets.

Omelet Pan

Akin to a frying pan, but made of heavy metal and with low, sloping sides. The weight of the metal keeps the eggs from cooking too fast, while the pitch of the sides lets you roll and fold the omelet or slide it out of the pan onto a plate. The development of Teflon has made a strong contribution to the cooking of omelets, although some cooks feel that it leads to using less butter, to the benefit of your health and the detriment of your omelet.

Onion

An aromatic edible bulb (*Allium cepa*). A native of Asia originally, it is now indispensable to most cooks everywhere in the world. It was brought to the New World by the Spanish via the West Indies and grows especially in rich, black, loamy soil throughout the North American continent (and elsewhere). Onions are easy to buy—they seem to sell from markets so fast they hardly have time to become perishable. Still, look for good, firm, dry ones with crackly skins and no sprouts. They are usually sold in two- or three-pound bags, which seems a sensible amount for most people. Onions keep well if left to themselves in a dry, airy space (don't pile them too massively on top of each other) or wrapped in plastic and refrigerated.

Onions come in various styles. They include the regular *yellow onion*, the one we use mostly in cooking; the *green onion* or SCALLION; the *pearl onion*, a small pickling onion; the *Vidalia*, from the American town of that name in Georgia; and the *Maui*, from Hawaii, all of which are much appreciated sliced atop hamburgers. *Pearl onions*, which are white, marble-sized, and mild, are best peeled by dropping them briefly in boiling water, then rubbing off the skins. *Boiling onions* are also white but run about an inch in diameter. Onions vary in color from white to yellow with a red strain that is mild and highly appropriate in salads.

One of the notable drawbacks to onions is their propensity for bringing tears to the eyes while they are being peeled and sliced. Try chilling them for upwards of an hour before preparing them. Some experts advise that they be prepared under running water. That hasn't been tried here, and sounds incredibly clumsy, but if it works for you, do it.

There are also various types of wild onions, some of which are overly harsh for culinary use, others acceptable if on the scrawny side.

Onion Flakes

Onion that has been dried and cut into flakes, used as a seasoning.

Onion Powder

Grated dehydrated onion.

Onion Salt

A combination of dried, powdered onion and salt.

Oolong

A TEA of dried and partially fermented tea leaves. It lies between the green (unfermented) and black (fermented) teas.

Opah

Also called *moonfish*. An enormous (up to several hundred pounds), rare, oval, open-ocean fish (*Lampris regius*) mostly preferring tropical seas but apt to be found anywhere. Anything this large would seem to lend itself to being cut into steaks and cooked as you would any fish steak. It is highly regarded as a food fish and can also be treated as you would salmon.

Open-Faced Sandwich

A sandwich variation consisting of a single slice of bread with some form of garnish—cheese, fish, meat. If it had a second slice of bread on top, it would be a true sandwich. Open-faced sandwiches are often cut to a very small size and in varying shapes for use as canapés.

Opossum

Also *possum*. A marsupial (*Didelphia virginiana*) of North America, eaten mostly in the southern United States, which was its original habitat although it has since extended its range all the way north to Canada. It is generally roasted either stuffed with or accompanied by yams or sweet potatoes. Opossums have glands on the back and inside the front legs that will spoil the meat if not removed quickly.

Orache

Also *orach*. A potherb (*Atriplex hortensis*) more popular in France than in North America except perhaps to the forager. It somewhat resembles spinach and is prepared in the same way.

Orange

A fruit to most of us (but a berry to botanists) that originated in China several millennia ago. Given that time frame, it has only been comparatively recently—in the last 2,000 years or so—that oranges made their way across Asia and Asia Minor to the Mediterranean and eventually to the Americas, especially California, Florida, and Texas.

Oranges, oddly enough, do not come by their color automatically. It seems to be a matter of climate—a spell of cool weather turns them orange; otherwise they remain green (or even return to a green color if the weather changes). In Florida, it is a common practice to treat the green oranges with ethylene gas to give them the requisite color, which suggests that if you are looking for orange peel, you would be well advised to select a fruit from California, where this step is seldom necessary, leaving the rind a little more pristine. Oranges are always picked ripe so they do not continue to mature once off the tree (although they may spoil if kept too long or too imperfectly).

When selecting oranges, pick those with plenty of heft to them (lightness is a sign they are insufficiently juicy). Pick thin-skinned oranges if for juice and thick-skinned oranges if for eating. Also, look for firm fruit that gives an impression of being heavy for its size. Smooth skin is usually to be preferred over skins that are thick or coarse and should not be puffy or soft or blemished. (An exception is for tangerines, which are by nature somewhat puffy.)

Oranges do not have to be kept chilled, but they will last longer if you chill them, especially if you plan on keeping them for more than a week. Eating oranges will taste better at room temperature, and slightly warmed juice oranges will give more juice, although it is cumbersome to chill them for keeping, then warm them for quantity, only to chill the juice all over again to make it taste better.

Oranges are generally subdivided into sweet and tart—the former used for eating and juice, the latter primarily for marmalade. Juice is far and away the prime use for oranges, but eating oranges show up on many a breakfast table, and they also surface in desserts, fruit cocktails, and salads. Oranges can also be baked (although no one seems to do this any more), made into bread, cake, cookies, custard, fruitcake, ice cream (or sherbet or sorbet), soufflés, or soup, and some would have you make them into a wine (it takes a year before you have anything that might be considered drinkable).

Citrus fruits tend to interbreed with facility, leading to crosses such as limequats (lime + kumquat) and many other variations. Some of the oranges you might encounter include:

Sour oranges (*Citrus aurantium*). Perhaps the ancestors of them all.

- *Bergamot.* A variety of sour orange cultivated for its rind, which is used for oil to be used as a flavoring.

- *Bigarade.* Probably the original orange; the overall name for bitter oranges in general.
- *Seville.* An almost inedible orange that provides the indispensable base for orange marmalade.

Sweet oranges (mostly *Citrus sinensis*). These form the bulk of our orange crop and are the source of all those reconstituted and not-from-concentrate juices you see in the supermarkets. Among them you may find:

- *Blood orange.* An anomaly in most North American markets, this orange has colored red fruit and juice (at its deepest, it has been likened to the color of Burgundy wine) and more often than not an elevated price tag. Blood oranges are said to be popular in Italy and are beginning to be grown in California and perhaps elsewhere in the United States. Should you run across them, a few segments might make an eye-catching addition to a fruit salad.
- *California.* Any orange grown in California, especially the navel orange (see below).
- *Clementine.* A tangerine (see below).
- *Florida.* Any orange grown in Florida, especially the juice orange.
- *Jaffa.* A distinguished (and somewhat pricey) sweet and juicy orange from Israel.
- *Mandarin.* A tangerine (see below).
- *Mineola.* It's called an orange but in fact is a cross between a grapefruit and a tangelo (see MINEOLA). It is also sometimes referred to as a *honeybell.*
- *Navel.* A large, thick-skinned eating orange grown mostly in California, but also in Arizona and Florida. The skin peels off easily and the flesh is juicy, seedless, and succulent.
- *Satsuma.* A variety of tangerine (see below).
- *Temple.* A sweet, juicy, seedless orange-and-tangerine cross.
- *Valencia.* A widely planted (in both California and Florida), somewhat late-blooming, juicy orange available in the late spring. (Food writer Waverley Root maintained that it was to be found in vast quantities everywhere except in its namesake, Valencia, Spain, where the Seville orange was preferred.)
- *Tangerine* (*Citrus reticulata*). Also *clementine* and *mandarin.* A fruit that probably originated in what is now southern Vietnam but derived its English name from its supposed origin around Tangiers, Morocco. Tangerines tend to be small with a slightly flattened look and many have a lacy sort of inner rind that must be peeled off. There are varieties with seeds as well as seedless ones. They are prime for eating, but the writer Marjorie Kinnan Rawlings (author of *The Yearling* and, more to the point,

Cross Creek Cookbook) reported that on the Florida citrus grove where she made her home, her tangerine ice cream was something more than special. Clementines are small, even for tangerines, and some botanists think they may represent a separate subspecies of their own. They are sweet and succulent.

Orange Bitters

A sweet-and-sour bitters used for flavoring drinks, especially the OLD-FASHIONED cocktail. Much was imported from those portions of Indonesia that were once under Dutch rule, but this is no longer the case.

Orange Flower Water

The blossoms of bitter oranges distilled in water to make a perfumed essence used particularly in cold drinks.

Orange Pekoe

A term signifying TEA leaves that are unbroken and of medium size.

Orangequat

A species of citrus composed of a cross between an ORANGE and a KUMQUAT.

Orange Roughy

A red, deepwater fish (*Hoplostethus atlanticus*) caught off New Zealand. Processed by factory ships and flown frozen to North America, it is a mildly flavored white-fleshed fish available in steaks and fillet-sized pieces. Orange roughy can be used as you would sole.

Oregano

An herb (*Origanum vulgare*) related to MARJORAM. The name is Spanish for *wild marjoram*, although in Mexico the plant is sometimes referred to as *Mexican sage*. It is particularly useful in Italian and Mexican cooking and resembles a coarser and somewhat more assertive version of MARJORAM and THYME. In addition to its contributions to pizza and spaghetti sauce, it makes a fitting companion for roasted and broiled meats (especially if used in a marinade) and for egg and cheese dishes.

Organ Meats

See VARIETY MEATS.

Orgeat

A sweet nonalcoholic syrup made from almonds and sugar with rosewater or orange flower water, used to flavor drinks or food. It was originally made with an almond–barley base.

Ormer
An Atlantic ABALONE (*Haliotis tuberculata*) found off the British Isles, especially around the Channel Islands.

Ortolan
A European bunting (*Emberiza hortulana*). It is served roasted or grilled and at one time was considered a great delicacy. In the United States and Canada, such birds are generally protected by law.

Orvieto
An Italian wine center known for its dry white table wines.

Orzo
A form of PASTA resembling an elongated, fat grain of rice (and cooked in similar fashion), although the name in Italian means barley. Try it in a soup.

Osso Buco
A dish composed of thick chunks of meaty veal shank, replete with marrow, braised in white wine and stock with vegetables (carrots, celery, garlic, onions, tomatoes) and seasonings (bay leaves, basil, thyme, parsley). The shanks are laid on end (so the liquid does not lap over the top and disturb the marrow) and the finished dish is traditionally served with the sauce known as GREMOLADA. This is the Milanese version—other methods leave out the vegetables, for example—and probably no two Milanese cooks would agree on either the list of ingredients or the exact proportions.

Ostrich Egg
An egg of the ostrich (*Struthio camelus*) eaten, to some extent, in Africa. One egg can weigh up to three pounds.

Ostrich Fern
A variety of FIDDLEHEAD fern.

Oswego
Also *bee balm* and *American melissa*. A plant (*Monarda didyma*), the dried leaves of which are used for TEA.

Ounce
A standard unit of measure—$\frac{1}{16}$ pound or 28 grams.

Ouzo
An anise-flavored Greek aperitif of the ABSINTHE type. Like other spirits of this sort, it turns milky when diluted with water.

Oven

A chamber in which food is cooked with dry heat. In addition to the traditional oven, we now have CONVECTION and MICROWAVE ovens as well.

Oven Fry

To place food (usually with a coating of some kind or at least brushed with margarine or an oil such as canola) in a hot oven to achieve a result that seems fried but uses far less fat.

Oven Roast

See ROAST.

Oven Temperature

Before the development of the (reasonably) accurate oven, cooks resorted to any number of ways of figuring out when an oven was ready for a dish to be cooked. Perhaps the experienced cook really could stick a hand in the oven and say "Now!," but failures must have outstripped successes then—or else the art of cooking is more forgiving than we give it credit for. And how in the world did you tell anyone else how hot an oven had to be before it was ready for a particular dish? Even fine cookbook authors tripped over their own definitions sometimes. One who defined "hot" and "moderate" and "slow" at the beginning of her book then threw in an undefined "quick" later on. ("Quick," of course, meant "hot," but if you knew that you probably didn't need her book in the first place.)

We owe our modern ovens in part to the manufacturers who engineered thermostatic controls in them (although even so, you'll be smart to check the heat with a separate oven thermometer) and in part most probably to the home economists who showed people how to use them.

Standard oven temperatures are as follows:

Description	Degrees Fahrenheit	Degrees Celsius
Warming	200	
Cool	225–250	107–121
Very Slow	250–275	121–135
Slow	275–325	135–163
Moderate	325–400	163–204
Moderately Hot	400–425	204–218
Hot	425–450	218–233
Very Hot	450–500	233–260

Oven Thermometer

A device designed to measure the temperature of your oven, based on the generally correct proposition that your oven dial is inaccurate, not only for the oven as a whole, but for different spots in that oven as well. There are two kinds of such thermometers, one based on a spring that heats up and moves a pointer across a face calibrated in degrees of heat, the other with a tube of mercury. The one with the spring is probably not worth even the smallish amount of money asked for it—it goes askew too easily and too early. The mercury thermometer is the better bet, even if it does cost a little more.

Oxtail

The tail of a beef critter. Oxtails are flavorful and are used in soup and can also be braised or incorporated into a stew. Red wine and dark beer make good braising liquids for oxtails.

Oyster

The oyster is a marine bivalve (of the family Ostreidae) that has been eaten by both primitive and sophisticated peoples the world over for just about as far back as we can see, as evidenced by the piles of oyster shells that once loomed along the shores of various seas and by the great mass of literature that has come down to us, especially from Greek and Roman writers.

Everyone knows (or at least has known since 1599) that oysters are not to be eaten in any month that doesn't have an "r" in it. Not everybody knows why. There is nothing hygienic about this rule; nothing different will happen to you if you eat a healthy oyster at such a time any more than it would if you should eat a similar oyster in the winter months. The oyster simply won't taste as good. Oysters spawn in warm weather, and, apparently, the act of reproduction is so wearisome, it takes all the pizzazz out of them and leaves them thin and drawn and almost devoid of taste. The time not to eat an oyster is when a raw oyster is offered to you from waters that are polluted, no matter how the month is spelled.

Most oysters are eaten raw, on the half shell, sometimes with a squeeze of lemon juice, although there has also developed a tradition of serving them with a piquant sauce that pretty much destroys any taste of oyster. This is true except in Asia, where despite the popularity of raw fish, oysters are usually cooked—in omelets or stir-fries or soups—or dried for use in other dishes or to go into the making of OYSTER SAUCE. Oysters are also cooked in the West, however. We see them baked (usually stuffed), broiled (as ANGELS ON HORSEBACK or OYSTERS ROCKEFELLER), grilled, poached, sautéed, smoked and sold in cans, put in soufflés, made into soups, and added to stuffings (especially poultry stuffings). Oysters may be transformed with butter, milk or cream, pepper, and salt into oyster stew and used in heartier stews (such as STEAK AND KIDNEY PIE). The one answer to the question of how to cook an oyster is "not long," as it becomes tough if overcooked.

The common oysters of North America fall into three categories: eastern (or Atlantic), Pacific, and king (or Japanese) oyster. They can be harvested the old-fashioned way (essentially by hand) or by oyster farming. The eastern oyster (*Crassostrea virginica*) is prevalent along the Northeast Coast as far as the Middle Atlantic states, but has gained special status along Cape Cod, New York's Long Island, and Chesapeake Bay. The original place-names are no longer used in commerce, but perhaps if you should happen to be in Cape Cod's Wellfleet, a Wellfleet oyster could possibly be local. Not so Long Island, where the indigenous bluepoint (originally from the Great South Bay, protected by the present resort area known as Fire Island) has extended its name to virtually all eastern oysters. And the Chincoteagues and Lynnhavens of the Chesapeake are all but a memory. For the most part, an eastern oyster is an eastern oyster today, although it may be labeled on the menu as "bluepoint."

The Pacific oysters are the delicious, tiny (no more than three inches) Olympia (*Ostrea lurida*) and the large Pacific oyster (*Crassostrea gigas*). The latter was brought from Japan around the turn of the twentieth century and has been successfully farmed ever since. It can be huge (up to a foot long) and is preferred to the far better Olympia because of its size and ease in handling. (It has been estimated that it may take as many as 200 shucked Olympias to make one solid pint.)

North America is of course not the only home of the oyster. Some of the European varieties are all but legendary. European oysters are almost all subspecies of *Ostrea edulis*. In Britain, these would include Blackwater, Colchester, Helford, and Whitstable oysters, all named for their home waters. Related French oysters include Armoricaines and Belons from Brittany, Gravettes d'Arcachon from the Bay of Arcachon southwest of Bordeaux, and Marennes from an area on the Atlantic between La Rochelle and Bordeaux. Other genera of French oysters (although not native to the area) include the Portugaise (*Crassostrea angulata*) and the imports from Japan found also along North America's Pacific coastline, the large pacific oyster (*Crassostrea gigas*).

While oysters are available fresh and in the shell, they are more likely to be found in small plastic containers, already shucked, sometimes frozen. You pretty much take your chances with the shucked ones (complain to the store if you are displeased with them). If you are interested in oysters in their shells, make sure the shells are shut.

Oyster Crab

A quite extraordinarily small crab (*Pinnotheres ostreum*) that commonly runs less than half an inch in width and makes its residence inside an oyster's (or mussel's) shell. Oyster crabs are sometimes sautéed (usually in butter) and eaten, shell and all— especially with oyster stew—providing a satisfying small crunch and very little else. George Washington was said to have been uncommonly fond of them.

Oyster Knife

A short, sharp blade—either pointed or round—on a small handle, intended for prying open your oyster. The trick is to hold the oyster in the palm of your hand with the bowl of its shell down and the hinge away from you and quickly insert the sharp part of the knife under the upper shell. You then twist it around to cut through the muscles holding the shells together. It's all a lot easier if you chill the oysters thoroughly beforehand. (You can also heat them in the oven, but they won't taste quite so good.)

Oyster Mushroom
A variety of MUSHROOM.

Oyster Plant
Another name for SALSIFY.

Oyster Sauce
A Chinese condiment and seasoning element made by cooking dried oysters with soy sauce and brine. It intensifies the flavor of the food to which it is added and is used in stir-fried dishes and with meats, poultry, seafood, and vegetables. It is sold in cans or small bottles and if not refrigerated after opening has a tendency toward moldiness.

Oysters Rockefeller
A recipe originating about 1889 at Antoine's, a famous New Orleans restaurant. It is composed, in at least one version, of chopped vegetables (celery, shallots, spinach) mixed up with butter, thyme, and Worcestershire sauce, cooked to the consistency of a thick sauce (perhaps informed with a little anise-flavored liqueur), poured over oysters on the half shell, covered with toasted breadcrumbs, and run under the broiler. It is served on a bed of cold rock salt, to keep the oyster shells from slipping around. All in all, it sounds like a dish more designed to show off the sauce than the oyster.

Paca

An edible rodent (*Cuniculus paca*) of the Andes, where the flesh is eaten and the skin used for leather.

Pacific Ocean Perch

A rockfish (*Sebastes alutus*), one of the various fish going by the name OCEAN PERCH.

Paddlefish

A fish (*Polyodon spathula*) of the Mississippi River related to the STURGEON.

Paddy

A name applied equally to the place where rice is grown and to rice before it has been dehusked.

Paella

A Spanish specialty (and, technically, the dish in which it is cooked) of rice with chicken and shellfish, usually seasoned with saffron and augmented with vegetables (especially garlic and onions and tomatoes) and sausage or other form of pork.

Paella Pan

A wide, shallow, unlidded metal (or earthenware) pan with two handles in which PAELLA is traditionally cooked and served.

Pain d'Épice

A spicy French GINGERBREAD especially informed by honey and ginger. It is a particular specialty of the Burgundian city of Dijon, famous also for mustard, wine, and CASSIS.

Pain Perdu

See FRENCH TOAST.

Pak Choy

See BOK CHOY.

Palette Knife

A British term for SPATULA. Indeed, when a good spatula for turning pastry or other dough is unavailable, an artist's palette knife (sold in art-supply stores) is said to make a useful substitute.

Palm

A family (Palmaceae) of tropical, woody plants, mostly tree-sized. Aside from their decorative aspect, various palms produce coconuts, dates, PALMETTO, palm oil and palm kernel oil, palm wine, and SAGO.

Palmetto

Also known as *hearts of palm*. The inner meat, shoots, and buds of the regal palm (*Roystonea regia*), cabbage palm (*Sabal palmetto*), and similar trees, found canned and sometimes fresh. Palmettos are used in salads, rice dishes, and vegetable combinations often flavored with pork or salt pork.

Palm Oil and Palm Kernel Oil

Oil derived from the fruit of the palm tree, or palm kernel oil, from the kernels. Palm oil is moderately high in saturated fat (49 percent of its fat is saturated as opposed to 9 percent for safflower and 13 percent for olive oil). Palm kernel oil is even higher at 81 percent. Neither is routinely seen in supermarkets but may be used in processing food. Palm oil is a common ingredient of both African and Brazilian cooking.

Palm Wine

An alcoholic beverage made from the fermented sap of the PALM, usually a coconut or date palm.

Pan

Any shallow utensil suitable for cooking.

Panada

A paste of fine breadcrumbs, flour, or rice mixed with stock, water, milk, or other liquid, used as a thickener or a binder for a stuffing or sauce.

Pan-Broil

To cook meat, for example, in a hot frying pan (especially one with ridges and troughs—the ridges to elevate the meat, the troughs to catch any juices) without any fat. Do it hot and fast or not at all, and be aware that some consider it frying, not really broiling.

Pancake

A quick bread cooked on a griddle, usually for breakfast but sometimes for dessert as well. Pancakes include such national favorites as crepes and blini (see CREPE and BLINI). They may be composed strictly of butter, egg, flour, milk, salt, and sugar, or may be enriched with a stuffing of seafood, fruit, or other ingredient. Buckwheat flour and cornmeal are sometimes used in place of regular wheat flour.

Pancetta

An Italian bacon that is cured but not smoked. It comes all rolled up and is used as a flavoring agent.

Pancreas

A digestive gland located in the abdomen. When taken from a calf or lamb, it is classified along with the thymus gland as SWEETBREAD.

Pandowdy

An early North American deep-dish dessert of sliced apples (usually, although other fruits may be used) with spices (cinnamon, nutmeg), sweetened with maple sugar, molasses, or sugar (usually brown sugar), and topped with a thick pastry crust. As both maple sugar and molasses were much used in New England, that area seems its likely place of origin.

Panettone

A cured Italian sausage made from the stomach of a pig, salted and air-dried.

Panfish

Almost any small, usually freshwater, fish big enough to eat and usually panfried.

Panfry

To cook in a frying pan or skillet with only a little oil or fat. The term can generally be interchanged with fry and sauté. It is perhaps best known as the preferred method of cooking a whole class of small, usually freshwater, relatively easily caught fish called panfish.

Panicum

A generic name for MILLET, *Panicum miliaceum*.

Panir

A type of Indian cheese made by adding some form of citrus to fresh milk or yogurt, suspending it in cheesecloth (or similar material) and letting the whey drip out. The remaining curd is pressed and cut into cubes and used in vegetarian cooking.

Panure

A French culinary term for a coating of very fine breadcrumbs bound to its object with melted butter or beaten egg, generally in preparation for frying.

Papain

An enzyme that has the digestive effect of breaking down protein. It is most notable as a component of the milky juice of the PAPAYA, which is used in tropical countries as a food tenderizer. Food tenderizers derived from it (and papaya milk itself) are also effective in easing such painful nuisances as insect bites, jellyfish stings, and sores and scratches of all descriptions.

Papaw

A tree (*Asimina triloba*) found naturally from Massachusetts to Mississippi and perhaps introduced wherever similar conditions prevail. It bears large, kidney-shaped, creamy-fleshed, sweet, and highly aromatic dark-colored fruit mostly eaten right off the tree. The poet James Whitcomb Riley described papaws as custard pies with no crust. Even so, you are unlikely to find any in the market.

Papaya

An orange or yellow subtropical fruit (*Carica papaya*) running up to about six inches in width (it can get bigger) and used both as a fruit and a vegetable. The unripe fruit—and indeed all parts of the tree—give forth a milky white liquid that contains PAPAIN.

When the fruit is still green, it can be picked and baked or boiled or otherwise treated like squash. The succulent, juicy ripe fruit enjoys widespread use as a melon, dressed with lemon or lime juice or simply salt and pepper and served for breakfast. The numerous black seeds are also edible, although most people don't bother. Papayas can be crystallized or made into jams, jellies, pickles, pies, and sherbets or added to compotes, especially with citrus fruits or pineapple.

Papayas are ripe when they are soft to the touch. Keep green papayas at room temperature while they mature; once ripe they can be held, but not for much more than a day or two.

Papillote

A paper frill used to decorate the bony ends of meats such as chops. It is more often encountered as *en papillote*, which is French for wrapping—indeed sealing—something in parchment paper or aluminum foil to seal in its aroma and flavor during the cooking process.

Pappadam

A form of bread from the Indian subcontinent made from lentil or potato or rice flour. Its preparation is so complex that even in India it is usually bought ready-made and completed at home. Pappadams are available in packages and once opened will keep for several months. When you open the package, each pappadam will resemble a thin, flat, round, saucer-sized piece of inedible plastic. Drop one in hot butter in a frying pan and it will "pop," transforming itself into a crisp, attractive slice of bread with bubbles in it. Pappadam is useful anywhere you might use bread or toast. It may also be crumbled into your food as you would common crackers into fish chowder or croutons into any number of dishes.

Pappardelle

A broad egg PASTA noodle served in northern Italy with game.

Paprika

A sweet, mild (there is a hot variety, too), and pungent, brilliantly red pepper found dried and powdered. The best comes from Hungary, where paprika is a way of life. Paprika from other climes has the color but not the savor, serving to add to the looks of your dish but not the taste. To get the real thing, make sure it is labeled as Hungarian; "imported" (Spain supplies a lot) is not enough.

Paraguay Tea

See MATÉ.

Paratha

A whole wheat, puffed bread from the Indian subcontinent. It is sometimes stuffed with a vegetable filling.

Parboil

To drop a food into a boiling liquid until it is partially cooked. It is much the same as blanching, except that in blanching, you don't leave the food in so long. A good recipe will give you the appropriate timing. It is a technique that is said to have also been used to help preserve foods before modern methods of preservation were available.

Parch

An old term indicating to dry or roast grain (such as corn) or coffee either over an open fire or on a wood stove. You would parch just enough coffee for immediate use; with grain, you would parch what you needed for a long journey, the dried variety being lighter and easier to carry than whole grain and easily reconstituted with a little water.

Parchment Paper

A paper specially treated for oven use. It is available in rolls or sheets as well as in precut rounds to fit cake pans. It is useful for lining cake and cookie pans to keep the ingredients from sticking and for wrapping fish and other dishes being cooked in the PAPILLOTE style. It has to some extent been superseded by aluminum foil.

Pare

To peel. A *good* paring knife is a necessity in any kitchen.

Pareve

In Jewish terminology, a food made without animal or dairy products. While strict Kosher law dictates that meats and dairy foods must be kept separate, to the extent that they must never be served at the same meal, fruit would qualify as pareve, for example, as would breads and pastries made with vegetable oil rather than butter or suet. (Lard, of course, would be unthinkable under any circumstances.)

Parfait

An ice-cream dessert consisting of small scoops of creamy, not completely frozen ice cream (sometimes of several flavors layered together) served garnished with fruits and nuts and syrups in a special tall, fluted glass.

Paris-Brest

A French ring-shaped pastry composed of puff pastry sprinkled with almonds and filled with an almond cream.

Parker House Roll

A light, yeast-risen breakfast or dinner roll folded over onto itself so that you can add your butter in the center fold. It was developed in the restaurant of the Parker House, a Boston hotel.

Parma

An Italian city that produces a very special prosciutto HAM as well as gives its name to PARMESAN cheese.

Parmesan

In northern Europe and North America, a hard, slightly sharp and salty cow's-milk CHEESE for grating, the kind known in Italy as *grana*. It takes its name from the city of Parma.

Parmigiano-Reggiano

What Italians think of when they speak of Parmesan cheese. By Italian law, Parmigiano-Reggiano is made only in an area of northern Italy between the cities of Parma and Reggio, using techniques essentially laid down in the Middle Ages. In addition to its use as a grating cheese, Parmigiano-Reggiano can develop into a superior table cheese as well.

Parr

A young (less than one year old) SALMON. It is recognizable by the dark, oval-shaped marks that develop along its sides. The name is sometimes extended to the young of other fish.

Parsley

Just about the most widely used and best known of kitchen and garden herbs, described by the French novelist and food enthusiast Alexandre Dumas as "the obligatory condiment of every sauce." Essentially, it comes in three varieties: curly, Hamburg, and Italian.

Curly parsley (*Petroselinum hortense* var. *crispum*) is what we see most often. It is bright green, and its leaves have, as the name implies, a pronounced curl. Italian, or plain-leaf, parsley (*Petroselinum hortense* var. *filicinum*) is darker and its leaves are flat and heavy. Although not so pleasing to the eye, it is tastier than the curly (and bear in mind that its stems are as flavorful as its leaves). The Hamburg variety

(*Petroselinum Hortense* var. *radicosum*) is the one least likely to be encountered; it is grown for its roots, which are white and resemble CELERIAC. These roots may be long (which is why it is sometimes called parsnip-rooted) or bulbous (for which it may be called turnip-rooted).

Parsley is most often used as a garnish or as a seasoning. As a garnish, it has the reputation of freshening the breath to the extent that it masks the aroma of onion or garlic, although that may be beyond even parsley's powers. The French FINES HERBES refers to the addition of parsley to a dish either by itself or with additional seasonings, and chopped or minced parsley is called for in innumerable recipes.

The uses of parsley, however, don't stop there. Fried parsley is a fine accompaniment for fried fish or other foods. Simply wash and dry it well and deep-fry it at 400°F for 1 minute, then drain and serve. And the roots of the Hamburg variety can be eaten like parsnips or added to soups or stews like any other root vegetable.

When buying leafy parsley, simply make sure that the leaves are fresh looking and green—stay away from any yellowing bunches. The springier the leaves are to the touch, the better. Wash the parsley well and, should you wish to keep it, refrigerate the moist leaves in a tightly lidded jar. You can keep them that way for a good two weeks. Parsley is also available dried, but it pales in comparison to its fresh counterpart.

Parsnip

One of our more maligned vegetables, parsnips (*Pastinaca sativa*) are long, yellowish brown, and carrot-shaped (although there is also a bulbous or turnip-shaped variety) with a woody central core that must be removed except in the very youngest specimens. Their characteristically sweet, delicate, nutty taste only truly develops in parsnips that have been touched with frost, making them distinctly a winter vegetable.

When you find parsnips that fit this description, steam them with the skin on and peel them while hot—they will retain more taste that way. They can then be creamed, mashed, pureed, sliced—even french fried. They are also, of course, an excellent vegetable for stews and braises—and used as you would pumpkin or squash, they make a pie filling that is generally highly appreciated while being at the same time almost unidentifiable. Parsnips are particularly favored in the British Isles, where a number of first-class ways of preparing them have been developed.

When selecting parsnips, choose firm, small, evenly colored ones without blemishes or soft spots, and stay away from any with a shriveled look. Store them in a plastic bag in the vegetable drawer of your refrigerator, and wash them only before using.

Parson's Nose

Also *pope's nose*. The fatty, edible tailpiece of a bird.

Partridge

Any of various gamebirds introduced to North America and much appreciated by wing shooters. The two species are the Hungarian or gray partridge (Perdrix perdrix) and the chukar or red-legged partridge (*Alectoris chukar*), although the name is loosely applied to grouse (especially ruffed grouse) and other upland fowl. Like other gamebirds, partridge are often roasted (braised if the birds are old), although many other ways to cook them exist. You would be well advised to plan on a single bird for each diner.

Pasilla

A hot dried CHILI pepper.

Passionfruit

A fruit of any of the various species of passionflower, a (mostly) South American plant so named because it reminded the conquering Spaniards of the Passion of Christ, thereby encouraging them to convert the native Indians to Christianity as brutally as they saw fit.

All of the passionfruit clan can be chilled and eaten with lemon juice as you would a melon, added to a salad, whipped up for a sweet drink (a little baking soda helps neutralize the acid), or used for flavoring cakes, candies, preserves, or sherbets.

The edible members of the passionflower family that you are likely to come across include:

Banana passionfruit (*Passiflora mollissima*). A small (three to four inches), oval, yellow passionfruit with a hard skin and a sweet taste.

Giant granadilla (*Passiflora quadrangularis*). A larger (8–10 inches or so) fruit with a yellowish brown outside and a gray pulp with lots of seeds. It is used mostly for juice.

Maypop (*Passiflora incarnata*). A smallish (about the size of a hen's egg) fruit of the southern United States with a slightly lemony flavor, sometimes consumed by children and foragers.

Passionfruit (*Passiflora edulis*). This is a purple fruit about the size of an egg with a smooth skin that wrinkles as it ages. Inside it contains a considerable number of small edible black seeds and orangy pulp characterized by a deep aroma and a tangy but still sweet taste. Once the skin starts to wrinkle, use it up, as it will dry out otherwise.

Passover Wine

A KOSHER wine served for the Jewish festival of Passover. In the United States, it is often a sweet, almost syrupy, heavy wine made at least partly from the Concord grape. A considerable number of Jewish households are beginning to prefer regular dry table wines made under rabbinical supervision for the Passover, many of which are imported from Israel.

Pasta

A flour-based paste made from flour, salt, water, and, in some cases, eggs. Macaroni, noodles, spaghetti—all that good stuff. Pasta is available in a bewilderment of styles and shapes and sizes, and one form or another of it comes from almost anywhere in the world. Italian pasta is what we are mostly familiar with, but Asian cooks were using their own equivalents long before Marco Polo left home. It is possible that Italy learned of it from Marco Polo's descriptions, although the Italian version seems to have been a Germanic version that the Romans may have stolen from the Ostrogoths.

Pastas fall into roughly three categories. There is dry pasta, made from flour and water; egg pasta, which includes most noodles; and filled pasta, which includes Chinese DIM SUM and Italian RAVIOLI. The Italian varieties are known by their shapes—so long as you know Italian.

In general, slim, long varieties adapt best to being served with a smooth sauce; irregularly shaped ones—bows, shells, squares—are better at picking up rich fulsome sauces replete with lumps of meat or bits of seafood. Filled pasta is usually poached and served with a sauce. The very small bits and pieces are most appropriate as a garnish in a soup.

Most pasta is dropped into boiling water (or simmering soup) until it is just at the bitable stage—known as AL DENTE. Some pastas, lasagna is an example, are then baked along with various other ingredients. There is something about the tomato that simply fits in with pasta, which is why so many pasta dishes feature tomatoes in one form or another.

Individual types of pasta are described under their own headings.

Pasteurization

A process for slowing the spoilage of MILK (although it was originally devised for wines and beer), developed in the 1860s by the French scientist Louis Pasteur. There are various methods of pasteurization, a common one being to heat milk to 145°F for 30 minutes; another is to keep it at 158°F for 15 seconds. Both have advantages and drawbacks. Ultrapasteurization applies a heat of 290°F for 2 seconds, but modifies the taste enough that it is rarely used for milk. Much cream, half-and-half, and eggnog is now ultrapasteurized, but there are some reports of it being unsatisfactory if you wish to make whipped cream with it.

Pastis

1. A French aperitif with a flavor of ANISE or LICORICE.
2. A French yeast-risen cake enriched with eggs and brandy.

Pastrami

A boneless piece of blade or flank steak that has been cured with salt and spices and smoked. It is used especially for sandwiches, served either hot or cold. Although beef is pastrami's common basis, turkey pastrami has also become popular.

Pastry

A rich dough made from flour and salt and water and some form of shortening (butter, goose fat, margarine, lard, or a hydrogenated vegetable shortening). Most pastry dough is unleavened but there are exceptions, as with Danish pastry.

Pastry dough has a multitude of uses ranging from piecrust to the topping for crusted meat pies to pandowdies to appetizers, snacks, and tea cakes to all the various pies and tarts that signal the end of a meal.

Pastry Bag

A washable, funnel-shaped bag with all sorts of interchangeable nozzles for dispensing creams, icing, frosting, or the like. With a pastry bag you can apply such decorative additions as rosettes (and even write messages if you're skillful enough).

Pastry Blender

A device for blending or cutting shortening into flour in pastry-making. It consists of a handle to which are connected several strips of wire bent into half circles. The wires are lowered into the mixture and rocked back and forth, cutting the shortening into tiny, flour-encrusted bits. Traditionalists prefer to employ two parallel knives, one held in each hand, the blades facing each other, or simply to use their fingers. If the finger method appeals to you, run your hand under cold water for a moment first and work fast so your body heat won't melt the shortening. In pastry-making, after all, you don't want the shortening to melt but to stay in tiny bits covered on all sides with the flour mixture. This is why pastry flour is worked cold and is chilled frequently between workings. But this can work in your favor, too. If you get tired cutting the shortening in, or if the muscles at the base of your thumbs start to protest, you can cover your bowl with plastic wrap and refrigerate it until you've had time to recover.

Pastry Brush

Not a single brush, but a whole family designed for chores ranging from tiny brushes for putting an almost infinitesimally thin glaze on pastries (cakes, cookies, pies) to sturdier specimens for greasing the griddle or buttering a baking dish. For the most delicate uses, a pastry brush of goose feathers is the choice of the professionals. Clearly, something that wears better (nylon, hog bristle) gives better service for the grittier jobs.

Pastry Cream

Also in French, *crème pâtissière*. Blended together butter, eggs, flour, salt, and sugar to which you add vanilla-flavored boiling milk, then allow to cool, stirring from time to time. It is used as a pastry filling.

Pastry Cutter

See COOKIE CUTTER.

Pastry Tube

A hollow metal tube with a plunger fitted into one end and an assortment of nozzles to fit on the other, used to dispense frosting, icing, and the like. Whatever ingredient you're planning to use to decorate your cake goes into the tube, the plunger keeps it flowing out at the rate you choose, and the nozzle you select determines what kind of decoration you're going to accomplish. All it takes is practice.

Pastry Wheel

A sharp wheel on a wooden handle for cutting or scoring pastry; it is much preferable to a knife, which tends to cut less evenly and to disrupt the dough. Some pastry wheels are flat, some fluted. They are also effective for slicing pizza.

Pasty

A nourishing meat pie developed for such hard workers as Cornish miners and North Woods lumberjacks. It is shaped like a turnover and the filling is usually some form of cooked meat, often with turnips and potatoes. It is usually pronounced *pass-ty* rather than *paste-ty*.

Pâte

Pâte (pronounced approximately *pot*) is French for pastry dough.

Pâté

A pâté (*pot-eh*) is a pie, but it usually refers to a special, discretely spiced preparation of ground liver and meat mixed with seasonings and baked surrounded by strips of bacon or pork fat. There are also fish and shellfish pâtés that are true pies, complete with dough. Pâtés can be served hot or cold. If comparatively roughly made and served cold, they are sometimes called terrines, after the receptacle in which they are cooked and served.

Pâte à Choux

See CREAM PUFF PASTRY.

Pâte Brisée

See SHORT PASTRY.

Pâté de Foie Gras

A PÂTÉ made from FOIE GRAS.

Patty

Any small, rounded pie or cake or similarly shaped item; a hamburger is a patty. There are also patty shells—small cupcake-shaped pastry shells to be filled with anything from a creamy main dish to a fruity dessert.

Pattypan

A variety of SQUASH.

Paupiette

A thin slice of meat or fish (especially sole) rolled up around some form of stuffing, wrapped in a piece of bacon, and braised.

Pawpaw

A name used for a number of fruits especially the PAPAYA, but in North America more appropriately assigned to the unrelated PAPAW.

Pea

The edible seeds and pods of a vine (*Pisum sativum*) and its variants. This group includes the garden pea (the English prefer a fairly large, somewhat wrinkled pea, the French a much smaller, more delicate *petit pois*, or "small pea," picked a little earlier, while it is still a bit immature), the sugar snap pea (or *mange-tout*), and the Chinese pea pod (*Pisum sativum* var. *Macrocarpon*). It also includes the green and yellow field peas (*Pisum arvense*) that are usually found dried and split. They are all variously related to other vegetables of the legume family, some of which share the name (blackeyed pea and chickpea, for example) but belong to differing genera.

Peas are probably as popular a vegetable as we have. They are not difficult to grow in a home garden, can be found fresh and succulent in farm markets, and are available in supermarkets but will not be quite so fresh and tender. They take well to freezing and reasonably well to canning. When choosing fresh peas, check the pods to ensure that the peas within are full and rounded, the pods plump and shiny with a good green color but not too large. Dried peas are usually sold in plastic bags and are difficult to check until you get them home. Just try to avoid any that look shriveled or have spots.

Cooked (more properly, steamed) in a very little water for a very little time, dressed with a little butter or margarine, fresh peas need little further attention unless you wish to add a sprig of fresh mint to the cooking water. (Some people also add a hint of sugar.) They also blend well with fennel, lettuce, and pearl onions, and peas with carrots are ubiquitous—if often overcooked—in institutional menus. Whether fresh or dried, peas also make wonderful soups—pureed as a base or added as an ingredient.

Pea Bean

A variety of BEAN.

Peach

A fruit of a tree of the rose family. From the way we use the word peach to refer to good tidings and positive people, it's pretty clear we're in favor of it. This love affair has been going on for some time, for the peach has been around more years than we can count. It probably arose in China (along with the apricot) and found its way west. The Romans called it the Persian plum, or *Prunus persica*, and the name has stuck as its scientific designation. Peaches are close kin to the NECTARINE, so close, in fact, that either one can be grafted onto the stock of the other.

Peaches come in a bewilderment of varieties with new ones constantly appearing. However, they will all have a more or less fuzzy skin. They will all also have flesh that is either yellow or white and will either adhere closely to the peach pit or stone (clingstone peaches) or freely drop away from that stone (freestone peaches). Either clingstone or freestone is fine for freehand munching, but the freestone is far easier when it comes to slicing. Most peach skins can be peeled off with little fuss, but some old-fashioned types are helped by being dropped quickly (20 seconds is ample) into boiling water first, as you would a tomato.

Look for peaches that are smooth and round and firm, free from any blemishes, with a good white or yellow color, and perhaps a slight blush. (The blush does nothing for or against the peach; it is simply a characteristic of some varieties and it looks attractive.)

Peaches are generally picked before they are ripe and are shipped slightly green. Look out for immature peaches. They will have a washed-out look and a somewhat plastic taste. Better by far to buy peaches that have a little give to them and eat them right up. (Even in the best of times, fully ripe peaches can't be expected to keep well for more than a day or two.)

In addition to fresh, peaches come canned, dried, and frozen. In one or more of their various manifestations, they can be used just as they are (or with cream and sugar) for dessert, baked into cobblers and pies and tarts, used to enrich fish and meat dishes, preserved in brandy or syrup, or made into chutney, preserves, or pickles of other sorts.

One of France's many elegant desserts features peaches that have been simmered in sugar syrup with a dash of vanilla extract, then removed to cool; the syrup is then reduced and flavored with a little kirsch; a bit of the syrup is combined with pureed raspberries; and the puree is then poured over the peaches, which are topped with a few fresh, whole raspberries. Extravagant but excellent.

Peacock

A spectacular bird (*Pavo* spp.) served forth on medieval tables but now confined to ornamental uses. It is related to the PHEASANT but apparently is more akin to TURKEY in taste.

Peanut

Also *earth nut*, *goober*, *goober pea*, *groundnut*, or *monkey nut* and formally known as *Arachis hypogaea*. Botanically it is a seed—not a nut—that grows underground on the roots of a plant native to South America. It has been transplanted, however, and is now of commercial importance the world over (Nigeria, for example, exports a lot). It is also one of our most versatile plants, with a host of industrial and other uses, as George Washington Carver so conclusively showed us, although a good half of the peanuts used in the United States goes into peanut butter. Peanut oil is also an invaluable kitchen aid.

Peanut Brittle

A candy made from cooking *raw* peanuts in a hot candy syrup and allowing it all to cool in thin sheets until firm and indeed brittle.

Peanut Butter

A spread composed of shelled peanuts that are then blanched, dry roasted, and ground into a smooth, creamy paste. Sometimes bits of peanuts are added to give it a chunky characteristic. Most peanut butter is used as a sandwich spread but it can also be used in prepared dishes, especially in Asia and Africa where peanuts in one form or another may pop up as an ingredient in a spicy dish, in a soup, or in a salad dressing or sauce.

Peanut Oil

A neutrally flavored oil obtained from peanuts and used in cooking and as a salad oil.

Pea Pod

A PEA, all of which is edible; the sugar snap pea or Chinese pea pod.

Pear

A fruit of the rose family. When we speak of something being "pear-shaped" we all envision a rounded ball getting smaller as it tapers upward. Not all pears fit this description. There are pear-shaped pears galore, but there are also pears that are long with only a slight taper, some that are oval, and pears that are simply round. Whatever their shape, they are all fruit (*Pyrus communis*) of the rose family found all over the temperate and subtropical parts of the world (they can grow in the tropics— they just won't produce anything worth eating). There are thousands of varieties of pears, but not too many that the average shopper is likely to encounter.

Pears have the characteristic of further ripening once off the tree, which means they are picked still green and hard and allowed to mature in transport, on the shelf, or in the home. When selecting pears bear in mind your intent. If you are looking for a pear to bake, you'll want one that is firmer than one for eating out of the hand. In the latter case, you'll want a little give, at least at the stem end. Don't pick one that is really soft, however. Pears ripen from the inside out, so if your pear is soft on the outside, it will probably be unpleasantly mushy inside. Color won't mean much in pear selection as some pears don't change color with age. Just make sure the skins are unbroken and unbruised. Let pears ripen on the kitchen counter, but once ripe, refrigerate them for no more than a few days. It would be unwise to try to freeze pears—they don't like it.

A well-ripened pear will be soft, juicy, and aromatic and can be sweet or spicy or even tart, depending upon the variety. Some of the older types, and some cooking ones as well, have a tendency to "woodiness, " but this is absent from the more popular eating varieties. Aside from eating out of hand, pears have a considerable versatility. They can be baked (in pies or tarts); are useful in chutney, juices, pickles, or preserves, as well as sherbets; and can even be distilled into brandy (*poire*), made into wine, or added to a spirit as a liqueur.

Some of the pears you might encounter include:

Anjou. A small, fall-to-winter (October–January) green or greenish-yellow pear with a sweet, spicy taste and lots of juice.

Bartlett. An autumn (September) pear known in Europe as the *Williams* or *Williams bon chrétien*. It is medium-sized and yellow (although there is also a red variety) with juicy, sweet, white flesh. In North America, it is the pear most frequently seen in markets and used for canning.

Bosc. A long-necked, brown or russet, autumn (October-November) pear with a smooth texture and a full flavor, suitable as a dessert pear (it combines particularly well with Brie) and equally good for cooking.

Clapp's favorite. An early (August) pear-shaped, green pear often with a rosy tinge on one side. It is aromatic and juicy. It is not much seen any more due to its poor keeping qualities, especially its propensity for getting mushy toward the core and doing so all too quickly.

Comice. In full, *doyenne du comice*. A fall (October–November), large, lumpy, greenish or greenish-brown pear for eating rather than cooking. It is juicy, mellow, and fragrant and is considered by many the best of the eating pears.

Nelis. Also *winter nelis*. A late (December–February), small, round or egg-shaped, russet dessert pear that also bakes well in a tart.

Seckel. A fall (September–October), round, yellow-to-red pear with yellow flesh. It is the smallest of the commercial pears as well as one of the sweetest and is used as a dessert pear and also for canning.

Pearl Barley

A BARLEY that has been husked and polished, or "pearled." It is excellent in Scotch broth and lamb and mutton stews, imparting a slightly nutlike flavor and an attractive suggestion of chewiness.

Pease

Pease porridge hot or cold or nine days old or whatever, it still refers to a concoction of dried peas, or what we might refer to as pea soup, with or without a hambone.

Pecan

A nut-bearing hickory (*Carya illinoensis*), native to the south-central United States, especially Texas and Oklahoma, and possibly Mexico (although Texans may have taken it there). The small oblong, thin-skinned pecan is especially good for baking (pecan pie being one of its specialties), and butter pecan ice cream has its advocates.

Pecans are available fresh, in the shell (just be sure the shells are intact and look healthy), or unshelled either loose or put up in vacuum-wrapped bottles, cans, and paper or plastic packets. Because they are so rich in fat, pecans are best stored under refrigeration (they'll last several months) or frozen. As with all frozen foods, don't just let them languish in the back of the freezer—use them up.

Pecorino

An Italian term for any CHEESE made from ewe's milk. Pecorino Romano is probably the most widespread, notwithstanding that what is sold in North America as Romano has very little chance of having ever been in the vicinity of a sheep. It is instead made with cow's milk.

Pectin

A carbohydrate found mostly in the skins and seeds of certain fruits that causes them to gel when boiled with sugar and some form of acid and then cooled. Apples, apricots, cranberries, and red currants are high in pectin. Some plants (elderberries, for example) are quite low, which is why home canners often add apples, crab apples, or apple jelly when making preserves from them. Commercial pectin is also available, but overreliance on commercial pectin and sugar can degrade the taste of the final product.

Peel

The outer skin or rind of fruits and vegetables as well as the act of removing it. Lemon and orange peel are often added to dishes to give them ZEST.

Peking Doily

Also *moo shu pancake*. Extremely thin, round pancakes about four to five inches in diameter on which MOO SHU is served.

Peking Duck

The more politically proper name being *Beijing duck*. It is not to be confused with *Pekin duck*, which is the breed otherwise known as *Long Island duckling*. The true, authentic Peking duck is one of the marvels of Chinese cooking. At its best, it consists of a special breed of duck, specially fattened and kept inactive to maintain its tenderness. Its feathers are drawn immediately upon slaughter, and its skin is left intact. Air is then blown between the skin and the flesh, the now ballooned duck brushed with a syrup and then hung up to dry until the skin is good and hard. The bird is then barbecued until golden reddish-brown. When done, the skin is cut into bite-sized pieces and served on soft, thin pancakes.

Pekoe
A grade of small-leafed TEA.

Pemmican
A trail food used by Native Americans, consisting of dried meat (bear, bison, or venison most likely) that has been pounded or ground and mixed with fat and with dried berries and then stuffed into cleaned animal intestines. If kept dry, it would keep seemingly forever.

Penne
Long straight tubes of PASTA, cut diagonally.

Pennyroyal
A European mint (*Mentha pulegium*) sometimes used as a (somewhat strong) flavoring. Its American counterpart (*Hedeoma pulegioides*) is not used in the kitchen but may be seen in gardens where it is thought to discourage mosquitoes.

Peperoncini
A variety of sweet pickling PEPPER.

Pepino
A Peruvian fruit that comes to us mostly from New Zealand. It ranges in size from that of an egg to a softball and has—when ripe—a golden sheen highlighted with violet. The flesh is pale yellow, tender, and aromatic—if somewhat elusive in taste. It can be eaten skinned (seeds and all) in fruit and seafood salads or served as a garnish. Should you find one, it should have a sweet smell, have a little give without being downright soft, and—as is true of most fruits—be free of spots or blemishes.

Pepitas
Pumpkin seeds—a favorite Mexican snack food. They may be roasted or raw, salted or plain.

Pepo
Any member of the gourd family, including cucumbers and squashes.

Pepper

Peppers come in two persuasions: the hot spice we cook and season with along with salt and the large family consisting in part of the sweet or mildly pungent vegetables we use otherwise in cooking, including their near relatives, the mild-to-explosively hot CHILI peppers we use as flavorings.

Piper nigrum. This is the botanical name of the pepper we use with salt as a spice or seasoning. It seems to have originated on India's Malabar Coast, the area from which most of the world's supply still comes. The pepper plant is a vine bearing clusters of peppercorn-filled pods. Its final product reaches us in one of the following ways:

- *Black pepper.* This is the pepper after it has been harvested, dried, and removed from its pods. It is sold either as whole peppercorns or ground up. Because pepper loses much of its punch after being ground, most authorities urge you to buy the peppercorns and grind them yourself as you need them.
- *Green peppercorns.* Peppercorns that have been picked before becoming fully ripe. They are soft enough to be converted to a paste, are extremely pungent, but are highly perishable and best kept refrigerated. They are, however, available freeze-dried.
- *White pepper.* Pepper ground from the inner kernel of the peppercorn only. The inner kernel is white, but as much of the pungency of pepper is contained in the husk, white pepper is markedly less strong than black.

Capsicum frutescens. These are a whole bunch of vegetables native to the Americas but transplanted the world over. They include:

- *Anaheim or Anaheim mild.* A long green or red pepper with a mild flavor resembling a bell pepper (see below).
- *Bell pepper.* Also *black, green, globe, red, sweet, white,* or *yellow pepper,* depending upon color, taste, or seeming shape. These are the peppers we grow in our gardens and use for stuffing, salads, pickles, and veal-and-peppers as well as half a hundred other dishes.
- *Chili pepper.* The truly hot members of the family, although there are some sweet ones, too. They are red and green and yellow and come fresh or dried or pickled. See CHILI.
- *Cubanelle.* A sweet green or red pepper suitable for roasting.
- *Holland.* Hydroponically grown peppers of various colors (purple, yellow) appropriate as an expensive variation on bell peppers.
- *Hungarian.* A sweet, mild yellow roasting pepper, not to be confused with the red variety that produces PAPRIKA.
- *Italian frying pepper.* Tapering, thin-skinned, light green peppers available in most supermarkets and appropriate for sautéing, veal-and-peppers, and similar dishes.

- *Peperoncini.* A small, sweet, green or red pepper mostly found pickled.
- *Pimiento.* A sweet, dark pepper usually sliced up and preserved for stuffing into olives or used in PAELLA and similar dishes.
- *Sweet cherry.* A round green or red pickling pepper.

Peppercorn
The seeds of the PEPPER plant.

Pepper Mill
A device used for grinding up peppercorns (or any small, berrylike herb, including allspice berries). Pepper mills range from fairly small to a foot or more high (used by waiters in restaurants where smaller ones left on the table tend to gravitate into a customer's pocket) and at their best can be adjusted for the size of the grind—finer or coarser.

Peppermint
A common MINT (*Mentha piperita*) used as a flavoring.

Pepperoni
A hard, spicy, air-dried Italian sausage made of beef and pork and informed with chili pepper. It can be eaten as is or used in cooked dishes such as pizza.

Pepperpot
1. Also *Philadelphia pepperpot.* A spiced, soupy stew of tripe, potatoes, and dumplings. Legend has it that it was created for the troops at Valley Forge and named for the cook's home town. Finding enough tripe to feed an army during a particularly harsh winter would seem to be a notable feat indeed.

2. A West Indian stew of meat or seafood (or both) and vegetables, all flavored with CASSAREEP.

Pepper Steak
1. In French cooking, a slab of fine beef into which coarsely ground peppercorns have been embedded. The meat is sautéed in butter; enriched with cream, meat stock, pan drippings, and wine; and then flamed with brandy upon serving.

2. In Italian cooking, beef cooked with green pepper, onion, and tomatoes in a flavorful sauce.

3. A Chinese mélange of strips of steak stir-fried with onions and peppers and flavored with soy sauce.

Perch
A name given to a goodly number of fish (perch, perchlike fishes, fishes that are not perch, bass, sunfish, ocean perch, freshwater perch, and on and on into the night),

but it can be limited here to the freshwater perch and pike-perch specimens. These include the European perch (*Perca fluviatilis*) and its North American near-clone the yellow perch (*Percaf lavescens*), the Iowa darter (*Etheostoma exile*), the logperch (*Percina caprodes*), the pike-perches, the sauger (*Stizostedion canadense*), and the walleye or walleyed or yellow pike (*Stizostedion vitreum vitreum*).

These perch are first and foremost panfish and, by that token, are excellent pan-fried. They are also amenable to baking, deep-frying, and poaching. They all have delicate and extremely tasty flesh but are inclined to be bony.

Percolator
A type of coffeemaker that forces boiling water to ascend a tube and percolate, or trickle down, through the ground coffee beans.

Periwinkle
An edible marine snail (*Littorina littorea* and *Littorina irrorata* and on the West Coast *Littorina scutulata*) almost entirely overlooked in North America. The shells are dropped in boiling salted water just long enough for the pearly foot protector (or operculum) to drop off, the shells are then removed, and the meat screwed out of the shell with a nutpick or even a pin. Periwinkles can be eaten as such or with a vinaigrette or mustard sauce or added to scrambled eggs.

Perloo
The name in the South for a down-to-earth, hearty rice dish (usually embellished with game or meat or seafood). It has been conjectured that the name is an adaptation of *pilau* (or PILAF).

Pernod
A proprietary French aperitif with an anise flavor.

Perrier
A proprietary French mineral water, more prized in North America than in France.

Perry
A pear cider, usually fermented.

Persian Melon
A MELON of the muskmelon group.

Persillade
Chopped parsley and sometimes garlic sprinkled over various dishes before serving.

Persillé
From the French for "parsleyed." A grouping of French cheeses that develop (or are inoculated with) scattered spots of edible mold resembling (to French eyes, anyway)

leaves of parsley. Such cheeses were originally made with goat's milk and still lean heavily in that direction.

Persimmon

A fruit of a tree of the ebony family that is more or less round in shape and ranges in color from yellow to a deep orange. What we see commercially is almost universally the *Japanese persimmon* (*Diospyros kaki*), but some lucky souls may grow or pick the native North American specimen (*Diospyros virginiana*), which grows naturally from the Gulf of Mexico north to Connecticut and west to the edges of Kansas. Its fruit is smaller and more flavorful than its Asian counterpart, and until it was crowded out somewhere near the middle of the twentieth century, it was found, in season, in many ordinary grocery stores. Now you pretty much have to have your own tree—or access to one.

Native persimmons rival walnuts in size and are for the most part ferociously astringent when green, so much so that the early colonist John Smith reported that an unripe one will "draw a man's mouth awrie with much torment." If cut not quite ripe from the tree (or selected fully ripe or even fallen to the ground), they will mature into a sweet and juicy treat that reminds some munchers of dates, whereas John Smith thought of apricots. The early settlers had numerous ways of making use of them—from eating them as they were, to putting them in breads and cakes and pies and puddings (it was only later that ice cream was added), and to drying them like dates or figs for later consumption.

The Japanese persimmon is larger—about the size of a medium apple—astringent when green but less so than the North American type. It is also pulpier in the middle and has a far less lush taste. The top can be cut off and the flesh dug out with a pointed spoon (a grapefruit spoon, for example) and eaten plain or enriched with a little wine (the Japanese use sake). Lemon or lime juice as well as kirsch or other liqueur is also a good addition.

Because persimmons become overripe so quickly, they are picked and sold green and must be ripened by the consumer. Get them when the fruit is firm and plump, the skin unblemished, and the color bright and uniform. Putting them in a brown paper bag with an apple will hasten their ripening, after which they must be eaten right up (or discarded). Both native and Japanese species have varieties that have the astringency bred out of them (either naturally or by the hybridizer's art), but make sure you know what you've got—you don't want to have your mouth, too, get drawn "awrie."

Pestle

A small, club-shaped utensil for grinding or pounding something in a MORTAR.

Pesto

A Genoese sauce consisting of a paste of basil and garlic and cheese in olive oil sometimes augmented with pine nuts. It is often added to a thick soup akin to MINESTRONE
and to other dishes as well, both in northern Italy and in neighboring sections of
Mediterranean France. Inventive cooks also make a pesto based on cilantro or
CORIANDER instead of basil, but make sure your cilantro is fresh before you try it.

Petite Marmite

A superior CONSOMMÉ served in an earthenware receptacle and usually topped with
a chunk of bread often spread with bone marrow and sometimes sprinkled with
grated cheese. It can provide a welcome warmth on a wintry day. The earthenware
receptacle is also called a petite marmite, being a smaller version of the cooking pot
known as a MARMITE.

Petits Fours

General name for various assorted French cakes and cookies and miscellaneous iced
pastries served especially with tea.

Petits Pois

A French term for *tiny green peas*, preferably fresh from the garden—but don't
count on it unless it's your own garden. The English preference is for larger peas,
and both types are available in North American markets canned, fresh, and frozen.

Petit Suisse

An unripened French cow's-milk cream cheese enriched with additional cream to
ensure richness.

Petrale Sole

A Pacific FLATFISH (*Eopsetta jordani*), considered among the best of the Pacific
flounders.

Pe-Tsai

A CHINESE CABBAGE. Also called *Chinese celery cabbage*, *napa*, and officially *Brassica
pekinensis*.

Pfeffernüsse

A spicy, peppery, hard, nut-shaped, German Christmas cookie.

Pheasant

Also *ring-necked pheasant*. A gamebird (*Phasianus colchicus*) originally of Eurasian
origin but naturalized in North America in the 1880s and right at home ever since.
It tastes somewhat the way a chicken might taste if it were allowed to run wild for
a few generations. Pheasant can be cooked any way that you would cook chicken
and is most usually roasted in some manner or other unless it is well along in age,

in which case it should be braised. It goes well with sour cream or yogurt. Figure one bird for two people.

Phyllo

Also *filo*. Sheets of dough rolled almost incredibly thin and built up, usually with various forms of flavorings or stuffings between the layers, into rich pastries, generally of Greek origin. The word is Greek for "leaf."

Picadillo

Essentially, a ground-meat relish, usually made with beef (although pork, veal, and venison are also appropriate) with garlic, onions, tomatoes, and other ingredients, at will. You can serve it with rice and bean dishes or use it as a stuffing.

Piccalilli

A form of CHUTNEY.

Pickerel

A small, freshwater and estuarine fish related to the PIKE.

Pickle

To preserve something in brine or vinegar (or a combination of both). The term also refers to anything so preserved. When we think of pickles, we usually think of pickled cucumbers, but many fruits and vegetables are commonly pickled including cauliflower, onions, peppers, tomatoes as well as pears and watermelon rind, some of them laid down in a thick mustard sauce. Even cod that has been cured in brine can be considered pickled as can certain cuts of meat, such as corned beef and pickled pig's feet.

All this notwithstanding, a pickle with no other qualification is a pickled cucumber.

Pickling Spice

A combination of herbs and spices used to PICKLE foods. The ingredients typically may include some combination of allspice, bay leaves, black pepper, cardamom, celery seed, chili pepper, cloves, coriander, dill seed, garlic, ginger, mace, mustard, and red pepper.

Picnic Ham

Also *picnic shoulder*. A pork shoulder cut that has been cured in the way that HAM is cured. It may be boned or not and is usually less expensive—and somewhat tougher—than regular ham.

Pie

Essentially, a dish composed of some form of stuffing surrounded by a pastry crust. There was a time in our chauvinist past when the marriageability of a young woman was judged on whether or not she had a "light touch" with a piecrust. A light crust will, of course, enhance any pie—especially a dessert pie—although we no longer deem it essential to a marriage.

Pies contribute much to good eating. We have meat pies and chicken pies as well as fruit pies. Pastry is not the only crust appropriate to a pie—lemon meringue pie is topped only with meringue, for example, and shepherd's pie is composed of a base of lamb with a topping of mashed potato. And some pies have a bottom crust but none on top. However, pies in general are made with pastry top and bottom, and in North America are most likely to contain fruit and be served for dessert.

Pie Bird

A small, hollow figurine in almost any shape but most often that of a singing bird (except in Wales, where a dragon is said to be preferred) to be put in the middle of a deep-dish pie as it goes into the oven. It acts as a vent or chimney for the steam that builds up under the crust during baking (and as a prop to keep the crust from sagging). In its absence, a funnel would suffice but wouldn't be anywhere near so much fun. Most pie-makers simply make slits or fanciful holes in their upper crust to serve the same purpose.

Pie Plant

See RHUBARB.

Pie Plate

A pan for baking pies—and serving them in afterward. Pie plates are traditionally round, 9–11 inches in diameter, and from 1 to 3 inches deep (the latter for deep-dish pies). Pie plates come in metal, ceramic, and glass. If a recipe calls for a 9-inch pie and you use a 10-inch plate, you'll still have enough dough but you'll have a skimpy amount of filling, because pie recipes are not calculated on the pastry (which can, within reason, be rolled out thicker or thinner according to need) so much as on what goes into that pastry.

Pierogi

A small, Polish crescent of noodle dough (sometimes yeast-risen) filled with a seasoned, minced mixture with various components that range from cheese to fruit to mashed potatoes to meat. Pierogi are dropped in a copious amount of salted boiling water. The cooked pierogi are then either sautéed in butter or rolled in a butter-and-breadcrumb mixture to serve as a first course or side dish.

Pig

A domestic hog or swine (*Sus scrofa*). Pigs seem to have been first domesticated some 5,000 years ago by the Chinese, and a good idea it was, too. Although forbidden in some cultures (Islam, Judaism), pigs have provided a relatively inexpensive form of meat usable in a wide variety of ways. The meat of the pig is referred to as PORK, and this applies whether the meat is fresh or cured. Among the bounty of the pig we can include, in addition to the chops, roasts, and spare ribs: BACON, BRAWN, FAT-BACK, HAM, HEAD CHEESE, LARD, PIG'S FEET, SALT PORK, SAUSAGE, and SCRAPPLE. A close relative of the pig is the wild BOAR, which is but infrequently seen on North American tables these days.

Pigeon

The familiar city pigeon as such is not eaten (although Parisians during World War II are reported to have tried them and found them unbelievably tough) but other members of the family (Columbidae) do appear on the table as DOVE and SQUAB. The word *pigeonneau* may show up in a recipe or menu; it is French for *squab*.

Pigeon Pea

A variety of BEAN.

Pignoli

See PINE NUT.

Pignut

A somewhat astringent nut of a species of HICKORY, *Carya glabra*.

Pig's Feet

You are much more likely to run across these in England (where they will probably be referred to as "trotters") or on the Continent than in North America, but they are available. They are sometimes pickled, sometimes added to long-braised dishes (they take a good deal of cooking), and sometimes simmered lengthily then covered with melted butter and fine, white breadcrumbs and broiled to a golden brown. They are also an ingredient of the Mexican specialty MENUDO.

Pike

A family of exciting freshwater game and food fish. Because of their voracious appetite and savagery—qualities that commend them to anglers—the pikes have been dubbed both "pirate kings" and "sharks" of fresh water. A few fish that are not pikes are called by that name. Some of the pikes include:

Muskellunge (*Esox masquinongy*). A large (up to 80 pounds) game fish of northern North American waters which, because of its size and fighting spirit, is something of an angler's dream.

Northern pike (*Esox lucius*). A greenish brown fish with yellow spots that inhabits the waters of northern and western North America. Northern pike run up to about 40 pounds.

Pickerel. Either the chain pickerel (*Esox niger*) or the redfin pickerel (*Esox americanus*), small, eastern game fish—not pikes but close relatives and, when big enough, treated the same way in the kitchen.

Sand pike. Another name for sauger (see below).

Sauger (*Stizostedion canadensis*). Not a pike; this fish is a PERCH.

Silver pike. A northern pike variant, but without the yellow spots.

Walleyed pike (*Stizostedion vitreum vitreum*). A misnomer; this fish is a PERCH.

Pikes, except in France, do not enjoy a high culinary reputation, mostly because they can be of an ungodly boniness, but also because the meat tends to be quite dry. Once boned, however, pike can indeed be palatable, if not overly flavorful; poaching and braising are handy ways to subvert its dryness, as is enriching it with a good stuffing and especially a good sauce. Pike can even be broiled (not usually a recommended technique for dry foods) if it is basted well enough and often enough. The French use it with great success for QUENELLES and MOUSSES and it is often made into GEFILTE FISH.

Pike-Perch

Various excellent food and game fish of the PERCH family that are commonly confused with the pikes.

Pilaf

An Oriental dish of rice or bulgur and usually fish or meat or poultry, also called *pilau.* It is seasoned either delicately or quite robustly depending upon the provenance of the recipe. The northern versions tend to be milder, the southern hotter and spicier. In preparing pilaf, the rice is generally sautéed in butter before being finished in the usual manner.

Pilchard

The young of the European sardine, a member of the HERRING family.

Pilot Cracker

A form of modern HARDTACK, but usually sweetened. Pilot crackers are sometimes crumbled into New England style chowders in lieu of COMMON CRACKERS, which are harder to come by.

Pilsner

Originally a BEER from Plzeň (or Pilsen) in Czechoslovakia, but now any light beer. Pilsner has its own glass as well, a tall tapering glass on a flat glass base.

Pimento

1. Also PIMIENTO.

2. In Jamaica, the name for the tree that bears ALLSPICE and for the spice itself.

Pimiento

A sweet, dark red PEPPER grown in the southern United States for canning. It is used as a stuffing for olives and to enhance the looks and flavor of a number of dishes, many (such as PAELLA) of Spanish origin. It is not to be confused with Jamaican pimento, which is what Jamaicans call ALLSPICE.

Piña Colada

A popular iced drink of rum compounded with coconut cream and pineapple juice. Without the rum, it describes a coconut/pineapple flavoring.

Pinch

An inexact cooking term usually meaning less than ¼ teaspoon; it is used when so little is needed that the exact amount is irrelevant.

Pineapple

The pineapple itself is not a single fruit but a conglomeration of small fruits that come together to form what we see in the market. It has a conelike shape covered with scales—the more scales the more pineappley the taste, the less scales the sweeter and juicier will it be—with a crown of leaves growing out the top. Pineapples come in various sizes (they will grow into monsters of some two pounds, but there being no market for such an entity, you're not likely to see one locally) and in any case the smaller ones tend to be tastier.

Pineapples have a drawback of not ripening once plucked. Hence, they are picked just before full ripeness and shipped by the fastest expedient method (air freight adds heavily to the cost). Look for a good plump one that is slightly soft to the touch with a sweet, pleasing aroma at the stem end. Avoid any that are bruised or show soft spots or blotches on the skin. You can refrigerate a whole pineapple for a day or so, but if cut, wrap it in plastic before you put it in the fridge. Pineapple, cut into serving-sized pieces, also freezes well.

You can find pineapple candied, canned, dried, frozen, whole, sliced raw, or sliced and packed in syrup or pineapple juice. You can find it in fruit juices (or concentrates) alone or with other components, in ice creams and sherbets, in yogurt, and in preserves. Although pineapple slices are a classic garnish for a ham, there is still nothing to quite match a fresh, ripe, whole pineapple. One elegant way to serve it is to trim the bottom to permit it to stand upright, slice off and discard the top, and, using a *sharp* knife, cut the pulp from the rind and remove it. You can then slice the pulp into serving sizes and replace them in the shell which is passed around, allowing guests to select pieces at will. If you've picked wisely, you will have an aromatic, sweet, juicy, delectable treat.

The pineapple is a semitropical delicacy (*Ananas comosus*) apparently brought to European attention at Guadeloupe on Columbus's second voyage to the New World in 1493 (although the contention is that pineapples first arose in Paraguay). It was distributed in Europe by Spanish and Portuguese explorers. It was called by various names—the Guarani Indians knew it as *nana ment*, "excellent fruit," a name that is reflected in its generic name and in, for example, the *ananas* of the French.

The Spanish preferred *piña*, from its resemblance to a pine cone, and our pineapple seems to have followed from there.

Pineapples have been cultivated throughout the Caribbean and in Central and South America and in the nineteenth century were widely grown in the Azores and Hawaii. Hawaiian land prices being what they are, most pineapples seen in the United States now come from Central and South America, those in Europe from southern regions of Africa.

Pineapple Guava
Another name for FEIJOA.

Pine Nut
Also *pignoli*, *pignolia*, and *piñon*. An edible seed that grows in the cones of various types of pines. Pine nuts add flavor and a little crunch to stuffings and can be used as you would almonds, for example, to give texture to vegetables such as green beans. They can also be added to stews and braised dishes. The pine nuts available in Oriental groceries are more pungent than those otherwise available. Most of the pine nuts you see have been roasted, as otherwise they tend to go rancid quite quickly.

Piñon
Another name for PINE NUT.

Pinot Noir
A wine grape (*Vitis vinifera*) responsible for all the fabled red table wines of France's Burgundy, the greater amount of its Champagne, as well as other mostly red table wines ranging from fair to extraordinary in other parts of the world, including especially California. Such wines, when truly from the pinot noir, will be expensive, as the vine bears but sparingly and sometimes the quality of its fruit does not produce the income inherent in lesser but more productive varieties. The vine also has its poor relations, the pinot blanc and pinot gris, and at one time the excellent CHARDONNAY was considered a member of the family but is no longer thought to be related.

Pint
A standard unit of measure amounting to 2 cups or .473 (or about ½) liter.

Pinto Bean
A BEAN usually found dried.

Pip
A British term for the seed or stone of a fruit.

Pipe

To force a substance, such as icing, through a PASTRY TUBE or pastry cloth in order to obtain a fanciful and attractive decoration or garnish.

Pipérade

A Basque concoction in which eggs, garlic, green peppers, onions, and tomatoes are scrambled in olive oil. It is sometimes gussied up with a little ham or bacon.

Piquant

Having the ability to whet the appetite; stimulating, pleasant, and tangy.

Pirogi

See PIEROGI.

Piroshki

A small, rich Russian TURNOVER with a seasoned filling usually of meat but sometimes of cheese, vegetables, or seafood.

Pisco

A BRANDY made in Peru and neighboring countries that is distilled from Muscat grapes and aged in clay or other neutral containers, from which it takes on no color. It is usually drunk young.

Pismo Clam

A variety of West Coast CLAM.

Pissaladière

A Provençale pizza—anchovies, olives, and onions in a circle of dough just like a pizza pie.

Pistachio

A greenish, almondlike nut (*Pistacia vera*) of Middle Eastern origin; pistachio shells are sometimes dyed red or blanched white before the nuts are put on sale. Besides being found in vending machines, pistachios are also used for ice cream and any baked goods that can be livened up with a touch of green. They can also give taste and crunch to stuffings as well as stews in the Middle Eastern style, which tend to incorporate dried fruit and nuts as well as meats and vegetables. You can find them fresh or put up in glass or plastic, shelled or unshelled, dry or salted, raw or roasted.

Pistou

A French variation of the Italian combination of a minestrone-like vegetable soup enhanced with PESTO or a sauce very much like it.

Pit

The kernel or seed or stone (or English pip) of a stone fruit such as apricot or cherry. Also, to remove such a seed or stone.

Pita

Also *pocket bread*. A flat, hollow Near Eastern white or whole wheat bread that when cut forms a pocket suitable for all manner of sandwich fillings. It can also be cut up to be used with various dips.

Pithiviers

A cake of puff pastry and rum-flavored almond paste from the French town of the same name, also famous for its lark pâté.

Pizza

A flat yeast-risen pastry shell filled or topped with a mixture of tomato sauce, cheese, and various other good things that may include anchovies, mushrooms, pepperoni, and almost anything else this side of the kitchen sink.

Pizza Cutter

A PASTRY WHEEL suitable for dividing a pizza pie.

Plaice

A name for several varieties of FLATFISH.

Planking

An early American technique of cooking and sometimes serving food on a plank or board. Meat and vegetables can be planked, but it is generally suggested for fish. The trick is to heat a hardwood board, oil it well, then place the usually half-cooked item on it to finish roasting it. Advocates of the technique insist that a much-used, well-oiled, carefully cleaned but never washed (and certainly not soaped) plank can impart a succulence that cannot be matched otherwise.

Plantain

1. A tropical fruit (*Musa paradisiaca*) closely related to the banana. It is, however, starchy rather than sweet and is used as a vegetable instead of a fruit. Unlike bananas, plantains must be cooked to be edible.

Plantains look like large green bananas at first, turning yellow and then black as they ripen.

Buy plantains green and keep them as you would bananas. You can bake them, broil them, fry them, or find a good tropical cookbook and follow it accordingly.

2. Any of a genus (*Plantago*) of plants used medicinally by early Native Americans and brewed into tea in medieval England. Now it is considered a tiresome weed, especially when it shows up in your lawn. The very young leaves can be used as a potherb and will supply a goodly amount of vitamin C.

Planter's Punch

A once popular rum punch noted for the mnemonic concerning its proportions: "one of sour, two of sweet, three of strong, and four of weak," referring to, respectively, lime juice, sugar syrup, rum, and water.

Plastic Wrap

A thin plastic sheet that clings to food or food containers to seal them from air or odors. Such wraps are made from various plastics, but that made from the one called polyvinylidene chloride (PVDC) and sold as Saran Wrap is markedly less permeable than others.

Plate

A meatcutter's term for the section of a beef critter's belly just between the BRISKET and the FLANK.

Plover

A family of birds (Charadriidae) some of which are considered gamebirds in England and on the Continent but protected, if not downright endangered, in North America. Some plovers are raised for the market in game farms and are consequently extremely expensive. Their flesh and their eggs are highly rated.

Pluck

1. To remove the feathers from a bird.
2. The heart, liver, lungs, and sometimes the windpipe of an animal. Only the liver and heart are commonly used for food these days.

Plum

A plethora of fruits of the rose family (especially the offspring of *Prunus domestica* and *Prunus salicina*) of distribution throughout the temperate world and with an ability to interbreed in various ways to confound classification. As a group, plums are small, stone-fruited, smooth-skinned fruit often of a purple hue but by no means always (they can also be black, blue, green, or yellow). One reason for the vast number of plum varieties is that one type will do well in one locale and fail utterly where conditions differ but where another plum will thrive. Growers like to go with what works.

Plums are used for compotes, desserts, jams, jellies, sauces, snacks, tarts, and dried as PRUNES.

When selecting plums, look for plump, shapely fruit that is well colored, firm to the touch, and without cracks or blemishes. If they are particularly soft or hard, look elsewhere. Plums generally have a powdery "bloom," but this is a characteristic of them and no cause for concern. If they are still somewhat hard, keep them out, but once ripe refrigerate them (they will hold for four or five days). Plums are also available canned and dried.

There are a few varieties of plum that might come your way. They include:

Agen. A French plum used only for excellent quality prunes.

Damson. A plum with a dark skin and flesh used only for preserves.

Friar. A large, black-skinned, amber-fruited, sweet, juicy, eating plum also recommended for preserves and sauces and tarts.

Greengage. A small, yellow-to-green, soft and juicy, very sweet plum with yellow flesh and a number of offspring forming the greengage (or gage) family.

Italian or prune plum. A small oval plum with bluish purple skin and firm golden flesh, especially used for prunes.

Mirabelle. A small, French, aromatic yellow plum good for cooking and making jams and the basis of the fruit brandy of the same name.

Red beauty. A plum with bright red skin and yellowish flesh used as a dessert or snack fruit.

Santa Rosa. A reddish purple plum with yellow flesh and a slightly tart taste.

Sloe. A bitter European plum used in jams and for flavoring gin.

Plum Pudding

A rich, steamed pudding filled with dried fruits, spices, brandy, and sometimes nuts, but not including plums. The "plum" referred to is traditionally fig, although plums may have been used originally.

Plum Sauce

A sweet-and-sour sauce made from the Chinese "plum" (considered an apricot rather than a true plum) and used as a dip with fried meats and with PEKING DUCK.

Plunge

To immerse something swiftly in water or other liquid.

Poach

To cook something in a liquid that is boiling so slowly that it almost seems not to be boiling at all, with bubbles that form but never quite make it to the surface. Poaching brings out the full delicate flavor of the matter being poached, whereas a more heady boil might serve to toughen it or break it into pieces.

Poblano

A dark green, even black, triangular CHILI. It is one of the milder members of the family with a rich and slightly bitter taste. The darker the color, the richer the taste. Dried poblanos are known as *anchos*.

Pochouse

A MATELOTE of freshwater fish cooked in red wine and flamed with brandy. It is thickened with BEURRE MANIE and augmented with bacon or salt pork, mushrooms, and small, glazed onions.

Pocket Bread

Another name for PITA bread.

Pod

The outer coating of certain seeds such as beans and peas.

Poi

A Hawaiian specialty of TARO root that has been cooked and pounded into a paste and usually permitted to ferment. It can be served as a sort of porridge or used as a condiment.

Poire

A BRANDY distilled from pears.

Pokeweed

A plant (*Phytolacca americana*) native to North America that bears masses of staining berries beloved by birds. The tender young shoots are gathered in the spring and cooked like asparagus. Foragers are warned to take care to get the shoots and no roots (the roots are strongly emetic) and to gather only the first, young growth as virtually all parts of the more mature plant are toxic.

Poland Spring

A natural spring in Maine that produces regular spring water and also a sparkling variety. The name is also used for a variety of spirits.

Pole Bean

A variety of BEAN cultivated on poles rather than allowed to grow freely on the ground.

Polenta

An Italian version of cornmeal mush (although barley and chestnut meals have been, and may still be, used). In addition to being served from the pot, it is often flavored with pan juices or augmented with grated cheese. When allowed to cool, it can be sliced and fried and the pieces served as a side dish.

Polish Sausage

See KIELBASA.

Pollack

A fish of the COD family.

Pome

A botanical designation for certain fleshy, seed-bearing fruits, such as the apple, pear, or quince.

Pomegranate

A tropical and subtropical shrub or bush (*Punica granatum*) with glossy leaves, bright coral-colored flowers, and a red to purple fruit that is lopsided, more or less round, leathery skinned, replete with seeds (613 according to one probably impeachable source). Pomegranates are widely referred to in mythology, perhaps the best known story being of Persephone, the Greek goddess of spring, who was abducted by the god of the underworld. Because she had eaten six pomegranate seeds while in captivity, she was compelled to spend six months of the year in the underworld, and six in the mortal world, endowing Greece with six months of growing season and six of fallow time. Whether it still works out that way is something you'd have to ask a Greek farmer.

Pomegranates are available from about October to January. Look for a good-sized one with good color—pink or red—with a little heft to it. If it is split or cracked or dusty, avoid it. When you bring it home, you can freeze it, refrigerate it, or keep it just at room temperature (if the room is dry). It will keep for a month or so in a cool dark place, for two months if refrigerated, and longer, of course, if frozen (up to a year). Pomegranates may be eaten raw but you must take care to eat around the white membranous part (known as *rag*) that forms a sort of inner rind. You could spit out the seeds, but that seems like an odd thing to do and most people chomp them quite happily. Try cutting the top off the fruit and breaking—rather than cutting—it to get at the pulp and seeds which you can eat with a spoon or strew over ice cream or other food of your fancy. Pomegranate juice is also highly regarded. Roll the whole pomegranate around on a table or other flat surface to break up its innards and stick a straw into it to get at the juice. You can also simply strain out the juice. Pomegranate juice is used commercially for the syrup GRENADINE.

Pomelo

Another name for GRAPEFRUIT but more properly applied to the SHADDOCK.

Pomerol

A wine-growing district of France's Bordeaux region noted for its generous red table wines that have a somewhat velvety feel in the mouth.

Pompano

A highly regarded food fish of the JACK family.

Pont l'Evêque

A semihard cow's-milk CHEESE from France's Normandy region with a long and distinguished pedigree. It has a yellow curd penetrated by tiny holes and has been made around the village from which it takes its name since medieval times. Cheese lovers insist that its special tang and distinctive flavor can only be achieved through fermentation by the bacteria native to the locale.

Pony
A small, balloon-shaped glass used for serving brandy.

Pony Beef
See BABY BEEF.

Pop
Another name for SODA (definition 3).

Popcorn
A variety of corn (*Zia mays* var. *everta*), which when heated in hot air or a little oil literally and quite noisily "pops," forming a tasty snack food that can be further flavored with butter, salt, soy sauce, cheese, caramel, or maple syrup, whether you're at the movies or just sitting around at home. Unflavored popcorn is favored by models and starlets who feel that the bulk appeases the appetite without adding weight.

Pope's Nose
Also *parson's nose*. The fatty, edible tailpiece of a bird.

Popover
A muffin with a hollow interior. When properly made, it will be somewhat crusty on the outside and moist on the inside. Popovers are composed of butter, eggs, and milk and are frequently baked in a special cast-iron popover pan.

Poppy
A plant (*Papaver somniferum*) that is the source both of opium and of poppy seeds. In Europe, the leaves are—or at least were—used in the same way as spinach (despite, as one source gently puts it, their "slightly narcotic effect") and the crunchy seeds are used mostly in baking, usually as a topping but sometimes as an ingredient of a rich pastry filling, and in salad dressings. Although the seeds themselves are not narcotic, even the small amount sprinkled on a poppy-seed bagel has been known to cause a positive reaction in blood tests for narcotics.

Porbeagle
Also *mackerel shark*. A SHARK of the North Atlantic that is of some commercial interest but more on the European side than the American. It has a somewhat mild flavor and when smoked is popular in Germany.

Porcini
An Italian name for the morel MUSHROOM.

Porcupine

A large, slow, dim-witted, arboreal rodent (of the family Erethizontidae) of North America (although there are Old World relatives as well) often found in deep woods, especially pine forests. Because of its slowness and lack of intellect, it is easy to take (walk up to it and bash it on the snout with a tree branch) and makes a welcome feast (it is said to resemble pork) for lost and hungry fishermen, hikers, hunters, and the like stranded in the woods without other means of sustenance. Its liver has been deemed a delicacy, apparently even by those not in dire need of sustenance. Like so many small animals, it has glands in the small of the back and under the forelegs that must be removed during the skinning process.

Porgy

An important food fish (family Sparidae) of worldwide distribution, often called *sea bream*. Porgies all share a more or less rounded, compact body, and their mild flesh ranges from palatable to excellent eating. They can be baked, fried, grilled over coals, or poached. Some of the more common ones include:

> *Jolthead porgy* (*Calamus bajonado*). Found roughly from Rhode Island to the Bahamas, it is at its best while still fairly small.
>
> *Red porgy* (*Pagrus pagrus*). This fish covers almost the whole range of both North and South America with close relatives in the Mediterranean. It may, if small, be treated as panfish, otherwise it is best baked or poached.
>
> *Scup* (*Stenotomus chrysops*). Common along the New England coast and down through the Carolinas. Bake, broil, or fry.
>
> *Sheepshead* (*Archosargus probatocephalus*). A tasty game fish found in the Atlantic from Nova Scotia to Brazil. Sheepsheads can be cooked almost any way appropriate for fish, although poaching seems to be preferred by many experts.

Pork

The meat of the pig. Most of the pork we eat comes from pigs slaughtered after about six months of age, excluding suckling pig, which has not yet been weaned and is of a clear white color and delicate taste. The pork you are likely to find in the market is a light-colored, finely grained, flavorful meat that may be slightly pink or grayish white. The number of cuts that can be taken off a pig carcass is almost infinite, but fortunately can be whittled down to a manageable few. Approaching from the rear, the hind legs essentially yield fresh leg roast or, if cured, HAM, either whole or in halves (butt end from closer to the body, shank end from closer to the foot) or in slices. From the center of the midsection comes the loin, which yields Canadian bacon, chops of various sorts, crown roast, and loin roast (the center cut is the pricey one, but the ham end and shoulder end also give good eating). From the sides come BACON, FATBACK, LARD, SALT PORK, and SPARE RIBS. From the front end of the pig comes the shoulder (also called *cala*) or picnic ham if smoked like ham. Just above that is the butt that can be cut into blade chops or left whole as a Boston butt roast. In front of the shoulder is the jowl, which gives more bacon. Leading it all off is the head, often used for BRAWN, HEAD CHEESE, and SCRAPPLE.

In addition to the above, there are also the spare parts: the brains, ears, feet, heart, kidneys, knuckles, liver, and tongue. Some of these parts are more available than others (unless you raise your own pigs) but all have been—and here and there still are—used for human consumption. And much of the meat that comes off a pig (and a good deal of the fat, too) is used in sausage-making.

When cooking pork, it is essential to cook it thoroughly. Pigs are capable of harboring a parasite known as the trichina worm, which can be disabling or worse for people. Cooking kills the trichina. This doesn't mean you have to burn pork to a dried-out crisp. The trichina die at about 137°F, so a roast that emerges from the oven at anything above about 150°F should be quite safe. Pork can not only be cut any number of ways, it also can be cooked in a multitude of styles.

Porpoise

An aquatic mammal (especially *Phocaena phocaena*), sometimes mistaken for the DOLPHIN, only sparingly used as food (it has, apparently, an oily taste not appreciated by most people).

Porridge

A cereal grain cooked in milk or water until thick, seasoned with salt and perhaps butter, and usually sweetened with molasses or sugar. It is usually served for breakfast.

Port

Perhaps the most prestigious FORTIFIED WINE. True port is produced in Portugal and appears in three types. The finest is vintage port, produced only in years when the harvest is considered good enough and laid down for aging before being brought to the table. You wouldn't want to cook with it. Closer to the average consumer is tawny port, a wine that has been blended and allowed to age until the color matures from purple to ruby to golden to tawny. Ruby port is the younger sibling of tawny and, having been aged for a shorter time, should be less expensive. All of these designations are used on ports made in parts of the world other than Portugal.

Port du Salut

An alternative name for PORT-SALUT.

Porter

A dark BEER.

Porterhouse Steak
A particularly choice cut of BEEF.

Port-Salut
A medium-soft, French, cow's-milk CHEESE originally made by Trappist monks in their monastery at Entrammes in Brittany beginning in the 1850s. The rights to the name were granted to a manufacturer with the result that the name is used widely throughout the world. It is said that the monks kept the secret of their cheese and continue making it in small amounts and sell it as Entrammes. A good Port-Salut will have a yellow paste and be mild and smooth and satiny.

Posole
An alternate spelling of POZOLE.

Posset
A hot beverage of spiced milk or cream augmented with beer, molasses, or wine (especially sherry). It is sometimes thickened with egg yolks or white breadcrumbs.

Possum
See OPOSSUM.

Pot
A utensil for cooking food.

Potage
A French term for a thick soup or broth known in early English as *pottage*. The "mess of pottage" for which the biblical Esau sold his birthright to his brother Jacob as described in Genesis was probably a form of dried pea or lentil soup.

Potato
An herb (*Solanum tuberosum*) of the nightshade family, which makes it an unlikely relative of the eggplant and the tomato. Potatoes are, however, used solely for their root, or tuber, which may be oval, round, or in some cases kidney-shaped. Potatoes arose in the high Andes where they have been a staple food for centuries. They were introduced to Europe by the Spaniards (probably in the late 1530s) but not much was done with them. Either Sir John Hawkins or Sir Francis Drake brought them to Britain about 1540, but not much happened until Walter Raleigh planted them on an estate in Ireland and began a vegetable love affair that continues to this day. They were known in France probably in the late 16th century, but were not much used as food until after 1770.

Some potatoes, even today but to a much lesser extent, have a greenish color caused by alkaloids (especially *solanine*) that in high quantities are toxic (and possibly carcinogenic). Early potato eaters would consume a suspect potato and break out in a rash that was feared to be the first sign of leprosy, which caused the planting of potatoes to be banned outright in certain areas of France. Potatoes were finally popularized by a French Army doctor, Antoine-Auguste Parmentier (with the result that, in France at any rate, any dish bearing his name contains potatoes). He had his potato patch on the outskirts of Paris closely guarded by French troops during the day, then withdrew the troops at night to allow people to come out and steal the crop, and potatoes soon became popular.

The uses of potatoes are vast. They can be baked, boiled, fried (either deep— or french—or homestyle), hashed, roasted, canned, made into chips or bread (with the addition of wheat flour to provide gluten) or flakes or flour or salad, or can be dried or frozen. Mashed potato, because of its digestibility, is often an early food for infants.

In selecting potatoes, consider your purpose and choose the appropriate kind. Make sure they have smooth skins and are firm to the grasp with no spots or blemishes and no sprouts. Avoid those with any hint of green (a giveaway for the presence of solanine), but if you have some that are greenish, peel then rigorously, as the solanine stays near the surface.

There are many varieties of potato, but those most available in North America break down to:

Long white. A popular potato originating in California. It has a thin skin, not a great deal of starch, and is good for boiling or homestyle frying.

Purple. Also called *black*, although the flesh is more purple than black and the skin a light violet. It is dry and mealy and is interesting baked or fried.

Round red. A round potato with a thin red skin and relatively little starch content. It is useful for boiling, in salads, and for frying.

Round white. The potato of the Northeast (especially northeast Canada, Long Island, and Maine). It is a smooth-skinned potato of all-round use.

Russet. Usually called the *Idaho* no matter where it is grown. This is a thick-skinned potato with a high starch content suitable for baking and for french fries.

Yellow. A fairly recent addition to our shelves, these thin-skinned, smooth, and creamy potatoes are usually best boiled or fried.

Potato Chip

A typically American snack food consisting of paper-thin slices of potato soaked in cold water, then deep-fried, dried, and salted. It originated in Saratoga Springs, New York, where it was known as a *Saratoga chip*. Potato chips are available plain or rippled and augmented with any number of flavorings.

Potato Flour

Cooked, dried potato that has been milled into a flour. It is useful as a thickener and gives a crispness when added to certain types of bread.

Potato Salad

A salad, hot or cold, composed of cubed, diced, or sliced cooked potatoes with a dressing. Celery, green peppers, hard-boiled eggs, and onions are frequent ingredients in such a salad which may be dressed with a bacon fat, boiled dressing, with mayonnaise, or with a classic VINAIGRETTE.

Pot au Feu

A French meal of a broth based on long-simmered beef (or on special occasions beef and a whole fowl) with root vegetables. The broth is served first, often with a crust of bread in the bottom of the bowl, followed by the meat and vegetables. It is a worthy antidote to a cold winter's day.

Pot Cheese

A form of COTTAGE CHEESE that has been more thoroughly drained of its whey, making it drier than regular cottage cheese.

Potherb

An HERB or other plant, the edible parts of which are used as a green or in soups.

Pot Liquor

Also *pot likker*. The liquid left over from simmering meat, especially in the southern United States, where the meat is more likely than not to be some form of pork.

Pot Marigold

An ornamental garden flower (*Calendula officinalis*) the petals of which have been picked, dried, and used as a flavoring or to impart a saffronlike color to soups and stews and sometimes to omelets. (The name marigold also applies to flowers of the *Tagetes* genus, not used in cooking.) It has been suggested that marigolds were used as something of a desperation measure and were an indication that the food being served had passed its prime, but if you want to use them I wouldn't let that deter you. Just don't overdo it—the herb can be quite strong.

Pot Marjoram

A strain of the herb MARJORAM.

Pot-Roasting

A cooking technique difficult to distinguish from BRAISING. Both terms refer to cooking a piece of previously browned meat in a closed pot with moist heat. Some say that if you put that pot in the oven you are braising, not pot-roasting, which must be done in a closed pot on the top of the stove. Some say that if you add little liquid or none at all, letting the item being cooked supply most if not all of the moisture, you are braising and if you add a substantial amount of additional liquid, you are pot-roasting. (Of course, if you add a great deal you will end up poaching, but let's not get into that.) So long as the food is good, it says here, you may call it what you like.

Pot-roasting is usually appropriate for older and tougher cuts of meat. A piece of fine top round steak (as opposed to chuck or bottom round), for example, would probably simply fall apart if cooked by this method.

Potted Foods

Cheese, game, meat, poultry, or seafood pressed into a small pot or terrine. Except for the cheese, the food is generally cooked, then minced, and pressed into the container and sealed with oil or clarified butter. Thus protected it will keep a goodly length of time and was often taken on voyages before other methods of preservation were commonplace. Potted foods are commonly spread on toast to be served as hors d'oeuvres.

Pouilly Fuissé

A light, dry white French table wine from vineyards around the city of Mâcon, in southern Burgundy. Much of the wine is marketed in North America under the name CHARDONNAY, the grape that goes into it.

Pouilly Fumé

See BLANC FUME DE POUILLY.

Poultry

A general term for domestic fowl—chickens, Cornish hens, ducks, geese, guinea fowl, squab, turkeys—raised for eggs or meat or both.

Poultry Needle

A hefty needle with a large eye used for sewing up the vent of a bird after the stuffing has been put in or for sewing the stuffing into other stuffable commodities. You can also use one to TRUSS your bird.

Poultry Seasoning

A commercial blend of herbs and spices—usually parsley, sage, marjoram, and thyme, but sometimes rosemary or others as well—intended for seasoning poultry stuffing.

Poultry Shears

A kind of sturdy and extremely heavy scissors that commonly break into two pieces (for cleaning) and are equipped with curved, serrated blades; they are used for cutting through the bones and joints of poultry to render them into desirably sized pieces for cooking.

Pound

A standard unit of weight equivalent to 16 ounces or .37 kilograms. Its abbreviation is *lb*.

Pound Cake

A cake originally made with one pound each of butter, eggs, flour, and sugar. You won't see it made that way today, although many light-textured cakes made from various ingredients still abound under the name.

Pousse Café

A mixed drink containing several different liqueurs added separately according to their specific gravity, so that each one forms a separate layer with the heaviest ingredient at the bottom, the others floating on top in order of lightness.

Poussin

A French term for a young (6–8 weeks), very small (12 ounces to 2 pounds) chicken. It is considered a delicacy by some, a tasteless bore by others. Rock Cornish hens or squab can be substituted.

Pozole

Also *posole*. A rich, Mexican, pork stew from the city of Guadalajara, where it might be made with a pig's head. Otherwise, it might include various cuts of pork (chops, loin), a whole dismembered chicken for festive occasions, garlic, hominy, and onions. It is often served with an accompanying relish including cheese, cabbage, lettuce, onions, and radishes.

Prairie Oyster

1. A raw egg ingested in one gulp usually with vinegar, salt and pepper, and perhaps Worcestershire sauce as a hangover cure.

2. Also *mountain oyster*. The prepared testicles of a beef critter or similar animal, akin to ANIMELLES.

Praline

1. A combination of nuts, usually almonds or pecans, glazed in a caramel sauce. It is eaten as a candy and used as a cake filling as well as a garnish or ingredient of, for example, ice cream.

2. A Louisiana cookie of almonds and brown sugar.

Prästost

Another name for the Swedish cheese PRESTOST.

Prawn

In North America, any large shrimp. In Europe, shrimplike shellfish including the common prawn of the northern Atlantic coast (*Palaemon serratus*), the deepwater prawn (*Pandalus borealis*), and the NORWAY LOBSTER (also called *Dublin Bay prawn* and *scampi*). Prawns can be cooked and served as you would shrimp.

Preheat

To bring something, an oven, for example, up to a certain temperature before putting the food in it.

Pré-Salé

A French term for lamb or mutton (less frequently beef) that has been grown in sea-side meadows and gained flavor from its salty pasturage. *Salt-meadow lamb* would be its English language equivalent, and at one time—before mass-production techniques took over the meat industry—such lamb was to be found, at least along the coastlines.

Presentation Pan

A fancy cooking utensil often of an attractive medium such as copper that is for flaming foods at the table or otherwise bringing hot foods to the table for serving. It is more of a restaurant than a household gadget.

Preserve

1. To prepare a food to prevent it from spoiling. Preservation methods include canning, distilling (colonial Americans, for example, quickly learned that whiskey kept better and was more easily transported than wheat), drying, freeze-drying, freezing, pickling, salting, and smoking. Preservation techniques may be used alone or in combination, as in salting food before smoking it.

2. A thick spread made from chunks of fruit cooked up with sugar and perhaps a little PECTIN; the result is akin to JAM and JELLY.

Pressure Cooker

An appliance for cooking food quickly with compressed steam. Most such cookers consist of a heavy aluminum or stainless-steel base with a perforated rack that fits just inside it and a cover that "locks" onto it, secured by some form of gasket. The top has a protuberance for a pressure valve, and there is usually an additional safety valve in case the other gets jammed somehow.

Pressure cookers work in about half the time it takes to cook the same food the regular way, yet enable the food to retain a great deal of its taste and freshness. Experts say, however, that there is a slight diminution of quality when compared to traditional cooking techniques. Special pressure cookers are made for use in microwave ovens, and extra large canning cookers are also available.

Prestost

Also *Prästost* and *Saaland Pfarr*, Prästost being Swedish for "priest cheese." It is a firm, creamy, cow's-milk CHEESE flavored with AQUAVIT or other ardent spirit.

Pretzel

A hard, brittle biscuitlike snack usually formed into the shape of a circle, a stick, or, especially, a loose knot. Pretzels usually consist of strands of leavened flour and water dropped into boiling water, then fished out and strewn with beaten egg and salt. The strands are then twisted into a desired shape and baked hard. There are, however, also soft pretzels. Pretzels are often considered an accompaniment for beer.

Prickly Pear

A prickly pear, also called the *cactus fig, cactus pear,* or *nopal,* is the edible fruit of various cactus plants of the genus *Opuntia,* native to the Americas (varieties can be found from Canada to South America) but cultivated in southern Europe, North Africa, and the Middle East as well.

The fruit themselves are pear-shaped in a lopsided sort of way with sharp spines that are removed in harvesting, leaving a few stinging hairs behind—so handle them with caution and peel them before use (soaking in cold water will soften and civilize the hairs). Prickly pears will range in color from green (when unripe) to orange or reddish brown (when ripe) and have a soft, somewhat bland bright red interior studded with seeds. Eat them well chilled when they are fully ripe.

Choose prickly pears that look dark enough to eat and get them when they are tender but carry no unseemly spots. You can keep them on the counter (if firm) or you can refrigerate them for a few days (if they are soft enough to eat).

Prickly pears can be eaten as is, used in salads, or served with ham and cheese as an hors d'oeuvre. Their juice looks spectacular, and deseeded it is served plain or in a mixed drink with vodka or rum.

Prime Rib

A rib roast of BEEF taken from an animal graded *prime* by governmental standards.

Processed Cheese

A method of making cheese by which the cheese is heated and mixed with emulsifiers into a coherent mass with colorings and flavorings. It is then cut up and the pieces put into airtight packages. It will keep far longer than natural cheese but cannot begin to compare in taste. Most cheese found in American markets (other than cheese specialty stores) is processed cheese.

Profiterole

A small mound of puff pastry filled with almost anything from PASTRY CREAM (with a chocolate sauce topping) to fish, meat, poultry, or variously flavored custards or ice cream. Profiteroles can be used as desserts or hors d'oeuvres, depending upon the filling.

Pronghorn

Also *pronghorn antelope*. A ruminant (*Antilocapra americana*) of western North America highly thought of for the quality of the venison it provides.

Proof

1. A way to test yeast for its effectiveness. When baking with yeast, the first step is often to combine the yeast with warm water and perhaps a little sugar or flour or other substance (for example, barley malt) that acts as food for the yeast. If after five or so minutes, the yeast froths and gives off a heady, somewhat earthy (it's known as "yeasty") aroma, it is working and usable. If nothing happens at all and you've had your water at the right temperature, your yeast is most likely a goner and you'd better get a new supply. Or maybe you're using brewer's, not baker's, yeast (it won't work in any modern recipe).

2. Alcoholic proof. In the United States it refers to double the alcoholic content (at 60°F) by volume of the spirit being tested (80 proof thus contains 40 percent alcohol). Figuring the degrees of British proof is so abstruse that even Winston Churchill once explained to the House of Commons that "when we speak of these degrees, what we mean is proof spirit; and what we mean by proof spirit is these degrees." If it's any help, British proof is 57.1 percent alcohol by volume, with overproof and underproof being figured from that standard. The French, in their logical way, compute proof as alcoholic content. Thus a spirit of 57 percent alcohol would be 114 proof (U.S.), at proof (U.K.), or 57 proof (France).

Prosciutto

An Italian type of HAM.

Provolone

A pale yellow, firm, southern Italian CHEESE from the milk of either buffalo or cow, usually pear-shaped, often hung in string nets. It is made other than in Italy, in which case it will certainly be of cow's milk. Provolone is a good table cheese (especially when allowed to age a few months), melts well, and when thoroughly aged becomes hard enough for grating.

Prune

A dried fruit of the PLUM, but only plums of certain varieties are usable for drying. Prunes have been known since ancient times and became popular in northern Europe as a fruit that could even be enjoyed in the winter. Prunes are available with their pits intact or, more seldom, pitted. They come in various sizes (small, medium, large, extra large, and jumbo) and can be eaten as is, soaked and stewed, or used in baked goods and puddings. Prune juice is also widely available. Prunes are noted for having a mild laxative effect.

Prunelle

A liqueur made from the pits of the blackthorn or sloe plum (*Prunus spinosa*).

Ptarmigan

A gamebird of the GROUSE family.

Pudding

A dessert that is boiled and steamed before being cooled, such as Christmas plum pudding. In the United States, it also generally refers to a sweet, flavored dessert, sometimes made with gelatin. In the United Kingdom, it can refer to a main dish cooked under a crust, such as a beef-and-kidney pie, or to the batter that is cooked in beef drippings to make a Yorkshire pudding. The word can also connote a blood sausage.

Puffball

An edible MUSHROOM.

Puffed Grain

Rice or wheat that has been heated until it expands and becomes light and fluffy. It is packaged as a commercial breakfast cereal.

Puff Pastry

An extremely rich, buttery, and flaky pastry. It is made by rolling chilled pieces of butter between layers of pastry, folding it in thirds, rolling it again, and repeating the process six or eight times. It is used for any number of pastries including croissants and napoleons.

Pullet

A hen less than one year old, the eggs of which are roughly half the size of that of the mature hen. Pullets' eggs were at one time fairly widely available, but now that eggs are mass-produced in factory-style environments, you would be hard put to lay your hands on any.

Pulque

The fermented juice of the maguey plant (*Maguey americana*), a popular stimulant in Mexico.

Pulse

A general word for the seeds (especially the dried seeds) of such legumes as beans and peas and lentils.

Pumpernickel

A dense dark German bread made of rye FLOUR sometimes augmented with wheat and often flavored with molasses and, perhaps, caraway seeds. The original pumpernickel was made from whole rye flour and was dark and heavy with a slightly sour taste.

Pumpkin

A large orange round vegetable (*Cucurbita pepo*) of the gourd family, best loved in North America as the indispensable ingredient for the Thanksgiving Day pie, especially now that the jack-o-lanterns that we used to cut out for Halloween are being so quickly replaced by dreary plastic facsimiles. Given Halloween and Thanksgiving, it follows that pumpkin is a fall phenomenon. Pumpkins appear in markets and roadside stands when the air is beginning to get nippy but before the first frost, usually sometime in September.

Select pumpkins that have a little weight to them, are free from spots and blemishes, and have a pleasing shape. That shape might be important should you wish to make a pumpkin soup and serve it at the table using the shell as a soup tureen. Otherwise, pumpkin can be used in any way you might use squash. Pumpkin seeds are also removed, dried, perhaps roasted, and served as a snack food called *pepitas*.

Pumpkinseed

A North American PANFISH.

Puree

1. To finely mash or sieve or—better yet—to run cooked food through a blender or food processor. Pureed vegetables (broccoli, for example) can be kept warm without harm, making them ideal when the main course requires some fancy finishing touches and the cook needs a dependable, undemanding vegetable to accompany it.

2. A soup thickened by having its ingredients pureed.

Puri

A deep-fried, whole wheat bread from the central and northern portions of the Indian subcontinent. It may be eaten with vegetarian meals or stuffed as a snack.

Purple Potato

Also *black potato*. A POTATO with a dark skin and flesh.

Purslane

A fairly ubiquitous weed (*Portulaca oleracea*), the young leafy growths of which are used in salad or in stews (they have a thickening quality, like okra) or as a green in the manner of collard or turnip greens. The related *winter purslane* (*Montia perfoliata*), a plant of moist soils, is also used in salads and sometimes is cooked briefly, like spinach.

Quahog
A large CLAM.

Quail
Also *bobwhite*. The quail, like the robin, is something of a misnomer. European settlers found quail here and named them for birds they were familiar with at home.
The American quail is no more related to its European counterpart than is our robin
(actually a thrush) related to its European counterpart.

American quail (of the family Galliforme) are small (six to seven ounces dressed)
and are of several species. The bobwhite is common in eastern and southern North
America, while California boasts the California quail, Gambel's quail, and the mountain quail, considered by most connoisseurs the best tasting of them all. Quail are
commonly roasted and served on toast. The usual serving is two per person.

Quarry Tile
An unglazed tile used as a floor in an oven to induce a crustier finish on bread products. (The tile absorbs the heat and diffuses it more evenly than is possible in a regular oven.) Quarry tiles are placed directly on the oven rack or floor while it is still
cold and allowed to preheat with the oven; bread dough or bread pans are then placed
directly on them. (When bread dough is placed directly on the tiles, the tiles are best
dusted with cornmeal first to prevent sticking.) A pan of boiling water may be
placed beneath to provide steam for an even crustier finish. Quarry tiles are available at most outlets that sell floor tiling.

Quart
A standard unit of measure amounting to 2 pints (or 4 cups, ½ gallon, or .95 liter—
close enough to 1 for most purposes).

Quatre Epices
A French spice mixture used in soups and stews. The name is French for "four spices"
(it is intended to taste somewhat like clove, ginger, nutmeg, and pepper), but the
generous French habitually add others as well.

Queen Anne's Lace
Another name for the wild CARROT.

Queensland Nut
An early name for the MACADAMIA nut.

Quenelle
A type of dumpling made of finely ground game, poultry, seafood, or veal mixed with egg, formed into an oval shape, poached in salted water, and usually served with a creamy sauce.

Quetsch
A small blue PLUM of Alsace used for tarts but especially for the plum brandy that bears its name.

Quiche
A small tart, either boat-shaped or round, filled with custard and usually some sort of flavoring—especially bacon and cheese and onion, although other fillings have become popular. From time to time quiche takes on the trappings of a fad, but like so many fads, if you hang in there long enough, it too will pass and the food will be just as good as it was before the trendy people heard about it.

Quick Bread
A non-yeast breadstuff—anything from a pancake to a full loaf of bread—that does not require the rising time of yeast and can consequently be mixed together and popped into the oven with a minimum of delay. The usual leavening agents are baking powder, baking soda, or sometimes simply eggs. Biscuits, muffins, and IRISH SODA BREAD are examples.

Quince
A yellow-skinned fruit (*Cydonia oblonga*) shaped somewhat like a pear but too tart to be eaten raw. Quinces have been known for centuries and probably hit their peak in the Middle Ages, especially around the Mediterranean Sea. The Portuguese called them *marmelo* and used them for a preserve we now know as marmalade, although we rarely make it with quince these days. Other quince jams and jellies are available, however. Fresh or canned quince can also complement lamb nicely when they are stewed together.

When selecting fresh quince, chose firm, round, or pear-shaped fruit with pale yellow, fuzzy skin. Quinces can be refrigerated, but try to use them within about two weeks.

Quinine Water
Also *tonic*. A somewhat bitter semisparkling, nonalcoholic beverage or mixer flavored with quinine (the bark of the chinchona tree) and citrus fruit. The British drank it to preserve their health in tropical climes (it is a treatment for malaria) and finding

it went well with gin invented the gin and tonic (and later the vodka and tonic). It is now taken for recreational, not medical, reasons.

Quinoa

A South American, herbaceous plant (*Chenopodium quinoa*) with grainlike seeds of prestigious protein content. Pronounced *keen-wah*, it is a fairly recent arrival in North America (although it has been a staple in the Andes for centuries) and can be highly expensive when you can find it at all. The plant (or shrub) bears an abundance of small seeds that look somewhat like rice, giving a crunchy texture and a nutlike taste. It has a variety of uses—plain in casseroles, salads, stews, and stuffings, and ground into flour for bread or pasta. It is available in many health food stores and increasingly in some supermarkets.

Rabbit

A mammal (*Oryctolagus cuniculus*) closely related to the hare. Although a quite common domestic food animal in Europe, it is far less so in North America where it is more likely to be considered either as a children's pet, as game, or as a tiresome garden pest. It can be cooked according to any of the methods appropriate for chicken—which it resembles—or following one of the more traditional European recipes including HASENPFEFFER, jugged hare, and CIVET. Rabbits are available frozen—more rarely fresh—in most supermarkets.

Raccoon

Also *coon*. A small, nocturnal North American mammal (*Procyon lotor*) distinguished by its "bandit's mask," ringtail, and habit of washing its food before eating. Raccoon-skin coats were fashionable in the twenties but are rarely seen now. Although hunted fairly extensively in rural parts of the southern United States, raccoons are now mainly excoriated by suburbanites elsewhere for their somewhat messy forays into garbage pails.

Once the musk glands in the "armpits" and alongside the spine in the small of the back are removed, raccoons (especially if not too old) are considered tasty fare. Skin the critter, remove its fat, then soak it overnight in salted water. You might then want to parboil a large one (in one or two changes of water) for up to an hour. Roasting (especially with a sweet potato stuffing) and (for the older ones) braising are recommended cooking methods. You'll want to take care with raccoons—they can, when they are around, transmit rabies.

Rack

1. A meatcutter's term for the section of a lamb's back between the shoulder and the loin; if you count the ribs with the first at the neck and the thirteenth at about midbelly, the rack comprises ribs six through twelve.

2. In wine-making, to decant a fermenting wine from one barrel to another, leaving any sediment, or lees, behind.

Raclette

A Swiss specialty whereby cheese is exposed to heat (traditionally toasted over open fire) and then served with small boiled potatoes and pickles—it is an après-ski spectacular.

Radicchio

An Italian form of CHICORY (*Cichorium intybus*). What we see is red with white ribs and has a tart, nutlike flavor. There are various subdivisions of radicchio, but all are interchangeable. Although mostly used in salads, radicchio can also be grilled or sautéed or even baked. Select radicchio as you would lettuce—select full, crisp, strongly colored heads. You can store them in plastic in the refrigerator for up to a week.

Radish

A small, tangy root of a plant of the mustard family. Radishes (*Raphanus sativus*) are the first vegetable that a youngster is usually encouraged to grow because they sprout so quickly the child can monitor the plant's progress from seed to harvest without getting overly bored. The taste can vary from quite mild to peppery, sometimes too much so for the young gardener. Most of the radishes we see are small, round, and bright red, although they can also be long and fingerlike or tapered and range in color from white through varying shades of red to black. The small, round, red kind are almost exclusively eaten raw, whereas the long, white kind are generally cooked, like turnips, which they resemble slightly in taste.

Make sure you select firm, evenly shaped radishes, clean and free from mold. Don't take them if they're cracked or show dark spots (although if they come from your own garden you're doubtless going to be more relaxed about this). If they come with tops, slice them off. Wash the radishes and either place them in a plastic bag in the vegetable drawer of the fridge or leave them out in an attractive bowl for snackers to snitch at will. There is also an Oriental variant known as DAIKON.

Ragout

A stew of pieces of meat, poultry, or fish cut into uniform size and shape and braised lengthily in liquid. Sometimes the item is browned, sometimes not. Vegetables or potatoes may be added. A typical ragout would be an Irish lamb stew, consisting of lamb, onions, and sliced potatoes simmered in water. And mighty good at that.

Rainwater

A type of MADEIRA wine.

Raisin

The dried fruit of the GRAPE. Raisins were originally sun-dried, but many are now dried by artificial means, in part to keep them more moist and plump. They are made only from sweet grapes, and it is felt that those from grapes with seeds are tastier than those from seedless varieties. Raisins make a fine snack and are widely used in baked goods, sauces, and stews. Once a package of raisins has been opened, seal it in plastic and keep it refrigerated. It will hold for up to a year.

Raita

A spicy yogurt salad from the Indian subcontinent, often made with thinly sliced cucumber, but other fruits and vegetables are also common.

Raki

Another name for ARRACK.

Ramekin

1. An individual baking dish.
2. A cheese-filled tart baked in a ramekin.

Ramen

A Japanese wheat (although other flours, such as buckwheat, may also be included) noodle, sold in North America as noodles with dried soup powder .

Ramp

A wild leek (*Allium tricoccum*), a variety of wild onion that grows from North Carolina upward through New England and westward to Minnesota. In Appalachia each year, ramp festivals are held, bringing leek lovers from all over the continent. Forager Euell Gibbons liked them in French onion soup, in tossed green salad, and pickled.

Rampion

A bellflower (*Campanula rapunculus*), the roots and leaves of which are used in salads, the young shoots cooked in the same way as asparagus.

Rancid

A term that refers to something rank, sour, or reeking of old oil and that has been allowed to go bad and is begging to be thrown out.

Rape

See BROCCOLI RABE.

Rapeseed

A seed of the rape plant (*Brassica napus*). When not processed as bird food, it can be made into a low-cholesterol cooking oil, generally sold as canola oil. A related oil, known as colza, is considered dubious or worse by nutritionists and health food experts.

Rapini

Another name for BROCCOLI RABE.

Rascasse
A scorpion fish (of the family Scorpaenidae), an ugly, essentially Mediterranean "trash" fish, said to be essential to the making of authentic BOUILLABAISSE.

Rasher
An individual slice of bacon (or ham), although it can also refer to a serving of several slices.

Raspberry
Another berry that is not a berry—it is a fruit composed of an aggregate of drupelets, which are like individual fruits all glommed together, although for culinary purposes, berry is fine. Raspberries are lush, flavorful, colorful (black, purple, red, yellow) and versatile. It has been suggested that despite the advocates of the strawberry, God doubtless did make a better berry upon the creation of this one. No opinion will be given here.

There is evidence of raspberries growing in Europe and Asia in prehistoric times, and North America has its own excellent emissaries. The European raspberry (*Rubus idaea*), naturalized quite early in North America, can be red or yellow whereas the raspberries of North America are either red (*Rupus strigosus*) or black (*Rupus occidentalis*, otherwise known as the blackcap raspberry). Variations on these plants have resulted in hybrids bearing purple fruit. The number of varieties of raspberries reflect in some sense the ripening time of the plant, differing ones being planted to ensure a continuous supply throughout the growing season. This has been obviated by the development of perpetual bearing varieties that provide enough to keep you happy unless you crave the changes in color that different plants can afford.

Raspberries—in addition to those you pick as you browse through a cultivated or wild raspberry patch—have a number of uses, mostly oriented toward desserts. They can be used, whole or crushed, as a filling for crepes. Raspberries also contribute to brandy, compotes (the ever-inventive French take large, perfectly formed raspberries and create a compote simply by dressing them with a few tablespoons of boiling sugar syrup), ice cream, jam, pies, sauces, soufflés, and tarts. You can also find them frozen, and while not quite like those off the bush, they're not bad. Raspberries are also used in a vinegar that was at one time particularly trendy but is nonetheless certainly worth having on hand. The brandy made with raspberries is *framboise* and is not a bargain item. For those who like being enveloped in an aroma of raspberry with their after-dinner liqueur, however, it is worth considering.

When selecting raspberries, remember the rule of berries: they lose their excellence virtually as they are being picked. If you can't pick your own, try a farm stand. If there are none in your area, look over the supermarket offerings and take only those raspberries that are plump and brightly colored and without any "bloom." Avoid those that are shriveled or moldy.

Ratafia

1. A cordial made by steeping fruit or the fruit and its cracked kernels in sugar and a spirit. It was popular in Victorian England, where it was customarily home-made. The name is also used for an Italian cherry cordial.

2. A tea cookie akin to a MACAROON.

Ratatouille

A French (especially Provençale) vegetable dish consisting of eggplant, tomatoes, and zucchini (or sometimes summer squash) embellished with bell pepper, garlic, onion, and spices, all simmered in lots of olive oil. It can be served hot or cold or some-where in between. It is good alone as an hors d'oeuvre or spread and as a canapé.

Rattlesnake

Any of various North American snakes (*Sistrurus* and *Crotalus* spp.), the meat of which is served usually at fancy game banquets but can sometimes be found canned in specialty stores. When tried here, many years ago, it did not make any lasting impression.

Ravioli

A small square of PASTA filled with meat, cheese, or spinach. Ravioli is usually poached and served with a tomato-based spaghetti sauce. It is a close kin to the Chi-nese WON TON.

Ray

See SKATE.

Razor Clam

A CLAM of the West Coast of North America.

Reblochon

A soft, French, cow's-milk CHEESE with a rich taste. Eat it young as it tends to turn bitter with age.

Red Beauty

A bright red PLUM eminently satisfactory for snacking.

Red Cheese

A Chinese seasoning made from fermented soybeans and red food coloring, some-times mixed with barley or rice. It can be flavored with chilis or rice wine. Red cheese is pressed into cakes and added to casseroles and stews.

Red Cooking

A Chinese cooking style in which foods (such as chicken) are browned in soy sauce, which imparts a deep red hue to the finished product.

Red Delicious

A bland red APPLE.

Red Eye Gravy

A camp gravy for ham. Angus Cameron and Judith Jones assert in *The L. L. Bean Cookbook* that it can be made by adding 1½ cups strong black coffee to the ham drippings to replace the water usually used in gravy-making. More haphazard cooks simply make it by adding plain water.

Redfish

See OCEAN PERCH.

Red Flannel Hash

A HASH made from the remains of a NEW ENGLAND BOILED DINNER (minus the cabbage). It gets its name from the beets that are cooked separately and thrown in as an afterthought. It can also be made from scratch. A recipe elicited in times long past from the late Arthur Lovell, Keeper of the Griswold Inn in Essex, Connecticut, called for hamburger hashed together with diced beets, onion, pepper, and potatoes, spiced only with salt and pepper, and bound with a little heavy cream. Others substitute bacon and whittle down the other vegetables to beets and onions and potatoes.

Red Grouper

A saltwater BASS.

Red Mullet

A European variety of MULLET.

Red (Pepper) Oil

See CHILI OIL.

Red Snapper

An important food fish (*Lutjanus* spp.) of the southern United States and the Gulf of Mexico, usually running about five pounds. It is highly thought of and can be cooked in any of the ways fish are generally cooked, including in a chowder or other fishy stew. The name is often applied to other fish of a more or less reddish hue.

Reduce

To BOIL DOWN, except when it refers to the unpleasant process of dieting.

Refresh

To stop something from further cooking by putting it under cold, running water. Spinach, for example, when wanted for salad, can be blanched in boiling water and then quickly refreshed and will come out more tender and with its greenness heightened.

Refried Beans

A Mexican specialty in which leftover, cooked, dried beans are mashed and then reheated, traditionally in lard. They are often served with tortilla chips or as a filling for tortillas.

Refrigerator Cookie

A type of cookie the dough for which is mixed, rolled into the shape of a log, covered with plastic wrap, and refrigerated for anywhere from a few hours to a few days before being sliced into rounds and baked.

Reggiano-Parmigiano

A superior Italian grating cheese known also as PARMIGIANO-REGGIANO.

Reindeer

A European branch of the CARIBOU and a traditional mainstay of the Lapps.

Reine Claude

A French name for a greengage PLUM, named for Claude, Queen of France and wife of Francis I.

Relish

Anything served on or with another food to perk it up somewhat. Carrot sticks, pickles, or radishes as a side dish can be considered relishes as can such flavorings as CHILI SAUCE and CHUTNEY.

Render

To leach out the fat from a fatty piece of meat or poultry for use as a cooking medium or flavoring. When applied to pork, the term is TRY OUT.

Rennet

A commercially available ferment used to curdle milk. Most rennet is made from the stomach of a calf, lamb, or kid, but a vegetarian substitute made from AGAR can be found as can one made from mushrooms and other plants. Rennet can usually be found in health food stores, most of which will get it for you if they don't regularly stock it. Most households have little desire to curdle milk, but may use rennet in JUNKET.

Reserve

Cookbook jargon for "don't throw it out, you'll need it later." Anyone writing in English instead of Recipe would no doubt suggest you set something aside rather than reserve it.

Retsina

A light Greek white or rosé wine flavored with pine pitch or resin. One conjecture suggests that early wines were carried about in goatskin bags (as in present-day

Spain), which needed pine pitch to keep them from leaking. The taste for resin then developed. While the very concept sounds unpleasant, a thoroughly chilled retsina can have a fresh, tangy effect, especially on a fiercely hot day.

Reuben Sandwich

A hearty sandwich of disputed origin containing slabs of corned beef layered with cheese and topped with sauerkraut, all on sourdough rye bread. You can serve it as is or run it under the broiler first.

Rex Sole

A Pacific FLATFISH.

Rhenish

A name once used (especially in the United Kingdom) for RHINE wines. It has since been displaced by the word *hock*.

Rhine

A white wine, ranging from dry to quite sweet, from grapes grown on the steep slopes of the Rhine River in Germany. The good Rhine wines are subject to a strict system of controls, all of which are—or ought to be—reflected on the label. The names to look for include the grape variety (such as Gewürztraminer, Riesling, Sylvaner), and, on the more expensive side, details of grape selection. These terms include *spätlese* (grapes that are left on the vine until late, when a special mold forms and results in a less juicy but far sweeter grape and consequently sweeter and more distinguished wine); the gradations of *spätlese*, which include *auslese* (selected bunches of grapes), *beerenauslese* (selected individual grapes), *goldbeerenauslese* (much like *beerenauslese* except the grapes are drier and of higher quality), and *trockenbeerenauslese* (the highest quality of specially selected grape and hideously expensive should you actually find one).

Rhône

A wine-growing district of southeast France, along the banks of the Rhône River from southern Burgundy to Avignon. The wines include the red and white (both dry and somewhat sweet) table wines of Châteauneuf-du-Pape, Condrieu, Cornas, Côte Rotie, Hermitage, and (for rosé wines) Tavel. As it traverses Switzerland on its way to France, the Rhône irrigates Swiss vineyards also, producing such wines as FEN-DANT and DOLE.

Rhubarb

A springtime field plant or year-round slightly less tasty hothouse plant (*Rheum rhaponticum*), the stalks of which are generally stewed or made into preserves and pies, for which the plant is also known as *pie plant*. Because rhubarb has such an almost mouth-puckering tartness, it is customarily combined with a fair amount of sugar. When picking out rhubarb, look for deep red stalks (they tend to be more fla-vorful), wrap what you're not using in plastic, and refrigerate not more than a day or so. Should you have your own plant, pick it just before using it. Use only the stalks—the leaves are toxic. Rhubarb has a special affinity for strawberries and can also be made into a sauce that—like a gooseberry sauce—goes excellently well with bluefish or mackerel.

Rib

Any of the bones that stiffen the body cavity of a bird or animal and the meat that adheres to it. Ribs (especially pork ribs) are barbecued, most flavorfully with a tangy sauce. Individual stalks of celery are also referred to as ribs.

Rib Roast

A standing roast of beef consisting of one or more ribs, often seen on menus as *prime ribs*, which is true only if the meat is prime beef. Lesser grades (especially choice) are more common outside of extremely high-priced establishments. A rolled rib roast is the same cut with the bones removed and the meat rolled and tied. Most beef lovers feel that when meat is removed from the bone before cooking, it loses some incre-ment of taste, although it is certainly easier to carve. The rib-eye is the choicest part of the cut, usually served as a steak.

Rice

1. A cereal grain (*Oryza sativa*) of Asian origin providing the mainstay of the diet for large portions of the world. While there are an estimated 7,000 varieties of rice, what we see comes in long, medium, and short grains, the names meaning just what they say. Long-grain rice separates into individual kernels more readily than the others; it is what the food flacks extol as "perfect rice," whether every time or not. Medium and short do not separate as well, and are more nearly perfect for Chi-nese dinners, especially if you plan on using chopsticks. While some rice is converted into FLOUR or made into vinegar or sake, most of it comes to the kitchen in one of the following forms:

Arborio. An Italian rice, from the northern area of Piedmont. It has the capac-ity of absorbing considerable moisture without becoming soggy, making it the rice of choice for RISOTTO.

Basmati. A delicate rice from the Indian subcontinent available either brown or white.

Brown. A rice removed from its hull and some of its bran but otherwise intact. It is tastier and far more nutritious than white rice and needs a longer cook-ing time.

Coated. Seldom seen, except perhaps if you buy it in bulk. This is a rice that has been coated with talc and sometimes glucose to help it keep. The coat-ing washes off readily or it can be soaked for a while. This is the only rice that needs washing before cooking—the others would lose whatever enrichments have been added if washed.

Converted. A rice specially processed to hold more of the nutrients than are found in regular white rice. It needs slightly longer cooking time but comes out the same color.

Glutinous. An Asian variety of a starchy short-grain rice. The Chinese use it for pastries and stuffings and Chinese children are said to use it as a sort of do-it-yourself modeling clay.

Instant. A rice that has been specially prepared to cook in the time it takes to boil water. It is ideal for those who don't have the twenty or so minutes it takes to make regular rice and can spare the extra expense; also for those who might need a handy, water-conserving shortcut when camping.

Puffed. A breakfast cereal caused by heating rice in a closed container until enough steam is generated to cause the rice to expand and become light and puffy upon exposure to the air.

White. The rice that most of us use most of the time. It has been stripped of hull and bran and germ. It is still a good source of starch, but most of its nutritional value has gone by the boards unless it is also labeled "enriched," in which case some of it has been put back again.

2. To force a vegetable, such as potatoes, through a device with small holes that cause the substance to emerge as small bits the size of rice. It is accomplished with a RICER.

Rice Flour

Rice that has been milled and ground. As it has no gluten, it is inappropriate for bread-making, but has some use in cakes and pastries and is widely used in the Orient for making noodles.

Rice Paper

An edible Asian paper used as a wrapping or in candy-making. It is made not from rice but from the pith of the rice-paper tree (*Aralia papyifera*), which is related to GINSENG.

Ricer

A kitchen device in which foods are pressed through tiny holes so that everything comes out in approximately the size and shape of rice. Essentially, a FOOD MILL.

Rice Stick

Or *rice noodles* or *rice vermicelli*. A flavorless Asian noodle made from RICE FLOUR. If deep-fried, it enlarges to far more than its original volume.

Rice Wine
Not truly a wine, as it is fermented from rice instead of some form of fruit, but usually given the name anyway. The two most prevalent are SAKE and MIRIN.

Ricotta
A cow's-milk WHEY CHEESE of Italian descent but now made fairly universally. The name translates from Italian as "recooked," and refers to the technique of cooking the whey left over from another, previously cooked cheese, or that whey augmented with additional milk. It can be fresh—in which case it somewhat resembles a slightly grainy cottage cheese and is often used in manicotti—or aged long enough to become firm. In Italy, ricotta is allowed to age to the point where it can even be grated.

Riesling
A wine grape (*Vitis vinifera*) widely grown in such places as Alsace, Austria, California, Chile, Italy, and Switzerland, but most tellingly in Germany, where it has been cultivated since Roman times. In California it is known as Johannisberg Riesling to differentiate it from other grapes that are called Rieslings but are not. A true Riesling produces a steely, dry, highly aromatic wine or—if left to mature on the vine—a still distinguished but sweeter wine, especially along the banks of the RHINE.

Rigatoni
A grooved tube of PASTA.

Rijsttafel
An Indonesian specialty, embellished by the Dutch into something of a smorgasbord-style extravaganza (the word is Dutch for "rice table"), consisting of plain boiled rice surrounded by up to 40 tangy, spicy side dishes of meat, poultry, sauces, and vegetables.

Rillette
A French form of potted pork but sometimes stretched to refer to other meats including game and poultry and even seafood.

Rind
The outer skin of something. Pieces of orange and lemon rind are useful flavorings; pork rind is often added to give body and some flavor to stews. Pork rind is also prime bait for some kinds of angling, and there are indeed people who derive pleasure from chewing it themselves.

Rioja
A wine district of northern Spain producing sturdy dry red wines that rank as the best of the Spanish table wines.

Risi e Bisi
Rice and beans.

Rising
To expand as the result of adding a leavening agent such as YEAST or BAKING POW-
DER to a dough or batter.

Risotto
An Italian style of cooking RICE in which it is first sautéed (sometimes with chopped
onions) in butter or margarine, then enriched with simmering broth, added only a
bit (about half a cup) at a time, the next addition being made only when the previous one has been fully absorbed. The result is a rice with a creamy consistency but
with each kernel remaining slightly firm. Risottos can be flavored with many additions—chicken, saffron, seafood, and vegetables are common. Although in theory
any kind of long-grained rice would suffice for the purpose, the Italian variety
(*arborio* is the most widely available) is in fact the only kind of rice that works well.

Rissole
A very thin pastry stuffed with FORCEMEAT or other filling, rolled into a half-moon
shape, and fried in deep fat.

Roach
A European fish (*Rutilus rutilus*) related to the CARP and prepared in the same ways.

Roast
To cook something uncovered in an enclosed space with dry heat. It wasn't always
this way—roasting began with cooking joints of meat on a spit over or near a hot
fire. Such a practice today would be considered spit-roasting or grilling rather than
the familiar placing of food in a hot oven and taking it out again when it is cooked.
    There are two principal schools of thought on roasting meats. One would have
you roast your meat at a constant, fairly low temperature—such as 325°F. The other
would have you start out at 450°F or even 500°F for up to half an hour, then turn
down the oven (to 325°F, for instance) for the balance of the cooking time. Advocates of the first claim that the meat roasts more evenly inside and out using their
method; those of the second claim that it gives a crustier outside and a juicier inside.
Unless you're already an advocate, try it both ways and stick with the one that suits
you. Otherwise, commute between the two as your mood (or the food) dictates.

Roaster
A chicken weighing roughly three to five pounds.

Roasting Rack
A metal rack that fits into a roasting pan and holds the meat being roasted above
the fat that drips from it during cooking.

Rocambole

The name of a couple of mild forms of garlic (*Allium* spp.) more likely to be found in Europe than the Americas.

Rock-and-Rye

A traditional American, spirituous drink of rye WHISKEY flavored with lemon, lime, or orange and embellished with a chunk of ROCK CANDY.

Rock Candy

Sugar syrup that has been allowed to crystallize either by evaporation or on sticks or pieces of string. It has the reputation of being soothing to sore throats. American author Damon Runyon writes about a character who focuses on rye whiskey and rock candy until the candy runs out and he settles for "rye whiskey and rock candy without the rock candy."

Rock Cornish Hen

A small domestic crossbred poultry that supplies about as much meat as one person would want. It needs marinating or spicing to have much taste and is generally roasted.

Rock Crab

A small (three to five inches) CRAB.

Rocket

Another name for ARUGULA.

Rockfish

A whole panoply of scorpion fish (family Scorpaedinae), including the OCEAN PERCH, which provide much sports fishing. Various members are frequently miscalled rockcod and red snapper. There is also a temptation here and there to call the totally unrelated striped bass a rockfish.

Rocky Mountain Oyster

See PRAIRIE OYSTER (definition 2).

Rodman's Mushroom

A fairly prevalent North American wild MUSHROOM much akin to the regular mushroom of commerce.

Roe

1. Fish eggs; the raw material of CAVIAR and when it comes from certain fishes (shad particularly comes to mind), a delicacy in itself. Roe can also refer to MILT.

2. A small deer (*Capriolus capriolus*) of Europe and Asia that is renowned for its succulence.

Rolling Pin

It's what you need to transform a blob of pastry dough into an elegant, thin sheet or to shape a mass of bread dough into the right size for your loaf pan. Some pins consist of cylinders with handles on each end; others are simply the cylinder, either straight or tapered. Pastry chefs say that the plain variety allows you to get the "feel" of the dough better. Using one well is something like playing the cello—it takes practice.

Rollmops

An hors d'oeuvre of sliced herring fillets with pickles and onions.

Roll Out

To extend—and thin—a pie crust or other pastry on your (usually) floured breadboard or marble slab using a lightly floured rolling pin.

Romaine.

A form of LETTUCE.

Romano

A very hard, sharp, popular grating CHEESE of Italian origin originally made with ewe's milk but more recently, and in the United States exclusively, with cow's milk.

Rome Beauty

A firm red, midseason, cooking APPLE.

Root Beer

A sweet carbonated soda flavored with herbs and roots including ginger, sarsaparilla, sassafras, wild cherry, and wintergreen, but also with additional artificial flavorings and caramel to add color.

Roquefort

A semisoft, blue-veined, sharp and peppery, ewe's-milk CHEESE made only around the village of the same name in southeast France. Receiving its blue veins from a special mold (*Penicillium roqueforti*), it is aged in special cellars where the cheese has been made at least since the first century. It is believed to be not only the oldest French cheese, but of blue cheese in general, the unquestioned monarch.

Rose

A plant and its flower (*Rosa* spp.), which can be used to some extent in the kitchen. Rose petals, for example, can be made into jam, a sweet syrup, vinegar, or other condiments. In addition, they can be added to honey or to stews (such as North African COUSCOUS), compounded into a sweet pudding, or crystallized into an elegant candy. ROSE HIPS make a preserve that is extremely rich in vitamin C. ROSE-

WATER is also of culinary importance, adding a delicate flavor and aroma especially to Oriental dishes.

Rosé

A pale pink—or rose-colored—wine made by partially fermenting the grape juice on the skins (which imparts the color). A substitute of sorts can be made by mixing red and white wines, but it doesn't work very well. Current fashion refers to rosés as *blush wines*.

Rose Apple

See JAMBO.

Rose Hips

The fruit of the dog rose (*Rosa canina*), a European plant now found wild in North America and elsewhere, especially along beaches. The hips can be made into a preserve rich in vitamin C.

Rosemary

Originally a Mediterranean plant, rosemary (*Rosmarinus officinalis*) is now found the world over, and not only in cooking; it has also been used in perfumery and soaps, in hair rinses and mouthwashes, to help flavor vermouth, as a replacement for incense, and in defense against witchcraft. In cookery, it can be used fresh or dried, the dried variety having, of course, more potency.

Fresh rosemary is most commonly used chopped (or snipped—cutting it up with a small pair of scissors is usually easiest); this is obviously not necessary with the dried variety. When adding dried herbs to a dish to be cooked, tying them in cheesecloth helps keep the dish clear of floating debris.

As a culinary herb, rosemary is protean. It adds flavor to salads and salad dressings, to soups and stews, to sauces and stuffings, and to roasts of beef, game, lamb, pork, poultry, and veal; it can be used (discreetly) in making jam, and it adds a special touch when mixed into the dough for baking-powder biscuits or dumplings.

Rosette

A rose-shaped pastry made by dipping a special iron (a *rosette iron*) into pastry batter and then into a deep-fryer. You can then sprinkle it with sugar and serve it for dessert.

Rosewater

A wonderfully aromatic essence of rose petals. Because of its delicate flavor and aroma, it is often called for in Oriental cookery and can also be added to almonds as you grind them, to keep them from getting all gummy.

Rösti

The national dish of Switzerland, rösti are grated potatoes sautéed and pressed into pancake form while cooking.

Rote

A PASTA in the shape of a wheel (some of which may be square). *Rotelle* are small wheels and *rotini* are tiny ones.

Rotisserie

A spit, usually with a pair of prongs for barbecuing meat. The chunk of meat is skewered on the spit, the prongs arranged on each side of the meat and screwed tight (to hold it in place) and the whole shebang set over (or next to) a fire for cooking.

Rouille

A *hot* sauce from the French Riviera made by crushing together garlic and hot red pepper and mixing it with breadcrumbs, fish broth, and olive oil. It has the consistency of a reddish-brown heavy cream and is used with fish and in fish stews (especially BOUILLABAISSE). Despite the overpowering ingredients, it has some odd ability to enhance the flavor of the foods to which it is added. But it is hot.

Roulade

A French term for a slice of meat or fish filled with something appropriate—cheese, chopped meat, vegetables—rolled up, tied, usually browned, and then baked or braised.

Round

The haunch of a beef critter and the cuts it supplies. These include the rump, top and bottom round, and sirloin.

Round Red

A thin-skinned red POTATO.

Round White

The northeastern variety of POTATO, as provided by Canada, Long Island, and Maine.

Roux

A French name for a mixture of equal parts of flour and butter used as the basis for a sauce or as a thickener. A standard approach is to melt two tablespoons of butter and stir in, gradually, two tablespoons of flour, letting it cook gently until it takes on a brownish color and the flour has had a chance to cook a bit. (Raw flour can be unpleasant.) Just keep stirring and don't let it burn and you have your roux. A brown, or long-cooked, roux (substituting lard for butter) forms the essential base of many CAJUN dishes.

Rowanberry
A European mountain ash (*Sorbus aucuparia*). It bears a small fruit that is the basis (when sufficiently sweetened) for a jelly to accompany cold meat and game.

Rugala
Another name for ARUGULA.

Rum
A spirituous liquor distilled from some form of fermented sugar cane. It may be flavored, diluted, or colored (with caramel, which imparts no taste). Most rum is distilled from molasses, but it can also be derived from raw sugar cane juice or concentrated sugar syrup. Rums can range in color from white through amber to dark brown and in body from light to heavy. Rum is used in a variety of cocktails and drinks such as daiquiris and hot buttered rum and moose milk but also has its place in the kitchen, flavoring various cakes and cookies, and embellishing a casserole of long-simmered black beans and ham hocks (rum and ham seem soul mates). Rum also works wonders in a New England equivalent of a pecan pie that uses maple syrup and a slight shot of rum in place of corn syrup and the optional drop of bourbon. Rum and maple also mingle happily in ice cream.

Rumaki
An hors d'oeuvre consisting of a bite of chicken liver with a slice of water chestnut rolled up and surrounded by bacon, pinned with a piece of toothpick, and run under the broiler until the bacon is crisp. The chicken liver is first marinated in soy sauce with garlic and ginger or soy sauce with curry powder, garlic, and olive oil.

Rump
A term sometimes applied to a cut from a beef ROUND.

Rusk
Bread sliced after baking and baked again until crisp and dry and a golden brown. Rusks may or may not be sweetened. They are considered easily digestible and are often recommended for young children. A well-known proprietary brand is Zwieback.

Russet
An Idaho POTATO.

Russian Dressing
A creamy salad dressing of American origin consisting of a mayonnaise base with catsup (or chili sauce) and pimiento among its ingredients.

Russian Mulberry
A variant on the Chinese MULBERRY giving somewhat insipid fruit.

Rusty Flounder

Another name for the yellowtail flounder, a FLATFISH.

Rutabaga

Also *swede* or *Swedish turnip*. A close relative of the TURNIP, the rutabaga (*Brassica napobrassica*) is a good two times the size of the average white turnip and is firm with a slightly sweet taste. Apparently, a cross between a cabbage and a turnip, it does not seem to have anything particular to do with Sweden. Rutabagas have a thinnish skin (peel it off before you cook it), and those we see have yellow flesh, although there is a variety with white flesh. See that they are firm without bad spots and store them in a cool place for up to a month. They can be used as you would use a turnip, but one satisfying way is to mix equal parts mashed rutabaga and mashed potatoes and dress it all with butter or margarine.

Rye

A cereal grass (*Secale cereale*), the flour of which is second only to wheat in importance in bread-making. As rye grows in more northerly areas than does wheat, it became a staple of northern and eastern Europe, where the granaries tend to be considerably to the north of their counterparts in North America. Rye flour has less gluten (see FLOUR) than does wheat and alone forms a compact, hard, dense loaf of bread, which is why most rye-bread recipes call for an addition of some wheat flour. Rye meal is also available for the experienced or adventurous bread-maker. In the United States, rye has also been used as a base for WHISKEY.

Saaland Pfarr

Another name for the Swedish cheese PRESTOST.

Sabayon

An alternate spelling for ZABAGLIONE.

Sablefish

Also called *blackcod*. A white-fleshed Pacific food fish (*Anaplopoma fimbria*) with velvety black skin. Its high oil content (too oily for some) gives the fish a buttery consistency (it sometimes masquerades under the name of *butterfish*) and a rich flavor. Sablefish is often grilled or steamed and much of it is smoked to be sold in delicatessens across the continent as *smoked sable*. Fresh sablefish has had a reputation for turning "mushy" on being cooked, but that is a seasonal problem. Understanding when to go after the fish has helped fishermen to bring in a more reliable catch. Fresh sablefish are at their best in August and September.

Saccharin

An artificial sugar substitute high in sweetening effect (400 times or more as sweet as sugar) and low in calories, but of disputed healthfulness. It also imparts a metallic taste.

Sachertorte

An impossibly rich Viennese pastry in the form of a chocolate cake layered (there are usually three layers) with apricot jam, iced with chocolate, and embellished with whipped cream.

Sack

A term for SHERRY in sixteenth- and seventeenth-century England, now used in a trade name for one specific sherry.

Saddle

A meatcutter's term for the upper part of an animal's back, including the loins.

Safflower

Sometimes called *Mexican saffron*. A thistlelike plant (*Carthamus tinctorius*) formerly grown for its almost nonexistent medicinal qualities but also for the bright, yellow-red flowers from which dyes were made, and which was and still is used to replace (or adulterate) SAFFRON. The seeds of the safflower plant yield a neutral-tasting highly polyunsaturated oil useful for cooking and other purposes calling for a light vegetable oil.

Saffron

The world's most expensive spice, it is composed of the stigmas—the threadlike flower parts that collect pollen—of a small, purple-flowered crocus (*Crocus sativus*) originally native to the Middle East, but introduced to Spain by the Muslims (or Moors) who invaded Iberia in A.D. 710 and stayed there until 1492. The best available saffron today remains Spanish. The stigmas are picked by hand and dried. To make a pound of the spice, the stigmas of some 70,000 to 75,000 plants are required.

Because the yield is so low and the work so manual, saffron has to be expensive. The threadlike filaments you find in the market are steeped in broth (or brandy or wine) before being added to the food at hand—breads, cakes, soups, stews, especially ARROZ CON POLLO, BOUILLABAISSE, COUSCOUS, and the TAGINE of North Africa. In addition to a pungent aroma and a slightly bitter taste (as well as a somewhat soothing feeling), saffron imparts a yellowish-orange hue to the dish. (If color is all that's wanted, marigold or safflower or turmeric are far cheaper substitutes.) A powdered form is also available but is not highly recommended. Because of the expense of saffron, the temptation to adulterate it is great, and all manner of other plants, including marigold and safflower, have been sold under the name. However, saffron that does not weave its magic for you is not necessarily fraudulent or adulterated— it may just be stale. If you don't get a sharp pungency when you open the saffron container, you can't expect much if any result in the cooking.

Sage

1. An herb (*Salvia officinalis*) of the mint family native to the northern Mediterranean. Its aromatic gray-green leaves are used in medicine and in cookery. Sage is one of our most potent herbs and restraint is advised in its use, or its somewhat musty, even bitter, taste will overpower the dish it is supposed to enhance. It is used especially in pork and sausage dishes and tends to be overused in poultry stuffings. Various experts have counseled replacing the sage in some (especially poultry) recipes with basil or regular dried mint or fresh summer savory. Sage is usually found ground or crumbled (or rubbed), but occasionally leaf sage is available as well.

2. An English cow's-milk CHEESE marbled with minced, fresh sage.

Sago

A starch derived from sago palms (*Metroxylon* spp.), native to Asia. It has some nutritional properties and is much used in tropical areas, most frequently as a thickener. It somewhat resembles TAPIOCA. If available at all, it will probably be labeled *pearl sago*.

Sailfish

A gamefish (*Istiophorus platypterus*) that excites only modest culinary interest and that mostly in Central America and the East Indies. Its excitement comes from its speed and acrobatic ability, but it can also be baked or broiled.

Ste. Maure

A French goat's-milk CHEESE from the Touraine. It has a red-dotted, bluish rind and comes in cylinders of about six ounces.

St. Emilion

One of the major districts of France's BORDEAUX wine-growing region. It produces dry red table wines noted for their fullness and body. Originally, the wines of two vineyards, Château Ausone and Château Cheval-Blanc, were alone at the top of listings, and while still on top, others have been added as worthy of distinction.

St. John's Bread

See CAROB.

St. Paulin

A mild, smooth French cow's-milk CHEESE somewhat similar to PORT SALUT.

Saithe

Another name for *pollack*, a fish of the COD family.

Sake

Also *saki* and sometimes *saké*. An Oriental (especially Japanese) alcoholic beverage brewed essentially from rice. Its culinary importance is in flavoring marinades and sauces. Sake is often referred to as *rice wine*, but as it is brewed not from fruit (such as grapes) but from grain, it is therefore technically a beer. Sake is smooth and potent with a somewhat sweet first impression followed by a tart, almost bitter, aftertaste. It is usually drunk warm in small porcelain cups, although in Okinawa and Korea, it may be served cold.

Salad

A combination of foods often confined to salad greens (perhaps with some extra ingredient to add flavor and interest and texture) but sometimes including all manner of foods—cheese, egg, fish, fruit, gelatin, grain, herbs, meat, nuts, pasta, poultry, sprouts, and vegetables all appear in salads of one sort or another. A green salad, potato salad, and the like may accompany a meal while a more formal one, such as a lobster salad, may be the main dish and a fruit salad the dessert. Salads generally have a dressing of some sort, even if it is only mayonnaise. There are many different dressings for salads, but the most common would be VINAIGRETTE or one of its variations. Most salads are served cold, but there are exceptions, especially German potato salad and spinach salad dressed with bacon drippings.

When to serve a tossed green salad seems to be a geographical decision. In California, it is served before the main dish (and swept away before the main dish is presented). In much of the rest of America it is served as a vegetable along with the main dish. In France it is served after the main dish. Take your pick.

Salad Burnet
See BURNET.

Salamander
In times past, a piece of iron on a handle that was placed over red-hot coals until red hot itself and then pressed onto the food in order to put a hot glaze on it. In modern restaurant parlance, a salamander is a section of the oven under which food goes to be heated or to be endowed with that last-minute glaze. The closest we get in home cooking is putting food under the broiler, as with a GRATIN.

Salami
A cured (generally by drying rather than smoking) sausage usually composed of lean beef, pork, garlic, and spices, and often either red or white wine. Genoa salami is quite rich and garlicky, and Kosher salami, of course, excludes pork or any pork product. A well-cured salami will keep almost indefinitely.

Salep
A yellowish powder derived from the roots of certain Asian orchids (*Orchis* spp.) and used in Oriental cookery. It combines both starch and a mucilaginous quality and is considered sufficiently versatile to be used in drinks intended as aphrodisiacs as well as soothing preparations for children and invalids.

Saleratus
A former name for BAKING SODA.

Salisbury Steak
Essentially, a lean HAMBURGER seasoned with chopped onion and other seasonings that has been broiled. It was devised in the nineteenth century by Dr. James H. Salisbury as a dietetic aid.

Sally Lunn
A sweet, buttery, yeast-risen cake or bun served with afternoon tea. It is said to take its name from its developer, Sally Lunn of Bath, England, who hawked it in the streets sometime during the eighteenth century.

Salmagundi
A word of obscure origin now denoting a carefully arranged salad composed of diced poultry or meat and perhaps anchovies with diced vegetables, marinated in some form of spiced vinaigrette sauce and dressed with mayonnaise.

Salmi

A dish from medieval times in which gamebirds were roasted until not quite done, sliced into serving pieces, and the cooking finished at the dining table with some rich, wine-based sauce. It now refers to a dish of leftovers, especially wild duck, reheated in an elaborately spiced sauce and most likely served over rice.

Salmon

A fish belonging to the same family as do CHAR and TROUT. Salmon is known as the king of fishes both for the excitement it gives the angler and for its succulence at the dining table. Most salmon are anadromous, spawning in freshwater but living most of their lives in the sea. There are others that have become landlocked, and some have made their homes in the Great Lakes, far from salt water.

Salmon is conventionally sold either whole or in steaks, depending upon the size of the fish. A whole fish can be stuffed and baked or it can, like steaks, be grilled. Fresh salmon can also be broiled or poached. At one time, there was a Maine tradition of greeting the Fourth of July with a meal of poached salmon, boiled potato, and green peas. Salmon is also eaten raw, especially if marinated in a combination of salt and sugar. GRAVLAX is prepared this way with the addition of dill. Salmon is also sold canned and frozen and smoked.

Some of the names you might encounter include:

Atlantic salmon (*Salmo salar*). Usually considered the tastiest of the tribe, especially if it has been caught in Iceland or Ireland or Scotland, but tasty enough when taken from Canadian waters. Atlantic salmon in the United States were at one time fished out, but are making a comeback of sorts. Otherwise, the fish ranges from Iceland to Maine and through Ireland and Britain to the northern reaches of Russia and down to Spain. The flesh is either orange or red and fairly oily.

Cherry salmon (*Oncorhynchus masou*). An excellent Asian fish important in Japan.

Chinook salmon (*Oncorhynchus tshawytscha*). An excellent Pacific salmon also found—although of not quite so fine quality—in the Great Lakes. Also called the *king salmon*.

Chum salmon (*Oncorhynchus keta*). A pretty good Pacific salmon found on both sides of that ocean and—again with a decline in quality—in the Great Lakes. It is the leanest and palest of the salmon. Also called the *dog salmon*.

Coho salmon (*Oncorhynchus kisutch*). A Pacific salmon found from California to Japan and also in Chile and the Great Lakes. Lighter than the chinook and less fatty.

Dog salmon. The chum salmon (see above).

Humpback salmon. The pink salmon (see below).

King salmon. The chinook salmon (see above).

Kokanee. A term of the western United States for landlocked sockeye salmon (see below).

Lox. Salmon cured in brine and cold smoked. It is slightly saltier than other forms of smoked salmon.

Nova. Smoked salmon, whether from Nova Scotia or prepared elsewhere.

Pink salmon (*Oncorhynchus gorbuscha*). A Pacific salmon found throughout the northern Pacific. It is mostly found canned, seldom fresh. Also called *humpback salmon.*

Sockeye salmon (*Oncorhynchus nerka*). An excellent deep red fish that can be superior fresh but is mostly canned.

Salpicon

A special French preparation of almost anything cut up fine, bound with a sauce, and used to stuff small pastries—eggs, fowl, fish, meat, what-have-you.

Salsa

A family of sauces with a TEX-MEX origin, usually some combination of chili pepper, coriander, and tomatoes (or tomatillos). Some inventive cooks are making it with fresh mangoes. The range is broad, however, and salsas can be smooth as well as chunky, cooked or uncooked. Salsa has overflowed from its area of origin to such an extent that its sales in the United States have overtaken that of catsup.

Salsify

Also called *oyster plant* or *vegetable oyster*. Salsify is a root vegetable looking much like a parsnip, with a mild flavor that reminds some diners of oysters. There are three related varieties: regular salsify (*Tragopogon porrifolius*), black salsify (*Scorzonera hispanica),* and Spanish salsify (*Scolymus hispanicus*). All may be used in the same way. It is hardy and seems to attain its best flavor after being touched with frost. Salsify can be baked, boiled, broiled, deep-fried, sautéed, or used in such combinations as soups and stews—so long as it is not overcooked, which makes it mushy. If you see it in the market, choose roots that are firm and crisp, not woody, and store them up to three or four days in the vegetable drawer of your refrigerator.

Wild salsify (*Tragopogon pratensis*, also called *goatsbeard*, and *Tragopogon dubius*) can be found by foragers, but the roots, while said to be delectable, are smaller than those of the cultivated variety.

Salt

Sodium chloride ($NaCl_2$)—the seasoning that adds savor to our foods, especially meat. Most salt has iodine added as a goiter preventative, and much table salt has other additives introduced to keep it flowing, because pure salt tends to form solid clumps when moisture gets at it. Coarse-grained types, such as Kosher salt, do not generally have this addition. Some individuals are restricted in their salt intake or forbidden it entirely. Thoughtful cooks bear these dietary necessities in mind when preparing food for such household members or guests.

Salt is the flavoring most likely to be included in the instruction "season to taste," an injunction that has been known to cause panic in the novice cook. Actually it means just what it says. Throw in a little salt (it's always better to under, than to oversalt), stir the dish around, and if you can, taste it (any one of us would be hard put to taste a soufflé without it being noticed). If it can't be tasted, make a note of how much salt you used (if the recipe is yours, write it in erasable pencil in the margin) and adjust for it next time (or if it works that way, write over your penciled annotation with ink). We all panic from time to time, but let's save it for something truly threatening.

Among the labels on salt you may find:

Celery salt. Table salt flavored with powdered celery seed.

Garlic salt. Garlic powder flavored with salt.

Iodized salt. Regular table salt with iodine added as a goiter preventative. Non-iodized salt may be preferred by those with thyroid problems.

Kosher salt. A coarse-grained salt acceptable for Jewish use and often preferred by those who do their own cooking and tend to be finicky.

Pickling salt. A finely ground table salt without additives that is used for curing and pickling.

Rock salt. A nonedible, grayish salt used in ice-cream-making machines and as a bed on which oysters or clams can be baked (or served) without their shells tipping.

Sea salt. Salt that has been evaporated from sea water. It tends to be costly and can mostly be found in health food stores.

Table salt. Regular, fine-grained salt with some additions (dextrose, sodium bicarbonate, potassium bicarbonate, for example) to keep its color or to increase flow. Most table salt is mined from sea beds that have long since dried out.

Saltimbocca

An Italian dish meaning "jump in the mouth." It is composed of thin slices of veal flavored with sage, either left flat or rolled up but either way augmented by pieces of prosciutto, sautéed in butter, and braised in Marsala. The name is an indication that the taste is supposed to be so compelling that you automatically, instantly, and without second thought, pop it right into your mouth.

Salting

Treating meat or fish (especially) with salt or a salt solution as a means of preservation. Nowadays we see it most in salt pork and to a lesser extent salt cod. If the salt pork is too heavily salted, BLANCH it for a few minutes before using. As to salt cod, it's almost always best to soak it overnight in cold water (changed once or twice if you get the chance) before using.

Salt-Meadow Lamb

A lamb that has been fed on seaside meadows, gaining flavor from the salty tang of the grass it feeds on. In French, *pré-salé*.

Saltpeter

A chemical, potassium nitrate (KNO_3), used to cure and redden meats, but which in high quantities makes it tough. There is a pervasive myth that it has the ability to lessen the sex drive, but modern science has found no basis for that belief.

Salt Pork

Pork fat taken from the belly and sides of a pig and salted, as opposed to FATBACK, which is unsalted. Salt pork may be heavily or lightly salted; if the former, blanching is usually called for to civilize it. It is sold in wrapped packages and will keep, refrigerated, for a month or so. Salt pork was a vital ingredient in the cooking of both colonial New England and the Old South.

Salt-Rising Bread

A time-honored bread-making technique that is being revived by home bread-makers. It doesn't really need all that much salt, but in earlier times the dough was kept warm in a bowl set into warm rock salt. (Today, a gas oven with a pilot light, a warming tray set on dead low, perhaps even a heating pad with a towel for a cover can save you from investing in a raft of rock salt.) What the bread needs is a true, stone-ground cornmeal, the kind with the germ intact. It does take a while. You begin with a starter (cornmeal, sliced potato, salt, sugar, and water) and let it work for 24 hours or so, proceed to make a "sponge," adding flour and milk and baking soda and leaving it for a couple of hours, then go on to the dough (more flour, shortening, and salt) and when that is ready you knead it, put it in pans, let it rise, then bake it. The result is heavier than conventional breads but has a texture and a flavor that makes all the time spent worthwhile.

Salt-Water Cooking

A French alternative to blanching when you're poaching a fish (see BLANCH). You simply add a tablespoon of Kosher (or other coarse) salt for each quart of water. If you have sea water available, use that by all means—as you would for steaming a lobster—and forget the additional salt.

Sambal

A Southeast Asian side dish of fruit, poultry, seafood, or vegetable, prepared with spicing that is sometimes mild but more often hot, even extremely so. A variety of different kinds of sambal is usually served at a sitting.

Samoosa

A snack food from India, Sri Lanka, and neighboring areas. It consists of a deep-fried turnover filled with spiced meat or potatoes.

Samovar

A large urn used for brewing tea. It is a major focal point of any Russian home.

Samp

Large pieces of HOMINY.

Samphire

1. A European coastal plant (*Crithmum maritimum*) with a taste mediating between licorice and iodine. It can be served as a salad or preserved in vinegar, usually with capers, and used as a condiment.

2. An American glasswort (*Salicornia europaea*) used much as its European counterpart.

Samsoe

A mild firm Danish cow's-milk CHEESE with holes; it has been called the *Danish Swiss cheese*.

Sand Dab

Another name for *dab*, a FLATFISH.

Sand Lance

Also *sand eel*. A minnowlike fish (*Ammodytes* spp.), found along the coasts of both the North Atlantic and North Pacific in shallow water, where they have a tendency to burrow into the sand when alarmed. They grow to a length of about six inches and are one of the fishes classified as WHITEBAIT.

San Domingo Apricot

See MAMMEE.

Sand Pike

Another name for *sauger*, a fish of the PERCH family.

Sandwich

We generally see it as two slices of bread with something in between. However, the sandwich is somewhat more complex than that. The Arabs were stuffing lamb and other good things into pita bread centuries ago, and the Mexicans were rolling tortillas around fillings long before they saw their first Spaniard. But there can hardly be an American child who doesn't equate a sandwich with bread and peanut butter. Some form of bread or roll, some form of lubrication (butter, margarine, mayonnaise), and some form of filling (cheese—whether toasted or not—chicken, corned beef, roast beef, tuna fish, the list goes on) still make up most of our sandwiches today. There are also triple-decker club sandwiches and single-layer open sand-wiches not to mention such variations as the hamburger and the hot dog.

Sangaree

An alcoholic beverage of varying ingredients. It seems to have started as port or sherry poured over ice with a little sugar. It was then augmented with a jigger of a spirit (brandy, gin, whiskey) with the port poured on top. It now seems to have been forgotten.

Sangria

A cooling Spanish wine punch consisting of red (sometimes white) wine, lemon or orange juice, sugar, and water or soda water. Sometimes slices of citrus fruits or berries or other fruit may be added as garnish, and once in a while, someone will add a tot of brandy.

Santa Rosa

A reddish-to-purple tart PLUM.

Sapodilla

A tropical evergreen tree (*Achras zapota*) that produces chicle, an ingredient of chewing gum, as well as a little round fruit with very sweet, yellowish-red pulp sur-rounding a few large, black, inedible seeds. It is usually peeled and sliced and eaten raw, but as it must be picked when ripe (it won't get any riper and will only go down-hill), it is not a good bet any distance from its growing area. In a pinch you might try keeping a ripe one for a few days refrigerated.

Sapsago

A hard, pungent, green, cone-shaped, Swiss, cow's-milk CHEESE flavored (and col-ored) with a type of clover (*Melilotus coerulea*) and usually used as a grating cheese.

Saratoga Water

A MINERAL WATER from a spring in the Adirondack Mountains of New York State.

Sardine

A fish of the HERRING family.

Sarladaise

According to the American food expert James Beard, a European delicacy consist-ing of sautéed potatoes and truffles, but only acceptable when the truffles are per-fectly fresh. You are not likely to find it in most restaurants.

Sarsaparilla

A carbonated soft drink and ingredient of root beer, originally made from various South American plants (*Smilax* spp.) and attempted from the roots of the North

American wild sarsaparilla plant (*Aralia nudicaulis*) but with dubious results. It is now synthesized.

Sashimi

A Japanese specialty of raw fish, specially cut (keep your hands and knife *cold* to preserve the delicacy of the fish or better yet, rely on a highly trained chef who specializes in this craft) and generally served with side dishes such as grated ginger, soy sauce, or WASABI. Only the freshest possible fish is appropriate for sashimi, and saltwater fish is much preferred. The appetite for sashimi also led to the development of SUSHI.

Sassafras

See FILÉ.

Satay

Sometimes *saté*. Spiced lamb (or fish or pork or poultry) kabobs from Indonesia, usually served with a peanut sauce often flavored with coconut.

Satsuma

A variety of mandarin ORANGE.

Sauce

Any liquid (or thickened liquid) seasoning for food intended to enhance its flavor. Sauces range from simple pan juices to complex concoctions appropriate only to a professional kitchen with a full-time chef, a large complement of assistants, and an all-but-unlimited budget. However, between these extremes there are a great many delights that can be cooked up with very little, some, or a great deal of fuss. Perhaps the most basic sauce is the WHITE SAUCE, on which so many variations can be made. A few other common sauces include HOLLANDAISE, MAYONNAISE, PESTO, and ROUILLE.

Saucepan

Probably the most important cooking utensil of any household. These pans are usually deep for their size and have sturdy handles and tight-fitting covers. They range in size from about one pint (smaller ones are available for melting butter and similar small jobs) up to four quarts. They may be made out of metal, ceramic, or glass.

Sauerbraten

A German method of preparing beef; literally, it means *sour roast*. To make it, a large piece of beef is marinated for three to four days in vinegar and water with carrots, celery, onions, bay leaves, cloves, peppercorns, and thyme. The meat is then browned and simmered in its marinade. It is finished with the addition of sugar, raisins, and crumbled gingersnaps simmered in some of the pot liquid and perhaps embellished with sour cream.

Sauerkraut

A white cabbage that has been shredded very fine, layered with salt, often flavored with juniper berries, and allowed to ferment under pressure (you put it in a crock with a heavy weight on top of it). It is, in other words, pickled. It is chiefly used with pork dishes and to accompany hot dogs. It is available canned or in plastic bags from most supermarkets, and if so, will probably benefit from a good rinsing before being used.

Sauger

A fish of the PERCH family.

Saury

An Atlantic and Pacific saltwater fish (*Scomberesox saurus*) similar to the GAR. The Pacific variety is caught, but chiefly by fishermen from Japan and Russia. It is not an important commercial fish in North America.

Sausage

Meat (at one time fish was also used and more recently poultry), chopped or ground, flavored and spiced, and, more often than not, stuffed into a casing. Pork is the most common sausage meat but is by no means the only one (beef, chicken, turkey, various types of liver, tongue, veal, venison, or other game are all ingredients of some sort of sausage). The original casings were made from the lining of the intestines—which sometimes added to the taste of the sausage. Sausages can be fresh, cooked, dried, pickled, salted, or smoked (either cooked or uncooked). They seem to have originated from a desire to make use of any and all parts of the animal in question but have also been bolstered by additions of all sorts—berries, bread, cereals, fats, flours, and just about any herb or spice you can imagine. Some sausages got their names from their real or imagined place of origin (bologna, frankfurter) others from their ingredients (liverwurst—in German literally "liver sausage") although some just seem incomprehensible, as the English bangers. Most sausages are packed into casings and tied off into links, others may present themselves simply as patties or even in bulk. They can be consumed at breakfast, lunch, or dinner, and added to other dishes such as paellas. What started as an exercise in thrift has blossomed into a virtual art, giving us much good and varied eating. Sausage varieties will be treated in this volume under their own headings.

Sauté

To fry something quickly in a small amount of fat. Classically, it is much more complicated than that, frying forming only a part of a complex cooking process that includes using the pan juices in a subsequent sauce. For most kitchen use the simpler definition will hold.

Sauté Pan

See FRYING PAN.

Sauternes

An exceptional sweet white wine from France's BORDEAUX region used as an after-dinner wine or an elegant midafternoon treat, although on its home turf it may be served at the dinner table with fish. It is usually linked with the similar—and just as exceptional—wines from the neighboring vineyards of Barsac. The name, usually without the terminal "s" is used elsewhere, especially in California, for any number of white wines that are usually somewhat sweet.

Sauvignon

Also *sauvignon blanc*. A wine grape (*Vitis vinifera*) that produces some extraordinary wines especially in France's Bordeaux and Loire wine-growing areas, but elsewhere as well, including California. Depending upon source and vinification, the wines can be dry or sweet and are usually distinctive and rewarding.

Savarin

A rich yeast-risen cake soaked in a syrup or spirit, baked in a special ring-shaped pan by the same name, and filled with pastry cream or other extravagance, sometimes including fruit. When made with raisins it is called a *baba*.

Savory

1. Either of two species of herb: summer savory (*Satureia hortensis*) and winter savory (*Satureia montana*). Summer savory, known as *bohnenplant* (beanplant) in Germany, is especially suited to dishes featuring beans or peas or lentils. Either of the two herbs will also improve meat dishes and soups. The winter savory is the less delicate of the two.

2. Also *savoury*. A British term for any unsweetened dish served usually at the end of a meal, sometimes as an hors d'oeuvre, and extended to anything (cheese or meat or what have you) that is not sweet and is served anywhere in or in between a meal.

Savoy

A type of CABBAGE.

Sbrinz

A Swiss cow's-milk, rich, yellow hard grating CHEESE also made in Argentina and Uruguay. It is also used as a table cheese.

Scad

A food fish of the JACK family.

Scald

To heat a liquid to just below its boiling point. Milk is scalded when a thin skin forms on the surface and just before it erupts and boils messily over. The term may also be used for BLANCH.

Scale

1. A device for measuring weight.
2. The thin flat growths that cover most fish; also to remove those scales.

Scallion

Also *green onion* and *spring onion*. A bulb (*Allium fistolosum*) of the onion family and the green leaves that go with it. The term is also sometimes applied to very young onions (*Allium cepa*) and fledgling leeks (*Allium porrum*) and even perhaps the SHALLOT, although this is considered misguided. Scallions have a mild onion flavor and are especially favored as a garnish and particularly a salad ingredient. Both the white bulb and the green leaves are usable. Just make sure they're fresh, and if you wish to keep them, refrigerate them in a plastic bag in your vegetable drawer.

Scallop

1. Also *scollop*. A slice of meat (usually beef or veal but chicken and turkey have been recently added) cut ⅛ inch thick or so and pounded even flatter. They were particularly favored in Victorian England.

2. A saltwater shellfish (family Pectinidae) of worldwide distribution but usually available in North American markets as bay scallops or sea scallops (the latter being larger and generally less sweet and tender). Calico scallops, which come from southern waters, are very slightly precooked to remove them from their shells, and tend to have the consistency of a pencil eraser. Scallops have a long and reverent history. During the Middle Ages, anyone bearing the scallop insignia (a ribbed, fan-shaped shell) was proclaiming a pilgrimage (either in progress or completed) to the shrine of the apostle Saint James the Greater at Santiago de Compostela, a cathedral in the northwestern Spanish city of Compostela, where the earthly remains of the apostle are said to be resting. (In a less pious age, it has served as the logo of a modern oil conglomerate.)

Scallops are a most unusual shellfish. Unlike others of their kind, they are quite mobile, relying on jet propulsion to move around. By squirting water through themselves and adjusting their valves accordingly, they are able to dart around through the water with considerable speed and a certain amount of directional ability. They also have a row of blue eyes, but as these are on the trailing, not the leading, edge, they serve no directional purpose but only to give warning to pursuing danger. (Or to paraphrase an old gag, they don't care where they're going but want to know where they've been.)

Whatever their history or biology, scallops are delicious. In North America, the muscle is removed and that is all that is eaten. In Europe, the whole critter (including both ROE and MILT (scallops tend to be hermaphroditic) are served forth. And Far Eastern sea scallops are dried under the name of *conpoy* and are (for those few who can afford such an expensive delicacy) shredded and added to slow-cooked dishes, usually at formal banquets. There are any number of ways to cook scallops. Just don't cook them too long (or, if they are fresh enough, not at all, should that be your inclination). Otherwise you can bread and deep-fry them, stick them with skewers and barbecue them, chowder them, cook them up with rice and green pepper and pimientos and Iberian sausage, or prepare them as the French do as coquilles St. Jacques, whereby the scallops are removed from their shells, braised briefly in white wine, lightly breaded, brushed with seasoned melted butter, run under the broiler, and served once again in the shells from which they came.

Scalloped

A method of preparing foods, especially potatoes, by slicing quite thin and baking them in a rich mélange of butter and milk and sometimes cheese. The casserole edges are also often ribbed to emulate a scallop shell.

Scallopini

An Italian dish made from a scallop of meat (especially veal) or poultry. They may be sliced thin, sautéed, and served with a wine or tomato sauce.

Scampi

A NORWAY LOBSTER, but in the United States it usually refers to a large shrimp.

Scarlet Runner

A pink and black pole BEAN used fresh or dried.

Schmaltz

A Yiddish term for rendered fat, usually referring to chicken fat. It may contain other flavorings, depending upon its intended usage.

Schnapps

A colorless, brandylike spirit originally distilled from potatoes. It is popular in the Baltics.

Schnitzel

A German word for SCALLOP (definition 1). *Wiener schnitzel* (or Viennese scallop) is traditionally a thin scallop of veal, breaded and sautéed in butter, often flavored with a wine such as Marsala.

Schnitz und Knepp

A Pennsylvania-Dutch specialty of dried apple slices (*schnitz*) cooked up with ham and brown sugar and served with dumplings (*knepp*).

Scollop

Another term for SCALLOP (definition 1).

Scone

A small crusty tea cake originally cooked on a griddle (but now more often oven-baked) and served in pie-shaped wedges with plentiful amounts of butter and various preserves. While the original scone was undoubtedly an oatcake, you will probably only find it made of wheat flour today.

Score

To cut or scratch lines on a food in order to decorate or tenderize it. Steaks are scored along the thin layer of fat you've left on the sides; it keeps them from curling during the cooking time. Ham, on the other hand, can be scored into a checkerboard effect which can be embellished with cloves and bits of pineapple or simply glazed without these additions.

Scorzonera

A black SALSIFY.

Scotch Broth

A lamb and barley soup (usually with carrots and other good things) native to Scotland. It is a good way to pay one's final respects to the bone left over from a roast leg of lamb (so long as you save some of the meat, too).

Scotch Eggs

An appetizer of hard-boiled eggs rolled in plenty of sausage meat, dipped in beaten eggs (a tablespoon of water is generally a recommended addition), covered with breadcrumbs, and deep-fried. They can be served hot, lukewarm, or cold, but are usually preferred cold. They are much easier to handle if they are halved or quartered.

Scotch Whisky

The distinct and unique distilled spirit from Scotland, deriving its taste, apparently, from the combination of Scottish water and Scottish Highland malt, although the Scots themselves would probably add the method of distillation (small "pot" stills instead of huge, industrial ones).

Scotch Woodcock

Another one of those wonderful English misnomers (like Welsh rabbit). This one is scrambled eggs flavored with anchovies and served on toast.

Scoter
A black WILD DUCK (*Melinita nigra*) with oily flesh. It demands careful cooking.

Scrapple
It is a Pennsylvania-Dutch dish made of pork scraps cooked with cornmeal (in some early recipes, buckwheat) in a broth seasoned often with sage, sometimes thyme, until it achieves a mushlike state at which point it is ladled into loaf pans and chilled. It is then sliced and sautéed, usually as a breakfast meat.

Scrod
A made-up name for the young of the cod or any similar fish, especially haddock. As the Boston restaurateur who coined the name did not know just exactly what the fishing fleet would supply, the name was a handy catchall for whatever turned up.

Sculpin
A family of broadheaded fishes, but the term refers especially to a Pacific food fish and gamefish (*Scorpaena guttata*) bearing spines that can cause considerable pain if one happens to jab you. The flesh is mild tasting and conducive to baking or broiling, perhaps over charcoal.

Scungilli
An Italian term for WHELK.

Scup
A fish of the PORGY family.

Scuppernong
A variety of MUSCADINE grape native to the southern United States.

Sea Anemone
A group of brightly colored marine polyps (order Actinaria) with tentacles resembling a flower. They are used mainly in France and usually in stews.

Sea Bass
A European saltwater fish of the BASS family.

Sea Cow
Another name for the MANATEE.

Sea Cucumber
See TREPANG.

Seafood
Fish and shellfish—a part of the human diet since well before recorded history, but only in recent decades have we had to take a close look at seafood as a health hazard. Striped bass in some areas are so full of PCB's that we're told not to eat them

under any circumstances; some bluefish have picked up sufficient pollutants that we are advised to curtail our eating of them—but not to the point where it would inconvenience anyone but a bluefish fanatic; we have been warned at one time or another that mercury levels in tuna and swordfish can render those fish harmful in any quantity; and some waters are so filthy that shellfish taken from them are illegal—and properly so. Until we clean up our waters, we're going to have problems with seafood, but even so most seafood is still perfectly healthy and is still an integral part of the diet of vast numbers of us.

Seafood has the advantage of being low in saturated fat and thus a healthier source of protein than meat or even poultry. It has the added advantage of being delicious. From raw clams and oysters to soups and chowders (the latter always better reheated the second day) to baked or broiled or fried or grilled or steamed whole fish (or fillets or steaks), seafood provides a huge gamut of cooking possibilities. Catch or collect your own if you can—it's not only more fun, it ensures fresher fish. Otherwise, buy it as fresh as you can (see FISH) and experiment. Even people who don't like fish usually find that they really do. They just didn't like the way it was cooked last time round. Try another way next time or another kind of fish and surprise them. They may surprise themselves.

Sea Kale
A European plant (*crambe maritima*) used as a potherb or added to salads.

Seal
A marine mammal (of the families Phocidae and Otariidae) and its Pacific relative the sea lion (*Zalophus* and *Otaria* spp.). They have been reputedly used as food: seals in 15th-century England and sea lions by Native Americans.

Sea Lettuce
A bright green, cellophane-like seaweed (*Ulva lactuca*) gathered by foragers from rocks. It is sometimes used as a nutritious addition to soups or salads. Natural foods expert Euell Gibbons reports that it is tasty but tough and needs to be chopped very fine.

Sea Moss
See DULSE.

Sear
To expose something to high heat in order to form a crust on the outside and by so doing enhance the flavor.

Sea Robin
Also *gurnard*. Any of a family of ugly little fishes (family Triglidae) found in Atlantic and Mediterranean waters. Mostly head and covered with scales simulating armor,

they are more favored in Europe than North America. Indeed, the *rascasse* that is considered so essential to BOULLABAISSE is a sea robin.

Sea Slug
See TREPANG.

Seasoned Salt
A commercial mix of salt with celery seeds, mace, mustard seeds, paprika, and sugar. It is useful in a number of recipes, such as stuffed cabbage.

Seasoning
Salt and pepper; also using salt and pepper in a dish. The word is sometimes extended to include herbs and other spices.

Sea Trout
See WEAKFISH.

Sea Urchin
A spiny denizen of the deep of the family Echinidae eaten in France and Japan but pretty much ignored elsewhere. The roe is usually scooped out and eaten with a splash of lemon juice.

Seaweed
Various forms of dried seaweed have been known and eaten in North America since Colonial days but have never attained the popularity they enjoy in Japan, the British Isles, or coastal France. In the 1970s, Japanese restaurants sprung up serving SUSHI and SASHIMI, the former encompassing rice wrapped in *nori*, the type of seaweed called *laver*. The important culinary seaweeds, usually available in health food stores, include DULSE, IRISH MOSS, and LAVER. A classical use of Irish moss is in BLANC-MANGE.

Sec
In wine-making, a term signifying that a wine is dry, or good for accompanying a meal. An exception is champagne, where it means "sweet" and for which the driest variety is labeled *brut*.

Seckel
A variety of PEAR.

Sekt
A German term for sparkling wine.

Self-Rising Flour

A FLOUR to which baking powder and salt have been added; it qualifies more as a mix than a flour and has the drawback that once opened, it loses its potency as baking powder does not last once opened.

Seltzer Water

Originally, an effervescent mineral water from the German village of Nieder Selters. It was broadened to include any carbonated water and now denotes one that is full of bubbles but free of salt.

Sémillon

A wine grape (*Vitis vinifera*) producing dry white wines, usually best mixed with another, such as sauvignon. It is also an important ingredient of the classic sweet wines of SAUTERNES.

Semolina

A flour ground from durum WHEAT and used especially for making pasta.

Sercial

A type of Portuguese MADEIRA.

Serrano

A hot, hot green (although also available in yellow and red) CHILI pepper. Approach it with caution.

Serviceberry

1. A group of shrubs (*Amelanchier* spp.) also known as *juneberry* and *shadbush*, many species of which bear juicy, purple-to-black berries not always appreciated raw, but considered first-class for pies. They may be found in the wild (often suffering from plant diseases and insect infestation) or cultivated as an ornamental but are not grown commercially for fruit.

2. Alternate names for the ROWANBERRY and its related SORB APPLE.

Sesame

Also *benne*. An East Indian herb (*Sesamum indicum*) providing small seeds with a strong, nutlike taste. These seeds can be used (often toasted) as a flavoring for breads and cakes and rolls or added to Oriental dishes. Raw sesame seeds are pressed into a flavorsome cooking oil or used in TAHINI. A dark sesame oil is also available, made from roasted seeds and giving a richer and tastier oil.

Seviche

A Latin American dish consisting of fillets of fresh, raw, ocean fish marinated in lime (or other citrus) juice, which has the effect of oxidizing (in effect cooking) it; it is generally marinated with onions and peppers and tomatoes.

Seville

A type of bitter ORANGE.

Shad

A fish of the HERRING family.

Shadbush

See SERVICEBERRY.

Shaddock

A precursor of the GRAPEFRUIT.

Shaggymane

An edible MUSHROOM.

Shallot

A small member (*Allium ascalonicum*) of the onion family, formed somewhat like a head of garlic but with a papery brownish skin and an inside that is white, sometimes tinged with purple. It has an oniony flavor, but is much more mild and tender. Shallots are mostly used in sauces, soups, and stews. In Oriental cooking, they are pickled for use in salads.

Shank

The upper leg of a meat-bearing animal. One of the best-known uses is the veal-shank dish osso BUCO.

Shark

A most interesting fish because it has cartilage instead of bones. Shark can also be delicious. A vendor at New York City's Fulton Fish Market, who was selling shark that morning, was of the opinion that good shark is a better bet (not so dry, apparently) than ordinary swordfish. The distinguished seafood authority Alan Davidson has given us a recipe equally useful for shark or swordfish—marinate the fish in olive oil, lemon juice, paprika, and bay leaves for the better part of the day, grill it, dress it with more lemon juice and olive oil, and enjoy.

Among edible sharks, the most widely seen in fish markets are the mako (*Isurus* spp.) sharks, but anglers will occasionally come across angel shark (*Squatina* spp., but sometimes confusingly referred to as MONKFISH) as well as DOGFISH. Porbeagle (*Lamna nasus*), also called mackerel shark, is also a possibility, especially in Europe.

In the Orient, shark meat, while eaten, is nowhere near so fancied as shark fins, which may be braised or served in a variety of rich soups. They are valued for their intermixture of flavor and gelatinous texture. Shark's fin is not the easiest commodity to prepare, which is why it is often sold in the form of chips or—at a price—as already cleaned strands. A whole fin is prepared by simmering it for a couple of hours, cooling it, rinsing it in cold water, refrigerating it overnight in more cold water, and then repeating the process the following day, and perhaps the day after that as well. It is then worked over to remove any pieces of skin, after which it is ready to use.

Sharkskin
Small squares of dried shark skin are placed in cold water and simmered for a couple of hours, drained, then simmered the same way again. The softened skin is then used as a flavoring.

Shashlik
See KABOB.

She-Crab Soup
A South Carolina specialty found in the spring when the crabs are mating. It requires a sponge crab, the female blue CRAB with her fertilized eggs attached to her swimmerets, giving her the appearance of a sponge. The soup is made with the meat or roe enriched with milk or cream or a combination of the two and butter, spices, and a dollop of sherry.

Shedder
A LOBSTER molting its shell or a soft-shell crab. Soft-shell crabs are a well-known delicacy, the shedding lobster less acclaimed. At the outset, the shedding lobster is limp and waterlogged, almost devoid of taste. As the shell hardens, the water dissipates and the flesh becomes firmer and remarkably sweet. You won't find them away from the coast, however, as shedders do not ship well.

Sheep
An animal (*Ovis* spp.) whether wild or domesticated that provides LAMB and MUTTON in addition to various variety meats (such as brains and kidney and tongue).

Sheepshead
A fish of the PORGY family.

Shell
1. A seashell-shaped PASTA in varying sizes. The largest, or giant shells, are often stuffed (cheese and prosciutto with egg, seasonings, and sugar are common, but more extravagant stuffings—such as lobster—also occur).

2. A PASTRY shell, such as a piecrust.

Shellfish
Any form of marine life with a shell. ABALONE, CLAMS, CRABS, CRAYFISH, LOBSTER, MUSSELS, OYSTERS, PERIWINKLES, PRAWNS, and SHRIMP are among those that qualify under this heading.

Shell Steak
A tender cut of beef taken from the loin.

Shepherd's Pie

A way of using up leftover meat, especially lamb. The meat is cut up small, heated in gravy (perhaps with carrots and onions), and covered with a crust of mashed potatoes. When made with beef, it is more frequently called *cottage pie.*

Sherbet

A form of ICE CREAM in which syrup or fruit puree is frozen while being beaten slightly during the freezing process (to promote a smoother consistency). It is then augmented with such additions as cream or white of egg or a combination of egg white and sugar syrup to impart sufficient softness that it can be readily scooped out of the freezer container.

Sherry

A selection of some of the world's most renowned FORTIFIED WINE originating in the area of southwest Spain around the town of Jerez de la Frontera, although the area was later broadened to include nearby Sanlúcar de Barrameda, giving its wine, known as Manzanilla, the right to be called sherry. The name *sherry* has also been adopted for wines of some similarity made elsewhere throughout the world.

Sherry is made by a method known as the *solera* system, by which barrels of the wine are stacked one above the other. The new wine is poured into the topmost barrel while an equal amount of the old is taken from the bottommost. By so doing, there is always a small amount of the oldest wine in each of the tiers of barrel, a technique that enhances each new vintage. Clearly, it doesn't really work until the solera has been in operation for a considerable time, giving the wine the aging it needs to make the system effective.

Sherry come in various types:

Amontillado. Somewhat dark, very slightly sweet, with a nutty taste. It is equally useful as an aperitif and a cooking wine.

Amoroso. Very dark, very sweet, originally created for the English market.

Cream sherry. Heavily sweetened and developed for a market in Bristol, England, which accounts for the brand names "Bristol Milk" and "Bristol Cream."

Fino. The driest of the sherries, especially appropriate as an aperitif.

Manzanilla. The driest and lightest fino (see above).

Oloroso. The prototype of all the sweet sherries.

Shiitake

A Japanese MUSHROOM.

Shin

The front part of the leg.

Shiner

A small saltwater fish, otherwise known as SILVERSIDE.

Shirr
To cook something—especially by baking—in a RAMEKIN.

Shish Kabob
See KABOB.

Shoat
A hog one year old or younger.

Shoofly Pie
A rich, molasses-based pie usually incorporating raisins, said to have originated in the Pennsylvania-Dutch country. Its fanciful name is given to several interpretations—either it was made to attract flies from other food and from people or it had to be constantly tended to chase them away.

Shortbread
A tender and crumbly pastry of Scottish origin made of flour and sugar enriched with a hefty proportion of butter (or shortening).

Shortcake
An American dessert made traditionally from biscuit dough, filled with fresh berries, and topped with whipped cream. Caloric but classy.

Shortening
The fat or oil—butter, goose fat, lard, any of the vegetable derivatives—used to give crispness to pastry and make it crumbly.

Short Pastry
A pastry containing a hefty amount of shortening. It is the basic pastry for piecrusts, tarts, and quiches, for example. Because of the amount of shortening in it, short pastry is baked on an ungreased sheet or pie plate.

Short Ribs
Cuts of beef, usually from the chuck, consisting of meat and fat clinging to a short (two- to three-inch) bone. They profit from long, slow cooking.

Shotglass
See JIGGER.

Shoveler
A broad-billed WILD DUCK (*Anas* spp.) that can make prime table fare, depending upon where it has been feeding.

Shred
To tear or cut something into strips—like Shredded Wheat before the pieces are molded back into biscuit shape. The shredding disk of a processor is helpful.

Shrimp

After lobster, certainly the most admired of the fruits of the sea, and in the greatest demand by far. Shrimp are technically crustaceans of the order Decopoda, meaning ten-legged. They range in size from quite small to fairly large. In general, the larger the shrimp the higher the price and the fewer, obviously, per pound. The general categories for shrimp are *giant* or *colossal* (less than 10 to the pound); *jumbo* (12–16 to the pound); *extra-large* (16–20); *large* (20–25); *medium* (25–35); *small* (35–45); and the *truly tiny* (as many as 100 to the pound). In North America, the largest are often referred to as prawns and sometimes scampi.

Shrimp are available canned, dried, fresh, or frozen. They may be whole or headless, cooked or raw. They may be peeled or still in the shell. (If peeled, they will probably have been deveined.) Shrimp come in a veritable rainbow of colors, including the striped tiger shrimp, although most that we see are green or gray until cooked, when they take on the familiar pink hue. The hundreds of varieties of shrimp can be broken down into two groups—cold water and warm water (including the tropical varieties). Shrimp, like their lobster cousins, are at their tastiest when taken from cold water.

Shrimp may be cooked in a variety of ways. The one simple rule when cooking shrimp is not to overdo it—three to five minutes will usually suffice. But there seem to be as many ways of preparing shrimp as there are people to think them up. Most frequently, shrimp will be boiled (and cooled for shrimp salad), broiled, fried, or grilled. Whole fresh shrimp are usually peeled and beheaded; sometimes they are deveined as well. The rule of thumb seems to be that small shrimp do not really need deveining, but the larger shrimp tend to contribute an unpleasant grittiness if it is not done.

When selecting fresh shrimp, sniff for a whiff of the sea. If the shrimp have an ammonia-like aroma, pass them by.

Shrub

A beverage of some antiquity. Up through the 18th century, shrubs were made on a spirituous base (rum, whiskey) with fruit juice, fruit rind, and sugar, steeped, strained, and aged slightiy. Today, if you see it at all, it will probably omit the spirits.

Shuck

To take a shellfish out of its shell or an ear of corn out of its husk.

Sieve

A large STRAINER.

Sifter

A form of strainer designed especially for flour and other dry ingredients of pastries and breads. Dating from the days when flour tended to be lumpy and in need of refinement, sifters are no longer strictly necessary for most purposes and when called for can often be replaced with a regular strainer or sieve. When they are called for, it is customary to measure your flour after, not before, being sifted.

Silver Pike

A western variant of the northern PIKE.

Silverside

Also *shiner*. Either the Atlantic sandsmelt (*Atherina presbyter*) or the Atlantic silverside (*Menidia menidia*), also called *whitebait*. They are small (three to four inches) and are deep-fried and eaten, bones and all.

Simmer

To cook a liquid over low heat so that it almost—but never quite—comes to a boil. This slight action is described by the French as making the surface of the liquid smile. See POACH.

Simple Syrup

A mixture of sugar and cold water (4 cups sugar to 1 water) for use, for example, in sweetening alcoholic drinks where sugar alone dissolves with difficulty or not at all.

Singe

To scorch something. It was once a necessary step in removing the last pesky pinfeathers of fowl being readied for cooking, but all this is now done before the consumer lays hands on the bird. And if you've ever taken the pinfeathers from a bird, you will be everlastingly grateful not to have to do it again.

Sirloin

A cut of beef from the loin of the animal. It is among the most tender cuts available.

Skate

Also *ray*. Sports fishermen have many other names for them, few of them fit to print. Skates are large triangular cartilaginous creatures (*Raja* spp.) only the wings of which are generally eaten, although very small ones are said to be just fine whole. This is one of the few (perhaps the only) fish that profits from a day or so out of the water before cooking (skate has a somewhat ammonia-like aura that takes a day or so to dissipate). The French recipe *raie au beurre noir* is perhaps the classic method of cooking skate: You poach the skate wings, then dress them with brown butter and a dash of vinegar. The recommended fashion for eating it is not to cut down through it, but to scrape along the top, taking the flesh in long strips.

Skewer

A long, sharp, needlelike device used as a LACER to close the vent on poultry being roasted, to TRUSS birds, and to thread pieces of meat and vegetables for grilling as shish kabobs or shashlik.

Skillet

See FRYING PAN.

Skim

To gently remove the upper part of a liquid while leaving the rest of it intact. It can refer to taking the cream off a bottle of nonhomogenized MILK, to removing the scum that bubbles up when a piece of meat is started for a soup or stew, or to removing a layer of fat from a simmering liquid. A slotted spoon or even a tea strainer will often get the job done, but specialized skimmers also exist. These are equally useful for retrieving dumplings or deep-fried foods that show their doneness by floating to the top of the hot cooking fat.

Skirret

A plant (*Sium sisarum*) of the parsley family with edible roots that can be boiled and buttered like beets or potatoes, but with a woody core that is best removed, as in the case of parsnips. If you should grow skirrets, you can leave them in the ground all winter and uproot them as the need arises.

Sliver

To cut something into long, thin pieces; also refers to any of those pieces.

Slivovitz

A Yugoslavian plum BRANDY.

Sloe

The *blackthorn*, a European plum (*Prunus spinosa*), and its small, somewhat astringent fruit used in preserves and as a flavoring for gin.

Slump

A fruit (usually berries) dessert with a top crust.

Smallage

See LOVAGE.

Smallmouth Bass

A freshwater BASS.

Smelt

A small fish (*Osmerus eperlanus*) originally caught from September until along about April, mostly as they came up rivers and streams and bays along the New England

and Canadian coastline to spawn. Now they are caught year-round in the Great Lakes as well. Smelt are delicious when spanking fresh and generally quite acceptable when not quite so pristine. They are usually decapitated and gutted, then deep-fried or sautéed. Maine poet R. P. T. Coffin, however, insisted that they be eaten whole—heads, innards (he called them "the works"), backbone—everything. He recommended layering them head to tail and tail to head in a greased oven dish and topping them with a crisscrossed lattice of strips of salt pork. The dish is put in a moderately hot (400°F) oven for half an hour, or until the smelts are fused with the salt pork into a slab resembling mahogany and tasting—to a Maine poet, anyway—like ambrosia. Only smelt caught in September will do, however, this being the only time that smelts "taste like themselves." The dish is untried here, mostly because fresh smelts have not yet found their way into this kitchen in September. The recipe is, however, one found traditionally in New England for such fish as salt and fresh cod, bluefish, or mackerel. Sometimes it is enriched with the last-minute addition of a little light cream or half-and-half, which is allowed to boil up just before serving, but whether Professor Coffin approved of this is unknown.

Smithfield Ham
A HAM native to Virginia.

Smoking
An ancient art of preserving and flavoring food with wood smoke. Ham and bacon only top a list that includes all manner of meat and fowl and fish and extends through sausages to cheese and nuts and even eggs.

Smorgasbord
A Swedish buffet (or "bread-and-butter table") consisting of a host of different hot and cold dishes, usually including at least cheeses, a dessert or two, various types of fresh or pickled herring, meatballs, salads, and sliced meats.

Smørrebrød
A Danish open-faced sandwich.

Smothered
In CAJUN cooking, *étoufée*, meaning in French "smothered." Something completely—or almost completely—covered with something else, such as a steak "smothered" in onions.

Snack
A mouthful or pick-me-up snatched between meals.

Snail
A snail (*Helix pomatia*) is not much used as food in North America, which is odd. As far as creatures with shells go, snails are certainly as attractive as any of their

marine counterparts, living as they do on the tender leaves and shoots of some of our most delicate crops—such as grapevines. In European outdoor markets, vast baskets of huge snails have traditionally been among the offerings, even in areas where the word *gourmet* would be greeted with a blank stare.

Most snails in North America are found canned and are prepared with garlic butter. Under this method, the snails are cleaned and blanched, then removed from their shells and simmered in seasoned broth for several hours. The cooled snails are then removed from the broth and replaced in the shells (which have been boiled to clean them thoroughly) and sealed with butter enriched with finely minced—even pureed—garlic and some breadcrumbs. They are then put under the broiler until heated through. (Of course with canned snails, many of these steps have been done for you.) Snails can also be deep-fried or chopped and cooked in fritters.

Snake
Not commonly eaten in North America, and if so usually confined to RATTLESNAKE.

Snap Bean
A familiar string BEAN.

Snapping Turtle
An edible TURTLE.

Snickerdoodle
A round cookie with a crisp exterior and a chewy inside, usually rolled in a combination of sugar and cinnamon before going into the oven.

Snip
To cut food (chives for example) into small uniform lengths using kitchen shears or a small pair of scissors.

Snipe
A bird (*Capella gallinago*) fairly common in North American boggy areas, marshlands, and riverbanks that is quite similar to a WOODCOCK.

Snook
Also *robalo*. A major gamefish (*Centropomis undecimalis*) of the Atlantic and nearby brackish water from Florida to Brazil. It provides a delicate, white-meated fish of superior quality, but you'll almost certainly have to catch it yourself.

Snow
A fruit dessert (apple, lemon) made on a foundation of egg whites beaten stiff with sugar, gelatin, and the fruit flavoring.

Snow Crab
A CRAB of northwestern North America.

Soak

To let an ingredient absorb a liquid. Some foodstuffs—dried beans come to mind—are so thirsty that the amount of soaking water must be generously more ample than the amount of beans to be soaked. (Otherwise, you risk having the beans absorb all the water yet remain merely soggy.) And if you're soaking something to rid it of a substance, as you soak salt cod to decrease its saltiness, it helps to change the water from time to time. Soaking differs from marinating in that a marinade is intended to flavor (and perhaps tenderize) whatever is being marinated.

Soave

A light, dry white Italian wine from the region of Verona.

Soda

1. BAKING SODA.

2. A concoction once common in drugstore soda fountains, consisting of plain SODA WATER with some form of flavored syrup and ice cream.

3. POP. Beverage made of soda water, flavoring, and sweetener.

Soda Bread

See IRISH SODA BREAD.

Soda Water

Any artificially carbonated water, sometimes with added salt. Another kind of SOFT DRINK.

Sofrito

Also *soffritto*. A name for a variety of related sauces. It can be made by simmering carrot, celery, and onion in oil or butter or a combination of the two (giving more a sauce base than the sauce itself). It can be made of bell pepper, garlic, onion, and pork, flavored with various herbs and spices, and simmered until quite thick. A Mexican variation is to start it out with ANNATTO seeds to give color before adding the meat and vegetables.

Soft Drink

A nonalcoholic, often carbonated, variously flavored beverage.

Soften

To prepare butter—or something similar—for use by leaving it out of the refrigerator for up to an hour or until it gets soft enough to be pliable but not runny.

Soft Roe

Another name for MILT.

Soft-Shell Clam

A variety of CLAM usually used for steaming.

Soft-Shell Crab

A blue CRAB in the molt, with a thin and edible shell.

Soju

An inexpensive, distilled Korean spirit made from grain other than rice and from sweet potatoes. It is an unaged, colorless beverage usually drunk straight. You'll probably have to go to Korea to find it.

Sole

A kind of FLATFISH.

Sonoma

A county in northern California notable for its high-quality wines.

Sorb Apple

A somewhat sour-tasting fruit (*Sorbus domestica*) seldom seen, but edible if picked after being touched with frost.

Sorbet

See SHERBET.

Sorghum

A cereal grain (*Sorghum vulgare*), varieties of which provide a distinctive pancake flour. The stalks of it make a light type of molasses. A staple food of large parts of Africa, it has been called, somewhat derogatorily, Kaffir corn, but the "corn" here reflects the older meaning of the word and refers to any important cereal grain rather than to the CORN (or maize) native to North America.

Sorrel

Also *sour grass*. A potherb (*Rumex acetosa*) with a pungent, tart, acid taste highly favored in the Old World. In most of North America it is benignly neglected (except in the extreme north, where an indigenous plant, mountain sorrel or *Oxyria digynia*, is used by natives and foragers). Sorrel leaves are used in salads and especially soups and are traditionally pureed as an accompaniment for shad.

If you find sorrel in the market, look for long, fresh, very green leaves and use them within two days at most. They will keep, briefly, in the refrigerator but even there will languish quite quickly. You are better advised to grow it yourself—in a garden or on a city terrace.

Soufflé

A delicate dish, often a dessert but also a main dish of fish, meat, poultry, or vegetables sustained by a foam of whipped egg whites. The base of a soufflé is a WHITE SAUCE that is enriched with the egg yolks and flavorings and into which the beaten egg whites are folded. It is baked in a special high-sided soufflé dish (a soufflé rises to almost three times its original size in baking) and has the well-earned reputation of collapsing if disturbed during the baking process or if the trip from oven to table takes longer than it likes. Oven temperatures for soufflés range from 400°F, for a dish with a firm outside and a creamy interior, to 325°F if a firmer, more even consistency is desired.

Soup
A BROTH that is usually augmented with some combination of meat and vegetables to form anything from a delicate first course to a hearty meal-in-itself. The term also embraces such variations as BISQUE and CHOWDER.

Sour
A family of alcoholic drinks made with some form of whiskey (or whisky) mixed with lemon juice and sugar and served cold with an orange or cherry garnish.

Sourdough
A bread leavened with fermented dough. The ferment occurs when flour or a potato or similar substance is mixed with water, milk, or a milk product and wild yeast is drawn from the air. The result is a tasty and indeed somewhat pleasantly sour-tasting bread or roll. San Francisco is the unchallenged home of sourdough breads in North America, but the practice is rooted in antiquity.

Sour Grass
Another name for SORREL.

Sour Mash
A technique of fermenting the MASH that is the raw material of whiskey. Sour mash is fermented from the leftovers from a previous fermentation, sweet mash from fresh water and yeast. The sour mash yields a more distinctive-tasting spirit, the sweet mash considerably more in quantity.

Sour Milk
See CLABBER.

Soursop
A fruit tree (*Annona muricata*) native to the West Indies. Its fruit is useful in conserves.

Soused
Pickled in brine or vinegar.

Souvlakia
A Greek specialty of lamb marinated in herb-flavored lemon juice and oil and then grilled on skewers.

Soybean

A protein-rich BEAN widespread throughout Oriental cooking and becoming an important North American cash crop as well. It provides flour, milk, oil, sauce, sprouts, and tofu. Young, fresh soybeans can also be cooked as you would fresh lima beans.

Soy Sauce

An ancient, sodium-rich, Chinese sauce made—much as it was 3,000 years ago—by mixing fermented soybeans with a roasted grain (wheat, usually, but sometimes barley). The mixture is fortified with yeast, salted, and left to mature. It is then filtered for commercial sale. Japanese soy sauce is somewhat more delicate than the Chinese variety. Soy sauce is used to flavor practically everything (fish, marinades, meats, vegetables, other sauces—such as its offshoot TERIYAKI) and to replace the use of table salt in Oriental dining.

Spaetzle

A German dumpling or noodle of eggs, flour, and milk or water, pressed through a large-holed colander, and dropped into boiling water. Spaetzles are served as a side dish, as you would noodles.

Spaghetti

Long thin solid PASTA strings. It is one of the glories of Italian cooking. Thin spaghetti takes well to light sauces (the oil clings better) whereas the thicker varieties seem to prefer something heavier, perhaps containing chunks of meat or seafood.

Spaghetti Squash

A peculiar SQUASH that cooks into long, spaghetti-like strands that can be dressed with a sauce and served as a combination vegetable and pasta substitute.

Spanish Mackerel

A large MACKEREL.

Spanish Pine

See AZAROLE.

Spanakopita

A Greek spinach pie made with PHYLLO pastry.

Spareribs

A cut of meat—pork but also game—consisting usually of the breastbone, rib bones, and rib cartilage. (There are also "country spareribs" or "back ribs" cut from the back end and including considerably more meat.) Spareribs are usually marinated and then barbecued, doused with the eater's favorite barbecue sauce.

Spätlese

A German wine term applied to special grapes in the vineyards of the RHINE valley. The grapes are left on the vines until some time after the regular harvest is over, and only then picked to be vinified into a naturally sweet wine.

Spatula

A handy and versatile flat, thin blade of metal, plastic, or rubber on a handle. This utensil is used for all manner of kitchen chores from scraping bowls to turning delicate pastry dough. In British usage, a spatula is referred to as a *palette knife*.

Spearmint

A common MINT (*Mentha spicata*) used as a flavoring.

Speckled Trout

An alternate name for the brook trout, which is a CHAR.

Spelt

A form of wheat (*Triticum spelta*) used in former times for human consumption, relegated to animal fodder, and now making a comeback as an alternative source of bread flour.

Spencer Method

A method of cooking fish devised by a U.S. government food expert. It entails taking fillets of fish, dipping them into salted milk then into breadcrumbs, placing them on a buttered baking sheet and anointing them with more butter, then baking them toward the top of a preheated 550°F oven for 10–12 minutes. The aim is a fillet with a crusty exterior and a moist inside.

Spice

A flavoring ingredient taken from a plant or tree. A spice may come from bark or flower or fruit or root or seed—whichever part is tastiest. What almost all spices—dried ones, too—have in common is that they will deteriorate with time. Keep them tightly covered and use them up before they lose their savor. Spice is one item that does not repay buying in bulk for later use. Individual spices are treated under their separate headings.

Spider

A three-legged SKILLET, but the term is often used for a regular legless skillet as well. The legs were originally intended to give stability when cooking over an open fire in camp or otherwise out-of-doors.

Spinach

A leafy vegetable (*Spinacia oleracea*) reputed to be disliked by children, possibly because it is so frequently cooked badly (when figuring cooking time for spinach, the adage "less is more" might well be kept in mind). In fact, spinach can also be served uncooked, as it often is in salads when the leaves are young and tender. Sometimes, however, it profits from being blanched quickly in boiling water, then refreshed by being run under cold water to stop the cooking. This gives it a slightly more tender edge as well as bringing out its full bright-green color.

Spinach grows best in sandy, gritty soil much of which tends to cling to the leaves. Thus, unless you like the taste or texture of grit, spinach must be thoroughly washed. Dropping it in a basin of warmish water and then rinsing it once or twice under cold running water does the best job. Even spinach that comes prewashed in clear bags will be aided by an additional rinsing.

Once washed, spinach can undergo various treatments. In the regular way of things, most cooks like to pinch off any tough stems and yellowed or otherwise unattractive leaves. Some then like to rip it into bitable pieces (others prefer to cook it first, then drain it and mound the spinach on a cutting board, slicing through the mound at quarter- or half-inch intervals, then give it a 90° turn and repeat the slicing, returning the vegetable to the now-empty pot in which it cooked—perhaps with a pat of butter or noggin of olive oil—to restore its heat). In either case, the spinach is cooked (covered) only with the water left on its leaves and only for 3–4 minutes from the time the water starts boiling. Mixing it around once or twice with a wooden spoon during the cooking won't do it any harm.

However, that is by no means the only way to accommodate spinach. The vegetable lends itself marvelously to croquettes, quiche, salad, soufflés, and soup and can serve as a foundation over which other food can be served, in which case the dish will be described as *florentine*. Spinach takes especially well to being flavored with nutmeg.

When buying spinach, look for fresh, crisp leaves, not too much stem, and a good green color (avoid any that is yellowing). A pound of spinach (or a 12-ounce package) should accommodate two quite nicely. Once you've bought it, keep it refrigerated if you must, but try to use it up within a day or two at the most.

Spinach also comes canned and frozen. Frozen spinach was once almost always pureed, but now can also be found as "leaf spinach." It freezes well.

Spiny Lobster

Also *rock lobster* and *crawfish*. A clawless marine crustacean found along both sides of the Atlantic, but more prevalent on the European and African side than the American, and along the coast of southern California and Mexico, although they can also be had off Australia and New Zealand. The European species (*Palinuris vulgaris*) frequently shows up in North American markets as South African lobster tail. The meat of the spiny lobster is dense and flavorful but not really a match for the American or the European LOBSTER.

Spirit

A liquid, alcoholic result of distillation of any number of fermented substances. Brandies are made, for example, from fruit (apples, grapes, plums. among others); gin and whiskies from grain; vodka, aquavit, and schnapps (at least originally) from potatoes; rum from sugar cane; and kumiss from sour mare's milk. Spirits have a long history in the kitchen, being useful as flavorings, as elements of a marinade, and for flaming.

Spit-Cook

To cook something on a spit over an open fire; SPIT-ROAST.

Spit-Roast

The original method of roasting meat and the prototype of the modern barbecue, where food is roasted on a spit over an open fire. Actually the matter being roasted need not be over the fire—it can be right alongside, assuming the fire is hot enough and the mechanism turning the spit reliable enough to ensure that all sides get equal time with the heat. In some respects this is preferred, as it allows the juices to fall into a special pan set there for the purpose rather than falling into the fire and causing flare-ups. Otherwise a DRIPPING PAN can be improvised.

Sponge

In bread-making, to allow the yeast and part of the rest of the ingredients to "work" until they form a spongy mass (usually four to six hours) and then to add the rest of the ingredients and proceed as with any other bread recipe. According to British cooking expert Elizabeth David, using a good half of the full amount of flour and letting the sponge develop for at least two hours are essential or the bread will be unable to develop the full taste that the sponge method can confer on it.

Sponge Cake

A joyously light and airy cake that gets that way largely because of eggs and air. Regular sponge cake has a yellow coloring due to the whole eggs used in its baking. Angel food cake, a special variation of sponge cake, has a pure whiteness on account of its being made only with the whites of the eggs. The egg whites must be well beaten, and once this is done—to prevent the air beaten into them from escaping—the preparation must continue not with unseemly haste, but with no undue loss of time or the whole thing may collapse.

Spoon Bread

A specialty of the southern United States made with white cornmeal, eggs, and milk. It has a soft consistency (eat it with a spoon) and is served as a side dish.

Spotted Bass

A freshwater BASS.

Sprat
A food fish of the HERRING family.

Sprig
A small branch of a leafy substance such as parsley or thyme.

Springerle
A German Christmas cookie that is yellow in color, flavored with anise, and decorated with elaborate embossed figures.

Springform Pan
A cake pan with sides that open at the release of a spring catch, making the bottom removable and, thus, saving you the need to invert the cake and urge it out of its cooking utensil.

Spring Onion
See SCALLION.

Spring Roll
A variation on the Chinese EGG ROLL.

Sprinkle
To scatter drops of water or lemon juice, bits of parsley, grains of salt, or whatever you want to add sparingly over your dish. The word (usually plural) also applies to the colored grains of sugar or chocolate used to decorate ice cream concoctions and cookies and other pastries.

Spritzer
A cooling, summer drink consisting of dry white or rosé wine mixed with seltzer or soda water in approximately equal quantities. It is served chilled with ice cubes.

Sprout
The small, young edible shoot of a BEAN or seed generally used raw in salads and sandwiches. The most widespread varieties are alfalfa, lentil, mung bean, radish, and soybean. If you see them in your supermarket, look for bright color and crisp texture. Sprouts will keep, refrigerated, for several days. There are also devices on the market that permit you to grow your own.

Spumante
An Italian term for sparkling wine, the most noted stemming from the northern Italian town of ASTI.

Spumoni
Also—in Italy—*spumone*. An Italian (more precisely, Neapolitan) ice cream often made in different layers containing various flavors as well as chopped fruits or nuts.

Squab

A young pigeon no more than four weeks old. They have (if still young enough) a flavorsome dark meat and can be broiled, roasted, spit-roasted, or split and fried. Squab is available in some specialty stores during the summer or year-round frozen. If unavailable, a Rock Cornish hen might fill the bill.

Squash

A whole family of edible gourds of the genus *Cucurbita*. They may be roughly divided into summer squash and winter squash (the latter developing later in the season and holding well over the winter, although in fact their seasons tend to overlap). They come in all shapes and sizes and colors and, in one form or another, will be available year-round. Squash lends itself to a variety of cooking methods. Depending upon the type, they can be baked, deep-fried, grilled over charcoal, sautéed, simmered, made into soufflé, used in soup, steamed, used in bread, or baked in a pie.

When selecting squash, look for firm, weighty selections with a skin you can dig a fingernail into. Avoid any with bruises or cracks. Summer squash will keep, refrigerated three or four days, winter squash—if kept in a dry, well-ventilated place—several months.

Among the summer squashes you are likely to come across (most of which are either species or subspecies of *Cucurbita pepo*) are:

Chayote. Not a *pepo*. See CHAYOTE.

Cymling. A disk or bowl-shaped, scalloped, pale green to white squash with a mildly sweet flavor. If more than four inches across, it tends to lose flavor.

Pattypan. Another name for *cymling* (see above).

Spaghetti. A large, oval, white squash with flesh that, when cooked, forms strands resembling spaghetti and can be served with a sauce to provide a vegetable spaghetti.

Yellow. Comes in straight or crook-necked shapes. It has a mild taste and is often steamed and mashed.

Zucchini. Most usually green but there are others. Small, very fresh zucchini are excellent sliced thin and sautéed in butter and chives, although there are myriad ways of preparing them. Very large zucchini are usually stuffed.

Among the winter squashes (most of which are species or subspecies of *Cucurbita maxima*) you are likely to see are:

Acorn. Actually a *Cucurbita pepo*. A deep dark green, it is shaped as you would expect with deep grooves running up and down the thick skin. It is often halved, the seeds removed, the indentations filled with maple syrup and butter, and then baked.

Banana. A large usually white, tapering squash that is typically sold in pieces.

Butternut. A light brown squash with a bulbous base, a hard skin, and sweet orange meat.

Hubbard. A large globular squash with a gray to bronzelike skin and rich, fla-vorful meat.

Turban. A round squash, bright orange with a blue "turban" at the stem end. This is a sweet, rich squash amenable to baking or steaming.

Squash Blossom

A large, yellow, trumpet-shaped flower of squash and pumpkins (*Cucurbita pepo*)—as well as the smaller flower of less extravagant squashes such as the zucchini—used especially in Mexican and Southwest cookery. In England, they were once stuffed with sausage, covered with batter, and deep-fried. In Mexico, they are fried in oil, made into soup, or stuffed with cheese. They also enhance salads and can be used as a garnish. They must be completely fresh, however, or will be limp and unat-tractive.

Squawbush

A high-bush shrub (*Viburnum trilobum*) that produces scarlet berries that look like cranberries but are not. They can, nevertheless, be made into excellent jams and jellies.

Squeateague

See WEAKFISH.

Squid

Also *calamari*. A marine cephalopod, the species most frequently seen in North American markets being *Loligo vulgaris*, which is found in Atlantic and Mediter-ranean waters. Squid are most popular among Mediterranean and Oriental peoples, but are catching on elsewhere as well.

Squid are small (they are at their best when two to five inches long), tubelike creatures with a white body containing an ink sac and a translucent "spine," topped by a head and 10 tentacles. Squid are available fresh (sometimes) or frozen. Should you buy them fresh, clean them by removing the "spine," cutting off the head and eyes, removing the ink sac, then turning the skin inside out and giving it a good washing. If you keep the skin intact, squid is excellent stuffed (the tentacles are usu-ally chopped up to form a part of the stuffing), but it can also be baked, boiled, deep-fried, stir-fried, or used in a seafood salad. In Japan, squid is one of the components of SUSHI.

Squilla

Also *mantis shrimp*. Small, burrowing crustaceans of the eastern Atlantic and Mediterranean. One of the more widely known varieties (*Squilla mantis*) resembles the praying mantis, whereby it gets its name. It is used for the most part in soups and chowders.

Squirrel

An arboreal rodent (family Sciuridae) once highly appreciated on North American dinner tables but not in much favor now. Squirrel meat is often compared with chicken and rabbit and can be cooked according to their recipes. Squirrel can also be stewed (as in a BRUNSWICK STEW) or roasted as with any other game.

Stagbush

A black HAW.

Stale

A term that refers to food that has gone by or lost its original freshness and flavor. It is not necessarily spoiled and can often be put to special uses. Stale homemade bread, for example, can be ground into breadcrumbs, although commercial breads often have additives that preclude this usage.

Star Anise

A star-shaped, eight-pointed Asian herb (*Illicium anisatum*) that carries a seed in each of its arms. It has a taste somewhat similar (albeit slightly more bitter) to European ANISE and is widely used in Oriental cookery.

Starch

In cookery, vegetable starches used as thickeners. Cornstarch, potato starch, and arrowroot are commonly used, but many other starches are available.

Star Fruit

Also called *star apple*. A long yellow fruit (*Averrhoa carambola*) with a cross-section in the shape of a five-pointed star. It started out in India and Sri Lanka, but most of those presently found in North America are grown in Florida or imported from Brazil or Israel.

When not yet ripe, they are slightly green, waxy looking, and almost translucent. There are two varieties, golden star, with a slightly tart taste, and Arkin, which is milder. Ripe star fruit can be used unpeeled in salads (although it is generally a good idea to peel them), the less ripe stewed as you would rhubarb. Sections of the star-shaped fruit are highly decorative atop desserts or slices of tomato.

If you buy them unripe, leave them at room temperature until they become ready; after that they will keep for about a week, somewhat longer if refrigerated.

Stayman

A crisp, tangy, midseason APPLE.

Steak and Kidney Pie

A hearty stew made with beef, or other meat, and kidneys chopped up with onions and mushrooms and perhaps oysters. It is covered with a crust to which some suet has traditionally been incorporated and baked.

Steak Tartare

A high-quality steak chopped fine and served raw with a garnish of chopped onions, hard-boiled egg, and other seasonings. A particularly lavish hors d'oeuvre is to serve steak tartare on a small round of dark bread and top it with caviar.

Steam

To cook something in a covered container in just a small amount of boiling liquid or placed atop a raised device resembling a strainer that holds it just above the boiling liquid. Particularly in the latter case, the steam has access to all sides of the matter being cooked and does equal work everywhere. The Chinese have special bamboo steamers in which they steam all sorts of food.

Steamer

1. A device for cooking with steam. Steamers range from a perforated basket that stands above the water level of a saucepan to a double boiler the top of which has a perforated bottom (a COUSCOUSIERE fits into this category) to a simple trivet with holes in it to tiers of perforated metal or lattice-bottomed bamboo that fit into a high-sided pot with a cover. There are as many of these components as foods to be steamed, one on top of the other, with the pot's lid keeping the steam inside where it will be effective.

2. A small variety of soft-shell CLAM.

Steep

To mingle something dry with something wet with the idea of extracting the flavor of the dry ingredient. You do this when you pour boiling water over tea leaves.

Sterlet

A species of STURGEON found in Russian, Asian, and Eastern European waters.

Stew

To cook something for a long time over relatively low heat. The stewing process not only extracts the flavors from the material being stewed, but also tenderizes such items as large fowl, overage game animals, and muscular pieces of domestic animals. Most stews, no matter how delicious they are the day they are made, become even more so the day after. Reheating simply enhances them.

Stilton

A firm, creamy yet slightly crumbly, blue-veined, British cow's-milk CHEESE considered one of the world's best. Originally made around the central English city from which it gets its name, it is now produced fairly widely around the world.

Stir

To mix something around with a spoon or other implement in order to blend it or, if over heat, to keep it from burning or curdling.

Stir-Fry

A cooking method devised by the Chinese and best suited to a WOK, although a frying pan will make a satisfactory substitute. Developed in a fuel-scarce land, it has the advantage of cooking quickly and efficiently and the added benefit of leaving most of the nutrients in the food itself instead of leaching them out, as so often happens with Western cooking techniques.

The technique consists of putting just enough oil in your pan so that when the oil is good and hot—but not quite smoking—you can roll the pan around and cover it completely with a thin layer. The material to be fried is then added and wafted gently about with a chopstick, a spatula, a wooden spoon, or similar utensil—that's the stir in stir-frying—so that all sides get covered with oil and are then quickly and uniformly cooked. Sometimes that's all, sometimes you'll want to add a little simmering chicken broth to finish, sometimes you'll add a small amount of CORNSTARCH dissolved in cold water to thicken it and impart a high sheen.

Inasmuch as stir-frying calls for ingredients usually cut quite small and ready at hand for instant use, it's essential that everything be cut or sliced or otherwise prepared beforehand and preferably lined up in small bowls in the order of use. It's a practice that comes in handy even when you're not stir-frying.

Stock

See BROTH.

Stockfish

A COD that has been dried but not salted.

Stockpot

A large, narrow cooking utensil for making soups and stocks. Stockpots begin in size at about 4 quarts and go up from there (20 quarts is considered a handy size for home use). They are made of thick metal, especially on the bottom, which must be exposed to long bouts of fairly strong heat. Their high sides permit foods to be placed inside and covered completely with water, while their narrowness exposes only a small amount of surface for evaporation. Most stockpots are made of sturdy metal (stainless steel and aluminum are common). Their sides may be less hefty than their bottoms (only the bottom gets all that intense heat, after all) and the good ones will also have a well-fitting lid.

Stollen

A German sweet bread that is chock-full of dried fruits and nuts and traditionally served on Christmas morning.

Stone Crab

A variety of CRAB only the claws of which are eaten.

Stoneground

An old-fashioned way of preparing cornmeal or whole wheat flour. It's also called *waterground* and refers to grinding the grist between two slowly rotating stone wheels or millstones, which were frequently run by waterpower. The result is generally coarser, and the stoneground flour or meal retains all the components of the grain in it—bran, germ, and all. As it spoils faster than its regular commercial counterpart, it should be bought in smaller quantities and used up in a reasonable time (a whole lot of it is not a great investment if you're only going to use it twice a year).

If you like gadgets and wish to grind your own flour from whole wheat berries, a home-style grinder is available for a price. It's said that some prefer to grind their wheat in the small amounts they need in an inexpensive coffee grinder kept just for that purpose, but it hardly seems like stoneground.

Store Cheese

A wheel of CHEDDAR that was once kept under a bell jar on the counter of the local general store and may still be found in small markets. By avoiding refrigeration, the cheese ripens slowly and at its own pace. In a more relaxed environment, this often caused much discussion and satisfying disagreement as to whether or not the cheese was really ready.

Stout

A form of BEER.

Strainer

A handy little device for keeping solids (such as tea leaves) out of liquids (such as tea). Strainers come in all sizes and an assortment of several can be awfully useful in the kitchen.

Strawberry

A ground-creeping plant (*Fragaria* spp.) that grows wild in large areas of Asia, Europe, and North and South America. The small, lush, red, wild berries can be a pest to pick, but they reward the picker with a taste that domestic strawberries can only approximate—and then only if freshly picked themselves. And as a special treat, there is a wild Alpine berry, a small one indeed, that the French call *fraise des bois* that is in a class by itself. For those with an insatiable appetite for strawberries, fresh berries are grown in gentle climes and distributed all over the continent, and frozen berries are also available.

One difficulty in flying strawberries all over the place is that once picked, they lose flavor, and unless picked when ripe they won't have the same appeal. Try one of the huge California berries right where they grow and you'll see how different they taste from the same crop shipped to an East Coast or Midwest supermarket.

The uses of strawberries defy the imagination. Eat them plain off the plant, with cream, in jams, jellies, mousses, and pies (in pies, strawberries combine especially well with rhubarb), not to speak of sauces and shortcakes and tarts. Cranberries, orange juice, and pineapple are among some other foods that complement strawberries. And a strawberry brandy (*fraise*), while expensive, has its advocates.

In selecting strawberries at the market, look for berries with a high color, ones with the caps still intact and no touch of white or green at the top. If they come in a box, make sure there are no red stains on the box—the berries may be overripe—and look out for any that do not have that pleasing plumpness that is a hallmark of a first-rate berry. If you manage to get them home without consuming them all, keep them cool and dry until ready for use (as early as possible). If they seem gritty, drop them briefly in a bowl of cold water and lift them out with your fingers. Hull them and they are ready.

It has been said many times since it first appeared in 1655, but bears repeating: "Doubtless God could have made a better berry, but doubtless God never did."

Streusel

A crumbly topping for breads, coffee cakes, muffins, and pies. It is composed of a mixture of butter (or margarine), flour, and sugar, often augmented with granola or nuts or spices of one sort or another. The name derives from the German verb *streuen* meaning "to strew" or "scatter."

String Bean

A common green BEAN.

String Cheese

A form of MOZZARELLA (sometimes combined with other cheeses) that is stretched into long ropelike strands during the cheese-making process, which sometimes includes soaking it in brine or vinegar.

Striped Bass

A fish of the BASS family.

Strudel

A crisp, fine, thin, European pastry case like a TURNOVER for fruits (particularly apples) and meats.

Stud

To place small bits of garnish or flavorings into something. You can stud a leg of lamb with slivers of garlic or a ham with cloves. In some cases (as with ham and cloves), the studding will protrude slightly; in others (such as garlic in lamb) it might be deeply embedded.

Stuffing

Whatever it is you put into your bird or breast of veal or suckling pig or whatever before you roast it. Stuffings are usually built around something bulky such as breadcrumbs or rice with something savory and good such as the giblets of the critter being stuffed, sausage, oysters, dried fruits, fresh fruits, nuts, vegetables such as onion and celery, spices, and often a FORTIFIED WINE. There are two schools of thought on how to treat stuffing. Revisionists claim that stuffing in a turkey, for example, gets soggy and that it's far better to cook it in a tightly sealed container in the same roasting oven. Traditionalists concede the possibility, but put more emphasis on the commingling of juices—and consequently of tastes—that takes place when stuffing is traditionally stuffed.

Sturgeon

A family incorporating the largest of the freshwater fishes (although sturgeon are also anadromous). Sturgeon have a virtual worldwide distribution and are commemorated mostly as the premier supplier of roe for CAVIAR. In fact, sturgeon has also been praised for its flesh, but this has been decreasing in volume over the years. Sturgeon are simply incapable of surviving in the polluted waterways which they prefer to inhabit. Sturgeon is firm and rich fare, has been likened to meat (especially veal, although Hudson River sturgeon was once known as "Albany beef"), and is often cooked in ways usually thought more fit for red meats than fish. Indeed, it can be cooked in almost any way that fish can be cooked; it can be baked, barbecued, sautéed like a steak, boiled, or smoked. Marinating it in white wine or brushing it with olive oil and grilling it are time-honored cooking processes. Some once-common species are now no more than a memory, others exist in diminishing numbers and probably on borrowed time. The sturgeons include:

> *Atlantic sturgeon.* There are two of them, one (*Acipenser sturio*) was once widespread on the eastern portions of the Atlantic as well as in the Baltic, Black, and Mediterranean seas, but it is now either nonexistent or quite scarce. The western variety (*Acipenser oxyrhynchus*) was once prevalent along the North American Atlantic coast and in adjoining rivers and estuaries but is now all but gone. The latter is the fish likely to show up in eastern markets of the United States.

> *Beluga* (*Acipenser huso*). Found in the Adriatic, Black, and Caspian seas and formerly in the Danube. It is particularly noted as a source for sturgeon caviar, although it is only about the third largest supplier of that delicacy.

> *Lake sturgeon* (*Acipenser fulvescens*). A sturgeon of the upper Mississippi and Great Lakes; like so many of its relatives it is found only in declining numbers, if indeed it is found at all.

> *Pacific sturgeon* or *white sturgeon* (*Acipenser transmontanus*). A monster of the North American Pacific coast that can achieve up to 400 pounds.

Russian sturgeon (*Acipenser gueldenstaedti*). A smallish fish of Russian waters
taken almost exclusively on its native grounds more for its flesh than its roe.

Sterlet (*Acipenser ruthenus*). One of the foremost suppliers of caviar, it inhabits the rivers emptying into the Black and Caspian seas from Russia and Eastern Europe.

Succotash

A dish of lima beans and corn often cooked in a little milk and sometimes flavored
with a dash of Worcestershire sauce. The American anthropologist and man of let-
ters Oliver La Farge reported that one version of the original American Indian dish
also included fish.

Sucker

A common name for a large variety of fish, most of which are scavengers. *Buffalofish*
and *carp* and *catfish* are often included in this category.

Suet

A hard fat that forms around the loins and kidneys of cattle and sheep. It has a variety of culinary uses such as in mincemeat, suet puddings (usually steamed or boiled
puddings using a suet base with bread and flavorings, often for dessert), or pastries
such as that used for a steak and kidney pie. It is also welcome in bird feeders.

Sugar

Sucrose—a refined product of cane (and sometimes beet). It is a universal sweetener. Other sources of sugar include corn, honey, maple sap, palm, and various fruits.
The sugar lobby describes it as wholesome and natural and calls for its extended use;
the health food lobby calls it deleterious if not downright hazardous to the health,
overrefined, and blatantly overused. Types of sugar include:

Barbados. A soft, moist, relatively unrefined brown sugar (see below).

Brown sugar. Originally, sugar refined less strenuously than white, but now
more likely white sugar to which a little molasses is added, the amount
depending upon the degree of brownness desired (more molasses = darker;
less molasses = lighter).

Castor sugar. A British term for sugar slightly finer than granulated; more like
powdered.

Confectioners' sugar. A very powdery sugar to which some cornstarch has been
added. It is mostly useful for frostings and icings, but try it also sprinkled
lightly over fresh—and freshly picked—strawberries or similar fruit.

Cube sugar. Sugar that has been pressed into cubes or dice of various sizes. They
dissolve quickly in your morning coffee.

Demerera sugar. Only slightly refined brown sugar from the area of the same
name in the former colony of British Guiana, now Guyana.

Granulated sugar. Sugar as we know and use it in the small gritlike particles.

Invert sugar. Sugar in solution heated with an acid or enzyme to produce a smoother, more easily assimilated result.

Powdered sugar. Sugar that is considerably more powdery than granulated, useful for demanding items such as angel food cake. In a pinch, you can fake it by putting granulated sugar through your food processor.

Raw sugar. In theory, sugar in the state in which it enters the refinery. In practice, slightly refined sugar to which molasses is often added to give it a brownish tinge.

Turbinado sugar. A very slightly refined sugar with a delicate brownish tinge.

Sugar Apple
See SWEETSOP.

Sugar Beet
A close relative of the garden beet from which SUGAR can be extracted.

Sugarberry
See HACKBERRY.

Sugarcane
The source of SUGAR and also of MOLASSES and RUM. The sugarcane (*Saccharum officinarum*) is a grass that originated somewhere in the Pacific area and wound its way around the world. The Spaniards brought it to the Americas (and with it the slave trade on which the great sugar plantations were built). Sugarcane is still of vital importance to the economies of several Caribbean nations as well as Brazil and India.

Suimono
A Japanese clear BROTH.

Sukiyaki
A Japanese dish of paper-thin slices of beef with noodles and mushrooms, cooked and served at the table.

Sultana
A type of RAISIN.

Sunchoke
A JERUSALEM ARTICHOKE.

Sundae
An ice-cream dessert with one or more scoops of ice cream topped with all sorts of good things—flavored syrups, fruits, nuts, whipped cream—any or all of the above.

Sunfish
A name variously applied to a group of freshwater panfish and to some marine fishes, such as the OPAH, as well.

Sunflower
Any of various flowering plants of the *Helianthus* genus native to North America but introduced into Europe and Asia. It was adopted particularly lovingly in Russia. The daisylike heads of the sunflower (they can run up to a foot across) contain masses of seeds that provide a nourishing cocktail snack as well as a popular cooking oil. Unhulled sunflower seeds are probably best set out in the bird feeder, but they are also available hulled, sometimes roasted and salted. The *Helianthus* genus is also responsible for the JERUSALEM ARTICHOKE.

Sunshine Bass
A hybrid of the STRIPED BASS, found in waters of the southern United States.

Suprême
An especially choice piece of game or poultry as, for example, a boneless and skinless chicken breast.

Surf
A somewhat tough species of CLAM used mostly minced for chowder or sliced up for frying.

Surimi
A paste composed of processed fish (especially a mild-flavored one like pollack). It can then be given whatever shape and texture is desired and sold as imitation crab, lobster, or shrimp. It is used especially in seafood salads.

Surinam Cherry
Also *Brazilian cherry* and *pitanga*. The juicy, red, soft fruit of a tropical and subtropical shrub (*Eugenia uniflora*). Somewhat acidic, the fruit is commonly used for jelly.

Surinam Spinach
A species of AMARANTH.

Sushi
A Japanese specialty of small ovals of rice flavored with rice vinegar, sugar, and salt and wrapped with a piece of raw fish. Sushi is frequently then wrapped in seaweed and often flavored with WASABI paste. In Japan, sushi can be hand-wrapped (*nigiri-sushi*), given its form by rolling it up in a bamboo mat (*makisushi*), or formed in a special box (*oshisushi*).

Swan

A graceful long-necked bird of the family Anatidae, beloved of readers of Hans Christian Andersen's *The Ugly Duckling* and heartily disliked by hunters in areas where they are protected.

Swans tend to uproot the aquatic plants on which ducks and geese feed, and they proliferate so fast they drive out any competition. While much prized as food in medieval times (white ones are still Crown property in Great Britain), they are not much eaten today. According to one veteran game warden, if you should wish to try eating a swan, choose a gray, rather than a pure white, one. The gray ones are younger and more tender.

Sweat

To cook something over low heat in a little oil in a covered pot or the oven in order to bring out the juices without browning it.

Swede

A yellow TURNIP.

Sweet and Sour

A type of dish in which a sweet element (pineapple, for example) is balanced against a sour one (perhaps vinegar). It is most visible in Chinese and Jewish cookery but crops up elsewhere as well, as in SAUERBRATEN.

Sweetbread

The thymus gland of a young (they tend to shrivel up as the animal grows older) animal such as a calf, lamb, or shoat, or a game animal. The term may also apply to the pancreas. The thymus is often referred to as *throat sweetbread*, the pancreas as the *stomach sweetbread*. Sweetbreads must be eaten fresh, or they tend to deteriorate. They are generally soaked for several hours in salted or acidulated water, blanched quickly, then set in cold water to harden. They are then ready to be cooked and are usually served with some rich sauce.

Sweet Cherry

A round, red or green, sweet PEPPER used for pickling.

Sweet Pepper

The bell PEPPER.

Sweet Potato

First of all, it's not related to the potato, but belongs with the morning glory. In the second place, it is not a yam—an entirely different vegetable—although it resembles one and often goes by that name. The sweet potato (*Ipomoea batatas*) is the edible tuberous root of a trailing vine probably of Peruvian origin, although it seems to have been pretty widespread across the Caribbean and Gulf of Mexico by the time

Columbus arrived. It now has a worldwide distribution and is much appreciated in parts of Asia, although Western Europe has never worked up any enthusiasm for it.

There are any number of sweet potatoes, but the ones we are apt to see are somewhat elongated and potato-like with orange skin and flesh. (Other varieties may be light yellow, red, violet, or white.) Most of them have a quite sweet taste, although there are others that are not sweet at all. In the northern United States, the preferred taste is for a sweet potato with a mealy consistency; in the South, a moister, sweeter one is preferred.

The uses of the sweet potato are somewhat limited. For many people, they are candied and served for Thanksgiving dinner and that's about it. However, they can also be baked or boiled (as with the regular potato), and sweet potato pie is a Southern tradition.

When looking for sweet potatoes, use the same guidelines as you would for any root vegetable. Make sure they are solid and unbruised and spring for the smaller rather than the larger ones. They'll keep about a week in a dry, well-ventilated place (they do not take kindly to refrigeration).

Sweetsop
Also *sugar apple*. A tropical American tree (*Annona squamosa*) related to the PAW-PAW, the fruit of which is amenable to jellies and conserves.

Sweet Woodruff
See WOODRUFF.

Swiss Chard
A green akin to the BEET.

Swiss Cheese
A cheese made just about everywhere and intended to resemble Swiss EMMENTHALER. If labeled "Swiss" it is probably domestic; if "imported Swiss," it could come from anywhere; if "imported from Switzerland," it is the real thing, but not necessarily of the highest quality.

Swiss Roll
A British nomenclature for JELLY ROLL.

Swordfish
One of the most important marine food and game fishes throughout the temperate world. They can be huge, but the pressure of the fishing fleets has made any fish over 500 pounds a rarity indeed. They congregate off the coast of New England each summer and can be found frozen year-round.

Swordfish is usually sold as steaks or simply chunks. The meat is firm, mild, not very "fishlike" in flavor, but in cooking does tend to dry out. It also loses its taste if overcooked. Cooking methods include broiling, charbroiling (marinate it first and baste it during cooking), or even frying. When selecting swordfish, try to seek out a specimen with a pinkish rather than the usual white hue. It will be tastier.

Syllabub

An old English drink consisting of milk curdled with sweetened wine or cider that is poured in from a height to cause the drink to foam. It developed into a sweet dessert made with cream beaten to a froth and augmented with brandy, rum, or wine.

Syrup

A liquid sweetener, predominantly made from maple, cane sugar, or corn.

Szechuan Peppercorn

A seed of an Oriental tree (*Xanthoxylum piperitum*) of the Ash family, which pre-dated the arrival of true peppercorns into China. They are typically used in concert with other herbs and spices, as in Chinese FIVE SPICES.

T

T.

A common abbreviation for TABLESPOON.

t.

A common abbreviation for TEASPOON.

Tabasco

1. An extremely hot green or red CHILI pepper found fresh or bottled.

2. A proprietary hot sauce from Louisiana made with CHILI pepper (but not made with the tabasco pepper) augmented with salt and vinegar. Use sparingly (a drop at a time).

Tablespoon

A standard unit of measure equaling ½ ounce or 15 grams (dry weight) or 15 milliliters (liquid measure).

Table Wine

Nonfortified wine intended primarily for accompanying food or as an aperitif.

Tabouli

Also *tabbouley* and *tabouly*. A Middle Eastern salad of BULGAR with parsley and olive oil but often mixed with mint and chunks of onion and tomato and dressed with lemon juice.

Taco

A deep-fried corn TORTILLA bent into a U shape and filled with meat, poultry, vegetables, or anything that strikes your fancy.

Taffy

A soft, chewy candy made of brown sugar or molasses. It is pulled and stretched continuously during its production and flavored with various substances, especially butterscotch. Saltwater taffy once had some saltwater incorporated into it, but this seems hardly the case anymore.

Tagine

A slowly cooked Moroccan stew. Almost anything—fish, fruit, meat, and vegetables—can go into a tagine.

Tagliatelle
A flat ribbon of PASTA with a width of ¾ inch.

Tahini
Also *sesame butter*. A spread made from ground SESAME seeds that is much used in Middle Eastern cookery. Although it keeps well unrefrigerated, it will tend to separate and need stirring to recombine the oil and the solids.

Tallegio
A soft, white- to straw-colored, Italian whole cow's-milk CHEESE with a pleasant, mild taste.

Tamale
A Mexican specialty of ground meat (usually, other fillings also occur) commonly flavored with chili, wrapped in cornmeal dough, placed in a corn husk, and steamed until done.

Tamari
A SOY SAUCE classically made from fermented soybeans alone, but now more likely a combination of soy and wheat. Some commercial varieties may be subjected to modern processing that decreases the cost but does nothing for the taste.

Tamarillo
Another name (especially in New Zealand) for the TREE TOMATO.

Tamarind
A tropical tree (*Tamarindus indica*) that produces a somewhat bitter pod used in chutneys, curries, drinks, and preserves. Although the name comes from the Arabic for "Indian date," it has nothing in common with the date either botanically or gastronomically.

Tandoor
A large clay oven of the Indian subcontinent used for cooking food (especially chicken) at an extremely high temperature. The food may first be marinated in a yogurt-and-spice marinade.

Tangelo
A cross between a TANGERINE and a POMELO.

Tangerine
A variety of ORANGE.

Tannia
See MALANGA.

Tansy

Also *mugwort*. An Old World plant (*Tanacetum vulgare*) that was introduced into North America and has since run wild. It has been used as a somewhat bitter flavoring for tea and, oddly enough, pastries, especially around Easter, perhaps as a reminder of the bitter herbs served at a Jewish Passover Seder. Tansy has also been included in stuffings for chicken or veal and is sometimes recommended with pork.

Tapas

A Spanish version of small cocktail snacks, although if you put enough of them together, they can constitute a meal.

Tapenade

A Provençale hors d'oeuvre made from green olives crushed to a paste with lemon juice or olive oil. It is sometimes embellished with anything from anchovies to capers to spices and, perhaps, tuna.

Tapioca

See CASSAVA.

Taramasalata

A Greek creamy pâté, served on crackers and used as a canapé. It is made from the salted and pressed roe of cod or mullet (or smoked cod roe) mixed together with bread or potatoes (or both), dipped in milk or water with oil and lemon juice and usually a little onion or scallion. Other ingredients can be added—cucumber, dill, tomato—at the whim of the cook.

Taro

A tropical vegetable (*Colocasia esculenta*) also called *dasheen*, among other names. It is a starchy tuber usually resembling a large yam, has white to somewhat yellow flesh, and tastes like a potato but less dry. Taro can be used any way that potatoes are used, including chips, and are a staple of the Dominican dish *sancocho*. They also form the basis for the Hawaiian staple *poi*, for which the taro is boiled and pounded into a paste then usually left to ferment slightly. Raw taro is said to be toxic, but cooking does away with that problem completely.

The word taro is often used as a catchall for various other similar plants (such as MALANGA), but the differences between them seem to be of more importance to the botanist than to the cook.

Tarpon

A sports fish (*Megalops atlantica*) par excellence but little seen on North American tables. In some areas, it is used for fish cakes.

Tarragon

An aromatic herb (*Artemesia dranunculus*) of Russian origin with wide culinary uses. Tarragon is fairly strong as herbs go and may dominate any herbal combination to which it is added. It has a slightly bitter flavor and greatly enhances chicken, fish, and vegetables. It is widely added as a flavoring for vinegar. Indeed, Alexandre Dumas contended that there could be no good vinegar without tarragon. Another strong-minded expert insisted that tarragon vinegar is the "only correct seasoning for steak tartare, but must never be put in soups as the taste is too strong and pungent."

Tart

1. Also *tarte*. A one-crust pie filled with fruit, preserves, custard, or a combination of these (apple-custard, for example).

2. Sour or sharp in taste.

Tartar

See CREAM OF TARTAR.

Tartar Steak

See STEAK TARTARE.

Tartar Sauce

A sauce based on MAYONNAISE with augmentations that might include capers, chives, dill pickles, onions, olives, and to moisten it, lemon juice, vinegar, or dry white wine.

Tarte Tatin

Also, *tarte des demoiselles Tatin*. A tart developed by the Tatin sisters of Orléans, France, in which sliced apples are placed in a buttered and sugared pan and topped with pastry dough. The sugar beneath the apple slices caramelizes during baking and when the tart is inverted out of its pan, forms the top. Essentially, an upside-down cake.

Tartlet

As the name suggests, a small tart; it is used as an hors d'oeuvre—and is usually called just a tart, its size notwithstanding.

Tautog

Also BLACKFISH. A western Atlantic food fish (*Tautoga onitis*) found from Nova Scotia to the Carolinas. It usually runs two to three pounds (but can be bigger) and has firm, tasty, dry, and delicate white flesh amenable to baking or broiling or as a base for a chowder.

Tavel
A full-bodied, dry rosé wine from France's Rhône River wine-growing area. It is generally considered the model for other rosés to aspire to.

T-Bone Steak
A cut of beef from the loin with a bone in just the shape you'd expect.

Tea
A beverage of great antiquity made from infusing the leaves of a somewhat demanding evergreen shrub (*Camellia sinensis*) grown for the most part in China and Southeast Asia, although it is cultivated elsewhere in Asia, and in Africa and South America as well. The tea plant needs heat and humidity yet achieves its best results at high altitudes, where the weather is cooler. It will grow unchecked unless pruned as severely as a grape vine, prefers shade to direct sunlight, and takes about four years before it produces a usable crop. (On the other hand, with proper care it can live and bear for a century.) At harvest time, the leaves must be picked with discretion, ensuring that they will all be of about the same size (when processed, uniformity of size is important). The production process releases certain elements in the leaf, chemicals that transform the beverage into the soothing, complex, elusive beverage that appears on our tables. How they are processed will determine what type of tea will ensue.

There are essentially three types of tea: fermented (*black*), semifermented (*oolong*), and unfermented (*green*).

Black tea is, of course, tea at the farthest end of the production process. The leaves are first withered, in order to cause them to lose some moisture and become dark and sticky; then they are "rolled" (the way each leaf curls seems to affect how it dispenses its flavor); after which they are fermented, which changes the chemical constitution of the tea, thereby affecting the taste and strength. Firing, essentially drying under heat, follows this step (in part to halt the fermentation at the desired point) and then the leaves are graded by size. (Tea leaves of different sizes do not seem able to work harmoniously together.) Black teas provide stronger brews than do the other teas, golden or red in color with a rich taste. Black tea is graded according to size (there is no connection between grade and quality), from flowery pekoe (the small, youngest leaves), to orange pekoe, to pekoe, to souchang, which is the largest.

The aim in making green tea is to avoid fermentation, thus allowing the tea to exude its own flavorings without the chemical changes that fermentation brings about. The leaves are steamed as soon as they are picked, then are rolled and fired but at a lower temperature than for black tea. The leaves emerge as green or perhaps gray. The grades of green teas generally follow the age of the leaf (the grade and quality of green teas are interconnected). They include gunpowder—it comes in tiny, rolled balls—and young hyson, made from young to slightly older leaves. Imperial is slightly older than young hyson and hyson is older yet. By and large, the younger the leaf the more delicate the tea.

The semifermented, or oolongs, fall in between black and green. They are withered for a short time, briefly fermented, and then fired, sometimes several times. Oolong is essentially the product of Taiwan and is labeled Formosa oolong with grades that run from standard through a tortuous hierarchy to finally achieve choice (which is even better than finest). Some oolongs are scented with gardenia or jasmine and are labeled pouchong.

Most teas are, of course, blends of different styles and grades, and as with any blended product, the blender attempts to replicate the taste year after year. Any number of blends can be found including Earl Grey and Irish breakfast tea and others under proprietary names.

Tea is available loose or in tea bags. Loose tea is both more economical and tastier, but tea bags are indisputably more convenient. There are any number of ways of brewing tea, all of them "correct." The Russians make tea in large samovars (or urns), the Chinese often make individual cups, and the British use the pot method. In this process, cold water (hot water from the tap and previously boiled water tend to lose air and become flat) is brought to a boil and poured over tea leaves that have been placed in the bottom of a teapot. The tea is left to steep and is poured out into preferably warmed cups and served with warmed milk, sugar, and lemon. If you don't have time for all this, just pop a tea bag in a cup, pour on some boiling water, and wait a few minutes. Or use instant tea.

Of course, hot tea is not the sole way of taking tea. Iced tea is becoming more and more popular, especially during the summer months. And flavored teas—anise, apple, cinnamon, cloves, gardenia, jasmine, mint (a North African and Middle Eastern staple), and lemon and orange flavorings (usually the rind) are among the flavorings that are widely available. In addition, a whole industry has blossomed producing herbal teas—teas that have no part of the tea plant in them but are predicated instead on herbs of various sorts. In any case, they fill a void for those who cannot tolerate caffeine.

Tea Bag
A small meshed bag holding enough tea for one cup. The bag itself imparts no taste and the cup of tea will be as good (or as mediocre) as the tea put in it.

Tea Ball
A metal container on a small chain. Tea is placed in the container, the container placed in a cup (or pot), boiling water is added, and the tea is infused into the water.

Teaberry
See CHECKERBERRY.

Tea Cozy

A cloth cover for a teapot intended to insulate the pot and retain the heat while the tea is steeping—or even keep it warm enough for a second cup.

Tea Egg

A hard-boiled egg, prepared by a Chinese method of cracking the shell (but not removing it), then simmering the egg for an hour with tea leaves and salt. The egg is allowed to stand in the water for another half hour. When removed from its shell, the egg will have a marbled effect where the tea has seeped through. It can be served for breakfast or lunch or just as a snack. Keeping it in its shell until it is eaten helps keep it moist.

Teal

A species of small freshwater WILD DUCK (*Anas* spp.).

Teaspoon

A standard unit of measure; three of them make a TABLESPOON.

Teflon

A trademarked name for a synthetic coating used on cooking utensils to keep food from sticking. It requires little or no fat but cannot withstand as much heat as non-Teflon pots and pans. Teflon is particularly helpful in an omelet pan.

Tellicherry

A town on India's Malabar Coast noted for the spice trade and especially the high-quality PEPPER it ships to the rest of the world.

Temple Orange

A variety of eating ORANGE with a thick skin.

Tempura

In Japanese cookery, seafood and vegetables (and sometimes chicken) dipped in an extremely light batter (egg yolks beaten in water and mixed with flour) and deep-fried. It is served with a dip consisting of soy sauce and DAIKON.

Tench

A Eurasian freshwater fish (*Tinca tinca*) reminiscent of CARP.

Tenderloin

A boneless cut of meat from along the backbone; one of the choicer cuts of meat, although there are those who consider it bland.

Tenpounder

Also *ladyfish*. A gamefish for the most part (*Elops saurus*) similar to herring but related to the tarpon. It rarely attains the weight its name implies. Should you catch one, try poaching or steaming it.

Tepid

See LUKEWARM.

Tequila

A Mexican spirit distilled from the fermented sap of the MESCAL plant.

Teriyaki

A Japanese sauce consisting of SAKE and MIRIN, simmered with dark soy sauce and sugar just until the sugar dissolves. It is used as a marinade for meat, poultry, and seafood.

Terrapin

One of a group of turtles (family Testudinidae) living in fresh or brackish water. Several classic terrapin recipes such as Terrapin Baltimore and Terrapin Maryland suggest a regional source, but the terrapin originally ranged from the Gulf Coast to New England. Both recipes call for the terrapin meat to be served in a rich sauce including butter, cream, eggs, and a little sherry. See also TURTLE.

Terrine

An earthenware cooking vessel, usually oval, usually with its own lid. It can be used to cook and serve a pâté, which then takes the name *terrine*, or for any hearty oven cooking you may wish to do, from braising a chicken to making a stew, depending upon its size.

Testicles

The sex glands of male mammals. They have been used as food, going under such names as ANIMELLES (in France) and PRAIRIE OYSTER (in the Old West). The customary cooking procedure is to slice them and sauté them in butter.

Tex-Mex Cooking

A style of cooking popular in the Southwest and Mexico. It relies heavily on CHILI peppers and such standards as TACOS and TORTILLAS. The name reportedly is not welcome in the area it describes.

Thickener

Something, such as flour or cornstarch, that makes a sauce, for example, a little thicker, such as flour added to pan juices to make gravy.

Thimbleberry
A name applied to various raspberry-like North American berries, especially the blackcap RASPBERRY (*Rubus occidentalis*) and the Great Lakes thimbleberry (*Rubus parviflorus*).

Thin
To dilute something. Also refers to something that has been diluted to the point of insipidity.

Thistle
A very broad term for a number of prickly plants, some of which are edible. The only one of overriding culinary importance is the ARTICHOKE, although Europeans would certainly add the CARDOON.

Thrush
Any of a number of smallish songbirds (family Turdidae) eaten in parts of Europe but protected by law in North America.

Thyme
An aromatic herb. In sailing-ship days, seamen returning to Genoa knew they were approaching land from the pervasive aroma of the wild thyme growing on the hillsides. You probably couldn't smell anything but oil fumes today and perhaps the wild thyme is also gone. But we do have an "improved" cultivated variety available everywhere that is simultaneously one of the most delicate and pungent herbs available. In fact we can choose between two. There is garden thyme (*Thymus vulgaris*) and lemon thyme (*Thymus serpyllum* var. *citriodorus*). Both varieties can add flavor to all manner of fish and meat and vegetable dishes as well as salad dressings, sauces, and soups and enrich a BOUQUET GARNI. The difference between them is that lemon thyme has a slight, but delightful, lemony aspect. Thyme is available dried as well as fresh and makes a fragrant addition to a kitchen garden. Wild thyme (*Thymus serpyllum*) is also recommended for feeding to rabbits to add to them an increment of taste.

Tian
A Provençale casserole dish and also its ingredients, which are composed of baked, sliced, or chopped vegetables (especially peppers of various colors) usually arranged in a dramatic fashion.

Tiger Lily
A somewhat showy lily (*Lilium tigrinum*) native to China or Japan but widely grown in North American gardens. In Chinese cooking, its delicate, light-golden buds are found fresh (they must be parboiled to remove any bitterness) and dried (in which

case they are soaked to soften them). They are added to stir-fried or slow-cooked dishes.

Tilefish

An Atlantic deep-water fish (*Lopholatilus chamaeleonticeps*) usually found in fillets or steaks. It is a versatile and tasty fish that can be cooked in a number of ways or eaten raw as in SASHIMI.

Tillamook

A cheese of the CHEDDAR style made in Oregon.

Tilsit

A semisoft mild cow's-milk CHEESE named for the German city of Tilsit, renamed Sovetsk by the Russians; the cheese is now widely made elsewhere.

Timbale

A French name for a tricky method of preparing just about any kind of ingredient—fish, fowl, fruit—by cooking and serving it in a large, rounded pastry crust.

Tinker Mackerel

A New England name for any small MACKEREL.

Tisane

Essentially, any herb tea. It is made by infusing flowers, herbs, or spices (especially balm, chamomile, mint, rose hips, but there are many others) in hot water and quaffing the result for medicinal effect or refreshment.

Toddy

A hot alcoholic beverage sweetened, sometimes spiced, and usually served in a mug of some sort.

Toffee

A British variant of TAFFY.

Tofu

A liquid pressed out of soybeans, it is the curd of soy milk. We used to call tofu "bean curd" and came across it when we dined out in Chinese restaurants. Then it was popularized under its Japanese name and now can be found everywhere and used for a dizzying number of uses.

Tofu is available in two varieties: soft and firm. The firm variety is simply soft tofu with the excess water pressed out of it. In addition to supplying the protein for a meatless dinner, tofu is usable in salad dressings, breads, pies, dips, shakes, and in countless other combinations for which there are whole cookbooks.

Togue
An alternate name for the *lake trout*, a CHAR.

Tokay
Hungary's contribution to the most highly esteemed wines of the world. Tokay (especially the extremely rare and outrageously expensive *eszencia*) is a rich, sweet dessert wine, and at its best, can hardly be equaled. The Tokay seen most frequently is *szamorodni*, which can run from quite dry to sweet. Both California and France's Alsace produce table grapes and wines labeled Tokay, but they have nothing in common with the Hungarian original.

Toll House Cookie
The original chocolate chip cookie. It was devised in the 1930s at the Toll House Restaurant in Massachusetts.

Tomalley
The liver of the lobster. It is of a green color and together with the coral (or roe) it forms a Christmasy delicacy.

Tomatillo
A small, green, tomato-like vegetable (*Physalis ixocarpa*). It is *not* an unripe regular tomato. The substitution does not work. Available fresh and canned, the tomatillo imparts a sour, some would say tobacco-like, taste. They are parboiled, peeled, and pureed to be added to Southwestern green chili recipes. Make sure the tomatillos you buy are firm, not mushy, and let them cook 15 minutes or so to civilize their sourness.

Tomato
A vegetable (technically it is a berry—*Lycopersicon esculentum*—but we use it as a vegetable) that is one of the joys of summer when "real" tomatoes fresh off the vine from backyard gardens or local farms become available, replacing the bulletlike supermarket mediocrities with the rubberoid skin that ship so well and have a taste that can politely be best described as blah. (Fortunately, fresh tomatoes take quite well to canning and in the off-season these supply our needs for such items as sauces and stews—albeit not for salads.)

Tomatoes come in a profusion of shapes and sizes and colors—red and yellow and some with no color at all. But there are cherry tomatoes and pear tomatoes and plum tomatoes, named not for taste characteristics but for their shape, and elongated and oval tomatoes in addition to the rounded ones that make up the bulk of the crop.

A native of Peru, the tomato was taken to Europe in the 16th century, but was considered an oddball, decorative plant. It was some time before anyone thought of eating one, and even then it took a while to catch on. Americans began eating tomatoes sometime in the 1860s and haven't stopped since. It is one of our favorite foods.

But this love affair seems to have caused a backlash. Because of the demand, strains of tomato were developed with the thick skin so frequently seen in supermarkets and with a greatly diminished taste. The problem is partly the need to develop a tomato that will stand shipping and retain some taste. A tomato picked when green (and reddened with ethylene gas) simply will not develop the taste it will if picked when ripe. And taste in a tomato is a tricky matter. Sugar is developed during the ripening process and a lack of sugar in an unripe tomato leads to a lifeless and sour product.

There are a number of tomatoes available from time to time. For salads, sauces, and stews the Italian plum tomato (or the sun-dried tomato) is usually recommended. For an hors d'oeuvre the small cherry tomato (with a bowl of salt for dipping) makes a cheerful and tasty sight.

When selecting tomatoes, follow the usual guidelines: Look for well-colored specimens that are firm and free of blotches and cracks. Stay away from any with a watery look or with sunken spots. Buy (or pick) them when they are ripe and use them up quickly.

Tomato Paste

Tomatoes cooked down to a rich paste. It is available in cans and tubes.

Tomato Puree

Tomatoes cooked and strained to form a thick gooey liquid.

Tomato Sauce

Tomatoes with such additions as garlic, peppers, perhaps some meat, and flavorings.

Tomcod

There is one in the Atlantic and one in the Pacific; both are members of the COD family.

Tom Collins

A tall, spirituous drink consisting of gin and sweetened lemon juice served over ice with seltzer or soda water.

Tongue

Tongue is a perennial occupant of the supermarket showcase but, even so, does not seem to be that popular in North America. Most of what we see are beef, lamb, pork, or veal (venison tongue is favored by those fortunate enough to come by one) and provide a good source of lean (albeit high-cholesterol) meat. Fresh tongue must be simmered and skinned and in the cooking provides a rich, nourishing broth. Tongue is otherwise available corned, pickled, and smoked.

Tonic Water

See QUININE WATER.

Tortellini

A type of PASTA made with the addition of eggs, shaped into small circlets, stuffed, and either poached and served separately or served in a broth. Tortellini are often seen frozen.

Tortière

A meat pie, once used as a lunch by lumberjacks and other woodsmen of French Canada and Maine who pulled it out of a handy pocket when the sun got high. It is made from meat—beef, game, pork, veal—already cooked and sliced up with potatoes and onions and sometimes turnips or carrots and baked. The pie can be round or in the half-moon shape of a turnover. To survive a morning's workout in the pocket of an active outdoorsman, the original crust must have been made out of something resembling Naugahyde, but for present-day use regular piecrust should suffice.

Tortilla

A traditional bread of Mexico, enthusiastically adopted in parts of the Southwest. It is made from corn lengthily soaked in a lime solution, then ground into *masa*. The masa is worked on a piece of stone (or metate), patted as thin as possible, and baked on a hot iron.

Tortoni

Also called *biscuit tortoni*. An Italian frozen dessert. It is made with sugar syrup and egg yolks, seasoned with sherry and heavy cream, garnished with chopped almonds, and served in a paper dish with sherry-soaked, broken-up macaroons.

Toss

To mix, as you would a salad. Gently lofting the greens very slightly into the air gives them a chance to mingle with the salad dressing and other ingredients to the benefit of all.

Tostada

A Mexican specialty consisting of a fried TORTILLA topped with a variety of ingredients including cheese, guacamole, lettuce, and tomatoes.

Tournedos

Thick slices of the best part of a beef tenderloin, sautéed or broiled. They are classically served on rounds of fried bread and with a topping, such as fluted mushrooms. *Tournedos Rossini*, a rich showpiece of French cookery, has slices of tournedos topped with foie gras and a slice of truffle.

Treacle

A British designation for MOLASSES.

Tree Ear

A Chinese cloud ear MUSHROOM.

Tree Tomato

Also *tamarillo*. A small, oval, one- to two-inch-long fruit (*Cyphomandra betacea*) that originated in Peru or Brazil but now comes mostly from New Zealand. It is no more than a distant relative of the true tomato. The fruit ripens to various shades of yellowish-orange to red to brownish-red and even to purple. It can be split and the flesh scooped out and eaten raw, used for dessert or fruit salads, or stewed. For use in other dishes, it is best skinned—drop it into boiling water for 2 minutes, refresh in cold water, and peel from the stem end.

Trepang

Also called *bêche de mer* or *sea cucumber*. It is a Pacific sea slug (*Actinopyga* and *Holothuria* spp.) highly prized by the Chinese who make soup of them and use them also in pork and poultry recipes. They come in dried form and must be soaked for as long as three or four days before using. They have relatives in the Caribbean but not of any great culinary quality.

Trifle

Originally, an elaborate British dessert for ceremonial occasions, but now reduced to sponge cake or ladyfingers soaked in sherry or other spirit, garnished with fruit or fruit preserve, and generally topped with custard or whipped cream.

Tripe

The lining of a beef critter's stomach, although lamb and (in France, at any rate) pork tripe may also be available. Beef tripe is divided into blanket tripe (the lining of the first of the animal's four stomachs), and then in order, honeycomb, book, and glandular tripe. In North America, honeycomb tripe is about all we see. Fresh tripe has been cleaned and parboiled before being put on sale, otherwise it may be canned or pickled.

Tripe has little or no taste of its own, but when simmered develops a gelatinous quality disliked by some, devoured by others. It is mostly seen in French and Mexican dishes, but also has a history of favor in New England and among cowboys in the Old West.

Triple Crème

A general name for any soft French CHEESE with a butterfat content of 72 percent or more.

Triple Sec

Any liqueur of the CURAÇAO type.

Triticale

A hybrid plant (wheat and rye) used whole in casseroles and for making a FLOUR that, while low in gluten, is high in protein. It is mostly available in health food stores.

Trivet

A flat, short-legged object used either over a burner to damp down the heat or on the table to hold hot serving dishes. It also raises the food being cooked in a pot above the surface of the cooking liquid, allowing it to steam.

Trockenbeerenauslese

A German wine term applied to special grapes in the vineyards of the RHINE valley. The grapes are left to literally rot on the vine, to be picked one by one as they appear ready. Each grape contains a minute amount of highly concentrated, exceptionally sweet juice that, when vinified, produces a sweet wine of great elegance. It is, however, of such astronomical cost that the wines have pretty much priced themselves out of existence.

Trotter

A mainly British term for a pig's (less frequently a calf's) foot.

Trout

A group of some of the world's most popular fish. Trout are of as much interest to the angler as to the cook, which gives them a double-barreled appeal. The "true" trout are close relatives of SALMON and share the same generic name, *Salmo*. One that does not is the brook trout, which to the scientist—if not the angler—is a CHAR, as is the lake trout found in the Great Lakes. Trout are never referred to as panfish, although they are probably the best subjects for panfrying that exist. Almost everyone agrees that "wild" (as opposed to farm-raised or even hatchery-bred) trout have an increment of taste that sets them apart, but even an inferior, supermarket, frozen, farm-raised trout can be a welcome addition to the diet. Unquestionably, trout is at its best immediately out of the water.

Trout lends itself to panfrying, but grilling and poaching are also worthy cooking methods, and smoking brings out some wonderful tastes. Trout *au bleu* has been described as a live trout dropped into simmering water, but in fact the trout has been killed first—and the method only really works at streamside when the trout has not yet shed its wetness. Trout with almonds is time-honored, but many feel the almonds overwhelm the delicacy of the fish.

Among the stream-dwelling trout are included: brown trout (*Salmo trutta*), cutthroat trout (*Salmo clarki*), golden trout (*Salmo aguabonita*), rainbow trout (*Salmo gairdneri*), and steelhead trout (usually considered the anadromous version of the rainbow trout).

Truffle

Pound for pound (ounce for ounce or fraction thereof more likely), the world's most expensive vegetable. A mysterious tuber, it grows according to no identifiable program, usually around the roots of oak trees where it can be sniffed out by trained dogs or pigs (or in former times, specially selected virginal women, the last of whom seems to have died of old age in France some years ago). Truffles come in two varieties, black and white, of which the black are by far the more prized. (The white variety is found only in the Piedmont section of Italy.)

Truffles are found in England (*Tuber aestivum*), France (*Tuber melanosporum*), and Italy (*Tuber magnatum*), of which the best are the French (from around Périgord) and the Italian (from Piedmont). Only the Piedmont truffles have any taste of their own (a slightly peppery tang) but the British and especially the French ones have a powerful aroma that transfers to whatever is cooked with them, improving them immeasurably. Eggs and *pâté de foie gras* are among the foodstuffs most pleasurably affected.

Truss

To tie up poultry before you roast it in order to preserve it in a compact form and avoid having the stuffing slop over into the oven.

Try Out

To brown salt pork, bacon, or the like in a frying pan to release the fat. Sometimes, but the phrase is considered misguided, fry out.

Tube Pan

A ring-shaped cake pan with a hollow tube arising in the middle. When the cake is turned out of the pan, it leaves a central core that can be filled with whatever delicacy appeals to the pastry cook.

Tule

See CATTAIL.

Tuna

A large, voracious fish of temperate marine habitat common throughout the Atlantic, Indian, and Pacific oceans and the Caribbean and Mediterranean seas. Its rich, tasty, somewhat fatty meat has variously been compared with that of chicken, beef, and veal.

There are variations among tunas, both in size and color and tastiness of the meat. The most delicate species is the albacore (*Thunnus alalunga*), also called "chicken of the sea" (before the name became a trademark), and the only species allowed to be labeled "white meat tuna" by U.S. regulations. This is one of the smaller members of the tuna clan, running around 3 to 4 feet and weighing in around 60–70 pounds. You're not likely to see fresh albacore in the market, as it is of prime interest to the canners. Of roughly the same size is the bonito (*Sarda* and *Euthynnus* spp.) but it is of hardly the same quality. Indeed in Japan, bonito is not eaten fresh but is dried to form the basis for soups and broths. The main Atlantic tuna species is the bluefin (*Thunnus thunnus*), a monster that can attain a weight of 1,000 pounds or more and feed the whole neighborhood. Its flesh is a deep red and more strongly flavored than albacore. In the Pacific, the resident tuna is the yellowfin (*Thunnus albaceres*), a smallish tuna with a delicate, light-colored flesh verging on pink.

Tuna tend to arise from the depths in great schools in the spring. They are caught in vast nets and considerable controversy has arisen around the use of drift nets, huge devices that float freely, enveloping not only tuna but also innocent dolphins, which are unable to survive the experience. Some canners now maintain that they buy only tuna that has been caught by methods that do not endanger dolphins. We can only hope that they are carrying through on this measure.

Canned tuna has all sorts of uses, including casseroles and salads and sandwiches. Fresh tuna (which profits from being marinated before cooking) can be baked, braised, broiled, or grilled.

Turban

1. Food, usually poultry or seafood, served in the shape of a circle (presumably resembling Turkish headgear), often prepared in a ring pan.

2. A variety of winter SQUASH.

Turbot

A superior species of FLATFISH.

Tureen

A large, covered, ceramic container, usually with a ladle, used for serving soup at the dining table.

Turkey

Benjamin Franklin wanted to name the turkey our national bird, but he was thinking of the wild turkey, a wily, active, and delicious bird. The domestic turkey, for all the vast amount of it we eat, is a pale imitation. The turkey (*Meleagris gallopavo*) is definitely a New World offspring. Native Americans were well aware of it and the Aztecs apparently had domesticated it before being decimated by the Conquistadors.

Originally, the domesticated turkey was huge, but nowadays a 25-pound bird for a tom (or male) or 16 for a hen (or female) is pretty standard as family size has shrunk and turkey is being pushed as an everyday staple rather than a splashy holiday treat. It is still the unusual household in the United States that does not feature turkey for Thanksgiving dinner, however, a custom said to date from 1621.

Turkeys are also being bred to provide as much white meat as possible, it being apparent that most Americans prefer the white to the dark. There is also a smaller turkey (5–10 pounds) for those with more timid appetites. Turkeys are available throughout the year either fresh or frozen or in parts (breast, drumsticks), as cutlets, tenderloins (the inside muscle of the turkey breast) and even ground or made into sausages and such lunch meats as turkey ham and turkey pastrami. Whole turkeys are almost invariably stuffed and roasted and the problem has always been to keep them from drying out in the cooking. Slow cooking and much basting is one answer and some producers are pushing their self-basting turkeys, which have been injected with butter or vegetable oil. Turkeys also smoke with distinction and may also be found boned and canned—appropriate for such dishes as turkey à la king.

It's difficult to do anything about selecting a turkey in the market as most of them are firmly encased in plastic and many of them are to be found in the frozen food section. Just make sure the plastic is unbroken and—if fresh—the bird has a little give to it, and hope for the best. If it doesn't work out, try another market (or another brand) next time.

Turk's Head Mold

A TUBE PAN with fluted indentations and a cover for steaming puddings (such as PLUM PUDDING) in the English fashion. Its somewhat fanciful name comes from its supposed resemblance to a Turkish turban.

Turmeric

An East Indian relative of GINGER used as a spice and dyeing agent. Turmeric (*Curcuma longa*) has a slightly bitter, pungent flavor and a bright yellow color akin to SAFFRON. Indeed, if you are looking only for color (rather than taste) you're better off using turmeric than saffron and saving yourself a bundle, but wear an apron because turmeric can inflict stains that are almost impossible to wash out. The most widespread use of turmeric is in curries and to give "ballpark" mustard its characteristic yellowness.

Turnip

A root vegetable (*Brassica rapa*) of the cabbage family. The root is used as a vegetable and the tops served as a green. Sometimes, especially when growers are thinning their plants, you can find turnip greens with tiny marble-sized turnips, which cooked together make a succulent combination.

Turnips arose in Asia Minor and spread from there. They provided the advantage of a plant that will grow sturdily even in poor soil and provide harvests where other crops will not. It being so easy and cheap to grow, it became something of a poor man's food and was also used as animal fodder.

Most turnips have white flesh, although one species (the RUTABAGA) is yellow. The outer skin is typically white with a top that is usually purple, but can also be black or green or red or white or yellow. They have a zesty tang, delicate when young and small, stronger as they grow older. When they get too large, the texture is apt to get woody.

Turnips are peeled and often then cut in the JULIENNE style. Or they can be used in stews and can be incorporated into a most interesting cream soup. They can also be boiled, steamed, or stir-fried.

When selecting turnips, look for small ones with intact, unblemished skins, heavy for their size. The greens should be bright and perky with no yellowing or wilting.

Turnip Cabbage
Another name for KOHLRABI.

Turnip-Rooted Celery
See CELERIAC.

Turnover
A pastry filled with meat, fruit, or almost anything good that comes to mind and folded over on itself into a half-moon or triangular shape.

Turtle
The Merriam-Webster *Webster's New Collegiate Dictionary* defines turtle as "any of an order (Testudinata) of land, freshwater, and marine reptiles with a toothless horny beak and a bony shell which encloses the trunk and into which the head, limbs, and tail usu. may be withdrawn." Fair enough. What the dictionary does not say is that of all these hundreds of species, a goodly number are edible and some are considered delicacies.

Among the most important turtles, gastronomically, are the TERRAPIN and the green sea turtle (*Chelonia mydas*), the base for the turtle soups that are served in a few restaurants here and there (some culinary experts consider its making so difficult that they do not recommend trying it at home) as well as steaks. The green turtle is not green but its fat is, therefore the name. It is a huge creature that browses on eelgrass along the Atlantic and Caribbean coasts and is collected either in nets or scooped up when it lumbers ashore to lay its eggs. It is not the only edible sea turtle. The loggerhead turtle (*Caretta caretta*) is another prized edible sea turtle.

Among other edible turtles are the snapping turtle (*Chelydra serpentina*), which ranges from Canada through Central America in freshwater and brackish ponds and rivers and the alligator snapping turtle (*Macroclemys temminckii*) found in lakes and pools in the southeastern United States. Although a good bet to stay away from in the wild, it makes superior table fare. There are also soft-shelled turtles and various varieties of land turtle that also make good eating. However, one naturalist has warned that land turtles often feed happily on plants poisonous to man, passing the toxins along to the discomfort (or worse) of the eater.

Turtle meat is available in some fish markets and can be dried, fresh, or frozen. Turtle soup can be made with dried turtle meat, but lacks some of the distinction of fresh. Turtle eggs are also favored, especially in France, as are turtle flippers, which are usually braised in some form of wine sauce.

Turtle Bean

A black BEAN used in black bean soup and other dishes.

Turtle Herbs

A mixture of basil, bay, marjoram, and thyme used to flavor soups. Turtle herbs can often be found commercially.

Tuscan

A hot, green CHILI pepper often used pickled.

Tutti-Frutti

It can be an ice cream or a dessert composed of diced mixed fruits (the name is Italian for "all fruits") compounded with brandy and sugar. The name also applies to a flavor of chewing gum.

Tybo

A firm Danish cow's-milk cheese similar to SAMSOE.

Tzimmes

A Jewish casserole usually composed of brisket of beef (although it may also be vegetarian) sweetened with honey and augmented by all manner of fresh and dried fruits and vegetables. It is traditionally served to mark the Jewish New Year, Rosh Hashanah.

UV

Ugli Fruit

An odd amalgam thought to be a natural cross between a grapefruit and a tangerine, although others sense another component—perhaps some form of bitter orange. The fruit is unprepossessing in looks. It resembles an oversized tangerine with a thick, loosely fitting yellowish-green skin and sweet orange flesh. Ugli fruit is generally eaten raw.

Ugli fruit is available during the winter months. Select one that's heavy for its size and gives a bit when gently pressed. You probably won't want to keep it more than a week unrefrigerated or two to three weeks refrigerated.

Upside-Down Cake

A cake (or tart) that is cooked with the fruit down and the pastry up and inverted once baked so that the top is bottom and the bottom is top. The idea is to line a cake pan with butter and sugar and top this with a layer of fruit over which you pour the batter. During the baking, the sugary fruit caramelizes. When the cake is inverted and removed from the pan, the glaze becomes the topping of the cake. A TARTE TATIN is an upside-down tart.

Usquebaugh

An ancient Celtic word for a spirituous beverage, from which is derived the word whiskey.

Utility Meat

Another name for VARIETY MEAT.

Vacherin

1. A dessert composed of a bowl of meringues decorated outside with piped meringue and filled with CRÈME CHANTILLY or ice cream or berries.

2. Any of several cow's-milk cheeses. Vacherin is a soft cheese made in Switzerland and France and usually eaten with a spoon; *Vacherin à la Main* (also called *Tomme de Montagne*) is similar with a firm rind and soft interior; *Vacherin du Mont d'Or* is a soft to semihard, French, cow's-milk cheese with a robust flavor.

Valencia

A variety of ORANGE.

Valpolicella
A dry red wine of Italy's Verona region.

Vanilla
A flavoring coming from the long, expensive pod or bean of the vanilla tree (*Vanilla planifolia*). We usually see either the whole bean (extensively processed) or its extract (the flavoring dissolved in a bit of alcohol), although an imitation is also available. It's usually better to spring for the true vanilla flavor, as the imitation gives you the aroma but not much of the taste.

Varietal Wine
A wine known for the principal grape used to make it rather than a place name from which it may or may not have come. A California or Australian Chablis tells nothing of the quality of the wine. A Chardonnay from the same area at least informs you that it is made from the same grape as is used in the French Chablis vineyards. A varietal wine usually has the edge over a generically named one.

Variety Meat
An overall term for those animal innards used for human consumption. The term is sometimes extended to include any edible portion not considered among our steaks and chops. A list might include: brains, ears, feet, heart, kidney, liver, lungs, marrow, muzzle, stomach, sweetbreads, tail, tongue, and testicles. And among Arabs and Eskimos, at any rate, you'd have to add the eyes. Variety meats are also sometimes referred to as *glandular meats*, *offal*, *organ meats*, and *utility meats*.

Veal
The meat from a young (less than three months old when slaughtered) calf. Meat from a calf less than six weeks is called "bob," or if more than about 16 weeks it is called "baby beef." Neither one has much to recommend it. If the calf is slaughtered at less than 12 weeks and is unweaned, it is *milk-fed veal*, or if weaned and fed a special diet of mother's milk and eggs, it is *formula-fed*. Regular veal has a creamy white color, a fine texture, and bones that display red at the marrow; specially fed veal may be more of a greenish pink. A great deal of the veal sold in North America is actually baby beef, which accounts for the toughness that is not there in true veal.

Veal is almost free from fat and can dry out if the cook is not careful. This is why a roast is generally barded with pork fat, which acts as a lubricant, and why moist heat is generally preferred to such dry-heat methods as broiling. The more available cuts of veal include bone-in roasts (breast, with a pocket for stuffing), boneless roasts (shoulder or breast), chops, cutlets, shanks, and sometimes steaks. Boneless roasts are sometimes roasted over a bed of diced carrots, celery, and sweet peppers, which can be defatted and pureed as a sauce. Cutlets, in Vienna as well as in Italy, are pounded thin, covered with some form of batter and sautéed. Veal shanks are the base for Italy's renowned osso BUCO. Veal seems particularly suited to being cooked with a fortified wine, especially Madeira and Marsala.

When selecting veal, look for white meat (redness means that it is getting long in the tooth), little or no fat, a dense, fine texture, and red marrow in the bones. If it meets all these criteria, it will probably be on the pricey side.

Vegetable

Essentially, a kitchen garden plant that supplies food. This definition excludes the herb garden, for example, and the orchard. As a matter of convenience, vegetables embrace certain species that botanists define as fruit, such as eggplant and tomato. The edible part of the plant may be only one component (tomato leaves, for instance, are toxic but the fruit certainly is not) or more than one (beets and beet greens both enter into the diet of many of us). The parts of vegetables that we place on our dining tables include flowers (broccoli), fruit (cucumbers or zucchini), leaves (lettuce, spinach), roots (including bulbs and tubers, all of which may be represented by carrots, onions, and potatoes).

One of the great drawbacks to vegetables is that they are often overcooked. Most need but little cooking before they get mushy and tasteless, and some need no cooking at all. An exception is collard greens which, in the Deep South, are cooked long and slow in plenty of water with some form of pork.

Individual vegetables will be treated under their own headings in this volume.

Vegetable Coloring

Dyes available as commercial preparations to give color to foodstuffs, the most obvious example being those we use on Easter eggs. They are derived from vegetable sources and have all sorts of applications, from making exotic pastries to (ugh!) dying your beer green for St. Patrick's Day.

Vegetable Marrow

A British term for zUCCHINI.

Venison

The meat of a deer or related species. Since the name comes from the Latin verb *venari* meaning "to hunt," it properly applies to any mammalian game, even though it is rarely used this way.

Verbena

See LEMON VERBENA.

Verdelho

A type of Portuguese MADEIRA.

Verjuice

Also *verjus*. The juice of unripened grapes (and sometimes crab apples or even sour oranges or lemons). It was used, especially by medieval cooks, to give tang to sauces that might otherwise be bland.

Vermicelli

Extremely thin SPAGHETTI. The name comes from the Italian and means "little worms."

Vermouth

An aperitif and mixer composed of wine fortified with brandy and infused with various herbs and plants. There are two varieties: French (pale white and dry) and Italian (dark-colored and sweet), although both countries make both varieties, as do a great many other countries as well. In addition to forming a component of a dry martini, vermouth has a number of culinary uses.

Viburnum

A widespread and extremely diverse genus of trees and shrubs that includes the misnamed highbush CRANBERRY.

Vichy Celestins

A naturally sparkling mineral water (there is a still variety, too) from the spa at Vichy, France. It is bottled and widely exported.

Vichyssoise

A creamy leek and potato soup served chilled and garnished with minced chives. It was developed around 1920 by Louis Diat, a French chef at New York's Ritz-Carlton Hotel from a venerable tradition of such soups well known in French households.

Vienna Sausage

A tiny Austrian sausage with blunt ends usually sold in cans. It is frequently wrapped in dough and cooked to form the hors d'oeuvre called *pigs in blankets*.

Vinaigrette

See FRENCH DRESSING.

Vindaloo

An extremely hot curry paste used with robust meats (duck, game) in parts of India.

Vinegar

Essentially, a weak solution of acetic acid used particularly in salad dressings, marinades, and pickling solutions. The word derives from the French *vin aigre*, meaning "sour wine," but vinegar is distilled not only from wine but from other sources as well. In addition to red and white wine, vinegar can be based on cider, grain alcohol, malt, and rice. Vinegar can be flavored with herbs (such as dill and tarragon) or fruits (such as raspberries). One impressive vinegar is balsamic, a sweet, dark, rich vinegar made in Modena, Italy. The true balsamic is aged for anywhere from 6 to 35 years and is expensive indeed. Most "balsamics" available today are the product of the factory and range from inexpensive, sweet, and harsh to a blend of the real thing with the mass-produced, which is better and smoother.

Vine Leaves
See DOLMA.

Violet
A small, flowering plant (*Viola* spp.) found in gardens, beside mossy stones, in dampish places in late spring, and in florist shops. Like rose petals, those of violets have been crystallized for adding to candies, pastries, and also salads.

Virginia Ham
A specially cured HAM from Virginia.

Vitello Tonnato
An Italian specialty of veal braised with tuna and a few anchovies, allowed to cool, then dressed with tuna-flavored mayonnaise and a little parsley, and served cold.

Vodka
A clear, colorless, practically odorless, and just about tasteless alcoholic spirit. It originated in Russia or Poland, in both of which countries it is considered the national drink. The first vodka was probably distilled from potatoes, but grain is the preferred source today. It became popular in the United States following World War II and remains so today, possibly because its neutral taste permits it to be combined with all manner of mixes.

Vol-au-Vent
Also called *bouchées à la reine*. Individual PUFF PASTRY shells, with lids, that can be stuffed with any filling that pleases you. Chicken, lamb, veal, and seafood preparations are traditional.

Wafer

A thin, crisp, disk-shaped candy, cookie, or cracker.

Waffle

A small, sweet batter bread cooked in a WAFFLE IRON and usually served for breakfast. The indentations made by the waffle iron's grid pattern trap the butter and syrup poured over the waffle and keep them from running off.

Waffle Iron

As you might expect, an appliance for making waffles. Most waffle irons these days are electric and have a removable (for ease in washing) element with a grid pattern on one side (for waffles) and a smooth surface on the other (for pancakes or grilled sandwiches). When you pour the waffle batter onto the gridded side and close the iron, the heat cooks the waffle while the weight of the iron impresses it with the pattern. You can also close it for sandwiches, toasting the sandwich on both sides and cooking the filling all at once. For pancakes, you leave the device open and use it much as you would a frying pan.

Wahoo

A species of MACKEREL.

Waldorf Salad

A salad created at New York's old Waldorf-Astoria Hotel before the turn of the century. It was originally chopped apples and celery dressed with mayonnaise. Chopped walnuts (or sometimes pecans) were added later.

Walleye

Sometimes called *walleyed* and *yellow pike*. A fish of the PERCH family.

Walnut

A nut-bearing tree of northerly temperate climates. It embraces the butternut (*Juglans cinerea*), English (more properly Persian, but credit was given not to its place of origin but to the nationality of the ships that first transported it) walnut (*Juglans regia*), and black walnut (*Juglans nigra*). Commercial walnuts are almost invariably English.

The nuts of each variety are known for being pleasant with a slight tang and for their oiliness—indeed the French press them for walnut oil, the distinctive taste of which is often favored for salad dressings. Walnuts are available whole in the shell, shelled, or shelled and broken up. The English make a pickle of them and otherwise, they are a delight to crack and eat whole, make a pleasant taste-and-texture contribution to stuffings (apple and walnut is classic), and are widely used in baking. Black walnuts, when you can find them, have a richer, slightly fermented taste.

Wapiti
Another name for the American ELK.

Wasabi
Often called *Japanese horseradish*, and although its taste and tang resemble true horseradish, the two are not related. Very hot and gray-green in color, wasabi (*Wasabia japonica*) is available mostly in Asian markets in the form of roots kept in pans of water. Avoid them if they are shriveled or sprouting. Otherwise keep them in a cool, dry place for three or four days at most and grate just enough for the use you have in mind and just before you are ready to use them. You can also find wasabi powdered in cans or envelopes. In this form it is mixed with water to form a paste and is traditional in Japan with SUSHI.

Washington Clam
Any of two species of West Coast CLAM (*Saxidomus nuttali* and *Saxidomus gigantea*), found in muddy shallow waters along the northerly shoreline.

Wassail
An early English form of punch (especially a Christmas punch) consisting of sweetened ale or wine flavored with spices and most often augmented with baked apples. The term also applies to the accompanying Middle English toast, "Wassail," which translates as "be well" or "be healthy."

Water Bath
See BAIN MARIE.

Water Buffalo
An Asian BUFFALO.

Water Chestnut
A small tuber of an aquatic plant (*Trapa* spp.) that seems to have originated in West Africa but has its widest use in Oriental cookery. It is crisp and slightly sweet and, peeled, is added mostly to give "crunch" to soups and other dishes. You can find water chestnuts canned, dried, fresh, whole, or sliced. Once opened, unneeded canned chestnuts can be refrigerated in water for up to a month if you change the water regularly.

Watercress

An herb (*Nasturtium officinale*) originally of European origin but introduced fairly early to North America and now often found wild in brooks and other running streams. Its mildly pungent flavor makes it a favorite salad ingredient and also a garnish. If you pick it yourself, make sure the water it grows in is unpolluted. If in doubt, head for the store. When you get your watercress home, take the leaves off the stems (which you can toss), wash them carefully, dry them, and refrigerate either wrapped in paper or in an airtight container.

Water Ice

A form of (usually) fruit ICE CREAM but made with water instead of milk (or cream). It has a hard consistency as opposed to the slightly mushy quality looked for in a GRANITA.

Watermelon

A MELON best loved by summer picnickers.

Waterzooï

Close to the national soup of Belgium, this Flemish dish is made with freshwater fish (saltwater variations can also be found) or with chicken. Celery and herbs and gobs of butter are essential. In either case, the ingredients are cooked very slowly and enriched with butter until the soup is thick and creamy. The chicken version has additional vegetables (leeks, onions) and a little white wine and, perhaps, egg yolks at the end.

Wax Bean

A yellow snap BEAN.

Wax Paper

A thin roll of translucent paper with a coating of wax on each side, used for covering dishes, lining pans, and more recently to cover foods being microwaved. Its use has been largely supplanted by aluminum foil and plastic wrap.

Weakfish

Also *sea trout* and *squeateague*. A fish (*Cynoscion regalis*) prevalent from Massachusetts to Florida. The name derives not from lack of strength, but owing to the tenderness of the mouth, which tears easily when hooked. The flesh straight from the water is fine and tasty but turns flabby the farther it gets from home. Charcoal grilling and panfrying are widespread cooking methods.

Weisswurst

A German white sausage made with pork and veal with bread and spices. Bake them, boil them, or steam them and serve hot or cold.

Welsh Rabbit

Also, as some would have it, *rarebit*. Melted Cheddar cheese, ale (or beer), and sometimes an egg, flavored with a little dry mustard and served on toast. There are many variations on this simple theme and many stories, including a medieval ethnic joke that has the Lord God so displeased with the clamor that His Welsh children are making in Heaven that He has Saint Peter move outside the Gates, shout out (in Welsh) "Roast Cheese!" and slam the Gates shut when all the Welshmen have stormed out in pursuit of their favorite snack. If you like cheese, you might be better off outside the Gates.

Wensleydale

A flaky, white, mildly sour, English cow's-milk CHEESE, some of which develops blue veins as it ages. The cheese was originally made with ewe's milk.

Western Sandwich

A sandwich composed of chopped ham, onion, and green pepper scrambled with eggs and placed between two slices of bread.

Westphalian Ham

A German specialty HAM.

Whale

An aquatic mammal of the order Cetacea much vexing to the social order. Whales have been used for food (the meat is reminiscent of beef, but with slightly fishy overtones), but their status as an endangered species has limited this use. At one time they were harvested for their oil as well as their meat. Only a few nations still persist in whaling, and they are subject to severe criticism for doing so.

Wheat

The Western world's most important cereal grain (*Triticum aestivum*), and the one from which our most important FLOUR is milled.

Whelk

Also known as *scungilli*. A large marine snail (*Buccinum undatum*) little known in North America (except in Asian and Italian neighborhoods) but much prized in Italy and Britain. The meat is tough and rubbery, but can be extracted from the shell by a half hour's boiling, then cleaned, and it's ready for slicing. Whelk is frequently served in a marinara sauce (lots of garlic and oregano), made into a cold salad, poured over spaghetti, or ground up for fritters. Cooked whelk is available canned or frozen.

Whey

A liquid in milk left over after the CURD has been removed. Whey is a by-product of cheese-making, but is mostly sold as food for pigs.

Whey Cheese

A CHEESE made from the WHEY rather than the curds of milk. Ricotta is about the best known of them.

Whip

To beat, as you would beat cream. You can use a fork or a whisk or an eggbeater, but an electric mixer or food processor beats them all.

Whisk

A marvelous gadget for beating and getting air into eggs and liquids of all sorts. It is equally useful for thoroughly mixing dry ingredients as in making bread or pastries. It consists of a number of looped wires the ends of which run up into a handle that fits nicely in the hand. Whisks range in size from almost too small to pick up to great monsters as long as your forearm, useful mostly in professional kitchens (which may be the only places to have room for them).

Whiskey

An alcoholic beverage distilled from grain (corn, rye, or wheat). Whiskey is the spelling in North America and Ireland.

Whisky

A distinctive spirit distilled in Scotland. This is also the spelling preferred for the spirit produced in Canada.

Whitebait

A small fish sometimes used as bait and sometimes fried and eaten whole, innards and all. They are traditionally small HERRING of various sorts but in North America can include massive infusions of SILVERSIDES (also called *shiners*) or sand eels (see SAND LANCE), neither of which are herring at all.

White Bass

A freshwater BASS.

Whitefish

A group of fishes, the best known of which are inhabitants of the Great Lakes, where they are sold fresh (usually filleted) or smoked. The lake whitefish (*Coregonus clupeaformis*) and the closely related cisco (also *Coregonus* spp.) are mostly what we see. Should you catch or come upon a fresh, whole whitefish, by all means grill it over charcoal if you can. Otherwise, it can be cooked virtually any way appropriate for fish.

White Lightning

See CORN LIQUOR.

White Perch

The name notwithstanding, a freshwater BASS.

White Sauce

Perhaps the most basic kitchen sauce—even the mother of sauces, as so many others are based on it. To make it, you might melt 2 tablespoons of butter and add, slowly, 2 tablespoons of flour with some salt and pepper, stirring all the time. Let it cook but not brown. When the flour has cooked a few minutes take it off the heat and add a little milk. Stir until smooth and add a bit more milk. Keep this up until you've used up a full cup of milk. There is your white sauce. Additional flour will make it thicker.

White Stock

A stock made from white meat (veal or the white meat of poultry) and vegetables that will not impart color to it. Unlike a BROWN STOCK, any bones used would not be browned first. (See BROTH.)

Whiting

In North America, a northern KINGFISH. In Europe, a relative of the COD.

Wholemeal

A flour that is ground from the whole grain (except the hull), bran and germ included.

Whole Wheat

A FLOUR either milled from the entire, hulled wheat kernel or having some of the components restored after milling. As it does not have the staying power of its white counterpart, whole wheat flour should be bought in small quantities and from stores with a fairly high turnover. It is best kept refrigerated.

Whortleberry

In North America, a nonspecific name for various berries related to the BLUEBERRY, sometimes even including the blueberry itself. In Europe, a berry (*Vaccinium myrtillus*) resembling and used in the same way as the blueberry.

Wiener Schnitzel

A Viennese method of cooking veal, although it seems to have originated in France. A veal cutlet is pounded to a thickness of a scant quarter inch, coated with flour, dipped in beaten egg, dredged with seasoned breadcrumbs, then dropped into hot oil (or oil and lard) just long enough to cook it through. It is served hot, traditionally with a salad.

Wild Boar

See BOAR.

Wild Cherry
See CHERRY and CHOKECHERRY.

Wild Duck
A wild duck is a slightly different proposition than domestic duck. Its flesh is richer, and it has less fat. As a result of both, a roasted (or spit-roasted) wild duck will call for a little marinating time, some sort of fat to BARD it, and a reduced roasting time vis-à-vis its domestic counterpart. Wild duck can also be braised or broiled with distinction, and a whole gamut of sauces can be used, including some form of orange sauce. Smoked wild duck is also a delicacy.

Wild ducks can really be divided into the large (roughly over 1¾ pounds) and the small (½ pound and up). The larger ducks (canvasbacks, gadwalls, goldeneyes, mallards, old squaws, and scoters, for example) will probably provide enough of a meal with one duck serving two people. The smaller ones (buffleheads, ruddy, shovelers, and teal are examples) will probably call for at least one per person. Because of the rich taste, some of the stronger root vegetables (such as turnip) are often recommended to go with them, and wild rice is also frequently served with them.

Wild duck is generally available only to hunters and friends of hunters, but sometimes farm-raised mallard can be found in specialty markets.

Wild Goose
It is a thrilling sight during the migration season to see those V-shaped formations of geese going about their business, sounding for all the world like a pack of hounds. Goose hunters seem to feel that having a goose on the table represents a formidable accomplishment, for the birds are wary, alert, and hard to bag.

Like duck, a wild goose cannot be addressed as one would a domestic fowl. It is considerably smaller, to begin with, and again is darker and richer and contain far less fat. Age must also be considered. A four-pound Canada goose (dressed weight) is appropriate for roasting. One over six pounds would probably be more delectable if braised. Cabbage and turnips (and sauerkraut) fit in well with wild goose as do all sorts of fruits including apples and apricots and oranges. Like wild duck, wild goose also takes well to smoking.

The wild geese most often encountered include the brant (*Branta* spp.), small (two to three pounds), dark birds that migrate from the Arctic southward, and the Canada goose (*Branta canadensis*), the common goose of North America running, depending upon subspecies, anywhere from six to twelve pounds (live weight, somewhat more than half that when dressed).

Wild Parsley
See LOVAGE.

Wild Rice

A cereal grass (*Zizania aquatica*) native to marshy areas of North America but transplanted to Europe and Asia as well. Despite its name, it has no kinship with rice or indeed with any other grain to which it is sometimes linked (the French call it "crazy oats"). Its nutlike taste and consistency make it a highly prized delicacy, especially with the darker meats (including duck and goose) and with game.

Williams

A European name for the Bartlett PEAR and the BRANDY (poire) made from it.

Windowpane Flounder

A thin, virtually translucent FLATFISH of eastern North America.

Windsor Bean

Another name for the broad BEAN.

Wine

A fermented juice of the GRAPE but extended to include the juice of other crops as well, such as dandelions and elderberries. Wines are classified as table wines (meant primarily for consumption with food, red, rosé, and white wines which may be dry, semisweet, or sweet); sparkling and semisparkling wines (such as Champagne and wines described as *pétillant* or "crackling"); fortified wines (such as port or sherry); and wine byproducts (including aperitif wines such as Dubonnet or vermouth).

Winesap

A late, dusky red APPLE that is slightly tart.

Winkle

A nickname for the PERIWINKLE.

Wintergreen

See CHECKERBERRY.

Winter Flounder

A widespread FLATFISH.

Winter Melon

A melon (*Benincasa hispida*) and thereby technically a fruit, but used by the Chinese and Japanese as a vegetable. It is large (up to eight inches) and round with a tough green skin that sometimes exhibits a waxy bloom. Peel off the skin, scrape out and discard the seeds, and use the delicate white pulp in stir-fried dishes (the Chinese parboil it first). It is also used in winter melon soup made with chicken broth, ground or cubed pork, and a beaten egg, enhanced perhaps with dried mushrooms and water chestnuts. For elaborate banquets, this soup may be cooked and served in the melon itself. Winter melon may also be braised, simmered, or steamed.

Winter melon is usually sold in slices that, wrapped in plastic, will keep in the vegetable drawer of the refrigerator for almost a week. Whole melons can be kept for weeks.

Witch Flounder

Also known as *gray sole*; a fairly common commercial FLATFISH.

Witloof

See BELGIAN ENDIVE.

Wok

A round-bottomed cooking utensil from China designed to cook its ingredients as quickly as possible while using the least possible amount of fuel. Woks are used in STIR-FRYING and are also useful for steaming and braising. While the round bottom is excellent for cooking over coals (you just nestle it into them), adjusting woks to gas and electric stoves calls for modification. A ring has been devised to fit over the burner of a gas stove (the wok fits right into it), and for electric stoves there are flat-bottomed woks. You can also find an electric wok at most department stores.

Most woks are composed of sheet steel and are wiped out after use or, at most, washed gently with warm, soapy water and dried immediately or set over a flame until all the water has evaporated.

Wonton

A small package of egg-noodle dough dusted with cornstarch and filled with a diced mixture of meat or seafood and vegetables. Wontons may be boiled, deep-fried, or steamed and are eaten as an appetizer, snack, or in soup.

Woodchuck

Also *groundhog*. A marmot (*Marmota monax*) of eastern North America much disliked by farmers for its habit of raiding the most succulent parts of the garden or field. They are not widely eaten, but reports have it that the young are as savory as rabbit or squirrel while older specimens serve well in stews.

Woodcock

A gamebird of Europe and eastern North America. The European species (*Scolopax rusticola*), known in France as *bécasse*, is somewhat larger than its American cousin. French gourmets consider it the finest of gamebirds and have devised any number of recipes for it, although most knowledgeable eaters prefer simply to remove the eyes and the gizzard and roast and eat the rest. The American bird (*Philohela minor*), though small, still packs a gustatory impact, being rich and strongly flavored to the point where fussy eaters face it with distress. Again roasting, including spit-roasting, is the cooking method that seems to gain the most approval. Because of its rich taste, and despite its small size, one bird per person is generally recommended.

Wood Ear

A Chinese cloud ear MUSHROOM.

Woodruff

Also *sweet woodruff* and *waldmeister*. A European herb (*Asperula odorata*) now naturalized throughout North America. It is used in a variety of drinks and teas, but its most noted use is in MAY WINE. However, especially in Austria, it is used to flavor candies, sausages, and other dishes.

Worcestershire Sauce

A condiment originally developed in India but first made commercially in Worcester, England, by the firm of Lea & Perrins. It advertises itself as being for "Soups, Sea Food, Steaks, Gravies, Barbecues, etc.," and with the possible exception of the "etc.," that sounds reasonable. It is a thin, pungent, dark sauce that includes in its formula anchovies (sometimes sardines or both), chili peppers, cloves, corn sweeteners, molasses, salt, onions, shallots, tamarinds, vinegar, and, of course, water. There are others on the market, including at least one firm (Harvey, in Great Britain) that produces a vegetarian version without the anchovies or sardines.

Wormwood

A genus of herbs or shrubs most notable for *Artemisa absinthium*, the plant from which was derived ABSINTHE and which is one of the flavorings that goes into the making of VERMOUTH.

Wrasse

An enormous family of mostly tropical, reef-dwelling fish, the most important—from the culinary point of view—being the TAUTOG.

XYZ

Xeres
The former name for Jerez (or Jeres de la Frontera), the Spanish center of the SHERRY trade.

Yak
A large bovine of the Himalaya Mountains, long domesticated in the higher elevations of India and in Tibet. It gives milk that is clarified into ghee, the Indian version of clarified butter, but is more important as a beast of burden than as a source of meat.

Yam
A tropical vine (*Dioscorea* spp.) that produces a tuber much resembling a sweet potato in shape and taste. Although the yam contains more sugar than a sweet potato, it does not generally taste so sweet. The yams we see in the market are but a drop in the bucket to the lavish variety that yams are capable of. They can be small or enormous and of varying hues.

When buying yams, treat them as you would potatoes—see that they are firm and unblemished. Store them in a dry, well-ventilated place but not for more than about a week. Cook them as you would potatoes or sweet potatoes, but they are especially good baked.

Yard-Long Bean
An Asian BEAN used when young and still tender. Its pods do not achieve a full yard in length.

Yarrow
Also *milfoil*. An herb (*Achillea millefolium*) that has been fermented into an alcoholic beverage, was once used to flavor beer, and may still show up in herbal teas.

Yautia
See MALANGA.

Yeast
A most remarkable microorganism responsible for all manner of wonders including making bread rise and transforming grape juice into wine and barley malt into beer. One form of yeast—brewer's yeast—is said to have healthful properties as a food additive.

In the kitchen, the yeast of interest is baker's yeast. It is most widely available dried, in small packages weighing ¼ ounce. Keep it cool and dry and use it before the date stamped on the back (usually a matter of months). Also available is compressed yeast (mixed with cornstarch) which comes in packages of ⁶⁄₁₀ ounce and must be used soon after purchase or it will lose its wondrous powers. Bulk yeast must be refrigerated and generally is programmed for use within about a year. To see if your yeast is still active, you simply PROOF it.

Yellow Bass

A freshwater BASS.

Yellow Pike

Another name for the fish known as the *walleyed pike*, or WALLEYE, which is not a pike but a PERCH.

Yellow Potato

A fairly new variety of POTATO.

Yellowtail

Almost any fish with a yellow tail will sooner or later get this name, but several stand out. One is simply the yellowtail, otherwise known as *California yellowtail* (*Seriola lalandei*), a mild, moderately fatty fish mostly of the Pacific and amenable to any method of cooking. Another is the *yellowtail snapper* (*Ocyurus chrysurus*), a southern Atlantic denizen that is an excellent all-round fish (at least when truly fresh) pan-fried, if small enough; otherwise either the whole fish or its steaks may be broiled or grilled. Also qualifying as good eating is the *yellowtail flounder*, a FLATFISH of the Atlantic from Labrador to New Jersey.

Yellow Turnip

See RUTABAGA.

Yerbe Maté

See MATÉ.

Yogurt

Sometimes *yoghurt*. A fermented milk product and one of the most popular items on any dairy shelf. It comes plain or sweetened and flavored or you can make it yourself (which tastes much better, really—less acid). Among its reassuring qualities is its ability to pinch hit for sour cream in many recipes that call for that delicacy but are intended for people who don't need all those additional calories.

Yogurt, whether plain or flavored (sometimes with fruit juice, sometimes with bits of fruit, sometimes with other flavors such as coffee or vanilla) has a creamy, rich, somewhat tangy, almost sour taste that commercial yogurt-makers sometimes get around by adding sweeteners. Yogurt has been around for millennia, especially among Balkan peoples and has always been considered a boon to good health—one claim is that it prolongs healthy life. Because of the ferments that turn it from milk into yogurt, even those with allergies to the lactose in regular milk can tolerate yogurt. There is also a frozen yogurt, but the health benefits—if any—disappear as the health-giving bacteria do not survive the freezing process. However, it's still fine for lactose-intolerant people.

Yorkshire Pudding

A traditional English accompaniment for roast beef. It is prepared from eggs, flour, milk, and salt, enriched with drippings from the roast and baked in the same oven. It is a thrifty way of making use of the whole roast and of satisfying the appetites of the diners with a less expensive side dish that tastes like the meat.

Youngberry

A huge (up to two inches long) hybrid berry reminiscent of the loganberry and the boysenberry. It is juicy with a red-to-black coloration and a tart taste.

Yuca

The Latin American name for CASSAVA.

Yucca

The young flowers of this plant (*Yucca* spp.) are used in the Southwest as a salad ingredient.

Yule Log

A French Christmas cake otherwise known as BÛCHE DE NOËL.

Zabaglione

Italy's great gift to the world of desserts. It is as simple as it is difficult to make. It consists simply of egg yolks, sugar, and wine—in this case MARSALA. (The addition of a touch of vanilla or the zest of some citrus fruit is permitted by some discerning chefs.) Prepared at the table at the time of serving, it requires simmering water over which the ingredients are set and whisked continuously until everything comes together to form a light, custardy, frothy perfection. It need not be a dessert—it can sometimes be used as a sauce for ice cream or pastries.

Zakuska

A Russian HORS D'OEUVRE.

Zarzuela

A winy Spanish fish stew that seems to include just about everything on the Spanish coast. It calls for some form of fish (perhaps haddock or a flatfish), shellfish (clams, mussels, maybe some shrimp), some eel and a little squid, all fried lightly in olive oil then stewed with almond paste, slightly sautéed onions, *garlic*, saffron, tomatoes, wine, and to top it all off, a hefty jolt of anisette. *Zarzuela* is Spanish for *operetta*, but heaven knows what you would do for an encore.

Zest
The rind of a citrus fruit—usually lemons or oranges—but *only* the rind. Get rid of the whitish pulp that forms the inner part of the rind (or the outer part of the meat). That is what gives it a bitter taste that is best avoided. The zest can be removed with a vegetable peeler or by a zester, a handy device that cuts thin strips of rind to whatever depth you wish (or have the dexterity to accomplish).

Zinfandel
A wine grape (*Vitis vinifera*) much used in California. Of obscure origin, it produces a pleasant, fruity red wine and also a white zinfandel of slightly less distinction.

Ziti
A PASTA in the form of a macaroni tube.

Zubrovka
A slightly pungent, green-colored, Polish VODKA flavored with a grass (*Hierochloe odorate*) that is the favorite food of the Polish bison, or *zubra*.

Zucchini
A popular SQUASH.

Zwieback
A bread that has been baked, sliced, then baked again to become brittle and crisp and dry. It is considered easily digestible and is often given to very young children and invalids.